3rd edition ———————————  **W9-BCU-960**

CONTEMPORARY SOVIET POLITICS
An Introduction

DONALD D. BARRY
Lehigh University

CAROL BARNER-BARRY
University of Maryland, Baltimore County

Prentice-Hall, Inc., Englewood Cliffs, New Jersey 07632

Library of Congress Cataloging-in-Publication Data

Barry, Donald D.
     Contemporary Soviet politics.

     Bibliography. p.
     Includes index.
        1. Soviet Union—Politics and government—1945-
2. Soviet Union—Social conditions—1970-
3. Soviet Union—Economic conditions—1976-
I. Barner-Barry, Carol.   II. Title.
JN6531.B35 1987   947.085   86-18694
ISBN 0-13-170317-X

Editorial/production supervision and interior design: *Marjorie Borden*
Cover design: *Lundgren Graphics, Ltd.*
Manufacturing buyer: *Barbara Kelly Kittle*

Printed in the United States of America

10   9   8   7   6   5   4   3   2   1

ISBN 0-13-170317-X   01

Prentice-Hall International (UK) Limited, *London*
Prentice-Hall of Australia Pty. Limited, *Sydney*
Prentice-Hall Canada Inc., *Toronto*
Prentice-Hall Hispanoamericana, S.A., *Mexico*
Prentice-Hall of India Private Limited, *New Delhi*
Prentice-Hall of Japan, Inc., *Tokyo*
Prentice-Hall of Southeast Asia Pte. Ltd., *Singapore*
Editora Prentice-Hall do Brasil, Ltda., *Rio de Janeiro*

To Irina

CONTENTS

III ECONOMIC POLITICS

IV PROBLEMS AND POLICIES

PREFACE

In preparing the third edition of this book, we have been impressed with the significant amount of high quality work on the Soviet system that has been published in recent years, both in this country and abroad. This scholarship has helped in the revision; and we have attempted to acknowledge, in the citations, our debt to a wide variety of colleagues.

Although there are many changes in this edition, the basic structure of the book remains the same. We have been gratified by the warm reception of the volume from many people, both students and professionals in the field. While the reader will find some changes in every chapter in the book, most of our effort has concentrated on the chapters about the Party and the government (Chapters 6 and 7) and on Parts III and IV (the six chapters on "Economic Politics" and "Problems and Policies").

Many of the people whose help we acknowledged in the first two editions provided advice and information on this revision. In this regard we would like to mention particularly Oles M. Smolansky, a long-time friend and colleague. Our son Dan used his computer skills to help create the charts found in Chapter 7. The people at Prentice-Hall, especially Liz O'Brien and Marjorie Borden, performed their professional tasks with great skill and thoughtfulness. Stan Wakefield, formerly Political Science Editor at Prentice-Hall, was instrumental in initiating the effort that led to this book, and we remain grateful for his years of encouragement and support. Professor Trond Gilberg of Penn State University reviewed the manuscript. The staffs of the Lehigh University and University of Maryland, Baltimore County, libraries facilitated our research in numerous ways. Word processing and other secretarial help was provided by Dorothy Windish, Chris Baran, Helen Pasquale, Sonya Horton, and Eileen O'Connor.

The book is dedicated to a long-time Russian friend, one of a number of people we have known in the USSR over the years who have helped us to better understand that country.

Donald D. Barry
Carol Barner-Barry

Major Administrative Divisions of the USSR

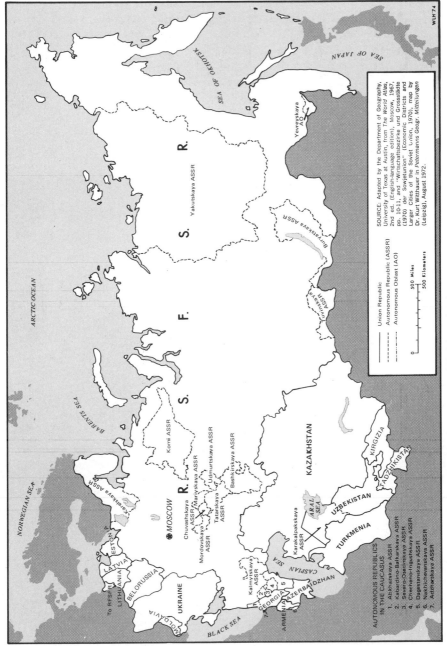

SOURCE: Adapted by the Department of Geography, University of Texas at Austin, from *The World Atlas*, 2nd ed. (English-language edition), Moscow, 1967, pp. 10-11, and "Wirtschaftsbezirke und Grosstädte (1970) der Sowjetunion" (Economic Districts and Larger Cities of the Soviet Union, 1970), map by Dr. Kurt Witthauer in *Petermanns Geogr. Mitteilungen* (Leipzig), August 1972.

Union Republic
Autonomous Republic (ASSR)
Autonomous Oblast (AO)

0   500 Miles
0   500 Kilometers

ARCTIC OCEAN

SEA OF OKHOTSK

SEA OF JAPAN

Yakutskaya ASSR

Buryatskaya ASSR

Yevreyskaya AO

Tuvinskaya ASSR

R. S. F. S. R.

NORWEGIAN SEA

BARENTS SEA

Karelskaya ASSR

Komi ASSR

Chuvashskaya ASSR
Mariyskaya ASSR
Mordovskaya ASSR
Tatarskaya ASSR
Udmurtskaya ASSR
Bashkirskaya ASSR

MOSCOW

To RSFSR
ESTONIA
LATVIA
LITHUANIA
BELORUSSIA
MOLDAVIA
UKRAINE

BLACK SEA

Kalmytskaya ASSR

GEORGIA
ARMENIA
AZERBAIDZHAN

CASPIAN SEA

ARAL SEA

Karakalpakskaya ASSR

KAZAKHSTAN

UZBEKISTAN
TURKMENIA
TADZHIKISTAN
KIRGIZIA

AUTONOMOUS REPUBLICS
IN THE CAUCASUS

1. Abkhazskaya ASSR
2. Kabardino-Balkarskaya ASSR
3. Severo-Osetinskaya ASSR
4. Checheno-Ingushskaya ASSR
5. Dagestanskaya ASSR
6. Nakhichevanskaya ASSR
7. Adzhaskaya ASSR

WLH 74

From *Problems of Communism*, XXIII, No. 3 (May-June 1974), 3, U.S. Information Agency.

xi

1

STALIN'S LAST JOURNEY:
Soviet Political Style

Observers were mildly surprised when Nikita Khrushchev, late in 1961, began again to harass Stalin's ghost. Khrushchev had first attacked his old boss in 1956, three years after the dictator's death. Calling Stalin a few uncomplimentary names, he assailed the "cult of personality" Stalin had built around himself, placed direct responsibility on him for the purge trials of the 1930s, and questioned the military judgment of the heretofore "infallible" leader. This "secret speech" set the tone for further criticism of Stalin by others and ushered in a "thaw," one of the most liberal periods in Soviet history. But at this point Khrushchev merely tarnished Stalin's image; he did not demolish it.

When he returned to the attack in 1961, Khrushchev unleashed (and no doubt engineered) a campaign that was not only intended to obliterate the Stalin *persona* from contemporary Soviet life but also to eliminate him as a factor in Soviet history. Khrushchev's remarks on Stalin, made early in the Twenty-Second Congress of the Soviet Communist Party in 1961, were taken up and expanded upon by succeeding speakers, with new crimes and treacheries constantly being revealed. The climax was reached when Madame Lazurkina, an Old Bolshevik,[1] rose to speak. She said that Lenin lived in her heart and that he had come to her and said that he did not want Stalin lying in state with him, that "it was unpleasant to lie beside Stalin, who had done so much harm to the Party."

It would not require much prescience to predict what would ensue

1

from a statement like this, made at a carefully rehearsed high Party meeting, where nothing occurs by chance.[2] What happened, of course, was that the Party Congress duly adopted a resolution calling for the removal of Stalin's embalmed body from its resting place beside the body of Lenin, where it had been viewed by literally millions of Soviet citizens and foreigners. The resolution was carried out with an efficiency quite remarkable for the usually sluggish Soviet bureaucracy. Early the next morning the crowds of people who gathered outside the Mausoleum found a small sign on a patch of grass in front of the tomb. The Mausoleum was "closed for repairs" (*zakryt na remont*).

For those of us who have lived in Moscow, and perhaps also for Soviet citizens with a sense of irony, this sign evoked a wry laugh.[3] Anyone who has lived and shopped in Moscow has had the frustrating experience of expending considerable time and energy to get to a particular store—only to find it "closed for repairs." This sort of thing can happen anywhere, but in Moscow it happens frequently enough to constitute a substantial source of annoyance. The problem is that a state-run establishment with no particular incentive to please customers can find any number of reasons for suspending regular working hours. Now the same expression was used to signify a basic change in the greatest shrine a communist can visit. The irony of it all was multiplied by the fact that the "repair" in question involved the jettisoning and desanctification of the person who was then the second most important saint of all communism.

By the next morning the deed had been completed. Stalin's body was gone from the tomb, moved to a spot at the foot of the Kremlin Wall, and people were allowed to view the solitary Lenin in the Mausoleum. In place of the granite monolith over the door to the Mausoleum with the insert letters in red stone reading Л Е Н И Н one found another block of granite, identi-
С Т А Л И Н
cal except that the inscription now read merely Л Е Н И Н. Even if the Kremlin stonemasons had been feverishly working overtime on this new stone, it surely would have required more than the available forty-eight hours to create. The removal would have had to be planned considerably in advance of public action. One cannot help wondering if some prescient archivist or janitor, sensing that the Lenin-Stalin Mausoleum was not to be a permanent arrangement, tucked away the stone used during Stalin's lifetime—the stone bearing only the name of Lenin?

In any case, the very act of removing Stalin from the Mausoleum and burying him below the Kremlin Wall reduced him to the mortal status of some of the other minor stars in the communist firmament, such as Dzerzhinsky, Zhdanov, Voroshilov, and the American John Reed.[4] But this was not the end of the process of "desanctification." It was only the beginning of a broad movement to obliterate his likeness and name from the Soviet citizen's awareness. Literally thousands of statues, bas reliefs, paintings, and other representations of Stalin had to be removed from public display, and this proceeded apace.[5] Stalin's image had been particularly ubiquitous in the Moscow subways, one of the proudest symbols of Soviet modernization. For a period of months after all other traces of the man—in the form of statues, paintings, bronze medallions, and the like—had been removed without a trace, a particularly intricate and colorful mosaic of Stalin situated in the ceiling of one of the main subway stations in Moscow was covered with a shroud. Apparently it was labored over by descendants of the masters of Kievan church mosaic work at night during the hours the subway was closed. When at last the mosaic was again displayed, Stalin had been replaced—but not with another identifiable Soviet personage.

The removal of the name of Stalin was—in and of itself—a stupendous undertaking. History books were changed to obliterate all mention of Stalin except when he was blamed for something. Stalingrad became Volgograd and, somewhat less successfully, the Battle of Stalingrad was transformed into "The Battle on the Volga."[6] But there were also the cities of Stalino, Stalinsk, Stalinabad, Stalinogorsk, and Staliniri, that required changed names as well as the urban districts and rural territories, schools, institutes, libraries, and countless other organizations *imeni Stalina* (named for Stalin), his speeches and writings in bookstores and libraries, and even card catalog entries in libraries. All of this and more had to be attended to, to be "normalized" (as the Soviets would put it).

Stalin's image has improved under the post-Khrushchev leadership. A large-scale rehabilitation of Stalin was planned for 1969 and was averted only by significant but private protests by some segments of the Party elite, supported by leaders of influential foreign communist parties.[7] But some members of the Soviet elite, including a number of important Party and military leaders, have continued to work toward a resurrection of the Stalin cult.[8]

Under recent Soviet leaders the Stalin image, if not the cult, has begun reappearing with significant regularity. This seems to be part of a more general effort to temper the rewriting of history that had cast many important Soviet leaders in the role of "nonpersons" after they died, left office, or were purged. Other leaders who have been at least partially rehabilitated include Nikita Khrushchev and Vacheslav Molotov.[9] More recently deceased leaders, such as Brezhnev and Chernenko, have been treated with relative respect. This was particularly apparent at the Twenty-Seventh Congress of the Soviet Communist Party in 1986 during which many of the policies of the Brezhnev era were criticized but Brezhnev himself was not scapegoated. It is important to note with respect to Stalin's rehabilitation, however, that recent publicity has focused on Stalin's revolutionary, military, and economic achievements; his crimes are being ignored. Thus, while older people still remember his atrocities, a significant number of Soviet citizens are—on the basis of this limited picture—making him into a popular hero.

This brief commentary on Stalin's role in Soviet political imagery suggests something about Soviet political style—about the basic political ground rules and the atmosphere in which Soviet politics operates. A number of considerations might be mentioned when discussing Soviet political style, but we will limit ourselves to what we think are the three basic ones. These factors, which are to some extent interrelated, are (1) that Soviet politics is "closed politics," rather than "open politics"; (2) that policy making in the Soviet Union is currently marked by tension between those who would (in the style of Brezhnev) preserve the status quo with only marginal changes and those who advocate more basic reform, especially economic reform; and (3) that the Soviet Union has a political culture organized around the imagery of Lenin. Let us consider these three basic characteristics in greater detail.

The term "political ground rules" was used in the previous paragraph. Some people might object that the Soviet system is one without ground rules. This is simply not true. Every political system that persists has to develop a set of basic understandings regarding how the "game of politics" is to be played. The alternative is anarchy.[10] Although these rules may change over time and although they may differ significantly from those of the Western democracies with which we are most familiar, it is safe to assume that they exist.

At least since Stalin consolidated his power in the late 1920s, Soviet politicians have accepted a primary ground rule: Soviet politics is closed politics.[11] What this means is that important political decisions ("who gets what, when, and how") are made behind the scenes with little or no advance public discussion or opportunity for direct public influence on the upper levels of the Soviet policy-making elite. There may be widespread discussions on policy proposals, such as that which centered around the draft Party Program in late 1985 and early 1986, but such discussions are more ritualistic than substantive, and few, if any, significant changes result. In the case of the draft Party Program, the goal of the public participation encouraged by the leadership seemed to be mainly a psychological one. It was intended to help to mobilize support for the Gorbachev regime's efforts to break the Soviet Union out of a prolonged period of stagnation.

It is from this closed political style that many of the other characteristics of Soviet politics flow: the structure and operations of the Party and the state, the uses to which the media of communication are put, the nature of the electoral and judicial systems, the extent of political participation of individuals and organizations in Soviet society. All of these things are designed to preserve the principle of closed politics. And since closed politics can be better maintained by fewer people than by many, this means that the group that controls the basic policy-making process has to be kept small.

The Soviet system has not always been closed to the same degree. Movement toward a more open discussion of political issues and some rather frank criticisms of shortcomings in the system were aired during the post-Stalin "thaw" periods (roughly 1956 to 1957 and 1961 to 1962). Both of these periods were relatively short and were followed by retrenchment. But even at the peak of the thaw periods there was no basic change in ground rule number one: Final decisions are made behind closed doors. Throughout the post-Khrushchev period right up to the present there has continued to be considerable opportunity for advance public discussion of policy recommendations (especially in less politically sensitive areas). The final decisions, however, are still made by a process removed from public scrutiny.

Several efforts to break out of this pattern have been made over the years, notably in some of the countries of Eastern Europe. For example, in Czechoslovakia in 1968 and in Poland in the early 1980s it looked for a while as though closed politics might be successfully challenged. In both cases, however, the initiatives were ruthlessly suppressed—by Soviet military force in Czechoslovakia and by conservative Polish military force in Poland.[12]

Turning to the second basic factor, a bit of historical discussion will clarify the evolution of the leadership's profound wariness of significant change in the status quo. Policy battles between conservatives and reformers were a feature of the Russian political scene long before the Soviet period. Perhaps the most obvious pre-Soviet case in point is the history of the reign of Peter the Great, who tried to open Russia to the West. Thus, in a basic sense the conservative-reformist tensions we see in the Soviet Union today have deep roots in Russian history.

When focusing on the Soviet period, it is necessary to begin with Lenin's death. Because he did not choose a successor, there took place a struggle for power waged according to the rules of closed politics. Stalin eventually won. The defeated politicians, rather than retiring—perhaps to try again later—were victimized. This victimization took various forms and went through several stages. For the most serious contenders (Trotsky, Zinoviev, Kamenev, Bukharin, and others) it almost invariably resulted in death by unnatural means and condemnation as "traitors," "wreckers," and "enemies of the people." They were blamed for the shortcomings of the Soviet system and, by extension, for the sorry lot of the average Soviet citizen. Victimization cum obliteration was a common fate of opponents or supposed opponents during much of the Stalin period and for a time after his death.

This was, to some degree, a simple reflection of the paranoid aspects of Stalin's personality. But there were also situational factors. Stalin was implementing policies, such as the collectivization of agriculture, that were radical departures from previous policies. Opponents of the new policies could easily be perceived as posing a threat to the success of reforms that Stalin saw as imperative. Why not get rid of them once and for all? This process of scapegoating acquired a momentum of its own and, in a sense, became an accepted method for dealing with political rivals in the Soviet system.

These events are close enough in time to be very real to the contemporary Soviet political elite. The perception of radical reform as diffusely threatening may lurk in the minds of many contemporary Soviet leaders, although no such dramatic scapegoating has taken place since the middle of the 1950s. Defeated or out-of-favor politicians have been allowed to remain alive after their fall from power but have lived in obscurity. The loss of the status and power that come with positions at the top, however, has no doubt been difficult for these former leaders, even though they have been allowed to live comfortable lives.[13] Another case in point that holds a message for contemporary Soviet leaders is the fate of Nikita Khrushchev. In the period from Stalin to Gorbachev, he was the boldest in initiating reforms. To a large extent, his reform efforts led to his ouster in 1964. Critics called him a "harebrained schemer," and his successors abolished most of his reforms.

That the style of closed politics facilitates such political scapegoatism is undeniable. Further, a major flaw in the Soviet system is the lack of any assurance that a top official can retire without loss of status and privileges. These factors create an incentive for those in power to hang on to their positions as long as possible. Staying in power to protect oneself, one's family, and one's associates is better than an insurance policy. Given the sad history of those like Khrushchev, who attempted reforms, there is a reluctance to be overly innovative because major innovations carry with them the possibility of great failures, as well as great victories.

This tendency toward self-protectionism and conservatism is not limited to the top leadership but permeates Soviet society. It is strongly reinforced by a number of other factors.[14] One is the bureaucratic and conservative tradition inherited from tsarist Russia and elaborated under Soviet rule. This has spawned a class of Soviet citizens who have both the desire and the means to defend their positions and privileges. Their imperative to do so is constantly fed by the persistence of the scarcity of goods and services. The deprivation that they desire to avoid is real and visible. Their efforts to protect their stake in the status quo are aided by the tendency of the ideological and propaganda systems to emphasize the felicity and essential rightness of the Soviet way of life. Finally, there is a history in Russia and the USSR of man-made and natural disasters that creates a situation of chronic anxiety on the part of much of the population and leads people to place a high value on security. The purges of the 1930s and the devastation of World War II, for instance, still occupy a large place in the memories of significant numbers of Soviet citizens. Known evils have the virtue of having been around long enough that most people have developed a strategy for adapting. Thus, the Soviet system is, at present, a highly immobile one in which it is difficult for new ideas to gain a foothold.

These factors have led to a certain sense of hopelessness in the Soviet populace in the face of strong indicators that major reforms are necessary. This can be seen in the following comments by three anonymous Soviet citizens made at the time of the Chernenko succession:[15]

> The USSR is in the middle of an economic crisis, although you never hear about it in the press. No matter who takes power, they won't be able to get us out of this mess.

If there were to be any changes for the better in the Soviet Union, it would be little short of miraculous! Admittedly, when someone new comes to power he sometimes throws a bone to the people, but in return he expects to be praised to the skies. . . . It makes no difference at all who takes power; changes are simply not possible . . .

There is no possibility for change in our country. It doesn't matter who is the general secretary [of the USSR Communist Party]. The point is that anyone who would use his power to make changes would not be given that power in the first place.

Still, it is clear that Gorbachev and the other members of the Soviet political elite recognize that some kind of reform, particularly in the economic sector, is of crucial importance. It is equally clear that there are differences within the top leadership regarding the extent and pace of such reform. A compromise currently seems to be in place. Experts are allowed considerable freedom to debate the merits of various reforms—from the marginal to the truly radical. Actual reform efforts, however, usually are approached in an incremental and cautious way.[16] The problems faced by the Soviet government are not the sort that can be dealt with quickly or easily. This, combined with the conservatism regarding change discussed previously, suggests that the debate over reform, as well as experimentation with specific reforms, will characterize the Soviet system for the foreseeable future.

The final ground rule has to do with the political culture of the Soviet Union. It is organized around the cult of Lenin.[17] The Soviet Union is officially atheistic and has a history of creating difficulties for those who choose to espouse some form of religion. There is, however, an official faith of sorts. It is secular, it is tied to the past, and it pervades political and social life. What is that faith? That faith is Lenin.[18]

Never mind that he was another "ends-over-means" politician (although the best the Russians have produced), that he sanctioned the purging of his enemies and instituted the concept within his own Party of equating opposition with disloyalty and, thereby, paved the way for the kind of regime Stalin built. His public image is larger than life and without human fault. It is part of Soviet mythology, propagated by the ideological network to induce the belief that in a truly religious sense Lenin lives on. Posters with a likeness of Lenin carry such slogans as "Lenin Lived, Lenin Lives, Lenin Will Live," "Lenin—more alive than all of the living," and "Lenin Is with Us." Madame Lazurkina, in asking that the body of Stalin be removed from the Mausoleum, said Lenin had recommended this to her.[19] No one took exception to her request or its rationale and, as mentioned, it marked the climax of the campaign to oust Stalin's body.

And then, of course, there is the Lenin Mausoleum itself. This shrine is the symbolic heart of the country (Red Square in front of the Kremlin Wall). Thousands of fervent worshipers come to view the Master—literally hundreds every day the Mausoleum is open. Then, there is the smart honor guard and, in the tomb, the utter silence (except for the muffled shuffling of feet). Lenin himself—his apparently well-preserved body encased in glass—is a spectacle worthy of any religion. What need for religious experience and emotional unity does the embalmed body of the spiritual leader of communism tap among the communist faithful in this atheistic state? It is not coincidental, probably, that the religious tradition of the Russian Orthodox Church provided for the embalming and public viewing of saints and other leaders of the Church.[20]

And if all of this were not enough to convince one of the immortality of Lenin, there is more. In somewhat the same way that the pantheist sees God in the trees and the birds and the very air, Lenin in the Soviet Union is also ubiquitous, albeit in more concrete forms. To illustrate this, let us take you on the trip from the suburban campus of Moscow University to the downtown campus—a trip we made hundreds of times when we were living at the university some years ago. First you would leave your dormitory, situated in a part of Moscow called Lenin Hills, and choose between taking a bus via Lenin Prospect or riding the subway named in honor of Lenin. If you were in a hurry you would opt for the subway, which is quicker. After the university station the first stop is the Lenin Hills stop, located on a bridge high over the Moscow River offering a panoramic view of Lenin Stadium through its huge windows. Since you have a paper to write, you get off at the subway stop "Library Named for Lenin" and enter Lenin Library, the Soviet equivalent to the U.S. Library of Congress. We could go on, but you probably get the picture.

This sense of the eternal Lenin is not accidental, of course, but is based on a long-term and highly orchestrated effort. Shortly after his death an "Immortalization Commission" was created to handle the embalming and to regulate development of the Lenin myth.[21] And even though under Stalin the Lenin cult "grew cold and lifeless" as the glorification of Stalin was enhanced, Khrushchev renewed the myth and "inaugurated the slick and cloying cult of Lenin still in evidence today."[22]

Is so ubiquitous a symbol really meaningful or effective as a counter to the grim realities of the present? For many people probably not. It is one of a number of examples of typical Soviet overkill that the reader will meet in this book. There is a strong tendency among Soviet bureaucrats to carry a good, or at least useful, idea to ridiculous extremes. The people who do this are zealots who have no effective checks on their power. Often the results are counterproductive. But that is another story.

Stalin's "last journey" from the Mausoleum to a patch of ground in front of the Kremlin Wall was, we said, spectacular but representative. It is closed politics in action, and it reinforced a profoundly conservative tendency in Soviet government. In order to understand these factors more fully, let us take a closer look at the Soviet system and how it works.

NOTES

[1]The Old Bolsheviks were members of the Leninist faction of the Communist Party prior to the 1917 Revolution and one of the prime targets of Stalin's purges in the 1930s.

[2]The dissident historian Roy Medvedev claims that Khrushchev took the other leaders by surprise both with his secret speech in 1956 and his renewed attack on Stalin in 1961. Medvedev states that with regard to the latter occasion, "the decision was taken not to broach the subject of Stalin" and when Khrushchev did so, the other speakers at the Twenty-Second Party Congress "hurriedly rewrote their prepared texts." See Roy A. Medvedev, "The Stalin Question," in *The Soviet Union Since Stalin*, eds. Stephen F. Cohen, Alexander Rabinowitch, and Robert Sharlet (Bloomington, IN: Indiana University Press, 1980), pp. 32–49. The quotations are from pp. 41 and 42. A more extended treatment of the subject by Medvedev is *On Stalin and Stalinism* (New York: Oxford University Press, 1979).

[3]See *The Washington Post,* Jan. 6, 1985, p. A25 for the reactions of an American journalist to the *remont* phenomenon.

[4]It took almost nine years, until June 1970, before a simple pillar surmounted by a bust of Stalin was erected to mark his burial place. This development was seen as one of the signs of a partial rehabilitation of Stalin carried out by Khrushchev's successors.

[5]Except in his homeland, the Soviet republic of Georgia. There the power of "hometown boy makes good" kept Stalin's image in public view long after it had been removed from the rest of the Soviet Union.

[6]This has been retransformed into "The Battle of Stalingrad," although the name of the city remains Volgograd. In 1973 *The Battle of Stalingrad* (in Russian) was published by the Lower Volga Publishing House, which is located in Volgograd.

[7]See Medvedev, "The Stalin Question," pp. 45–50.

[8]Ibid.; see also Elena Klepikova and Vladimir Solovyov, "The Secret Russian Party," *Midstream,* 26, No. 8 (Oct. 1980), 14.

[9]Elizabeth Teague, "Molotov Rehabilitated: A New Approach to Soviet History?" *Radio Liberty Research,* No. 262/84, July 5, 1984; Alexander Rahr, "Signs of a Rehabilitation of Nikita Khrushchev," *Radio Liberty Research,* No. 292/84, July 31, 1984. In neither of these cases was the rehabilitation complete. Molotov's reinstatement in the Communist Party, for instance, was not announced in the Soviet Union but was reported in the Italian Communist newspaper *L'Unita.* See *The New York Times,* July 6, 1984, p. A1. On Khrushchev, see *ibid,* Aug. 22, 1984, p. D23.

[10]Phillip Brickman, *Social Conflict: Readings in Rule Structures and Conflict Relationships.* (Lexington, MA: D. C. Heath, 1974).

[11]"Closed politics" could no doubt be traced to an earlier point in Soviet history, but this will not be undertaken here.

[12]A liberalization of similar proportions might have been underway in Hungary in 1956, but its duration prior to the Soviet invasion was much shorter.

[13]Michael Vozlensky,*Nomenklatura: The Soviet Ruling Class* (New York: Doubleday, 1984), p. 35.

[14]Stephen F. Cohen, "The Friends and Foes of Change: Reformism and Conservatism in the Soviet Union," *The Soviet Polity in the Modern Era,* eds. Erik P. Hoffmann and Robbin F. Laird (New York: Aldine, 1984), pp. 85–104.

[15]Elizabeth Teague, "Soviet Citizens' Perceptions of the Andropov and Chernenko Accessions to Power," *Radio Liberty Research,* No. 250/84, June 25, 1984.

[16]A notable exception seems to be the drive against alcoholism.

[17]For a more extended treatment of this topic see: Nina Tumarkin, *Lenin Lives! The Lenin Cult in Soviet Russia.* (Cambridge, MA: Harvard University Press, 1983).

[18]Ibid., pp. 1–23, and *The Washington Post,* Sept. 23, 1984, p. C5.

[19]The name Lazurkina suggests interesting but certainly unintentional parallels with the biblical Lazarus. Lazurkina in a sense "rose from the dead" like Lazarus in returning from years in a Stalinist prison camp to initiate the call for Stalin's final disgrace.

[20]Peter Wiles's discussion of this point and of the general matter of Lenin's immortality is especially relevant here. Wiles discusses Lenin in the context of what he concludes is "an inordinate interest in physical immortality on earth: much deeper in both theory and practice" in Russia and the Soviet Union than elsewhere. He states that the embalming and public viewing of Lenin is attributable to Stalin, "the pupil of the seminary, the self-constituted repository of Great Russian tradition," who "insisted on burying him like an Orthodox saint." "On Physical Immortality," *Survey*, Nos. 56 and 57 (Jul. and Oct. 1965). The quotations are from No. 56, p. 127, and No. 57, p. 159.

[21]For example, the Immortalization Commission in 1924 prohibited the display of Lenin's likeness on candy wrappers and other labels. This was done after complaints about a cigarette package carrying Lenin's portrait that when dropped on the pavement resulted in pedestrians "unwittingly stepping on Lenin's face." This example and other information in this passage is from Tumarkin, *Lenin Lives!* p. 237.

[22]Ibid, p. 206.

SELECTED BIBLIOGRAPHY

BINYON, MICHAEL, *Life in Russia*. New York: Pantheon Books, 1983.

BYRNES, ROBERT F., ed., *After Brezhnev: Sources of Soviet Conduct in the 1980s*. Bloomington, IN: Indiana University Press, 1983.

HOFFMANN, ERIK P., ed., *The Soviet Union in the 1980s*. New York: The Academy of Political Science, 1984.

———, and ROBBIN R. LAIRD, eds., *The Soviet Polity in the Modern Era*. New York: Aldine, 1984.

KLOSE, KEVIN, *Russia and the Russians: Inside the Closed Society*. New York: W. W. Norton & Co., 1984.

SHIPLER, DAVID K., *Russia: Broken Idols, Solemn Dreams*. New York: New York Times Books, 1983.

TUMARKIN, NINA, *Lenin Lives! The Lenin Cult in Soviet Russia*. Cambridge, MA: Harvard University Press, 1983.

VOZLENSKY, MICHAEL, *Nomenklatura: The Soviet Ruling Class*. New York: Doubleday, 1984.

2

HISTORICAL FACTORS:
The Soviet Political Heritage

Why is closed politics the basic identifying characteristic of the current Soviet political system? There are many ways of approaching this question and one of the most obvious is the historical. How did the Soviet Union get to where it is today? Given this perspective, much of the explanation is to be found in the persons who fashioned Soviet Russia, their beliefs, and their actions. It is from them that the present system evolved. But the Soviet system was not a complete break with the past, no matter how much its originators claimed that it was. They themselves were products of the Russian political tradition and were influenced by it. Much of contemporary Soviet politics has some relationship to the nature of Russian politics as it developed in the centuries before the October Revolution of 1917.

To note this relationship is not an argument in favor of historical determinism. That is to say, it should not be asserted that the Soviet Union was somehow "destined" to evolve as it has because of inevitable historical forces pushing it in a certain direction. The historian's understanding of history is not complete enough to allow the explanation of historical developments with that degree of precision. Willful human behavior *can* affect social and historical developments; we are not merely prisoners of our past or of inevitable historical forces. Nor are we saying that the present Soviet Union is merely pre-Revolutionary Russia in contemporary guise. The French have a saying, *Plus ça change, plus c'est la même chose*" ("the more things change, the more they stay the same"). Popularizers of history use this idea as the starting point for theories about historical developments, and the concept has been widely applied to Russia and the Soviet Union.

What we *are* saying is that there are certain factors in Russia's past that have predisposed her to develop in the way she has rather than in a way more typical of most of modern Western Europe. This is not the place to attempt a comprehensive analysis of Russian history. Many thorough studies of the relation of the Russian past to the Soviet present are listed in the bibliography at the end of the chapter. What we will do in the short space of this chapter is to sketch the broad outlines of the historical factors that are particularly relevant to the way Soviet politics has developed.

Recorded history in the territory of Russia dates from the ninth century. Kievan Rus, as the state was known, was a feudal state in every way. Its main outside contacts were not with feudal Europe, however, but with the Byzantine Empire in what is now modern Turkey. Byzantine influence on Russia was pervasive and strong. Its legacy included the Cyrillic alphabet (rather than the Latin alphabet used in Western Europe); the imperial title of "tsar," a corruption of "Caesar"; Orthodox Christianity; and the concept of the God-Emperor, who combined in his person the authority of the Pope and the Emperor. After the seat of the Byzantine Empire, Constantinople, fell to the Turks in the fifteenth century, the Grand Dukes of Moscow proclaimed their city the "Third Rome," asserted leadership of the Orthodox Church, and adopted the Byzantine double-headed eagle, which became the symbol of Russia's tsars.

In the meantime, the state of Kievan Rus had been destroyed in the thirteenth century by the Mongol invaders who maintained their control for the next two centuries. Under this particularly cruel despotism the Moscow princes emerged to prominence as the tribute collectors for the Mongol-Tatar overlords. The Moscow princes treated their subjects, and the other princes of Russia over whom they gained influence, with the same barbarism they had come to expect in dealing with the Mongol-Tatar khans.

Ivan III finally overthrew the khans in 1480 and established Moscow's control over wide areas of Russia. His rule was marked by a strong centralization of control and the use of force against any challengers to his authority. These characteristics were, to a greater or lesser extent, typical of the reigns of all his successors.

Russia thus emerged from two hundred years of Mongol domination that had reinforced the Byzantine inclination toward centralism and autocracy. It had been cut off for centuries from contact with Western Europe, missing in particular the liberating effects of the Renaissance and the Reformation. The latter was particularly important in that it stimulated the questioning of authority as an outgrowth of the development of conflict between church and state. This questioning, in turn, led Western Europe down a path basically different from that of Russia, where authoritarian absolutism and a church in the service of the state existed right up until the time of the 1917 Revolution.

The centralized autocracy of the tsars was not accompanied by notable predictability in succession to the throne, even after the establishment of the Romanov dynasty in 1613. Heirs often were eliminated as more powerful contenders seized power. To take the eighteenth century as an example, the century began during the reign of Peter the Great, who ruled from 1682 to 1725. It ended with the reigns of Catherine the Great (1762 to 1796) and her son Paul (1796 to 1801). Between these two periods, as Sidney Harcave has put it, there were "six rulers, three female and three male. Of the women, the first was amiable but incapable, the second neither amiable nor capable, and the third reasonably acceptable. Of the males, the first was a child, the second an infant, and the third an adult with the personality of a child."[1] What is equally interesting to note is the means of accession and the fates of these rulers. Like Ivan the Terrible, Peter the Great had slain his son, so there was no clear heir to the throne. Peter's second wife Catherine, who had been a peasant girl from Livonia on the Baltic Sea, seized power by force and held it until she died in 1727. She was succeeded by Peter's grandson, twelve-year-old Peter II, who died of smallpox three years later. Then came Peter's niece Anna, who died in 1740, to be succeeded by her six-week-old grandnephew Ivan VI. The latter was dethroned and later murdered by Peter's daughter Elizabeth, who was succeeded in 1762 by her nephew, a German prince crowned as Peter III. He was dethroned six months later by his wife—who became Catherine the Great—and was murdered in prison by friends of Catherine. The century was ended under the reign of Catherine's inept son Paul, who was strangled by high officials in his own court in 1801.

The nineteenth century saw greater regularity in succession to the throne. But this century of revolutions was not a calm one for Russia, nor one in which stability of political development could be achieved. There were only five more tsars. None of them could be called enlightened, with the possible exception of Alexander II, the "reforming tsar" who had emancipated the serfs and effected other reforms in the early part of his reign. Subsequently, he pursued reactionary policies until he was assassinated by a terrorist bomb in 1881.

The instability of succession in the eighteenth century hardly permitted the kind of continuity and calm necessary for the gradual development of constitutional traditions or popular institutions. And, indeed, no effective opposition to the monarchy developed during the eighteenth century. As early as 1550 Ivan the Terrible had established the *Zemsky Sobor* (Assembly of the Land), an assembly of lesser nobility, clergy, and urban bourgeoisie. Although it possessed only meager powers, it did succeed in limiting the authority of the boyars, powerful nobles who were contending with the tsars for ascendancy. It also was instrumental in electing Michael, the first of the Romanovs, as tsar in 1613. Thereafter its power declined, and it was eventually abolished by Peter the Great.

Peter, in his effort to westernize and modernize the autocracy, created a bureaucratic system founded on merit and established an Imperial Governing Senate, a body that was designed to serve in the capacity of an executive cabinet. But none of Peter's reforms pointed in the direction of popular representation. Elective city councils *(dumas)* were established in 1785 under Catherine the Great. The conditions for representation and voting were severely restricted to the more affluent classes, and the *dumas* constituted no important reform.

Shortly after the emancipation of the serfs in 1861, Alexander II signed a law establishing the *zemstvo,* an assembly for rural self-government. It provided for indirect and unequal suffrage and was deliberately weighted to allow the nobility to dominate. But, in spite of their shortcomings, the *zemstvos* provided popular initative for change, and their accomplishments in such areas as primary education, health, and the application of progressive argicultural techniques were impressive. In later years the powers of the *zemstvos* were reduced, however, and the proportion of noble representation was increased. *Zemstvo* meetings held in secret were broken up by the police, with repressive action taken against *zemstvo* leaders. This promising reform was thus gradually neutralized by the reactionary forces in power, in spite of its positive accomplishments in a number of areas.

What we have described so far is a picture of Russian political developments extending well into the nineteenth century and exhibiting two basic characteristics: first, a repressive autocratic tradition based on despotic political rule with roots traceable not to Western Europe but to the Byzantine Empire and two centuries of Mongol hegemony in Russia; and second, growing out of this tradition, an uncongenial atmosphere for the development of self-government at a time when movement in this direction had become well established in the West.

A small number of foreign observers wrote about life in Russia during this period, and some of them commented on these two broad characteristics. Perhaps the most well known is the Marquis de Custine, a French nobleman who traveled through Russia in 1839. Custine's sketch of Russia *(Journey for Our Time,* first published in 1843) parallels the work of his countryman Alexis de Tocqueville on the United States a few years earlier *(Democracy in America,* first published in 1835), although Tocqueville's analysis is much more flattering to its subject. Custine relates that he "went to Russia in search of arguments against representative government" but "returned from Russia a partisan of constitutions." He admires the picturesque sights of Moscow, Petersburg, and Nizhni Novgorod; comments favorably on the beauty of Russian churches, particularly St. Basil's in Moscow; characterizes Russians as a "naturally engaging people"; and praises their intelligence, adroitness, and ingenuity. But on matters political his comments are almost unrelievedly negative. They often relate to the particular implications for everyday life of the despotism and lack of self-government then prevailing. He returns again and again to themes such as Russia's insulation from the outside world and its suspicion of foreigners, coupled with attempts to show outsiders a false picture of conditions. He notes an absence of personal liberty and the repression of all opposition (by, among other means, declaring dissidents to be insane and incarcerating them). There are the familiar prevalence of police officials and government informers and the all-pervasive secrecy engendered by the regime, which prevents official discussion of accidents and disasters and discourages Russians from talking with strangers. Finally, Custine comments on the necessity of people to lie, feign, and dissimulate in the course of their everyday lives and the attempt of the government to dominate everything.[2] A good case can be made, then, that a significant part of Soviet political culture can be traced to the political situation in mid-nineteenth century Russia and earlier.

Integrally connected with the characteristics of despotism and an absence of representative institutions is a third great theme of Russian history which manifested itself conspicuously in the nineteenth and early twentieth centuries: the development of a revolutionary tradition growing out of frustration with the apparent impossibility of effecting change by peaceful means. The Decembrist Revolt in 1825 is an early milestone. This attempt to replace Nicholas I by his brother Constantine, accompanied by the demand for a constitution, was put down by force. The prominent leaders of the revolt were hanged. More relevant, perhaps, is the anarchism that developed in the middle years of the nineteenth century. The strands of intellectual movements in Russia during this period are many and complex, but among them were elements of populism *(narodnichestvo)*, some adherents of which became committed to insurrectionary means in desperation over the failure of other methods. A terrorist organization known as People's Will *(Narodnaia Volia)* emerged in the 1870s with the aim of assassinating government officials. Its successes included the killing or wounding of a number of important persons, among them Tsar Alexander II in 1881. The members of the movement genuinely believed that the "revolution of the deed" would lead to popular uprisings which would, in turn, overthrow the old regime. Instead, their efforts brought even more severe repression from the government, and the resistance movements were driven further underground.

A major instrument in effecting this repression was the political police. Though theoretically a part of the bureaucracy, this "eyes and ears of the emperor" in fact operated largely independently and without check. A strong political police force dates from 1826, when Nicholas I created the notorious "Third Section" (of the tsar's Imperial Chancellery) in reaction to the Decembrist Revolt of the previous year. Its agents were everywhere, watching other government officials, regular citizens, and foreigners; attempting to infiltrate dissident organizations; supervising political prisons and places of exile. Later placed in the Ministry of Interior and called the *Okhrana,* the autonomous political police became an important instrument of all succeeding tsars. This reliance on secret-police methods was learned by the Bolsheviks in their experiences with the tsarist *Okhrana*. Its carry-over into the post-Revolutionary period under various titles* was a logical consequence of the political battles the Bolsheviks fought to gain power.[3]

A notable event in the late nineteenth century struggle between the tsarist regime and its opponents was the execution in 1887 of a member of the People's Will, Alexander Ulyanov, for participation in a plot to assassinate Alexander III. The conspiracy had been detected and foiled by the *Okhrana*. Ulyanov's younger brother Vladimir later took the name Lenin and became the founder of the Soviet Union. Lenin is said to have understood from his brother's fate that the terroristic approach of the People's Will was doomed to failure. Out of this came his more systematic efforts to effect change based on the writings on Marx and Engels.

The works of Marx began to be translated into Russian shortly before Lenin's birth in 1870. The first Russian Marxist organization was founded in 1883 by Georgii Plekhanov, a former populist, and others. Lenin became a Marxist during the following decade and visited Plekhanov in exile in Geneva in 1895. Later that year, after his return to Russia, Lenin was arrested for subversive activities and spent the next four-and-one-half years in prison and Siberian exile. Such incarceration and exile was a common fate of Russian revolutionaries. Infiltration of revolutionary movements by police agents and informers—leading to the arrest of movement leaders— was frequent. Lenin's understanding of this problem no doubt reinforced his determination to establish a movement based on a small group of professional revolutionaries working in secret in order to minimize the chances for infiltration.

Though at first considered a follower of Plekhanov, Lenin later broke with him and other older Russian Marxists over several important matters of doctrinal interpretation and Party organization. On the latter, Lenin advocated not a mass parliamentary party but an elite core of revolutionaries who could seize power. They would then organize a "dictatorship of the proletariat" on behalf of the workers. His famous and oft-quoted passages in the 1902 pamphlet "What Is To Be Done?" contain the essence of Lenin's views. He said that "no revolutionary movement can endure without a stable organization of leaders maintaining continuity" and that because of the need to combat the government and the political police, "such an organization must consist chiefly of people professionally engaged in revolutionary activity" and "must perforce be not very extensive and must be as secret as possible." Lenin returned again and again to the ingredients of small size and secrecy, holding that the latter element could never be achieved by a mass organization. In another passage he proposed "to concentrate all secret functions in the hands of as small a number of professional revolutionaries

---

*The Soviet secret police have gone under the following names: Cheka (1917–1922), GPU (1922–1923), OGPU (1923–1934), NKVD (1934–1938), NKVD/NKGB (1938–1945), MVD/MGB (1945–1954) and KGB (1954–present).

as possible."[4] Finally, Lenin felt that the party must act with unity, not divisively. For this purpose, he formalized the concept of "democratic centralism," which prohibited dissent from established party policy.

Thus, the main elements were an elite party of professional revolutionaries whose policies are adopted in secret behind a façade of complete unity. Under vastly different conditions in the 1980s, one can still recognize these elements in the mode of operation of the Soviet political system.

Revolutionary agitation continued after the turn of the century, culminating in the Revolution of 1905. Although finally put down, the Revolution, combined with the Russian defeat in the war with Japan, led a frightened tsar to issue the October Manifesto (1905). This document promised the establishment of a popular assembly or *Duma,* a constitution, and free rights of political participation.

To balance the *Duma,* a Council of State was created as an upper house, half of whose members were appointed by the tsar. No proposal of the *Duma* could become law without the approval of both the Council of State and the tsar. The tsar's ministers in the Council of Ministers were responsible only to him. Although the beginnings of constitutional government had been created, the balance of power still lay strongly on the side of the monarch.

When the first *Duma,* elected in 1906, clashed with the tsar's ministers and outspokenly advocated further reforms, the tsar dissolved it. The same fate met the second *Duma,* convened the next year. Before elections for the third *Duma* were held, the tsar unilaterally changed the electoral law to reduce the electorate and further favor the propertied classes over other voters. This *Duma* (1908 to 1912) and its successor (1912 to 1917) were much more conservative in composition. But the efforts of minor parties, particularly the Constitutional Democrats or Cadets, to criticize the government and fight inefficiency led to hope in some circles that a genuine constitutional monarchy might yet evolve.

A severe blow to this hope was the First World War, which proved to be a military disaster for Russia. The fourth *Duma* looked into the incompetence of the government in prosecuting the war, but its proposals for wide-ranging reforms were ignored. Exhausted by the war, with widespread food shortages, transportation difficulties, and other disruptions at home, the country drifted toward anarchy. Great crowds of striking workers filled the streets of Petrograd (formerly St. Petersburg, later to be Leningrad) in early and mid-March 1917, and when troops employed to disperse the crowds decided to join the demonstrators, a critical point in the Revolution was reached. The *Duma* had again been ordered dissolved by the tsar, but it elected a temporary committee to aid in the restoration of order. This temporary committee, on securing the abdication of the tsar, formed the Provisional Government, which attempted to assert its authority in the country. However, it was overthrown by the Bolsheviks, the wing of the Russian Social Democratic Labor Party led by Lenin, later in the year. It should be emphasized that neither the March Revolution nor the abdication of the tsar had been engineered by the Bolsheviks. Their leaders, including Lenin himself, were in exile or prison at the time.

During the early days of the March Revolution, soviets, or local revolutionary councils, were established across Russia. The most important of these was in Petrograd. The soviets included representation from various sectors of the populace and were very different in character from the middle-class Provisional Government with which they were at odds almost from the start. Alexander Kerensky, the Vice-Chairman of the Petrograd Soviet and a member of the Social Revolutionary Party, joined the Provisional Government to handle liaison with the Petrograd Soviet. He was the Provisional Government's only socialist and was to become its last head. The Provisional Government chose to continue Russia's participation in World War I, which brought it considerable condemnation at home. This, combined with its ineffectuality in coping with urgent economic problems and demands for reform, helped spell its end. The Bolshevik strategy was to gain control of the soviets and thereby oust the Provisional Government. In August, General Kornilov, the army commander, attempted to overthrow the government, abolish the soviets, and establish a right-wing government. The attempt was repulsed, but only with the help of revolutionary troops and a union of the various parties in the Petrograd Soviet. This further divided those who had supported the Provisional Government. When the Bolsheviks moved to take power by force in November,* the Provisional Government was too weak to resist successfully. Power came to the Bolsheviks not so much because they had widespread popular support but because the majority had lost confidence in the Provisional Government.

After gaining power the Bolsheviks still had to face several years of bitter civil war against a combination of forces bent on their overthrow. And because after the March 1917 Revolution they had clamored so vociferously for a constituent assembly, they felt compelled to hold elections shortly after the seizure of power. The Bolsheviks gained only 25 percent of the vote in the election; after one day, when they were unable to compel the constituent assembly to do their bidding, armed guards under their control closed the session. Thus ended the only genuinely elected legislative body during the whole period of Soviet rule.

Clearly, then, the Bolshevik leaders took power by force and were determined to maintain it that way. Little in the background of Lenin or his comrades—or, for that matter, in the prevailing currents of Russian history—pointed in the direction of the establishment of a liberal democracy. Lenin purported to believe in mass participation; he once remarked that "every cook must learn to administer the state." However, this would clearly be *controlled* participation under the leadership of the elite band of

---

*By the old Russian (Julian) calendar the Revolution occurred in October. The Bolsheviks soon adopted the Gregorian Calendar used in the West. But in the Soviet Union it is still referred to as the October Revolution.

Bolsheviks. Such mass participation has been a characteristic of the political and social system that survives to the present day, but it has little in common with democracy as the term is generally understood.

So the Bolsheviks brought with them in their accession to power the practices learned from their long years of conspiratorial struggle against the tsarist adversary. In the absence of an alternative tradition of open, pluralistic politics, this mode of operation has maintained its dominance right up to the 1980s. The scholar-diplomat George Kennan brilliantly analyzed the importance of this heritage for this system. Noting the lack of accountability or of formal procedures for establishing authority, Kennan observed that these faults were compounded by the absence of "a clear code of personal and collegial ethics" to which the leaders might have referred in solving the problems of personality and issue conflict that faced them in administering the state. The "traditional rules of revolutionary ethics," he stated, were deficient for men in power. Thus, after destroying the edifice of the tsarist state and the political forces of the center and the right (to some extent this struggle continued until the end of the civil war in 1921), the Bolshevik leaders turned to eliminating the other revolutionary socialist parties, the Mensheviks and the Social Revolutionaries, and then to victimizing their members. So the code of ethics of the revolutionary period, which had implied fair treatment of other revolutionaries of the left since they were fighting a common enemy, now was narrowed to the Bolsheviks alone. But it didn't stop there. Asks Kennan, "[i]f the Socialist-Revolutionary deserved death, what did the Bolshevik deserve who leaned to Socialist-Revolutionary or Menshevik, or other unacceptable views?" This question was not answered in Lenin's lifetime, though he suggested forebodings of trouble in his famous "Testament," written in late 1922 and early 1923, when he recommended that Stalin be removed from the post of General Secretary of the Party because he had accumulated immense power and because of his rudeness toward comrades. The matter of whether it is permissible to apply the death penalty to Party comrades was settled at the end of 1934 when Stalin arranged the murder of Kirov and set off the period of the great purges.[5]

The period of political murder ended soon after Stalin's death, and discredited leaders began to be treated in a milder fashion. A debate has gone on for years as to whether Stalinism was a logical outgrowth of the system Lenin had created or some terrible aberration. In defending the latter point, for instance, the dissident Soviet historian Roy Medvedev, a Leninist, has written that "[i]t was an historical accident that Stalin, the embodiment of all the worst elements in the Russian revolutionary movement, came to power after Lenin, the embodiment of all that was best."[6] Certainly nothing dictated that a person of Stalin's paranoid mentality *had* to succeed Lenin. But as Western biographers of the latter have shown, Lenin did not eschew terror and the murder of opponents of the Bolsheviks.[7] And, to maintain Bolshevik control in a country facing increasing unrest due to economic difficulties, he engineered changes in intra-Party practices that effectively eliminated opposition voices in the name of Party unity and paved the way for the victimization of opponents. Resolutions drafted by Lenin and adopted at the Tenth Party Congress in 1921 in effect forbade the existence of factions within the Party and seriously limited freedom of criticism. There is evidence that secret-police methods began to be used against intra-Party opposition almost immediately thereafter.[8] In other words, Lenin laid the basis for the end of intra-Party democracy. It was only a short step from the tactics Lenin condoned to the practices Stalin employed after the former's departure from the scene.

Leaders since Stalin have avoided his excesses in the treatment of opponents. But they have been unwilling to question the Leninist principles that provided the touchstone for Stalinist rule. These principles have proved invaluable in providing an organizational framework for the maintenance of oligarchical rule.

NOTES

[1]Sidney Harcave, *Russia: A History* (Chicago: Lippincott, 1953), p. 88.

[2]The edition of Custine used here is *Journal for Our Time: The Russian Journals of the Marquis De Custine*, trans. and ed. Phyllis Penn Kohler (Chicago: Henry Regnery Co., 1951). The quotations are from pp. 23 and 148. The particular traits mentioned as being ascribed to Russia by Custine may be found throughout the book; particularly useful references are on pp. 57–68, 97, 151–52, 265, 332–33, 339–40, 352–53, and 372. For a commentary on the parallels between the Russia of Custine's day and the twentieth-century Soviet Union, see Walter Bedell Smith's Introduction to Kohler's edition, pp. 7–20.

[3]The most complete analysis of the political police of the Russian and Soviet periods is Ronald Hingley, *The Russian Secret Police* (New York: Simon and Schuster, 1970).

[4]V. I. Lenin, *Collected Works* (Moscow: Foreign Languages Publishing House, 1961), V, 452–53 and 464.

[5]George Kennan, "Introduction," in Boris I. Nicolaevsky, *Power and the Soviet Elite*, ed. Janet D. Zagoria (New York: Holt, Rinehart & Winston, 1966), pp. xiv–xvii.

[6]Roy A. Medvedev, *Let History Judge: The Origins and Consequences of Stalinism*, trans. Colleen Taylor, ed. David Joravsky and George Haupt (New York: Knopf, 1971), p. 362.

[7]See, e.g., Louis Fischer, *The Life of Lenin* (New York: Harper and Row Publishers, Inc., 1964), pp. 20–21, 247–48, 278, 375 and passim.; David Shub, *Lenin* (Garden City, NY: Doubleday, 1948), pp. 303–11; Robert Conquest, *V.I. Lenin* (New York: Viking, 1972), pp. 98–102.

[8]On these points see Leonard Schapiro, *The Origin of Communist Autocracy* (Cambridge, MA: Harvard University Press, 1960), pp. 322–23, 334–36, 358–60.

SELECTED BIBLIOGRAPHY

BROWN, ARCHIE, and others, eds., *The Cambridge Encyclopedia of Russia and the Soviet Union.* Cambridge: Cambridge University Press, 1982.

CARRÈRE D'ENCAUSSE, HÉLÈNE, *A History of the Soviet Union*, 2 vols. London: Longman, 1982.

CLARKSON, JESSE D., *A History of Russia*, 2nd ed. New York: Random House, 1969.

CUSTINE, MARQUIS DE, *Journey for Our Time: The Russian Journals of the Marquis De Custine*, trans. and ed. Phyllis Penn Kohler. Chicago: Henry Regnery Co., 1951.

DANIELS, ROBERT V., *The Roots of Confrontation*. Cambridge, MA: Harvard University Press, 1985.

DMYTRYSHYN, BASIL, *USSR: A Concise History*, 3rd ed. New York: Scribner, 1978.

DZIEWANOWSKI, M.K., *A History of Soviet Russia*. Englewood Cliffs, NJ: Prentice-Hall, 1979.

HARCAVE, SIDNEY, *Russia: A History*. Chicago: Lippincott, 1953.

HINGLEY, RONALD, *The Russian Secret Police*. New York: Simon and Schuster, 1970.

———, *The Tsars, 1533–1917*. New York: Macmillan, 1968.

MCCAULEY, MARTIN, *The Soviet Union since 1917*. London: Longman, 1981.

MCKENZIE, DAVID, and MICHAEL W. CURRAN, *A History of Russia and the Soviet Union*. Homewood, IL: Dorsey Press, 1982.

PIPES, RICHARD, *Russia Under the Old Regime*. New York: Scribner, 1974.

RAUCH, GEORG VON, *History of Soviet Russia*, 6th rev. ed. New York: Holt, Rinehart & Winston, 1972.

RIASANOVSKY, NICHOLAS, *A History of Russia*, 2nd ed. New York: Oxford University Press, 1969.

SCHAPIRO, LEONARD, *The Origin of Communist Autocracy*. Cambridge, MA: Harvard University Press, 1955.

———, *The Russian Revolutions of 1917: The Origins of Modern Communism*. New York: Basic Books, 1984.

TREADGOLD, RONALD W., *Twentieth Century Russia*. Chicago: Rand McNally, 1964.

ULAM, ADAM, *A History of Soviet Russia*. New York: Holt, Rinehart & Winston, 1976.

WESSON, ROBERT, *Lenin's Legacy: The Story of the CPSU*. Stanford, CA: Hoover Institution Press, 1978.

WOLFE, BERTRAM D., *Three Who Made a Revolution*, 4th rev. ed. New York: Dial Press, 1964.

3

AN OFFICIAL IDEOLOGY:
Does It Make Any Difference?

The main issue to be raised in this chapter is simple to state: What role does ideology play in contemporary Soviet politics? The answer is not nearly as easy to supply. In fact, it can be argued that it is impossible to supply, because it is impossible to read the minds of the Soviet leadership or survey any reasonable sample of the Soviet populace. We can look at what the leaders say, compare it to what they do, and try to come to some conclusions about the extent to which their actions were influenced by the ideological precepts that they continually enunciate. But reasonable persons can, and do, differ in their conclusions on this point. Correspondingly, we can talk to those Soviet citizens who are accessible to us, but we cannot know whether what they say is typical or even if they are being honest with us. Thus, of all the aspects of Soviet politics that attract the attention of Western writers, none has been less satisfactorily treated than ideology—in spite of the fact that the amount of scholarly and journalistic writing on the subject is enormous.

Why, one may ask, should I care about the relationship of ideology to politics? If we examine political *action* with sufficient care, we ought to find out a good deal about how the Soviet political system operates. True enough. And such an approach is sufficient—if one is not tempted to ask "why?" as well as "how?" But to limit attention to the "how?" is more of a problem in the study of the Soviet Union than it would be in a study of many other countries. This is because the Soviet Union has an "official ideology," an authoritatively approved set of political ideas to which all Soviet citizens are supposed to subscribe. This set of ideas not only provides the framework for current political behavior, but it is also said to contain within it the key to understanding the future development of societies, that is, it has predictive value as well. An authoritative Soviet source describes these two features succinctly:

> The Marxist science of the laws of social development enables us not only to chart a correct path through the labyrinth of social contradictions, but to predict the course events will take, the direction of historical progress and the next stage of social advance . . .[1]

The source adds elsewhere that "Marxist Leninist theory is not a dogma but a *guide to action*."[2] One can see, then, the much greater importance ascribed to ideology in Soviet politics than is common in Western politics.

One may not agree that political ideas in the Soviet Union are all that important: Most non-Marxist Western scholars are dubious about the predictive value of Marxian ideas; even Soviet leaders acknowledge occasionally that citizen behavior does not always measure up to ideological exhortations. But Soviet spokespersons continue to maintain the overriding importance of ideology. This makes it necessary to examine the relevance of ideology to elite and mass beliefs and actions and to determine the functions it serves in the Soviet system.

THE OFFICIAL NATURE OF SOVIET IDEOLOGY

Much scholarly effort has been expended on defining and discussing the term ideology, and a great deal of disagreement surrounds its use.[3] The vagueness and lack of accepted definition of the term has led some writers to discard it entirely in favor of "belief system," "value system," or other expressions. We have not chosen this alternative both because ideology is the term that Soviet writers themselves use and because it is so pervasive in the writings of Western analysts of Soviet politics.

We referred earlier to a political ideology as a "set of political ideas." A more elaborate definition would be "a belief system that explains and justifies a preferred political order for society, either existing or proposed, and offers a strategy (processes, institutional arrangements, programs) for its attainment."[4] This definition is somewhat open-ended, in that one could consider under it a *personal* belief system ("my ideology," "x's ideology") or a broader concept embracing the prevailing belief system of a whole class, race, or nation. Although the collective connotation of ideology embodies the more common usage of the term, the word is employed in both ways in the West. The American political scientist Robert Lane, for instance, in his book *Political Ideology*, "undertook to discover the latent political ideology of the American urban common man" through in-depth interviews with fifteen American males. He describes ideologies as "group beliefs that individuals borrow."[5] The Soviet conception of ideology, by contrast, emphasizes the term's broader application. The authoritative *Political Dictionary* defines ideology as "the totality of political, legal, moral, religious, artistic, and philosophical views which express the interests of one or another class." Ideology arises, the *Political Dictionary* continues, "as a reflection of the conditions of the material life of the society and of the interests of certain classes . . . The ideology of the working class and its party is Marxism-Leninism—the revolutionary weapon in the struggle for the overthrow of the exploitative system and the building of communism."[6]

Thus, Marxism-Leninism is the "official" ideology of the Soviet Union, the lone repository of permissible political thought in the orthodox Soviet belief system. All political systems to some extent possess an official ideology of this kind. The difference is a matter of degree. In Western countries, we like to think that the political ideas that individuals subscribe to are freely arrived at. Although research in political psychology, particularly that having to do with socialization and peer-group influences, might cast doubts on this belief, at least we can say that there is a considerable difference in the amount of effort expended by Western governments as compared with the Soviet Union to inculcate an approved set of political ideas. The official Soviet ideology is an "imposed" ideology, which is impressed upon the citizenry with a thoroughness that has no parallel in the West. Is this imposition successful? To answer that question we would have to determine what the aims of ideological imposition are, that is, the functions the ideology is designed to perform. This is a matter to which we will return at the end of the chapter. But for the present we can say that a great many citizens appear to accept the official ideology as the basis for their political judgments. Yet it is equally clear that a considerable number do not. Most obviously, this can be seen in some of the statements that emanate from the dissident movement. It also can be seen in official complaints about the "highlifeism" and cynicism of Soviet youth.[7] Ideological indoctrination may have considerable influence, but it does not completely blanket out competing ideas.

In any case, it should be clear by now that there are two aspects of the concept of ideology that we have been discussing: the set of political ideas a person *has,* and the set of ideas that some outside source, in this case Soviet political authority, is trying to impose.

How does one acquire an ideology? The briefest answer is "through socialization," that is, through one's life experiences, those events by which one comes to understand one's place and role in society. Along with such understanding comes a set of attitudes toward life, society, and politics. Some of this socialization takes place informally, perhaps even unconsciously, "through the skin." For example, a person builds up attitudes toward authority on the basis of treatment by parents and other authoritative figures. Much socialization is more "formal," however, and involves learning in schools, reading in newspapers and books, and so forth. It is primarily within these more formal avenues of socialization that organized attempts to manipulate one's political belief system—one's ideology—take place. Thus the second use of the term mentioned above: The official Soviet ideology is propagated largely through the official socialization channels.

THE SOURCES AND CONTENT OF SOVIET IDEOLOGY

As the quotation from the *Political Dictionary* shows, Marxism-Leninism is considered to be the ideology of the Soviet state. A brief outline of some of the fundamental concepts of Marxism-Leninism should be of help to the reader with no prior acquaintance with these ideas. Marxism as a social theory is designed to provide a framework for the understanding of human history as well as present and future social developments. It also sets forth an image of a better society to be achieved at some unspecified point in the future. The key element is the relationship between labor and the instruments of production.

History, in Marx's view, proceeds according to a dialectical process. The concept of the dialectic, borrowed from the philosopher Hegel, refers to a process of disputation by which higher truth is reached by confronting the contradictions of a given statement: Thesis confronted by antithesis produces synthesis or higher truth. Marx's adaptation of Hegel's concept of the dialectical movement of society was his positing of the economic factor as the key ingredient in the dialectical process of historical development; thus, the terms *dialectical materialism* and *historical materialism*. His was an economic interpretation of history based on the class struggle. As Marx put it, "the history of all hitherto existing societies is the history of class struggle." According to the laws of historical development, societies move through successive stages from primitive communalism to slave-based society to feudalism to capitalism to socialism, ultimately culminating in the building of an ideal communist society where the means of production belong to all and the laborer works both for himself and for society as a whole. Each of the stages prior to communism carries within itself as part of the dialectical process the seeds of its own destruction—its own inherent contradictions which will eventually destroy it. With the rise of capitalism to replace pre-existing societal forms, the main antagonistic classes were the proletariat, or urban workers, and the bourgeoisie, or capital producers. In the capitalist state the exploitation of the former by the latter was the key dialectical element that would eventually lead to socialism, under which exploitation of man by man would cease. Socialism, however, is but a stage in the development toward communism. Although there are no hostile social groupings under socialism, there still may be certain contradictions and survivals of the past in the minds of citizens that must be eliminated. Communism implies the overcoming of these problems, the institution of complete public ownership and self-government, and the achievement of a sufficient economic and technological level of development to guarantee abundance.

Lenin's contributions to Marxism were most important in his appli-

cations of the theory to the conditions existing in Russia early in the twentieth century. Marx had treated the dialectical movement of history as
inevitable. Although he aspired to participation in movements for political
change—he once wrote: "the philosophers have *interpreted* the world in
various ways; the point however is to *change* it"—his contributions were
largely in setting down the basic theoretical framework. Lenin, by contrast,
both conceived the organizational basis and strategy for revolution and led
the successful struggle to establish the Bolshevik regime. His most important
theoretical contributions involved his ideas on party organization and his
theory of revolution. Lenin's writings on party organization were discussed
in the previous chapter. He favored a small group of disciplined professional
revolutionaries operating in secret rather than the mass organization advocated by some of his fellow Russian socialists. He also argued with them
about the possibility of revolution in Russia at that time. Marxian precepts
seemed to require a mature capitalism before a socialist revolution could
take place, and Russia was only at a primitive stage of capitalist development.
Lenin argued, however, that on the organizational base that he devised, it
was not necessary to await the full maturation of capitalism in Russia before
taking power. The party could act for the proletariat and thus speed up the
inevitable process. Lenin's practical genius, along with his ability to persuade
his comrades of the possibility of telescoping the revolution, helped bring
the Bolsheviks to power in 1917.

These ideas of Marx and Lenin are among their most important
theoretical contributions. But they concentrate largely on the historical
processes and tactical procedures leading up to the creation of the socialist
state rather than on guidelines for running the state. The writings of Marx in
particular were sketchy on practices to be used after the seizure of power. As
Louis Fischer put it, for the Bolsheviks trying to maintain their position after
November 1917, "Marx was no Baedeker."[8]

The concept of a Soviet ideology for running a modern state must
perforce go beyond Marx and Lenin and embrace other authoritative statements. How can the limits of Soviet ideology be reasonably defined? A brief
but acceptable cataloging of the elements of Soviet ideology is that of the
American political scientist Alfred G. Meyer, written some years ago to
initiate a discussion of the uses of ideology in the USSR:

> [The] doctrine consists of the following parts:
> 1. a philosophy called Dialectical Materialism;
> 2. generalizations about man and society, past and present, called Historical
>   Materialism;
> 3. an economic doctrine called Political Economy, which seeks to explain the
>   economics of capitalism and imperialism on the one hand, and of socialist
>   construction on the other;
> 4. a body of political thought, or guidelines, now called Scientific Commu-
>   nism, which deals, first, with the strategy and tactics of communist revolu-
>   tions, and, second, the political problems of socialist states; and

5. the official history of the CPSU (Communist Party of the Soviet Union). To this one might add the shorter-range pronouncements made by the Party interpreting current affairs and determining goals and priorities.[9]

If these are the main categories of Soviet political ideology, where is one to find the details, the specific ideas and values? The volume of such material is truly stupendous, and this is where the problem of the content of Soviet ideology begins to get difficult. There are, as mentioned, the works of the fathers of Soviet ideological thought such as Marx, Engels (Marx's collaborator on much of his work), and Lenin, as well as the writings of numerous less important political thinkers and actors who were their followers. The latest official edition of the collected works of Lenin amounts to fifty-five volumes.[10] The Second Edition of the works of Marx and Engels in Russian totaled fifty volumes plus several volumes of indexes. Then there are the Soviet leaders after Lenin. To take only the recognized top leaders: Stalin's collected works filled thirteen volumes; Khrushchev's amounted to eight volumes; and by 1982, nine volumes of Brezhnev's collected works plus a number of other individual volumes had been published; several volumes of the writings and speeches of Andropov and Chernenko have appeared more recently.

The quotation from Meyer mentioned the official history of the CPSU; but it is relevant to ask "which history?" The history written during Stalin's time, and attributed to him, known as the *Short Course*, was repudiated and withdrawn several years after his death. It was replaced by a multivolume history begun under Khrushchev, the first volume of which had to be recalled after Khruschev's removal. A policy shift caused the recall and revision of the third edition of a one-volume Party history several years later.[11] And so it goes.

The Meyer passage also mentions "scientific communism" as an ideological source. This is a relatively new concept, introduced officially with great fanfare as an independent part of Marxism-Leninism only in 1962. Since then a great number of books on the subject have been written, including the textbook *Scientific Communism,* the seventh edition of which was published in 1985 with a first printing of one-half million.[12]

Of a slightly different character is the Party Program. Several programs have been adopted during the history of the Bolshevik movement—the first in 1903, years before the assumption of power, and the second in 1919. In 1961 a third Program was approved. This document, the size of a 150-page paperback book, was a utopian tract that bore the strong stamp of the Khrushchev era. Described as "a program for the building of communist society," it purported to define "the main tasks and principal stages of communist construction." Many of its specific provisions were so closely associated with Khrushchev that the Program was seldom mentioned after his removal in 1964. In the 1980s the intention to adopt a revised document was announced, and this was done at the Twenty-Seventh Party Congress in 1986.

Although termed merely a revision of the 1961 Program, the 1986 version is considerably shorter and contains numerous significant changes. Much of the utopian language, such as the statement in the 1961 version that "the present generation of Soviet people shall live under communism," was dropped in the 1986 version.[13]

The 1977 USSR Constitution is another recent document that is relevant to ideology. It is known as the Constitution for developed socialism, the stage that the Soviet system is said to have reached in the 1980s. The Constitution will be discussed in more detail in Chapter 5.[14]

Finally, there is the last sentence of the quotation from Professor Meyer concerning the "shorter-range pronouncements made by the Party interpreting current affairs and determining goals and priorities." Such pronouncements might include any of a number of statements made at plenary meetings of the Party Central Committee, to which at least short-term obeisance is paid by all. Recent examples would include an emphasis on the importance of continuity and collective leadership, as well as the drive to recruit more blue-collar workers and collective farmers into the Party. Professor Meyer's view notwithstanding, these pronouncements really amount to concrete interpretations of the basic ideology rather than constituting additions to the central core of the Soviet belief system.

This quick review of the sources of Soviet political ideology and its main categories should make two things clear: First, the volume of ideological materials is truly great; second, it is not always certain what in this mass of writing is currently accepted and approved. One might look upon the mass of ideological materials as a great archive of potentially useful materials that can be drawn on as the need arises. It has been said of the Bible that some part of it can always be found as justification for almost any religious point of view. Or, more poetically,

> One day at least in every week
> > The sects of every kind
> Their doctrines here are sure to seek
> > And just as sure to find.[15]

If this is true of the Bible, it is also true of the classics of Marxism-Leninism in the sense that their volume is so great and that in considerable part the writing is vague and ambiguous. Even where the writing is reasonably clear, Soviet leaders are not above distorting the meaning of a phrase or passage from Marx or Lenin to serve their own ends. Soviet history is replete with such instances. One of the best known and most important is the identification of Lenin with Khrushchev's campaign for "peaceful co-existence," which became known as "the Leninist principle of peaceful coexistence." Even the Chinese Communists claim that Khrushchev distorted Lenin's intention in using the term, and some Western analysts think this point is sound.[16]

As mentioned before, a considerable amount of the material in this ideological archive has fallen into disuse, either because certain concepts have become embarrassing or no longer useful, or because they were associated with discredited leaders like Stalin or Khrushchev. But the Soviet approach to these matters is extremely flexible. Concepts and ideals can always be revived again, as is occasionally done with long-forgotten statements by Lenin. In fact, "new" ideas of Lenin which were not known previously but which support current Soviet policies are sometimes published.[17] Ideas of discredited leaders may be revived with a leader's rehabilitation or they may be used when necessary without identification with the leader. Whatever practice is used, great effort normally is made to emphasize that new developments are consistent with orthodox doctrine and amount at most to "creative adaptations" of it.

If this is the totality of the Soviet ideological repository, so to speak, what parts of it can be said to be of real importance in the 1980s and how do they affect the way current Soviet leaders behave?

THE DOCTRINAL NUCLEUS

The casual reader of Soviet writings might conclude that Soviet politicians are fond of quoting Marx and Lenin. Over the years the habit of quoting the "founding fathers" of Soviet ideology has become expected behavior. Nor does this practice extend only to politicians: Journalists, lawyers, historians, economists, in fact all people writing in what may be broadly defined as the humanities and social sciences (and, in Stalin's heyday, many of those in the natural sciences as well) establish their orthodoxy by citation. Especially in a book or scholarly article, appropriate references are considered *de rigueur*. Failure to include them would be seen as an important omission. For both politicians and nonpoliticians, such citations afford protection by reminding all who care that the writer's devotion to ideological orthodoxy is complete and fervent.

In many cases the bows to the fathers of communism seem most perfunctory: a quote or two in the first couple of pages and nothing more for the rest of the book or article. But the bows are made nevertheless. When carried to extremes, such citationism leads to sterile discourse, a fact even Soviet authorities have complained about.[18] But if Soviet writers, especially politicians, are expected to quote Marx and Lenin, what can one say about the sincerity with which they do so and the degree to which ideological principles determine the content of the ideas that they attempt to translate into behavior? These matters are at the heart of the controversy about Soviet ideology among Western scholars, whose views diverge widely. What follows, therefore, is our view, accompanied by references to some of the leading statements by other scholars.

A Western author often cited as a proponent of the view that doctrine determines behavior in Soviet politics is Dr. Fred Schwarz, head of a California-based "anticommunist crusade." The title of his best-selling book indicates the position he takes: *You Can Trust the Communists (. . . to do exactly as they say!)* [19] In a more scholarly vein the British economist Peter Wiles has written: "Communists are governed by their sacred texts" and that it "is more than seeking doctrinal justification for what they want or are forced to do." [20] For example, according to Wiles, tasks like the collectivization of the peasantry are inherently both difficult and disagreeable. He goes on to point out: "No one is forced to perform them; no one in his right mind would want to perform them. Yet they have been achieved . . . The reason is of course that the Communist leaders are not in their right mind; they are in Marx's mind." At the other end of the scale from these views is that of the historian Robert Daniels. In his numerous writings on the subject, Daniels has taken a rather cynical view about the sincerity with which ideological pronouncements are held. He has written, for instance, that ideology "is an instrument for rationalizing after the fact." [21] Similarly, France's Emmanuel Todd has written: "We must not think . . . that the Russian Communists are 'ideologically motivated.' Rather, we should see them as perfect cynics." [22] And the Soviet dissident Academician Andrei Sakharov has remarked that the present regime is characterized by "ideological indifference and the pragmatic use of ideology as a convenient 'facade.' " [23]

Most Western writers reject these extremes. Our own position is that since the leaders of the Soviet state have spent their adult lives living within the system and have received most of their education under it, it seems likely that, to varying degrees, [24] they accept the basic principles of the doctrine and have a view of the world that is shaped by Marxism-Leninism. Just by its influence on the thought processes of Soviet leaders, in other words, the ideology has an impact on their behavior. This idea has been captured best by Paul F. Cook, a U.S. State Departmental official:

> If one looks upon ideology, however, not as the operational code of the international communist conspiracy, not as a blueprint for the attainment of world communism, but rather as a system of thought in a more restrictive sense, as *Weltanschauung*, especially one increasingly imbued—or contaminated if you will—by traditional Russian values, then it retains its relevance as a determinant of Soviet policy. [25]

This view of ideology does not suggest a very rigidly held faith. One of the characteristics of recent Soviet leaders has been their flexibility with regard to doctrine. A difficulty in sorting out the impact of ideology on action stems from the Marxist-Leninist penchant for fusing the two, for discussing "the unity of theory and practice." As Khrushchev once put it,

"Marxism-Leninism teaches that theory divorced from practice is dead, and practice which is not enlightened by theory is blind." So doctrinal changes are evident from time to time in spite of efforts by Soviet authorities to portray the consistency of the doctrine. Within these shifts in interpretation and variations in the way certain principles are realized in practice, however, there remains a small nucleus of precepts that communist leaders seem determined to live by or, perhaps more accurately, to live with.[26] There is some controversy as to which precepts belong in this group; we would offer the following as ones that the leadership has made a conscientious effort to implement throughout the Soviet period.

The Sanctity of the Communist Party

The sanctity of the Party is the supreme article of faith. "The Party" is above criticism, as are its top leaders, except when a campaign is orchestrated against one or a small group of them, in which case they are distinguished from the Party and designated as an "anti-Party group" or castigated for "harm to our Party." The realities of political power in the Soviet Union confirm the place of the Party in the belief system, as does the prominent mentioning of the Party in such documents as the Party Program and the USSR Constitution. And the concept of "democratic centralism," the cornerstone of Party and state operations in the country, seeks to ensure that the prime position of the Party leadership will be maintained. As Daniel Bell has put it, "the doctrinal core . . . is not any specific theoretical formulation, *but the basic demand for belief in the Party itself.*"[27]

Socialist Ownership of the Means of Production

What this principle implies at the present time is state ownership and control of virtually all economic activity in the country, centralized planning of the economy, and a prohibition of "private property," meaning property that could be used for "speculation" or illegal economic gain.*

Collectivism

If the hallmark of Western liberal thought is individualism, it is collectivism that reigns in Soviet theory. Some writers suggest that collectivism found a congenial setting in Russia because *sobornost'*, a sense of community or togetherness, was widely held to be a positive virtue in the Russian past.[28] But whether or not this link is a reasonable one, the collective idea is firmly

---

*"Personal" *(lichnoe)* property is distinguished from "private" *(chastnoe)* property in Soviet law and is sanctioned. Personal property includes things used for personal consumption or enjoyment (for example, clothing, books, an automobile, a house) which are not used for the economic exploitation of other persons. For a description of the limited categories of "private property" allowed under Soviet law, see F.J.M. Feldbrugge, G.P. Van den Berg, and William B. Simons, eds., *Encyclopedia of Soviet Law*, 2nd rev. ed. (Dordrecht, the Netherlands: Martinus Nijhoff, Publishers, 1985), p. 585.

imbedded in Soviet theory and practice. A whole battery of related Russian words is used to describe the phenomenon: *kollektivizm* (collectivism), *kollektivnost'* (collectivity), and, most important, *kollektiv* (the collective or peer group). Broadly speaking, the term *kollektiv* refers to the peer group of the individual, but a peer group that operates in a way with which most Westerners will not be familiar. One writer who has understood its role is Allen Kassof, who writes:

> The peer group—or, to use the Soviet term, the collective—is the setting for group pressure. The Large Soviet Encyclopedia defines the collective as "a joining of people who are linked together by common work, general interest, and goals. (A collective of workers in a factory, a collective of employees of an institute, a collective of scientific workers at a higher educational institution, a collective of the students of a school)." The task of the collective is to instill in Soviet citizens habits of collectivism—that is, to discourage "egoistic striving" and to foster an acceptance of group control over values, attitudes, and behavior, not only during the formative years but throughout adult life as well.[29]

The doctrinal tenet of collectivism has extremely wide implications. It means no less than the superiority of the peer group's norms over those of the individual. The peer group norms, in turn, may well be inspired from higher up in the political system or may amount simply to the interpretation of the responsible Party representative in the group.[30] Such norms involve matters such as the work *kollektiv*'s censure of a person who habitually reports late for work or the student *kollektiv*'s warning to persons who talk to foreigners. They may also involve matters as serious as one's right to speak or write. It was, after all, Solzhenitsyn's professional *kollektiv*, the Ryazan branch of the Writers' Union, that officially blocked publication of his work. The *kollektiv* expelled him and thus terminated his membership in the Union of Writers of the USSR. Since such membership is necessary for the authorized publication of one's writing, Solzhenitsyn could no longer have his works published legally.

Atheism

A longstanding tenet that is traceable to Marx, atheism remains a principle fully supported by the Soviet leadership. The degree of toleration and harassment of believers and religious organizations has varied over time, but the basic opposition remains. No overt believer would be allowed to occupy a position of political responsibility in the country.

Antagonism Toward Other Social Systems

Khrushchev's endorsement of the idea of peaceful coexistence between antagonistic socioeconomic systems marked a significant change in Soviet doctrinal tenets. For although, as mentioned, Khrushchev traced the idea of peaceful coexistence to Lenin, his interpretation of the concept amounted to a revision of the Leninist thesis concerning the inevitability of wars under imperialism. This did not imply complete relaxation of tensions between capitalism and socialism, because economic competition between the two camps was to continue in order to demonstrate which system was superior. Moreover, Soviet leaders have consistently held that peaceful coexistence does not extend to the ideological sphere. As Khrushchev put it, "ideological differences are unbridgeable, and they will continue to exist."[31] Thus, the value systems and principles identified with countries in the capitalist world are not to be endorsed or tolerated either by Soviet leaders or by Soviet citizens. A basic gulf between the two camps remains.

This list of elements for a doctrinal nucleus is short when one considers the volume of doctrinal writing. But others who have attempted similar listings have come up with little or no more.[32] Perhaps the most obvious omissions involve the doctrines of historical and dialectical materialism and associated concepts such as the class struggle. But these are really of little relevance to the 1980s. As the foundation of the whole edifice of Marxist-Leninist doctrine, they undoubtedly affect the way Soviet leaders look at the world and act as the prism through which they see and understand social phenomena. But such concepts appear to have little obvious influence on the way they react to events or on the policies they adopt. According to Richard Lowenthal, "there are vast parts of Communist ideological structure, such as the scholastic refinements of dialectical materialism or the labor theory of value which in their nature are so remote from the practical matters to be decided that their interpretation cannot possibly affect policy decisions."[33] This point appears to apply to Soviet leaders and followers alike. As Boris Shragin, a philosopher and 1974 emigrant from the Soviet Union, has put it: "Practically no one in the Soviet Union takes Marxism seriously. Its basic theses, let us say the 'dictatorship of the proletariat,' have absolutely nothing in common with contemporary Soviet political reality."[34] The dissident emigré Vladimir Bukovsky put it more bluntly: "From top to bottom, no one believes in Marxism dogma anymore, even though they continue to measure their actions by it, refer to it, and use it as a stick to beat one another with: it is both a proof of loyalty and a meal ticket."[35]

THE FUNCTIONS OF IDEOLOGY

What purposes does ideology serve in the Soviet system? Certainly all of the items listed above make political control easier for the Soviet leaders. That is to say, since the *Communist Party is above criticism*, it is subject to no challenges in running the country. The *socialist economic system* means that there will be no powerful economic aggregations competing with the state. *Collectivism*, controlled by the state, facilitates the propagation of "correct" political ideas to the populace, and *antagonism toward other social systems* justifies the exclusion of "harmful" and "alien" ideas from outside. Finally, *atheism* serves to discourage people from the attraction of competing faiths or loyalties within the country. Obviously, then, political control is one of the major functions of the ideology. In fact, we would maintain that it is the most important. All other functions enhance the control aspect and none contravenes it. Let us look at these other functions.

The Communications Function

Soviet leaders speak the language of Soviet ideology, using its categories and key terms as a framework for discourse. It is probably no exaggeration to say that one would be denied a political role in Soviet society if one could not or would not manipulate the language of ideology. Western foreigners are sometimes surprised to find that ordinary Soviet citizens on occasion also employ this language, as in the following conversation between a Moscow taxi driver and an American:

> "Communism isn't a fairy tale, like God. For centuries people talked about God—my mother most of all. And there wasn't one; there was never any such thing as God; no one has a scrap of proof. But you can *see* Communism being built. It isn't a matter of faith or fairy tales, but of work. Look at our university. Look at Moscow, building itself up. Look at our steel mills."
> [The American replies:] "Look at *our* steel mills."
> "Ah, son, that's just the point. It's the system that counts. Can't you see that? You have capitalism there, so that your steel mills, even if they are ahead of ours, mean profits and greed. It's the law of capitalism, the rule of whoever can grab most. But the law of socialism is sharing; our building means progress for everyone and for civilization. It's not just the factories that count, but who owns them and what is done with them and how people feel about them. Our factories are *ours,* so we are building Communism, not selfishness."[36]

It is through the ideological code of communication that political differences of opinion are often expressed, and one must be aware of the subtle distinctions and nuances of that code to catch the differences.[37] In addition, the need to pay homage by citing ideological sources like Marx and Lenin, coupled with this tendency to use the approved formulations, places useful restraints on discussion.

The Legitimizing Function

Taken as a whole, the ideology serves to legitimize current political and economic arrangements in the Soviet Union. If the Soviet people must work hard, as is suggested by the taxi driver's remarks, their work is in the service of a higher goal. The means used to arrive at that goal have less importance than the goal itself. The Party, as the speaker for the proletariat, claims that its rightful role is running the system—determining the best means to achieve the goals set by the ideology. As the sole interpreter of historical truth (that is, where both the world and the Soviet Union have been and are going), it can assure that its primacy is maintained.

The Social Integration Function

Social integration involves the shared internalization of values by a group of people. This sharing helps to enhance group feeling and cohesion. As Brzezinski and Huntington have put it:

> For citizens to share in certain beliefs they must make almost automatic responses to certain key notions, symbols, or aspirations. Such responses create social cohesion and make the functioning of the system possible. Political indoctrination of the citizen, by making him nationally conscious, integrates him socially and politically, and this inevitably makes for the further spreading of the elite's ideology or political beliefs.[38]

The Unifying Function

Soviet ideology is unifying in its attempt to rise above and gloss over religious, nationality, and other differences. This has both international and domestic relevance. It supplies doctrinal cohesion with foreign communist parties and socialist movements. And it justifies the maintenance of the international socialist system against threats to any of its members (the rationalization for the 1968 invasion of Czechoslovakia). The emphasis on a classless society attempts to dignify manual labor and mitigates the divisive problems of class distinctions. Being anti-nationalist, Marxism-Leninism justifies the repression of "bourgeois nationalism" on the part of nationality groups within the country in favor of rule by the party that represents all workers of all nationalities.[39]

There has been much talk in recent years about the "erosion of ideology" in the Soviet Union.[40] If the major role that ideology plays in the system is the enhancement of political control, will the erosion of ideology mean the erosion of control? We doubt it. The Soviet leaders have been quite successful in adapting doctrinal concepts to practical needs and in keeping ideology in its "proper" place. They are likely to go to great lengths to insist on its continued relevance, no matter how devoid of content ideological rhetoric becomes. As a medium of communication, ideology serves as a kind of early-warning system. Those who are unwilling to communicate within the ideological framework are exposed and denied any role in politics. This is a positive factor in helping to maintain control, no matter how empty the ideology might become. It is a feature that other authoritarian systems lack. As used in the 1980s, it can be looked upon largely as an asset.

NOTES

[1]Clemens Dutt, ed., *Fundamentals of Marxism-Leninism* (Moscow: Foreign Languages Publishing House, 1961), p. 17.

[2]Ibid., p. 19.

[3]A good short review of the concept of ideology, and a number of definitions of it, may be found in Willard A. Mullins, "On the Concept of Ideology in Political Science," *American Political*

Science Review 66 (1972), 498–511. See also Alexander J. Groth, *Major Ideologies* (New York: John Wiley, 1971), pp. 1–18, and Reo Christenson and others, *Ideologies and Modern Politics* (New York: Dodd, Mead, 1971), pp. 1–35.

[4]Ibid., p. 5.

[5]Robert E. Lane, *Political Ideology: Why the American Common Man Believes What He Does* (New York: Free Press, 1962), pp. 3, 15.

[6]B. N. Ponomarev, ed., *Politicheskii Slovar'* (Moscow: Gosudarstvennoe Izdatel'stvo Politicheskoi Literatury, 1958), pp. 199–200.

[7]Vladimir Tolz, "The Party and Youth: Old Remedies for New Problems," *Radio Liberty Research*, No. 335/84, Sept. 5, 1984.

[8]Louis Fischer, *The Life of Lenin* (New York: Harper and Row Publishers, Inc., 1964), p. 254.

[9]Alfred G. Meyer, "The Functions of Ideology in the Soviet Political System," *Soviet Studies*, 17 (1966), 273.

[10]In addition, there are three supplementary index volumes to Lenin's collected works. The title suggests that Lenin's collected works are "complete" *(Polnoe Sobranie Sochinenii)*, but it is clear that a number of available items have been partially or completely omitted for political reasons. See R. C. Elwood "How Complete is Lenin's *Polnoe Sobranie Sochinenii?*" *Slavic Review*, 38 (Mar. 1979), 97.

[11]See Sidney I. Ploss, "Soviet Party History: The Stalinist Legacy," *Problems of Communism*, 21 (Jul.–Aug. 1972), 32–41.

[12]*Nauchnyi Kommunizm* (Moscow: Izdatel'stvo Politicheskoi Literatury, 7th ed., 1985).

[13]At the time of this writing (early 1986), Western analyses of the 1986 version of the Party Program have only begun to be published. *Radio Liberty Research* published a number of articles on the draft version of the new program. See, e.g., Elizabeth Teague, "Draft of New Party Program Published," *Radio Liberty Research*, No. 358/85, Oct. 28, 1985.

[14]One of the most thorough analyses in English of the 1977 Constitution refers to it as "a major ideological statement." F.J.M. Feldbrugge, ed., *The Constitutions of the USSR and the Union Republics: Analysis, Texts, Reports* (Alphen aan den Rijn, the Netherlands: Sijthoff & Noordhoff, 1979), p. 3. See also Alfred B. Evans, Jr., "Developed Socialism in Soviet Ideology," *Soviet Studies*, 29 (1977), 409–28.

[15]Augustus De Morgan, "Matter to Spirit: Preface," in *The Home Book of Quotations*, 5th ed., rev., ed. Burton Stevenson (New York: Dodd, Mead, 1947), p. 159.

[16]On this point see Leonhard, *Three Faces of Marxism*, pp. 64–66, 146, 231; Christenson and others, *Ideologies*, p. 138; Robert C. Tucker, *The Marxian Revolutionary Idea* (New York: W.W. Norton, 1969), pp. 173–79.

[17]For instance, in September 1962, *Pravda* published a theretofore unknown version of an article by Lenin (written in 1918) that argued that "victory over the bourgeoisie" must come by economic means. This was interpreted as having both domestic implications, in connection with a pending change in economic planning and management, and foreign-policy implications, in connection with the Soviet Union's doctrinal dispute with the People's Republic of China. *Pravda*, Sept. 28, 1962, p. 1. See also the analysis in *The New York Times*, Sept. 29, 1962, p. 1. In 1975, 487 new documents attributed to Lenin were published, among them a previously unknown writing of 1920 which welcomed trade links between Soviet Russia and the capitalist West. See *The International Herald Tribune*, Aug. 9–10, 1975, p. 1.

[18]See the discussion of this point in Donald D. Barry, "Law and Social Science: Recent Developments," in *Social Thought of the Soviet Union*, ed. Alex Simirenko (Chicago: Quadrangle, The New York Times Book Co., 1969), p. 157.

[19]Dr. Fred Schwarz, *You Can Trust the Communists (. . . to do exactly as they say!)* (Englewood Cliffs, NJ: Prentice-Hall, 1960).

[20]This and the subsequent quotation are from Peter Wiles, *The Political Economy of Communism* (Cambridge, MA: Harvard University Press, 1964), p. 356.

[21]As quoted in Daniel Bell, "Ideology and Soviet Politics," *Slavic Review*, 24 (1965), 601. In his treatment of the subject as a whole, Robert V. Daniels presents a more balanced view than the quotation suggests. In his *The Nature of Communism* (New York: Random House, 1962) Daniels states, along the lines of the quotation, that "the actions of Marxists are not determined by Marxist theory, but only ornamented by it" (pp. 17–18) and that ideology "is only an

instrument to justify what the Communists feel are their practical interests" (p. 373). But he also discusses (p. 356) "the actual substance of lasting Communist belief," indicating that not all is expendable. Among other writers who have suggested that ideology has very little influence on political action are Samuel L. Sharp and Dan N. Jacobs. See Sharp's "National Interest: Key to Soviet Politics," in *Soviet Conduct in World Affairs*, ed. Alexander Dallin (New York: Columbia University Press, 1960), p. 46. Jacob's view is developed in Christenson and others, *Ideologies*, pp. 95–141, wherein he states (p. 137) that the acts of Soviet leaders "must be verbally squared with Marxist theories. But it is the 'acting' that comes first and the 'squaring' that comes after."

[22] Emmanuel Todd, *The Final Fall*, (New York: Karz Publishers, 1979), p. 132.

[23] Andrei Sakharov, "On Aleksandr Solzhenitsyn's Letter to the Soviet Leaders," in *The Political, Social and Religious Thought of Russian "Samizdat"—An Anthology*, Michael Meerson-Aksenov and Boris Shragin, eds. (Belmont, MA: Nordland Publishing Co., 1977), p. 294. This quotation by Sakharov is made in the context of a critical analysis of Solzhenitsyn's views on ideology. A more thorough and critical treatment of Solzhenitsyn on ideology is an essay by Lev Kopelev in the same volume: "The Lie Can Be Defeated Only by the Truth," pp. 302–42. Solzhenitsyn has written frequently about Soviet ideology. He is clearly of the opinion that it plays a very powerful role in the Soviet system. See, for instance, his discussion of ideology in "Letter to the Soviet Leaders" (1973), reprinted in *East and West* (New York: Harper and Row, 1980), pp. 120–29. Solzhenitsyn has a particular view of ideology, however. As Geoffrey Hosking has put it: "He sees it not simply as an external imposition, a mere propaganda, but as a spiritual force (albeit of a base sort) which remoulds men's conceptions of themselves and of those around them, and which therefore affects every single action they perform." Geoffrey Hosking, *Beyond Socialist Realism* (New York: Holmes & Meier, 1980), p. 119. See Hosking's discussion of Solzhenitsyn's view of ideology, especially as expressed in *The Gulag Archipelago*, p. 117.

[24] The degree of acceptance of ideological precepts among Soviet leaders is surely not uniform. Propositions concerning the levels of strength of leaders' belief may be found in the writings of Merle Fainsod and Alfred Meyer, among others. Fainsod, in *How Russia is Ruled*, rev. ed. (Cambridge, MA: Harvard University Press, 1963), discusses three categories of leaders (pp. 595–96): those for whom ideology is a matter of "deep commitment," embraced with "the righteous self-assurance of a true believer"; those for whom ideology "is almost a matter of pro-forma faith"; and those for whom ideology "may be a matter of cynical adjustment, where inner doubts are suppressed in the interest of career making." Meyer, "The Functions of Ideology," p. 283, borrowing categories suggested by Robert Presthus involving "modes of psychological adjustment to bureaucratic systems," discussed the "upward-mobile" who "accept values positively and actively," the "indifferent" who are passive in their attitudes toward ideology, and the creative individuals who are "ambivalent" about ideology.

[25] Paul F. Cook, "The Soviet Union in the Year 2000," seminar notes from a talk delivered at the Russian Research Center of Harvard University, Dec. 19, 1974, p. 4.

[26] Although most Western writers seem to accept the idea, few have attempted to spell out the elements of such a doctrinal nucleus. Among the exceptions are Robert V. Daniels, mentioned in note 21; Daniel Bell, who examines "the doctrinal core" of Soviet ideology in "Ideology and Soviet Politics," p. 602; and John S. Reshetar, Jr., who discusses "the hard core of doctrine," in *The Soviet Polity*, 2nd ed. (New York: Harper & Row, 1978), p. 93.

[27] "Ideology and Soviet Politics," p. 602, italics in the original. Other writers expressing this point of view include Daniels, *The Nature of Communism*, p. 356; Reshetar, *The Soviet Polity*, p. 93; Fainsod, *How Russia is Ruled*, p. 596; Richard Lowenthal, "The Logic of One-Party Rule," in *Soviet Conduct In World Affairs*, p. 60; and Hélène Carrère d'Encausse, *Confiscated Power: How Soviet Russia Really Works* (New York: Harper & Row, 1982), pp. 16–17.

[28] See, for example, John Maynard, *Russia in Flux* (New York: Macmillan, 1948), passim; Harold J. Berman, *Justice in the USSR*, rev. ed. (New York: Vintage Books, 1963), p. 221; Robert G. Wesson, *The Russian Dilemma* (New Brunswick, NJ: Rutgers University Press, 1974), p. 79.

[29] Allen Kassof, *The Soviet Youth Program* (Cambridge: Harvard University Press, 1965), p. 42. Kassof's extended discussion of the *kollektiv*, of which the quoted passage is a part, is excellent. See also Frederick Barghoorn's discussion in *Politics in the USSR*, 2nd ed. (Boston: Little, Brown, 1972), p. 99.

[30] As Barghoorn put it in *Politics in the USSR*, p. 142, it appears that the *kollektiv's* functions remain "firmly in the hands of party executives."

[31] Speech of Nov. 6, 1957, *Pravda*, Nov. 7, 1957, p. 2.

[32]See the sources listed in note 21.

[33]*Soviet Conduct in World Affairs*, p. 59.

[34]The International Conference of Slavists at Banff, Canada," *Radio Liberty Dispatch*, No. 330, Oct. 9, 1974, p. 4.

[35]Vladimir Bukovsky, *To Build a Castle: My Life as a Dissenter* (New York: Viking Press, 1978), p. 73.

[36]An Observer, *Message From Moscow* (New York: Knopf, 1969), pp. 188–89.

[37]See William E. Griffith, "On Esoteric Communications," *Studies in Comparative Communism*, 3 (1970), 47.

[38]Zbigniew Brzezinski and Samuel P. Huntington, *Political Power: USA/USSR* (New York: Viking, 1964), p. 47.

[39]Robert G. Wesson suggested the unifying function of ideology. See his *The Soviet Russian State* (New York: John Wiley, 1972), pp. 142–45.

[40]See, for example, Meyer, "The Functions of Ideology," especially pp. 283–85; Bell, "Ideology and Soviet Politics"; Zbigniew Brzezinski, ed., *Dilemmas of Change in Soviet Politics* (New York: Columbia University Press, 1969), especially the first chapter, by Brzezinski, "The Soviet Political System: Transformation or Degeneration," pp. 1–34.

SELECTED BIBLIOGRAPHY

ANDERSON, THORTON, *Masters of Russian Marxism*. New York: Appleton-Century-Crofts, 1963.

BESANÇON, ALAIN, *The Soviet Syndrome*. New York: Harcourt Brace Jovanovich, 1976.

CAREW HUNT, R. N., *The Theory and Practice of Communism*, 5th ed. New York: Macmillan, 1961.

CARRÈRE D'ENCAUSSE, HÉLÈNE, *Confiscated Power: How Soviet Russia Really Works*. New York: Harper & Row, Publishers, 1982.

CHRISTENSON, REO, and others, *Ideologies and Modern Politics*. New York: Dodd, Mead, 1971.

DANIELS, ROBERT V., *Marxism and Communism: Essential Readings*. New York: Random House, 1965.

GILISON, JEROME M., *The Soviet Image of Utopia*. Baltimore: Johns Hopkins University Press, 1975.

JAWORSKYJ, MICHEL, ed., *Soviet Political Thought: An Anthology*. Baltimore: Johns Hopkins University Press, 1967.

KUX, ERNST, "Contradictions in Soviet Socialism," *Problems of Communism*, XXXIII, No. 6 (Nov.–Dec. 1984), 1–27.

LEONHARD, WOLFGANG, *Three Faces of Marxism*. New York: Holt, Rinehart and Winston, 1974.

MEYER, ALFRED G., *Communism*, 3rd ed. New York: Random House, 1967.

———, *Leninism*. Cambridge, MA: Harvard University Press, 1957.

———, "The Functions of Ideology in the Soviet Political System," *Soviet Studies*, 17, No. 3 (Jan. 1966), 273–85.

MULLINS, WILLARD A., "On the Concept of Ideology in Political Science," *American Political Science Review*, 66 (1972), 498–510.

REJAI, MOSTAFA, *Comparative Political Ideologies*. New York: St. Martin's Press, 1984.

SCHAPIRO, LEONARD, ed., *The USSR and the Future*. New York: Holt, Rinehart & Winston, 1963.

SEROKA, JIM, and MAURICE D. SIMON, eds., *Developed Socialism and the Soviet Bloc: Political Theory and Political Reality*. Boulder, CO: Westview Press, 1982.

TUCKER, ROBERT C. *The Marxian Revolutionary Idea*. New York: W. W. Norton, 1969.

WILES, PETER. *The Political Economy of Communism*. Cambridge, MA: Harvard University Press, 1964.

4

POLITICAL SOCIALIZATION:
On Becoming and Being Soviet

Political socialization involves the whole process by which an individual becomes a functioning (even if passively) part of his or her political system. There are two basic perspectives on this process.[1] First, there is the perspective of the individual. From this point of view, socialization is the process through which a person acquires political orientations. Second, there is the group or institutional perspective. From this point of view, socialization is the process by which persons or groups attempt to influence the development and evolution of political beliefs, attitudes, and behavior in others. Usually, this is a status-quo oriented process. The current political regime aided by other segments of the society, such as the schools or patriotic organizations, attempts to mold and maintain "good citizens." It need not, however, be status-quo oriented. For example, some families or groups may consciously attempt to produce nonconformists or to convert individuals into "rebels" or "dissidents." Second, there is the inescapable fact of selective perception and retention. People are diverse and they process incoming information in diverse ways. Therefore, each individual takes the political materials supplied and creates his or her own personal political orientation.

Our attention in this chapter will be focused on the formal channels of socialization, the avenues by which the Soviet state attempts to influence the development of its citizens' political beliefs and behavior. We will look first at the characteristics and aims of the socializing process and then at the institutions through which the process is carried out.

"Propaganda" is not a dirty word in the Soviet Union. This makes it fairly easy to identify the nature and direction of conscious efforts by the state to socialize its citizens. In its efforts to bring about homogeneity in the political attitudes and behavior of the Soviet population, the leadership sees to it that wide publicity and exhaustive discussions focus on the characteristics and values of the "new Soviet person."* Substantial deviations from the centrally endorsed line are clearly not permissible, though there is much discussion of variations on the major theme. Thus, it is not difficult to identify what the Soviet leaders are trying to accomplish in the way of political socialization.

Finding out what they actually do accomplish is far more difficult because such research in the Soviet Union is, as a practical matter, impossible for non-Soviet scholars and very restricted and ideologically controlled for Soviet scholars. Therefore, in the following discussion, assertions about what the Soviet government is trying to do can be made with considerable assurance, but assertions about how well they succeed must depend mostly on the educated intuition of ourselves and others who have been able to live for extended periods of time in the Soviet Union.

Generally speaking, we think that the "overkill" nature of the Soviet approach is to some extent counterproductive; large numbers of persons in the Soviet population appear to tune out much of the socialization effort directed at them. But this phenomenon is probably not nearly as pronounced for the Soviet population at large as it is among Soviet intellectuals, the group with which we and other foreign observers most often come into contact. Moreover, we will argue that even if socialization efforts have only limited success in the total population, they probably are effective in convincing the purveyors of the socialization messages of the rightness of their views—socializing the socializers, as it were. In addition to educated guesses on these matters, we will also draw upon the findings of social-psychological research on attitudes and behavior in the United States to support our conjectures as to the possible effects of socialization efforts on Soviet citizens. But because of the paucity of hard data on the actual effects of the socialization process, our description in this chapter will be much more one of the propagandist's hopes than of their accomplishments.

MAIN CHARACTERISTICS OF THE SOCIALIZING PROCESS

It is almost impossible for the average Westerner to appreciate how blatant some Soviet efforts at political socialization are. These efforts are characterized by an intensity and focus that have no real parallels in a country like

---

*The term *"novyi sovetskii chelovek"* is generally translated "new Soviet man." It is not merely the heightened consciousness of the authors in this day of women's liberation that bids us to substitute "person" for "man." Russian–English dictionaries offer "person" as an alternative to "man" in translating *chelovek* (we are using Smirnitsky's third edition), and it is clear that in discussing the *novyi sovetskii chelovek*, Soviet publicists have in mind *all* Soviet citizens, regardless of sex. Therefore, "person" seems the more appropriate of the alternative translations.

the United States. Since certain approaches are pervasive in Soviet life—being found in schools, offices, factories, social organizations, and all the other loci of socialization efforts—they will be discussed separately here in order to set a framework. This will be followed by a more concrete discussion of what happens to the average Soviet citizen in the course of growing up and functioning as an adult in a political system with leaders who are determined to mold him or her into the "new Soviet person."

Pervasiveness of Political Symbols and Messages

November seventh, it is clear
Is the reddest day in all the year.
Through the window look ahead,
Everything outside is red!

—Soviet child's nursery school rhyme[2]

In terms of the visual dimension alone, the ubiquity of politics is staggering. Particularly during national holidays, Soviet cities and villages take on a highly political aspect. But to a lesser extent this is true the year around. The color red is everywhere. There are banners lauding the glory of the Communist Party and the Soviet People and exhorting everyone to try harder for the greater glory of the Soviet Union. There are pictures of the great heroes of communism—Marx, Engels, and Lenin—as well as less conspicuous pictures of the leaders of the current regime. There are also pictures, albeit much smaller, of ordinary people—that is, people who are ordinary in most respects but who may have distinguished themselves in service to the Soviet State by manufacturing more screwdriver handles than anyone else in the factory or by performing an equivalent feat in other walks of life. There are often pictures of dead or living foreign heroes, together with expressions of solidarity with their struggle against the oppressors of their peoples. It cannot be overemphasized that these pictures and slogans are everywhere—in subways, in schoolrooms, in ships, in offices, on billboards, on the sides of buildings, on book covers, and in store windows. In short, they are so ubiquitous that it is difficult to go about daily life without seeing one at frequent intervals.

If you add to this the same sort of message in the audio dimension—from radio, television, and loudspeaker—the effect is overwhelming and, we suspect, probably deadening for many Soviet citizens. Does the average Soviet citizen simply tune it out most of the time? A young Soviet soldier who defected in Afghanistan suggested as much when he made the following remark: "Propaganda has reached a saturation point. Nobody wants to listen to it any more."[3] Based on our experience and the rapidity with which we learned to tune it out, we suspect this to be the case. On the other hand, the possible subliminal effects of all this should not be discounted. Even when blocking the propaganda out on a conscious level, the average Soviet citizen may continue to absorb a good deal on an unconscious, emotional level, only to have it pop out again when needed—as in a moment of crisis.

Manipulation of Information

The teacher at nursery school is giving the children a little talk. She hangs a map of the world on the wall and explains: "Look, children, here is America. The people there are very badly off. They have no money, therefore they never buy their children any candy or ice cream and never take them to the movies. And here, children, is the Soviet Union. Everybody here is happy and well off, and they buy their children candy and ice cream every day and take them to the movies." Suddenly one of the little girls bursts into tears. "What's the matter, Tania, why are you crying?" "I want to go to the Soviet Union," sobs the little girl.[4]

The way in which people view their world and their role in it is conditioned to a large extent by their information about the immediate environment and the larger world of which it is a part. Compared to people in North America, Soviet citizens live in a pretty cut-and-dried world. What they learn about their own country and the rest of the world is what the Party leadership has decided they should learn. There is little of the clamor of competing and often contradictory information that constantly assaults us. Certainly the more thoughtful persons, like some of the Moscow University students among whom we have lived, know it is not all that simple and realize the implications of the periodically occurring minor shifts in what is "true." It is misleading, however, to generalize from these few elite and intellectually gifted members of the society to the entire population. There is little doubt that such mammoth changes in the "truth" as the overnight shift of Stalin— from God to devil and the current more gradual move back in a positive direction probably gives pause to even the most uneducated and apolitical collective-farm worker. But short of these relatively rare permutations of the "truth," it is safe to assume that the average person does not think much about whether he has an accurate picture of the world. Moreover, when these thoughts do occur, it is a sure bet that the issue is seldom seen as being particularly salient and, thus, is unlikely to arouse strong feelings.

In a technologically advanced country like the Soviet Union the educational system is the chief source of information about the world, and the Soviet educational system is tightly and centrally controlled. Only books and teachings that inculcate the "correct" attitudes and information are allowed. The process begins early and extends widely through the curriculum. David Shipler, former *New York Times* correspondent in Moscow, came to the following conclusions after observing Soviet schools:

Nowhere in the younger years are the style of education and the matrix of expectations more clearly visible than in the approach to art. The stress is on drawing, painting, or modelling realistically, often according to a rigid pre-scription. In one class, youngsters made clay roosters all looking the same. The teacher was quite proud. . . . Teachers display considerable uneasiness about artwork that is out of the well-defined groove. An American friend, watching a class of eight-year-olds in Moscow copy a drawing of a snowman with such precision that their work might have been paper tracings, noticed one boy coloring his snowman yellow. The youngster received a stern re-primand.[5]

The teacher who encourages students to question and probe is not likely to last long—at least outside of the most advanced and elite scientific institutions. This does not mean that Soviet students are taught nothing but lies and distortions. There are disciplines—like physics, mathematics, and geology—in which the curriculum differs little from the norm in other parts of the world. This can also be true of substantial subfields within disciplines, such as those areas of law that are not politically sensitive.

There are other fields, however, like Soviet history, in which scholarship is expected to reflect the Party line of the moment. Attempts to achieve a balanced and factually based presentation of significant historical events is condemned as "bourgeois objectivism." To present more than one side of the story is thought to aid the enemies of communism. Since much history is not firmly based on the documentary record, it can easily be changed rapidly when there are sudden major shifts of the Party policy, and there was a time when the whole population was periodically enlisted in the job of "correcting" history books by penciling out unacceptable passages and substituting acceptable ones. Recently, however, there are signs that the Soviet leadership may be moving toward more accuracy in the recording and reporting of Soviet history.[6] That this is not a total change, however, can be seen in the fact that while Stalin is mentioned more and more often, his crimes are being ignored and only his accomplishments discussed. This cavalier approach to history must engender in many Soviet citizens a deeply rooted scepticism toward any and all of the "truths" that the regime wishes to inculcate.

What is true of the formal education system is true of the media—newspapers, television, radio, books, periodicals, and other forms of mass communication are strictly and centrally controlled. As in the case of Soviet history, their role is seen as one of bringing the Party's policy to the people; objectivity is viewed as anticommunism. In a sense, this could be seen as less insidious than the bias in the media in a country like the United States, since the Soviet media's bias is openly and proudly acknowledged and, with some exceptions, can easily be detected and allowed for by the least perceptive reader. This benefit of openness, however, is more than canceled out by the lack of competing sources of information. As a result, the reader who might wish to discount for some of the bias has no obvious way of finding out what other possible sides of the story may be. Coupled with the indoctrination role of the media, there is the agitation and propaganda apparatus (about which more later) which supplements the already overwhelming mass of official policy messages with speeches as well as person-to-person and small-group exhortation.

Finally, information is controlled by strict limitations that the government puts on contact with persons and ideas from outside the Soviet Union. There is virtually a constant campaign to discourage informal contacts between Soviet citizens and foreigners, and the campaign becomes more or less strident as the situation demands. Those with friends in the Soviet Union can measure it by the rise and fall of Soviet mail. Only the foolish disregard these messages. For the foreigner to ignore them may mean inconvenience—being thrown out of the Soviet Union or not permitted to return. For a Soviet citizen it can be worse.

These messages are not only conveyed by the media. When we were at Moscow University we lived in a large wing of the university where virtually all of the noncommunist foreigners were assigned rooms. There was only one entrance to the wing, and the entrance was flanked—day and night—by as many as five or six persons who simply sat and watched all who entered and left. If they did not recognize you, they stopped you, asked to see your student pass, and inquired as to your business in that wing of the dormitory. The message was clear to us and, if possible, even clearer to our Soviet friends, who used to plan their entry carefully and would never walk in with a foreigner.

The other side of this coin is the fact that it is virtually impossible for most Soviet citizens to gain permission to travel outside the Soviet Union. Even travel to other communist countries presents problems, though not as many as travel outside the communist bloc. Thus, there is no way for the Soviet citizen to see for himself what the world is like.

All of this creates an overwhelming hunger for information and curiosity about the outside world among more thoughtful and educated people. Those who by dint of considerable bravery and perseverance do manage to gain access to information via other than official sources often find it difficult to assimilate this information. This was made clear to us time and again in our discussions with students, when the information we gave them was interpreted in Party-line fashion by even those who were the most open-minded.

"Voluntary" Participation

And maybe the tramps living off handouts can be said to exist outside the Soviet system (although in the camps they have to work). All the rest, whether they wish it or not, are building communism. The State doesn't give a tinker's damn what theories they use to justify their participation, or what they think or feel. So long as they don't resist, protest, or publicly disagree, they suit the Soviet State. Nobody says they have to like it, everything is quite simple and cynical. Do you want a new apartment? Make a speech at the meeting. Do you want to earn an extra twenty or thirty rubles, or get a responsible job? Join the Party. Do you want to keep your privileges and avoid unpleasantness? Vote at meetings, keep your nose to the grindstone and your mouth shut. Everyone does it. Who wants to spit into the wind?

—Vladimir Bukovsky[7]

Experimental and other research by Western psychologists in the area of role playing is only in its infancy, but there are tentative conclusions that are suggestive with regard to Soviet political socialization. As Daryl Bem has put it, "it would seem very difficult to play a particular role all of one's life without 'internalizing' part of it, that is, without beginning to believe part of it."[8] This effect can be seen in the following anecdote by a former Soviet citizen:

> I knew, for instance, a student who was Russian. Very bright. I remember his reading Solzhenitsyn during our second year. I knew about it: we sort of trusted each other. But then he joined the Party, and is making a big career. But at the same time, in the depths of his heart he disliked the regime very much. But you can't live with a split personality. It's very difficult. You have to justify what you are doing. You can't be disgusted with yourself. *You have to readjust your philosophy to your way of life.*[9]

This adds considerable significance to the fact that one of the hallmarks of Soviet society is the pressure for Soviet citizens to participate in a great number and variety of politically significant activities.[10] They are not paid to participate; they are probably not harmed physically if they do not. But the subtle pressure of expectation is everywhere, and it falls disproportionately on the young, on Party members, and on non-Party members occupying key positions. One learns at an early age that to "get ahead" one has to do some things "voluntarily."

From cradle to grave, political activity—whether motivated by sincere belief or sheer opportunism—seems to be necessary for a share of the better things life has to offer, such as leadership positions in school, attainment of coveted educational opportunities, the best jobs, good housing, and so forth. These rewards, however, are not direct and immediate. Rather, they seem to come when they come, but it is a good calculated risk that they will—sooner or later. The Soviet citizen who volunteers more or less opportunistically, then, may hope that the rewards will come; but there is no guarantee.

If Bem and his fellow psychologists are right, a person in this position will be more likely to change attitudes than one who can count on a direct and immediate reward. In addition, there is a wealth of social-psychological evidence suggesting that actively playing a role is more likely to socialize a person to a given set of beliefs than if that person were merely the passive receiver of someone else's indoctrination efforts. Seldom is the Communist Youth League *(Komsomol)** member paid off directly and immediately for volunteering to give Party-line lectures at a factory. This person is most likely, however, to be pushed unconsciously a little further in the direction of believing the political message that these lectures contain. At the very least, the Soviet system of "volunteer" work replaces unstructured free time with structured efforts at political indoctrination.

What are some of the most common jobs for which "volunteers" are expected? A Communist Youth League member might be put in charge of

---

*The Communist Youth League is an organization for people from fifteen to twenty-seven years of age.

the program for a group of Young Pioneers.* Members might volunteer for work details at their school or university, to do such jobs as cleaning lab equipment or painting walls or doing needed factory or farm work during the summer or on holidays. Allen Kassof cites the example of a group of Young Pioneers that was set to work collecting relics of the Revolution which they then discussed and turned over to the local museum.[11]

Perhaps the classic type of "volunteer" labor is the *Subbotnik* (from the Russian word for Saturday, *Subbota*). As the name implies, it involves voluntary unpaid work on Saturdays and began in 1919 or 1920 when the new Soviet Union was in a state of civil war, "as a contribution to the fund for the defense of the young Soviet Republic.[12] Currently, a *Subbotnik* is celebrated with great fanfare on the Saturday nearest the birthday of Lenin (April 22), though they may take place at other times of the year.[13] All workers are expected to do an extra day of work; the money earned or saved is collected and spent on some socially beneficial project, such as a research center. There is a tremendous media "hype," and some celebrities contribute labors that are little more than symbolic and inspirational. For example, during the 1980 *Subbotnik* the Soviet cosmonauts orbiting the earth symbolically vacuum-cleaned their spaceship. The average Soviet citizen, however, does nothing more glamorous or exciting than work an extra day for no pay. For example, *Izvestiia* noted that during the April 1984 *Subbotnik*, over 2 million people in Lithuania manufactured goods worth over 8 million rubles.[14]

For Party members and non-Party activists, lifelong study in the adult political instruction system is expected. These students have full-time jobs and family responsibilities, so that meeting classes and doing assignments can take up a substantial portion of their leisure time. Also, from time to time they may be assigned to give a political presentation to an outside group, to go to a theoretical conference, or to visit a collective farm to provide the proper political interpretation of some current problem. The instructors in this adult political instruction system are intellectuals and officials from industrial organizations who are also "volunteering" their free time to teach in the system.[15]

Much of the agitation and propaganda network runs by means of volunteer labor, mostly of Party members who are concurrently improving their political knowledge in the adult political instruction system. Even voting in elections is not "voluntary" in the sense that it is in the United States. It is no accident that Soviet elections regularly turn out 99 percent of the eligible electorate. Careful records are kept of who voted, and the person who has not voted yet may find himself being escorted to the polls. Refusal to vote, under these circumstances, is rare.

Collective Responsibility

The Soviet citizen is definitely his brother's (or sister's) keeper. Your behavior is everybody's business. One of the authors can recall the following experience:

*An organization for children age ten to fifteen.

I was sitting in a trolley car, nose buried in a book, when I heard an imperious "DEVUSHKA!" ("YOUNG WOMAN!") It soon became clear that it was directed at me, so I looked up—into the face of a righteously indignant middle-aged Soviet woman. Having finally gotten my attention, the woman began abusing me for my lack of courtesy. When I protested innocence (after all, I was quietly sitting and reading and bothering no one), I found that my sin was one of omission. Unnoticed by me, an elderly woman had gotten onto the trolley and, in the opinion of the indignant woman at least (and no one contradicted her), I should have made it my business to notice this fact and leap up, offering my seat. The fact that I had not seen the old woman was irrelevant. Sheepishly, I got up and offered my seat—there was little else to do, since ignorance was obviously no defense and it was equally obvious that the old woman did need to sit more than I did. I soon came to dread the sound of that imperious "DE-VUSHKA!" It invariably meant an embarrassing incident in which I would be hard put to defend myself, but it *did* make me much more guarded in my behavior than I ever had been in the United States. More recently, a visiting journalist observed that "complete strangers will come up and tell you that you must tie your shoelaces, that you mustn't swim in the river after a picnic, that your car is dirty and you should clean it."[16]

This phenomenon, which might be regarded as an officially sanctioned busybodyism, is one of the most difficult things for Westerners to adjust to in Soviet life. Whereas we are taught to mind our own business, Soviet children are taught responsibility for their playmates' behavior. This lesson is begun in the earliest school years,[17] when classroom teachers are supposed to encourage competition between the rows of children in the classroom to achieve the highest standards of behavior and achievement. Large charts are posted in the school where the standings of the rows are given, both for individual and overall kinds of activities. Later the children "graduate" from membership in rows to membership in Young Pioneer and *Komsomol* groups or "links." This system covers a wide range of behavior. For example, a superior student may be assigned to help one who is behind in his or her studies. This is probably fairly common. However, there have been some more extreme cases.[18] In one, the *Komsomol* group took it upon itself to try to resolve a situation where a male member had left his wife (also a member) for another woman. This interference was enthusiastically endorsed in an editorial in *Komsomolskaia Pravda*, the official newspaper of the Communist Youth League.

When we lived in the dormitory at Moscow University, we heard rumors of night inspections of dormitory rooms but never experienced them ourselves (perhaps our status as a married couple helped). We were, however, subject to periodic unannounced cleanliness inspections by our *Komsomol* floor committee. The results of these inspections were posted in the lobby for all to read.

The special impact of such experiences on young people grows out of the particular vulnerability of children and teenagers to peer-group influences. Embarrassment can be doubly painful if it is in the presence of one's peers. This form of socialization is not limited to youth; it continues throughout life when the school *kollektiv* is replaced by a housing *kollektiv* or a

work *kollektiv*. These groups, unknown in the United States, are very powerful in the Soviet Union. They have the capacity to supervise and interfere in
almost all facets of a member's life, be it relations with his or her spouse, the
discipline of children, or the diligence with which a job is done.[19] The central
role of the collective in Soviet life can be seen in the following quotation from
a Soviet book on social psychology:

> The moral foundation of the personality is laid in the family, but the full
> flowering and formation of the personality of human beings can be achieved
> only in the working collective. That is, in the working collective, where common
> labor is carried out on the principle of comradely cooperation and mutual aid
> and where the unity of state, social and individual interests is assured, a person
> can completely realize himself and have the sensation of being a participant in a
> common cause—the building of communism.[20]

This emphasis on the centrality of the work collective to the organization of
Soviet life has recently received attention in Soviet law. Special mention was
made of the work collective in the 1977 Constitution (Article 8), and a law
"On Work Collectives and Increasing their Role in the Management of
Enterprises, Institutions and Organizations" was adopted in 1983. The
thrust of the law is on consultation of workers in periodic mass meetings. But
actual worker participation in management does not seem to be intended.[21]

All of this emphasis on collectivism may seem alien to those who place a
high value on individualism. But a positive side may also be discerned in
collectivism's contribution to preserving public order. Jane Jacobs in her
landmark book *The Death and Life of Great American Cities* makes the point that
the safety of city streets is directly related to the extent to which there are
"eyes upon the street, eyes belonging to those we might call the natural
proprietors of the street."[22] Recently, the Soviet police have begun distribu-
ting cards called "check lists for lawbreakers."[23] These cards can be used by
Soviet citizens to report the name and address of anyone they think has
committed one of a list of crimes printed on the card or any other breach of
public order, including "the rules of Socialist communal life." The name of
the person filling out the card need not be appended.

A neighborhood in which there is a sense of community responsibility
for what happens on the streets and in the corridors will be much safer than
one in which there is none. Persons who have lived in the USSR for any
length of time overwhelmingly report that they feel safer in Moscow and
Leningrad than in comparable American cities. While a good bit of this
impression may be accounted for by the false sense of security engendered
by the failure of the Soviet news media to report crimes, this censorship does
not explain it all away. Especially in the case of youth, there is much less
temptation to misbehave because the street does have eyes upon it and the
persons behind those eyes feel free to make your business their business.
According to a Soviet commentator:

The collective's demands upon its members, its inculcation of a sense of responsibility in each person play a tremendously important role. No specialised control agencies can replace the wealth of comradely, friendly influence that the collective can bring to bear. There is no greater power of influence on human behavior than the power of the collective.[24]

Though this is not the whole story,* the positive features of collective responsibility should not be overshadowed by its all-too-obvious potential for abuse.

The Carrot and the Stick

In Western commentaries more emphasis has been placed on the punishments that threaten Soviet citizens than on the rewards that lure them. Thus, Westerners who follow the news media tend to be quite well informed on the mistreatment of those Soviet citizens who do not conform to the wishes of the leadership. They are much less aware of the benefits to be derived from going along with the system.

In part, this is a result of the information that is made available in the West; we, too, are prone to have our opinions molded by the selection of information that is fed us by the mass media. The saving grace is that this selection is not as tightly controlled from the center as is the Soviet version. Our bias is much more related to the fact that prison camps and other punishments make much more spectacular copy for newspapers, magazines, and television as well as far better speech material for up-and-coming politicians. But that is not the whole story. There is also the fact that it is easier for North Americans and Western Europeans to understand the punishments. The attractiveness to Soviet citizens of many of the rewards is difficult to comprehend because the conditions of Soviet life are so much different.

To take one example, it would seldom be effective to bribe an American to compromise beliefs or behavior by promising an opportunity to rent a desirable apartment. In the Soviet Union, however, most people live in housing that would be considered distinctly substandard by Americans. Even some of the newest and "nicest" apartment complexes resemble nothing so much as crudely built public housing in the United States. These, though, are an improvement over a single room (or curtained-off corner) in a drafty wooden hut or a crumbling relic of prerevolutionary Russia. Coupled with this is the fact that rents in the Soviet Union are so low that almost anyone can afford a desirable apartment—the trick is to find one to rent. The effect of this on some persons' value choices is made clear in an excerpt from the Burg and Feifer biography of Solzhenitsyn.

---

*The apparently greater safety of Soviet cities is also a function of such things as a relatively less acute drug problem, the lack of ghettoized minorities in urban centers, strong gun controls, and the pervasive formal control network.

Three writers supported Matushkin. But the fourth, Yevgeny Markin, hesitated. He suggested that the praise–censure pendulum had swung too often and was troubled by the lurching from one extreme to the other. "If we expel Solzhenitsyn today but may have to readmit him later," he concluded, "I want nothing to do with this business."

In the end, Markin did vote against Solzhenitsyn. Later, it became known that he had been persuaded before the meeting by the offer of a new flat. (He hinted broadly at his extremely cramped living conditions during the meeting itself.) During the next few days, according to Ryazan residents, he roamed wildly drunk through the town, repenting loudly, cursing himself and bemoaning his weakness. Two years later he published some poems which many interpreted as condemning himself and other members of the establishment intelligentsia for acting against their consciences in the Solzhenitsyn affair.[25]

The system of rewards tends to be an interlocking affair in which the acquisition of some of the rewards significantly increases a person's chances for further rewards. First, and perhaps most crucial, is educational opportunity.

When I was fourteen, which is when they start taking everyone into the Komsomol, I refused to join. "What's the matter? Do you believe in God?" they asked me curiously, but I refused to give any explanation. They pressed me for a very long time, because I was a good student and it was the accepted thing for all the good ones to be in the Komsomol, but they didn't get anywhere and in the end gave up. "Watch out," said my friends, "you'll find it harder to get into the university."[26]

In the Soviet Union to a much greater extent than in the West, higher education or advanced training of some sort is the key to upward mobility and the good things of life. In order to reach the pinnacle represented by the academician or the prima ballerina, one must first be admitted to one of the top universities, institutes, or training schools. Known "troublemakers" will find the path strewn with obstacles, as will the children of known "troublemakers." No matter what your aspirations (unless they are for relative solitude and spartan living), being a member of the Communist Party or *Komsomol* will help. If you are zealous in your organizational activities—so much the better. Such things may lead to a good job in a desirable location—preferably Moscow or Leningrad. Good jobs pay well and the pay may be augmented by bonuses for fulfillment or overfulfillment of plan. If the job is prestigious enough it may also carry with it access to special shops which are closed to the general public and which carry those luxuries that make for the good life—Soviet style. Also included may be the opportunity to travel outside the Soviet Union, posh (by Soviet standards) housing accommodations, a country home, household help, automobiles, and numerous other luxuries.

Though all of the above rewards tend to hinge on the possession of special skills or learning as well as political activism, there are others that are accessible to the humblest factory or collective-farm workers. There are awards for brigades of shopworkers who have overfulfilled their plans, there are medals for outstanding activists and workers, and there are titles (like "Heroine Mother" for bearing and raising ten or more children). In addition, for real political standouts, there may be membership in the Supreme Soviet, which does not carry much power but which is prestigious and which offers those from remote parts of the Soviet Union the periodic opportunity to taste the cosmopolitan delights of Moscow.

If this describes a sampling of the rewards, what of the punishments? Never when we lived in or visited the Soviet Union were we particularly aware of fear "as an ever-present reality of Soviet Life."[27] It is likely that this was the case in the worst of the Stalin era and may still be the case for a narrow sector of the Soviet populace that is actively engaged in political dissent. The prevalent atmosphere, however, seems to be one of caution. For some, this caution is sprinkled with striking instances of what can only be regarded as bravery or foolhardiness. At times we found ourselves much more concerned about the welfare of our Soviet friends and acquaintances than they seemed to be about themselves. This apparent recklessness appears to be a development stemming from the death of Stalin and the demise of the strength of Stalinism which coincided with the Khrushchevian thaw. There is relatively little chance of someone's being taken to Lyubanka prison and summarily shot nowadays. The current leaders have tried to put the lid back on, but the effort is not nearly as firm or frightening as it was before.

The punishments are often the opposite of the rewards. You may be denied admission to a university, institute, or trade school. If graduated, you may be assigned to an inappropriate or low-status job in some undesirable and remote place. This can, in turn, bring low pay or good pay in a situation where there is nothing worthwhile to spend it on. Needless to say, there is no chance for travel, and your lack of priority will probably result in inferior housing conditions. Although these are some of the milder punishments, they are not to be scoffed at, since they can affect life in almost all its facets.

More ominous are the punishments reserved for the more difficult cases—such as those of the dissidents. First, and perhaps mildest, is the constant harassment experienced by nonconforming Soviet citizens and, on occasion, their families or friends. Measures in this category include dismissal from one's job or the voiding of one's residence permit to live in a desirable location. More extreme are incarceration in a prison or commitment to a mental institution. Capital punishment is still used for a wide variety of crimes, but it is not overtly used as a sanction against political dissenters. Some of the latter have died or had their health broken in prison, however, allegedly as a result of mistreatment. One of the most extreme current measures is simply getting the person out of the Soviet Union permanently. Trotsky was exiled in this way in 1929, but the measure was not used again until 1974, when the Nobel Laureate Solzhenitsyn was arrested, questioned, and summarily flown out of the Soviet Union. A variation on this practice has been used a number of times in recent years. A dissident is allowed to go abroad for a time (or encouraged to do so on threat of worse treatment if he refuses). While he is abroad his citizenship is taken away and he is barred from returning to the USSR.

Cases such as these receive wide publicity in the West. But it is not as it was in Stalin's time when severe punishment or death could happen to anyone, even the most blameless and loyal. The people who are being punished now know that they are defying written or unwritten laws or that they are associated with those who are. If a Soviet citizen is discreet and conservative in behavior, it is possible to go about the business of living without fear of undue retribution. Those who choose to do otherwise apprehend—whether vaguely or with clarity—that they are running risks which may have grave consequences.

The punishment-reward approach is probably the least effective of the characteristic Soviet approaches to political socialization. Why? A person clearly threatened with punishment or enticed with rewards is more likely to be openly defiant or go along with what is expected without altering basic attitudes and values. If successful political socialization is to be defined as something more than eliciting external compliance, and we think it should be, compliance without conviction is not the most desirable outcome of the socialization process. As indicated previously, however, there is evidence that if a person plays a role for a long enough period of time, there is a good chance attitudes will change to become more in tune with the role.

"THE NEW SOVIET PERSON"

Now that we have an overview of the major characteristics of the socializing process in the Soviet Union, it is time to take a closer look at the message. In essence, the entire thrust of the political socialization process is a conscious effort to create a new kind of person, a Soviet citizen tailored to the needs of the regime, a "Builder of Communism." In her monograph on Soviet information networks, Gayle Durham Hollander has drawn the following concise portrait of the ideal Soviet citizen:

> The composite ideal citizen is totally politicized, yielding to the judgment of the Party even in the most personal aspects of life; a lover of labor and an enthusiastic contributor to the Soviet economy; always an activist, participating on cue in civic activities such as demonstrations and agitation and propaganda sessions organized by the Party. The ideal citizen is also politically literate, possessing a firm grasp on ideology as a guide for thinking and living (such education is a mandatory part of all education, even at the most specialized levels); unspontaneous and self-disciplined; vigilant against enemies of the Party and state (even among one's own family members or friends); totally patriotic; has a strong sense of solidarity with workers in other countries (as long as this agrees with the current Party line), and finally, is primarily collectivist and anti-individualist. There is also a whole set of virtues which are not specifically political, but associated with the "good citizen": honesty, sobriety, modesty,

courage, egalitarianism, intolerance of injustice, and so on. Obviously, this is a tall order.[28]

Note that the emphasis here is on the public image one must present, on the role one must play when in the presence of others. Assuming that the role is played by most people, the extent to which it is internalized is another matter. It can hardly fail to be internalized to some extent, however, by anybody who bothers to play it. On the other hand, from the point of view of the leadership, a fairly thorough effort to be the kind of person described above is a practical substitute for absolute belief.

Although some Soviet authorities maintain that human nature has changed in the Soviet Union,[29] even a short stay in Moscow is bound to bring the foreigner into contact with persons who seem quite unreconstructed. There are many Soviet citizens who are honestly trying to live up to the ideal of the "new Soviet person," and a few who seem to succeed, but the conditions of life in the Soviet Union today make this a difficult task. Undoubtedly, life in the Soviet Union is easier now than it has been for most people at any time in the past. Material conditions have improved enormously, and there is no longer widespread fear of arbitrary and unjust arrest and imprisonment. However, by Western standards, the situation is far from ideal.

Many consumer goods are in short supply or unavailable most of the time. Consequently, besieged salespersons are among the rudest and most arbitrary in the world. The system used in most stores—a buyer must pay one person and pick up the purchase from another—is a monument to distrust. Inadequate and substandard housing crowds people together so closely that friction is bound to develop over shared facilities, such as communal kitchens, and the lack of considerateness among neighbors. A high level of civic and political activity is difficult to maintain when one works a full day and then has to spend another hour or so standing in line to get food for dinner—coupled perhaps with another hour in line because some scarce clothing item is suddenly being sold and will be gone tomorrow. Conditions such as this foster an ethic which holds that a person's first task is to take care of Number One—by any means possible. It also seems to encourage the notion that stealing from the state is acceptable as long as you do not get caught. The jokes and songs that circulate in private express the opposite of an uncritical and enthusiastic acceptance of all Party pronouncements and orders.

In short, although many people occasionally exhibit the characteristics of the "new Soviet person" some of the time or most of the time (at least around foreigners), upon close examination it is difficult to conclude that human nature has changed. There is outward conformity, coupled with a certain amount of inward acceptance of the norms and values of the regime. But human nature in the old-fashioned sense of the word still seems firmly entrenched in the Soviet Union.

MAJOR SOCIALIZING INSTITUTIONS

Now that we know the message and the way it is conveyed, it is time to look at the medium. In a sense, it is virtually impossible to single out a small group of institutions that can be said to do the job of political socialization in any country. This is even more so in the Soviet Union, where virtually every facet of life brings a person into contact with political messages. The only reasonable thing to do is to concentrate on those institutions that bear the brunt of the socializing task. This will be done here on an institution-by-institution basis in the approximate order in which the average Soviet citizen might come into closest contact with them during his journey from cradle to grave.

The first and most obvious institution in a person's life is the family. In the Soviet Union families come in a variety of compositions and sizes, ranging from the extended family of the Central Asian republics to the tiny family of the unwed mother. The most common type of family is the urban nuclear family composed of mother, father, and one or two children. There was a time in the Soviet Union when there was considerable conflict over child-rearing methods and values between the young Soviet regime and the traditionally oriented families of the various Soviet nationalities. This friction has gradually declined over the years, as most Soviet parents are now persons born and raised well after the Revolution.

For example, the practice of religious training was once a major source of tension between families and the government. Now, although there are doubtless many exceptions, a much smaller proportion of Soviet parents has strong religious beliefs.[30] Attachment to old customs and traditions of child care is also fading—rapidly in the cities and slowly in rural areas and ethnic strongholds such as Central Asia. For these and many other reasons revolving around the consolidation of power in the Soviet regime, the conflict between family and state is no longer a major problem. In the future, the child-rearing practices of Soviet parents will be further influenced by a new course, introduced in a 1984 school reform, that focuses on "the ethics and psychology of family life."[31] Thus, the family has largely become an ally of the state.

The evidence is strong that a majority of Soviet parents are—for a complex of reasons including expediency, ideological agreement, and ambition—more than willing to shift responsibility to the state. That is, they view political socialization as the responsibility of the educational system and the youth groups. Their role is seen as supportive rather than central. The most common form of parental participation in political socialization is the discussion of domestic and foreign current events, as well as of the ideological and political content of art and literature. According to a recent report,[32] more than 40 percent of older schoolchildren regularly discuss political news with their fathers. Another 31 percent hold such discussions periodically. These discussions are based primarily on newspaper, radio, and television news reports.

Before proceeding to an outline of the educational system and youth group structure, which provide the basic socializing experience for Soviet children, it should again be emphasized that the process is centrally controlled and that certain guiding principles are uniformly applied. These have been summarized by Urie Bronfenbrenner:

1. The peer collective (under adult leadership) rivals and nearly surpasses the family as the principle agent of socialization.

2. Competition between groups is utilized as the principle mechanism for motivating achievement of behavior norms.

3. The behavior of the individual is evaluated primarily in terms of its relevance to the goals and achievements of the collective.

4. Rewards and punishments are frequently given on a group basis . . .

5. As soon as possible, the task of evaluating the behavior of individuals and of dispensing rewards and sanctions is delegated to the members of the collective.

6. The principle methods of social control are public recognition and public criticism, with explicit training and practice being given in these activities. Specifically, each member of the collective is encouraged to observe deviant behavior by his fellows and is given opportunity to report his observations to the group. Reporting on one's peers is esteemed and rewarded as a civic duty.

7. Group criticism becomes the vehicle for training in self-criticism in the presence of one's peers.[33]

Although preschool institutions are not, technically speaking, part of the Soviet educational system, for many children they are the setting for the first extrafamilial educational experiences. Since about half of the Soviet work force is composed of women, the need for child care is substantial. Soviet parents usually solve child-care problems in one of two basic ways. One solution is the *babushka,* or grandmother. The mother of one of the parents lives with the family and takes over the main burdens of housekeeping and child care. This solution has been very important in the past and still plays a role, as one can easily see in Soviet parks frequented by black-coated *babushkas* and their small charges. This method of child care is bound to diminish in importance in the future, however, as today's professional and skilled mothers become tomorrow's professional and skilled grandmothers. This will reduce even more the traditional influences in the socialization of young people.

The child-care institutions, which are destined to increase in importance in the future, are the child-care centers *(yasli),* which accept children up to the age of four, and the nursery school-kindergartens *(detskie sady),* which accept four- to six-year-olds. By the end of 1978, preschool institutions had enrolled 13,177,000 children. The majority of these (7,567,000) were in the Russian Soviet Federated Socialist Republic. This represents a considerable expansion, since it more than triples the 4,428,000 children (3,038,000 of which were in the RSFSR) enrolled in preschools in 1960.[34]

Up to five years of age the emphasis is on simple physical care, entertainment, health-promoting activities, and the learning of basic skills, such as feeding and dressing oneself.[35] At five, however, begins the process of instilling patriotic feelings in the children. There are simple lessons on their local community, the Soviet Army, and Lenin. At age six these are supplemented by lessons on the international situation and on other nationalities. Respect for Soviet national symbols, such as the flag, is also inculcated.

At age six or seven the child enters the first grade and can expect to continue in school for the following eleven or twelve years. At this point begins a much more pronounced emphasis on the *kollektiv*. The Soviet child immediately finds himself a member of many groups that are in a constant state of competition.[36] Rows in a classroom compete, classrooms in a school compete, and schools in a region compete. In this context it is not hard to understand why the notion of competition between social systems and competition between nations comes easily to a Soviet citizen. For them, it is part of the natural state of things.

In short, competition is certainly not discouraged in the USSR. If anything, it receives more official emphasis in Soviet schools than in American schools. But there is one key difference—the competition is between groups, not individuals. Among individuals in a group, cooperation and mutual aid are encouraged. "Individualism" is a dirty word in the Soviet Union. And the intermixture of competition and cooperation becomes even more complex when competing groups at one level (for example, the rows in a classroom) become part of a cooperating collective at another level (for example, the classrooms in a school building).[37]

Superimposed on this structure and further increasing its complexity is the competitive relationship between and among the "links," which are the smaller units of Soviet youth groups. The earliest youth group that a child may join (and virtually all do) is the Young Octobrists. This accepts children from seven to ten years old. At ten the children may become Young Pioneers and, again, membership is almost universal. From the Pioneers the next step is the *Komsomol*. Here, however, universality of membership ceases. A degree of selectivity is introduced that is similar to, though less stringent than, the admission process necessary for Communist Party membership. At this level, persons are admitted only on an individual basis, not by whole classrooms, as is sometimes the case with Young Pioneers. Young people from ages fifteen to twenty-seven are eligible to become *Komsomols*, but aspiring members must be sponsored by either *Komsomols* of two-years' standing or by Communist Party members. They must also give evidence of desirable character traits.

Together with the regular school courses in civics, history, and social studies, the members of these youth organizations get additional citizenship training in their activities outside the school. Let us take the Young Pioneers as an example, since their activities are probably formative for the largest number of Soviet adults. The network of their extramural institutions include Young Pioneer Palaces and Houses; Young Technicians' stations;

Young Naturalists' stations; Young Tourists' stations; children's libraries; sports, art, and music groups; and Young Pioneer camps. Within this framework of institutions the Young Pioneers both learn and teach younger members of the organization.

The political content of the ideological framework of the Young Pioneers is clear in the ceremony of admission to membership. In the presence of older Pioneers, *Komsomols*, teachers, leaders, and parents, the new members take the following pledge:

> I, a Young Pioneer of the Soviet Union, solemnly promise in the presence of my comrades
> to warmly love my Soviet motherland
> to live, to study, and to struggle as Lenin willed and as the Communist Party teaches.[38]

Then the new member promises to observe the rules:

> The Pioneer loves his motherland and the Communist Party of the Soviet Union. He prepares himself for membership in the Komsomol.
> The Pioneer reveres the memory of those who have given their lives in the struggle for the freedom and the well-being of the Soviet motherland.
> The Pioneer is friendly with the children of all the countries of the world.
> The Pioneer studies diligently and is disciplined and courteous.
> The Pioneer loves to work and to conserve the national wealth.
> The Pioneer is a good comrade, who is solicitous of younger children and who helps older people.
> The Pioneer grows up to be bold and does not fear difficulties.
> The Pioneer tells the truth and guards the honor of his detachment.
> The Pioneer strengthens himself and does physical exercises every day.
> The Pioneer loves nature; he is a defender of planted areas, of useful birds and animals.
> The Pioneer is an example for all children.[39]

The political content of the Pioneer program is also clear from such activities as participation in the November 7 and May Day Parades as well as ritual visits to lay flowers at monuments to Lenin. Indeed, the combination of attractive facilities and programs with a strong collectivist and patriotic message makes these youth groups potentially powerful agents of political socialization.

All Soviet education has political content, but some courses have more than others. As N. P. Kuzin, a Soviet educator puts it:

> Under the present conditions of the school, the task of inculcating a scientific Marxist-Leninist world view, which is founded on a position of Communist Party-mindedness (*partiinost'*), is part of the process of instruction in every subject. However, subjects in the social and political cycle—history (domestic and world), economic and political geography, social studies—hold special

significance in the formation of the pupils' understanding of the laws of social development and in their inculcation with strong civic feelings and with a sense of social standards in conformity with the norms of socialist society.[40]

In 1984, the Supreme Soviet approved a school reform plan.[41] The goal of this reform was to change the school from an institution whose primary objective is education into a place where children can be more overtly molded into "new Soviet persons" and where they can be prepared for productive work by age sixteen.[42] These goals are to be realized by approximately 1990. Innovations are to include new textbooks and courses, such as a new social studies course designed to inculcate communist ideals, socialist internationalism, and pride in the USSR. Also, there will be a new group of elective courses on ideology.

Vocational training is to be given increased importance. Starting in the second grade, vocational training will occupy an even larger proportion of the school week, and many more children will be channeled into vocational-technical schools upon completing the ninth grade. This aspect of the reform seems aimed at enlarging the size of the labor pool and decreasing the number of students aspiring to higher education. It also seems to be designed to improve the productivity of Soviet workers.

A heavy dose of political material is continued in the post-secondary educational system, whether the student goes on to some form of vocational education or to a university or institute. In order to be admitted to an institution of higher education, for example, one must have graduated from a general education school or the equivalent. One must also pass a set of examinations. These entrance examinations include Russian language and literature, a foreign language, and specialized subjects according to the projected field of concentration of the aspiring student. For social science and humanities majors this means a test in the history of the USSR. Once the student is admitted, he or she will take more than six hundred hours of instruction in socio-political topics and several hundred more on military and civil defense training.[43]

In adulthood the collectivist influence of the school and youth groups is continued. Reminiscing about his young adult years, Sergei Zamascikov, a former Soviet citizen, has observed:

> The net of primary Komsomol organizations and committees that exists in every factory, institution and educational establishment places the young Soviet person in a situation where on every important issue in his life—from acquiring an obligatory recommendation for university admission to obtaining a ticket to the local disco—he has to deal with the Komsomol, and, in one way or another, to conform with its ideology.[44]

Supplementing the influence of the *Komsomol* is the influence of the *kollektiv*. Those who go on for higher education become members of the *kollektiv* at their university or institute. For those who enter the work force directly from the general education schools or vocational-technical schools, the *kollektivs* are at their places of work and their places of residence. In either case, their lives are considerably influenced by the cooperative efforts of their *kollektiv* and local *Komsomol* organization.

For the elite group who are *Komsomol* members or who become Party members, the role of political socialization activities in their lives looms even larger. They are expected to engage in constant political work among their non-Party colleagues and neighbors, both to enforce and to inculcate the values inherent in the ideal of the "new Soviet person." Aside from active efforts, they are expected to lead exemplary lives themselves in order to demonstrate to others how a "new Soviet person" should conduct his or her affairs. Finally, Party members are expected to be working constantly to upgrade their own ideological level, not only by keeping up with Party and government activities in the mass media, but also by participating in agitation and propaganda activities and by attending political schools.

News, both in the broadcast media and the written media, is what the Party says it is. As a practical matter this means mostly stories highlighting current Party policy or Soviet economic advances. Ultimate control over content rests with higher Party authorities. Day-to-day decision making on all but the most sensitive issues is usually done by lower-level officials.

In cases involving highly trusted people, this can amount to self-censorship. For example, in an interview[45] Boris Kalyagin, a senior political commentator on Soviet television, described his work in the following way:

> Of course we have to express views which are official in our country. It's quite a responsibility, because no one [no censor] reads what we are saying before we go on the air. There's no revision. Our second bulletin comes on at 11 P.M. and there's no one around to ask or to check. . . . So we have full responsibility for what we say.

Notable here is, first, his total acceptance of censorship as the norm and, second, his lack of ambivalence about functioning as a spokesperson for the government.

The government agency responsible for publishing is the State Committee on the Press of the USSR Council of Ministers, whose Main Administration for the Preservation of State Secrets in the Press *(Glavlit)* apparently handles censorship functions.[46] The number of subjects that are prohibited from being mentioned in the Soviet press is formidable. A former Soviet citizen who had direct contact with Soviet censorship operations has described the *Index of Information Not to Be Published in the Open Press,* a thick book informally referred to as the "Talmud." This three-hundred page, small-print volume covers every conceivable forbidden topic, including general information, military information, industry, construction, agriculture, transport, economics, and finance. A partial list of prohibited topics in the section on general information includes the following:

1. Information about earthquakes, avalanches, landslides and other natural disasters on the territory of the USSR;
2. Information about fires, explosions, aeroplane, naval and mine disasters, train crashes;
3. Figures about the earnings of government and Party workers;
4. Any comparison of the budget of Soviet citizens and the prices of goods;
5. Information about even seasonal or local price increases;
6. Reports about increased living standards anywhere outside the socialist camp;
7. Reports of food shortages in the USSR (it is possible only to speak about local bottlenecks in the delivery of specific items);
8. Any kind of average statistics about the country as a whole not taken from Central Statistical Bureau reports;
9. The names of any KGB operatives apart from the Committee's Chairman;
10. The names of employees of the former Committee for Cultural Relations with Foreign Countries, again, apart from the Chairman of the Committee;
11. Aerial photographs of Soviet cities and the precise geographical coordinates of any populated point on Soviet territory;
12. Any mention of Glavlit organs and the jamming of foreign radio broadcasts;
13. Names of political figures on a special list, to which belong five of the eight Soviet "prime ministers," Rykov, Molotov, Malenkov, Bulganin, and Khrushchev.[47]

As this short extract from the "Talmud" shows, the forbidden subjects include not only military information and other data that a vigilant government bureaucrat in the West would probably want to keep secret but also anything that might conceivably reflect negatively on the USSR. Any Westerner who gains even a cursory acquaintance with the Soviet press quickly perceives this unorthodox (to us) approach to the news. The American correspondent Hedrick Smith put it well when he wrote an article on Soviet journalism entitled "In Moscow, the Bigger the News, the Smaller the Story."[48]

Aside from this formal censorship, Soviet journalists have to cope with an informal accountability structure as well. Foremost in this connection is the Union of Journalists which, instead of functioning as a representative of the workers to the management, functions to keep journalists in line should they show a tendency to stray. A journalist intent on defying central control can be removed from Union membership for breach of a professional code that is vague enough to be interpreted in many convenient ways. Such removal effectively closes a journalist out of the profession. In addition, editors can also be called to account by the local Party organization. Last, but not least, the journalists' trade magazine, *Zhurnalist*, is used to keep tabs on media professionals, mainly by means of the publication of critical articles that convey official displeasure not only with the journalists involved but also with Party officials in that locale.

To some extent, this system may be in the process of change—albeit somewhat marginal change from a Western point of view. In his speech at the Twenty-Seventh Party Congress in 1986, General Secretary Gorbachev called for more openness in the mass media. This new openness *(glasnost')* had actually been discussed in the media prior to the Party Congress. In part it seems to be intended to support Gorbachev's campaign against corruption. In fact, reported resistance to this new policy at the local level has been attributed in the national media to the reluctance of local Party officials to allow criticism of local Party activities and officials in newspapers under their control. There have, however, also been calls for openness of other types, such as the reporting of natural disasters and details of current events (for example, a methanol-drinking tragedy in which there was loss of life). It is too early yet to ascertain the boundaries of this new media policy, but it seems to herald only a more flexible censorship system, not its abolition.

Censorship, however, is not only a negative matter of forbidding journalists to print or broadcast certain messages. It is also a matter of setting standards as to what they are expected to publish. These standards are expressed most comprehensively in the "Basic Principles of the Soviet Press," which are discussed at length in the official handbook for Soviet journalists. These "Basic Principles" are

1. Party-mindedness or unconditional Party loyalty (Partiinost)
2. High ideological content (Idéinost')
3. Patriotism (Otéchestvennost')
4. Truthfulness (to Leninist theory) (Pravdívost')
5. Having a popular character (Naródnost')
6. Accessibility to the masses (Mássovost)
7. Criticism and self-criticism (Krítika i Sámo-Krítika)[49]

According to Gayle Durham Hollander, who has done extensive research on the Soviet press, a "good part of the Soviet journalist's training is devoted to teaching him how to apply them in various situations." She adds, "How well he uses these guidelines is one measure of his success."[50]

This system of censorship not only involves journalists. It affects anyone attempting to publish or produce anything, including books, films, and plays. Everything has to be written with an eye to ideological, as well as artistic, requirements. Along with normal editorial duties, Soviet editors must make sure that manuscripts conform to the dictates of socialist realism. This means that they "must have a positive hero, that the (from the Communist point of view) good must defeat the (from the Communist point of view) evil, and that the general thrust and tone of the work must be optimistic."[51] There must be no criticism, expressed or implied, of the Soviet system, and life in capitalist systems must be presented negatively.

Of course, what is in a paper, book, or magazine is of little moment if no one reads it. For the Soviet Union mass literacy is a relatively recent phenomenon, and people read constantly and proudly. One of the things which first strikes a Westerner is the fact that most people carry books, magazines, or newspapers with them constantly and use odd moments to read—standing at a bus stop, swaying in a subway car, or waiting in one of the ubiquitous lines. *Izvestiia,* the official government newspaper, proudly proclaimed in 1974 that the Soviet people were the "Readingest People in the World."[52]

Large numbers of newspapers and periodicals are published, and the degree of central control is great—though not absolute. Many agencies have their own newspapers, including the Party Central Committee *(Pravda)*, the Soviet government *(Izvestiia)*, the *Komsomol (Komsomolskaia Pravda)*, the military *(Krasnaia Zvezda)*, and the Union of Soviet Writers *(Literaturnaia Gazeta)*. These are among the most important, but there are approximately eight thousand newspapers in the entire Soviet Union. So many newspapers does not mean that there is a great deal of diversity. First of all, the physical appearance of most of these newspapers is characterized by a monotonous sameness that makes it hard to distinguish among them without reading the name. Second, the differences in content tend to be more subtle than striking. Many papers will carry the full text of the same leader's speech on the same day; often smaller newspapers will print full editorials from *Pravda* or one of the other central papers. Further uniformity is provided by the use of materials provided by TASS, the governmental news agency, and *Novosti,* which is technically nongovernmental but is subject to governmental control. The most authoritative newspaper is the Party's *Pravda* (the name means "truth" in Russian). With approximately eleven million copies printed daily it claims to have the largest circulation in the world. Like other Soviet papers, it is small in physical size, normally consisting of only six pages, and inexpensive, costing only four kopecks (about five cents).

Apparently more newspapers and periodicals are published than the people are willing to buy. As a result, they are sometimes pressured by local officials to subscribe to papers and magazines they would not ordinarily buy—in spite of the fact that this practice is frowned upon by the Party. Hollander reports the following example:

> The prevailing strategy is "Get the periodical into the home at any cost." An example of such "violations of the principle of voluntariness," as this phenomenon is euphemistically called in the Soviet press, was reported in 1960 from Byelorussia. Noticing that many people at the Minsk brick factory did not subscribe to periodicals, the local Komsomol organization became alarmed. It decided to launch a campaign; all young workers who did not subscribe were listed and each was subjected to a series of "personal talks" by Komsomol activists. As a result, subscriptions increased by five hundred copies.[53]

More common, we suspect, are the people who subscribe for reasons of expediency. They ostentatiously buy and carry around the correct publications, and it is assumed that they are ideologically sound.

Among the most avid consumers of the media are Party members. They have a greater-than-average need to keep up with the current Party line because they must act as ideological resource persons and behavior models. Aside from Party members, who are the major media consumers in the USSR? This is difficult to ascertain precisely, because Soviet research efforts to date have been selective and methodologically questionable. However, they do furnish the basis for an educated guess. It seems that education, occupation (level of skill), and income have the greatest effect on press exposure. When the level of any of these increases, the amount of reading also tends to increase.[54] In the case of radio and television, residence in an urban area seems to be crucial, with persons in Leningrad, Moscow, and the capitals of the Baltic states probably having the greatest broadcast exposure.[55] Since consumer preferences have a limited influence over publishing and broadcasting decisions in the Soviet Union, such exposure will inevitably lead to ingestion of substantial amounts of "ideologically sound" information.

The limited nature and central direction of the press create a starvation for information on topics considered unacceptable by Soviet journalism. One source of such information is word of mouth or rumor. Certainly the rumor network thrives in Moscow, and most of our Soviet friends indicated to us at one time or another that they rely on it for some kinds of information. The failure to publish news on homicides and other unpleasant events sometimes encourages rumors about murder waves or maniacs on the loose. On occasion the press has even felt compelled to deny the substance of such rumors.[56] Are the rumors reliable? This is almost impossible to ascertain. But research conducted on former Soviet citizens indicates that a substantial number considered them highly reliable.[57] More recent impressions tend to support this conclusion.[58]

The word-of-mouth network is mainly valuable for information about the Soviet Union.* For information about the outside world many Soviet citizens rely on foreign radio broadcasts as well as an occasional Western newspaper or magazine.** Broadcasts specifically intended for the Soviet Union originate in a number of countries, including the United States, Great Britain, France, and West Germany, and more discerning Soviet citizens speak with some authority about the relative reliability of the various countries' broadcasts.*** Citizens of Tallinn, the capital of Estonia, have another

---

Samizdat, the underground press, can be regarded as a variation on this theme. However, since it is to be discussed later with reference to the dissident movement, it will not be discussed here.

**Noncommunist newspapers and magazines from Western countries are not freely available for purchase in the Soviet Union. Many Soviet citizens who can read Western languages are anxious to get such publications from foreign tourists. Limited numbers of Western noncommunist newspapers are sold to foreigners in the large tourist hotels reserved mainly for foreigners.

***Parenthetically, it should be mentioned that for many listeners it is not the news about the outside world that is the main incentive for listening to foreign radio broadcasts. Rather it is the chance to hear (and perhaps record) contemporary music which is considered ideologically harmful by Soviet authorities.

outside source for news—one that is not specifically intended for them. By means of tall antennas on the tops of their houses, they can watch television programs from Helsinki, Finland, fifty miles across the gulf of Finland. The Finnish and Estonian languages are sufficiently similar that the Estonians can understand the programs. There is no doubt that for the intelligentsia these foreign broadcasts are a significant socializing factor, but whether they are very important for other strata of Soviet society is difficult to tell.[59]

Aside from the media, the agitation and propaganda network is the main socializing force brought to bear on Soviet adults. It is difficult to imagine many Soviet citizens who are not exposed to some agitation and propaganda on occasion. Most attend meetings or have contact with agitators or propagandists on a relatively regular basis.

One of the main settings for agitation and propaganda activities is the Club or House of Culture. By the beginning of 1984, the USSR had more than 138,000 such institutions.[60] They provide a center for a wide range of social and cultural activities and seem to be heavily used as social centers by the Soviet people. The agitation and propaganda apparatus takes advantage of this by scheduling such events as political lectures in conjunction with a social event. At the students' club in Moscow University, we attended both concerts and dances which were preceded by political presentations of some sort. Often attendance at the political part of the program was necessary for attendance at the featured entertainment. Many students would busy themselves with reading or talking during the political lecture, making it clear that they were there for the dance or concert and that the rest was a necessary evil.

In addition to clubs and community centers, virtually every Soviet institution of any size from factory to hospital has its agitation and propaganda center. The most modest of these are called "red corners" and may consist simply of a picture of Lenin placed on a red cloth (usually with flowers) and some reading material. The more elaborate are called "agitation points" (*agitpunkty*). They commonly service whole neighborhoods. Here one can find political literature of all sorts, posters, and the equipment for movies, records, and tapes. They furnish facilities for lectures, meetings, exhibitions, consultations, and political campaign activities as well as serving as polling places in Soviet elections. Finally, many agitation activities are carried out less formally in field, factory, park, and housing complex.

As a practical matter, the difference between agitation and propaganda is not always clear. A theoretical distinction was drawn many years ago by the Russian Marxist theoretician G. B. Plekhanov and is still cited approvingly in the Great Soviet Encyclopedia: ". . . the propagandist conveys many ideas to one person or a few people while the agitator conveys only one or only a few ideas, but he conveys them to a mass of people."[61] In practice, however, the distinction between the content of the presentation is more important than the distinction between the number of people. Agitators often speak to individuals or small groups, and propaganda lectures frequently have large audiences. However, propaganda "tends to be more theoretical, working toward a series of interrelated ideas that form a systematic world outlook," whereas agitation "is directed toward the understanding and acceptance of policy, with the intent of producing fairly specific behaviors and attitudes."[62]

Personnel for the agitation and propaganda network are drawn from the ranks of Party members and non-Party political activists. They may be appointed by the local Party organization or may volunteer. Their training for agitation and propaganda work is also under the aegis of the Party.

The Communist Party of the Soviet Union has several systems of political schools. One is for Party officials who are employed full time in the Party apparatus. In addition, more than half of the editors of republican, territorial, regional, city, and district newspapers have completed this form of political education.[63] There is a corresponding higher school for the training of *Komsomol* officials. This is a relatively recent innovation, and administratively it is under the *Komsomol* Central Committee.

For Party members who are not Party or *Komsomol* professionals and non-Party activists—the groups from which most agitators and propagandists are drawn—there is another set of schools. These feature three levels of courses geared to the needs of students with varying educational backgrounds and abilities. The most elementary is the political school *(politshkola);* the middle level is the circle *(krug);* and the most advanced is the theoretical seminar. Related to this is the Evening University of Marxism-Leninism, where the teachers for the political schools are trained. These teachers, called "propagandists," are Party members who do such teaching without pay during their leisure time.

How effective is all this effort at agitation and propaganda? For some of the people some of the time it is probably highly effective. Certainly for the ambitious Party member or non-Party activist, attendance at agitation and propaganda events is essential to successful career progress. However, most of the Soviet people we have observed at such events seemed to take them in stride as part of life, without evincing any great interest or enthusiasm. In his novel *The Girl from Petrovka,* George Feifer captures the mood nicely in a passage about the visit of the narrator and Oktyabrina (the girl from Petrovka) to Gorky Park in Moscow:

> Oktyabrina and I found ourselves entrapped in a monumental jam behind the open air auditorium, where a political agitator with a microphone was delivering a deafening harangue. The subject was "The Victory of Leninist Proletarian Internationalism in the Yemen." To this hymn, weary hundreds were gratefully dozing in their seats. At least they'd found *some* kind of entertainment, and a place to rest.
>
> Elsewhere the noise was equally devastating: caterwauling babies racked with thirst, charwomen shouting in snack bars, a public address system blaring Sunday Leniniana . . . Yet the extraordinary thing was that most people were enjoying the day not as something camp, but at face value. Just being in the park was a treat; it was enough to watch the lucky few who had secured places on the ferris wheel, and were now ooh-ing and ah-ing in appreciation

and alarm as their gondolas swung upward towards cleaner air and a splendid panorama of the baking city.[64]

NOTES

[1] For a more extended discussion, see Carol Barner-Barry and Robert Rosenwein, *Psychological Perspectives on Politics* (Englewood Cliffs, NJ: Prentice-Hall, Inc., 1985), pp. 80–81.

[2] Vladimir Bukovsky, *To Build a Castle: My Life as a Dissenter* (New York: Viking, 1979), p. 60.

[3] *U.S. News and World Report,* Sept. 24, 1984, p. 32.

[4] Ibid., p. 62.

[5] David K. Shipler, *Russia: Broken Idols, Solemn Dreams* (New York: New York Times Books, 1983), pp. 60–61.

[6] Elizabeth Teague, "Molotov Rehabilitated: A New Approach to Soviet History?" *Radio Liberty Research,* No. 262/84 Jul. 5, 1984.

[7] Bukovsky, *To Build a Castle,* p. 76.

[8] Daryl J. Bem, *Beliefs, Attitudes, and Human Affairs* (Belmont, CA: Wadsworth, Brooks/Cole Publishing Company, 1970), p. 66. Also see: Arthur R. Cohen, *Attitude Change and Social Influence* (New York: Basic Books, 1964), pp. 81–99; Carl I. Hovland, Irving L. Janis, and Harold H. Kelley, *Communications and Persuasion* (New Haven, CT: Yale University Press, 1953), pp. 215–40; and Philip Zimbardo and Ebbe B. Ebbesen, *Influencing Attitudes and Changing Behavior,* rev. ed. (Reading, MA: Addison-Wesley, 1970) pp. 56–60. Kurt Vonnegut's book *Mother Night* (New York: Avon, 1966) puts the same theme into a literary framework.

[9] Michael Swafford, "Political Attitudes and Behavior Among Soviet University Students" (Washington, DC: Office of Research, U.S. International Communication Agency, 1979), p. 32.

[10] N. Sh. Kozhokar' and S. N. Markiman, "Vozrastanie Obshchestvenno-Politicheskoi Aktivnosti Mass v Sovremennyknsloviiakh," in *Formirovanie Novogo Cheloveka-Stroitelia Kommunizma* (Kishinev: Izdatel'stvo "Shtiintza," 1973), p. 7.

[11] For a more complete discussion of this topic, see Kassof, *The Soviet Youth Program,* pp. 76–119.

[12] Georgi Smirnov, *Soviet Man: The Making of a Socialist Type of Personality* (Moscow: Progress Publishers, 1973), p. 177 and Timothy W. Luke, *Ideology and Soviet Industrialization* (Westport, CT: Greenwood Press, 1985), p. 130.

[13] *The Washington Post,* Dec. 28, 1983, p. A12.

[14] April 22, 1984, p. 2.

[15] For a comprehensive treatment of the political-instruction system, see Ellen Propper Mickiewicz, *Soviet Political Schools* (New Haven, CT: Yale University Press, 1967); also see Nigel Grant, *Soviet Education* 4th ed. (New York: Penguin, 1979), p. 188; Seymour M. Rosen, *Education and Modernization in the USSR* (Reading, MA: Addison-Wesley, 1971), pp. 110–11.

[16] *The Washington Post,* August 9, 1982, p. A1.

[17] For a more detailed discussion see Urie Bronfenbrenner, "Theory and Research in Soviet Character Education," *Social Thought in the Soviet Union,* ed. Alex Simirenko (Chicago: Quadrangle/The N.Y. Times, 1969), pp. 269–99.

[18] Kassof, *The Soviet Youth Program,* pp. 134–35.

[19] For a more extensive discussion along these lines, see Herschel Alt and Edith Alt, *The New Soviet Man* (New York: Bookman Associates, 1964), pp. 53–56.

[20] V. E. Semenova (ed.), *Sotsial'no-psikhologicheskie problemy nravstvennogo vospitaniia lichnosti* (Leningrad: Izdatel'stvo Leningradskogo Universiteta, 1984), p. 84. For discussion of a law on this subject passed by the Supreme Soviet in 1983, see: *Izvestiia,* Jun. 18, 1983, pp. 2–5. The text of the law is in *Izvestiia,* Jun. 19, 1983, pp. 1–2.

[21] Elizabeth Teague, "The USSR Law on Work Collectives: Workers' Control or Workers Controlled?" *Radio Liberty Research,* No. 184/84 May 10, 1984.

[22] Jane Jacobs, *The Death and Life of Great American Cities* (New York: Random House,

1961), p. 35. Also see E. S. Savas and J. A. Kaiser, *Moscow's City Government* (New York: Praeger, 1985), p. xxix.

²³Julia Wishnevsky, "A New Milestone in the Soviet Practice of Denunciation," *Radio Liberty Research*, No. 148/84, Apr. 11, 1984.

²⁴Smirnov, *Soviet Man*, p. 169.

²⁵David Burg and George Feifer, *Solzhenitsyn* (New York: Stein and Day, 1973), pp. 185–86. Markin was expelled from the Writers' Union immediately after publishing one of the poems mentioned (pp. 341–42).

²⁶Bukovsky, *To Build a Castle*, p. 97. Also see Mervyn Matthews, *Education in the Soviet Union: Policies and Institutions since Stalin* (London: George Allen & Unwin, 1982), pp. 162–64.

²⁷This was the conclusion of Herschel and Edith Alt, *The New Soviet Man*, p. 47. That the Alts had a different impression from ours might be due to the fact that although their second trip to the Soviet Union (1959) and our first period of residence (1961 to 1962) roughly coincided, they spent much more of their time with members of the Soviet Jewish community. Also, that time period was one of rapid and profound change in the Soviet Union. In any case, we did not find a comparable atmosphere among those Soviet citizens with whom we were in daily or occasional contact.

²⁸Gayle Durham Hannah, *Soviet Information Networks* (Washington, DC: Center for Strategic and International Studies, Georgetown University, 1977), p. 4.

²⁹For example, Smirnov, *Soviet Man*, pp. 189–90.

³⁰Hannah, *Soviet Information Networks*, pp. 74–75 and "The Two Faces of State Religion," *Soviet Analyst*, No. 20 (Oct. 13, 1977), p. 8. This may be changing due to a strong revival of religious belief and practice among Soviet young people. *The Washington Post*, Sept. 24, 1984, p. A14; *Komsomol'skaia Pravda*, Mar. 22, 1984.

³¹*The Washington Post*, Sept. 1, 1984, p. A26.

³²Semenova, *Sotsial'no-psikhologicheskie problemy*, pp. 45–46.

³³Bronfenbrenner, "Theory and Research," p. 279.

³⁴*Vestnik Statistiki*, No. 1 (1980), p. 79.

³⁵The information on preschool curriculum in this paragraph is from "Brief Guidelines on the 'Preschool Education Program,' " *Soviet Education*, 16, No. 8 (Jun. 1974), 54–91.

³⁶*The New York Times*, Jun. 13, 1979, p. A10.

³⁷For a more extensive discussion of this phenomenon, see Bronfenbrenner, "Theory and Research," pp. 272–79.

³⁸Kassof, *The Soviet Youth Program*, p. 79.

³⁹Ibid.

⁴⁰N. P. Kuzin, "Certain Problems of Social and Political Education in the Soviet Schools of Today," *Soviet Education*, 16, No. 6 (Apr. 1974), 46–47.

⁴¹*Izvestiia*, Apr. 13, 1984, pp. 1, 4.

⁴²*Izvestiia*, May 4, 1984, pp. 1, 3.

⁴³Swafford, "Political Attitudes," p. 7.

⁴⁴*The Washington Post*, Sept. 11, 1983, p. C2.

⁴⁵*The Baltimore Sun*, Jan. 31, 1984, p. B1.

⁴⁶Hannah, *Soviet Information Networks*, p. 61.

⁴⁷The former Soviet citizen is Leonid Finkelstein and the quotation is from Martin Dewhirst and Robert Farrell, eds., *The Soviet Censorship* (Metuchen, NJ: Scarecrow, 1973), p. 546. A more recent confirmation of this situation comes from another former Soviet citizen and writer, Vladimir Voinovich ("Sidelights on Soviet Censorship," *Radio Liberty Research*, No. 255/84, Jun. 29, 1984). Voinovich also asserts that the lists of forbidden topics continually becomes longer.

⁴⁸Hedrick Smith, "In Moscow, the Bigger the News, the Smaller the Story," *The New York Times Magazine*, Nov. 23, 1975, p. 32.

⁴⁹Gayle Durham Hollander, *Soviet Political Indoctrination* (New York: Holt, Rinehart & Winston, 1972), p. 39.

[50]Ibid.

[51]Voinovich, "Sidelights," p. 3.

[52]*Izvestiia,* September 19, 1974, p. 5.

[53]Hollander, *Soviet Political Indoctrination,* p. 58.

[54]Ibid., pp. 73–74. For more detail see also pp. 52–74.

[55]Ibid., p. 110.

[56]*The New York Times,* Apr. 10, 1978, p. 1.

[57]Alex Inkeles and Raymond A. Bauer, *The Soviet Citizen* (Cambridge, MA: Harvard University Press, 1959), pp. 172–77.

[58]*The New York Times,* Apr. 10, 1978, p. 1.

[59]It should be noted that the jamming of foreign broadcasts increased significantly in 1980. Although this jamming is not technologically sophisticated enough to completely blanket them out, it does make it more difficult for Soviet citizens to listen to broadcasting from outside the Soviet Union.

[60]*SSSR v tsifrakh v 1983 godu* (Moscow: "Finansy i statistika," 1984), p. 225.

[61]*Bol'shaia Sovetskaia Entsiklopediia,* 3rd ed. (1970), I, 181.

[62]Hannah, *Soviet Information Networks,* p. 35.

[63]B. Moralev, "The Training and Retraining of Managerial Personnel," *Soviet Education,* 15, No. 1 (Nov. 1972), 14.

[64]George Feifer, *The Girl From Petrovka* (New York: Viking, 1971), pp. 148–49.

SELECTED BIBLIOGRAPHY

ALT, HERSCHEL, and EDITH ALT, *The New Soviet Man.* New York: Bookman Associates, 1964.

BRINE, JENNY, MAUREEN PERRIE, and ANDREW SUTTON, eds., *Home, School and Leisure in the Soviet Union.* London: George Allen & Unwin, 1980.

BRONFENBRENNER, URIE, *Two Worlds of Childhood.* New York: Russell Sage Foundation, 1970.

BROWN, ARCHIE, ed., *Political Culture and Communist Politics.* Armonk, NY: M.E. Sharpe, Inc., 1985.

———, and JACK GRAY, eds., *Political Culture and Political Change in Communist States.* New York: Holmes & Meier, 1979.

BUKOVSKY, VLADIMIR, *To Build a Castle: My Life as a Dissenter.* New York: Viking, 1979.

CROUCH, MARTIN, and ROBERT PORTER, eds., *Understanding Soviet Politics Through Literature: A Book of Readings.* London: George Allen & Unwin, 1984.

DEWHIRST, MARTIN, and ROBERT FARRELL, eds., *The Soviet Censorship.* Metuchen, NJ: Scarecrow, 1973.

DUNSTAN, JOHN, *Paths to Excellence and the Soviet School.* Berk, England: NFER Publishing Co., Ltd., 1978.

FITZPATRICK, SHEILA, *Education and Social Mobility in the Soviet Union. 1921–1934.* New York: Cambridge University Press, 1970.

FRIEDGUT, THEODORE H., *Political Participation in the USSR.* Princeton, NJ: Princeton University Press, 1979.

GEYER, GEORGIE-ANNE, ed., *The Young Russians.* Homewood, IL: An ETC Publication, 1975.

GRANT, NIGEL, *Soviet Education,* 4th ed. New York: Penguin, 1979.

HANNAH, GAYLE DURHAM, *Soviet Information Networks.* Washington, DC: Center for Strategic and International Studies. Georgetown University, 1977.

HARASYMIW, BOHDAN, ed., *Education and the Mass Media in the Soviet Union and Eastern Europe.* New York: Holt, Rinehart & Winston, 1976.

HOLLANDER, GAYLE DURHAM, *Soviet Political Indoctrination.* New York: Holt, Rinehart & Winston, 1972.

HOPKINS, MARK W., *Mass Media in the Soviet Union.* New York: Pegasus, 1970.

JACOBS, EVERETT M., ed., *Soviet Local Politics and Government.* London: George Allen & Unwin, 1983.

JACOBY, SUSAN, *Inside Soviet Schools.* New York: Hill and Wang, 1974.

KREUSLER, ABRAHAM A., *Contemporary Education and Moral Upbringing in the Soviet Union.* Ann Arbor, MI: University Microfilms International, 1976.

LANE, CHRISTEL, *The Rites of Rulers: Ritual in Industrial Society—the Soviet Case.* New York: Cambridge University Press, 1981.

MAKARENKO, A. S., *The Collective Family: A Handbook for Parents.* New York: Doubleday, 1967.

MATTHEWS, MERVYN, *Education in the Soviet Union.* London: George Allen & Unwin, 1982.

O'DELL, FELICITY ANN, *Socialization Through Children's Literature: The Soviet Example.* Cambridge, MA: Cambridge University Press, 1978.

SMIRNOV, GEORGI, *Soviet Man: The Making of a Socialist Type of Personality.* Moscow: Progress Publishers, 1973.

TOMIAK, J. J., ed., *Soviet Education in the 1980's.* New York: St. Martin's Press, 1983.

TUMARKIN, NINA, *Lenin Lives!* Cambridge MA: Harvard University Press, 1983.

WHITE, STEPHEN, *Political Culture and Soviet Politics.* London: Macmillan, 1979.

———, "The Effectiveness of Political Propaganda in the USSR," *Soviet Studies,* 32 (1980), 323–48.

5

THE CONSTITUTION:
Form Without Substance

Armenian Radio* asks: What is the difference between a good constitution and an excellent constitution?

Answer: A good constitution guarantees freedom of speech, while an excellent constitution guarantees freedom *after* speech.
   —current Soviet joke related to the authors by Irina Minkova

For the person studying American politics, the U.S. Constitution is a document of great importance. Semester-long or year-long courses devoted to the interpretation and development of the Constitution are given in both universities and law schools. And the U.S. Supreme Court, the conclusive interpreter of constitutional provisions, is an organ of great power and prestige in the American system.

The USSR Constitution holds no such place in the Soviet system, and it is rightfully given little attention by most analysts of Soviet politics. Constitutional development in the Soviet Union has gone through several phases. The first Constitution, of the "Russian Soviet Federated Socialist Republic" (RSFSR), was adopted in July 1918 and served as a model for the documents adopted in the areas of the former Russian empire, such as Byelorussia, the Ukraine, Azerbaidzhan, Armenia, and Georgia, as they were gradually

---

*The mythical Armenian Radio is used as the opening line for many Soviet jokes, signaling to the listener that the topic is political.

taken over by the Bolsheviks in the years after the Revolution. Formal federation among the states associated with the RSFSR was achieved late in 1922 with the creation of the Union of Soviet Socialist Republics (USSR). Its Constitution went into effect in January 1924.

The details of these first two documents need not detain us here.[1] They did not differ greatly from each other, and except in detail and terminology they did not set up essentially different systems of government from that provided in the 1980s. The third Constitution, dating from 1936, was in force for over forty years. In October 1977 it was replaced by a new Constitution,* a much longer document but one with many similarities to the 1936 charter. The adoption of this new Constitution was preceded by a much publicized period of discussion of a draft version of the Constitution. Over 140 million Soviet citizens took part in the discussion, 1.5 million meetings were devoted to it, and about 400,000 proposals for changes in the draft were received.[2] In the end, however, the changes in the final version of the document resulting from the discussion were not very important. Soviet authorities are fond of claiming that the discussion "testifies to the genuinely democratic character of the Soviet system." Closer to the mark, however, would seem to be the conclusion of a Western analyst that what took place was "a public debate of gigantic proportions and minimal depth."[3]

The 1936 Constitution was adopted in the midst of the "great terror" which existed from 1936 to 1938, the greatest political purge in Soviet history. It has been suggested that the introduction of a new constitutional document at this time was an attempt on the part of Stalin and his cohorts to convince the world that the Soviet Union was, after all, a state run according to law. It was not only a matter of the purges giving the Soviet Union a bad name that influenced the adoption of a new Constitution. There was also the growing fascist threat, which the Soviet Union was attempting to combat. Stalin needed the cooperation of communist parties of foreign countries with other parties of the left in "united fronts" against the fascists. To have the Soviet Union, then the only communist state, appear to be more democratic than had heretofore been thought would not hurt. The introduction of a more democratic constitutional document, moreover, was welcomed at home. The Soviet Union was a country to which Western ideas were not completely alien. Marxism, after all, was a Western import. Many Soviet intellectuals, in particular, were strongly attracted to the West. Thus, the introduction of "progressive" ideas from the West, such as a set of democratic constitutional provisions, would help in gaining legitimacy for the regime both at home and abroad.

Whatever the actual importance of these considerations, the adoption of the Constitution was justified primarily on other grounds. Socialism, it was said, had been achieved in the USSR, and this was the "constitution of victorious socialism." Since antagonistic classes had been eliminated, leaving

*For the reader's convenience the text of the current Constitution is included as Appendix A.

only workers, peasants, and intellectuals as different varieties of "toilers," and since, with the abolition of private employment, a socialistic economic system had been established, new state arrangements consonant with these achievements could be made. It was also the "Stalin Constitution," so named supposedly because Stalin was the titular chairman of the document's drafting commission, but really so designated to provide another jewel for the leader's diadem. This designation ceased to be used when Stalin's star went into decline.

Stalin called the Constitution "the only thoroughly democratic Constitution in the world." While that is arguable, its provisions were impressive and represented considerable improvement over previous Soviet documents. Universal suffrage by secret ballot replaced a system of limited suffrage in which priests and other former members of the bourgeoisie had been disfranchised. The representatives of the new bicameral Supreme Soviet were directly elected, whereas the old Congress of Soviets had been indirectly elected. The 1936 Constitution was also slightly more realistic than its predecessors in that it mentioned, although only briefly, the important place of the Communist Party in the Soviet system. Finally, a detailed and extensive listing of "Basic Rights and Duties of Citizens" was included for the first time in a federal Constitution. Among the rights were several that would have been novel for Western constitution writers of the time, including the "right to work," meaning "guaranteed employment," as well as rights to rest and leisure, education, and maintenance in old age. In addition, more familiar provisions were included that guaranteed freedom of expression, separation of church and state, the inviolability of the person and the home, and equality of nationalities, races, and the sexes. The duties were closely tied to the socialist nature of the system. Citizens were expected to abide by the Constitution and the laws, to maintain labor discipline, to perform public duties honestly, and "to respect the rules of socialist community." They were charged with safeguarding public property" as the sacred and inviolable foundation of the Soviet system." They were pledged to defend the Motherland. These passages stressed the citizen's obligation toward the state and the community and effectively reversed the emphasis found in many Western constitutional documents—on the rights of the individual against the state.

The 1977 Constitution bears many similarities to its 1936 counterpart. True, it is considerably longer (174 articles and some 13,000 words, as against 146 articles and 8,000 words); but in large part the additions and changes are cosmetic. A long prologue, missing in the 1936 document, contains some keys to the theoretical underpinnings of the new Constitution. Why a prologue of this sort is necessary requires some background explanation. In the Marxian-socialist world a constitution has come to serve as a kind of signpost, indicating where a country has been and where it is going. It represents the fulfillment of past objectives and the promise of future achievements. Marxian thought dictates looking at the world in terms of stages of development. This is a "given" of historical analysis. It applies, of course, to the history of the Soviet Union as well. Thus, it has been seen as fitting that new constitutions be adopted to regulate affairs in the successive important stages of Soviet history. There is abundant evidence that Soviet constitutional experts hold to this point of view. For example, the most complete compilation of Soviet constitutional documents states that each constitution "represents a stage in the continuing historical path" of the Soviet state and is "the legislative basis of the subsequent development of the life of the state."[4]

In line with this reasoning, the prologue to the 1977 Constitution speaks of the Soviet Union as a "developed socialist society" which is "an objectively necessary stage on the road to communism" and a higher stage than the socialism proclaimed in the 1936 Constitution. Accordingly, it is said that the tasks of the dictatorship of the proletariat have been fulfilled and a new kind of state, "the state of the whole people," has been created. With this "socio-political and ideological unity" achieved, the superior position accorded to workers can be abandoned; thus, the elective representative bodies are now "soviets of people's deputies" rather than "soviets of workers' deputies."

In the articles of the 1977 Constitution itself, perhaps the most important change involves the more prominent position accorded to the Communist Party. In the 1936 document it was mentioned twice briefly. These references are basically repeated, but Article 6 of the 1977 Constitution goes much further, calling the Party "the leading and guiding force of Soviet society and the nucleus of its political system, of all state and public organizations." The party is charged with determining "the general perspective of society's development and the line of domestic and foreign policy of the USSR."

The 1977 Constitution has a separate chapter on foreign policy which did not exist in the 1936 document. The three articles in this chapter list the elements that are currently important in foreign policy and manifest a commitment to objectives which will surprise no one who has studied recent Soviet pronouncements. Thus, the doctrine of peaceful coexistence is endorsed. Yet in the same sentence support for wars of national liberation is affirmed. As discussed in Chapter 14, it is this seeming ambivalence that causes Western countries to be unsure of Soviet intentions. Among other formulations, the Constitution reaffirms the commitment to "comradely mutual assistance" among socialist countries and "socialist internationalism," phrases that were used to justify the invasion of Czechoslovakia in 1968.

The section on rights and duties of citizens is near the beginning of the 1977 Constitution, although it was close to the end of the 1936 document. The new provisions repeat the notable ones from the latter but also contain a number of new guarantees, including a whole chapter on the equality of citizens as well as new rights to housing, to the "use of the achievements of culture," to criticize the shortcomings of officials and organizations, and others. There are significant conditions attached to some of these rights, however, a matter that will be discussed subsequently.

Some subtle shifts in power to the Presidium of the USSR Supreme Soviet, at the expense of the USSR Council of Ministers, have been written into the 1977 Constitution, which also seems to give the central government somewhat more power over the constituent republics. These and several other differences from the 1936 Constitution, as they pertain to the governmental and legal operations of the Soviet state, will be mentioned in the following chapter.

Let us now look at the place the Constitution holds in the Soviet system. A political system may be described as *constitutional,* or as having *constitutionalism,* when the exercise of political and governmental power therein is *defined* and *limited.*[5] It is precisely this lack of definition and limitation on political powers that characterizes the Soviet Constitution. As Carl Friedrich has put it, "(a)s a political process, the constitution can be described as analogous to the rules of the game insuring fair play."[6] But as pointed out in Chapter 1, aside from the uniform commitment of Soviet leaders to closed politics, it is a lack of recognized rules that characterizes the way Soviet politics is played.

Let us look at the two elements of constitutionalism separately. To be sure, the USSR Constitution describes the formal organs of government and lists their powers. But even in the 1977 Constitution, in which the Communist Party is mentioned more prominently than in previous constitutions, no attempt is made to define its formal powers. Yet everyone accepts the fact that the Party is the focus of power in the Soviet system. Since the formal governmental organs described in the Constitution exercise almost no independent political power, the Constitution's defining of political and governmental powers amounts to an empty gesture.

What about the matter of limiting political power? It stands to reason that since the formal governmental organs *have* little power, there would be little that really could be limited by the Constitution. But, since Party policies are often channeled *through* the governmental apparatus, the Constitution might serve as a limitation on the formal implementation of Party policy. There are a number of constitutional provisions that might limit state power. To take one of the most obvious examples, Article 50 of the Constitution guarantees citizens "freedom of speech, of the press, and of assembly, meetings, street processions and demonstrations." Several factors detract from or condition this guarantee, however. First, the guarantee of the rights mentioned in Article 50 is prefaced by the phrase (also present in the 1936 Constitution), "in accordance with the interests of the people and in order to strengthen and develop the socialist system." This might be interpreted to limit the objectives for which the rights might be used. Even more ominous is the provision in Article 39 that the "enjoyment by citizens of their rights and freedoms must not be to the detriment of the interests of society or the state or infringe the rights of other citizens," a formulation that could be used to justify repression of dissident activities. As mentioned, the 1936 Constitution balanced a whole set of duties of citizens against their rights. This list of duties has been expanded in the 1977 Constitution, and one in particular suggests a potential limitation on the exercise of freedom of expression as spelled out in Article 50: the provision in Article 59 that the exercise by citizens of their rights and freedoms "is inseparable from the performance of their duties and obligations."

In spite of these conditions, the guarantee of freedom of expression does exist, and it would seem that one might have a case against the government if one could show that any of these constitutional rights had been infringed upon, by, say, the police or security officials. After all, an authoritative Soviet statement on the subject says that the Constitution "not only proclaims the rights and freedoms of the individual and the citizen, but comprehensively guarantees them."[7]

But the fact is that the Soviet Constitution does not serve the latter function. One cannot go to court to show that one's constitutional rights have been violated and enjoin further violation. The Constitution, despite its designation as "the basic law," does not serve as a basis for litigation. Thus, the major way in which the U.S. Constitution can be implemented to limit the exercise of governmental power does not exist in the Soviet system. One of the interesting things about the recent dissident movement in the Soviet Union has been that some dissenters have attempted to invoke the Constitution to support claims that their rights have been violated. No Soviet court appears thus far to have ruled on such complaints, however.[8]

The lack of judicial attention to constitutional rights is not merely a matter of repressive practices on the part of the Soviet authorities. It is that, to be sure, but it is also a manifestation of a more general ambivalence which runs like a thread through the Soviet system. It is trite but apt to observe that Russia lies between East and West and does not know which way to turn. Historians and political scientists have long used this theme as a key to the interpretation of Russian and Soviet history.

Thus, as a country without a history of gradual nurturing of respect for the rule of law, prerevolutionary Russia still relied heavily on Western Europe for the development of legal codes. A similar admiration for the progressive ideas of the West persuaded the Bolshevik leaders to adopt the concept of a written constitution. But it was the form that was adopted, not the substance. A constitution defines the powers and duties of governmental organs because some contention, some conflict in the way the country is to be governed, is expected. So the rules of conflict management are set out from the start. But the stated Soviet assumption about the way the governing process will work has been not one of conflict but one of unity of views, and this is particularly the case with regard to the bodies mentioned in successive Soviet constitutions.

Since conflict among governmental bodies is not contemplated, Soviet theorists reject the principle of separation of powers. They see no need for balancing the power of one branch of government against that of another. Thus, the concept of judicial review of governmental enactments or actions is also rejected. As mentioned, constitutional guarantees do not serve as a basis for court action. Nor has the constitutional provision that judges and people's assessors (lay judges) "are independent and subject only to the law" (Article 155) provided any kind of an opening wedge for such development.

If there is any body responsible for maintaining the constitutionality of state action, it would be the nominal legislature, the USSR Supreme Soviet, which is designated by the Constitution as the highest organ of state power in the country. However, this organ has no genuine political or legislative power. Moreover, the Supreme Soviet itself has on occasion acted casually toward constitutional provisions, adopting laws in technical violation of the Constitution and then changing the Constitution (by two-thirds vote of both houses, as provided in Article 174 of the Constitution) to conform with the new laws.[9]

The only avenue for the individual who believes that his constitutional rights have been violated is the informal complaint apparatus. This mechanism seems to have proved to be of dubious usefulness at best, and in any case rests heavily on the discretion of the procurator or other official with whom the complaint is registered.

In sum, then, the Constitution provides no limitation on the exercise of state authority; it defines the functions of a governmental apparatus that is essentially powerless but fails to spell out the powers and procedures of the Communist Party, the really dominant force of the system.

One other aspect of the Constitution remains to be discussed, the relationship of recent constitutional development to the political process. Since the Constitution does not define or limit political power, it might be thought that Soviet politicians would be indifferent to it. This has not been entirely the case. The issue of the adoption of a new Constitution has to some extent been the focus of contention among high Soviet political leaders over the years. As early as 1959, Nikita Khrushchev promised that basic revision of the Constitution would take place. In 1961 he indicated that a whole new Constitution was being drafted. Khrushchev was named Chairman of the Constitutional Drafting Commission in 1962, a position that Brezhnev took over after replacing Khrushchev in 1964. Like Khrushchev, Brezhnev seemed committed to the adoption of a new Constitution yet incapable of bringing the project to fruition. In 1966 he promised that the document would be completed by the Fiftieth Anniversary of Bolshevik rule in November 1967. In 1972 he promised that a text of the Constitution would be released before the Twenty-Fifth Party Congress in 1976. Both of these dates came and went without a new Constitution, and it was clear that sufficient opposition existed to block the project.

During all of these years, Brezhnev had been gaining strength relative to his Politburo colleagues, however, and by 1977 the time was ripe for the issue to be resolved. At a Party Central Committee meeting on May 24, two important developments took place: A draft of the new Constitution was approved and Nikolai V. Podgornyi, Chairman of the Presidium of the Supreme Soviet, was dropped from the ruling Party Politburo. As subsequent events were to show, these developments were connected. The next month Brezhnev took over Podgornyi's post of Chairman of the Supreme Soviet Presidium, a position that is equated with being the ceremonial president of the country. Some analysts have suggested that Podgornyi opposed the new Constitution because of disagreement with certain of its provisions. Whether or not this is so is not clear. It does seem likely, in any case, that he resisted being replaced in the Presidium Chairmanship by Brezhnev and so was removed from both the Politburo and the Presidium in what amounted to a forced retirement. A new provision in the 1977 Constitution made it more convenient for Brezhnev, who was seventy at the time, to assume the Presidium Chairmanship while keeping the post of Party General Secretary. This is Article 120, which provides for the first time for a Presidium First Vice-Chairman who can relieve the Chairman of many of his ceremonial duties. Subsequent leaders followed the Brezhnev example. Shortly after having become General Secretary of the Party, both Andropov and Chernenko also assumed the Presidium Chairmanship. This trend was ended by Gorbachev, who chose not to assume the Presidium Chairmanship. Instead, he used the post as a vehicle for the honorable semiretirement of Andrei Gromyko, the powerful and longtime Minister of Foreign Affairs.

It is not constitutional trappings, however, that carry crucial weight in the system. For the really salient aspects of Soviet politics one must look elsewhere, to the "real Constitution." The late Tibor Szamuely put it brilliantly several years ago, in a quotation that is equally applicable to the situation of the 1980s:

> The Stalin Constitution, of course, is a meaningless scrap of paper, but the USSR *does* have a genuine constitution—unwritten, or rather, unpublicized, yet perfectly well understood and recognized by all concerned. This real constitution contains the actual rules of Soviet political life: the rules of Party management of the country, of *nomenklatura* and *Glavlit,* of the organization of elections and of the passport system, of "doublethink" and "thought-crime" (to use Orwellian shorthand). Every intelligent Soviet citizen is familiar with these rules and acts in accordance with them.
>
> The important thing about these "constitutional laws" is not that they are unpublished but that they exist and are strictly adhered to, by government and subjects alike. The stability they provide may be very different from ours—but it is nonetheless stability (they are already older than many of the laws on our own statute books).[10]

After describing formal governmental operations in the next chapter, we will move on to an examination of the "real Soviet Constitution."

NOTES

[1] The texts of the 1918 and 1924 Constitutions may be found in James H. Meisel and Edward S. Kozera, eds., *Materials for the Study of the Soviet System*, 2nd ed. (Ann Arbor, MI: The George Wahr Publishing Co., 1953), pp. 79, 153. A concise constitutional history of the Soviet Union may be found in F.J.M. Feldbrugge, ed., *Encyclopedia of Soviet Law*, I (Leiden, the Netherlands: A. W. Sijthoff, 1973), p. 151.

[2] Brezhnev made these statements in his speech at the time of the adoption of the Constitution on October 4, 1977. This speech is translated in F.J.M. Feldbrugge, ed., *The Constitutions of the USSR and the Union Republics: Analysis, Texts, Reports* (Alphen aan den Rijn, the Netherlands: Sijthoff & Noordhoff, 1979). See pp. 202–203. This book is the most complete analysis of the 1977 Constitution in English and also contains the texts of the 1978 Constitutions of the fifteen union republics. A thorough analysis of the public discussion of the 1977 Constitution as well as the text of the document may be found in Robert Sharlet, *The New Constitution of 1977: Analysis and Text* (Brunswick, OH: King's Court Press, 1978).

[3] Feldbrugge, ed., note 2, p. xi.

[4] *Istoriia Sovetskoi Konstitutsii (V Dokumentakh), 1917–1956* (Moscow: Gosudarstvennoe Izdatel'stvo Iuridicheskoi Literatury, 1957), p. 3.

[5] See Carl J. Friedrich, *Constitutional Government and Democracy*, 4th ed. (Waltham, MA: Blaisdell Publishing Company, 1968), pp. 24–26; also Charles Howard McIlwain, *Constitutionalism Ancient and Modern*, rev. ed. (Ithaca, NY: Cornell University Press, 1947), pp. 21–22.

[6] Friedrich, *Constitutional Government*, p. 123.

[7] V. B. Chkikhvadze and others, ed., *Entsiklopedicheskii Slovar' Pravovykh Znanii* (Moscow: Izdatel'stvo "Sovetskaia Entsiklopedia," 1965), p. 198.

[8] The provision in Article 58 which gives citizens a right to compensation for damage caused by unlawful activity of state or public organizations or by officials may be a potential test of this point. In the draft version of the Constitution this provision allowed the right to such compensation "in the manner and within limits established by law." In the final version this phrase was dropped. Soviet lawyers writing on this point have expressed different views as to whether this means that the provision could be used as a direct basis for a damage suit. It should also be mentioned that Article 173 of the Constitution states that "The Constitution of the USSR shall have supreme legal force." So far as is known, however, neither of these provisions has so far been used by a court as the basis for a decision in a case.

[9] This is a fairly frequent practice. See *Encyclopedia of Soviet Law*, p. 155. As a recent example, in May 1975 the Presidium of the USSR Supreme Soviet adopted an edict creating two new ministries out of the former Ministry of Heavy, Energy and Transportation Machinery Construction. At the Supreme Soviet meeting in July 1975, the Supreme Soviet adopted a statute amending the Constitution to accommodate this change. So the *de facto* change preceded the *de jure* amendment, even though Article 146 of the Constitution requires a two-thirds vote of the Supreme Soviet to amend the Constitution. For details on this example see *Izvestiia*, July 10, 1975, pp. 3, 4.

[10] Tibor Szamuely, "Five Years After Khrushchev," *Survey*, 72 (Summer 1969), 59–60.

SELECTED BIBLIOGRAPHY

BARRY, DONALD D., WILLIAM E. BUTLER, and GEORGE GINSBURGS, eds., *Contemporary Soviet Law*. The Hague: Martinus Nijhoff, 1974.

BERMAN, HAROLD J., and JOHN B. QUIGLEY, JR., eds., *Basic Laws on the Structure of the Soviet State*. Cambridge, MA: Harvard University Press, 1969.

CHALIDZE, VALERY, "Human Rights in the New Soviet Constitution," in *Social Engineering Through Law*, Part II of *Soviet Law After Stalin*, eds. Donald D. Barry, George Ginsburgs, and Peter B. Maggs. Alphen aan den Rijn, the Netherlands: Sijthoff & Noordhoff, 1978.

FELDBRUGGE, F.J.M., ed., *The Constitutions of the USSR and the Union Republics: Analysis, Texts, Reports*. Alphen aan den Rijn, the Netherlands: Sijthoff & Noordhoff, 1979.

FRIEDRICH, CARL J., *Constitutional Government and Democracy,* 4th ed. Waltham, MA: Blaisdell Publishing Co., 1968.

GILLISON, JEROME M., "Khrushchev, Brezhnev and Constitutional Reform," *Problems of Communism,* 21, No. 5 (Sept.–Oct. 1972), 69–78.

HAZARD, JOHN N., "A New Constitution for 'Developed Socialism,' " in *Social Engineering Through Law,* pp. 1–34.

LURYI, YURI, "The New Constitution of the USSR from Draft to Law: An Analysis of the Changes Adopted," in *Social Engineering Through Law,* pp. 35–66.

MEISEL, JAMES H., and EDWARD KOZERA, eds., *Materials for the Study of the Soviet System,* 2nd ed. Ann Arbor, MI: The George Wahr Publishing Company, 1953.

SCHNEIDER, EBERHARD, "The Discussion of the New All-Union Constitution of the USSR," *Soviet Studies,* 31, No. 4 (Oct. 1979), 523–41.

SHARLET, ROBERT, *The New Soviet Constitution of 1977: Analysis and Text.* Brunswick, OH: King's Court Press, 1978.

UNGER, ARYEH L., *Constitutional Development in the USSR: A Guide to the Soviet Constitution.* London: Methuen, 1981.

6

THE GOVERNMENT:
The Fringes of Power

It is no secret that the focus of policy-making power in the USSR is not located in the government; it is in the Communist Party of the Soviet Union, particularly in its top organs, the Politburo and the Secretariat. This concentration of policy making does not mean that all parts of the government are equally powerless, however. It is necessary to distinguish between two kinds of government organs, the representative institutions and the bureaucracy.

In the first category are the legislative bodies, the USSR Supreme Soviet and its counterparts at lower governmental levels. It is considered an honor to be elected a deputy to a legislative organ; but while the formal authority of these bodies is great, little real power or influence is wielded by them. Their contribution is limited under their considerable formal powers to the highly efficient processing of state business. The acts that are passed, however, have their origins elsewhere and are not modified in any significant way during the formal legislative process. Thus the chief role of the legislative bodies is to carry out Party policy and, to a limited degree, to impart a certain legitimacy to the overall political system.

The bureaucracy is another story. In the USSR the bureaucracy is found largely within the organs that make up the USSR Council of Ministers and analogous bodies on lower governmental levels. These organs are charged with implementing and executing policy decisions. As any student of administration knows, the distinction between policy and administration is a fluid one and is not always easy to define. Because of this fact, considerable leverage resides in the hands of bureaucrats. They are charged with implementing and coordinating policy, but their central position in executing decisions of a general nature handed down from above often enables them to initiate policy as well. As Franz Schurmann has put it in discussing the Soviet and Chinese bureaucracies, "policy is not always made at the top. Sometimes impulses come from the middle and lower levels of organization, and are only legitimized by the executives at the top."[1] The potential for this kind of initiative among Soviet bureaucrats probably is heightened by the fact that it is common for responsible administrators in the state apparatus to hold positions simultaneously in important Party bodies. The state bureaucracy, then, occupies a considerably more significant position in the Soviet scheme of things than do the legislative bodies.

THE SUPREME SOVIET

Parliamentary Sessions

The presiding officer at a joint session of the two houses of the Soviet national legislature, the Supreme Soviet, asked members of each house to vote on a law in question. To each house he said: "Those who are for adoption of this law please raise their hands. Please lower them. Who is opposed? None opposed. Who abstains? No abstainers. The law has been adopted."[2] One probably could find analogous practices in representative bodies in Western countries, but it certainly is not what we would consider the norm for Western parliamentary democracy in action. Yet it is an epitome of Soviet procedures in the formal legislative organs of the Soviet state and is consistent with the mythology erected by Soviet ideologues to justify such procedures.

According to this mythology, the Soviet Union is a state that has long since reached socialism and has eliminated antagonistic classes. One would not expect great differences to be manifested in legislative voting. The same kind of justification suffices for the absence of contested elections, as we shall see. The result is that such institutions as legislatures, which carry on their work relatively in the open (in the sense that supposedly verbatim reports of their proceedings are available but not in the sense that it is easy for foreigners or other "outsiders" to observe their proceedings), are incredibly efficient in the amount that they accomplish. According to the USSR Constitution (Article 108), the USSR Supreme Soviet is the "highest body of state authority"; it is "empowered to deal with all matters within the jurisdiction of the Union of Soviet Socialist Republics." In exercising this high authority the Supreme Soviet completes all of its business while meeting an average of less than a week per year.[3]

Although unanimous voting helps in achieving this efficiency, it is not the only device enlisted to this end. The fact is that the Supreme Soviet has been "rationalized" to the point where its functions can easily be handled during a few days each year (or dispensed with entirely if necessary, as in the war year of 1943). They amount merely to the ceremonial completion or ratification of the policy-making process, on which all of the essential work has been done elsewhere. The main purpose of collecting 1,500 Supreme Soviet deputies in Moscow for a few days each year is not to sound them out on popular views in their constituencies and get their opinions on policies. The time allotted is too short for this. Everything connected with the Supreme Soviet in action shows that the function of representing constituency interests is virtually unperformed. The main function of Supreme Soviet meetings seems to operate in the other direction, to carry "the word" outward from the center. Yet, almost incidentally, some "localism" does creep into Supreme Soviet discussions, and this can be looked upon as a primitive form of constituency representation. Most often this takes the form of mild complaints against the low level of capital investment in the budget for a given republic or the failure of certain economic enterprises or ministries to supply the area with certain kinds of goods. Although such complaints may be no more than republican-level elites objecting to USSR-level elite decisions, they indicate that the Supreme Soviet is regarded as a forum for the expression, however tentative and covert, of the political interests of localities.

If one looks to some of the Soviet Union's East European neighbors, one can find greater manifestations of such independence in legislative sessions. Not only are differences of opinion sometimes more openly expressed, but on rare occasions such differences may be carried to the point of voting against party-sponsored measures, as was the case in East Germany in 1972 in connection with the government-sponsored abortion reform legislation.[4] No Soviet legislator has gone this far, but the airing of local interests observable now could possibly point in that direction.

Composition

That the USSR Supreme Soviet is a different kind of legislative body from what we are accustomed to in the West can be seen in part from its composition. Its two houses are the Soviet of the Union (750 members elected every five years from electoral districts based on population size) and the Soviet of Nationalities (750 members elected every five years as representatives for the various national territorial units).[5]

As befits a political system that claims to have been created by a rising of the proletariat, the proportion of workers and collective farmers in the Supreme Soviet is high, about 50 percent in recent years. The significance of this figure is somewhat diminished, however, when one considers other figures suggesting a more elitist character for the body: For instance, it appears that over half of the members of the Supreme Soviet typically have partial or complete higher education and that about three fourths of them are either Communist Party members or candidate members. Soviet commentators are also fond of pointing out that turnover of the membership of the Supreme Soviet is high: more than 50 percent and as high as 65 percent in recent elections. But this turnover still leaves some 500 to 700 deputy slots for returnees from previous legislatures, including a significant number for high political leaders who have been members for many years.[6]

Women deputies have made up about 30 percent of the Supreme Soviet in recent years. Although this percentage is well under their 53.1 percent of the total Soviet population, it is high when compared with the proportion of women in legislatures in the West. But the Supreme Soviet is by no means the most elitist of Soviet political bodies. In other parts of the political hierarchy the picture is different. In the Communist Party, for instance, women are much more under-represented. Their numbers are negligible in the higher Party bodies, and they comprise less than one quarter of the general Party membership. Not one woman was appointed to the 115-member USSR Council of Ministers chosen in 1984. On the other hand, in the elected legislative bodies below the national level, the proportion of women is larger, as is the proportion of non-Party members and (with minor exceptions) young people. Table 6–1 shows the trends in these areas. As the Table indicates, there has been, in most cases, a steady growth in the representation of these groups at all levels, suggesting a coordinated effort to raise what probably amounts to quotas. With each lower level of government, the proportion of persons in the nonfavored categories (that is, younger persons, women, non-Party members, persons without higher education) increases. It is significant that only at the local soviet level do non-Party deputies outnumber those who are Party members. This suggests that the lower levels serve both as a training ground for these categories of people and as an avenue for broadening political participation (or at least a sense of participation) without much risk by the authorities of diminishing their political control.

What is the basis on which individuals are selected for Supreme Soviet membership and what are the rewards for those selected? Since it is a body that meets only for a few days each year, it is clear that there are no full-time legislators, as is common in the West. Rather, Supreme Soviet deputies perform other full-time jobs, and this other work serves as a basis for their election to the Supreme Soviet.

Election to the Supreme Soviet may be a reflection of the position one has achieved in Soviet society. All of the most important Party and governmental officials and a number of top scientists and intellectuals (such as the President of the USSR Academy of Sciences) are always members. For these persons membership amounts to yet another affirmation of their status. In addition, being chosen to serve in the Supreme Soviet can provide a reward for good work, an honor bestowed on less exalted Soviet citizens who have distinguished themselves in their fields of endeavor. A local factory will give great attention to one of "its" workers elected as a deputy,

TABLE 6 –1   Representation of Selected Groups in Elective Bodies (Soviets) at Different Levels of the Soviet State Structure (in percent)*

PARTY MEMBERS OR CANDIDATES	WOMEN	NOT ELECTED AT PREVIOUS ELECTION	COMPLETE OR INCOMPLETE HIGHER EDUCATION	WORKERS OR COLLECTIVE FARMERS	DEPUTIES BELOW AGE 30
Supreme Soviet of USSR:					
Elected in:					
1970 72.3	30.5	55.8	51.4	50.3	18.5
1974 72.2	31.3	55.8	53.0	50.7	18.4
1979 71.7	32.5	55.4	52.9	51.1	21.1
1984 71.4	32.8	n.a.†	n.a.	51.3	22.0
Supreme Soviets of Union Republics:					
Elected in:					
1971 67.6	34.8	63.6	49.0	50.4	17.2
1975 67.5	32.5	65.6	50.8	50.5	18.3
1980 67.2	35.9	63.2	52.2	50.6	19.9
1985 67.1	36.2	n.a.	n.a.	30.6	20.3
Supreme Soviets of Autonomous Republics:					
Elected in:					
1971 63.5	38.0	64.2	50.3	47.9	18.5
1975 63.8	39.1	66.1	49.3	50.1	22.0
1980 63.3	39.9	66.2	49.8	50.5	22.9
1985 63.0	40.3	n.a.	n.a.	50.6	23.6
Local Soviets:					
Elected in:					
1971 44.5	45.8	50.1	18.1	65.3	25.7
1973 43.9	47.4	46.2	n.a.	67.3	28.2
1975 43.8	48.1	44.8	20.6	67.7	30.1
1977 43.2	49.0	n.a.	n.a.	68.4	32.4
1980 43.1	49.5	46.7	23.8	68.7	33.3
1982 42.8	50.1	54.2	n.a.	69.2	34.0
1985 42.8	50.3	n.a.	n.a.	67.3	34.3

*On the basis of the 1977 USSR Constitution (Article 90) the interval between elections for the USSR, union-republic, and autonomous-republic supreme soviets was changed from four to five years, while that for the local soviets was changed from two to two-and-a-half years.
†**Note:** n.a. = not available

Sources: *Spravochnik Partiinogo Rabòtnika* (Moscow: Izdatel'stvo Politicheskoi Literatury) 1976, No. 16, pp. 471–73, and 1981; No. 2, pp. 505–508. *Izvestiia,* Jun. 17, 1970, p. 1; Jun. 20, 1971, p. 1; Jun. 23, 1973, p. 1; Jun. 19, 1974, p. 1; Jun. 21, 1975, p. 1; Jun. 25, 1977, p. 1; Mar. 7, 1979, p. 1; Mar. 1, 1980, p. 1; Jun. 26, 1982, p. 1; Mar. 7, 1984, p. 1; Mar. 2, 1985, pp. 1–2.

and considerable local prestige is attached to the honor. Almost invariably the worker chosen has an excellent work record, is active in party or *Komsomol* affairs, and is attempting to improve himself through further training or education. He is also typically depicted as a "good comrade." To the extent that Supreme Soviet deputies do serve as the "media for the message" from Moscow, of course, it is important that such persons command the respect of their coworkers.

In addition to the prestige and the chance for political advancement that such election affords, other nonmaterial incentives should also be mentioned: the feeling of being in the "in group," of mixing with the "real" leaders, and of spending a few days a year in Moscow at government expense. For the lathe operator from far-off Sakhalin Island, in the Pacific Ocean, this last matter may be a particular incentive. Let us look at the process by which these people make it to the ranks of the highest Soviet legislative institutions, the electoral system.

Elections

To those familiar with parliamentary or presidential elections in the West, the Soviet electoral process has to be considered the ultimate mark of hypocrisy and sham in Soviet governmental operations. One has to wonder why they bother with elections at all. On the one hand there is the constitutional guarantee—again echoing the best progressive provisions of Western democracies—of "universal, equal and direct suffrage by secret ballot" (Article 95). On the other hand there is the whole of Soviet electoral practice since elections began to be held under this provision in 1938. The basic features of Soviet elections will be familiar to most readers: one person running for each seat in an uncontested election and over 99 percent of the electorate participating, with virtually all of them voting for the unopposed candidate (rather than voting against him by crossing out his name, the only other act envisaged in Soviet electoral practices). In this most pro forma of arrangements, only a miniscule number of candidates do not receive the required 50 percent of the votes cast, and this *never* happens in the national or republic-level elections, only at the local levels.[7] Even where such a defeat takes place there is no possibility of simultaneously electing another person by means of the write-in vote, because a write-in is considered to invalidate the ballot. Election, therefore, depends upon nomination, and this process is also suitably controlled to allow only "desirable" candidates to be put forward.

Almost 2.3 million persons are elected to legislative-type institutions in the USSR, from the local soviets to the Supreme Soviet. At each level the process is similar. Six kinds of bodies are allowed to nominate candidates. Since all of these bodies—communist-party organizations, trade unions, *Komsomol*, cooperatives and other public organizations, work collectives, and meetings of servicemen in their military units—are sanctioned by the regime, they provide an initial screening process. Although it is possible for more than one candidate to be nominated for a single seat—indeed, such a practice would seem to be implied in allowing a number of kinds of organizations to make nominations—somehow it always has worked out that only one candidate runs for each legislative seat. Obviously, by some informal behind-the-scenes process a single candidate is chosen. This need not mean that in all cases it is a matter of Party dictate; but we know too little about the process of candidate "emergence" to say how it typically works.

The actual casting of ballots is a similarly orchestrated arrangement. After obtaining a ballot paper at the local voting place by presenting identification, the voter casts a valid ballot simply by placing the paper in the ballot box *(urna)*, which is usually suitably located under a giant portrait of Lenin. In other words, no marks at all need be affixed by the voter. It is a simple act of transference from election officials to ballot box, with the voter as medium. And the typical individual's participation in the whole Soviet political process is summed up in the hollowness of this act. Of course the individual may mark the ballot by crossing out the name of the candidate, and several curtained booths are usually provided for those who wish to use them. Some Western analysts have suggested that the very act of using the booth might be considered suspicious, and that those who went into booths would be reported to the authorities. While this suggestion makes some sense, given what we know of the Soviet system, it is a kind of safeguard that even suspicious Soviet authorities do not consider necessary, at least on a systematic scale. In our observations of voting practices in several polling places in Moscow, it was true that very few people bothered to use the booths. But some did, and as far as we could tell no one paid them the slightest attention.[8]

In spite of the seeming emptiness of the whole thing, it must be said that the Soviet Union expends considerable efforts and funds on the electoral process. From all outward appearances, at least, the election rules are followed scrupulously. A vast network of election commissions, from the Central Election Commission to those on the lowest voting level, is set up to handle all phases of the elections. In addition to the nominating process, a campaign of sorts is run in which the nominee's name is made known to the people of his or her constituency. The candidate even makes a preelection speech to a meeting of voters. Although a candidate may run only in one constituency, some are offered seats in more than one in what is apparently meant to be interpreted as a sign of the popularity of the top leaders. With profuse thanks the leaders decline all offers but one.

Why do they go to all this trouble? Probably for several reasons. First and foremost, the elections serve as a legitimizing device for the people in power. No matter how meaningless they may appear to us, they can provide some basis for the claim that the people are behind the leaders. How many leaders or people the elections actually convince of this fact is an open question; but at least the elections do not serve as a manifestation of opposition, and the near unanimity of the results is no doubt comforting to the leaders. Likewise, the results can offer no encouragement to would-be opponents of the regime, since they indicate how completely the present leaders are in control. Moreover, while the election process appears a great waste of time to us, this is not to say that it would be so considered by the Soviet populace at large, most of whom have never known anything else.

The Soviet schools and other socialization channels have strongly emphasized the positive character of the process and have made great efforts to rationalize its particular characteristics.

It is said, for instance, that since Soviet society does not contain the inherent contradictions of capitalist society (classes, the profit motive, and so on), there is no need to have contested elections. More telling criticisms are made of the role that money plays in the electoral process of Western countries, particularly the United States. And whatever else can be said about Soviet elections, it is certainly true that individual candidates need not raise great amounts of money for their campaigns. So by a combination of pointing out the negative aspects of Western electoral politics and showing how the Soviet mode of election fits in so well with the classless, nonantagonistic nature of Soviet society, voting is transformed into a positive, meaningful act. This attitude has even found its way into what some Western analysts consider respectable contemporary Soviet literature. Consider this excerpt from the story "The Old Guys" by the liberal Soviet writer Yuri Kazakov:

> Tikhon [the "positive hero" in this story] loves to vote. Before an election he goes to the voting place practically every day and reads the magazines and newspapers, and listens to the speeches attentively, his ear cocked to one side. He's always the first one to vote; if he's on duty that day and can't come, they bring the ballot box to him first thing in the morning. Putting on his glasses, he reads the ballots over at length, asks all about *the candidate* [emphasis added]—who he is, where he's from, who his father and mother were—and then he orders them to come into the booth, and holding the ballot carefully in his fleshy fingers, he drops it into the box.[9]

All that has been said points to the lack of any personal relevance for the individual voter. But the very "passion for unanimity" exhibited by Soviet leaders with regard to the electoral process apparently can provide a means for limited voter leverage, even if only on a personal level. A Soviet acquaintance related the following story: He became so disgusted at his failure to get a new apartment for his family after repeated promises from the local authorities that he decided to refuse to vote in the coming election. When election day was nearly over and he and his wife had not voted, local Party activists came to get him to vote, and when he still refused, they sent more important Party officials. After "negotiations" with the officials, the couple agreed to vote, having been promised that they would have their apartment at the earliest possible time. Shortly thereafter the friend and his family moved into the new apartment, and he is convinced that his election-day activities were largely responsible for this. Obviously this is not a tactic that everyone in need of an apartment could use successfully. But other Soviet citizens, in discussing this incident, have confirmed its plausibility: Since the performance of local Party authorities is judged in part on how effectively they can reach and mobilize the citizens within their jurisdiction—including getting them to vote—it would be possible to exercise influence via the electoral process by refusing to be mobilized.[10]

More meaningful influence through the electoral process depends, of course, on the voter's being able to exercise some choice. This the Soviet authorities have never been willing to allow. What is interesting to note is that there have been rare recommendations in recent years that at least a limited choice be provided to the voter in legislative elections.[11] If this were to be done, the Soviet Union would be following the lead of several of its East European neighbors, where limited electoral choice is combined with the absence of alternative governments or policies.

Is actual Soviet voting really at the level indicated by official statistics; that is, typically more than 99 percent of eligible voters? Earlier the tendency among Western analysts was to accept this high figure, seeing it as evidence of the successful manipulation of the masses by the authorities. But more recently some doubt has been expressed about the validity of the official figures. Information from recent emigrés suggests that the need felt by local Soviet officials to produce the appearance of a high rate of voter turnout is sufficiently great that they often condone practices that considerably inflate such participation. Examples of such practices include the occasional stuffing of the ballot box; one member of a family voting for all members; and, more frequently, the widespread covert avoidance of voting. The last is accomplished by a voter claiming that he expects to be away from his voting district on election day, obtaining a certificate allowing him to vote elsewhere, and then not voting. Taking into consideration such practices, a former member of a Soviet local election commission concluded: "A much closer approximation to reality is that about three-quarters of Soviet electors vote."[12]

The Standing Committees and the Presidium

Where should one look for the "real" policy-making power? One who considers himself a realist about these things probably would suggest immediately the top of the Party hierarchy, that is, the Politburo or the Secretariat. Although this suggestion might be accurate so far as ultimate political power is concerned, including the ultimate power to veto any legislative proposal, it is certainly not realistic to think that all policy is initiated at the top. Policy making (which often ends in the adoption of formal legislation) is more complex than this. We can quickly eliminate the Supreme Soviet from any meaningful role in the adoption of legislation by virtue of the short duration of its meetings and the size of the body (1,500 members). What about bodies connected with the Supreme Soviet? There are two such bodies that merit mention: the committees (or commissions) of the Supreme Soviet and the Presidium of the Supreme Soviet. Each house of the Supreme Soviet has sixteen standing committees made up of thirty-five deputies each (the Planning Budget Committee of each house has forty-five members each). They include committees on "Legislative Proposals," "Foreign Affairs," "Agriculture," and "Health and Social Security." Although it is likely that these committees receive proposed legislation before it is presented to the whole legislature for approval, it is also clear that they play little part in the formulation of legislative proposals. The reason is the same one that applies to so many supposedly representative bodies in the Soviet Union, whether they be in the Party structure or the government-used structure: Such bodies are not composed of people who can devote full-time attention to this work. Rather, their members hold down other jobs full time, directing minimal attention to the functions of the governmental or Party bodies of which they are members. This is true not only of members of the Supreme Soviet and its committees (as well as the soviets or legislative bodies at lower levels of the Soviet governmental apparatus) but also of members of such theoretically important Party bodies as the Party Congress (according to Party Rules the supreme organ of the Party) and the CPSU Central Committee.

Supreme Soviet committees simply do not meet frequently enough to perform serious work in the formulation of policy. It is likely, however, that the committees' advisers from specialized state organs (for instance, the Ministry of Justice and the various law institutes) play a considerable role in drawing up alternative policy proposals, always subject, of course, to veto from somewhere in the Party apparatus. Moreover, the committee chairmen are typically responsible officials from a fairly high level of the bureaucratic apparatus who may play an important role in policy discussion *in lieu of* the committees that they head. In whatever form, however, the contributions of Supreme Soviet committees to policy making must be considered modest.[13]

The Presidium of the Supreme Soviet is far more important than are the standing committees, although in terms of the total picture of Soviet political power it should be described as "useful" rather than "influential." The Presidium is made up of thirty-six members, in addition to a Chairman, a First Deputy Chairman, and a Secretary. As a bow to the Soviet principle of federalism, fifteen of this number are designated as Deputy Chairmen and represent the fifteen union republics. Although the Constitution does not require it, in practice these Deputy Chairmen have chaired the supreme soviet presidiums of the republics they represent. The other members include a mixture of well-known and obscure personages in the Soviet political hierarchy.

The Presidium has an impressive list of powers and duties granted by Articles 121, 122, and 123 of the Constitution. These include the typical functions performed by the heads of states in other countries, such as granting pardons, awarding orders and titles of honor, and certifying diplomatic representatives; they also include some little-used powers such as issuing interpretations of laws. The most important power is that of issuing edicts. In this capacity the Presidium serves as a kind of continually functioning legislature, allowing for the extremely short sessions of the regular legislature, the Supreme Soviet. When there is a need for a legislative-type act to have the force of law and the Supreme Soviet happens not to be in session (that is, about 98 percent of the time), such a measure can be adopted by the Presidium in the form of an edict *(ukaz)* and will be fully enforceable by the executive branch and the courts. Typically, the Supreme Soviet, the next time it meets, will transform the edict into a statute *(zakon)* in one of its regular votes. In fact, much of the time in Supreme Soviet sessions is spent in this process of transforming edicts into statutes. In terms of the total volume of Soviet legislation, relatively little of it is adopted initially as statute by the Supreme Soviet. This procedure is normally reserved for basic pieces of legislation, the immediate adoption of which is not a pressing matter, such as the "Basic Principles" of criminal law or civil law, or for routine and recurrent legislation such as that on the annual budget or economic plans.

Thus, the basic law-making function is performed by the Presidium, in spite of the constitutional provision giving sole legislative power to the Supreme Soviet. But is it actually the whole Presidium that performs this function? It seems unlikely that this is the case, because there is very little evidence that the whole Presidium meets very frequently at all.* And this stands to reason, since nearly 40 percent of its membership (the chairmen of the fourteen union-republic supreme soviet presidia located outside of Moscow) have full-time jobs hundreds or thousands of miles away from where the Presidium is supposed to meet. It is often announced in the press that the Presidium has met on the day before the session of the full Supreme Soviet, apparently to take up matters of planning for the Supreme Soviet meeting. And on rare occasions when an extremely important action such as the ratification of a treaty takes place, there is evidence that the Presidium actually has met. On most other occasions it is likely that edicts are adopted in the name of the Presidium by a very small number of its members. When such edicts are announced in the press, the names of the Chairman and the Secretary are listed. Since the Chairman has in recent times been a member of the ruling Party Politburo, it can be assumed that initiative for the edicts comes largely from the Politburo or, perhaps in the case of less important edicts, from some lower level of the central Party hierarchy.

To summarize, then, the law-making function resides formally in the 1,500-member legislature, the Supreme Soviet, but is largely exercised by the 39-member Presidium of the Supreme Soviet. Since this body seldom meets, its lawmaking function appears to be mostly performed by the Presidium's Chairman and Secretary. The edict-making power exercised by these two officials gives the force of law to policies approved in the actual Soviet power center of the Soviet system, the Communist Party of the Soviet Union.

*Some recent evidence suggests that the Presidium meets once a month. See Gordon Wightman, book review, *Soviet Studies*, 32, No. 4 (Oct. 1980), 598. But if this is the case, it does not appear that regular monthly meetings of the Presidium are routinely covered in the Soviet press.

THE COUNCIL OF MINISTERS

The other major organ in the Soviet state apparatus is the Council of Ministers. It is appointed by and formally responsible to the Supreme Soviet or, between Supreme Soviet sessions, to the Presidium. Analogous to a cabinet in Western parliamentary or presidential systems but of considerably larger size, the Council of Ministers is described in the Constitution (Article 128) as "the highest executive and administrative organ" of the USSR. Also consistent with Western usage, it is referred to as "the Government" *(Pravitel' stvo)* and its chairman, the equivalent of prime minister, is head of government.

In a way, the status of the Soviet Council of Ministers reflects *in extremis* a situation that is increasingly evident in the West, the bypassing of the Cabinet and rule by a small, less formal coterie surrounding the head of government.[14] The Council of Ministers' power and importance are meager enough as it is, with the Communist Party having such a strong role in policy making. The Council's large size and the nature of its composition add further to its impotence.

The USSR Council of Ministers now has more than one hundred members.* Fifteen of these members chair the union-republic councils of ministers, performing their major functions on a completely different level of government, for the most part, outside of Moscow. Even without these fifteen, a body of ninety-five to one hundred members is much too large to meet either frequently or with efficiency. In recent years this fact has received official acknowledgement, accompanied by a more realistic assessment of the importance of the Council. A law regarding the USSR Council of Ministers was adopted in 1978 and provides (Article 28) that meetings of the Council will take place "not less than once per quarter," which is probably about as often as it actually meets.[15]

Under these circumstances it is hardly possible that the Council of Ministers can act as the "executive organ" it is indicated as being by the Constitution. The more important policy-making and executive organ of the government is the Presidium of the Council of Ministers. Said to have existed since 1953 but given official recognition only with the adoption of the 1977 Constitution, this body is composed of the Chairman, First Deputy Chairmen, and Deputy Chairmen of the Council of Ministers; it numbered fifteen members when it was chosen in 1984. Its members typically have broad experience, and some have considerable political influence. The same cannot be said for most of the rest of the members of the Council of Ministers. With few exceptions they are career specialists of rather narrow

---

*The number was 115 for the Council of Ministers chosen by the Supreme Soviet in Apr. 1984. The composition was as follows: one Chairman, three First Deputy Chairmen, eleven Deputy Chairmen, sixty-two ministers, nineteen Chairmen of USSR State Committees, three other heads of agencies of the Council of Ministers, one Administrator of Affairs of the Council of Ministers, and the chairpersons of the fifteen union-republic councils of ministers serving *ex officio. Izvestiia,* Apr. 13, 1984, p. 1.

experience in the state apparatus and have little or no voice in overall governmental policy.

A realistic view of the importance of the Presidium of the Council of Ministers was given in 1980 by the Soviet legal scholar B. M. Lazarev: "it is not an advisory body but a determinative body . . . Its decisions are considered decisions of the USSR Council of Ministers itself . . . The great bulk of questions within the competence of the government are decided by the Presidium of the USSR Council of Ministers." Lazarev points out another recent legal provision that affirms the insubstantial role of the Council of Ministers: Article 29 and the 1978 Law on the Council of Ministers, which provides that in urgent cases the Chairman of the Council may make decisions in its name. The Chairman's powers are further enhanced by the provision allowing him to recommend to the Supreme Soviet the slate of candidates for ministers as well as to recommend the naming and discharge of individual ministers.[16]

The reason for the large size of the Council of Ministries is the large number of economic ministries included therein (for example, ministries of gas industry, cellulose-paper industry, electro-technical industry, food industry, and so on) in addition to the traditional ministries found in Western countries, such as foreign affairs, defense, and justice. It is understandable that the central government in a socialist system would have considerable responsibility for running the economy, and in the Soviet Union this responsibility is handled largely through the economic ministries.

A word of explanation might be useful about the structure of ministerial-level departments of the Council of Ministers. There are three basic types of such bodies: all-union ministries, union-republic ministries, and state committees and other departments. All-union ministries are, in theory, more centralized bodies than union-republic ministries, since they exercise direct control throughout the country of the branch of administration within their jurisdiction. Corresponding ministries on the union-republic level do not exist. Union-republic ministries, on the other hand, normally administer their affairs through corresponding bodies of the same name at the level of the fifteen union republics. It is difficult to state a general rule delineating the kinds of ministries that are all-union and those that are union-republic. At the time of the adoption of the 1936 Constitution there were few ministries of strictly economic purpose. Heavy industry was put in the all-union category whereas light industry was union-republic. But with the proliferation of economic ministries over time, such a heavy industry–light industry dichotomy has become largely meaningless, Of the "traditional" ministries found in most Western countries, defense and foreign affairs were all-union until 1944, when they joined justice, finance, and health, among others, in the union-republic category. The Ministry of Defense was returned to the all-union category in 1978. Foreign trade, another original ministry, remains to this day of the all-union type.[17] Since Khrushchev's regime there has been a considerable growth in the number of all-union ministries, suggesting an increase in authority at the national level at the expense of the union republics.[18]

Like ministries, USSR State Committees are identified as "central organs of state administration and all-union or union-republic." But although ministries are said to be responsible for "branch administration" (that is, a branch of the economy such as the oil industry), state committees carry out "interbranch administration," meaning that they are responsible for activities common to several branches of administration. A good example is the State Planning Committee *(Gosplan)*. The number of such agencies rose from five in 1936 to over twenty in the 1980s (including nineteen actual state committees, the State Bank of the USSR, the Central Statistical Administration, and the People's Control Committee).

Under Article 133 of the Constitution, the Council of Ministers has the power to issue "decrees," *(postanovleniia)*, acts that are considered legal norms, and "resolutions" *(rasporiazheniia)*, which are normally of a routine rather than normative nature, pursuant to laws already on the books. This provision is the vehicle for the policy-making power exercised in the name of the Council of Ministers. Sometimes exceedingly important policies are adopted as decrees or resolutions. An act of particular importance, or one for which special public attention is desired, may be issued as a joint decree of the USSR Council of Ministers and the Party Central Committee. It is not unknown for such a document to serve as the basis for and to be followed by edicts adopted by the Presidium of the Supreme Soviet or statutes adopted by the Supreme Soviet itself. Thus, the constitutionally mandated order of things is reversed: Rather than a Council of Ministers' action being adopted "in pursuance of" laws or other acts of the Supreme Soviet or its Presidium, laws sometimes "pursue" Council of Ministers' decisions.

Western commentators have often noted the lack of distinction between the various kinds of acts that issue from agencies of the Soviet state, and even Soviet lawyers at times have acknowledged this problem. But it is unlikely that this is a top item on the Soviet authorities' agenda of things in need of reform: The confusion and messiness of the present system may be anathema to the legal mind, but legal minds do not run the USSR. Although the authorities appear to follow very precisely the legal formalities on some aspects of state operation (for instance, with regard to the running of the largely meaningless popular elections), they pay little attention to legal niceties in other areas. This works to their advantage in the sphere of legislation, for they have an extremely flexible procedure whereby they can transform policy decisions into law. Nor is this all: Substatutory acts of various governmental agencies (including the Council of Ministers) do not have to be published unless they are of general significance or of normative character. Since it is the governmental agencies themselves that determine if their acts are general or normative, a good deal of "secret legislation" is thought to be in existence. One Western specialist has concluded that the "number of 'unpublished' legal acts far exceeds that which is published."[19]

As suggested above, even though general, overall policy comes from the Party leadership, and thus ultimate political power resides there, this centralization of policy making does not mean that the state bureaucracy is completely powerless. Far from it. The *elected* representatives have little power, but the members of the state apparatus are in a more strategic position. Although they may not have much responsibility for *initiating* policy (and this is probably true all the way up to the level of the USSR Council of Ministers), they are in charge of administering it. This can be an exceedingly important part of the overall governing process. To offer just one example, the discretion of the ministers and other officials of the USSR Council of Ministers in managing the nationalized economy is substantial.

In any society, administrators exercise great control over policy implementation. Anyone who has had occasion to deal with Soviet bureaucratic officials knows the great power they can wield (most often, it would seem, to say "NO!") and how little recourse one has when dissatisfied with their decisions. The Soviet public at large has little control over the bureaucracy, and the political leadership spends a considerable amount of time trying to maintain its control.

SOVIET GOVERNMENTAL STRUCTURE BELOW THE NATIONAL LEVEL

Up to now, only the national level of the state apparatus has been considered. There are other levels of government as well. Local governments are organized around the "local soviets of workers' deputies," or local soviets. And since the Soviet Union is a federal system, there are also intermediate levels of government to consider.

For two reasons, the examination of these governmental structures and operations can be treated briefly. First, in many respects the subnational governments are merely microcosms of the national government, so that a full description would involve considerable repetition of what has been said above. Second, there is a consensus among Western observers that on most counts the Soviet brand of federalism is a sham federalism.[20] Thus one can find little in the way of significant initiatives or departures from national policy on the republic level. Still, the structure of the system is federal, and even if it is not very meaningful, a few words should be said about it.

Federal Structure

As far as units in the federal system go, below the all-union or national level are four levels representing nationality groups which populate given territorial areas. These are the union republic (also called "soviet socialist republic" or SSR), the autonomous republic ("autonomous soviet socialist republic" or ASSR), the autonomous province, and the autonomous district.

As mentioned earlier, representatives from these units make up membership of the Soviet of Nationalities, one of the houses of the bicameral national legislature, or Supreme Soviet. The union republics, fifteen in number, are the most important and embrace territories in which most of the country's major nationalities are concentrated. Union republics vary greatly both in territory and in population. The largest by far is the giant Russian Soviet Federated Socialist Republic (RSFSR), with almost three fourths of the total land area of the country and more than 52 percent of the total Soviet population. Thus, the RSFSR is more than twice as large as the continental United States and has as many people as Great Britain, France, and the Benelux countries combined. The remaining union republics range down in size to tiny Armenia, which is approximately the size of the state of Maryland, and Estonia, which is slightly larger but which has a much smaller population.

Unlike units on the three lower levels, union republics possess the theoretical right under the USSR Constitution (Article 72) "freely to secede from the USSR." Of course this right has never been exercised, and, like many other constitutional guarantees, it is not to be taken seriously. Moreover, Article 75, a provision not in earlier constitutions, seems to dilute the right of secession in stating that the territory of the USSR "is a single entity and comprises the territories of the union republics" and that "the sovereignty of the USSR extends throughout its territory." Another pseudoright of union republics, designed to impart greater theoretical independence to these units than to lower levels of the federal system, is the right under Article 80 to enter into diplomatic and other relations with foreign states. But the right of union republics in the 1936 Constitution to have their own military formations does not appear in the 1977 Constitution.

It used to be said by Soviet authorities that a union republic possessed three distinguishing characteristics: that it is not surrounded on all sides by other union republics; that the nationality for whom the republic is named constitutes a "compact majority" of the republic's population; that it has a population of at least one million persons. These characteristics would be necessary, it was suggested, should the republic choose to secede from the USSR. In recent years, however, Soviet sources have stopped mentioning these three "objective characteristics,"[21] perhaps because the Kazakh and Kirghiz peoples no longer constitute a majority of the populations of "their" republics.[22]

As far as governmental structure goes, the union republics very much replicate the national level. Each has its own constitution and elects a supreme soviet (but made up of one house rather than two) which chooses its presidium and a council of ministers. Each republic has a supreme court as well as lower courts. Within their areas of jurisdiction, these organs operate in the same ways as their national-level counterparts.

The autonomous republics (ASSRs) represent concentrations of nationality groupings within union republics. The ASSRs are designed to give a limited amount of autonomy to the medium-sized nationality groups of the country; each possesses its own constitution and its own elected supreme soviet which appoints its presidium and a council of ministers. These "organs of state" are apparently meant to accord limited attributes of statehood or sovereignty to the ASSRs (Soviet sources refer to the ASSR as a "Soviet socialist national state"). Unlike union republics, however, autonomous republics do not possess even theoretical rights of independence such as the right of secession and the right to maintain foreign relations. They are clearly under the jurisdiction of the union republics in which they are located.

Very little autonomy, even of the theoretical variety, is accorded to governmental units on the two lowest levels, the autonomous province and the autonomous district. Both types of units have elected soviets or representative councils which name their executive committees as well as the district courts. But in these respects they are no different from regular local governments. Except for the nationality basis for these units, they appear to differ very little from the other administrative subdivisions in the Soviet Union which are run by local soviets.[23]

Local Governments

Local governments may be considered those that do not possess even theoretical statehood or sovereignty. This category would include the two lower units in the federal structure just discussed, the autonomous province and the national district, as well as the strictly territorial units. The last group includes a confusing array of names and types.[24] Suffice it to say that they cover all of the territorial-administrative subdivisions of the country down to the level of the village or big-city district, and that they all have essentially the same structure. It consists of an elected local soviet (council) which typically meets more often than its big brother, the Supreme Soviet, but which still meets rather infrequently. The local soviet elects an executive committee to handle its business during the intervals between local soviet sessions.

It is the chairman of the executive committee of the local soviet that Western journalists often refer to as the "mayor" (for example, the "Mayor of Moscow"). The local soviet possesses full rights to exercise the powers granted to it, such as they are. As it happens, local authorities in the Soviet Union have very few powers guaranteed to their exclusive competence. Higher authorities can interfere rather freely at the lower levels, if they choose to.[25]

A number of Western analyses of Soviet local politics have been written in recent years. One of the common conclusions in many of these studies is that Soviet politics, when viewed at close range, appears to be a considerably more complex and subtle process than many Western writings have suggested. One study, for instance, challenges the view of the state apparatus as merely a façade for complete Communist Party control. The author sees the overlapping membership of Party and state organs at the local level as ensuring ultimate Party control but providing the potential for more effective political decision making at the same time. This point is no doubt applicable with regard to the whole of the Soviet political structure.[26]

Our view of governmental structure and operations, as espoused in this chapter, basically emphasizes the one-way nature of the operation, serving the purposes of the rulers rather than the ruled. In some ways, however, popular "input" can be achieved through the governmental process, and this we have only touched on lightly so far. It is in the potential expansion of such areas that prospects for change in Soviet politics may be looked for. We return to this matter in Chapter 11.

NOTES

[1] Franz Schurmann, "Politics and Economics in Russia and China," in *Soviet and Chinese Communism: Similarities and Differences*, ed., Donald W. Treadgold, (Seattle, WA: University of Washington Press, 1967), p. 299.

[2] *Zasedeniia Verkhovnogo Soveta SSSR*, 10th Sozyv, 8th Session, 16–17 Jun. 1983; Stenographic Record (Moscow: Verkhovnyi Soviet SSSR, 1983), p. 139.

[3] In the 47 years between the first session of the Supreme Soviet and the end of 1984, the Supreme Soviet met for a total of 300 days, or about 6.2 days per year. The average is inflated by relatively long sessions from 1938 to 1940 and 1955 to 1960. Subsequently the Supreme Soviet met even less frequently. In the 19 years from 1966 through 1984 it met an average of about 5 days a year. Article 112 of the Soviet Constitution provides for Supreme Soviet meetings twice a year. These sessions, normally in June or July and November or December, usually last 2 to 3 days each.

[4] *The New York Times*, Mar. 10, 1972, p. 2.

[5] The apportionment by territorial unit is as follows: thirty-two deputies for each union republic, eleven deputies for each autonomous republic, five deputies for each autonomous province *(oblast')*, and one for each national district *(okrug)*.

[6] For instance, Kunaev was continuously a deputy since 1962, Ponomarev since 1964.

[7] Jerome M. Gilison, "Soviet Elections as a Measure of Dissent: The Missing One Percent," *The American Political Science Review*, 62 (1968), 820. For a minor exception to this statement (that is, an example of a candidate for a seat in a union-republic supreme soviet not receiving the required absolute majority of votes), see Ger P. van den Berg, "A New Electoral Law in the Soviet Union," *Review of Socialist Law*, 4 (1978), 356.

[8] On the basis of his study of the matter, Friedgut concludes: "The main reasons for using the booth, other than to cross out the candidate's name, appear to be a desire to bait the authorities in a way that is relatively safe, and an instinct to preserve the vestiges of choice, with those who do not wish to vote negatively protecting by their use of the booth the identity of those citizens who vote against the candidate." Theodore H. Friedgut, *Political Participation in the USSR* (Princeton, NJ: Princeton University Press, 1979), p. 113.

[9] Yuri Kazakov, "The Old Guys," in *Going to Town and Other Stories*, trans. Gabriella Azrael (Boston: Houghton Mifflin, 1964), p. 241.

[10] A 1978 discussion of Soviet elections by a former member of a local election commission confirms that elections sometimes "permit the population to bargain with the authorities over minor matters." Victor Zaslavsky and Robert J. Brym, "The Functions of Elections in the USSR," *Soviet Studies*, 30 (1978), 367. See also Friedgut, *Political Participation*, pp. 101–102.

[11] See the discussion of one such recommendation in *The New York Times*, March 22, 1966, p. 2; another was made by the Soviet lawyer A. I. Lepeshkin in 1965. See the *Current Digest of the Soviet Press* (hereafter cited as *CDSP*), 17, No. 14 (1965), 5. For more recent examples see Van

den Berg, "A New Election Law," p. 358. Van den Berg concludes that the new law on elections to the Supreme Soviet of the USSR adopted in 1978 will have little impact on actual electoral practices.

[12]Zaslavsky and Brym, "The Functions of Elections," p. 366. See also Friedgut, *Political Participation*, pp. 115–30. As Ann Sheehy put it in 1979, "it is difficult to believe the Central Election Commission's claim that in Uzbekistan only fourteen voters out of a total electorate of over seven million failed to show up at the polling station this year." "Soviet Electorate Edges Closer to Complete Unanimity," *Radio Liberty Research*, No. 87, Mar. 15, 1979, p. 2.

[13]Shugo Minagawa has shown that numerous regional Party secretaries serve on these committees and suggests that their roles on the committees may be significant. See "Regional First Secretaries in Parliamentary Committees," *Soviet Union*, 6, Pt. 1 (1979), 1–40.

[14]With regard to Great Britain on this point, see Anthony Sampson, *The Anatomy of Britain Today* (New York: Harper and Row, (1965), pp. 129–32. Among many writings that have commented on the declining significance of the Cabinet in the U.S. political system, see Thomas E. Cronin and Sanford D. Greenberg; eds., *The Presidential Advisory System* (New York: Harper and Row, 1969), especially pp. 25–28, 61, 330.

[15]Although no figures are published on the frequency of USSR Council of Ministers meetings, the Dutch scholar Ger P. van den Berg has found figures indicating that the Uzbek Republic's Council of Ministers meets infrequently (for example, an average of fewer than five times per year between 1969 and 1975), and the smaller Presidium of the Uzbek Council of Ministers meets quite frequently (over thirty times per year in recent years). Van den Berg concludes on the basis of a study of a number of writings on the institution of the council of ministers: "These studies . . . reveal that the Council itself is not of importance as a working institution, but that its inner cabinet—the Presidium of the Council of Ministers—is of primary importance for an understanding of the political and state structure of the Soviet Union." Book Review, *Review of Socialist Law*, 6 (1980), 103.

[16]The 1978 Law on the Council of Ministers is the first such piece of legislation regarding that body. It spells out in greater details than was previously the case the Council's powers and duties. It was adopted on July 5, 1980, and was first published in *Izvestiia*, July 6, 1980, p. 2. The Lazarev quotations are from B. M. Lazarev, *Sovet Ministrov SSSR* (Moscow: "Znanie," 1980), pp. 60–61.

[17]A typical, if not very meaningful, explanation by a Soviet authority for the all-union–union-republic distinction in ministries is that the all-union variety "control[s] those branches and spheres of administration that are fully granted to the Union [that is, the national government]," whereas union-republic ministries operate in those areas where both the national and the union-republic governments are competent. See, for example, A. I. Denisov and others, *Osnovy Sovet-skogo Stroitel'stva* (Moscow: Iuridicheskaia Literatura, 1968), p. 73. This statement does not explain, of course, why there has been such frequent shifting of ministries from one category to the other over the years.

[18]See Boris Lewytzkyj, "Sources of Conflict in the Top Levels of Soviet Leadership," *Radio Liberty Dispatch*, No. 3, Jan. 3, 1975.

[19]Harold J. Berman, *Justice in the USSR*, rev. ed. (New York: Vintage Books, 1963), p. 235. Although Soviet lawyers have little power in the strictly political operations of the Soviet system, they do seem to have been exercising increasing influence on those aspects of law that do not fall into the category of "political justice." Among the areas where their recommendations have borne fruit is in the increased publication of acts having the force of law that emanate from various governmental organs. See Donald D. Barry, "The Development of Soviet Administrative Procedure," in *Soviet Institutions and the Administration of Law*, Part III of *Soviet Law After Stalin*, eds., Donald D. Barry, F.J.M. Feldbrugge, George Ginsburgs, and Peter B. Maggs (Alphen aan den Rijn, the Netherlands: Sijthoff & Noordhoff, 1979), pp. 4–11. A Soviet lawyer writing in 1978, while noting the progress made in this area, deplores the fact that "even now there are some cases when acts [of the USSR Council of Ministers] remain unpublished." *Opublikovanie Normativnykh Aktov*, ed. A. S. Pigolkin (Moscow: Iuridicheskaia Literatura, 1978), p. 73.

[20]See, for instance, the discussion by L. G. Churchward, *Contemporary Soviet Government* (New York: American Elsevier Publishing Company, Inc., 1968), pp. 151–71. This author contrasts the Soviet practice of federalism with the way in which the term is generally under-

stood in the West. See also Chapter 12, where we return to the discussion of federalism in connection with Soviet nationality problems.

[21]Compare, for instance, two authoritative Soviet legal dictionaries. The 1956 *Iuridicheskii Slovar'* 2nd ed., P. I. Kudriavtsev (Moscow: Gosudarstvennoe Izdatel'stvo Iuridcheskoi Literatury, 1956), p. 435–36, under "union republics" mentions the three characteristics, whereas the 1984 *Iuridicheskii Entsiklopedicheskii Slovar'*, eds. A. Ya. Sukharev and others (Moscow: Izdatel'stvo "Sovetskaia Entsiklopediia," 1984), pp. 347–48, does not. Some Western writers still discuss the three characteristics as if they were *de rigueur*, but we have found no recent Soviet source that does so.

These three characteristics were apparently first mentioned by Stalin in his speech on the draft of the 1936 Constitution, November 25, 1935. Stalin said that an SSR should be a "border republic to be in a position logically and actually to raise the question of secession," adding that "of course none of our republics would actually raise the question of seceding from the USSR." An English translation of Stalin's speech may be found in James H. Meisel and Edward Z. Kozera, eds., *Materials for the Study of the Soviet System*, 2nd ed. (Ann Arbor, MI: The George Wahr Publishing Co., 1953), p. 231. The quotations used in this note are from pp. 239–40.

[22]According to the 1979 Census, the Kazakhs constitute only 36 percent of the Kazakh Republic population, with Russians comprising 40.8 percent. The Kirghiz are the largest ethnic group in their republic, with 47.9 percent of the population.

[23]For more details on the characteristics of the federative-nationality units in the USSR, see F.J.M. Feldbrugge, ed., *Encyclopedia of Soviet Law*, II (Leiden, the Netherlands: A. W. Sijthoff, 1973). This source lists eight autonomous provinces and ten national districts and describes both types as "administrative units with a nationality-geographical basis" (p. 426). See this source also for a discussion of the differences between the autonomous province and the national district. An important article on legal aspects of Soviet federalism, by a former Soviet lawyer, is A. Shtromas, "The Legal Position of the Soviet Nationalities and Their Territorial Units According to the 1977 Constitution of the USSR," *The Russian Review*, 37, No. 3 (Jul. 1978), 267.

[24]For example, Bratus', ed., *Entslikopedicheskii Slovar' Pravovykh Znanii*, p. 230, lists under "local organs of state power in the USSR" the following categories: *krai,* province *(oblast'),* autonomous province, national district, district, city, settlement, and village. In addition, as varieties of the last category it lists the Russian terms *stanitsa, derevnia, khutor, kishlak,* and *aul.* For an explanation of most of these categories, see Feldbrugge, ed., *Encyclopedia*, p. 426 ff., under "local authorities."

[25]See ibid.

[26]Ronald J. Hill, *Soviet Political Elites: The Case of Tiraspol* (New York: St. Martin's Press, 1977), esp. pp. 105–18. Hill's bibliography, pp. 216–21, contains many relevant references to English-language works on Soviet local politics.

SELECTED BIBLIOGRAPHY

ARMSTRONG, JOHN A., *Ideology, Politics and Government in the Soviet Union: An Introduction,* 4th ed. New York: Holt, Rinehart & Winston, 1978.

BYRNES, ROBERT F., ed., *After Brezhnev: Sources of Soviet Conduct in the 1980's.* Bloomington, IN: Indiana University Press, 1983.

CARRÈRE D'ENCAUSSE, HÉLÈNE, *Confiscated Power: How Soviet Russia Really Works.* New York: Harper and Row, 1982.

CARSON, GEORGE BARR, JR., *Electoral Practices in the USSR.* New York: Holt, Rinehart & Winston, 1955.

DI FRANCEISCO, WAYNE, and ZVI GITELMAN, "Soviet Political Culture and "Covert Participation" in Policy Implementation," *American Political Science Review,* 78, No. 3 (1984) pp. 603–21.

FRIEDGUT, THEODORE A., *Political Participation in the USSR.* Princeton, NJ: Princeton University Press, 1979.

GILISON, JEROME M., "Soviet Elections as a Measure of Dissent: The Missing One Percent," *The American Political Science Review*, 62 (1968), 814–26.

HARDING, NEAL, ed., *The State in Socialist Society*. Albany, NY: SUNY Press, 1984.

HAZARD, JOHN N., *The Soviet System of Government*, 5th ed. Chicago: University of Chicago Press, 1980.

HECHT, LEE, *The USSR Today*, 2nd ed. Springfield, VA: Scholasticus Publisher, 1982.

HILL, RONALD J., *Soviet Political Elites: The Case of Tiraspol*. New York: St. Martin's Press, 1977.

———, "The CPSU in a Soviet Election Campaign," *Soviet Studies*, 28, (1976), 590–98.

JACOBS, EVERETT M., ed., *Soviet Local Politics and Government*. Boston: Allen and Unwin, 1983.

MOTE, MAX E., *Soviet Local and Republic Elections*. Stanford, CA: The Hoover Institution, 1965.

OSBORN, ROBERT J., *The Evolution of Soviet Politics*. Homewood, IL: Dorsey Press, 1974.

RESHETAR, JOHN S., JR., *The Soviet Polity*, 2nd ed. New York: Harper & Row, 1978.

ROTHMAN, STANLEY, and GEORGE W. BRESLAUER, *Soviet Politics and Society*. St. Paul, MN: West Publishing Co., 1978.

SAVAS, E. S., and J. A. KAISER, *Moscow's City Government*. New York: Praeger, 1985.

SCHAPIRO, LEONARD, *The Government and Politics of the Soviet Union*, new rev. ed. New York: Vintage Books, 1978.

SHIPLER, DAVID K., *Russia: Broken Idols, Solemn Dreams*. New York: New York Times Books, 1983.

SHTROMAS, ALEXANDER, *Political Change and Social Development: The Case of the Soviet Union*. Frankfurt, Germany: Verlag Peter Lang, 1981.

SIEGLER, ROBERT W., *The Standing Commissions of the Supreme Soviet: Effective Cooptation*. New York: Praeger, 1982.

VAN DEN BERG, GER P., "A New Electoral Law in the Soviet Union," *Review of Socialist Law*, 4 (1978), 353–62.

VANNEMAN, PETER, *The Supreme Soviet*. Durham, NC: Duke University Press, 1977.

ZASLAVSKY, VICTOR, and ROBERT J. BRYM, "The Functions of Elections in the USSR," *Soviet Studies*, 30 (1978), 362–71.

7

THE COMMUNIST PARTY:
The Focus of Power

A Soviet friend was having trouble keeping his apartment in the university housing complex where he lived. He had gotten the apartment because his wife was a student at the university, but now her studies were completed. His work was in a research institute under the jurisdiction of a different government ministry from that of the university, and the university was trying to evict them to make room for university people. The housing problem being what it is, the friend was fighting tooth and nail to keep the apartment. He had appealed to the director of his institute for help and was returning for the last time to try to reason with university officials. "If this doesn't work," he said, "I'll go to the Party." He said this with an air that suggested both assurance and finality. As a loyal Party member in good standing, he was confident that the Party would resolve the matter in his favor (and he was not above using his Party position to this end, incidentally). Moreover, he looked upon the Party as a kind of court of last resort, the organization that would have the final word.

Our friend kept his apartment—with the Party's support. As is the case in any country in the world, influence and connections count. In fact, in a country such as the Soviet Union, where there is such a shortage of things that people want—housing, cars, quality clothing, home appliances, and the like—connections may be considerably more important in everyday life than in a country of relative abundance like the United States. The Russian word for this influence or "pull" is *blat,* and it is a very important word in the language.

In addition, since the Communist Party of the Soviet Union (CPSU) is the real focus of power in the Soviet system, it wields the greatest amount of influence. Any Party member, no matter how lowly his rank, is somewhat set apart from the approximately 94 percent of the Soviet population who are not "communists," that is, members of the Party. Some importance and potential power attaches to this status.[1]

This does not mean that every Party member abuses his status for personal advantage or that the local Party organs can or will intervene on a member's behalf in all cases. But such use of Party position has existed in some measure since the beginning of the Soviet state. It is a problem common to all modern societies and organizations, where elites are bound to emerge in one form or another. How the Soviet authorities have dealt with this problem is a matter to which we will return.

PARTY MEMBERSHIP

It may be surprising to some that Party members comprise such a small percentage of the total population. But this is in line with the Leninist idea of a small, highly disciplined group of revolutionaries who would win the revolution and direct the new state. Lenin's insistence on this kind of party was one of the major factors leading to the split of the Russian Social Democratic Party into the Bolshevik wing, led by Lenin, and the Menshevik wing, led by Martov, who advocated a mass party. Many analysts maintain that it was only the Leninist type of organization that could have achieved success in the Revolution.[2]

In any case, were Lenin alive today he would no doubt be astonished that the Party is so *large.* Although Party members comprise only about 6.5 percent of the total population and 9 to 10 percent of the adult population, the proportion of members is much higher than in Lenin's day. Throughout the Lenin period, Party members made up considerably less than 1 percent of the Soviet population. Gradual growth since then saw the percentage surpass 3 by 1950, 4 by 1960, and 5 by 1965. By 1986, there were more than 19 million members, about 6.5 percent of the Soviet population.

During the post-Stalin years Party membership has not grown at a consistent rate. During the Khrushchev period and for two years thereafter (that is, from 1956 through 1966) Party membership grew at an average annual rate of about 5.3 percent. After Khrushchev, however, the leadership decided that this rate was too high and steps were taken to slow the growth. From 1967 to 1976 the average growth rate was about 3 percent, from 1976 through 1980 it was just over 2 percent, and from 1981 through 1985 slightly under 2 percent. The Party has also taken other measures to affect the size and character of Party membership. Two of these are the so-called "exchange of Party cards" and the attempt to bring a greater proportion of workers and collective farmers into the Party. The result of the latter effort will be to make it more difficult for white-collar workers, especially intellectuals, to join. We shall discuss both of these measures in greater detail.

There has never been any idea of having the Communist Party embrace the whole Soviet population. Admission standards are rather strict. Persons may join the Party at age twenty-five or, if they are members of the *Komsomol,* at age eighteen. Applicants must have recommendations from three Party Members of five or more years' standing who have known the applicants for at least a year. Such recommendations presumably are not given lightly, for the Party Rules (see Appendix B) provide that those making recommendations will be considered responsible by the Party for the impartiality of their endorsement. Persons admitted to the Party serve a probationary period of one year as candidate members before being accorded full membership.

The document known as the Party Rules is a kind of constitution of the Party. It sets out the general principles of admission to the Party and requirements of members and describes the principles of Party operation as well as its structure and organization. Like the USSR Constitution, it is basically a statement of ideals or seemingly desirable principles rather than an accurate reflection of actual Party operation. According to the Rules, which list numerous duties of Party members, communists are expected to "master Marxist-Leninist theory," "provide an example of a conscientious and creative attitude toward labor," "firmly and steadfastly put into effect the general line and directives of the Party," "take an active part in the political affairs of the country," "boldly lay bare shortcomings and strive for their removal," and so forth. In short, whatever a Party member's full-time job, he or she is expected to be ever active in pursuing the Party's interests as well.

It is not surprising, then, that being a Party member is not every Soviet citizen's desire. It means giving up some portion of one's free time and, for the young and politically ambitious, perhaps virtually all of it. Moreover, the profile of the good communist suggested in the Rules involves a member's being always "on guard" to detect shortcomings and to correct them. Even in a society that has long encouraged the idea that being a busybody is a positive trait, this can get to be something of a bore. In some circumstances Party membership can interfere with a person's ability to perform conscientiously in one's profession. Dina Kaminskaya, a former Soviet lawyer who was involved in the defense of several important dissidents, found that not being in the Party gave her slightly more room for maneuver in some of her professional activities. For instance, she writes that when she found herself almost alone in supporting a colleague whose professional work with dissidents had brought him into disfavor with the authorities, "I thought to myself for the nth time, thank God I'm not in the party."[3]

But for many, the advantages of Party membership—the sense of belonging to the elite, no matter how low one's position, and the chances for job advancement and material rewards that membership implies—outweigh these disadvantages. Not that Party members are blatantly favored in the distribution of jobs and the good things of life. Apparently, the special stores for Party members where scarce goods were sold no longer exist,[4] and housing, automobiles, and other things in short supply are now supposed to be distributed in a scrupulously fair manner on the basis of need and/or one's place on a list. But to some extent, at least, Party membership suggests connections, or *blat*, and, as the old Soviet saying goes, "*blat* is stronger than the government."* Regarding jobs, it is simply a fact of Soviet life that a large number of jobs are only open to Party members. These include key positions in politics, the military, diplomacy, and internal security. Party membership is also an advantage to the person seeking any number of other responsible positions. And, of course, with regard to such matters as travel (especially abroad), Party members, as the most trustworthy people, receive preferential treatment.

· It is not surprising, therefore, that the Party attracts certain persons who are not "politically active and conscious" and who are not wholly "devoted to the communist cause" (Party Rules, Article 4). The Party is engaged in a continuous campaign, sometimes more intensely pursued than at others, to weed out the unworthy: the lax, the incompetent, those pursuing their own selfish interests. For the last the Soviet political lexicon contains two appropriate epithets. These happen to be cognate words and are easily translatable: *kar'erist* (careerist) and *opportunist* (opportunist); but the derogatory connotation of these terms is much stronger than in English. In addition to the regular expulsion procedures, the Party from time to time carries out a thorough membership review procedure to eliminate members who are not fulfilling their Party duties. This process, known as the "exchange of Party cards," was done most recently in the early 1970s, and it was reported in 1976 that some 347,000 people were dropped from the Party in the exchange.[5] Even without an exchange of Party cards, it was reported in the early 1980s that almost 300,000 Party members had been removed from the Party in the past five years for "acts incompatible with the designation communist."[6]

Another aspect of Party membership worth examining is social composition. Available data indicate that the Party is typically a somewhat more elite organization that the governmental bodies, particularly the soviets, examined in the last chapter. Information on social groups in the Soviet Union typically includes only three broad groups: workers, collective farmers, and employees. The last category embraces all white-collar workers up to and including high Party, government, and economic functionaries, as well as intellectuals. Workers and collective farmers comprise almost 74

*See the Glossary for a further discussion of *blat* and other important Soviet political terms.

percent of the Soviet population and about 56 percent of the Party membership.

One of the misleading aspects of this breakdown is that the statistics are based on the status of individuals when they joined the Party and generally do not reflect changes that result from an individual's advancement in occupation or education. Thus, most of the members of the high Party leadership are still listed in the worker or collective farmer categories, their status when they joined the Party many years ago.[7] This practice may hide the fact of a Party membership overwhelmingly composed of persons who are not workers or farmers. And it may also explain the strenuous efforts of the Party since the mid-1970s to recruit more workers and farmers and to reduce the proportion of intellectuals.

Those with partial or complete higher education number about 8 percent of the Soviet population but almost one-third of the Party; those with primary or no formal education comprise more than 31 percent of the Soviet population but less than 10 percent of the Party. Women now number more than 53 percent of the Soviet population but about 27 percent of the Party membership. Finally, a small handful of nationality groups, most notably the Russians, are overrepresented, whereas a number of others, mostly concentrated in the Baltic area and Central Asia, are grossly under-represented.[8] All these discrepancies increase in the upper levels of the Party hierarchy.

PARTY ORGANIZATION

The lowest level of Party organization is the primary Party organization (PPO). PPOs are normally organized at members' places of work, but they may also be established on a residential basis in villages or large housing complexes. At least three Party members are required to create a PPO. There are more than 425,000 such PPOs, which are said to exist in almost all "workers' collectives" in the country. This is the basic organization, to which every Party member belongs, and for most members it is the main point of contact with the Party. Several million members of PPOs serve in leadership capacities as members of PPO committees and bureaus or as PPO secretaries, but by no means all of these persons are full-time Party functionaries. Most are given time off from their regular jobs to perform Party duties. Normally only a PPO with 150 or more members is entitled to have full-time paid workers.

Obviously not all PPOs are equal in size. About 40 percent of the more than 425,000 PPOs have 15 or fewer members, more than 80 percent have fewer than 50 members, and only several hundred have over 1,000 members. The complexity of the leadership organization of the PPO varies with its size (see the Party Rules, articles 53–57, Appendix B). The highest organ of the PPO is theoretically the general meeting of all members, which is supposed to be convened at least once a month. Soviet authorities have acknowledged, however, that in many PPOs this rule is often ignored.

Above the PPO level, the Party is organized on approximately the same territorial basis as the state administration. The levels are the rural or urban district *(raion)*, the city *(gorod)* or autonomous district *(avtonomnyi okrug)*, the province *(oblast')* or territory *(krai)*, the union republic, and the national Party organization.[9]

As with the governmental structure discussed in the last chapter, there is considerable similarity between the lower and national Party structures. Our emphasis in this chapter will be on national Party structure and operations. We will discuss the central Party organs in some detail below, but for now let us merely mention that the main parts of the central Party organization are the Party Congress, the Central Committee, the Politburo (called the Presidium from 1952 to 1966), and the Secretariat (headed by the General Secretary of the CPSU). Organs or positions analogous to these are present at lower levels of the Party system. All levels have their Congresses—called conferences[10] below the union-republic level—their committees, their bureaus, their secretariats, and their first secretaries. At all levels the formal hierarchies of organs are the same: The congress or conference is the highest body,[11] and it elects the smaller committee, which elects the even smaller bureau as well as the secretariat or individual secretaries. And at all levels the actual power hierarchy is precisely the opposite of what the Party Rules and the organization charts suggest. The best way to demonstrate this is to discuss in more detail the relationship between the various Party organs at the all-union level.[12]

THE NATIONAL PARTY ORGANS

The Party Congress

The major Party organs at the all-union level are the Congress, the Central Committee (CC), the Politburo, and the Secretariat.* The Party Congress is referred to as the supreme organ of the CPSU, but it is so only in a formal sense. As with other bodies of large membership and infrequent meetings, its actual powers are meager. Delegates to Congresses represent subordinate territorial Party bodies in numbers determined by the CC CPSU. Those numbers grew continuously until the 1980s, and then stabilized at about 5,000 (the capacity of the Palace of Congresses in Moscow's Kremlin, where Congresses are held). Over the years, the intervals between Congresses have gradually been widened through changes in the

---

*Another central organ is the Central Auditing Commission. This body, whose members are named by the Congress, handles administrative matters and is charged with auditing Party financial accounts. It appears to be a largely honorary body whose members are somewhat less important in the Party hierarchy than those chosen to the Central Committee.

relevant provisions in the Party Rules. Only recently have Congresses regularly been convened at the prescribed intervals. No Congresses took place between 1939 and 1952, when they were supposed to be held every three years. From 1952 to 1971 the prescribed interval was four years, with Congresses actually being held in 1956, 1959, 1961, 1966, and 1971. In 1971 the interval was lengthened to five years, ostensibly to provide the Congress with the opportunity of reviewing each new Five-Year Economic Plan before its adoption, but also perhaps in recognition that (except for the "Extraordinary Congress" in 1959*) the Soviet leaders have seldom been able to get around to holding a Congress more than once in five years.

If the above suggests that Party Congresses are without significance, that impression would be wrong. As a body, the Congress possesses virtually no political power, and this has been the case at least since Stalin consolidated his power in the mid-to-late 1920s. But Congresses do serve as a backdrop for the presentation of some of the important programs and objectives of the Party and as a forum for the discussion (such as it is) of these matters. They are held with great fanfare, including saturation media coverage just before and during the ten-day period of the Congress. They thus perform the function of mobilizing Party members and the populace at large to follow the direction indicated by the Party leaders. The proceedings of the Congress serve, in other words, to provide the "line-cues" and instructions as to what the Party leadership considers important for the present and immediate future.** And there are sometimes hints of serious policy differences among influential Party leaders that are played out behind the scenes at Congresses. The Soviet press does a good job of covering up these differences, but careful students of Soviet politics have made impressive analyses of several of these conflicts. Viewed in these terms, recent Party Congresses serve as convenient benchmarks with regard to developments in some of the major aspects of Soviet policy. To take only the post-Stalin Congresses as examples:

1. The Twentieth Party Congress, February 1956. The major theme of the Congress was de-Stalinization, initiated by Khruschchev's "secret speech." Open, published attacks on Stalin date from this point.

2. The Twenty-First Party Congress, January–February 1959. This was an "Extraordinary" Congress, called before the prescribed interval between Congresses had elapsed. It was called to adopt the first Seven-Year Plan (1959 to 1965), under which the Soviet Union aimed to "overtake and surpass" the United States in many basic areas of economic activity. This plan was scrapped shortly after Khrushchev's ouster in late 1964 and a return was made to Five-Year Plans. A minor theme of the Congress was the discussion of increased use of so-called *obshchestvennye* or "social" organizations, such as the volunteer people's guards, which would supplement the regular police.

*The Congress held in 1959 is officially designated as an "Extraordinary" Congress, called for special purposes before the time interval for the convening of another Congress had elapsed.

**The collected speeches and resolutions of the Congresses are published in book form and the most important individual speeches in pamphlet form soon after each Congress.

3.   The Twenty-Second Party Congress, October 1961. The major event at this Congress was the adoption of the new Party Program, which was to serve as a guide for the "comprehensive building of communism" in the Soviet Union. A second important event, already discussed in Chapter 1, was the continuation of the attack on Stalin which culminated in the removal of his body from the Mausoleum on Red Square.

4.   The Twenty-Third Party Congress, March–April 1966. This first post-Khrushchev Congress set the tone for subsequent ones. Less spectacular and revealing of Party problems than its immediate predecessors, this Congress was carried on in a businesslike, almost dull way. A number of changes in the Party Rules were made. The most important were a return to the terms used during most of the Stalin period of "General Secretary," rather than "First Secretary" of the Party, and "Politburo," rather than "Presidium," and the abolition of the requirement, only adopted at the previous Congress, that a certain proportion of "renewal" or turnover in Party leadership organs take place at each new election of Party leaders. The general principle of renewal was retained but the setting of fixed percentages of turnover was deleted. In addition, considerable attention was devoted to the new Five-Year Plan.

5.   The Twenty-Fourth Party Congress, March–April 1971. This Congress continued the tone set in the previous one. Among important Party developments was Brezhnev's call for an exchange of Party cards, mentioned earlier in this chapter. The most emphasized aspect of the Five-Year Plan was the increased growth rate in the production of consumer goods, which, for the first time since the launching of Five-Year Plans in 1928, were to increase at a higher rate than producers' goods.

6.   The Twenty-Fifth Party Congress, February–March 1976. Brezhnev's position at this Congress appeared more secure than ever. Rather than retiring, as some had predicted, he was reelected to the Politburo and continued as Party General Secretary. Adulation of Brezhnev by a number of colleagues was particularly fulsome. The discussion of the new Five-Year Plan indicated a return to the dominance of heavy industry after the failure to achieve a faster growth for the consumer sector, as envisaged in the Five-Year Plan adopted in 1971. This Congress was also notable for the independent line taken by several foreign communist leaders (the Italian, French, and British, in particular) regarding the paths their countries should take toward socialism.

7.   The Twenty-Sixth Party Congress, February–March 1981. Noting that twenty years had passed since the adoption of the Party Program in 1961, Brezhnev proposed that a new version of the Program be adopted. He indicated that the USSR's movement toward communism would be through the present stage of developed socialist society, "a necessary, natural and historically lengthy period." What he did not mention was that this stage had not been anticipated in the 1961 Program, which had predicted both that the "technical basis of communism" would be created by 1981 and that the USSR would overtake the U.S. in per capita production by 1971.

The most important result of the Congress was its affirmation of the status quo. No new ideas of significance were proposed and, symbolically of greater importance, not a single personnel change was made in the aging Politburo or Secretariat.

8.   The Twenty-Seventh Party Congress, February–March 1986. Three Party General Secretaries (Brezhnev, Andropov, and Chernenko) had passed from the scene since the last Congress, and the new General Secretary, Mikhail Gorbachev, had been in office less than one year when the Twenty-Seventh Congress commenced. The Congress marked the culmination of a consid-

erable turnover in leadership ranks, not just in the central Party and government but in the provinces as well, that had been put into motion after Gorbachev came to power.

Gorbachev's five-and-one-half hour "Political Report" touched on all major aspects of domestic and foreign policy. While he and others called for "radical reform" of the economy, policy proposals in this area were left vague. Gorbachev reaffirmed his commitment to *glasnost'* (openness) in discussing the country's problems, and a slight increase in openness and spontaneity was perhaps noticeable at the Congress, in comparison with those of the Brezhnev period.

A revision of the Party Rules was approved, and a new Party Program, which toned down utopian statements of the document promulgated under Khrushchev, was adopted. The Congress also endorsed the Twelfth Five-Year Plan (1986–1990) and a document that charts economic and social planning to the year 2000.

A very important, if routine, function taking place at every Congress is the choosing of the Party leadership. It is routine because, although the Congress is supposed to "elect" the Central Committee (which then "elects" the Politburo and the Secretariat), the election is really a matter of approving the list of CC members, and it is carried out so as to insulate the leadership selection process from the mass membership of the congress as much as possible.[13]

An important psychological way of insulating the top leaders from the rank-and-file delegates to the Congress is the seating arrangement. The top one hundred or so people sit on the stage of the Palace of Congresses in Moscow; the rest of the delegates sit in the "audience" and watch the performance. No less a student of legislative assemblies than Winston Churchill has commented on the psychological importance of the shape and arrangement of representative assembly halls. When the House of Commons was to be rebuilt after being damaged by bombs during World War II, Churchill argued peruasively for retaining the small, rectangular-shaped hall with an aisle down the middle to separate the Government from the Opposition. This, he felt, would help maintain the two-party system as well as the sense of importance of members and of legislative proceedings. He opposed the "semicircular assembly, which appeals to political theorists, enables every individual or every group to move around the center adopting various shades of pink according to the weather changes."[14] No doubt Churchill would have recognized the symbolism of the theater arrangement in the Soviet Union (which is used at Supreme Soviet meetings as well as at Party Congresses) as well as the unified, if passive, support of the "audience" for the "actors" which the arrangement suggests.

The Central Committee

In electing the Central Committee, the Congress in effect vests its supreme power in a smaller leadership body. In theory, the Central Committee plays a very important role, for it provides the main link between the

Congress and the even more elite Politburo and Secretariat. And, at least on paper, it is provided with a set of really formidable powers.

According to the Party Rules, the CC "directs the activities of the Party" between Congresses, "selects and appoints leading functionaries, directs the work of central government bodies and social organizations of working people, sets up various Party organs, institutions, and enterprises and directs their activities, appoints the editors of the central newspapers and journals operating under its control, and distributes the funds of the Party budget and controls its execution" (Article 35). Thus, the Central Committee is given a leading role in directing not only the Party but also the work of all other governmental and social organizations in the country through the Party members in these groups. From what Western scholars know of the operation of the Central Committee, however, it has only rarely risen to the level of playing a really significant decision-making role with regard to these matters.

Meetings of the CC (called plenary sessions or plenums) are required at least every six months by the Party Rules, and in fact that is about how often they are held. As an aspect of the rationalization of Soviet politics, CC meetings in recent years have often been timed to take place just before Supreme Soviet meetings, which also typically are held twice a year. This not only facilitates the coordination of business processed by the two bodies, but it also means that the considerable number of persons who belong to both organs, many of whom live great distances from Moscow, can attend both meetings in one trip.

There are, however, considerable differences between the meetings of the Supreme Soviet and those of the Central Committee. The former, as mentioned in the last chapter, usually take two to three days and are accompanied by considerable press coverage of both the important speeches made and the formal actions taken, such as the adoption of laws. It is, relatively speaking, an open proceeding. The CC plenary session is usually completed in one day. Beyond reporting that the meeting has been held, press coverage is minimal. Speeches at plenary meetings are seldom carried in the press, even when it is announced that a Party leader made an important speech. In moving from the façade to the substance of Soviet politics, the characteristic of closed politics discussed in Chapter 1 comes more and more into play.

But is the Central Committee really so important in Soviet politics? Yes and no. Yes, symbolically, potentially, and in the sense that enormous powers are exercised in its name. No, in that the Central Committee *as a body* does not and cannot exercise continuous control over Party policy making and implementation. Let us be more specific about these matters.

The Central Committee is of great *symbolic* importance because it is the membership body of the top four hundred to five hundred communists in the country. It includes not only all the members of the supreme Party organs—the Politburo and the Secretariat—but also most of the important leaders of republic and regional Party organizations as well as Party leaders in many other walks of life, from governmental administration to the communications media to the military, the arts, diplomacy, the sciences, and the economy. It brings together, even if for only a few days a year, the most important Party members in the country.

It is of *potential* importance in terms of the power and authority that *could* devolve upon it some day, given the right circumstances. With its considerable theoretical powers, especially regarding the activities of the Party and the selection of Party leaders, it is not inconceivable that a nucleus within the Central Committee could unite to oppose the leadership. This opposition could be on matters of policy or personnel, or even on the subject of more genuine participation of the Central Committee in running the Party. The basic principles of Party operation (for example, democratic centralism and the prohibition against "factions") militate against such a development, it is true. But if devolution of political authority is to take place anywhere in the Soviet system, the Central Committee is a likely place for it to happen.

There has been one occasion in the post-Stalin period in which the Central Committee appears to have opposed a majority of the Politburo and to have prevailed. As Khrushchev explained it, a majority of the Politburo (at that time called the Presidium) in June 1957 opposed Khrushchev's leadership and demanded his resignation as First Secretary of the Central Committee. Khrushchev insisted that he had not been appointed by the Politburo to this position and that that body could not oust him. He quickly was able to assemble much of the Central Committee in Moscow and to receive their support, thus affirming his position according to Party Rules. He was then able to have his opponents, whom he labeled the "anti-Party group," removed from their positions.[15]

If this can be looked upon as an example of the exercise by the Central Committee of its authority, it is surely not typical CC activity. Nor does it suggest much actual power in the CC itself. Initiative did not come from the CC. It was clearly manipulated by Khrushchev and his allies. And one looks in vain for repeat performances. There is some controversy as to whether the Central Committee even met when Khrushchev was ousted in 1964.[16]

Another situation in which the Central Committee might be able to exercise power involves disagreements in the Politburo that fall short of clear attempts to oust leaders from power. Some Kremlin watchers see such disagreements as a more-or-less constant part of Soviet politics. In such situations, it is suggested, a bloc of Central Committee members siding with one of the contesting factions in the Politburo may succeed in frustrating the adoption of policies favored by the other faction. There is some evidence to suggest that such activity does take place at CC plenary meetings, but the information is much too sketchy for us to conclude that it even approaches being an institutionalized pattern of CC operations.

An enormous amount of activity takes place under the third category, policies and actions carried out in the Central Committee's name. Authoritative policy can emerge in a number of interrelated forms, from a speech of a Party leader at a CC plenary meeting to a CC plenary meeting decree (*postanovlenie*) to a simple CC decree. The simple decrees are interesting for two reasons. First, they are sometimes issued as joint decrees with the USSR Council of Ministers.[17] This form seems to be used to give added authority to important government programs or regulations. Second, they are issued and dated at times when the Central Committee is not meeting as a body (indeed, they are *not* identified as decrees of the plenary sessions, as some others are), and one must wonder how they do come into being. It appears that they are issued *in the name of* the Central Committee on the instruction of either the Politburo or the Secretariat. These decrees of the Central Committee far outnumber the decrees of the Plenum of the Central Committee.[18]

But the very fact that most such Central Committee decrees are not adopted at Central Committee meetings indicates the relative insignificance of the body. Although a much smaller body than the Supreme Soviet, it is a kind of Party equivalent of the Supreme Soviet; its size (307 full and 170 candidate members were named by the Twenty-Seventh Party Congress in 1986, for a total of 477) is prohibitively large for genuine discussion and policy making, particularly in light of the fact that it meets infrequently and for short periods of time. So it is basically relegated to a position of providing the medium through which Party decisions are channeled by more important Party bodies and officials. But to reiterate a point made earlier, the Central Committee is made up of the most important Party members in the country. In this sense it is not only a far more significant body that the Supreme Soviet, but it is also both a "talent pool" from which top leadership emerges and a stepping stone to (and, in some cases, down from) the top leadership. This is a point to which we will return later in the chapter in connection with the discussion of political elites.

The Politburo and the Secretariat

At the apex of the Party structure are the Politburo and the Secretariat. Students reading about CPSU structure for the first time are often confused about the relationship between these two bodies and want to know which is the more important and powerful. Answering such questions is not a simple matter. The two organs are charged with different responsibilities. The importance of their functions and the power that results from them are not easily comparable, although at times it appears that they compete for power. Suffice it to say that they are both extremely important organizations.

Another way to discuss the two is to ask whether membership in one or the other body carries more prestige. It seems fair to say that it would be more prestigious to be a full member of the Politburo than to be a Secretary of the Secretariat. At the same time, the person typically recognized as the single most important official in the country has been the leader of the

Secretariat, the General Secretary. But the General Secretary is also a member of the Politburo and is sometimes even referred to unofficially as the "leader" of the Politburo. It is most prestigious, then, to have a position on the Politburo *and* on the Secretariat, as several men* typically do. Finally, it can be said that losing a position on the Secretariat normally would be considered a demotion but not the complete collapse of a political career if a seat on the Politburo were retained. Loss of a seat on the Politburo, however, would surely spell political demise.

The provision in the Party Rules on the Politburo and the Secretariat (Article 38) is extremely brief:

> The Central Committee of the Communist Party of the Soviet Union elects a Politburo to direct the work of the Party between plenary meetings and a Secretariat to direct current work, chiefly the selection of personnel and the verification of the fulfillment of Party decisions. The Central Committee elects a General Secretary of the CC CPSU.

On the basis of this bare statement and whatever else analysts have been able to discover about these bodies, it is generally said that the Politburo is the policy-making body of the Party and the Secretariat is the administrative or bureaucratic arm. The Secretariat supervises the execution of policy and, as the Rules suggest, handles day-to-day problems, including the selection of personnel to fill Party jobs. The Secretariat may also play an important role in shaping policy when it researches questions subsequently discussed in the Politburo and when it drafts resolutions which are then passed by the Politburo.

There is no set number of members of either the Politburo or the Secretariat. In recent years the Politburo has been a body of about twenty members, several of whom have only candidate (nonvoting) status. The Secretariat, as the administrative branch of the Party, may employ as many as several hundred thousand persons, a figure that includes paid workers in Party organizations around the country.[19]

As one gets closer to the center of power, the information about actual operations becomes vaguer. Not a great deal is known about the conducting of Politburo or Secretariat business. During their tenures as Party leaders, both Khrushchev and Brezhnev gave interviews to Western correspondents about Politburo proceedings.[20] And at Party meetings Brezhnev and others provided a few further details which were reported in the Soviet press. Since the death of Brezhnev brief descriptions of Politburo meetings have regularly been carried in the Soviet press. On the basis of this information the following can be said: the Politburo meets in a building in the Kremlin on a regular basis, usually once a week; typically the meeting day is Thursday, with meetings lasting three to six hours; discussions deal with a variety of

*Very few women have ever served on either the Politburo or the Secretariat.

domestic and foreign-policy problems, with a consensus of the whole Politburo eventually being reached; only rarely is it necessary to take a formal vote, but when that happens, a majority vote carries; in some cases the Politburo creates special commissions to study particular problems or to implement particular decisions.

This rather bland description of Politburo proceedings may be typical of some meetings, but it is not likely that things are always so peaceful. Many Western analysts look upon Soviet political structure and tradition as inherently involving more or less continuous conflict among the leaders.[21] Since the most important body is the Politburo, this conflict must surface most often among Politburo members (although not necessarily always at Politburo meetings). But the paucity of information on this aspect of Soviet politics leaves us only with a vague partial sketch rather than a full picture.

One of the much-endorsed principles of Soviet politics is that of "collective leadership" *(kollektivnoe rukovodstvo)*. The term embraces the idea that no single person should hold the top posts of Party chief and head of the government (Chairman of the Council of Ministers) at the same time. This principle was disregarded by both Stalin and Khrushchev. After Khrushchev's fall the Central Committee resolved that the two positions should not be held simultaneously by the same person.[22] When Brezhnev, Andropov, and Chernenko assumed the Chairmanship of the Supreme Soviet Presidium while keeping the Party General Secretary's position, they did not violate the letter of this resolution.

Another facet of collective leadership involves the way—previously described—in which Politburo decisions are supposedly reached. An implicit aspect of the principle is that there is no formally designated leader of the Politburo. It is a collective body in which all full members are theoretically equal. In practice, of course, it is unlikely that such theoretical equality can be maintained. The General Secretary normally chairs Politburo meetings, and a sign of Brezhnev's ascendance in the early 1970s was the reference to him by several other Party notables as "the leader of the Politburo."

But it may be perilous for a leader to dispense completely with collective leadership, or at least with Politburo consultation. Apparently one of the reasons for Khrushchev's ouster was the feeling that he was arrogating too much power to himself and a small coterie of personal advisers.

Although the Politburo is the prime decision-making body in Soviet politics, few formal decisions are taken in its name. Traditionally, press coverage of Politburo meetings has been minimal. But after Brezhnev's tenure as General Secretary, the veil of secrecy surrounding Politburo activities was lifted slightly. In late 1982 regular reports began to be published in the Soviet press entitled "In the Politburo of the Central Committee of the CPSU." These reports have appeared almost weekly since then, usually in the Friday or Saturday issues of certain newspapers (suggesting, as indicated, that the Politburo does indeed meet usually on Thursdays). The reports do not really add much to our knowledge of Politburo operations.

One Western analyst sees the reports "more as a public relations exercise than as a genuine attempt to inform the Soviet population of the concerns of their leaders.[23]

Secretariat operations are less publicized than those of the Politburo. Its meetings are virtually never announced and it was not until 1971 that it was even indicated that regular meetings were held. At that time Brezhnev stated that the Secretariat, like the Politburo, meets once a week. The normal meeting day is Wednesday, the day before the regular Politburo meeting. In his speech at the Twenty-Sixth Party Congress in 1981, Brezhnev stated that the Secretariat had met 250 times since the Twenty-Fifth Congress. This number is slightly higher than that of Politburo meetings for the same period (236) and amounts almost precisely to one meeting per week. Brezhnev's description of functions of the Secretariat amounted to little more than a reiteration of the statement in the Party Rules: "The selection of personnel, the organization and checking of the execution [of decisions], practically speaking, all current questions of Party life—such, basically is the circle of problems handled by the Secretariat of the Central Committee."[24]

These words suggest a preoccupation in the Secretariat with day-to-day matters of Party concern. This does not mean, however, that the work of the Secretariat is unimportant. The impact of the Secretariat's activities is felt throughout Soviet society. The General Secretary heads a group of "Secretaries of the Central Committee of the CPSU," several of whom also serve on the Politburo. The General Secretary is responsible for execution of overall Party policy; the other secretaries are in charge of administering and overseeing certain broad areas of activity of interest to the Party. This list of areas is nowhere officially designated and is subject to change. During recent years it has included the following subjects: Ideology and Culture, Cadres, Party Affairs, Agriculture, Foreign Policy, Foreign Relations with Ruling and Non-Ruling Communist Parties, Heavy Industries, and Defense Industries. In addition to the specialized responsibilities of the Secretaries, the Secretariat contains a number of departments, several headed by Secretaries, the others headed by lesser Party functionaries. These departments, more than twenty in number in recent years (see Chart 7–1), cover all of the major areas of economic activity and foreign affairs as well as culture, propaganda and agitation, science and education, governmental administration, and personnel. It is the staff workers in these departments who constitute the large number of central-Party-apparatus employees.

Thus, it is difficult to think of an area of contemporary Soviet life that is not supervised by some part of the Secretariat. Public policy in these areas must be strongly influenced by the Secretariat, even if it is not formally granted policy-making powers. Just by virtue of its ability to appoint persons to fill important Party and non-Party posts, the power that can be exercised by the Secretariat is enormous. Moreover, it is fair to say that departments in the Secretariat have general responsibility for supervising the work of specific ministries within the governmental apparatus. An example of how this process is said to work in the foreign affairs area is provided by Valentin Falin, Deputy Head of the International Information Department of the Secretariat:

> The process is about as follows. The Ministry of Foreign Affairs prepares a paper that deals with the issue in question on the basis of concrete facts. If the issue includes national security aspects, then the Ministry of Defense and possibly other Ministries are drawn into the preparation of the paper, and a summary of views is drawn up. This summary is then handed to the relevant Department of the Central Committee, which employs its own experts and consulting staff, who check the facts before it is submitted to the Politburo.[25]

The number of people employed in the Party apparatus is not known, but it must be sizable. It has been estimated that several thousand persons are employed in the Secretariat alone; the total number of full-time paid Party workers in the country may be 250,000 to 300,000.

THE PARTY-GOVERNMENT RELATIONSHIP

Much of what has just been said about the functions of the Party apparatus suggests that it plays an important role in *governing* the country. What, then, is the Party's relationship with the government, and why should two hierarchies of organs—Party and government—exist side by side (see Charts 7–2 and 7–3)? Such questions are not easy to answer. They are matters that confuse some Soviet citizens, even though it is recognized that the Party is the ultimate authority in the system. And Soviet leaders and political scientists, though denying that there is any basic problem in the duality of hierarchies, sometimes allude to small difficulties in the management of administrative and governmental affairs that stem from the parallel set of organs.

The standard Soviet position on Party-government relations is that the Party plays a "leading role" and "guides" governmental and social organizations, and the latter carry out their functions under Party guidance.[26] This suggests a rather neat division of responsibilities, somewhat reminiscent of the "policy-administration" dichotomy long familiar to students of public administration in the West. But it is clear that to treat policy and administration as completely distinct categories is a futile exercise because of the unavoidable mixture of the two functions in practice. The late Leonard Schapiro, long a student of Soviet affairs, saw the problem clearly as it applied to the Soviet system: "The borderline between policy and administration is never easy to draw. The party cells in the government machine were supposed to 'guide' but not 'interfere.' But where does guidance end and interference begin?"

The concept of *podmena* ("substitution" or "supplanting"), Party organs acting in place of government organs, is a source of longstanding concern for the Party. Although it has been recognized as a problem since at least

Chart 7–1 CPSU Central Committee Departments

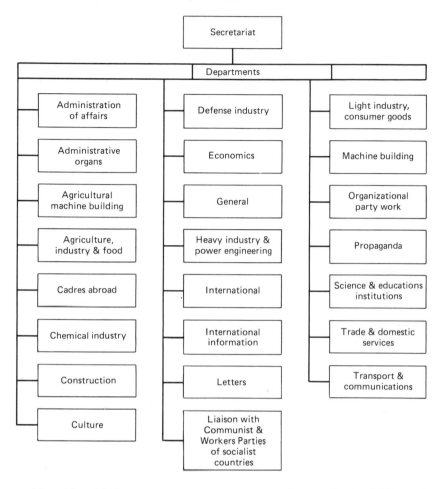

Source: Adapted from Joint Economic Committee, Congress of the United States, *Soviet Economy in the 1980s: Problems and Prospects*, Part 1 (Washington, DC: U.S. Government Printing Office, 1983), p. 18.

1919 and is prohibited by the Party Rules (Article 60),[27] it is still a widely discussed phenomenon. And specific examples of the Party's performing functions clearly delegated to the government are sometimes aired.

Given the pervasiveness of the Party role, it is not surprising that suggestions were made during the public discussion of the 1977 Constitution to give direct legislative power to the higher Party organs. Brezhnev, in his speech at the time of the adoption of the Constitution, called such proposals "deeply erroneous," creating "confusion as to the role of the Party" and obscuring "the meaning and functions of the organs of Soviet power." As suggested, however, such confusion is understandable, given the extensiveness of Party activity in the Soviet system.

Chart 7–2 Organizational Structure of the Communist Party of the Soviet Union

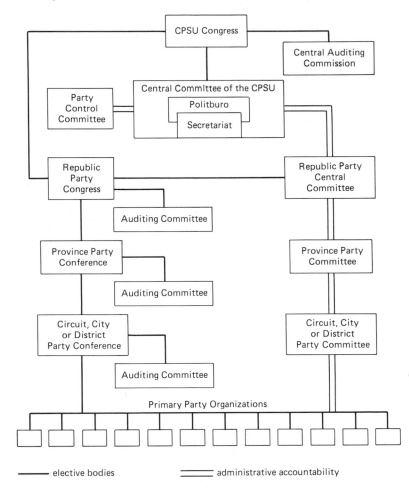

Source: *SSSR: Entsiklopedicheskii Spravochnik* (Moscow: "Sovetskaya Entsiklopediia," 1982), p. 179.

PRINCIPLES OF PARTY OPERATION

Two principles of Party operation already noted are collective leadership and the principle of renewal. The first involves a sharing of top Party and government posts, rather than their being held by one man. The second involves the regular turnover of leadership in Party bodies. As shown, both of these principles have been subject to some modification or dilution in practice.

Several other principles of Party operations are worth discussing. By far the most important, "the guiding principle of the organizational structure and of the entire life and activity of the Party" (Party Rules, Article 19),

Chart 7–3 Governmental Structure, USSR Level

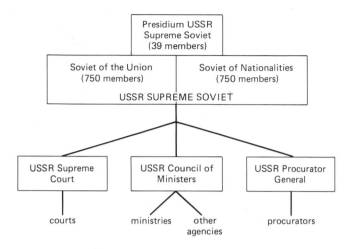

Source: Adapted from *Politicheskaia Organizatsiia Sovetskogo Obshchestva* (Moscow: Izdatel'stvo Politicheskoi Literatury), pp. 19 and 23.

is "democratic centralism." The term is said to embrace four subprinciples, the first two of which might be looked upon as democratic, the last two as centralist.

1. Election of all leading Party bodies, from the lowest to the highest.
2. Periodic reports of Party bodies to their Party organizations and to higher bodies.
3. Strict Party discipline and subordination of the minority to the majority.
4. The obligatory nature of the decisions of higher bodies for lower bodies.

But the actual interpretation of "democratic centralism" is much more restrictive and "centralist" than the four elements imply. We have already shown, through the example of the central Party organs, what the "election" of leading Party bodies involves. And although it is clear that periodic reports of Party bodies do take place, the occurrence of such reports does not imply that they provide the occasion for free debate. Moreover, other sections of the Party Rules can be looked upon essentially as negating the democratic elements of the principle. Particularly relevant is a passage from the introduction to the Rules:

> Ideological and organizational unity, monolithic cohesion of its ranks, and a high degree of conscious discipline on the part of all Communists are an inviolable law of the CPSU. All manifestations of factionalism and group activity are incompatible with Marxist-Leninist principles, and with Party membership.

If there is any democratic substance remaining to the principle, it is this: On some issues Party members appear to be accorded the right to free discussion "until a decision has been made" (as an earlier formation of the concept of democratic centralism put it).[28] Continuation of opposition on an issue beyond that point would be completely improper and would make the individual or group subject to sanction.

Another principle which is referred to several times in the Party Rules is "criticism and self-criticism." In one passage the term is mentioned in connection with free discussion of Party policy (Article 26) and in another with the laying bare of shortcomings in Soviet society (Article 2i). The principle was obviously created to help the Party check and eliminate abuses of power, both within and outside the Party. But the limitations on free discussion mentioned above restrict somewhat the extent to which this device can be implemented. It probably comes into play in criticizing Party operations at the lower levels, but public criticism of high Party leaders, especially at the national level, is forbidden; unless, of course, a campaign against a high Party leader is being orchestrated by his colleagues.

It is the self-criticism aspect of the term that appears to have been more important during the past few decades. Especially during the Stalin era, public self-criticism was frequently practiced by individuals who, for one reason or another, had fallen from favor.[29] They were expected to admit all of their errors and acknowledge the correctness of the criticism against them. And, in a way, one can see how this practice fits in with democratic centralism: If a decision is made that a person is to be criticized, Party discipline would require that that person not go against the Party line on the matter. If he were to speak out in public at all, it would have to be to go along with the criticisms against himself.

Although this form of public self-denunciation has been much less prevalent in the post-Stalin era, this does not necessarily imply that self-criticism is a thing of the past. It is more likely that the Party now finds such washing of dirty linen in public in bad taste. If a Party decision to criticize a member has been made, he is probably still required to acknowledge his errors but within Party meetings rather than in public.

A final matter to be discussed in this section is not really a principle of Party operation. It is, rather, an arrangement that facilitates central control within the Party and Party control in the society at large. In that sense it bears some similarity to the principles just discussed. The name of this system or practice is *nomenklatura*. The term *nomenklatura* refers to a list of positions for which Party approval is required before a person holding one of those positions can be removed or a replacement can be named. Every Party organ above the PPO has its *nomenklatura* list. In general, the more important the position, the higher the Party organ on whose list it appears. Many, but by no means all, positions on *nomenklatura* lists are Party posts. Such lists contain, as one writer has put it, "the most important leading positions in all organized activities of social life,"[30] including high positions in the military, soviets, the administrative apparatus, economic enterprises, the communications media, and all of the semipublic social organizations (for example, the *Komsomol* or youth organizations, trade unions, women's organizations, and scientific and cultural societies). Appointment of Party members to *nomenklatura* positions is not required, but communists clearly predominate in such posts.

Thus, the Party maintains control over all aspects of Soviet society in part through the *nomenklatura* system. And greater power flows to the central Party apparatus because its list covers all of the strategic positions in the country. Within the central apparatus, most decisions on *nomenklatura* appointments take place within the Secretariat, which helps to explain why the General Secretary's position is such an important one in Soviet politics.

Most analysts agree that although *nomenklatura* implies only Party approval or confirmation of personnel decisions, in fact the Party often takes the initiative in filling positions on the list. Moreover, even lower level positions in various organizations are subject to Party scrutiny through the so-called "accounting nomenklatura" *(uchetnaia nomenklatura).* Changes in such positions do not require Party approval, but the Party must be kept informed.

Like many systems of rules of this kind, the *nomenklatura* system has given rise to some unintended consequences. A measure of prestige in Soviet society has become whether one's job is "nomenklatured" or not, and by what level of Party organ. It is said that a person on a sufficiently high *nomenklatura* list cannot be subject to criminal prosecution without Party approval. Persons having a *nomenklatura* position may be removed from it for incompetence but appointed to other similar work, because they have retained their *nomenklatura* status. This status, once conferred, provides a kind of permanent tenure to those who hold it, and the Soviet press provides occasional examples of persons' going to great lengths to keep from losing *nomenklatura* status.

At times, then, the *nomenklatura* system has been criticized for providing a haven for incompetents. But other likely consequences of the system are not publicly discussed. Harasymiw, a leading Western student of *nomenklatura,* believes that it facilitates the maintenance of the following characteristics of Soviet leadership:

> The fact that the CPSU functions more as a simple "transmission belt" than as a political party in the accepted sense; the ability of one man with authority over a *nomenklatura* to build a power base in the party or elsewhere and consequently the necessity for purges; and the tendency of Soviet leadership as a whole to become inbred and conservative.[31]

This characteristic may actually inhibit reformist impulses and even restrict the ability of the leadership to implement policy decisions made at the top. Michael Vozlensky, a former Soviet citizen and the author of the authoritative book *Nomenklatura* (1984), asserts that "only an outside observer could suppose all power in the Soviet Union to be in the hands of the Politburo . . . In fact, the Politburo, though immensely powerful, has only a limited field of action. This limitation of its power has nothing to do with democracy and everything to do with the division of labor inside the nomenklatura class." He goes on to suggest that district and local Party leadership groups have control over most *nomenklatura* appointments at those levels and that the Politburo finds it prudent to interfere only rarely in their activities. This puts considerable power in the hands of local Party officials. Vozlensky finds parallels between this aspect of the Soviet system and medieval feudalism: "The nomenklatura is a bastard kind of feudalism; every nomenklaturist is granted a fief, just as every vassal was granted a fief by the crown."[32] The ability of "nomenklatured" officials to hold on to their positions for long periods of time helps to impede the admission of younger persons to high positions. This is related, therefore, to what is one of the most important traits of the top Soviet leadership in recent years: advanced age.

PARTY LEADERS: BACKGROUND AND CAREERS

If we know little about the proceedings of the Politburo and the Secretariat, there is more to be said about the activities of the individual members of these bodies. Not that information about them is so very plentiful: Compared with a president, prime minister, or cabinet member in the West, most Soviet politicians are anonymous bureaucrats. But relatively speaking the members of the Politburo and the Secretariat are the best-known politicians in the country. The names and pictures of the top several leaders appear frequently in the Soviet press in connection with speeches, travel abroad, meetings with foreign leaders, and the like. Thus, a reasonably full picture of their careers and background characteristics can be sketched.

There are basically two ways in which a leadership group of this kind can be described. One is to sketch the broad characteristics and trends with regard to the group as a whole, perhaps over some set period of time. The other is to provide information on individual personalities. The latter approach may be more interesting, but it is also of less long-term interest because of turnover in the membership of the leadership group. Our emphasis, therefore, will be on the group as a whole, with individual leaders mentioned only for illustrative purposes. What is referred to as the top leadership group is composed of full members of the Politburo, who have numbered between eleven and sixteen in recent years; the candidate Politburo members, who typically number six to eight; and perhaps five more CC Secretaries who are not also either full or candidate Politburo members.

The top leadership, then, is normally comprised of twenty to twenty-five members.*

One of the reasons for the relatively substantial amount of available information on Politburo members is that almost all hold other responsible posts. Their presence in multiple important political, economic, and quasi-public positions gives some suggestion as to how political power is exercised and maintained in the Soviet Union. Table 7–1, "The Interlocking Directorate," provides some of the information relevant to this point. The table should be studied carefully. It describes leadership arrangements only at one point in time, and not all aspects of the interlocking directorate pattern will always be the same. In recent years, however, the holding of certain positions seems by convention to go along with full Politburo membership. Among these would be the Party General Secretary, the Premier (Chairman of the Council of Ministers), the Chairman of the Presidium of the Supreme Soviet, and the First Secretary of the Ukrainian Party Organization.** These people have "seats" on the Politburo, as it were, although such seats are not guaranteed in any written rules. New incumbents in these posts have, in recent years, been either full Politburo members or have been elevated to that status on being appointed to one of these posts. The other places on the Politburo (there is no set number of full or candidate members) are held by persons who hold other significant posts; there are usually one or more Secretaries of the Central Committee (but usually not so many as to constitute a majority of the full Politburo membership***), perhaps on or two First Deputy Premiers, and several first secretaries of union-republic Party organizations. Usually heads of government ministries are not important enough as politicians to qualify for Politburo membership, but in the mid-1970s the heads of the Ministries of Foreign Affairs and Defense and of the KGB were named full Politburo members, a move that was thought to have been based on the growing Soviet role in world affairs.

The status of candidate members of the Politburo is interesting but somewhat ambiguous from the standpoint of career patterns. They are not mentioned in the Party Rules (which state only that the CC selects a Politburo); but on the analogy with the functions of candidate CC members—who are mentioned in the Rules—it would seem that the candidate Politburo members have the right to speak but not to vote in Politburo proceedings.

Candidate Politburo membership can be a stepping-stone to full Politburo membership, although this stage is sometimes skipped. Moreover, a

---

*The number was twenty-six after the Twenty-Seventh Party Congress in March 1986.

**The Ukraine is the second most populous Soviet republic and a key agricultural and industrial area. No other republic has been accorded the more or less permanent representation on the Politburo that its First Party Secretary has had almost continuously since the 1930s. The largest union republic, the RSFSR, has no separate Party organization as do the other fourteen republics. This is no doubt because the Russians dominate the national Party structure.

***This is in contrast to the Politburo of the fourteen union republics, where CC secretaries often constitute majorities of these bodies.

large number of candidate members never attain full Politburo membership. For these people, candidate membership is the high point of their careers. Some slip back to more modest positions rather quickly, whereas others hold candidate membership as a relatively permanent status. P. N. Demichev (USSR Minister of Culture since 1974) was appointed a candidate Politburo member in 1964 and still occupied that position more than twenty years later.

A number of other relevant characteristics of the top leaders are not covered in Table 7–1. Among these are sex, nationality, education, and age. The only woman ever to serve on the Politburo was the late Ekaterina Furtseva (candidate member, 1956 to 1957; full member, 1957 to 1961). Furtseva was also the only female CC Secretary until Alexandra Biriukova was named a Secretary in 1986. The top organs have always been strongly dominated by members of the three major Slavic nationalities, the Russians, Ukrainians, and Byelorussians, with only token representation of other nationalities. Unlike earlier generations of Soviet leaders, virtually all of the present top leaders have complete higher education.[35] For the overwhelming majority of leaders, this education has been of the highly specialized, technical variety. The norm has been to have training in one of the engineering specialities rather than in the humanities or social sciences.*

Although most of the leaders spent some time working at their professions, by and large they got into political work fairly early in their lives. For only a few was this political work in organizations other than the Party apparatus, such as the state apparatus or the army. The dominant career pattern for the top political leadership is fairly clear, then: Slavic ethnic background (preferably Russian), graduation from a higher educational institution with a technical specialty, early transfer to professional Party status, and a process of working up through Party ranks.

That the major characteristics of the top twenty to twenty-five leaders can be summed up in so few words is in itself extremely significant. It suggests a deliberate attempt to minimize diversity and to bring like-minded individuals into the top leadership group. One might reasonably ask if this narrowness is suitable for a large and complex system where the leaders have so many political and economic responsibilities. Western analysts who have raised this question have suggested that the leadership pool is kept exclusive to maintain ideological orthodoxy and to prevent "revisionism." The danger is that the kind of leaders who rise to the top under this kind of an arrangement will not have the competence or experience to cope with the increasing demands placed on them. The system, in the long run, thus must either "degenerate" or "transform."[36] Such a thesis, which has been challenged by a number of analysts, is not easy to prove or disprove. Since "degeneration" is

---

*Lenin, the founder of the Soviet state, studied law, and Gorbachev graduated from the Law Faculty of Moscow University in 1955. But almost no other high Soviet political leaders have had legal training.

TABLE 7—1   The Interlocking Directorate, March 1986

POLITBURO	SECRETARIAT	COUNCIL OF MINISTERS	PRESIDIUM OF SUPREME SOVIET	OTHER POSTS
Full Members:				
Gorbachev (1980)*	Gorbachev, General Secretary (1985)		Gorbachev (1985)	
Aliev (1982)				First Deputy Chairman USSR Council of Ministers (1983)
Vorotnikov (1983)				Chairman, RSFSR Council of Ministers (1983)
Gromyko (1973)			Gromyko, Chairman (1985)	
Zaikov (1986)	Zaikov (1985)		Zaikov (1983)	
Kunaev (1971)			Kunaev (1962)	First Secretary, Kazakh Party Organization (1964)
Ligachev (1985)	Ligachev (1983)			
Ryzhkov (1985)		Ryzhkov, Chairman (1985)		
Solomentsev (1983)				Chairman, Party Control Committee (1983)
Chebrikov (1985)		Chebrikov, Chairman, KGB (1982)		
Shevardnadze (1985)		Shevardnadze, Minister of Foreign Affairs (1985)		
Shcherbitsky (1971)				First Secretary, Ukrainian Party Organization (1972)
Candidate Members:				
Demichev (1964)		Demichev, Minister of Culture (1974)		
Dolgikh (1982)	Dolgikh (1972)			

*The list of leaders in this table is in the order in which they were announced after their election, March 6, 1986. See *Izvestiia,* March 7, 1986, p. 1. Except for Gorbachev, the order is alphabetical according to the Russian alphabet. The dates in parentheses represent the year in which the person achieved the position indicated.

POLITBURO	SECRETARIAT	COUNCIL OF MINISTERS	PRESIDIUM OF SUPREME SOVIET	OTHER POSTS
El'tsin (1986)				First Secretary, Moscow Party Organization (1986)
Sliunkov (1986)			Sliunkov (1983)	First Secretary, Byelorussian Party Organization (1983)
Sokolov (1985)		Sokolov, Minister of Defense (1984)		
Solov'ev (1986)				First Secretary, Leningrad Oblas Party Organization (1985)
Talyzin (1985)		Talyzin, Chairman, Gosplan (1985)		
	Birukova (1986)			
	Dobrynin (1986)			
	Zimianin (1976)			
	Medvedev (1986)			
	Nikonov (1985)			
	Razumovskii (1986)			
	Yakovlev (1986)			

a long-term development, and since its signs are not clearly defined, it is difficult to say if it is underway or not. If transformation can counter degeneration, is it taking place? In the present context, transformation would seem to mean, among other things, bringing persons of more diverse backgrounds and skills into the Party leadership. At the level of the Politburo and the Secretariat there is no particular evidence of this process. But is it underway at a less exclusive level of the Party hierarchy? The answer to this question is not yet clear. Two studies published in the 1970s suggested that the proportion of "coopted specialists" (persons with special skills or education who have spent considerable periods of time in nonpolitical work) had been rising.[37] If this was true of the 1960s and part of the 1970s, however, the trend seemed to alter its course thereafter. Bialer, in his 1980 study (based on a sample of middle-level Party leaders), found a "highly pronounced" decline in cooptation. And he and other scholars have noted the high levels of continuity in the middle and upper leadership posts in the Party which, of course, has left little room for the cooptation of specialists into responsible Party posts.[38] At the same time, it is clear that within the middle-level leadership group the number of persons with some kind of special, nonpolitical training has become far greater than the now relatively small number of nonspecialist professional politicians. The latter, who either lack formal higher education or were educated at higher Party schools and spent virtually all of their adult lives in political work, used to dominate the higher Party ranks. In 1980, however, Bialer is able to write of "the total disappearance" of these "party generalists" who have been supplanted not by coopted officials but by individuals who, through long experience in certain specific spheres of activity, "are highly specialized in their generalized areas of responsibility." This he considers "a functional substitute for coopting outside specialists into the Party apparatus.[39]

Whether this new effort at specialization will be sufficient to avoid the degeneration previously discussed is not clear. Certainly the Party leadership recognizes the great challenges facing the country and the need to have knowledgeable specialists available to help solve practical problems. Soviet leaders have referred to a "scientific-technical revolution" now underway throughout the world, and of the necessity for skilled experts to deal with its problems. Their clear intention, however, is to keep these specialists "on tap" rather than "on top" and to continue directing the overall course of Soviet society.

By all counts the high Party leadership is an old group. The purges of the Stalin period had helped keep down the average age at the top of the Party, but after Stalin much greater stability characterized this group, particularly during Brezhnev's tenure (1964–1982). Under Brezhnev and his successors, dismissal in disgrace has occurred less frequently, but graceful retirement has not quite become institutionalized. So many leaders seem to try to hang on to power as long as possible. Thus, the average age of full Politburo members (this generalization could be made about other high Soviet political bodies as well) rose from about 50 in 1939 to 55 in 1952 to 61 in 1964 to over 70 near the end of the Brezhnev period. The Brezhnev-era gerontocracy probably approached the limit in terms of an average that one could reasonably expect in a collegial body of a dozen or so members; and after Brezhnev's death the average dipped somewhat. In spite of the considerable turnover in top positions in the first year of Gorbachev's tenure as Party General Secretary, however, the average age of the twelve full Politburo members elected at the Twenty-Seventh Party Congress in March 1986 was still over 65. Only two of these twelve (Gorbachev and Foreign Minister Shevardnadze) were under 60, and Presidium Chairman Gromyko was the oldest at almost 77.

Until Gorbachev, the tendency in recent years was toward older persons holding the top Party position (General Secretary). The age factor was clearly connected with the remarkable turnover in that post in the early to mid-1980s. While there were only four top leaders during the first 65 years of the Soviet regime (Lenin, Stalin, Khrushchev, and Brezhnev), four also occupied the top post in the 28 months between November 1982 and March 1985 (Brezhnev, Andropov, Chernenko, and Gorbachev). Lenin and Stalin were in their forties when they assumed the reins of power, while Khrushchev and Brezhnev were in their late fifties. Andropov was 68 and Chernenko was 72. None of these leaders left voluntarily, all dying in office except Khrushchev, who was removed by his colleagues at age 70. Mikhail Gorbachev, in assuming the General Secretaryship just a few days after his fifty-fourth birthday in March 1985, became the youngest Soviet leader since Stalin.

Many of the same characteristics of the top leadership just described are to be found at the lower levels of the Party leadership as well. Next to the Politburo, the body most studied as to elite characteristics is the CPSU Central Committee. Since the CC is the main promotion channel to higher Party rank, it is understandable that its members would bear similarities to the top leaders. As with the Politburo, a considerable proportion of CC membership is apportioned on the basis of status. That is, the holding of a position more or less automatically qualifies one for a seat on the CC. For full CC membership such positions include:

1. *Party:* the top twenty to twenty-five Party leaders discussed earlier, all first secretaries of union-republic Party organizations, thirty to fifty first secretaries of important regional Party organizations, and the first secretaries of the Moscow and Leningrad Party organizations.
2. *Government:* the chairman and first deputy chairman of the USSR Council of Ministers, the ministers and first deputy ministers of several key ministries, including Foreign Affairs and Defense; the chairmen of several republican councils of ministers, including those of the RSFSR, the Ukraine, Byelorussia, and probably Georgia and Uzbekistan.
3. *Other:* The First Secretary of the USSR *Komsomol,* the Chairman of the All-Union Trade Union Council and at least one deputy of that council, the editor of *Pravda,* and the President of the Academy of Sciences.

To some extent, at least, this process of status appointments also applies to CC candidate members.

This "automatic" membership constitutes less than half of the full members of the CC; the internal politics of the Party, the bargaining and competition among various leadership groups, determines the remainder of the members. Whatever the final composition in terms of individuals, the proportion of various hierarchies represented on the CC has remained fairly constant in recent years: 40 to 45 percent are full-time Party workers, about 35 percent are from the governmental apparatus, about 10 percent from the military and security bureaucracies, with the remainder made up of plant directors, outstanding workers, and people from the arts, sciences, and other fields.[40]

Regarding other background factors, the parallel between the CC and

the top leadership is maintained. Women have made up about 4 percent of CC members in recent years (as against about 25 percent of the total Party membership). Although the level of education has not been as high in the CC as in the Politburo-Secretariat, the former is dominated by persons with engineering and technical training. Also, the CC is disproportionately dominated by ethnic Slavs. As to age, the Central Committee naturally has a lower average than do the Politburo and Secretariat. But as in those two bodies, its average age shows a tendency to increase over time. From an average age of 49 in 1952, full members of the Central Committee rose gradually in age to an average of 56 in 1966, 58 in 1971, and 60 in 1976.[42] gradually in age to an average of 56 in 1966, 58 in 1971, and 60 in 1976. After drifting higher thereafter, it returned to 60 in 1986.[41] Moreover, there is evidence to show that the Central Committee's age structure is high when compared with other countries.[42]
patterns tells only part of the story, of course. Beyond the traits that we have described, political success depends on a person's performance on the job and his luck or skill in backing the right policies. Finally, as in any political system, connections are important. A politician must have the astuteness to associate himself with the "right people," those who succeed rather than fail.

Regarding job performance, since so many future leaders come from at least a few years in responsible production assignments, they must have demonstrated at least minimal competence in their professions. Those who got into Party work at an early age likewise probably exhibited some level of political and managerial skill in order to work up through Party ranks. Thus, obvious incompetents would probably not rise very high in Party circles.

Personal connections, developed and cultivated to help one's career, are prevalent in most countries. Yet the peculiar nature of Soviet political processes may make such contacts especially important there. The late Franz Borkenau explained this phenomenon over thirty years ago in a passage that is still basically sound:

> Here, as in most other things, life in the USSR is different only in degree, not in kind, from life everywhere else, and it is just as hard to draw a line between the personal and the political factor. Both have to be taken into account, and especially their interaction. Yet certain peculiarities do attach to the Soviet case. Prominent among them is the instituion or practice called *Shefstvo*, which gets its name from the French word *chef*, meaning "leader" or "boss." This system is not confined to the Soviet world, but the absence of political economic, and intellectual freedom in that world endows it with much greater importance there, making it in effect the only way in which a Soviet citizen can rise to power and eminence. No matter what his pursuit or field, if he is ambitious, he must choose a protector or patron among those already in power, and put himself in the relation of "client" to him and rely upon him for favors indispensable to advancement.
>
> The universality of this practice creates a rather complicated and extensive system of patronage on the various echelons of Soviet power that has to be deciphered before the personal factor in Soviet politics can be given, in each case, its due importance. Difficult though this may seem, it is not always an

insuperable task. The very scale on which the *Shefstvo* system functions in Soviet Russia provides the observer with leads aplenty.[43]

Much analysis by Western scholars about power relationships in the Kremlin ("kremlinology") over the past four or five decades has been based on assumptions about such patron-client relationships. Yet these relationships need not be permanent: A *shef* may abandon his protégé or the latter may turn against the former. Crucial to the downfall or continued success of a Soviet politician may be his ability to see the direction things are going and to shift alliances or modify policies. Moreover, seeing *shefstvo* relationships as permanent may mislead the Western analyst in his conclusions about the strength of a leader's position or other aspects of Soviet politics. Brezhnev was almost universally seen by Western scholars as a protégé of Khruschev—which he surely was for a considerable period of time—until he replaced Khrushchev as General Secretary of the Party in 1964. Brezhnev obviously had been able to disassociate himself from Khrushchev to some extent and be recognized as a leader in his own right; in contrast, others closer to Khrushchev, such as Leonid Ilichev and Khrushchev's son-in-law Alexei Adzhubei, both lost their positions soon after Khrushchev's removal from office.

In addition to everything else, there is surely a measure of luck in the ebb and flow of political careers. Being in the right place at the right time or backing the policy whose time has come (or gone) appears at times accidental rather than calculated. A number of brilliant political careers were helped along when rivals or superiors were removed in large numbers during Stalin's purges. And being connected with the virgin-lands program during times of bumper harvests (as Brezhnev briefly was) could be very good for one's career. But numerous political fortunes have been hurt by association with the much more frequent experience of mediocre or poor agricultural production. And being on the wrong side of the issue of détente with the West in the early 1970s is thought to have been a major reason for the demise of at least one Politburo member.[44]

The game of Soviet politics should be viewed not just as a clash of personalities who make alliances and cynically manipulate issues merely in order to increase their power. It surely is this in part. But it also appears to involve genuine disagreements about policies and issues. Such differences are not easily ascertainable by the nonexpert or the casual reader of the Soviet press. Soviet leaders set great store by the "monolithic unity" of their views, and they sometimes go to great lengths to obscure their differences. The appearance of unity justifies, among other things, the claim that there is no need for more than one political party. But careful analysts of Soviet politics have long been aware of both personal and policy differences among members of the Soviet elite.

The appropriate question to ask here is, "Is there any discernible pattern or relationship between the background characteristics of members of the Soviet elite and their policy views?" One of the purposes of the study of background factors and career patterns, beyond mere description, is to seek a link between the background and life experiences of political leaders and their political behavior. But this kind of analysis requires a large amount of both background data and attitudinal data on a significant number of leaders, so that quantitative measures of association can be made. The results of such efforts in the study of elites in Western countries, where data are much more available than in the Soviet Union, have been modest so far.[45] Regarding the Soviet Union, almost no progress has been made.[46] By and large, studies of Soviet elites have been limited to a cataloging of background data on persons who reach high political status, as well as the pathways they follow in getting there.

All of the matters discussed in this section, personal background characteristics, career patterns and experience, acquaintances and connections, luck, and positions on important issues count for something in determining how an individual fares in Soviet politics. Our problem is one of the scarcity of reliable information on these crucial matters. Because we can rarely get anything like a full picture of these variables, we are thrown back on assumptions and speculation to complete our analysis. It is on this that the imprecise science of kremlinology is based. We will have something more to say about the information problem in the final chapter.

NOTES

[1]On the perceived importance of being a "communist" or Party member, see Harvey J. Pitcher, *Understanding the Russians* (London: Allen and Unwin, 1964), p. 36; Robert G. Wesson, *The Russian Dilemma* (New Brunswick, NJ: Rutgers University Press, 1974), p. 158; Robert G. Wesson, *Lenin's Legacy: The Story of the CPSU* (Stanford, CA: Hoover Institution Press, 1978), p. 274.

[2]See, for example, Thornton Anderson, *Masters of Russian Marxism* (New York: Appleton-Century-Crofts, 1963), pp. 90–100.

[3]Dina Kaminskaya, *Final Judgment* (New York: Simon and Schuster, 1982), p. 217.

[4]Jerome M. Gilison, *British and Soviet Politics* (Baltimore: Johns Hopkins University Press, 1972), p. 25. But if such shops no longer exist for ordinary Party members, they do exist for the highest-ranking individuals in the state, Party, military, and police hierarchies, as well as for individuals such as writers, musicians, and others who legally possess hard foreign currency and can shop in the foreign-currency stores.

[5]*Pravda*, Feb. 25, 1976, p. 7.

[6]*Izvestiia*, Feb. 24, 1981, p. 4. At the Twenty-Seventh Party Congress in 1986, Gorbachev stated that there was no need for a special purge of Party members at that time. *Izvestiia*, Mar. 26, 1986, p. 10.

[7]See *The New York Times*, Nov. 10, 1974, p. 4.

[8]For instance, the Russians constituted 52.4 percent of the Soviet population in 1979 but provided 60.5 percent of the CPSU membership in 1977, and the Tadzhiks amounted to 1.1 percent of the Soviet population and provided 0.4 percent of CPSU members in the same years. The sources for these data are "The All Union Census of 1979 in the USSR," *Radio Liberty Research Bulletin*, No. 123/80, Mar. 27, 1980, p. 14; and "KPSS v Tsifrakh," *Partiinaia Zhizn*, 1977, No. 21, p. 31. For further discussion see Jerry F. Hough and Merle Fainsod, *How the Soviet Union is Governed* (Cambridge, MA: Harvard University Press, 1979), pp. 351–54. On other

matters discussed in this paragraph see ibid., pp. 340–51 and *Narodnoe Khoziastvo v SSSR v 1979 g.* (Moscow: Statistika, 1980), pp. 8 and 32.

[9]No special status in Party organization has been accorded to autonomous republics (ASSRs). This difference from state organization has been little discussed either by Soviet or by Western writers. An *oblast'* (province) Party organization parallels the governmental organization of the ASSR. At the union-republic level there are only fourteen Party organizations, the RSFSR not having a separate organization. This is presumably because communists from the RSFSR play such a central role in the national Party organization. An "RSFSR Bureau" of the national Party organization was abolished in 1966.

[10]Since 1966 the Party Rules have provided for the convening of Party conferences at the all-union and union-republic levels in the intervals between Party congresses. So far, such conferences have not been held.

[11]At the first two levels above the PPO, that is, the rural or urban district *(raion)* and the city or autonomous district, the Party Rules provide that a general meeting of the Party organization (that is, all Party members) may replace the conference as the highest Party body.

[12]Party organization practices at the national level are not mirrored in all respects at the levels below. On Party activities below the national level, the interested reader could consult the following sources: Jerry Hough, *The Soviet Prefects: The Local Party Organs and Industrial Decision-Making* (Cambridge, MA: Harvard University Press, 1969); Hough and Fainsod, op. cit., Chap. 13, "Provincial and Local Politics," pp. 480–517; Ronald J. Hill, *Soviet Political Elites: The Case of Tiraspol* (New York: St. Martin's Press, 1977).

[13]The information provided in the press on the proceedings at Party Congresses makes it unclear as to whether a formal vote, even of the pro forma variety, actually is taken at the Congress on election of the leadership bodies. Relevant information from the Twenty-Fourth Congress in 1971 will illustrate this point. After the completion of discussion of the Five-Year Plan, *Izvestiia* informs us: "Then the Congress turned to a consideration of the next point on the agenda—elections of the central organs of the Party." No further information on the subject was given. The next day's issue of the paper states: ". . . Then the Congress heard the announcement of the Chairman of the Accounting Commission G. V. Romanov on the results of the election of the central organs of the Party." Although there was no further information on Romanov's report, the paper did contain a list of the new members of the Central Committee, an announcement that this new Central Committee had met the previous day, and a list of members (with pictures) of the Politburo and Secretariat that had been elected by the new Central Committee; *Izvestiia,* Sept. 9, 1971, p. 1, 2. A similar procedure was used at the Twenty-Sixth and Twenty-Seventh Congresses; see *Izvestiia,* Mar. 3, 1981, p. 1; Mar. 4, 1981, pp. 1 and 2, Mar. 6, 1986, p. 1, and Mar. 7, 1986, p. 1. That this function is routine does not mean that careful preparation does not go into it. Jerry Hough suggests that this aspect of the Congress is a crucial stage in "the circular flow of power." As Hough puts it, the General Secretary strengthens his position through "his ability to appoint and remove the provincial party secretaries," who "in turn, control the selection of delegates to the all-Union Party Congress." Hough concludes: "Even when there is no contest at the Congress, the loyalty of the bulk of the delegates to the regional party secretaries is a decisive factor preventing the old Politburo members from challenging the list of new Central Committee members prepared by the General Secretary"; Jerry F. Hough, "The Soviet Political System: Petrification or Pluralism," *Problems of Communism,* 21, No. 2 (Mar.–Apr. 1972), 42.

[14]Churchill's statements may be found in "Rebuilding the House of Commons," in Arend Lijphart, ed., *Politics in Europe* (Englewood Cliffs, NJ: Prentice-Hall, 1969), p. 85.

[15]The most complete account of the events described in this paragraph is found in Roger Pethybridge, *A Key to Soviet Politics: The Crisis of the Anti-Party Group* (New York: Holt, Rinehart & Winston, 1962).

[16]Most accounts suggest that the Central Committee did meet and ratified Khrushchev's removal. Myron Rush, *Political Succession in the USSR,* 2nd ed. (New York: Columbia University Press, 1968), p. 210, doubts that the Central Committee could have been assembled in the short time between Khrushchev's return from his Black Sea vacation and the public announcement of his resignation. But other sources state that the Presidium majority opposed to Khrushchev took the initiative and summoned CC members before Khrushchev's return, and that the CC met and approved his ouster a few hours thereafter. If this were the case, it is still clear that the CC played only a passive role, going along, in effect, with the orders of those who had

summoned them. Two sources that give accounts of this Central Committee meeting are Martin Page, *The Day Khrushchev Fell* (New York: Hawthorn, 1965), pp. 55–65, and William Hyland and Richard Wallace Shryock, *The Fall of Khrushchev* (New York: Funk and Wagnalls, 1968), pp. 188–97. A thorough account of Khrushchev's fall, including a Central Committee meeting, is given by Michel Tatu in *Power in the Kremlin* (New York: Viking, 1969), pp. 399–423. The Medvedev brothers report that "the very well briefed full membership" of the Central Committee met for a short time and voted to drop Khrushchev "*unanimously* and without debate" (emphasis in the original). Roy A. Medvedev and Zhores A. Medvedev, *Khrushchev: The Years in Power* (New York: Columbia University Press, 1976), p. 175.

[17]Or, occasionally with other bodies, such as the All-Union Council of Trade Unions.

[18]For a quick confirmation of this point, see any listing of Party resolutions and decisions as to the breakdown between these two types of decrees. See, for instance, *Spravochnyi Tom k Vos'momu Izdaniiu "KPSS v Resoliutsiiakh i Resheniiakh S'ezdov, Konferentsii i Plenumov TsK"* (Moscow: Izdatel'stvo Politicheskoi Literatury, 1973) or *Voprosy Ideologicheskoi Raboty KPSS: Sbornik Documentov, 1965–1973*, 2nd ed., enl. (Moscow: Izdatel'stvo Politicheskoi Literatury, 1973). An excellent and thorough discussion in English of the differences between these two kinds of CC actions, and of formal Party decisions in general, may be found in Robert McNeal's introduction to *Guide to the Decisions of the Communist Party of the Soviet Union 1917–1967* (Toronto: University of Toronto Press, 1972), especially pp. x–xviii. McNeal states that about 89 percent of the total number of decisions listed in his book are nonplenary session CC decrees, whereas less than 5 percent are CC plenary session decrees.

[19]Western estimates of the size of this apparatus range from about 100,000 to about one-half million. See Rolf H.W. Theen, "The Soviet Political System Since Stalin," *Problems of Communism*, 30 (Jan.–Feb. 1981), 76.

[20]Khrushchev's interview was with Turner Catledge of *The New York Times* in May 1957. It may be found in N. S. Khrushchev, *Speeches and Interviews on World Problems* (Moscow: Foreign Languages Publishing House, 1957), pp. 53–57. Brezhnev's interview was described by a number of correspondents. See the AP dispatch of June 16, 1973, as carried in the *Rome Daily American*, p. 1; also see *The New York Times*, Jun. 15, 1973, p. 3.

[21]Carl A. Linden, *Khrushchev and the Soviet Leadership, 1957–64* (Baltimore: The Johns Hopkins Press, 1966), especially pp. 1–9; Robert Conquest, *Russia After Khrushchev* (New York: Holt, Rinehart & Winston, 1965).

[22]The resolution has not been published openly but is referred to in several sources. See the discussion in *Resolutions and Decisions of the Communist Party of the Soviet Union* (Toronto: University of Toronto Press), Vol. 4, ed. Grey Hodnett, pp. 316–17 (1974) and Vol. 5, ed. Donald V. Schwartz, p. 3. (1982).

[23]Elizabeth Teague, "A Month in the Life of the Politburo," *Radio Liberty Research*, No. 379/83, Oct. 10, 1983, p. 7. From their inception until early 1986 these press reports did not include the date of Politburo meetings but merely referred to that body's "regular meeting." In Mar. 1986, shortly after the Twenty-Seventh Party Congress, the dates of the meetings began to be included.

[24]*Izvestiia*, Feb. 24, 1981, p. 8.

[25]Henry Brandon, *The Washington Star*, July 15, 1979, as quoted in Elizabeth Teague, "The Foreign Departments of the Central Committee of the CPSU," *Radio Liberty Research Bulletin*, Oct. 27, 1980, p. 4.

[26]The following paragraphs rely heavily on Donald D. Barry, "The *Spravochnik Partiinogo Rabotnika* as a Source of Party Law," in *Ruling Communist Parties and Their Status Under Law*, ed. D. A. Loeber and others (The Hague: Martinus Nijhoff, in press). See this source for relevant citations. Several chapters in this volume deal with problems of bringing the Party within the ambit of the law.

[27]The prohibition on *podmena* seems to have been strengthened in the Party Rules adopted in 1986. In this new version of the Rules the prohibition has been placed in a separate article (it had been part of a more general Article 42, on lower level Party organizations). And, in addition to the statement on *podmena*, a new stipulation, that "Party organizations operate within the framework of the USSR Constitution," was added. See Appendix B, Article 60.

[28]Abdurakhman Avtorkhanov, *The Communist Party Apparatus* (Chicago: Henry Regnery Co., 1966), p. 100.

[29]Examples of such self-criticism, although not limited to intra-Party matters, may be found in J. M. Bochenski, *Soviet Russian Dialectical Materialism* (Dordrecht, Holland: D. Reidel, 1963), pp. 123–28 and the section "Criticism and Self-Criticism," pp. 154–55.

[30]Bohdan Harasymiw, *"Nomenklatura:* The Soviet Communist Party's Leadership Recruitment System," *Canadian Journal of Political Science*, 2, No. 4 (Dec. 1969), 506. Other useful sources on *nomenklatura* include Hough, *The Soviet Prefects*, pp. 114–16 and 150–55, and Michael Vozlensky, *Nomenklatura: The Soviet Ruling Class* (New York: Doubleday, 1984). Estimates on the number of "nomenklatured" workers varies considerably. Vozlensky, p. 95, estimates the figure at 750,000, while T. H. Rigby gives a figure of "something over 2 million." T. H. Rigby, "Introduction," in *Leadership Selection and Patron-Client Relations in the USSR and Yugoslavia*, eds. T. H. Rigby and Bohdan Harasymiw (London: George Allen & Unwin, 1983), p. 3. See Rigby's discussion of possible reasons for this discrepancy, p. 9, note 10.

[31]Harasymiw, *Nomenklatura*, p. 506.

[32]Vozlensky, *Nomenklatura*, p. 71.

[33]As far as is known to the authors, the term "interlocking directorate" was first used to describe the overlapping nature of Soviet elite representation in important bodies in *Staffing Procedures and Problems in the Soviet Union* (study submitted by the Subcommittee on National Security Staffing and Operations to the Committee on Government Operations, U.S. Senate, Washington, DC, 1963), p. 9.

[34]On this point see John H. Kress, "Representation of Positions on the CPSU Politburo," *Slavic Review*, 39, No. 2 (Jun. 1980), 218–38.

[35]Hough raises reasonable questions concerning the quality of the higher education of some of these individuals. See Hough and Fainsod, op. cit., pp. 469–70.

[36]This thesis is most closely associated with Zbigniew Brzezinski. See his "The Soviet Political System: Transformation or Degeneration?" *Problems of Communism*, 15, No. 1 (Jan.–Feb. 1966), 1. For an updating of the original degeneration thesis see Brzezinski, "Soviet Politics: From the Future to the Past?," in *The Soviet Polity in the Modern Era*, eds. Erik P. Hoffman and Robbin F. Laird (New York: Aldine, 1984), pp. 77–82.

[37]Frederick J. Fleron, Jr., "System Attributes and Career Attributes: The Soviet Political Leadership System, 1952 to 1965," in *Comparative Communist Party Leadership*, eds. Carl Beck and others (New York: David McKay, 1973), pp. 57–58; Michael Gehlen, "The Soviet Apparatchiki," in *Political Leadership in Eastern Europe and the Soviet Union*, ed. R. Barry Farrell (Chicago: Aldine, 1970), pp. 146–54.

[38]Seweryn Bialer, *Stalin's Successors: Leadership, Stability and Change in the Soviet Union* (Cambridge: Cambridge University Press, 1980), pp. 117–20 and 91–92. Robert E. Blackwell, Jr., "Cadres Policy in the Brezhnev Era," *Problems of Communism*, 28 (Mar.–Apr. 1979), 31–37.

[39]Bialer, op. cit. The quotations are from pp. 120, 121, and 122.

[40]For an independent analysis of several of the points made in this and the previous paragraph, see Hough and Fainsod, pp. 455–59.

[41]Michel Tatu, "The Central Committee Elected at the Twenty-Seventh Party Congress: Halfway Towards Rejuvenation," *Radio Liberty Research*, No. 106/86, Mar. 10, 1986.

[42]John D. Nagle, *System and Succession: The Social Bases of Political Elite Recruitment* (Austin, TX: University of Texas Press, 1977), Chap. 4, pp. 77–91.

[43]Franz Borkenau, "Getting at the Facts Behind the Soviet Facade," *Commentary*, 17, No. 4 (Apr. 1954), 394. Among the metaphors used to describe the personal relations among political clients and patrons in the Soviet system, a novel and interesting one recently put forward is that of "political *seilschaften.*" *Seilschaft* is a mountaineering term that refers to a " 'roped party' of climbers whose mutual aid, protection and support enable them to scale heights that would be beyond their individual powers." See the theoretical and empirical analysis based on this concept in Gyula Jozsa, "Political Seilschaften in the USSR," in Rigby and Harasymiw, eds., pp. 139–73. The quotation is from p. 139.

[44]The member was P. Y. Shelest. *See The New York Times*, May 22, 1972, p. 1.

[45]See the discussion of this point, as well as the results of the data analysis, in Lewis J. Edinger and Donald D. Searing, "Social Background in Elite Analysis: A Methodological Inquiry," *American Political Science Review*, 61, No. 2 (June 1967), 429, especially pp. 429, 444–45.

[46]In two studies attempts have been made to analyze the relationship between background characteristics of Soviet leaders and their attitudes as expressed in published articles and other writings. In both studies acknowledgement is made of the problems associated with the small number of accessible writings by Party leaders, which serve as the data base for the attitudinal part of the studies. Philip D. Stewart and Kenneth Town, "The Career-Attitudes Linkage Among Soviet Regional Elites: An Exploration of Its Nature and Magnitude" (paper prepared for delivery at the 1974 Annual Meeting of the American Political Science Association, Chicago, IL, August 29–September 2, 1974); and Robert E. Blackwell, Jr., "Political Generation and Attitude Change Among Soviet Obkom Elites" (paper prepared for delivery at the 1974 Annual Meeting of the American Political Science Association, Chicago, IL, August 29–Sept. 2, 1974).

SELECTED BIBLIOGRAPHY

ARMSTRONG, JOHN A., *The Politics of Totalitarianism.* New York: Random House, 1961.

AVTORKHANOV, ABDURAKHAMAN, *The Communist Party Apparatus.* Chicago: Henry Regnery, 1966.

BIALER, SEWERYN, *Stalin's Successors: Leadership, Stability and Change in the Soviet Union.* Cambridge: Cambridge University Press, 1980.

BUNCE, VALERIE, *Do New Leaders Make a Difference? Executive Succession and Public Policy Under Capitalism and Socialism.* Princeton, NJ: Princeton University Press, 1981.

COHEN, STEPHEN F., ALEXANDER RABINOWITCH, and ROBERT SHARLET, eds., *The Soviet Union Since Stalin,* Bloomington, IN: Indiana University Press, 1980.

GEHLEN, MICHAEL P., *The Communist Party of the Soviet Union: A Functional Analysis.* Bloomington, IN: Indiana University Press, 1969.

GELMAN, HARRY, *The Brezhnev Politburo and the Decline of Detente.* Ithaca, NY: Cornell University Press, 1984.

HARASYMIW, BOHDAN, *Political Elite Recruitment in the Soviet Union.* New York: St. Martin's Press, 1984.

———, "Nomenklatura: The Soviet Communist Party's Leadership Recruitment System," *Canadian Journal of Political Science,* 2, No. 4 (Dec. 1969), 505–12.

HILL, RONALD J., and PETER FRANK, *The Soviet Communist Party,* 2nd ed. London: George Allen & Unwin, 1983.

HODNETT, GREY, *Leadership in the Soviet National Republics: A Quantitative Study of Recruitment Policy.* Oakville, Ontario: Mosaic Press, 1978.

HOUGH, JERRY F., and MERLE FAINSOD, *How the Soviet Union is Governed.* Cambridge, MA: Harvard University Press, 1979.

———, *Soviet Leadership in Transition.* Washington, DC: The Brookings Institution, 1980.

———, *The Soviet Prefects: The Local Party Organs and Industrial Decision-Making.* Cambridge, MA: Harvard University Press, 1969.

JONES, ELLEN, "Committee Decision-Making in the Soviet Union," *World Politics,* XXXVI, No. 2 (Jan. 1984), 165–88.

LOWENHARDT, JOHN, *The Soviet Politburo.* New York: St. Martin's Press, 1982.

MILLS, RICHARD M., "The Soviet Leadership Problem," *World Politics,* XXXIII, No. 4 (July 1981), 590–613.

MOSES, JOEL C., *Regional Party Leadership and Policy-Making in the USSR.* New York: Holt, Rinehart & Winston, 1974.

———, "The Impact of *Nomenklatura* in Soviet Regional Elite Recruitment," *Soviet Union,* 8, Part 1 (1981), 62–103.

RESHETAR, JOHN S., JR., *A Concise History of the Communist Party of the Soviet Union,* rev. ed. New York: Holt, Rinehart & Winston, 1964.

RIGBY, T. H., ARCHIE BROWN, and PETER REDDAWAY, eds., *Authority, Power and Policy in the USSR: Essays Dedicated to Leonard Schapiro.* New York: St. Martin's Press, 1980.

RIGBY, T. H., and BOHDAN HARASYMIW, eds., *Leadership Selection and Patron-Client Relations in the USSR and Yugoslavia*. London: George Allen & Unwin, 1983.

RYAVEC, KARL W., ed., *Soviet Society and the Communist Party*. Amherst, MA: The University of Massachusetts Press, 1978.

SCHAPIRO, LEONARD, *The Communist Party of the Soviet Union*. New York: Random House, 1960.

Soviet Succession (Hearings, Senate Select Committee on Intelligence, Sept. 29, 1982, 97th Congress, 2nd Session).

TATU, MICHEL, *Power in the Kremlin: From Khrushchev to Kosygin*. New York: Viking, 1968.

VOZLENSKY, MICHAEL, *Nomenklatura: The Soviet Ruling Class*. New York: Doubleday, 1984.

WESSON, ROBERT G., *Lenin's Legacy: The Story of the CPSU*. Stanford, CA: Hoover Institution Press, 1978.

8

THE LEGAL SYSTEM:
What Is "Socialist Legality"?

"Is there any law or justice in the Soviet Union?" A course on the government of most countries would not even touch on such a question. It would be assumed that there was a viable legal system and that the job at hand was to explore its basic structure and characteristics. Such assumptions are not so easily made with reference to the Soviet Union. Westerners are likely to be most knowledgeable about the more irregular events in Soviet legal history such as the purge trials and recent attempts to intimidate and silence dissidents by use of the legal process. Although such events are an undeniable indicator of the nature of the Soviet legal system, taken alone they present a distorted picture.

Most Soviet citizens experience their legal system in terms of the humdrum of banal disputes that is the grist of legal systems everywhere in the world. Unless there is something highly unusual (for a Soviet citizen) in their behavior, they no longer fear the knock on the door at night. Their contact with the legal system is more likely to be of the divorce court–parking ticket variety; it seldom causes more than a ripple in the surface of their day-to-day lives. Correspondingly, it is in this less spectacular aspect of the Soviet legal system that we can recognize law and justice in the forms to which we are accustomed.

And this should not be surprising. On reflection, it is clear that any society so highly organized as the Soviet Union cannot be governed entirely on the basis of arbitrary fiat. There must be some system of regularized rules to take care of the great majority of disputes—those that are not sufficiently sensitive to be given individual political attention. Otherwise, Soviet leaders would be unable to focus their attention on the relatively small number of disputes that do have significant political implications.

How, then, can one characterize such a system—part arbitrary and part ordinary? Ernst Fraenkel,[1] writing of Nazi Germany, characterizes such a system as a "dual state." In some aspects, it can be a "prerogative state" which is governed arbitrarily with no effective limits on the jurisdiction of state organs. In other aspects, it can be a "normative state" in which government is limited by legal norms that delineate the boundaries of permissible government action. The areas of jurisdiction covered by the "prerogative state" and the "normative state" are not fixed. Rather they are constantly expanding and contracting as the situation demands. Thus, the period of the Stalinist purges can be viewed as a period when the ambit of the "prerogative state" was greatly expanded. Correspondingly, the period after Khrushchev's "secret speech" denouncing Stalin to the Twentieth Party Congress—generally termed a period of "thaw"—can be regarded as a period when the "prerogative state" contracted and the "normative state" expanded to fill the void. It was during this latter period, as we shall see later, that Soviet jurists became actively involved in an effort to define and establish in practice workable principles of "socialist legality."

Therefore, in studying the Soviet legal system at any particular point in time, one must strike a balance that takes into account the relative strengths of those forces that are characteristic of the "prerogative state" and those that are characteristic of the "normative state." To focus exclusively on one or the other distorts the picture. In addition, to generalize on their relative strength from one point in time to the entire history of the Soviet Union is to construct a highly inaccurate picture of the Soviet legal system.

KEY PRINCIPLES

There are certain principles that can be regarded as hallmarks of the Soviet legal system in that one cannot progress far in the study of Soviet law without meeting them. They are basic in the sense that, at the very least, they are given lip service and at times efforts are made to fashion them into working parts of the system. Three of the most important of these will be discussed in detail: (1) socialist legality, (2) the educational function of law, and (3) the relation between economic planning and law. All of these embody principles that are heavily influenced by the Soviet environment and Soviet history and, thus, can form the basis for some key distinctions between the Soviet legal system and those of the noncommunist world with which the readers of this book will be most familiar.

Socialist Legality

Soviet officials and writers use the words "socialist legality" in more than one way. First, and less important for this chapter, is the use of the term "socialist legality" to distinguish law and justice under the Soviet regime from the "bourgeois legality" that held sway in the various parts of the Soviet Union before the communist takeover. Second, "socialist legality" can be defined as the "unwavering fulfillment of laws and related legal acts by the organs of the state, officials, citizens and public organizations."[2] All subsequent references in this chapter will assume the second definition of the term "socialist legality."

Observance of the law by Soviet officials, particularly those of the organs of state security such as the KGB (Committee for State Security), has never been as "unwavering" as the above definition suggests. The general pattern has been for prominent Soviet leaders, beginning with Lenin, to make public statements calling for strict observance of legal norms while allowing or encouraging Soviet government organs blatantly to violate certain of these norms when political expediency demanded it. An early example of this tendency is given by Samuel Kucherov:

> After the seizure of power by the Bolshevists, Lenin had already declared to the Second All-Russian Congress of Soviets on November 8, 1917: "The problem of land may be solved only by the All-People's Constituent Assembly. . . . Even if the peasants will further follow the Socialist Revolutionary Party, let it be so. . . . Let the peasants from one end and us from the other, solve this question" (Lenin, XXII, pp. 22–23). But when the Bolshevists gained only 175 of the 707 seats of the Constituent Assembly, Lenin dispersed it with the help of the bayonets of sailors and Red Guards. It must be stressed that the elections to the Constituent Assembly were conducted when the Bolshevists were already in power, that they accepted the results of the election in advance and that the forcible dispersal of the Assembly was a clear breach of legality.[3]

The extent to which there has been a gap between words and deeds has changed over time. The nadir was probably the Stalinist purge period, during which the Special Boards of the NKVD sent thousands of Soviet citizens into forced labor camps—frequently on the flimsiest of evidence. The high point of concern with the establishment of "socialist legality" as a working force in the administration of justice came after the Twentieth Party Congress in 1956. Khrushchev had denounced the excesses of the Stalin period and called for reforms which would rule out the possibility of such abuses in the future. The Party Congress had also passed a resolution that charged all Party and government organs with the "watchful guard over legality and the resolute and severest suppression of any expression of illegality, arbitrariness and the violation of socialist order."[4] Thus there ensued a period, lasting to the early 1960s, when both scholars and political leaders talked about socialist legality in a way that approached the "rule of law" idea in the West—the idea that countries ought to be governed by laws not by men. But, as the sixties wore on, the pendulum began to swing the other way, and in official pronouncements the idea of "socialist legality" has come to be coupled with the idea of "socialist law and order" (*sotsialisticheskaia zakonnost' i pravoporiadok*). At least initially, this change in emphasis was connected with the campaign against "hooliganism" and, as is often the case in the West, the call for "law and order" implied a certain disregard of the niceties of legal protections and procedures.

Although socialist legality is supposed to characterize the legal behavior of all Soviet citizens and organizations, one institution has the principal responsibility for maintaining socialist legality. This is the USSR Procuracy. The activities of this government organ and of other legal institutions will be discussed later in this chapter.

The Educational Function of Law

In the Soviet Union, much more than in most Western countries, the law is regarded as an active force molding and channeling individual behavior in ways considered desirable by the Soviet leadership. There are few arguments as to whether changing the law can change people's behavior and attitudes. It is assumed that it can—if only the people are brought into contact with the law and the legal system in the proper way. Thus, the emphasis is not on whether the job can be done but rather on how to go about doing the job.

There are three overlapping themes[5] that emerge from Soviet efforts to "do the job." First, and in some ways most basic, is "legal upbringing" (*pravovoe vospitanie*). This refers to the process of legal socialization which begins during early childhood and continues throughout life. Here the emphasis is both on inculcating a knowledge of the provisions of the law and of its demands on the individual and on the nurturing of a value system that stresses law-abiding behavior and attitudes. It has as its aim the creation of responsible, law-conscious, and law-abiding adults. Second, and most obvious to a foreigner, is the continuous effort by the media, the adult education system, and the *agitprop* structure to propagandize knowledge of the law among the Soviet people. This theme, referred to as "legal propaganda" (*pravovaia propaganda*) by Soviet writers, focuses on adults and, in effect, reinforces and continues to build on the base created by "legal upbringing."

The third theme, the educational role (*vospitatel'naia rol'*) of the legal process, is not unlike what is referred to as the deterrent role of the law in some Western countries, notably the United States. It goes much further, however, than an emphasis on the harshness of sentencing, and it is different in some very basic ways. First, there is a considerable reliance on the effect on individual Soviet citizens of exposure to actual court processes or trials. Media coverage of court trials is scant and highly selective—the standard being their value for educational purposes as perceived by the Soviet leadership. Thus what the average Soviet citizen knows about actual court proceedings is either what he or she is supposed to know and nothing more or what he or she personally has experienced from involvement in a trial process. This brings us to the second point—that much of Soviet procedure is designed with its educational role in mind. For example, some Soviet trials are held in "circuit sessions" *(vyezdnye sessii)*. "Circuit sessions" are trials that are held not in courtrooms but in the places of work or residence of the people involved. Thus, the trial process reaches and presumably educates not only the persons directly involved but also their families, coworkers, and neighbors. Sometimes official representatives of their *kollektiv* participate in the trial itself on behalf of one or the other side of the case. Also, the procedural rules that govern Soviet trials allow Soviet judges much more freedom to act pedagogical roles—lecturing, cajoling, and scolding. George Feifer conveys this relationship between the judge and the participants in the following dialogue between a judge and a criminal defendant:

> The judge clears her throat, flips the pages of the record and finds her place with a stout finger . . .
> "Have you been reprimanded for truancy at the factory?"
> "Yes."
> "Absent from work with no good reason—that is your attitude toward your work, toward your responsibilities. And rebukes for appearing drunk in the factory—did you get any of these?"
> He does not answer.
> "*Did* you?"
> "I think . . . well, yes."
> "How many?"
> "I don't know. I don't remember."
> "Four?"
> "Maybe. I didn't count. Sometimes it was on a holiday, when everyone was drunk."
> "Four reprimands! That's an unheard-of-attitude toward work and life in our socialist society. Disgraceful! It started with disinterest in work; then drinking and hooliganism—and led from that to stealing; of course it led to stealing, naturally to stealing—do you understand that? Why were you repeatedly late? Why did you continue to violate work discipline in spite of your warnings? You ignored them. You drank on the job. You were truant. And then you stole. Logical."[6]

Popular participation in the administration of justice also serves to enhance the educational role of law. Such participation may take a variety of forms. The use of lay judges, known as people's assessors, to hear cases in court along with the regular professional judge, will be described below. Other kinds of popular participation may be included under the Russian term *obshchestvennost'*. This untranslatable word is often rendered as "the public" or "society," with the adjectival form *obshchestvennyi* as "public" or "social." It refers to the use of Soviet citizens to perform unpaid services which supplement the work of the state bureaucracy.

Thus, when a person is accused of a crime or has another kind of legal problem involving adjudication, colleagues at his place of work, acting as a *kollektiv*, might send to court a "social defender," a lay colleague of the accused, to testify as to the defendant's good moral character. If his work record is not good or he has exhibited other negative traits, his *kollektiv* might send a "social accuser" to present the bad side of the defendant's extrajudicial record.

Another form of *obshchestvennost'* is the volunteer people's detachment or *druzhina* (from the word *drug,* meaning "friend") made up of citizens who, in nonworking hours, perform a kind of auxiliary police role, helping the regular police to patrol and keep order in places. Perhaps the best known form of popular participation of this kind is the comrades' court. This body is not part of the regular court system. It is a lay body made up of representatives of the *kollektiv* in a place of work or residence. It hears cases of minor importance not within the jurisdiction of regular courts such as a worker's chronic absenteeism or drinking on the job, or a person's slovenliness or rude behavior in the communal areas of an apartment house. The comrades' court has the right to levy minor sanctions against the accused, such as a censure or a small fine, or to transfer the case to the regular court system if the alleged infraction warrants it. But the main function of the comrades' court is the educational one: to achieve the desired behavior in the community at large by bringing the force of organized public opinion to bear on those who commit minor infractions.

Social or *obshchestvennye* organizations received much more attention under Khrushchev than they have under his successors. But the enabling legislation for these organizations is still on the books, and one can read from time to time that they are performing the functions for which they were designed.

Thus, the role of the law, and with it the court process and the legal profession, is not only to settle disputes but also to reinforce and elaborate on the messages coming from other sectors of Soviet society. The good Soviet citizen forms the habit of law-consciousness *(pravosoznanie)* and law-abiding behavior. With the cooperation of the media and the educational system, this concept is introduced to the Soviet citizen at an early age, and what he or she learns is continually reinforced in a myriad of ways. The goal, of course, is the creation of the "new Soviet person."

Economic Planning and Law

The fact that the Soviet economic system is highly socialized, with almost no private economic activity permitted, suggests a much wider range of legal regulation of the economy than is the case in the West. There is a large number of forbidden economic activities for which there are legal sanctions. Some of them, such as counterfeiting, are also illegal in the West. But others, such as private entrepreneurial activity and the practicing of a wide range of forbidden professions, find no analog outside the socialist bloc. The Soviet authorities have carried on a long campaign against prohibited economic activities. As a sign of the seriousness of their efforts (and perhaps of the lack of success in stamping out such practices as well), several economic crimes, if committed on a large enough scale, may be punished by the death penalty. One of these is speculation, which is defined in Soviet law (Article 154 of the RSFSR Criminal Code) as the "purchase and resale of goods or other articles for gain." But a more fundamental way in which law penetrates the economic sphere is with regard to planning. As will be discussed in more detail in Chapter 9, the economic system is highly centralized and directed. The mechanism for achieving optimal economic results is planning and, in a quite literal sense, the plan *is* law. Annual plans and five-year plans are adopted by the Supreme Soviet of the USSR as statutes and thereby have an obligatory character.

This does not mean that if plan targets are not fulfilled by a factory its manager will be considered to have broken the law.* Nonfulfillment of plan would constitute a career liability to a manager, not a legal liability. The adoption of the plan as law denotes both the official character of the plan and the serious intentions of the leaders with regard to economic performance. And the details of plan fulfillment are legalized by converting plan assignments into legal relationships among participating parties. Thus, state economic enterprises (the producers and sellers of goods and services in the USSR) are invested with legal personality, allowing them to enter into contracts, administer property, and sue and be sued. These enterprises contract with each other for sale and purchase of goods and supplies necessary to fulfill plan assignments. Breach of contract and other legal problems between and among economic enterprises are handled by a system of arbitration tribunals called *Gosarbitrazh*, which is completely separate from the regular court system.

Even employer-employee relationships are based in part on a legal premise. Factory laborers and other workers have work quotas they must fulfill, and in that sense they are part of the overall economic plan. In addition, in each plant there is a collective contract (*kollektivnyi dogovor*) between management and labor concerning the mutual obligations of both sides relevant to fulfilling production plans and other matters.

All able-bodied persons in the USSR are expected to work, and this principle finds expression in the law as well. Article 12 of the Constitution provides: "It is the duty of, and a matter of honor for, every able-bodied citizen of the USSR to work conscientiously in his chosen, socially useful occupation, and strictly to observe labor discipline. Evasion of socially useful work is incompatible with the principles of socialist society." Legal teeth for

---

*Although, if the factory repeatedly produces poor quality products or does it on a large scale as part of its plan fulfillment, the manager may be subject to a criminal sanction for that offense (Article 152 of the RSFSR Criminal Code).

this constitutional principle are found in the so-called antiparasite laws. These laws have been in existence since the late 1950s. In their earlier versions in the various republics they provided that persons who "avoid socially useful work" or derive nonlabor income that allows them to lead a "parasitic way of life" may be tried by a court (or, in some instances, by a workers' collective). Those convicted were banished to specially designated locations to perform obligatory work. The exceedingly broad language of these statutes led to abuses, and in 1965 the law was revised to eliminate the worst of these. Thereafter, only courts could try such cases, and only parasites from Moscow and Leningrad would be subject to resettlement.

In 1970 and 1975 further changes finally made the antiparasite law part of the criminal law (Article 209 of the RSFSR Criminal Code). Previously it had been designated as an "administrative measure," to avoid calling the punishment a criminal sanction (which, incidentally, removed the necessity of following settled criminal procedure). Under this arrangement, resettlement in other parts of the country is not possible. But if a person chooses to lead a "parasitic way of life," he may be punished by a sentence of up to one year in prison or in corrective labor (up to two years for repeaters). Thus, the requirement to work, with legal sanctions for able-bodied persons who avoid it, remains part of the system.

Another means of legal or quasilegal influence in the economic sphere is through so-called "people's control." The USSR Committee on People's Control reports to the USSR Council of Ministers. Its chairman is a member of the Council of Ministers. Below this level, there are people's control committees at the union-republic, autonomous-republic, territorial, province, autonomous-province, autonomous-region, district, city, and borough levels. There are also people's control groups and posts under settlement and rural soviets as well as at enterprises, on collective farms, and in institutions and organizations. The 1977 Constitution enhanced the importance and authority of the people's control apparatus.[7] It was followed by a 1979 law entitled "Concerning People's Control in the USSR." Under it, the people's control organs are charged with carrying out "systematic checkups to verify the implementation of Party directives, Soviet laws and government decisions."[8]

The inspections of the people's control committees are carried out by professional Party *apparatchiks* helped by ordinary citizens who volunteer to monitor the performance of labor and management "in enterprises and farms across the country, in ministries, in construction, in transport and communications, in consumer services, and in health, educational, and military establishments."[9] By the end of the 1970s over ten million volunteers were said to be involved in people's control. This is an example of the voluntary participation discussed in Chapter 4 which, in theory at least, serves to socialize the participants to the norms of the Soviet system. Lacking reliable data, it is difficult to say with assurance the degree to which such participation is actually taking place, and Western views on this matter diverge. One recent source accepts the Soviet figures on participation and asserts that as a result of drawing the masses into control work, "the participants practice and internalize the official norms of Soviet society."[10] Another writer, a Soviet emigré who had personal experience with people's control, is more skeptical. He mentions, for instance, a nineteen-member people's control committee at a certain Moscow factory: "I spoke to each of the persons; not one knew that he was a people's controller."[11] His conclusion: "The truth is that the control groups are a fabrication. The figure of ten million is unreal, and the principle of public control is an empty phrase."

Soviet sources assert that people's control makes a significant contribution to the economic well-being of the USSR. For example, in 1979 it was claimed that people's control inspectors in Moscow had been instrumental in saving 130,000 tons of ferrous and nonferrous metals and increasing the production of silk fabric to more than 2 million meters over what had been planned. The government newspaper *Izvestiia* frequently devotes a whole page to people's control activities, describing how various posts and groups have uncovered and corrected economic problems. This publicity is obviously designed to put all economic administrators on notice that their frailties and inefficiencies are being watched.

COURT STRUCTURE

In the Soviet Union, as in most other developed countries, if you have a legal problem, the first thing you must do is get yourself a lawyer. Soviet citizens with formal legal training usually pursue one of a number of law-related careers, including notary, advocate, jurisconsult (legal adviser to an enterprise, government agency, or other organization), judge, member of the Procuracy, or legal scholar. For the person accused of a crime or party to a civil suit, recourse is to his local law office, where he selects or is assigned an advocate to represent his interests and to advise him. If the case is one that must be taken to court, it is most likely to be tried in the people's court of that district. The people's courts hear 90 to 95 percent of all civil and criminal cases of the first instance. If it is one of a limited number of important criminal cases, however, it may be first heard in a court of the next level, a regional court,* or, if it is adjudged by certain key officials to be a case of extreme importance, it may get its first hearing in the supreme court of that union republic.

Cases of the last two degrees of importance, however, are relatively infrequent, so let us follow the path of an ordinary case, one which starts at the lowest level of the system, in a people's court. In the Soviet Union, courthouses are not the prominent, often imposing, edifices that they are in

---

*The term "regional court" as used here includes provincial *(oblastnye)* courts, territorial *(kraevye)* courts, courts of autonomous provinces, supreme courts of autonomous republics, courts of national districts, and some city courts (for example, Moscow and Leningrad).

countries like the United States. Rather, you are likely to go with your lawyer to a quiet street somewhat removed from the mainstream of daily activity and to enter a small, often dingy prerevolutionary building. You take your place on a bench in a dark hallway among other patient souls who are also waiting for their cases to be tried. When your case is called, you enter a small courtroom presided over by a portrait of Lenin hanging above a long table with three chairs behind it. People involved in your case may not be the only ones in the courtroom. There may also be some curious onlookers, probably senior citizens who use the entertainment the court affords to add zest to their retirement years in much the same way that some retired persons in the United States religiously follow their favorite soap operas. Your case will be tried before a court consisting of a judge and two people's assessors. The judge, who presides over the sessions of the court, is elected in the general election of the area served by the court. His term of office is five years and, in theory, anyone over twenty-five years of age is eligible. As a matter of practice, however, the overwhelming majority of judges are lawyers (the proportion had reached 97 percent by the mid-1970s). This represents a change from the early Soviet years when many judges had little or no formal training.

Unlike the judge, the people's assessors hold full-time jobs elsewhere. Every *kollektiv* that has more than one hundred members elects one people's assessor. During their 2½-year terms, people's assessors serve in this capacity for only two weeks per year. The rest of the time they are at their regular places of work. Thus there is little opportunity for a people's assessor to accumulate any great store of legal knowledge or experience and, consequently, unless the assessors are particularly assertive types, they will probably play a rather passive and pro forma role in the hearing of your case. Their symbolic importance is considerable in that they represent the wisdom of the common man, the voice of the peer: Their role is not unlike the symbolic role of the jury in Anglo-Saxon legal systems. But observation of court proceedings indicates that the judge's professional knowledge gives him sufficient leverage over the people's assessors so that they seldom challenge his view of the merits of the case before the court.

Soviet court sessions, in keeping with the buildings in which they take place, are much less formal, ritualistic, and impressive than those in the West. There is usually a good bit of give and take between the bench and witnesses. It is not at all unusual to hear a judge or, less frequently, a people's assessor carry a large portion of the burden of questioning witnesses. One might even scold or lecture on morals and conduct, as in the following exchange between a people's assessor and an alleged victim of an attempted rape:

> "With whom do you live?" It is one of the lay assessors, her spreading breasts resting on the desk, come to life.
> "With my mother!"

"She gives you permission to stay out until three in the morning?"

"No."

"Well, what do you think about such behavior now? About the way you treated your mother—is that the way to treat a Soviet mother?"

"No, I behaved very badly, of course."[12]

As a result of the relatively unrestrained style of courtroom discussion, the general direction of the opinions of the three members of the court is sometimes quite easy to guess before they retire for deliberation. The conference in which the judge and people's assessors reach their decision, however, is always secret. The decision, which includes both the verdict and the sentence, must be in written form. If there is a minority point of view it is not announced publicly, although it can be written down and attached to the file of a case.

If you are being accused of a crime, the case against you will be presented by an official of the local office of the USSR Procuracy *(Prokuratura)*. But trying such cases is not the only function performed by the Procuracy. It is a huge and highly centralized governmental body which operates on a nationwide basis. Unlike judges and people's assessors, procurators are not elected by the voters of the district that they serve. All procurators are appointed, beginning with the Procurator General of the USSR, who is appointed for a five-year term by the Supreme Soviet of the USSR. He, in turn, appoints his immediate subordinates for five-year terms, and so on down the line, with all procurators being appointed for five-year terms by those superior to them. Therefore, the local offices of the Procuracy function independently from all local government organizations, with all subdivisions and personnel directly or indirectly responsible to the Procurator General of the Soviet Union. The 1979 law on the Procuracy charges the Procuracy with supervising precise compliance with the laws of the Soviet Union. It specifically provides for:

1. supervision over the execution of laws by agencies of state administration, enterprises, institutions, organizations, officials, and citizens;
2. supervision over the execution of laws by agencies of inquiry and preliminary investigation;
3. supervision over the execution of laws during court trials;
4. supervision over the observance of laws in places of detention, in places of pretrial custody, and during the enforcement of penalties and other measures of a compulsory nature prescribed by courts.[13]

Let us assume for purposes of the discussion that you lose your case. Where do you go from there? In the larger Soviet republics the judgment of a people's court may be appealed to the next level court, the regional court. In the smaller republics in which there are no regional courts, appeal is to the republic supreme court. Correspondingly, if your case were one of those important criminal cases that are heard in the first instance in the regional court, appeal would be to the republic supreme court. In any event, no matter on which level your case is heard, it is your one and only chance for an appeal in the usual sense of the word. In other words, you have only one appeal.

But the appellate process is not the only way a case may be reconsidered. There is also supervision review *(proizvodstvo v poriadke nadzora)*. In this, the president of the people's court or an official of the Procuracy may protest a decision. Frequently, a protest is made at the request of a party to the case, but it can be made independent of the wishes of the parties. Such a protest can also be made in the regional courts, the republican supreme courts, and even the USSR Supreme Court. Thus, a case may go through a lengthy series of reconsiderations in which only the decision of the Plenum of the USSR Supreme Court is truly a final judgment. It should be noted, though, that although such a protracted process is theoretically possible, in practice it is extremely rare.*

Finally, a word about the USSR Supreme Court, which plays a much more modest role in the Soviet government than is played by the U.S. Supreme Court. The members of the Court are appointed by the Supreme Soviet of the USSR for a term of five years, and the chairmen of the supreme courts of the union republics are *ex officio* members. The Court can act as a whole (the Plenum) or in separate panels of judges (the Civil Chamber, the Criminal Chamber, and the Military Chamber). Under the 1979 Law on the Supreme Court of the USSR, The Plenum of the Supreme Court has two main tasks: to hear appeals from decisions of republican supreme courts and to issue guiding explanations to the lower courts. The latter are published[14] statements concerning the interpretation and application of the law and are written by the Supreme Court Plenum on the basis of an examination of current court practice and judicial statistics. The Civil and Criminal Chambers hear protests concerning cases that come up from the supreme courts of the union republics when these decisions are alleged to violate federal legislation or impinge on the interests of other union republics.

THE LEGAL PROFESSION

In the 1930s more than half of all judges and procurators had no legal education whatever. Since World War II, however, the situation has changed drastically, and by the late 1970s the overwhelming majority of members of the legal profession had at least incomplete higher legal training. Today it is all but impossible to enter any branch of the legal profession without completing such education. It is only older legal personnel who have not completed law school.[15]

---

*There are people's assessors for every level of the court system who are available to hear cases of original jurisdiction. But when a case goes from a lower court to a higher court by appeal or supervision, only professional judges participate.

Legal education may be pursued in two ways, on a part-time or a full-time basis. Full-time study is offered at university law faculties and at law institutes. The curriculums of the two differ somewhat, with the institutes being less theoretical in emphasis. The basic courses of study, however, have many more points in common than differences. It is also possible to study law by means of correspondence or evening-school courses designed for persons wishing to study without becoming full-time students. The correspondence program is administered by the All-Union Institute of Soviet Law Teaching by Correspondence, which has branches in many cities, especially those where there are no institutions of higher learning. The curriculum and examinations in both these part-time programs are the same as those for full-time students, and correspondence students are given paid leave from work to take examinations or to do special projects in connection with their studies. Though some Soviet and Western commentators have raised questions as to the quality of correspondence education, there are many more law students in correspondence or evening courses than there are in the full-time programs of the universities and institutes.

How does one become a law student? First and foremost, in order to be admitted to the law programs a person must have completed secondary education. Second, he or she must be under thirty-five years of age and have had two years of work experience in production. Finally, a successful applicant must have passed the entrance examinations which cover Russian language and literature (or the local language if classes are conducted in that language), the history of the USSR, and a foreign language. Once the applicants have fulfilled these requirements, selection for admission is competitive, with the available places going to those applicants who have the highest scores in their examinations and the best records from their secondary schools. Once a person has been accepted at a university or institute there is no tuition, and for most university students and all institute students there is a stipend to cover living expenses.[16]

Graduate work in law is open on a competitive basis to those who have completed the basic program of legal education and who have had two years of practical work after graduation (there are exceptions to the latter requirement). Again, there are competitive examinations, and the aspiring graduate student must present a paper on his special subject. The three-year full-time graduate curriculum (there is a four-year curriculum for evening and correspondence students) leads to a degree of "Candidate of Legal Sciences." The degree "Doctor of Legal Sciences" is only awarded to mature scholars who have made a significant contribution to research in some area of legal studies.

What career options are open to the newly graduated jurist? Most jurists go into one of several major branches of the legal profession, becoming advocates, jurisconsults, procurators, judges, law teachers, or legal scholars. Each of these represents a distinct career pattern which will be discussed in more detail subsequently. However, many jurists work in a wide variety of other positions. For example, some serve as notaries or work as investigators for the police, the Procuracy, or the KGB. Also, jurists comprise the legal staffs of a wide variety of governmental and paragovernmental organizations, ranging from the USSR and republican supreme soviets to trade unions.

Jurists who represent private citizens in court and who give them legal advice are called "advocates." On occasion, an advocate may represent an economic enterprise, but the advocate's main function under the law of 1979, concerning the *Advokatura* of the USSR, is to supply legal services to citizens and organizations. Soviet advocates are organized into associations of advocates which serve specific geographical regions. Each association elects a presidium that governs its affairs.

The advocate is paid according to a fee schedule that is issued by the republican ministry of justice, although in special cases where extra work or special expertise is required, an advocate may obtain permission to charge more than the schedule allows. Fees, however, are still very low— approximately 25 rubles per case[17]—and many advocates apparently succumb to the temptation to ask a bit more "under the table." This practice is illegal and can lead to disbarment, but it is evidently quite widespread and constitutes an almost accepted part of the legal process.[18] It compensates somewhat for the relatively low career status of the advocate in the Soviet Union. It also leads to a certain cynicism about the legal profession among the general population.

One of the major problems for the advocate in practicing his profession stems from the fact that he has a duty to society as well as to his client:

> The bar in the USSR furthers the protection of the rights and legitimate interests of citizens and organizations, the administration of justice, the observance and strengthening of socialist legality, and the fostering in citizens of a spirit of precise and undeviating execution of Soviet laws, a solicitous attitude toward the people's property, observance of labor discipline, and respect for the rights, honor and dignity of other persons and for the rules of the socialist community.[19]

This can create problems for the individual advocate in preparing his case. Should he make the strongest possible case for his client, as do American lawyers, or should he present a more balanced view of the issues being litigated? If he does the former, he may be accused of putting his client's welfare above the welfare of society—a very serious charge in the Soviet context. On the other hand, it is difficult to engage in advocacy and be balanced and objective at the same time. This is a dilemma that is constantly being discussed and has not yet been definitely resolved. But in spite of their relatively low status, low pay, and somewhat ambiguous role, there are many excellent and dedicated advocates. Among these are advocates who have worked hard to defend the interests of clients who were highly unpopular, including such political "untouchables" as dissident writers and economic criminals.

Although some advocates do advise or represent economic enterprises, most large economic enterprises employ legal specialists known as jurisconsults. They are jurists whose job it is:

1. to check on the legality of all the activities of the ministries, department, enterprises, organizations, or institutions in which they work;
2. to work to strengthen the economic accounting of management;
3. to make sure that all contractual obligations are fulfilled;
4. to defend the legal rights and interests of the management and employees;
5. to engage in legal propaganda (which involves delivering lectures, making reports, working in social-law consultation offices and being constantly available for consultations with employees).[20]

Many jurisconsults appear to exert considerable influence over management policy making as a result of their legal expertise. Jurisconsults have also played key roles in the preparation of economic legislation and in bringing the legal problems of state enterprises to the attention of policy makers in the Party and government.

Unlike the U.S. judiciary, in which a judgeship is often the capstone of a successful legal career, the Soviet judiciary is a career alternative for the newly graduated jurist.* Thus, the Soviet judiciary is run along civil service lines in that it is composed mainly of persons who become judges at or near the beginning of their careers and who are promoted from lower courts to higher courts on the basis of performance. If this seems strange in view of the fact that judges in the Soviet Union are elected, it is necessary to remember that under the Soviet system there is only one candidate on the ballot for each position. The choice of a candidate for judge is made on the basis of the person's professional and political qualifications. Since judges must be elected every five years and since the Party controls the nominations, political dependability is expected of Soviet judges. Almost all of them are Party members. This control over judicial nominations usually keeps judicial decision making in line with Party policy and makes more crass forms of direct interference in specific cases rare. Party influence, including that exerted by individual Party members with personal interest in the outcome of particular cases, is not, however, unknown. Information from former Soviet lawyers and other recent research suggests the existence of more of this kind of interference than could heretofore be documented.[21]

Another career option open to the graduating jurist is entry into the ranks of the Procuracy. As with the judiciary, most procurators begin their work in the Procuracy soon after completion of their legal education. Their

---

*As with so many other features of the Soviet legal system, this pattern reflects the continental European tradition. From a European perspective, it is the United States that has the unusual method of choosing judges.

careers advance mainly by means of promotion within the organization. A former Procurator General of the USSR, Rudenko, entered the Procuracy at the age of twenty-two and rose to eminence through its ranks. As in the judiciary, political commitment is essential to success. The overwhelming majority of procurators are Party members. Normally the Procurator General is the only jurist who is a member of the Central Committee of the Communist Party of the USSR*—a fact that indicates both the relatively high status of procurators within the legal profession and the importance of the Procuracy within the Soviet government.

Finally, the branch of the Soviet legal profession commanding the highest status and the highest pay is made up of the academic jurists, the teachers and scholars. These are the jurists who teach in the four law institutes and the forty-five university law departments as well as those who engage in research and graduate training in legal research institutes.[22] It is the academic lawyers who have been most active in the post-1956 campaign for legal reform. Their influence has been greatest in the drafting and discussions that preceded the adoption of the All-Union Fundamental Principles on which the new codes of the union republics are based.**

Although jurists play important roles as legal advisers, consultants, judges, prosecutors, administrators, and police investigators, their impact on the political system is much less than in the United States, where law is the foremost access route to a political career. One reason is that there are far fewer jurists in both absolute numbers and in proportion to the total population. If the United States has sufficient lawyers for the population's needs, the same may not be the case in the USSR. Increasing legal regulation of Soviet life, especially of economic relationships, appears to have resulted in a shortage of lawyers. This seems to be particularly true in rural areas and other less desirable places of residence in the USSR.[23]

Jurists in the USSR almost invariably choose career patterns within the legal profession. Seldom are they found in top political posts. Legal training and practice do not serve as the springboard into active political life that they do in many countries of the West, most notably the United States. Although Lenin and several other early Soviet leaders had legal training,[24] General Secretary Gorbachev is the first post-Lenin top leader to have had a legal education.

Thus, jurists in the Soviet Union tend to stick pretty close to the practice of law in one form or another. Their political influence—such as it is—stems almost entirely from their mastery of the fine points of the law and from the fact that many occupy key positions from which they can participate in both the drafting and the administration of the law.

*The Party Central Committee selected in 1986 included Procurator General Rekunkov and Supreme Court Chairman Terebilov among its full members, and Minister of Justice Kravtsov as a candidate member.
**There is a more detailed discussion of the All-Union Fundamental Principles and the codification process in the following section.

THE FORM OF SOVIET LAW

The Soviet Union is like most other countries in that it has a very complex system of law—especially if one includes substatutory rules which can issue from both governmental and semigovernmental sources.[25] In this section only those of the most general significance will be considered in order to outline the form of Soviet law in its broadest dimensions.

At the base of Soviet law is, of course, the USSR Constitution, which was discussed in Chapter 5. The statutory law of the Soviet Union takes two forms: the codes and the statutes *(zakony)*. There are many varieties of substatutory rules, which are too numerous and complex to be discussed here, but two of the most significant are edicts *(ukazy)* of the Presidium of the Supreme Soviet of the USSR (many of which are enacted into statutory law at the subsequent session of the Supreme Soviet) and decrees *(postanovleniia)* originating in the Council of Ministers of the USSR. Finally, there are court opinions. The most important of these emanate from the USSR Supreme Court and the union-republic supreme courts. These bodies may issue both decisions in specific cases and broader "guiding explanations." Although these do not constitute precedent in the sense that they would in a common-law system, like that of the United States, they are used as guides by lower courts in deciding cases.

Like the legal systems of many continental European countries and unlike the common-law systems of Great Britain and the United States, the Soviet system of law is built around a comprehensive set of codes. These codes, the basic statutory law of the USSR, cover such areas as criminal law and procedure, civil law and procedure, family law, land law, labor law, and corrective labor law. Most such codes are union-republic legislation, meaning that each union republic has its own separate code for each of these areas of law.* This does not mean that the codes differ greatly from each other. Generally speaking, codification is a two-step process.[26] First, the USSR Supreme Soviet adopts All-Union Fundamental Principles in those areas slated for codification. These principles, shorter and less detailed than the republican codes, set down basic legal provisions to which all republican law must conform. They ensure fundamental uniformity in the republican codes, although allowing differences on matters of detail or on matters involving adaptation to local conditions. For example, the republic of Georgia, unlike the other union republics, permits the making of wine at home. Quite obviously, this permission is related to the fact that the Georgian SSR is the wine-making center of the country.

The practice of enacting comprehensive codes goes back to tsarist Russia. But in order to keep the law contemporary, there is the need to write new codes from time to time. Currently, the Soviet government is coming to

---

*There are also some USSR codes, such as the Air Code, the Customs Code, and the Merchant Shipping Code.

the end of what has been a period of extensive codification activity which has stretched over a period of approximately thirty years, beginning in the 1950s. Prior to this time the legal system had been operating on the basis of codes that dated back to the early years of Soviet rule.

For example, the Criminal Code that was in force before the new Criminal Code was adopted in 1960 dated back to 1926—despite the fact that work on a new code had been started in 1939. Thus, for decades there had been the gradual "accumulation of irregularities, anomalies and obsolete norms,"[27] culminating in a situation where a new, more adequate code was seen as absolutely essential. The impetus came in the wake of the new concern with socialist legality that followed Khrushchev's denunciation in 1956 of the excesses of the Stalin period. And in subsequent years the adoption of principles and codes had been preceded by considerable discussion of the drafts of such documents by many legal experts and other interested persons.

The second type of statutory act, the statute *(zakon)*, is legislation passed by the Supreme Soviet. The codes and fundamental principles are, technically speaking, statutes too, but the laws generally referred to as statutes are legislative acts of a narrower application. Since the Supreme Soviet meets for only a short time each year, the statutes that it can adopt are relatively few in number and constitute only the most important legislative enactments. Examples from recent years include the annually adopted budget and the 1979 statutes on the Procuracy, the USSR Supreme Court, and the *Advokatura* (legal profession) which were passed following the adoption of the new Soviet Constitution.

Far more common is the Supreme Soviet practice of transforming substatutory law into statutes. Many of the documents adopted by the Presidium of the Supreme Soviet as edicts *(ukazy)* between Supreme Soviet sessions must be transformed into statutes by the full Supreme Soviet. This routine exercise requires very little time and helps explain why Supreme Soviet sessions can be so short. Some Presidium edicts, concerning such matters as the awarding of decorations and honors, remain in force as edicts.

Decrees *(postanovleniia)* adopted by the USSR Council of Ministers are much more numerous than edicts. Dietrich A. Loeber has estimated that there "is one statute for every 50 edicts and 285 decrees."[28] Decrees are the main vehicles for determining the direction of the economic and cultural development of the country and are, therefore, the major device used by the Soviet leadership to exert its will in the form of legal norms.[29]

It has long been the conclusion of scholars that a certain number of enactments of Soviet governmental organs are not published. There is a definite requirement that statutes *(zakony)* be published, and it is probably safe to assume that most or all of them are published. Edicts are also supposed to be published as a general rule, but there are provisions for nonpublication if they are not of "general importance" *(obshchee znachenie)* or are not "normative" in character. It is probably safe to assume that most but not all edicts are published. Since a majority of Soviet laws passed by the Supreme Soviet originate as edicts, the modus operandi is probably for an edict that the leadership does not wish to have published to be left as an edict that is deemed not to be of "general importance" and not "normative."[30]

Unlike edicts, it is the unusual decree that gets published. There is no specific requirement for publication unless the Secretary of the Council of Ministers decides that publication is necessary. Dietrich A. Loeber has estimated that more than 80 percent of the decrees remain unpublished[31]—a fact of considerable importance because decrees have a substantial practical impact on economic and cultural life in the Soviet Union.

In addition, the Soviet Union is in the continental European law tradition in that only selected decisions of higher courts are published. Although those decisions that are published can be studied for what they indicate about the nature of Soviet justice, it is impossible to say what proportion they are of the total decisions of higher Soviet courts. It is equally impossible to know if they are typical. Even guiding explanations to the lower courts which are issued by the USSR Supreme Court may not always be published. During research on guiding explanations issued by the USSR Supreme Court from 1962 to 1971, the authors found evidence that there may be a small group of guiding explanations that are not published (that is, 10 out of a total of 141).[32]

Thus, it is reasonably easy for a government enactment having the force of law or having a considerable impact on the enforcement of the law to remain more or less "secret"—accessible only to a small group of persons inside or close to the government. Relatively few of these enactments have come to the attention of Western scholars, so it is impossible to estimate their impact on the Soviet legal system. What are the protections against abuse of this power to keep legal enactments "for internal use only"? Neither the Procuracy nor the courts has any power to interfere with a government decision not to publish. Theoretically, only the Presidium of the Supreme Soviet could act as a check on decisions made at the Council of Ministers level; correspondingly, the Supreme Soviet could overrule its own Presidium. However, there are no known cases where a decision not to publish was overruled.[33]

NOTES

[1] Ernst Fraenkel, *The Dual State: A Contribution to the Theory of Dictatorship*, trans. E. A. Shils and others (New York: Oxford University Press, 1941).

[2] *Iuridicheskii Entsiklopedicheskii Slovar'* (Moscow: Sovetskaia Entsiklopedia, 1984), p. 101.

[3] F.J.M. Feldbrugge, ed., *Encyclopedia of Soviet Law*, II (Leiden, The Netherlands: A. W. Sijthoff, 1973), p. 620.

[4] Ibid., p. 621.

[5] "Foreword," *Soviet Education*, 14, Nos. 11–12 (Sept.–Oct. 1972), 6–8. For a much more detailed discussion of the educational function of Soviet law see Harold J. Berman, *Justice in the*

U.S.S.R.: An Interpretation of Soviet Law, rev. ed. (New York: Vintage Books, 1963), pp. 277–384. Also: Harold J. Berman, "The Use of Law to Guide People to Virtue," in *Law Justice and the Individual in Society*, eds. J. L. Tapp and F. L. Levine (New York: Holt, Rinehart and Winston, 1977), pp. 75–84.

[6]George Feifer, *Justice in Moscow* (New York: Simon and Schuster, 1964), p. 30. Copyright 1964 by George Feifer, reprinted by permission of McIntosh, McKee and Dodds, Inc.

[7]*Izvestiia*, Dec. 1, 1979, p. 3.

[8]Ibid., p. 2.

[9]Jan S. Adams, *Citizen Inspectors in the Soviet Union: The People's Control Committee* (New York: Holt, Rinehart & Winston, 1977), pp. 1–2.

[10]Ibid.

[11]Boris Bichshtein, "The Reality of People's Control," *Radio Liberty Background Report*, Dec. 27, 1979, p. 3.

[12]Feifer, *Justice in Moscow*, pp. 212–13.

[13]*Encyclopedia of Soviet Law*, pp. 546–47.

[14]A selected few may be circulated internally to a limited number of persons and not published for the general public. Circumstantial evidence of this is discussed in Donald D. Barry and Carol Barner-Barry, "The USSR Supreme Court and Guiding Explanations on Civil Law, 1962–1971," in *Contemporary Soviet Law*, ed. Donald D. Barry, William E. Butler, and George Ginsburgs (The Hague: Martinus Nijhoff, 1974), pp. 71–72.

[15]Donald D. Barry and Harold J. Berman, "The Soviet Legal Profession," *Harvard Law Review*, 82, No. 1 (Nov. 1968), 10–11. As recent evidence of the changed situation with regard to legal education, a 1977 Soviet source claims that 96.8 percent of all Soviet judges have completed higher legal education. See V. Terebilov, *Sotsialisticheskaia Zakonnost'*, No. 10 (Oct. 1977), 3–12.

[16]*Encyclopedia of Soviet Law*, p. 391.

[17]On fee schedules for various legal services see *Soviet Statutes and Decisions*, 10, No. 1 (Fall 1973), 38–48, and "Interview with D. I. Kaminskaya and K. M. Simis," *Radio Liberty Special Report*, No. 10, Jan. 11, 1978, p. 17.

[18]The slang term in Russian for these supplementary fees is *mixt*. A thorough discussion of the practice may be found in Dina Kaminskaya, *Final Judgment* (New York: Simon and Schuster, 1982), pp. 29–30.

[19]"Law of the Union of Soviet Socialist Republics on the Bar in the USSR,"*Pravda*, Dec. 3, 1979, pp. 2–3, translated in *Current Digest of the Soviet Press*, 32, No. 1 (Feb. 6, 1980), 16.

[20]For more detail, see Yuri Luryi, "Jurisconsults in the Soviet Economy," in *Soviet Law After Stalin*, Part III, *Soviet Institutions and the Administration of Law*, eds. Donald D. Barry, F.J.M. Feldbrugge, George Ginsburgs, and Peter Maggs (Alphen aan den Rijn, the Netherlands: Sijthoff and Noordhoff, 1979), pp. 182–96. Also see V. I. Chudnov, *Polpredy Zakona: O Rabote Iuriskonsul'ta* (Moscow: "Iuridicheskaia Literatura," 1977), pp. 9–11.

[21]See Kaminskaya, *Final Judgment*, especially p. 57, where she states: "Sadly, I must say that in all my years as a practicing lawyer I never encountered a truly independent judge. The judiciary's complete subjection to Party and governmental directives on penal policy has always existed in the Soviet Union and remains unchanged to this day. As for a judge's impartiality in trying specific cases, here the degree of dependence on higher authority fortunately has lessened with the years." See also Louise Shelley, "Party Members and the Courts—Exploitation of Privilege," in *Ruling Communist Parties and Their Status Under Law* (Martinus Nijhoff: The Hague), forthcoming. Shelley's chapter, based on interviews with former Soviet lawyers, provides several examples of Party members attempting to influence the legal process.

[22]M. Vyshinskii, "Kadry Iuristov," *Pravda*, Nov. 20, 1979, p. 3.

[23]See A. Sukharev, "Key Problems of Training Legal Cadres," *Sotsialisticheskaia Zakonnost'*, No. 2 (Feb. 1974), p. 3, translated in *Current Digest of the Soviet Press*, 26, No. 26 (July 24, 1974), 9; also Vyshinskii, "Kadry Iuristov," 3.

[24]Among the few persons with legal training besides Lenin who played leading roles in the early years of the Soviet state were N. N. Krestinsky, V. R. Menzhinsky, P. I. Stuchka, and N. V. Krylenko. See Donald D. Barry, "Leaders of the Soviet Legal Profession: An Analysis of

Biographical Data and Career Patterns," *Canadian-American Slavic Studies,* 6, No. 1 (Spring 1972), 73.

²⁵Examples of semigovernmental sources would be the Central Committee of the CPSU and the Presidium of the All-Union Central Council of Trade Unions. For more information, see *Encyclopedia of Soviet Law,* pp. 420–24, 739.

²⁶An exception to the two-step codification process involves those areas in which codes are adopted on the all-union level. Examples are the Air Code and the Merchant Shipping Code.

²⁷Robert Conquest, ed., *Justice and the Legal System in the U.S.S.R.* (New York: Holt, Rinehart & Winston, 1968), p. 130.

²⁸Dietrich A. Loeber, "Legal Rules: For Internal Use Only." *The International and Comparative Law Quarterly,* 19 (Jan. 1970), 76.

²⁹Ibid., p. 75.

³⁰The publications of Soviet dissidents have in recent years cited numerous examples of unpublished edicts. An example of this genre is the edict of the Presidium of the USSR Supreme Soviet of Nov. 3, 1972, removing the limitations on choice of residence earlier enforced against certain categories of Soviet citizens (those of former German citizenship) and certain persons without citizenship. This edict carried the statement "not subject to publication." See *Khronika Tekushchikh Sobytii,* No. 34, Dec. 1974 (New York: Khronika Press, 1975), p. 87.

³¹Loeber, "Legal Rules," p. 77.

³²Barry and Barner-Barry, "The USSR Supreme Court," pp. 71–72.

³³Loeber, "Legal Rules," p. 80.

SELECTED BIBLIOGRAPHY

ADAMS, JAN S., *Citizen Inspectors in the Soviet Union: The People's Control Committee.* New York: Holt, Rinehart & Winston, 1977.

BARRY, DONALD D., WILLIAM E. BUTLER, and GEORGE GINSBURGS, eds., *Contemporary Soviet Law.* The Hague: Martinus Nijhoff, 1974.

BARRY, DONALD D., F.J.M. FELDBRUGGE, GEORGE GINSBURGS, and PETER MAGGS, eds., *Soviet Law After Stalin.* Part I, *The Citizen and the State in Contemporary Soviet Law,* 1977. Part II, *Social Engineering Through Law,* 1978. Part III, *Soviet Institutions and the Administration of Law,* 1979. Alphen aan den Rijn, the Netherlands: Sijthoff and Noordhoff.

BASSIOUNI, M. CHERIF, and V. M. SAVITSKI, *The Criminal Justice System of the USSR.* Springfield, IL: Charles C. Thomas, 1979.

BERMAN, HAROLD, J., *Justice in the U.S.S.R.: An Interpretation of Soviet Law,* rev. ed. New York: Vintage Books, 1963.

————, and JAMES W. SPINDLER, trans. and eds., *Soviet Criminal Law and Procedure,* 2nd ed. Cambridge, MA: Harvard University Press, 1972.

BUTLER, WILLIAM E., *Soviet Law.* London: Butterworth, 1983.

————, comp. and trans., *The Soviet Legal System: Selected Contemporary Legislation and Documents.* Dobbs Ferry, NY: Oceana Publications, 1978.

CAMERON, GEORGE DANA, III, *The Soviet Lawyer and His System: A Historical and Bibliographical Study.* Ann Arbor: MI: Michigan International Business Studies, No. 14, 1978.

FEIFER, GEORGE, *Justice in Moscow.* New York: Simon and Schuster, 1964.

FELDBRUGGE, F.J.M., G.P. VAN DEN BERG, and WILLIAM B. SIMONS, eds., *Encyclopedia of Soviet Law.* Dordrecht, the Netherlands: Martinus Nijhoff, Publishers, 1985.

HAZARD, JOHN, N., *Managing Change in the USSR: The Political-Legal Role of the Soviet Jurist.* Cambridge, Cambridge University Press, 1983.

————, WILLIAM E. BUTLER, and PETER B. MAGGS, *The Soviet Legal System,* 3rd ed. Dobbs Ferry, NY: Oceana Publications, Inc., 1977.

IOFFE, OLIMPIAD, *Soviet Law and Soviet Reality,* Dordrecht, the Netherlands, Martinus Nijhoff, Publishers, 1985.

————, and PETER B. MAGGS, *Soviet Law in Theory and Practice.* New York: Oceana Publications, Inc., 1983.

KAMINSKAYA, DINA, *Final Judgment.* New York: Simon and Schuster, 1982.

KUCHEROV, SAMUEL, *The Organs of Soviet Administration of Justice: Their History and Operation.* Leiden, the Netherlands: E. J. Brill, 1970.

LOEBER, D. A., and others, eds., *Ruling Communist Parties and Their Status Under Law.* The Hague: Martinus Nijhoff, forthcoming, 1985.

MAGGS, PETER B., GORDON D. SMITH, and GEORGE GINSBURGS, eds., *Law and Economic Development in the Soviet Union.* Boulder, CO: Westview Press, 1982.

NEZNANSKY, FRIDRIKH, *The Prosecution of Economic Crimes in the USSR, 1954–1984.* Falls Church, VA: Delphic Associates, Inc., 1985.

SHELLEY, LOUISE, *Lawyers in Soviet Work Life.* New Brunswick, NJ: Rutgers University Press, 1984.

SMITH, GORDON B., *The Soviet Procuracy and the Supervision of Administration.* Alphen aan den Rijn, the Netherlands: Sijthoff and Noordhoff, 1978.

ZILE, ZIGURD L., ed., *Ideas and Forces in Soviet Legal History,* 2nd ed. Madison, WI: College Printing and Publishing, Inc., 1970.

9

ECONOMIC PLANNING AND MANAGEMENT: The Central Organization of Scarcity

In the preceding chapters a number of comparisons between Western systems and the Soviet system have been suggested. Although some similarities have been found (the use of basic codes of law in the USSR and the continental European countries, for instance), differences have predominated. But the area where the differences are perhaps the greatest is in economic organization and operation. All of the "private enterprise" systems of the West have a generous component of government participation in the economy. They are "mixed" systems in varying degrees. But none begins to approach the level of state control over the economy that exists in Eastern Europe; and among the East European socialist countries, the Soviet Union probably embraces this principle most completely.

What *is* so different about the Soviet economic system? Virtually every aspect of the economy contains basic differences from the Western types. First and foremost, almost everyone holding a job in the Soviet Union is an employee of the state. This applies even to those employed by so-called "cooperative organizations" such as collective farms, which possess a technical (but fictitious) independence from state control. This degree of state control is unparalleled in the noncommunist world, and from it flows all of the other characteristics of the economy.*

*Alongside the regular state-controlled economy is an important and thriving "second economy." The wide variety of illegal and semilegal activities that characterize this sector grew out of chronic problems and shortages in state economic operations. This second economy will be discussed in the next chapter.

159

BASIC ECONOMIC ORGANIZATION

It was suggested in the previous paragraph that all working Soviet citizens are state employees. This is not quite true according to the letter of Soviet law. There are four types of legally sanctioned organizations in the Soviet Union: institutions *(uchrezhdeniia)*, enterprises *(predpriiatiia)*, cooperatives, and *obshchestvennye* or "social" organizations; only the first two are, strictly speaking, state organizations.

Institutions are of two types, those with administrative or authoritative functions and those without. In the first category are the traditional governmental organizations described in Chapters 6 and 8—the soviets, councils of ministers (including the ministries and committees within the councils), the courts, and the Procuracy. Those without authoritative functions include such organizations as scientific and research institutes, schools and all other educational institutions, hospitals, and museums.

The primary distinction between institutions and enterprises centers around the basic economic purpose of the enterprise. Most of the production or other economic functions in the country, from restaurants and hotels to local bus and taxi systems to steel plants and coal mines, are organized as enterprises. Each enterprise is recognized as an entity with some degree of autonomy. It possesses certain property; it may enter into contracts to further its economic purposes; it may sue and be sued. In legal terminology, it is a "legal person." In addition, the enterprise operates on the basis of "economic accountability" *(khozraschet)*, meaning that its performance is judged on the basis of the relationship between what it produces and the cost of its operation.

In spite of this partial autonomy, the degree of control by higher state organs is evident. Enterprises are created by state charters and are managed under rules approved by the government. Property is "allotted" to them but they do not own it—even jointly—since "the state is the sole owner of all state property."[1] Moreover, these agencies perform work specified by the government, fulfill governmental plans, and are run by personnel chosen by the government. Attempts since the mid-1960s to give enterprises somewhat greater autonomy for the sake of economic efficiency have been met with great resistance from the central bureaucracy. Since the mid-1970s great emphasis has been placed on merging enterprises into "production associations," larger units made up of numerous enterprises that manufacture related products and are located reasonably near to each other. The objective of creating these associations, which possess somewhat greater autonomy than do enterprises, is to enhance the efficiency of Soviet industry.

The foremost type of cooperative is the *kolkhoz*, or collective farm. Among others are fishing collectives and cooperatives of artisans. When a cooperative is created it is chartered by the government and land and other socialized state property are transferred to it. The cooperative is then supposed to be controlled democratically by the full membership of the organization. The "general meeting" of the cooperative is supposed to elect a chairman and other full-time management personnel and make the most important decisions concerning the governing of the organization.

In practice, however, the technical legal autonomy of the cooperative is not of great significance. For example, it is fairly generally acknowledged by Soviet sources that the collective-farm chairman is in fact selected by Party or governmental officials. Moreover, the *kolkhoz*, like every other production cooperative, is included in the government's plan and is expected to fulfill its part of the plan.

The term "social organization" covers a wide variety of organizations, including trade unions, sports clubs, unions of writers and artists, and many others. Any formally recognized organization that does not fall into one of the previous categories would be a social organization. These bodies are voluntary and, like the cooperatives, are supposed to be run by their general membership. Clearly, however, they are controlled in important ways by the Party authorities and they wield no important independent power. Unlike the cooperatives, most social organizations are not primarily economic in function, and so their activities need not detain us further in this chapter.

SUPERIOR GOVERNMENTAL ORGANS

The economic ministry is the link between the factory or farm and the central organs of economic control. At the national level there are two kinds of ministries: all-union and union republic, and economic ministries may be found in each category. As might be expected in a country where the state has such great control over the economy, the governmental apparatus is heavily populated with economic administrators. About 80 percent of the ministries and state committees presently represented in the USSR Council of Ministers have a primary economic purpose. Most of these are charged with rather narrow production areas such as automobiles, oil, chemicals, coal, and construction.

But several have broader economic objectives. The Central Statistical Administration is charged with the collection of economic and social statistics. In addition to taking the census of population, it prepares and publishes periodic reports on economic accomplishments and plan fulfillment. The main responsibility of the Ministry of Finance is the preparation of the annual budget. The portion of the budget that is published for the general public is quite brief, but it appears that the Ministry keeps much more detailed budgetary information for restricted use. The State Bank Administration is the apex of the centralized governmental banking monopoly. Among other functions, it is charged with enforcing detailed rules concerning banking and credit with which every economic institution in the country must comply. The most important central agency of general economic concern, whose precise analogue is to be found in no country in the West, is the State Planning Committee *(Gosplan)*. France may have her *Commissariat du Plan* and Britain her National Economic Development Council, but no Western planning effort has approached the extensiveness or detail of Soviet planning, and none bears the compulsory character of the highly centralized Soviet system. The distinction is often made between "indicative planning" on the Western side and "imperative planning" on the Soviet side.

The USSR *Gosplan* is responsible for the coordination and direction of all economic planning in the country. It works with the USSR ministries as well as the republican-level councils of ministers. They, in turn, deal with the enterprises and other economic organizations. The way in which this planning effort is said to work will be discussed in the following paragraphs.

PARTY CONTROL

In theory at least, the Party exercises a high level of supervisory control over economic activities. This control is achieved in a number of ways, several of which have been mentioned previously. First, virtually all the important economic administrators, from ministers to managerial personnel at the factory level, are Party members. And a great many economic posts are on one or another *nomenklatura* lists, suggesting further Party influence. At the all-union level the holders of the most important economic positions are likely to be members of the CPSU Central Committee or even of the Politburo. The same holds true at the union-republic level with regard to party bodies at that level. Thus, economic administration is not divorced from political administration; it is integrated into the political sphere by virtue of the Party status of those who hold responsible economic positions.

The Party also has a more formal role in running the economy. Within the Secretariat of the Central Committee there are some twenty departments responsible for various substantive areas of activity that are of interest to the Party. About half of these departments cover economic areas: agriculture, chemical industry, construction, defense industry, heavy industry, light and food industries, machine building, trade and domestic services, transport and communications, planning and financial organs.[2] The size of the staffs of these departments is not known, but it may run into the thousands. Thus, in addition to the regular governmental economic bureaucracy, there is also a Party economic bureaucracy of considerable size. The function of the Party bureaucracy is to oversee economic operations and to enlist the aid of lower levels of the Party hierarchy in correcting economic problems at their source. The Party economic bureaucracy is not supposed to supplant state economic management but to guide and aid it. Excessive Party interference in state operations goes under the term *podmena* ("substituting" or "supplanting") in Russian. It has long been a matter of concern, and although it is prohibited by Article 60 of the Party Rules, the temptation of the Party to play a large and direct role in the Soviet economy is one of the persistent themes of economic administration.[3]

A separate function is performed by the Party control organs. Although apparently not of great importance in recent years, these bodies have been charged with an independent checking function at the production level, with power to report plan violations and other problems to higher Party authorities for correction.[4]

Another formal mode of Party participation is in the review of plans and budgets. In most recent years the December Supreme Soviet meeting, at which the plan and budget for the next year are approved, has been preceded by a Central Committee plenary meeting, at which reports on the plan and budget are made by responsible officials. Nor are these meetings merely pro forma. Kremlinologists suggest that in recent years these sessions have been characterized by acrimonious debate about economic priorities and the role of Party organs in economic administration.[5]

THE PLANNING FUNCTION

The Soviet Union works with economic plans of varying durations. The most well known to outsiders is the Five-Year Plan. The period of 1986 to 1990 is covered by the twelfth of these Five-Year Plans. The Five-Year Plans are broken down into annual plans and quarterly plans, and at the actual production level monthly plans are used as well. Finally, the Soviet leaders are attempting planning of a much longer term. The "Complex Program for the Development of Consumer Goods Production and the Service Sector for 1986 to 2000" is an example.

In the beginning stages the planning process is referred to as "negotiated planning" or "counter planning" (*vstrechnoe planirovanie*) in that it runs in two directions, from the top down and from the bottom up. The enterprises provide estimates of their production output and input requirements. These are collected, coordinated, and revised by the planning agencies and sent still higher in the planning hierarchy, where a preliminary plan is drafted. Relevant parts of this draft are sent back down the planning chain to the enterprises, which may comment on and request changes in the plan. By this procedure the final plan is achieved.

Although this description might suggest considerable influence on planning from the grass roots, this is not likely the case. The most important planning decisions are made at the center, and the production units can only hope to have a minor effect on the targets set by higher officials. Thus, a preponderance of control in the planning process is with the central planners. A frequent response of factory managers has been to circumvent the plans or to seek devious ways of fulfilling them. These methods have been described in a number of books in English.[6] Among the most popular of such devices are falsifications of production statistics, illegal transfer of funds from one use to another, and the concealment of full production capacity from superiors. Another frequent practice has been to take advantage of the way in which plan targets are stated to fulfill the plans in the easiest manner possible, regardless of the needs of the economy. An oft-quoted passage from a Khrushchev speech illustrates this well:

> It has become traditional to produce the heaviest chandeliers possible rather than just beautiful chandeliers to adorn homes. This is because the heavier the chandeliers manufactured, the more a factory gets since its output is figured in tons. So the plants produce chandeliers weighing hundreds of kilograms and fulfill the plan. But who needs such a plan? . . .
> Furniture factories have plans stated in rubles. Hence they find it best to make a massive armchair since the heavier the chair the more expensive it is. Formally the plan is fulfilled since the furniture makers add various details to the armchair and make it more expensive. But who needs such armchairs? . . . Everybody knows this. Everybody talks a good deal about this, but still the armchairs win.[7]

It is problems such as these that led the Soviet political leadership in 1965 to embark on an ambitious economic reform designed to provide higher quality products of the kind needed in the economy. The *quid pro quo* was to give the enterprises more autonomy in operation combined with higher material incentives in exchange for increased efficiency. The success of this reform will be discussed later.

This description of the process of negotiated planning does not begin to suggest the complexity of the operation. There are some 45,000 enterprises and production associations in the Soviet economy, some 48,000 collective and state farms, and many other economic units, as well as a total work force of some 130 million people. All the essential economic operations of all these organizations and people must be embraced and coordinated by the plan. A leading Soviet economic scholar has commented that without thorough automation of the planning process, the entire Soviet population would soon be needed to fulfill the routine tasks of planning and management.[8] This is the reason why so much attention has been given in recent years to mathematical models and computer applications in the planning process. The introduction of these innovations, however, has been met with considerably less than full acceptance. Traditionalists in the planning bureaucracy (and probably in the political leadership as well) have resisted the efforts of the new planners, in part perhaps because of fear that the specialists will come to appear indispensable and thereby wield excessive leverage over the direction of the economy.[9]

But the present planning system has serious problems and will eventually have to involve the mathematical economists in a more significant role. And in spite of the undoubted success of the Soviet economy in recent years, the record regarding fulfillment of plans shows that not all aspects of the economy are progressing well. Attempts have been made in recent years to give higher priority in Five-Year Plans to the lagging consumer sector than to heavy industry. But plans and performance do not always coincide, and primary emphasis on the growth of heavy industry has remained. Even in this sector, however, recent performance has not been strong. Dissatisfaction with overall economic results is behind the recurring attention paid by Soviet politicians and economists to economic reform.

ECONOMIC REFORM

The Soviet leaders are inveterate reformers in the economic sphere. Although they have not changed the basic socialized nature of the economy, they have carried on a restless effort, especially in the years since Stalin, to create a more suitable economic organization and structure. Each new leader has pledged to make progress in combating the country's economic problems, and reforms of varying complexity and magnitude have been the result. The foremost reform during the Khrushchev period was the change from the "production principle" to the "territorial principle" in economic organization. What this involved was the elimination of many highly centralized economic ministries of narrow purpose and the creation of over one hundred economic councils *(sovnarkhozy)* throughout the country. Each was to have responsibility for substantially all economic activities within its region. This regionalization did not conflict with the federal system, for regions did not cut across union-republic boundaries. But the future of the federal system, according to the Party Program adopted during the Khrushchev period, appears to have been in doubt.[10]

The main purpose of this reform seems to have been to enhance the country's economic efficiency. This was to have been done by eliminating the centralized ministries, which, Khrushchev charged, had become self-contained economic empires, and by creating more rational units for the supply of materials and for overall economic coordination, as well as by cutting down on transportation costs and other economic inefficiencies. It is likely that the reform also had a political motivation involving Khrushchev's efforts to outmaneuver his opponents and place his lieutenants in strategic positions.

As things worked out, the *sovnarkhoz* reform did not bring about substantial decentralization. Most important economic decisions were still made above the regional level. And it did not result in obviously great increases in economic efficiency. In early 1965, within a few months after Khrushchev's ouster, the whole reorganization was scrapped and the system of specialized economic ministries was reinstated. If anything, economic control through the ministries has now become even more centralized than before the Khrushchev reform. The *sovnarkhoz* arrangement was one of the "hare-brained schemes" for which Khrushchev's successors castigated him. It is of little more than historical importance now. Another development that began during the Khrushchev period did outlive him, however. Under Khrushchev, limited experiments were begun that would give greater responsibility and less central direction to individual enterprises in order to enhance their economic efficiency and production. This general idea was publicized in the West under the name of "Libermanism," after Evsei Liberman, a Soviet economist and a strong advocate of reform.

In September 1965, Khrushchev's successors instituted some of the measures reform economists had been advocating. The much-publicized economic reform of 1965 incorporated a number of principles. One of these was the abolition of the *sovnarkhozy*, just mentioned, with the resulting return of significant powers to *Gosplan* and the recreated economic ministries. In addition, it was envisaged that:

1. Enterprises would have a greater voice in planning and production decisions;
2. the enterprises' "success criteria" (the indicators by which their performance is judged) would be changed to enhance economic efficiency;
3. a greater share of their "profits" could be kept and distributed as material incentives to the workers;
4. wholesale prices would be reformed;
5. interest charges on capital stock would be instituted to provide incentives for efficient use;
6. the industrial and commercial supply system would be reorganized to enhance the possibility of direct relations between buyer and seller.[11]

The job of executing the economic reform was entrusted to the economic bureaucracy, including many bureaucrats with a vested interest in the *status quo*. A number of Western analysts predicted that this inertia would have a retarding effect on the reform's development. Within several years it was clear that even the more modest goals of the reform had not been achieved, and it was quietly abandoned.[12] Apparently it was concluded by the leaders that the autonomy and decentralization implied in the reform constituted a greater threat to their political control than they were willing to risk. The next reform was in the mid-1970s. It was intended to create "production associations" to which the smaller economic enterprises would be subordinate. In some respects, this amounted to an increase in centralization, since it involved taking power from enterprises and giving it to production associations. It has been called a "restructuring that moved the system back from economic dependence to economic subordination."[13] At the end of the 1970s a further reform put greater emphasis on long-term and more detailed planning in order to anticipate and facilitate technological change.[14]

None of these reforms (not even the 1965 reform, because of the way it was implemented) has addressed what many Western analysts consider the major problem of the Soviet economy: overcentralization and excessive direct-planning controls.[15] It is not that this problem has gone unrecognized in the USSR. A number of economists have spoken in favor of greater decentralization.[16] Resistance to such a move amounts in large part to a *political* decision, which asserts, in effect, that the risks to the political system from the unforeseen and unintended consequences of decentralization are not worth the increase in economic performance that might result. It is thought that this resistance comes largely from the middle and upper levels of the political and economic bureaucracy, and even the highest political leaders may have trouble implementing economic reforms when recalcitrant subordinates refuse to cooperate.[17]

Gorbachev's accession to power in 1985 seemed to signal a serious attempt to deal with the conservative economic bureaucracy. Within a year he had succeeded in removing a large number of ministers and other responsible officials, and at the Twenty-Seventh Party Congress in 1986 he and others called for "radical reform" in the economy. But specific changes have been slow to come, and the question of whether Gorbachev can succeed in effecting important change in the economic machine, where his predecessors have failed, remains open.

SOVIET ECONOMIC PERFORMANCE

If the foregoing discussions of planning and reform suggest the existence of serious problems in the Soviet economy and dissatisfaction among leaders with economic performance, then the correct impression has been conveyed. But the genuine achievements of the Soviet economy over the years should also be recognized. An impressive industrial base has been constructed, economic growth rates until recent years have been impressive, and a military machine of great force has been created. If economic plans are perennially underfulfilled for many products on the consumer goods side, plan quotas are often impressively exceeded in other areas. In several important areas production figures have been consistently high over a number of years; and in certain recent years, Soviet output of a number of significant products has surpassed that of the United States. These include steel, oil, coal, pig iron, and fertilizers.

Even if the consumer sector is neglected relative to the development of the rest of the economy, the Soviet citizen still sees improvement in his standard of living from one year to the next. Average wages have been rising slightly every year. Prices are not completely stable but neither is there the raging inflation that has characterized Western countries in recent years. Frequent visitors to the Soviet Union invariably remark that Russians are better dressed than they used to be, and many Soviet citizens move into new apartments each year. All of this suggests nothing about the quality of consumer goods and, generally speaking, it is below the norm in the West. In fact, compared with the standard of living in the West, all of these accomplishments may appear to be quite modest. But the Soviet citizen is more likely to judge his economic situation with regard to what he knows best, that is, how he used to live or how his parents lived. And there is no doubt about it, for millions of Soviet citizens things have never been better. A more detailed analysis of the situation of the Soviet consumer will be made in Chapter 10.

A look at a sampling of official data on the Soviet economy and at the conclusions Western economists have derived from these data will give a fuller description of the parameters of Soviet economic performance. It will also indicate the guarded way in which economic figures are publicized and the relative paucity of the information released.

One example is the Soviet budget. Published budget figures are extremely scanty and indicate only the barest outline of economic activity. By the mid-1980s the Soviet budget amounted to about 400 billion rubles in both revenues and expenditures. More than 30 percent of this amount is obtained from deductions from enterprise profits. Less than 10 percent (about 8 percent in recent years) comes from personal-income taxes. Soviet publicists are very proud of the fact that the income tax constitutes such a small share of total income. The mildly progressive income tax ranges from 0 percent of personal income for persons earning up to 70 rubles per month to 13 percent for salaries of more than 100 rubles per month, with somewhat higher rates for authors, certain self-employed persons, and others deriving income from outside of the regular wage and salary system.[18] Khrushchev, in fact, once proclaimed that the Soviet regime would soon bring about "an end to all taxes," meaning, of course, an end to visible taxes; that is, those on income. But it would have required a considerable rearrangement of consumer prices to recover the revenue lost from the elimination of the income tax, and this the leadership apparently could not bring itself to do.

The remainder of budget revenues comes from several other sources, the most important of which is the turnover tax. In recent years this tax has provided more than one quarter of total revenues. Soviet authorities have been cryptic in discussing the turnover tax. This is not surprising, since the existence of the tax is one of the main reasons why income taxes can be so low. It is an indirect tax levied largely on consumer goods. Although the rates of turnover tax on individual products are seldom publicized, they are known to be quite heavy on some goods, amounting to 100 percent and more of the wholesale price. This not only serves to raise considerable amounts of revenue for the state, but it is also designed to sop up extra purchasing power in the hands of Soviet consumers and discourage demand for certain products (for example, passenger cars and vodka). For instance, the turnover tax on one model of a Soviet passenger car was reported in 1979 to be almost 60 percent of the car's retail price.[19]

The trends with regard to these three main taxes as a proportion of total revenue are interesting to note. The turnover tax was introduced in 1930 and once provided nearly 60 percent of all revenues. Recently, deductions from enterprise profits as a revenue source have grown considerably, and at present they provide about 30 percent of total revenues, slightly more than the turnover tax. The personal-income tax rose from about 5 percent of total revenues in 1940 to about 8 percent in 1985.

The Soviet budget is a balanced budget. Deficit financing is not practiced, and typically a small surplus of revenues over expenditures is shown.[20] A selection of figures on the breakdown of spending by major categories is given in Table 9–1. As the table makes clear, the category of national economy has grown steadily, both in ruble amount and as a percentage of total expenditures. The other categories have also grown in rubles but have constituted a smaller percentage of the total budget as expenditures for the economy have grown.

Whatever credence Western analysts place in other budget figures, they are almost unanimous in agreeing that the defense expenditure data are grossly understated. This understatement is achieved in a number of ways. For one thing, the overt defense budget covers only part of total defense expenditures. It is said to pay for the salaries and subsistence of the armed forces plus military construction and procurement. It is thought to exclude the financing of military research and development, civil defense, strategic stockpiling, internal security forces, and other expenses that are partly or wholly included in the defense budgets of Western countries. These costs are assumed to be hidden in other budget allocations, such as national economy and science, or to constitute part of the unexplained budget "residuals."* Another relevant consideration is the pricing system. Since prices are state controlled, it is likely that they are arbitrarily set low for military goods and services, which would underrate to some degree the economic commitment to this area.

Western specialists have expended great efforts over the years in considering these and other matters relevant to Soviet military spending. Although complete agreement as to conclusions is lacking, specialists appear to agree that Soviet defense spending is much higher than the amount stated in the budget. Some estimates put it at four times the listed amount.[21]

In translating such ruble amounts into meaningful assessments of the value of the military product achieved, further disagreement is generated. Until the mid-1970s it seemed generally accepted that the Soviet Union was producing "in comparison with the U.S., an annual defense package of roughly equal value."[22] In 1976, however, the CIA revised previous estimates of Soviet defense expenditures, concluding that the USSR commitment to its armed forces was considerably larger than was thought to be the case earlier. Since then other studies, including ones completed by the CIA

---

*Residuals are the difference between the listed total budget expenditures and the sum of the expenditures for the individual categories. See Table 9–1. For more discussion of defense expenditures as part of "residuals," see Franklyn D. Holtzman, *Financial Checks on Soviet Defense Expenditures* (Lexington, MA: D.C. Heath and Company, Lexington Books, 1975), pp. 13–20.

TABLE 9—1 Major Categories of Soviet Budget Expenditures for Selected Years

	1940 B.R.*	%	1960 B.R.	%	1980 B.R.	%	1986 B.R.	(PLAN) %
Total Expenditures	17.4	100	73.1	100	294.6	100	414.2	100
A. National Economy	5.8	33.5	34.1	46.7	161.0	54.6	235.7	56.9
B. Social-Cultural and Science**	4.1	23.5	24.9	34.1	98.8	33.5	131.8	31.8
C. Defense	5.7	32.6	9.3	12.7	17.1	5.8	19.1	4.6
D. Administration	.7	3.9	1.1	1.5	2.6	.9	2.9	.7
Sum of Individual Expenditure Categories***	16.3	93.5	69.4	95.0	279.5	94.8	389.5	94.0

*B.R. = billions of rubles

**Soviet statistical handbooks provide a more detailed breakdown of the social-cultural and science category. For purposes of the present discussion this breakdown will not be necessary. All other expenditure categories listed in the table are as given in the handbooks.

***The totals on this row are not the same as those given above because of "residuals," which are explained in the text.

Sources: Narkhoz, 1972, pp. 724–25; Narkhoz, 1982, p. 520; Izvestiia, Nov. 27, 1985, p. 3.

in 1980 and 1983, have confirmed this general conclusion and have led to increased defense expenditures on the part of the United States.[23]*

THE SPECIAL PROBLEM OF AGRICULTURE

Several areas of activity compete for the title of "domestic problem number one" in the Soviet Union, but all analysts place agriculture at or near the top of the list. It is a long-standing problem, one that has baffled generations of Soviet leaders and contributed to the demise of a number of political careers. The long-term inflexibility of Soviet leaders regarding expansion of the tiny private sector in the economy undoubtedly contributes to the depth of the problem, but it must be said that the Soviet Union starts out with serious inherent disadvantages. Only about 10 percent of the Soviet Union's vast landmass is designated as arable, and much of this is not ideal for farming. One Soviet source has stated that "almost two thirds of all arable land on the country's state and collective farms lies in zones categorized as suffering at least to some degree from water erosion, and over 40 percent has 'significant' erosion problems."[25] Moreover, undependable weather conditions make crop yields uncertain even on the better lands.

As a result, even bumper-harvest years do not produce great surpluses of food, and in years when natural conditions are particularly unfavorable, a near disaster can result. In spite of these problems, the agricultural situation did not reach its present serious proportions until the 1970s. During the 1960s, the USSR was a net exporter of grain and had to import it only during one year. But the 1970s were a turning point in the Soviet agricultural situation. From then on, "reliance on imports from the West became what now appears to be a permanent part of the Soviet foreign trade picture."[26] In recent years there has been a "stagnation or decline in per capita production of most basic food products."[27] Food rationing has become common in large parts of the country. And the leadership has advanced an enormous number of (essentially conservative) proposals and decrees on agriculture—which suggests the urgency with which they view the situation.[28]

While grain production is only one aspect of the agricultural picture, it is taken as a significant measure of Soviet agricultural success. For the first half of the 1980s, the plan target was for about 240 million metric tons of grain per year (even though the all-time record crop, in 1978, was only 235 million). When less than 200 million tons are produced, it is considered a poor harvest, and as much of the difference as possible must be made up by using imports from the West. Suffice it to say that from 1980 to 1984, the 200 million ton level was not reached once, and large annual imports of grain have constituted a substantial drain on Soviet hard currency holdings.[29] The

---

*Not all Western specialists accept these analyses of Soviet defense spending, however. Some responsible studies have suggested that flaws in the CIA's methodology overstate the level of spending by a considerable amount.[24]

poor agricultural results have had a serious effect on the economy as a whole, not only depressing the overall level of economic growth, but also draining investment funds from other sectors of the economy.

What is the leadership doing about the agricultural problem? Although it is a considerable simplification, it can be said that the important elements on the input side of Soviet agricultural policy (or any other area of economic activity, for that matter) are exhortation, organization, and investment. The relative emphasis on each of these elements appears to have some relationship to the level of agricultural success.

The exhortation element has always played a major role in agricultural efforts, and Soviet society is well set up for such activity. The media, the *kollektivs*, the various organizations in Soviet society can be efficiently mobilized to call attention to agricultural achievements and problems and to seek mass support for agricultural activities (such as calling for volunteers to help with the harvest). And the political organs regularly exhort farmers to greater efforts by calling national attention to agriculture. Numerous plenary sessions of the Party Central Committee in recent years have been devoted exclusively to agricultural problems, as have many speeches of top leaders, and in each recent year a "harvest decree" has given special attention to agricultural shortcomings and has proposed changes to improve the situation. Exhortation alone, however, is incapable of solving agricultural problems, and during large parts of the Stalin and Khrushchev eras it was not accompanied by the necessary financial and organizational support.

As suggested earlier, Soviet leaders have shown themselves to be restless reorganizers, fitfully seeking *the* administrative arrangement that will provide optimal economic results within the socialist framework. This penchant for reorganization has not been so evident in agriculture as in the rest of the economy; but the record shows a considerable amount of organizational evolution, and more change is likely in the future. The present economic organization of agriculture can be traced to the late 1920s and Stalin's drive for collectivization to replace individual peasant households. The collective farm, or *kolkhoz,* quickly became the dominant form of agricultural organization, and by 1936 more than 90 percent of the peasants had been forced into *kolkhozes.* Although accomplished at great cost in terms both of lives and of agricultural production, this "revolution from above" achieved Stalin's end of gaining control over the countryside and eliminating the "capitalist elements" there.

As mentioned earlier, the *kolkhoz* is a cooperative organization and is supposed to be run democratically by its membership. Although this is generally recognized as fiction, other aspects of *kolkhoz* operation have in the past set it off from regular state-run institutions. For many years members of the *kolkhoz* were not paid wages but received a partnership-type share in the profits of their cooperative organization, the share being based on the level of skill of the worker and the amount of his work. Particularly for peasants living on poorer collective farms, this system resulted in a very low level of remuneration. This method of payment has largely been replaced by a regular wage system. Although the average wages of collective farmers are still far lower than those of industrial workers, collective farmers are better off than before as a result of the guarantee of regular wages.

Another result of being outside the regular state system was that until 1964 persons working on collective farms were not within the state system of social insurance. A collective farm might have its own social insurance, but the benefits were on the whole inadequate, especially in the poorer *kolkhozes*. Reforms of 1964 and 1970 basically changed the system, so that now a uniform system of social insurance has been created.

In these two respects—the paying of wages and social insurance—the *kolkhoz* has taken on the characteristics of the other major agricultural organization the *sovkhoz,* or state farm. But the *kolkhoz* is still a cooperative organization and as such is considered to be at a lower stage in the development toward socialism than the state farm, which is state owned.

The *sovkhoz* can be looked upon as a kind of rural enterprise. It is a state institution run by a director appointed by the state. Its employees are paid regular wages. Although created during the 1920s, the *sovkhoz* did not become of great importance to Soviet agriculture until after Stalin's death in 1953. During the Khrushchev era the number of *sovkhozes* in the country more than doubled, and the amount of land under their jurisdiction increased greatly. Since Khrushchev, this tendency has continued at a less rapid rate. By the mid-1980s there were more than 22,000 state farms, which cultivated over 53 percent of the country's sown area. Many of the *sovkhozes* were created from former collective farms. Along with this development a great number of *kolkhozes* were consolidated to make larger *kolkhozes*. As a result, the total number of *kolkhozes* has fallen steadily, from a high of nearly 240,000 in 1940 to about 25,000 by the mid-1980s. At that time, *kolkhozes* accounted for about 44 percent of sown land.[30]

Another category of land under cultivation, and one of particular interest, is the "personal subsidiary undertakings of the population" (as it is called in the official statistical yearbook). These are, of course, the "private plots" so coveted by Soviet citizens. This land constitutes less than 3 percent of the total sown area, and yet its production figures in certain areas are disproportionately great: At the end of the 1970s some 63 percent of potatoes, 32 percent of vegetables, 30 percent of meat and milk, 31 percent of eggs, and 24 percent of wool came from private plots.[31] In all, their output amounted to nearly one-quarter of the total agricultural product.[32]

It is no wonder, then, that the present leadership continues to tolerate the existence of the private plot. Even though it is considered by the authorities to be a survival of the past that will die out with the achievement of abundance eventually produced by the collective and state farms, it is a necessary, if undesirable, feature of the agricultural scene for the present.

Many nonspecialists in the West associate the private plot exclusively with collective farmers. But such plots may also be provided to *sovkhoz* employees, professional people living in the countryside, and even urban workers, who frequently travel to the country to tend their plots. In fact, it has been estimated that some 30 million such plots exist, aiding the livelihood of over 100 million Soviet citizens.[33] Nikita Khrushchev, as a pensioner after his fall from power, tended such a plot at his country home near Moscow. He brags in his memoirs about the corn he managed to grow in his own private plot.[34] As a rule, the plots of urban workers are controlled by the factories and other institutions that employ them. An administrative measure instituted in 1974 to cut down on labor turnover provided that a worker who gives notice of quitting his job loses his right to his plot, no matter how long he may have tended it or what improvements he may have made on it.[35]

The most recent major innovation in agricultural organization is the emphasis since the early 1970s on "agro-industrial complexes" and other forms of interfarm cooperation. The creation of these institutions is intended to reduce overhead, enhance specialization, and increase output through economies of scale. By the end of the 1970s, more than nine thousand of them were in existence. These combinations are basically of two kinds: single service or single crop organizations and broader aggregations encompassing a range of crops and different stages of production. The latter type appear to have been created largely in connection with fruit, wine, meat, and vegetable production. They are most prevalent in the Moldavian republic, which is serving as a large-scale experiment in this new arrangement for administering agriculture. The Soviet leadership has given its full support to the development, and it can be expected that the two types of interfarm cooperation will be increasingly introduced around the country. One might wonder whether Soviet agriculture is not already encumbered by agricultural organizations that are too large and unwieldy; some Soviet agricultural specialists have urged caution in implementing the reform. But the continued commitment of the leaders to it suggests that for the present the emphasis will be on increased interfarm cooperation.[36]

A third area of Soviet agricultural efforts, in addition to exhortation and reorganization, involves investment. Until recently, it had been clear that the Soviet leadership was unwilling to commit to agriculture a level of investment necessary to guarantee significant improvement. But under Brezhnev genuine efforts to correct the investment imbalance were made. Between 1965 and 1980, for instance, the agricultural share of total investment rose from 28 to 38 percent.[37] Still, this investment has only involved a decrease in the traditional investment advantage of industry over agriculture. It has not brought agriculture up to a parity with industry. The increases in agricultural investment have been concentrated in the state rather than the collective sector. This means that the leadership probably will continue to favor the *sovkhoz* as well as continue to move toward the industrialization of the agricultural system. In any case, it is beginning to look as though the *kolkhoz*—at least in its traditional form—may be the wave of the past.

Investment in agriculture takes a number of forms, only several of which will be mentioned here. One of these is farm machinery. Production of tractors has increased considerably in recent years, but Soviet farming is still plagued by gross undermechanization. For instance, in the mid-1980s the Soviet Union had just over half as many tractors as the United States (2.6 million compared with 4.4 million) with an area of cultivated land one-third larger than that of the United States.[38] Moreover, because of the perennial lack of spare parts in the country, many of these Soviet tractors stand idle for long periods of time. Given these problems in the domestic economy, it might seem surprising that Soviet tractors are a popular export item. About one fifth of the production of the rugged Belarus tractor made in Minsk is for export not only to the other socialist countries but also to France, Canada, Great Britain, and the United States.

Another traditional problem in Soviet agriculture involves the production and use of mineral fertilizers. Soviet farmers have applied much less fertilizer in their farming than their Western counterparts typically do, and this is perennially reflected in lower outputs. In recent years the Soviets have made really impressive advances in fertilizer production. But in spite of these advances problems remain: The quality of the fertilizer is somewhat poorer than that typically produced in the West; packaging remains poor or nonexistent, sometimes allowing the fertilizer to deteriorate; the lack of roads or trucks to transport the fertilizer means that what is produced is not always used; and there seems to be a general resistance to its use among farmers.[39]

The Soviet government has become involved in a system of price supports or subsidies. In order to stimulate production, the state, in 1970, began to pay higher prices for certain agricultural goods while allowing the retail prices of these products to remain constant. The state has absorbed the resulting loss in what amounts to an agricultural subsidy. The economic solution to this matter would be simply to raise the retail price of food. Politically, this is a step the authorities are reluctant to take, given their much-touted comparisons between raging inflation in the West and stable prices at home. But the subsidy bill is large and growing. By 1983, the subsidies had reached the annual sum of 195 rubles per capita across the USSR, a figure larger than per capita expenditures for health and education. A single example of a subsidy shows the lengths to which the leadership has gone to keep from increasing prices: In 1983 the subsidy on one kilogram of meat amounted to 2.8 times the retail price of the meat.[40] With the projected increase in output of meat provided in the economic plans, the bill could grow considerably more. Soviet authorities have hoped to combat this growth through increases in productivity; but failing that, undesirable increases in retail prices may be the only answer.[41]

In spite of considerable effort and great infusions of money, agriculture remains a most pressing problem. While there are some positive sides to recent developments,[42] Soviet leaders cannot be pleased with the present situation. Where is Soviet agricultural policy falling short? Many Western observers, while acknowledging the problems of climate and land quality mentioned earlier, would suggest that the real culprit is the socialized nature of Soviet agricultural organization. Others, while not denying that this may be a contributing factor, see the problem as more complex. They believe that even in an essentially socialized system, considerable improvement in agricultural production could be achieved by (1) overcoming excessive centralization in planning and management; (2) adopting appropriate pricing policies (which means, essentially, higher agricultural prices); and (3) creating meaningful incentives for farm managers and workers.[43]

These proposals have been heard not just from Western analysts but from some Soviet scholars and leaders as well. Lately, a good deal of attention in the Soviet Union had been paid to Hungarian agriculture as a possible model for Soviet agricultural development. Hungary has adopted a flexible market-type system based on just those factors mentioned above: administrative decentralization, rational pricing, and meaningful incentives.[44] While Brezhnev himself recommended studying Hungarian methods,[45] it is not likely that the USSR would embrace the Hungarian system without considerable modification. For decentralization—whether economic, administrative, or political—seems to be anathema to Soviet political style.

Given all of the problems discussed in this chapter, it would be easy to conclude that the Soviet economic system is a failure. And not even the Soviet leadership would deny the existence of problems. But the question of success or failure depends upon ultimate objectives or values: What is *most* important? Some analysts suggest that while the Soviet economic system may be *economically* dysfunctional, it is *politically* functional. From this standpoint, the comments of former Soviet professor O. S. Ioffe are worth noting:

> The Soviet economy, built on the principle of state monopoly, supports state power better than any economic system that has ever existed. No other regime in history has had at its disposal material resources as rich as those held by the Soviet dictatorship, and hence no other regime has possessed such absolute political power. . . . In this regard, Soviet economic policy has never suffered a real failure. . . . The Soviet economy is inefficient only as a source of material well-being. This criterion, however, has nothing to do with real Soviet economic efficiency.[46]

NOTES

[1] Article 21 of the Principles of Civil Legislation of the USSR and the Union Republics, *Izvestiia,* Dec. 9, 1961, p. 2.

[2] A full list of the departments of the Secretariat may be found in Herwig Kraus, "The Apparatus of the Central Committee of the CPSU," *Radio Liberty Research,* No. 9/78, Jan. 5, 1978.

[3] Fyodor Kushnirsky reports that recently Gosplan has become more controlled by the Party bureaucracy than by its ostensible parent organization, the USSR Council of Ministers. Fyodor I. Kushnirsky, *Soviet Economic Planning, 1965–1980* (Boulder, CO: Westview Press, 1982), pp. xvi, 57–58, 81–83.

[4]On Soviet control organs generally see Jan S. Adams, *Citizen Inspectors in the Soviet Union: The People's Control Committee* (New York: Holt, Rinehart & Winston, 1977).

[5]See, for instance, the *Radio Liberty Dispatches* on the subject written by Christian Duevel and dated Jan. 7, 1975 (No. 23), Jan. 24, 1975 (No. 41), and Jan. 31, 1975 (No. 54). See also the report by Paul Wohl in *The Christian Science Monitor* (Boston), Feb. 20, 1975, p. 2.

[6]See, for instance, Harry Schwartz, *An Introduction to the Soviet Economy* (Columbus: OH: Chas. E. Merrill, 1968), pp. 56–68.

[7]*Pravda*, July 2, 1959, p. 2.

[8]*The New York Times,* Dec. 13, 1973, p. 12.

[9]For an enlightening discussion by a former insider of the political aspects of the debate over mathematical economics in the USSR, see Aron Katsenelinboigen, *Soviet Economic Thought and Political Power in the USSR* (New York: Pergamon, 1980).

[10]See the Program of the Communist Party of the Soviet Union, adopted Oct. 31, 1961, Part Two-IV, "The Tasks of the Party in the Field of National Relations." The copy of the Program used by the authors is from *The Road to Communism* (Moscow: Foreign Languages Publishing House, n.d.), pp. 559–63.

[11]For more details on the reform see Schwartz, *An Introduction,* pp. 59–64, and Gertrude E. Schroeder, "Soviet Economic Reform at an Impasse," *Problems of Communism,* 20, No. 4 (Jul.–Aug. 1971), 36–37. This analysis relies heavily on the latter source.

[12]A thorough analysis of the demise of the 1965 reform and the incentive system that replaced it may be found in Jan Adams, "The Present Soviet Incentive System," *Soviet Studies,* 32 (July 1980), 349–65.

[13]Olympiad S. Ioffe, "Law and Economy in the USSR," *Harvard Law Review,* 95, No. 7 (May 1982), p. 1623. See also Franklyn D. Holtzman, "The Performance of the Soviet Economy: Past, Present and Future," Occasional Paper No. 160, Kennan Institute for Advanced Russian Studies, 1982, p. 23.

[14]Holtzman, "The Performance," pp. 23–24.

[15]Holtzman, "The Performance," pp. 66–68; Ioffe, "Law and Economy," pp. 1624–1625; Alec Nove, *The Economics of Feasible Socialism,* (London: George Allen & Unwin, 1983), p. 113; Fyodor I. Kushnirsky, "The Limits of Soviet Economic Reform," *Problems of Communism,* 33, No. 4 (Jul.–Aug. 1984), pp. 33–43.

[16]See, for instance, the descriptions of the polemics in 1984 carried out in two Soviet journals: Elizabeth Teague, "Further Polemics over Economic Reform," *Radio Liberty Research,* No. 476/84, Dec. 12, 1984.

[17]On this point, see Boris Rumer's discussion of the opposition to Andropov's initiatives in this direction in 1983. Boris Rumer, "Structural Imbalance in the Soviet Economy," *Problems of Communism,* 33, No. 4 (Jul.–Aug. 1984), p. 25.

[18]Andreas Tenson, "Rates of Income Tax in the Soviet Union," *Radio Liberty Research,* No. 452/83, Dec. 1, 1983.

[19]Toli Welihozkiy, "Automobiles and the Soviet Economy," in *Soviet Economy in a Time of Change* (Washington, DC: Joint Economic Committee, Oct. 10, 1979), Vol. 1, p. 821.

[20]But the emigré economist Igor Birman, after a careful analysis, has concluded that Soviet budgets may have had quite considerable deficits in recent years. See his "The Financial Crisis in the USSR," *Soviet Studies,* 32 (Jan. 1980), 96, and his more complete study, *Secret Incomes of the Soviet State Budget* (The Hague: Martinus Nijhoff, 1981).

[21]See, for instance, Table 2, "Alternative Estimates of Soviet Military Expenditures, 1955–1976," in Abraham Becker, "The Meaning and Measure of Soviet Military Expenditure," in *Soviet Economy in a Time of Change,* Vol. 1, p. 362.

[22]Herbert Block, "Value and Burden of Soviet Defense," in *Soviet Economic Prospects for the Seventies* (Washington, DC: Joint Economic Committee, Jun. 27, 1973), p. 176.

[23]For a review of the 1976 CIA study and other analyses, see Becker, "The Meaning and Measure of Soviet Military Expenditure," pp. 352–66; on the 1983 CIA study, see *The New York Times,* Mar. 3, 1983, p. 1.

[24]A good review of several studies of Soviet defense spending, and of the methodological problems involved in this kind of assessment, is Donald F. Burton, "Estimating Soviet Defense Spending," *Problems of Communism,* 32, No. 2 (Mar.–Apr. 1983), pp. 85–93. See also a report on a

1984 NATO study which asserts that previous Western studies have exaggerated Soviet military spending. *The New York Times,* Jan. 30, 1984, p. A2. Some sources conclude that the CIA studies *under*estimate actual military spending. See, e.g., Igor Birman, "Professor Holtzman, the CIA, Soviet Military Expenditures and American Security," *Russia,* no. 10 (1984), 35–56.

[25]As quoted in Philip R. Pryde, *Conservation in the Soviet Union* (London: Cambridge University Press, 1972), p. 36.

[26]Holtzman, "The Performance," p. 19.

[27]Philip Hanson, "Recent Developments in Soviet Agriculture: A Statistical Note," *Radio Liberty Research,* No. 157/83, Apr. 18, 1983, p. 1.

[28]Rumer, "Structural Imbalance," p. 29, reports that "a stream of approximately 250 resolutions (by this author's count) flowed forth from the Central Committee and the USSR Council of Ministers during Brezhnev's 18 years at the helm."

[29]*The New York Times,* Aug. 28, 1984, p. A1.

[30]*Narkhoz,* 1982, pp. 188, 212.

[31]*Narkhoz,* 1982, p. 192.

[32]Karl-Eugen Wadekin, "Policies and Prospects for the Private Sector of Soviet Agriculture," *Radio Liberty Research,* no. 352/79, Nov. 23, 1979, p. 11.

[33]F.J.M. Feldbrugge, ed., *Encyclopedia of Soviet Law, I* (Leiden, the Netherlands: A. W. Sijthoff, 1973), p. 537; see also pp. 312–14.

[34]N. S. Khrushchev, *Khrushchev Remembers: The Last Testament,* ed. and trans. Strobe Talbott (Boston, MA: Little, Brown, 1974), p. 134.

[35]*Radio Liberty Research,* no. 188, May 2, 1975, p. 6.

[36]A thorough analysis of recent agricultural integration policies may be found in Robert F. Miller, "The Politics of Policy Implementation in the USSR: Soviet Policies on Agricultural Integration," *Soviet Studies,* 32 (Apr. 1980), 171–94.

[37]Rumer, "Structural Imbalance," p. 29.

[38]*Narkhoz,* 1982, p. 202; U.S. Department of Agriculture, *Agricultural Statistics,* 1979 (Washington, DC: U.S. Government Printing Office, 1979), p. 427.

[39]Keith Bush, "Soviet Agriculture: Ten Years Under New Management," *Radio Liberty Research Paper,* May 23, 1975, pp. 14–15.

[40]Gale Johnson and Karen McConnell Brooks, *Prospects for Soviet Agriculture in the 1980s* (Bloomington, IN: Indiana University Press, 1983), p. 202; Rumer, "Structural Imbalance," p. 30.

[41]Ibid., pp. 18–21. On increases after 1973 see David M. Schoonover, "Soviet Agricultural Policies," in *Soviet Economy in a Time of Change,* Vol. 2, p. 110.

[42]For instance, "an important accomplishment of the past three decades has been that the threat of famine no longer exists in the USSR." Johnson and Brooks, "Prospects," p. 200.

[43]On these points see, for example, Johnson and Brooks, "Prospects," p. 198; Rumer, "Structural Imbalance," p. 30.

[44]See, on these and other aspects of the Hungarian system (and Soviet attention devoted to them), the following: *The New York Times,* Oct. 19, 1982, p. A2; *Radio Liberty Research,* no. 89/83, Feb. 22, 1983, and no. 116/83, Mar. 14, 1983.

[45]*The New York Times,* Oct. 18, 1982, p. A2.

[46]Ioffe, "Law and Economy," p. 1625.

SELECTED BIBLIOGRAPHY

BARTOCCI, ENZO, and FRANCO FERRAROTTI, *Industrial Relations in the USSR.* Lexington, MA: Lexington Books, 1975.

BERGMANN, THEODORE, *Farm Policies in Socialist Countries.* Lexington, MA: Lexington Books, 1975.

BERGSON, ABRAM, and HERBERT S. LEVINE, eds., *The Soviet Economy Toward the Year 2000*. London: George Allen & Unwin, 1983.

BERLINER, JOSEPH, *Factory and Manager in the USSR*. Cambridge, MA: Harvard University Press, 1957.

BIRMAN, IGOR, *Secret Incomes of Soviet State Budget*. The Hague: Martinus Nijhoff, 1981.

CLARKE, ROGER A., and DUBRAVKO J.I. MATKO, *Soviet Economic Facts, 1917–1981*, 2nd ed. New York: St. Martin's Press, 1983.

COLLINS, JOHN M., *U.S.–Soviet Military Balance: Concepts and Capabilities, 1960–1980*. New York: McGraw-Hill, 1980.

FRERIS, ANDREW, *The Soviet Industrial Enterprise: Theory and Practice*. New York: St. Martin's Press, 1984.

GOLDMAN, MARSHALL I., *U.S.S.R. in Crisis: The Failure of an Economic System*. New York: W. W. Norton, 1983.

GREGORY, PAUL, and ROBERT C. STUART, *Soviet Economic Structure and Performance*, 2nd ed. New York: Harper and Row, 1981.

HEDLAND, STEFAN, *Crisis in Soviet Agriculture*. New York: St. Martin's Press, 1984.

HOLZMAN, FRANKLYN D., *Financial Checks on Soviet Defense Spending*. Lexington, MA: Lexington Books, 1975.

HUNTER, HOLLAND, ed., *The Future of the Soviet Economy: 1978–1985*. Boulder, CO: Westview, 1978.

HUTCHINGS, RAYMOND, *The Soviet Budget*. Albany, NY: SUNY Press, 1983.

——, *Soviet Economic Development*. Albany, NY: SUNY Press, 1982.

JOHNSON, D. GALE, and KAREN M. BROOKS, *Prospects for Soviet Agriculture in the 1980's*. Bloomington, IN: Indiana University Press, 1983.

KUSHNIRSKY, FYODOR I., *Soviet Economic Planning. 1965–1980*. Boulder, CO: Westview, 1982.

LEE, WILLIAM T., *The Estimation of Soviet Defense Expenditures, 1955–1975: An Unconventional Approach*. New York: Holt, Rinehart & Winston, 1977.

MILLAR, JAMES R., *The ABCs of Soviet Socialism*. Urbana, IL: University of Illinois Press, 1981.

NATO-Directorate of Economic Affairs, *The USSR in the 1980's: Economic Growth and the Role of Foreign Trade*. Brussels, Belgium: NATO-Directorate of Economic Affairs, 1978.

NOVE, ALEC, *The Economics of Feasible Socialism*. London: George Allen & Unwin, 1983.

——, *Political Economy and Soviet Socialism*. London: George Allen & Unwin, 1979.

——, *The Soviet Economic System*. London: George Allen & Unwin Ltd., 1977.

PRYDE, PHILIP R., *Conservation in the Soviet Union*. London: Cambridge University Press, 1972.

ROSEFIELDE, STEVEN, *False Science: Understanding the Soviet Arms Buildup*. New Brunswick, NJ: Transaction Books, 1982.

SCHAPIRO, LEONARD, and JOSEPH GODSON, eds., *The Soviet Worker: Illusions and Reality*. New York: St. Martin's Press, 1981.

Soviet Economy in a Time of Change (prepared for the Joint Economic Committee, U.S. Congress). Washington, DC: U.S. Government Printing Office, 2 vols., Oct. 10, 1979.

YOUNG, BRIGITTA, *Prospects for Soviet Grain Production*. Boulder, CO: Westview, 1983.

10

THE SOVIET CITIZEN:
Worker and Consumer

In the previous chapter we discussed economic operations, achievements, and problems in the Soviet system. Attention to the economic situation of the Soviet citizen was intentionally omitted in order to give it separate treatment in this chapter. Here we take a look at basic aspects of the individual's economic and social status: work, remuneration, standard of living, and typical consumer problems, with particular attention to housing. The concluding section of the chapter examines three areas of citizen preferences that are related to the individual's status as worker and consumer: developments regarding the birth rate, labor turnover, and internal population migration. In each of these areas citizen preferences conflict to some extent with the desires of the political authorities. These conflicts constitute long-term problems for the political leadership.

In an analysis such as this one, comparisons of the economic situation of Soviet citizens with those of other countries, especially the United States, are desirable and useful. The reader should be aware, however, of the problems such comparisons present. In many cases the comparison is best made in terms of money. But the official relationship between the Soviet ruble and the U.S. dollar is a very misleading one. The ruble is not "hard" currency; that is, unlike the U.S. or Canadian dollar, the British pound, the West German mark, the French franc, the Dutch guilder, and other Western currencies, it is not freely convertible on the open market. Although some rubles are smuggled out of the country and may be bought in the West (at lower prices than the official rate), rubles are not supposed to be available outside of the USSR. The rate of exchange, therefore, can be and is set by the Soviet authorities at a level as advantageous as possible to the Soviet Union.

As of January 1986, the official rate of exchange was 100 U.S. dollars = about 76 rubles (a ruble is made up of 100 kopeks); thus, a ruble at that time was worth about $1.32. This dollar rate against the ruble is much higher than in recent years and reflects the relatively strong international position of the dollar against other "hard" currencies. But most analysts agree that this rate is still considerably inflated in favor of the ruble. The Soviet authorities are able to maintain this rate because the sale of dollars for rubles is illegal under Soviet law. There is, however, a thriving black market for dollars, the rate being approximately four to five rubles to the dollar—considerably above the official rate. Just as the official rate is depressed with regard to the dollar, though, the black-market rate is somewhat inflated. The reason is that the dollar and other "hard" currencies are subject to strong demand pressures, for they can be used to buy items in stores that the Soviet government maintains for foreigners and Soviet citizens who have a legitimate right to possess foreign currency. The attraction of these "hard currency" stores is that they sell items that are either difficult to obtain or totally unavailable in the stores where rubles are the medium of exchange. Thus, if one could determine the "real" value of the ruble, it would no doubt fall somewhere between these two figures. But no level for the "real" value of the ruble is generally accepted.

A second, less tangible problem of comparison involves the consideration of quality. A single measure of the differences in quality of goods available in the Soviet Union and in the West would obviously be very difficult to calculate. No such measure is available. Generally speaking, most people familiar with the situation agree that the quality of most Soviet consumer goods is below the typical level in the West. Thus, the reader should keep qualitative considerations in mind when consumer goods and services are compared in the course of the following discussion.

WORK

Of the total Soviet population of approximately 275 million, an excess of 115 million are classified as "workers" and "employees." But these categories include the state sector only. When collective farmers and persons employed in the small private sector are added, the figure totals more than 135 million. About three quarters of those employed are involved in production, with the remainder in nonproduction or services. As in other industrialized or industrializing countries, the service industries have been accounting for an increasing percentage of the labor force in recent years. But the Soviet proportion is still much lower than in the United States, where some two thirds of working people were in the service industries in 1980. The disparity is even greater in the percentage of the labor force in farming: Over one fifth of the total Soviet labor force is in farming, as against less than one twentieth in the United States.[1]

The proportion of women in the labor force is high: 51 percent in 1982 compared with about 42 percent in the United States. As in the United States, certain types of employment are considered "man's work" and "woman's work," although the fields may not be exactly the same in the two countries. A small proportion of women work in construction and transportation, whereas retail trade, banking and insurance, and the health professions are overwhelmingly populated by women. In most areas, however, it appears that women are underrepresented in management and supervisory positions. As noted in Chapter 7, the paucity of women in the upper reaches of the Party and state apparatuses is even more striking. Only one woman has ever been on the Party Politburo.

The conclusions one can draw about the status of women in professional life, then, are decidedly mixed. The proportion of women in the labor force is high, and in certain professions their numbers far surpass those of women in like professions in the West. The most obvious example is the medical profession. Nearly 70 percent of Soviet doctors are women, as against about 12 percent in the United States. Moreover, women hold 59 percent of all positions in the Soviet Union occupied by specialists with either higher or intermediate education. But as suggested, women are generally underrepresented in supervisory positions.[2] And this subordinate job status is reflected in earning power. Alastair McAuley, in his study of working women in the USSR, came to the conclusion that, overall, women's gross earnings in the 1970s were 60 to 65 percent of men's earnings. He found that for the most part these disparities could be attributed to the kinds of occupational segregation described.[3]

Part of this is no doubt due to the traditional dominance of men in leadership posts. But it may also be attributed to the differing roles played by men and women in Soviet domestic life. One Soviet specialist on family matters determined that a husband's workweek (including housework) is about fifty hours and that of the working wife is eighty hours. Another speaks of women having "literally a double working day—seven to eight hours on their jobs, and between four and six at home." Soviet experts associate this heavy burden with a variety of social problems the country is now facing, including an increasing divorce rate and a dropping birth rate in many parts of the country. One writer has even concluded that women are "rebelling" against the status quo of the "patriarchal family, with complete and unconditional primacy of the husband." A manifestation of this rebellion has been the appearance of feminist literature in the unauthorized publications of the dissident community.[4]

And even the official Soviet press has lately allowed the expression of remarkably frank views on the subject—the assertion, for instance, that a man's refusal to share household chores amounts to "moral parasitism and sponging."[5]

Women are accorded certain benefits under Soviet law. Article 122 of the Constitution prohibits employment discrimination against women, and the criminal law provides sanctions for refusal to hire a woman because of pregnancy. Provisions of the labor law exempt women from heavy work, work in unhealthy circumstances, underground work, and, in most cases, night work.[6]

In spite of these provisions, it appears that in fact women carry on their share of heavy, unpleasant work. Soviet authorities have not published hard information on this subject in recent years, but figures from the 1970s indicate that nearly half of all jobs requiring mainly physical labor were held by women.[7] And even the casual observer in the Soviet Union is bound to note women performing unusually heavy tasks. The frequent sight of women shoveling snow into a piece of snow-removal equipment while the driver—a male—sits and smokes, or the railroad repair gang made up entirely of female laborers are pictures that make the foreigner do a double take. Even legislative committees of the Supreme Soviet were moved in 1975 to object to the unhygienic conditions some women experience in doing heavy factory work. The committees also called for an end to required overtime and advocated the establishment of more child-care facilities.[8] At the same time the government adopted a law lowering by five years (to age fifty) the age at which women performing one of the more arduous production jobs, that of machinist, will be allowed to retire.[9] This concern for female labor is justified on further grounds than a generalized desire to improve working conditions for women. The economy depends greatly on its womanpower, and that reliance will increase, if anything, in coming years.

While the normal working week for most of the labor force is a five-day week with two days off, about one sixth of workers put in a six-day week. In a sense, the six-day week is the legally mandated norm, because paid vacations are figured on the basis of the six-day week. The minimum paid vacation for all workers (except *kolkhozniki*) is fifteen days—two weeks and three days as calculated according to the six-day work week. This vacation time increases with one's length of service. A seven-hour workday goes with a six-day workweek. Those working fewer days usually work 8.25 hours a day. The average workweek in 1982 was 40.6 hours, several hours more than in the U.S.

This average workweek does not include overtime, which may amount to a considerable number of hours in some Soviet industries. In certain fields, in fact, it is clear that production plans would not be fulfilled without the use of overtime. Soviet workers are paid straight wage rates for overtime rather than time-and-a-half or some other form of enhanced compensation, as is common in the United States. Under Soviet law, overtime work is supposed to be allowed only as an exceptional measure and only with the consent of the trade unions. In practice it appears to be a much more common occurrence than the law suggests. As noted earlier, there have been complaints about requiring women to work overtime, and it would appear that trade unions are normally acquiescent on the matter of overtime work.

If there are complaints by workers about overtime work, this is not the only area of job dissatisfaction of which Soviet leaders are aware. A revival of sociological research in the USSR since the 1960s has pinpointed problems in many areas of Soviet life, including that of satisfaction with one's job. A number of studies have uncovered quite significant findings on this question. For one thing, workers appear increasingly to be expressing dissatisfaction with the boredom and lack of creativity of assembly-line work. This, of course, is not a uniquely Soviet phenomenon but has been reported recently in numerous Western countries as well. Other findings indicate that (at least at the factories where the surveys were carried out), there are dissatisfactions with unsanitary working conditions, with inferior working equipment, with the hectic organization of factory life, and with the phenomenon of "storming"—that is, the practice of crash production at the end of a month, quarter, or year in order to meet plan targets. Satisfaction or dissatisfaction with wages, although an important factor, is by no means completely determinative with regard to job satisfaction.

Another area of criticism discussed in one of the Soviet sociological studies is "socialist competition." It was started in the 1920s under Stalin and recently was revived under Brezhnev. Following the examples of "shock workers" and others with excellent production records, individuals and work collectives "voluntarily" revised their production plans upward and compete against others having similar work assignments. This is designed to increase economic efficiency and production and is not inconsistent with other practices in Soviet political socialization (see Chapter 4). The campaign has received much publicity in the press since 1971, including personal endorsements by Brezhnev and others. But it apparently has not been uniformly well received at the factory level. In one study the following answers were among those received to questions about socialist competition: "It exists only on paper"; "Our brigade doesn't have competition; there is just a daily quota we have to fulfill"; "The whole thing is just a fiction in our factory."

The official figures on socialist competition in the factory studied indicated that 81 percent of the workers participated in individual competition, whereas the finding of the study's survey was 13 percent. The authors of the study ask why the factory management bothers to concoct such figures and send them to the Ministry, but the reason is quite clear: A campaign has been mounted and all participants must conform to its dictates. The authors condemn the "formalism" of inventing figures on socialist competition, concluding that "the high figures in the records create the illusion of well-being" so that one will say "why take steps to change things if everything is in order?"[10] Clearly this kind of "formalism" is not limited to the one factory in the study.

Nor is the matter one that affects factory production alone. "Campaignism" is a part of Soviet life and can be observed in such widely diverse areas as economics, law enforcement, artistic and cultural policy, and many others. Because of the Soviet power structure and the limitations on criticism of high officials, some policies handed down from on high are slavishly carried out (or made to appear to be fulfilled, as in the case of the invented figures just described) without regard for the consequences in individual cases. In his memoirs Nikita Khrushchev describes the problem very accurately:

> Unfortunately, under our Soviet way of life, it sometimes happens that people overreact in implementing the recommendation of a man who holds a high post; and a new measure which starts out as an improvement goes too far.[11]

When a policy decision is said to come *s verkhu* (from above) implementation of that decision, actual or apparent, is assured.

Given the taut Soviet labor market, it is understandable that the authorities should turn to devices such as socialist competition to increase production. As they themselves have said, if growth in output can no longer be achieved by the introduction of new labor resources, it must come from the increased productivity of the present labor supply. Part of the productivity increase can be achieved by providing workers with improved tools, technology, and automation, which are being introduced where possible. But the authorities also constantly exhort workers to increase production on their own, and the campaign for the socialist competition is part of this general effort.

Another aspect of the drive for greater work productivity is the renewed emphasis on Stakhanovism. Alexei Stakhanov was a Donets Basin coal miner who, in August 1935, was reported to have cut 102 tons of coal by hand in a single work shift, about 14 times the regular quota of 7 tons. This achievement, which appears to have been at least partially staged by providing Stakhanov with all manner of auxiliary aid, was given wide publicity. Thus began the Stakhanovite movement, involving the recognition of similar achievements in other fields of work and the raising of output norms for regular workers. Stakhanov became an instant celebrity. He was admitted to the Party by a special decree without having to serve candidate status and was elected to the Supreme Soviet. Books were published in his name. After World War II much less attention was given to the Stakhanovite movement. But in 1970 a revival of sorts took place when Stakhanov, then sixty-four years old, was designated "Hero of Socialist Labor," the highest civilian award. And in 1985, the fiftieth anniversary of the Stakhanovite movement was celebrated with a reception honoring veteran Stakhanovites at Central

Committee headquarters, hosted by Party Secretary Gorbachev. Media coverage emphasized the relevance of Stakhanovism in Gorbachev's drive for labor productivity.[12]

It was mentioned earlier that trade-union permission is required for overtime work but that such permission did not appear to be a serious obstacle for a factory's management to overcome. This fact is related to the place and role of trade unions in the Soviet system. During the latter years of the tsars, unions had come to be positively associated with the goals for which workers were striving, and so their retention became a necessary part of postrevolutionary Russia. But in the early 1920s the unions became the focus of a struggle that could have challenged Party control,[13] and before the decade was over trade unions had been effectively neutralized as an independent force. It was declared that there was no basic antagonism between unions and management because the latter was representative of the state, which was a dictatorship of the proletariat, that is, of the workers. Management and unions were to work hand in hand, with all decision-making power in areas related to production on the side of management and the union playing a subordinate role. Under this kind of philosophy, it is clear that the ultimate weapon of trade unions of the West—the strike—is strictly forbidden.[14]

This is not to say that unions have no role to play. As John Hazard has shown, the unions have come to perform some of the functions normally associated with a Ministry of Labor (which was abolished in the USSR in 1933).[15] Thus, the observance of safety rules is controlled by trade-union committees, as is much of the social-insurance system. In addition, the grievance procedure mechanism, by which an individual worker may appeal decisions of management that affect him adversely, involves a commission for labor disputes made up of representatives of the local union and management. In such situations it appears that, at least on occasion, the unions genuinely attempt to support the worker's point of view.

Unions also serve as a kind of social focus for workers' lives, managing the factory "club" and other social and cultural events. Twenty-one large national unions are affiliated in one central organization, the All-Union Central Council of Trade Unions (ACCTU). Workers are not required to join a union, but the overwhelming majority do. There are more than 130 million trade unionists in the USSR, making the ACCTU the largest mass organization in the country.[16] Membership dues amount to 1 percent of a worker's wages. Membership confers on the worker some minor advantages in the social-insurance system as well as payment or partial payment for stays at health and vacation resorts maintained by the factory.

But the unions have only an advisory voice in matters of output and efficiency, which are controlled by management; they have no role in setting wage rates, which are established by the government. References by Soviet spokesmen to unions as "a force to be reckoned with"[17] should be considered in the light of such constraints. It is no wonder that the leadership of the

ACCTU is not considered a position of great political significance. The transfer of Alexander Shelepin in 1967 from a Party secretaryship to head of the trade unions was seen by all observers as a clear demotion, and it presaged his ultimate removal from political power a few years later.

One of the benefits provided by some of the larger labor unions in the United States is a supplemental unemployment benefit. No unemployment compensation of any kind is provided in the Soviet Union because unemployment was declared to have been abolished in 1930. Each year the Central Statistical Administration reports full employment. In an overall sense this is undoubtedly true, and it is much to the credit of the Soviet system that a consistently high level of employment has been achieved. The feeling of lack of worth based on being unable to find work is not a recurrent feature of the lives of large numbers of Soviet citizens. In many parts of the country there is a critical shortage of workers, giving rise to a policy of encouraging retired workers to return to productive labor.

But it appears that in some parts of the country there are more workers in certain job categories than there are jobs—workers who do not choose to move to less desirable parts of the country where jobs in their specialty would be available. In the West such workers would be classified as unemployed, but in the USSR, since vacant jobs await them, they are not.[18] Aside from this, there is so-called "frictional unemployment," that is, workers who are between jobs because of lack of knowledge that jobs exist or lack of knowledge by employers that workers are available. Time lost in such situations has usually averaged about one month in recent years, but a worker receives only two weeks' severance pay. Because of the financial hardships associated with such periods of unemployment, some Soviet writers have cautiously proposed in recent years that some form of unemployment benefit might be introduced.

Wages and Other Benefits

By 1984 the average monthly wage or salary in the Soviet Union was about 185 rubles, a rise of more than 40 rubles or more than 30 percent from 10 years earlier.[19] The fact that this is an *average* wage means, of course, that not everyone is paid this much. As a matter of fact, income disparities in the Soviet Union are quite great. The minimum wage, increased during the 1970s from 60 rubles to 70 rubles per month, is the floor for a wide-ranging wage system.

Ever since the early Stalin period, any notion of equality with regard to wage rates has been clearly disavowed. "Equalitarianism has nothing in common with Marxist Socialism," said Stalin in 1931. Thereafter much steeper wage differentials than had theretofore existed were introduced.[20] In official Soviet wage figures one can observe considerable differences in wage payments among various branches of the economy. Thus, workers in the building industry average about 20 percent more than the average wage;

those in transportation 18 percent more; those in industry 10 percent more. If one examines certain subcategories of these branches of the economy, the salaries are even more impressive: Engineering-technical workers in construction receive 32 percent more than the average wage, and workers in water transport 42 percent more.

There are, of course, a number of categories of workers that receive less than the average wage. The less-favored sectors include agriculture (11 percent less than the average wage), retail trade and housing and communal services (23 percent), and health and social security (27 percent less). And within these general sectors wide disparities may exist. For instance, among agricultural workers, agronomists and other technical personnel receive 16 percent more than the average wage; whereas office personnel receive 24 percent less than the average.[21]

In regard to these disparities, it must be noted that since Stalin's death in 1953 the range of wage differentials has been gradually narrowed. People receiving lower incomes are now living much better relative to high-salaried citizens than was the case in the past. This improvement is in part attributable to the rise in the minimum wage, which has increased from 22 rubles a month in 1950 to 70 rubles a month. Generally speaking, large increases at the lower end of the wage scale have been accompanied by relatively modest increases at the upper end. The group that has benefited most from these developments is the farmers. Although a farmer's income is still low relative to that of the typical city worker, the average wage in agriculture rose faster in the decades of the 1950s and 1960s than in any other branch of the economy. This improvement was accomplished not only through straight pay raises but also by means of converting collective farmers into higher-paid state farmers and changing the occupational structure of agriculture in the direction of more high-paying jobs.[22]

The wage levels discussed so far involve only *legal* money earnings, of course. To judge from conversations with Soviet citizens, articles in the press, and reports of court cases a considerable number of Soviet citizens manage to supplement their regular income by a wide variety of illegal or improper practices, including hiring out for private business the state-owned truck one drives, short-weighting the product one sells and keeping the difference, hiding one's actual income from driving a taxi, and many others. John Scott explains how the taxi driver may supplement his regular wage:

> His [Scott's taxi driver at one point in his travels] salary is 75 rubles a month, plus about 25 in bonuses and premiums, for working five eight-hour shifts a week. He shares his Volga with two other drivers, and they decide the shifts themselves. He gets no cut on the meter. "But . . . er . . . I usually net 500 to 600 rubles a month take-home pay." I expressed my astonishment, and he explained a bit awkwardly: "You see, by plan each taxi is supposed to bring into the base 23 rubles per eight-hour shift on the meter take. But, actually, if you do a good job—if the customers are satisfied—you bring in much more. So we

turn in maybe 25 or 26 rubles a shift—enough to get an overfulfillment of plan bonus—and well, we don't throw the rest away. After all, to give it to the base would upset their planning and make all sorts of trouble." It was clear that Soviet taxi drivers constitute a sort of new aristocracy.[23]

Such practices as these are illegal, of course. They constitute "stealing of state property" (Articles 89–96 of the RSFSR Criminal Code), and if committed on an especially large scale they can result in the death penalty (Article 93.1). Whether or not such harsh measures have cut down on the practice is hard to determine. The Soviet legal literature and the media continue to give it attention, however, and Soviet emigres claim that increasing numbers of well-educated citizens are leaving the learned professions for the more lucrative rewards of "semilegal private enterprise."

Such developments are part of a significant and apparently growing "second economy" in the USSR. This second economy embraces many aspects of the shortage-prone consumer sector of the regular economy and takes many forms: privately arranged home repairs, "moonlighting" for pay by physicians, acquiring state-owned gasoline for use in private cars, buying and selling items on the black market such as Western-made blue jeans, and literally hundreds of other common practices.

How extensive is the second economy? In spite of the considerable attention devoted to the phenomenon both in the Soviet Union and in the West, reliable estimates of its magnitude do not exist. But observers appear to agree that it touches, in one way or another, the great majority of families in the country. James Millar states that "the attainment of a comfortable standard of living in the Soviet Union depends as much on reciprocity as on markets." By reciprocity he means "an exchange of goods or services which is conducted on the basis of relationships other than those of the marketplace." And the ability to participate in such exchanges depends upon one's access to scarce commodities, whether they be caviar, high-quality vodka, theater tickets, or countless other goods and services that can be provided to others for reciprocal favors.[24] Apparently, millions of persons in the USSR take advantage of such access. The sheer volume of this activity suggests that some aspects of the second economy are tolerated and even encouraged by the authorities. On the basis of an analysis and cataloging of a wide variety of "shadow economy" practices in the USSR, Professor F.J.M. Feldbrugge foresees "a gradual extension of the area of toleration for activities which are not considered threatening to the system.[25]

There are other, perfectly legal, ways to supplement one's income. Such supplements can contribute significantly to the wide disparity in real income among Soviet citizens. Needless to say, the supplements largely go to the more favored members of Soviet society. University professors are among the best-paid people in the country. A full professor holding a doctorate and working at a university receives 450 rubles a month. If he or she heads a department, 50 rubles more is received. A scientist or scholar is better off if he can maintain an affiliation with a university *and* a research institute, a fairly common practice. In such a case, a person is entitled to one-and-a-half times one's rate of pay. For instance, a scholar who holds the directorship of a research institute might receive 500 rubles a month for that position and also receive 250 rubles for half-time as a university professor.

The most elite group of scholars are the few hundred who belong to the USSR Academy of Sciences. Full members of the Academy are entitled (in addition to whatever salary they may earn from their regular jobs) to 500 rubles a month tax free for life and a chauffeur-driven automobile. Corresponding members receive 250 rubles per month and the automobile. There are also hundreds of other full and corresponding members of the republican academies of science who receive monthly stipends of 350 and 175 rubles, respectively.[26]

It is no wonder, then, that advanced degrees are valuable commodities in the Soviet Union. It is said that some well-placed Party and governmental officials have arranged for scholars to write dissertations for them, thus providing the backup security of an academic career to the uncertain future of a political career.[27] A former insider in the Party apparatus reported that at the time when he had direct knowledge of the situation (the 1970s), 63 percent of the CPSU Central Committee members and 73 percent of union-republic central committee members as well as 56 percent of responsible officials of the state apparatus held research degrees, with the implication that many of these degrees were based on dissertations written for the recipients.[28]

The middle level of government and Party officials (republican-level minister, USSR deputy minister, department heads in the CC, CPSU, and so on) earn salaries roughly equivalent to that of a university professor but are not eligible for affiliation with a research institute and, therefore, extra pay. Higher-level government and Party officials (heads of republican government and Party organizations, USSR ministers, Central Committee secretaries) earn 600 rubles to 800 rubles per month, and the highest officials—the Party General Secretary, the Prime Minister, and the Chairman of the Presidium—receive 900 rubles or more.[29]

Nor are these pay levels limited only to scholars and high government and Party workers. Many performers, actors, and artists command high salaries. For example, the foremost television news announcer was reported in 1980 to be receiving the equivalent of $1500 per month, about six times the starting pay of a beginning reporter.[30] Mervyn Matthews has estimated that the elite in terms of income (400 to 500 rubles per month and more) amounts to some 227,000 people, about 0.2 percent of the labor force.[31]

For the really important members of the elite, however, the base salary is only the beginning of material advantages. Many important employees in the political apparatus are entitled to extra material privileges of various kinds through a system that goes under the general name *kremlyovka* (from the word Kremlin). It includes special dining rooms, food stores, and snack bars in selected important Party and government buildings, at which all manner of high-quality food, drink, and other products are available at greatly reduced prices to the select few who are entitled to receive purchase vouchers. As Konstantin Simis explains it: "People with access to the *kremlyovka* are divided into two categories: those in the first are given monthly vouchers of 80 rubles, and those in the second in the amount of 140 rubles. . . . With the 80 rubles worth of vouchers . . . an official can buy enough food for a month (including caviar and other expensive delicacies such as brandy, wine, and high-grade vodka)."[32]

Large numbers of high state and Party workers also receive an extra month's pay, the so-called "thirteenth month," to cover vacation expenses. The same people may also be eligible for admission to special sanatoria and rest homes maintained for the elite, which they attend free or at greatly reduced cost. And medical care for them is in superior facilities maintained by the Fourth Directorate of the Ministry of Health.

Finally, any politician of considerable importance—as well as a number of scientists, scholars, artists, and others in good repute with the regime—is likely to be a member of the USSR Supreme Soviet, a republican supreme soviet, or both. Membership in the first of these carries a monthly salary of 200 rubles; the second pays 120 rubles a month.[33] Each deputy to such a legislative session or on legislative business receives free hotel accommodations. And each deputy to a soviet, at whatever level, receives free transportation anywhere within the jurisdiction of that soviet by any means of public transportation except taxi. Needless to say, the duties associated with Supreme Soviet membership are extremely light. This payment can be looked upon, therefore, as a further advantage bestowed on certain favored members of Soviet society.

Official position in the Soviet Union carries with it not only power but also the opportunity for additional material advantage. This is achieved in countless ways. The higher senior officials in the Party and state apparatus are entitled to *dachas*, or country homes, maintained by the state. The most luxurious of these go to the top people in the Party hierarchy. Travel expenses for senior officials on official business are covered by local Party organs in the areas where the travel takes place. Officials "buying" things on such trips apparently do not have to pay for them, as this cost is also absorbed by local organizations. It is said that officials receiving gifts on trips abroad may keep them for their own use rather than turning them over to the state.[34]

Is the disparity in income and wealth as great as in the countries of the West? Certainly not. Occasionally one reads about a Soviet "millionaire," but such reports are usually in connection with the trial of someone accused of illegal economic activity. The opportunities for huge accumulations of wealth through capital gains, real-estate operations, ownership of large manufacturing plants, and the like simply do not exist. But in the Soviet context, that of a country that began with a conscious effort to eliminate the vast gulf between the rich and the poor, the disparity is surprisingly great. In spite of a number of leveling features of the Soviet system—such as free education, inexpensive medical care, cheap public transportation, and low-rent housing—money means a great deal. If seventy years of Soviet power have eliminated classes from the scene, then there still exist several "levels" of population, based on income, wealth, and comfort, and the levels are easily discernible. To some extent the advantages enjoyed by the higher-income citizens can be passed on to offspring. High income appears to be positively correlated with high education, and the children of higher-educated Soviet citizens are more likely to receive higher education than are the children of less-educated citizens. For the less-able child of the richer family there is a thriving system of private tutoring to aid in the passing of university entrance examinations. The reported fees are such that few families of modest income could afford to pay the price.

The pension system is consistent with the principle of differing income levels in that it is based on the income earned during the productive lives of pensioners. Pensions are paid to retired and disabled workers as well as to dependent survivors of income earners. To qualify for full old-age pensions, men must have worked for at least twenty-five years and have reached the age of sixty; for women the respective figures are twenty and fifty-five years. For both sexes the age limits are lowered for those who are in certain arduous occupations or who have worked in certain inclement regions of the country. The size of the pension is based on a percentage of the worker's average pay during high-earning years, with the minimum pension set in 1981 at 50 rubles a month and the maximum at 120 rubles. But personal pensions may be awarded to distinguished citizens, and these may exceed the maximum, as may the pensions of certain other categories of workers, such as scientists and test pilots. Pensions are tax free, and because of the tight labor market, pensioners are permitted to work while drawing part or all of their pension allowances.

Temporarily disabled workers receive 100 percent of their base pay, while workers with long-term or permanent disabilities receive a percentage of base pay calculated according to their number of years of work. Pensions for survivors of income earners are calculated on the same basis as those for permanently disabled workers.

Until 1965, collective farmers were not covered by state pensions. Collective farmers could have their own "mutual-aid" pensions, but only a small percentage of eligible *kolkhozniki* were actually receiving funds. Finally, in that year, the social-insurance principle was extended to collective farms. Although the pension benefits of *kolkhozniki* are somewhat lower than those of other workers, this extension means that virtually all workers in the country are covered by the state pension system.

In terms of adequacy of coverage, however, even Soviet sources have begun to raise serious questions. An authoritative source stated in 1978 that "the level of well-being of non-ablebodied citizens in our country has begun to fall perceptibly behind the living standard of the population as a whole . . . The current scale of pensions requires serious readjustment." One of the main reasons for this is that pension levels have increased only slightly since 1956, although overt and hidden inflation has eaten away at fixed incomes.[35]

With an average monthly wage of 185 rubles, how well off is the typical Soviet consumer? This can be looked upon in various ways. By any calculation, it appears that the minimum family budget for a family of four well exceeds that figure.[36] In other words, in a family where the principle provider earns only the average wage or less, the working wife is not just a convenience but a necessity. This is no doubt part of the explanation as to why a higher percentage of married women in the Soviet Union maintain full-time jobs than is the case in Western countries.

Although Soviet authorities have not adopted the concept of a "poverty level," such as has been done in the United States and other countries of the West, there has been some talk about the "underprovisioning" *(maloobespechennost')* of some segments of the population. A careful Western study published by Mervyn Matthews in 1985 attempted to analyze the dimensions of the problem. Using categories comprising a "minimum budget" devised by Soviet scholars and his own analysis of Soviet data, Matthews came to the surprising conclusion that "the 'poor,' as defined by Soviet statistical parameters, must have numbered no less than two fifths of the entire Soviet population in 1981."[37]

A relatively high percentage of the family budget goes for food. Official Soviet figures for 1984 on the budget for industrial workers give the percentage spent on food as 30 percent.[38] Other Soviet figures, as well as Western estimates, however, suggest that the proportion is considerably higher, perhaps 50 percent or more.[39] Official estimates on food as a proportion of the U.S. family budget for the same period are lower, ranging between about 21 percent and 31 percent, depending upon the level of income.[40]

On the other hand, the typical Soviet family will spend a considerably smaller proportion of its budget than the American family on such things as housing, transportation, and medical care.* What this all adds up to is a substantially different pattern of spending in the Soviet Union, based on a different social and economic setting. It is time, therefore, to introduce another aspect of the Soviet worker's compensation not yet discussed. This is what official Soviet publications refer to as "payments and benefits from the social consumption funds," which were said to amount to more than 75 rubles per worker per month for 1984.[41] This fund covers both direct

---

*Even approximately comparable data on these matters are extremely hard to find. But as a rough comparison on housing, official Soviet figures for 1982 list 2.6 percent as the proportion of family budget spent on "apartment rent, communal services, and maintenance on private homes." The 1983 figure on housing for an urban family of four persons in the United States ranges between 19 percent and 23 percent of the annual budget, depending upon the level of income involved. The data are from *Narkhoz*, 1982, p. 385, and *Statistical Abstract of the United States* (Washington, DC: U.S. Government Printing Office, 1983), p. 492.

payments, such as pensions, disability, vacations, and student stipends, and benefits received without direct payment, such as medical care, educational costs, and housing subsidies. Thus, if the typical Soviet family spends considerably less of its disposable income than the American family on housing, it is in part because most Soviet housing is heavily subsidized, and this subsidy is counted as part of the employee's total compensation. But to count the total 75 rubles per month as actual compensation is misleading. It may be reasonable to include medical care, education, and housing subsidies in a worker's compensation, but such direct payments as pensions, disability allowances, and student stipends usually go to people without full-time jobs. These payments certainly are compensation but not compensation for gainfully employed persons. Therefore, only part of the social consumption fund (and the smaller part at that)[42] should be considered as contributing to workers' incomes.

How does the Soviet worker benefit from the social consumption fund compared with so-called "transfer payments," that is, social security, welfare payments, and such, in Western countries? Several Western scholars have considered this matter and have concluded that data are not now available to make precise comparisons. But tentative conclusions suggest that for several Western European countries transfer payments as a percentage of total income may not be very different from that in the Soviet Union.[43]

Such benefits aside, how does the Soviet worker's income compare with that of his Western counterparts?* Radio Liberty over a number of years has made analyses of earnings and prices in the Soviet Union. Their data are relevant here. As of December 1981 the average monthly take-home pay (after taxes) in the USSR and four Western countries (converted to U.S. dollars at the prevailing rates of exchange) was as follows:[44]

USSR	$237.90
USA	$983.98
Federal Republic of Germany	$893.49
France	$786.92
United Kingdom	$737.74

STANDARD OF LIVING

Moving from income to expenditures, one finds comparisons equally difficult to make. We have already mentioned that housing costs are considerably lower in the Soviet Union than in the West, and we will have more to say on the quality and availability of housing later in this chapter. Medical and dental expenses for the Soviet citizen are negligible (most Soviet citizens have to pay for drug prescriptions and other medicines, for instance, but for

---

*The reader is reminded of the problems of converting rubles to dollars. Yet if any comparisons are to be made, this conversion seems to be the only reasonable way to approach the matter.

little else), whereas they can be major costs in the United States. The cost of public transportation (five kopecks or less for subways, buses, and trolleys) compares very favorably with similar services in the West. Finally, the price of a good loaf of dark or white Russian bread cannot be approached in the West. But these are only individual examples, and overall they are misleading.

Radio Liberty researchers have attempted a more comprehensive comparison of food and other costs in the Soviet Union and the West. Their analysis is based on a "Weekly Basket of Consumer Goods" containing twenty-three items—including meats, vegetables, fruits, beverages, dairy products, and grain products—which are available in the West and usually available in the Soviet Union. The items in the food basket are based on an estimated Soviet level of consumption, and the results of the survey for March 1982 for Moscow and four Western cities are expressed in hours of work required to purchase the basket.[45]

Moscow	46.8
Washington	16.3
Munich	20.4
Paris	19.4
London	22.5

What the overall comparison hides is that while prices on such staples as bread, carrots, and cabbage are generally lower in the Soviet Union than in the West, prices of meat, poultry, dairy products, and fruit are more or less equivalent. The result is that the purchase of this quantity of food places a greater burden on the lower Soviet wage levels. The prices included in the survey reflect much of the inflation that has occurred in the West since the 1970s, and in this respect the Soviet citizen is considerably better off in relation to his Western counterparts than he used to be.

In spite of the high cost of food relative to income, it is without question that Soviet citizens are eating better now than they did some years ago, perhaps better than they ever have before. Soviet citizens in 1950 consumed about 3100 calories per day on the average. By 1977 this figure was 3300, roughly similar to the average in the United States. The number of calories, however, is not an indicator of the kind or quality of food being consumed. In the case of the Soviet citizen there has been a dramatic change during these years. In 1950, 71 percent of these calories came from grain products and potatoes, but in 1977 the figure was 46 percent. And the Soviet citizen who was eating about 57 pounds of meat a year in 1950 was eating almost 125 pounds by 1978.* This figure may still be low in comparison with some of the

---

*As impressive as these figures are, it should be noted that they are *average* figures and are Western estimates based on official Soviet data. They indicate little about the availability of meat in various parts of the country and to various levels of the Soviet population. Against these averages one should take account of widespread reports of meat shortages and the use of ration cards for the purchase of meat and other products in certain parts of the country.

other industrialized countries (the average American consumed 186 pounds of meat in 1978, the average French citizen about 165 pounds, the average Pole about 200 pounds), but they show a dramatic change from the recent Soviet past.[46]

Another area in which the Soviet consumer has made progress relative to his Western counterpart involves price inflation. Most Western countries experienced serious and continuing inflation throughout the 1970s and early 1980s. To some extent, this inflation cut into the purchasing power of almost all workers. Although it is not quite true, as Soviet analysts would have it, that recent world-wide economic troubles "stopped at the Soviet frontier,"[47] it is true that the Soviet economy is fairly well insulated against certain international economic problems, including inflation. Retail prices are fixed by the state, except for prices at the collective farm markets, which may vary according to supply and demand. By and large, the fixed prices have not changed much in recent years, and at least some price changes appear to be related to goals of the Soviet leadership not directly relevant to internal economic operations. For instance, increases in the price of vodka have been attributed to the government's drive against alcoholism; and increases in the prices of caviar, champagne, furs, and other products seem connected with the aim of discouraging domestic demand in order to increase export potential—especially to hard-currency markets. On the other hand, the decrease in some prices seems directly related to internal demand: Certain goods such as small-screen television sets and some domestically produced clothing were not selling, so the price cuts in the 1970s were designed to move such items.

That prices are fixed does not mean that there is *no* inflation, however. In addition to the price increases just mentioned, what amounts to hidden inflation can manifest itself in several ways. A frequent practice is to introduce a new model or type of a long-available item and accompany some minor changes with a large increase in price. This technique is used on many consumer goods, from automobiles to vodka. Some goods simply become unavailable for long periods of time, so that the consumer must purchase more expensive substitutes. If the more expensive items are not available at fixed state prices, they might be purchased at higher prices at collective farm markets or on the black market. The ratio between state retail prices and collective farm market prices has been steadily rising for most recent years. Although the kind of inflation described here cannot be documented in Soviet sources or studied by traditional social science techniques, it is real inflation nevertheless. No doubt it is not of the magnitude experienced in Western countries in recent years; but according to many people familiar with the Soviet economy, it is a real problem for heads of Soviet households trying to make ends meet.

Perhaps more characteristic of the Soviet system than inflation is what economists call "repressed inflation." Repressed inflation occurs when prices cannot rise according to the laws of supply and demand because of the lack of supply (and, in the Soviet case, because of fixed prices). That is, goods in demand are not available for purchase, and a great deal of purchasing power remains unused. A sign of this situation is large amounts of money in savings accounts, which has been very characteristic of the Soviet Union in recent years. In 1982 more than 174 billion rubles were held in such accounts, nearly ten times as much as in 1965. Although the rate of accumulation of such savings seems to be dropping, the sum is still indicative of great amounts of unused purchasing power.[48]

A typical way in which the state seeks to cope with this excess purchasing power is by putting extremely high prices on certain items that are in great demand. Of a number of possible examples of this practice, the privately owned automobile is the best.

The privately owned passenger car occupies an interesting position in the Soviet Union for a number of reasons. The government has long had an ambivalent attitude toward it, at times openly labeling the private car an unsocialist manifestation of privatism. In addition to setting high purchase prices, the authorities have tried to discourage ownership in various ways. These include the unwillingness to provide liability insurance for car owners (which several socialist countries of Eastern Europe do allow their citizens to buy) and sporadic attempts—with little success so far—to provide a car-rental system as a substitute for private ownership. Furthermore, the Soviet highway system is not developed to the extent that widespread car travel is easy, and the network of filling stations, repair shops, and other service facilities is notoriously inadequate. The difficulties car owners face in getting spare parts are legendary.

The reasons for the underdevelopment of the private car industry are not difficult to adduce. In addition to ideological considerations, the investments necessary to develop the system would be tremendous, and the authorities have many higher-priority objectives for their investment funds. In addition, a well-developed private transportation system would compete with (and possibly financially undermine, as has happened in the United States) the public transportation system. On purely economic grounds, there is no question as to which mode of transportation the Soviet authorities see as more rational.

It was not until 1972 that more passenger cars than trucks were produced. The Soviet Union still has an unusually high ratio of trucks to passenger cars on its roads. And even though much progress has been made in providing the public with private automobiles, the USSR, comparatively speaking, lags far behind many other countries. In the mid-1980s the ratio of passenger cars to persons in the USSR was one to more than 30. In sixteen countries of the world, it was one car to fewer than four people. In this respect, the Soviet Union lags far behind not just the developed West but most of the East European countries as well.[49]

Yet public demand for passenger cars is longstanding and intense. Although this demand cannot be transmitted to government officials via the political process in ways with which we are familiar in the West, there is no doubt that Soviet authorities are aware of it. And notwithstanding the ideological and other considerations mentioned above, the authorities to some extent have submitted to this pressure by increasing automobile production significantly in recent years. Since the beginning of the Eighth Five-Year Plan in 1966, the Soviet Union has undertaken a major effort to boost car production. During this time they have gone from a production of slightly more than 200,000 passenger cars to more than 1,300,000 in 1984. Not all of these, of course, will go to private purchasers. Many will still be used for official state and Party purposes and as taxis, and an increasing number will be exported, especially to Western countries, in exchange for hard currency. But by 1980 the great majority of automobiles produced were going to private parties; it is here that the car's use to absorb excess purchasing power and to fight repressed inflation comes into play.

Four models of passenger cars are available for purchase by private citizens: the Volga, the Zhiguli (based on the Italian Fiat), the Moskvich, and the Zaporozhets. All are in the subcompact class, but they range in size from the Volga (98 horsepower and about the size of a Ford Grenada) to the Zaporozhets (40 horsepower and about the size of a Honda Civic). The prices of Soviet passenger cars have risen considerably. As of the mid-1980s their selling prices in the Soviet Union (and the dollar equivalents at the then rate of exchange) were as follows:

Model	Price (Rubles)	Price (Converted to U.S. $)
Volga	15,000	20,860
Moskvich	7,300	10,150
Zhiguli 2101	6,600	9,175
Zhiguli 2103	8,600	11,950
Zhiguli 2106	9,100	12,650
Zhiguli 21011	7,300	10,150
Zaporozhets	5,375	7,500

Most of these prices are well above the prices for roughly equivalent vehicles sold in the West. Some great percentage of the purchase price, therefore, amounts to turnover tax and is designed to absorb excess purchasing power and discourage demand.[50] Some clue as to the actual cost of production of these vehicles may be indicated by prices charged when they are sold for hard currency. Under these circumstances, the cars mentioned above have typically sold at about 35 to 40 percent of the domestic ruble price.[51]

In spite of these prices, the demand for private cars remains extremely high. Autos must be fully paid for at time of delivery, and there is a waiting list two to three years long for most models. Even substantial price rises have failed to discourage consumers. Used cars are also extremely high priced. Since they may sometimes be obtained without the long waiting period required for new cars, it is not unusual for a late-model car to sell for substantially more than its original purchase price. Since even the cheapest new car costs over two years of the average worker's salary, it is clear that the high demand for cars is found almost exclusively among the more favored members of Soviet society.

With regard to other consumer durables, supply problems are not nearly so critical. The percentage of families possessing refrigerators, television sets, washing machines, and other appliances has steadily increased, and waiting periods for such items are the exception rather than the rule. Besides the automobile, the other basic commodity in high demand by large numbers of Soviet citizens is improved housing.

HOUSING

To say that the Soviet Union has a housing problem should surprise no one. Nor is the problem one that characterizes the Soviet Union alone. Much of the world is ill housed, and even among the industrialized countries a critical housing situation exists. The Soviet Union has made truly impressive gains in housing construction in recent years. If differences between promises and reality still remain, there is no doubt that many millions of Soviet citizens have recently acquired adequate housing for the first time in their lives.

And yet the problem remains a critical one. Both the leaders and the man in the street agree on this. The great recent efforts in housing construction began only in the 1950s. Prior to that time, the housing record was mediocre at best. And the housing situation inherited by the Soviet regime was a poor one, among the worst in Europe by some accounts.[52] Added to this was the widespread destruction of housing in the European part of the USSR during World War II. So the present generation has a great deal to make up for in housing construction. And there is no doubt that as the average citizen's standard of living rises in other aspects of his life, his expectations as to what constitutes adequate housing rise too.

One index of the housing situation is the so-called "sanitary housing norm," that is, the amount of per capita "living space" supposedly guaranteed by Soviet law to those residing in cities and urban settlements. The minimum norm, first set in the Russian republic in the 1920s, is 9 square meters (a space about 10 feet by 10 feet square). In spite of the fact that this figure has been written into law for more than six decades, the sanitary housing norm was apparently only achieved for the country as a whole by the early 1980s.[53] The present level of housing space is far more than that achieved in earlier years (6.8 square meters in 1964, 4.7 square meters in 1950) and testifies to impressive recent improvements. The Soviets built an average of over two million apartments per year over the last twenty-five years, and they annually provide new apartments or improved living conditions for approximately ten million people. Although the plan targets for housing construction are usually underfulfilled, Soviet authorities claim that they are building more housing than any other country in the world.[54]

It is when one examines more closely a comparative claim such as this one that the Soviet housing situation looks less impressive. If more total housing units are produced in the USSR than elsewhere, the same does not hold with respect to population size. Per thousand population, many Western European countries and Japan have produced more housing units than the USSR in recent years. And in terms of total housing floor space per capita, the results are even more unfavorable to the USSR. Moreover, if one compares the stock of housing per unit of population, the USSR is lower than several East European countries as well as the United States, Japan, and most of Western Europe.[55]

The Soviet authorities have long promised to solve the housing problem. As far back as 1961, in the Party Program adopted that year, it was stated that by 1980 every family would have its own "comfortable apartment in accordance with the requirements of hygiene and everyday life." When it became clear that this timetable could not be met, the date was pushed back to 1990, and more recent evidence suggests that the turn of the century may be a more realistic date. As one Western expert concluded in 1985, "even today, 40 years after World War II, the USSR has the worst housing shortage of any industrial nation."[56]

By general consensus among Western observers, the quality of housing construction in the USSR is inferior to most housing construction in the West. Homes built in the early years of the push to solve the housing problem—the late 1950s—sacrificed quality for quantity. Such apartments quickly took on a shabby appearance. Since then, quality has been improved (accompanied by a drop in the construction rate) but is still inferior to most urban housing in the West. In 1969 and again in 1975 the Party Central Committee was moved to condemn the low quality of housing construction and to demand improvement from responsible officials and ministries.

Although most housing is now being built with the standard amenities (such as running water), a large part of the stock still in use lacks such facilities. In terms of average size, the housing units built in the Soviet Union in recent years are smaller not only than those in the West but also than those in virtually all East European countries as well.[57]

Most housing now being constructed in the Soviet Union is built by the state, about two thirds of the total in recent years. But this has not always been the case. Until the early 1960s, over half of the housing constructed every year was privately built, and even in the 1970s private and cooperative housing comprised over half of the total housing stock.[58]

As the last sentence suggests, the other forms of housing are private and cooperative. Much of the private housing is the rude one-story structure so prevalent in the Soviet countryside. The predominance of that type of structure in urban areas has long since passed. Great numbers of small private structures have been torn down in recent years, and in many larger cities the building of private homes has been forbidden. As much as the Soviet authorities might find the private home an ideologically objectionable artifact of the past, however, it remains a much-needed factor in the total housing picture. As Henry Morton remarked in his thorough study of Soviet housing, it is ironic that the first socialist state continues to have a basic dependence on private housing; whereas in the capitalist states of the West private enterprise has failed to provide adequate housing for large numbers of people, requiring the construction of great amounts of public housing.[59]

Official disapproval of privately built housing is thinly veiled and is expressed in a number of ways. Credit is difficult to get and is limited in amount; the private house is restricted in size to 60 square meters of floor space (except for certain privileged categories of persons and citizens with large families); building materials are in chronically short supply; a family may only own one home; and, as the Soviet press frequently indicates, private homeowners are sometimes treated like second-class citizens by local bureaucrats.[60] Yet because personal home-building eases the housing shortage so much, there are signs that the authorities have moved in recent years to minimize the ideological stigma attached to this form of private property.

Less ideologically objectionable is cooperative housing. This arrangement was experimented with early in Soviet history and then abandoned for several decades. During the 1960s it was revived and officially encouraged. The cooperative scheme allows groups of citizens to combine forces and become shareholders in building a multiapartment complex for their own occupancy. In the law on cooperatives, the authorities have carefully avoided using the word "ownership." The shareholder is "granted" an apartment for his "permanent use," although most of the rights of ownership accrue to him. Although this wording mitigates the emphasis on private property for official purposes, there is no doubt that cooperative shareholders consider that they "own" their apartments. Cooperative housing has other advantages over private housing. Cooperative buildings tend to be large and are therefore well suited to densely settled urban areas. They also provide a means of channeling significant amounts of money directly from the populace into housing, thereby somewhat relieving the burden on the state. And finally, they serve as a means for drawing off excess purchasing power from those wealthy enough to afford cooperative apartments.[61]

Cooperative apartments cost considerably more than state apartments. As mentioned, the rents in the latter are extremely low, and even with the cost of utilities, tenant payments amount to no more than 4 to 5 percent of the typical family income. State apartments are heavily subsidized. It is said that the state pays two thirds of the maintenance cost of apartments in addition to financing the initial construction cost.[62] A shareholder in a cooperative, by contrast, must make a down payment of 40 percent of the cost of the apartment, which could amount to several thousand rubles. The remainder may be paid over 10 to 20 years in equal monthly shares at an interest charge of 0.5 percent. These monthly payments, which include maintenance costs, are considerably higher than for state apartments. In spite of these higher costs, the cooperative idea has been popular, perhaps because one can avoid the waiting line by joining a cooperative; a wait of perhaps several years will be faced by the ordinary citizen seeking a new state apartment. Cooperative apartments of much higher quality and cost are increasingly being built by members of the various Soviet elites. Such people, who have large amounts of money available, find the cooperative apartment an ideal way to improve housing conditions in a relatively short period of time.

Like other branches of housing construction, cooperative apartment building has usually not met plan targets in recent years. Its share of total housing construction has remained well under 10 percent for a number of years. As comments in the press frequently indicate, in spite of official approval of cooperative housing, support and cooperation by local authorities has not always been what it should be. It looks as though it will be some time before cooperative housing becomes a major contributor to solving the problem.[63]

CITIZEN PREFERENCE AND GOVERNMENT POLICIES

Birth Rates, Labor Turnover, and Migration

The relationship of housing to other economic and social problems has not been widely explored by Soviet scholars. But recent Soviet sociological research has generated information that tends to support the impressionistic views of a number of Western specialists. Regarding crime, the classical Soviet view is that it is a remnant of the past and will disappear when all traces of capitalism are eliminated from Soviet society. But in the limited amount of crime statistics published in the USSR, one can find cautiously presented evidence suggesting that contemporary social factors in the USSR, including poor housing conditions, may be related to the incidence of crime.[64] Soviet authorities are more open about the relationship of housing to such problems as the falling birth rate, labor turnover, and underpopulation in certain parts of the country.

Soviet demographers are concerned about the drop in the birth rate in the European part of the USSR. Population is growing at a much faster rate in the non-European republics, particularly in Soviet Central Asia. Thus, before the year 2000, ethnic Russians are expected to constitute less than a majority of the Soviet population, and such a shift in population balance would have considerable symbolic significance.* Demographers attribute

---

*According to the 1979 Census, Russians constituted 52.4 percent of the Soviet population, as against 53.4 percent in 1970. Murray Feshbach projects a figure of 48 percent by the year 2000. "Population and the Labor Force," in *The Soviet Economy: Toward the Year 2000*, eds. Abram Bergson and Herbert S. Levine (London: George Allen & Unwin, 1983), p. 80.

part of the drop in birth rate to inadequate housing. Survey data directed at this problem support the demographers' conclusion.

The housing situation is not the only reason for the low birth rate, of course. For low-income families more children means a general drop in the level of material comforts. The state tries to encourage population increases by various means. Until 1981 a woman received four months' paid maternity leave for each child, and she could take up to one year unpaid leave after a baby was born. In that year, a decree was adopted increasing benefits. Under its terms, a working mother receives 35 rubles a month for a year while remaining home with the child (50 rubles in certain remote parts of the country). Moreover, one-time payments, which used to be awarded only on the birth of the third child, now begin with the first child, at considerably higher levels than before.[65] Then there are the well-known awards of "Maternal Glory" for giving birth to and raising seven, eight, or nine children; and "Heroine Mother" for ten children.* While the increased benefits in the 1981 decree are notable, it should be emphasized that childbearing incentives have been in existence for many years, while the birth rate has continued to drop. Whether these new benefits will make a difference remains to be seen.

High labor turnover is a matter of considerable concern to Soviet authorities and planners. From 1940 to 1956, Soviet law made it a crime to leave one's job, and presumably labor turnover was relatively well controlled thereby. Since 1956, workers have been free to change jobs; and although this freedom is of definite benefit to workers, it is of great concern to planners. Since 1957, the rate of labor turnover has stabilized at about 20 percent per year. This degree of turnover causes considerable loss of work time; and since a high proportion of job changes are accompanied by changes in occupation, there are enormous costs in retraining as well as in wasted skills. Moreover, these problems are particularly acute in certain parts of the country, most notably Siberia and the Far East, where labor shortages have definitely held up development plans. It is reported that labor turnover runs about one third higher than the country average in these areas.[66]

A third, and related, development is population migration. The two aspects of this problem of most concern to Soviet leaders are the move from the countryside to the city and the difficulty of persuading people to settle in the less attractive parts of the country. A long-term and countrywide aspect of population movement has been the rural exodus. Between 1939 and 1961 the proportion of the Soviet population living in cities rose from about one third to more than half. By the mid-1980s the urban proportion had reached about 65 percent. The migration of people from rural areas to the cities,

---

*According to a Soviet publication, the Heroine Mother award had been given to about 200,000 women and the 3 degrees of Maternal Glory to more than 3.5 million mothers between the time the awards were instituted in 1944 and the beginning of 1981. G. A. Kolesnikov and A. M. Rozhkov, *Ordena i Medali SSSR*, 3rd ed. (Moscow: Voennoe Izdate'stvo, 1983), pp. 104–7.

which makes up a great part of this urban growth, has been officially encouraged or condoned, at least until recently. The authorities have long looked upon this development as being naturally related to their high-priority goals of economic growth and urbanization.

This encouragement has been selective, to be sure. For quite a few years the government has tried to prevent migration to the larger cities. As early as 1931, for example, the Party Central Committee adopted a resolution prohibiting the location of new industries in the main urban centers. And in Moscow, Leningrad, and a number of other major cities, regulations have been adopted to prevent out-of-towners from establishing permanent residence. This has led many persons to circumvent the law by contracting marriages of convenience with urban citizens in order to gain resident status. The failure of the authorities' efforts is most evident in Moscow, where the population has grown from slightly more than six million in 1959 to almost eight and one-half million by 1983.

But these are measures that have been applied largely to the big urban centers in the Western part of the country. It is only in recent years that the authorities have come to understand and react to the more general problems associated with the rural exodus. Aided by data from sociological surveys, they have found that the most desirable rural residents, the young and the skilled, are the ones who tend to leave; that the areas of greatest rural manpower shortage are the ones that are losing the most rural workers; and that the general influx into the cities is adding to the burgeoning number of urban problems the country is facing.

By the 1980s the situation had reached a stage that many Soviet leaders must have considered critical. In spite of a crash campaign to train tractor drivers, only a small proportion of those receiving such training remain in agricultural work. And one study showed that three quarters of the rural youth in a large section of the country left the countryside after receiving higher or secondary education.[67]

These problems characterize many rural areas of the USSR. But they are most critical in a few regions located farthest from the great urban centers of Western Russia. The areas of largest rural out-migration naturally include those that are least desirable as places to live and, incidentally, those where underpopulation has long been most severe: Siberia and the Far East.

The Soviet Union has waged a long and largely unsuccessful battle to increase the population in the part of the country east of the Ural Mountains. This large territory is made up of two basic parts, the five Central Asian republics (the Kazakh, Uzbek, Kirghiz, Tadzhik and Turkmen SSRs) and the three eastern regions of the RSFSR (Western Siberia, Eastern Siberia, and the Far East). It is the three latter regions that will concern us here. Taken together, this vast territory comprises 57 percent of the whole USSR and about three-quarters of Russia (the RSFSR). Yet, its 29 million people as of the mid-1980s amounted to only 11 percent of the USSR population and 20 percent of the RSFSR population. The main reason for this low population is not hard to ascertain: It is extremely difficult to get people to stay in this part of the world because life there is so unpromising and uncomfortable. This problem contributes to the low birth rate for the Russian Republic as a whole, which was only 6 percent for the period from 1970 to 1979 as against 8.6 percent for the entire USSR. On the other hand, in the Central Asian republics there is an indigenous population living in cities that were established in ancient times. These people have strong cultural attachments to that part of the country. There is no problem with keeping them on their land. When attachment to the land is coupled with a cultural emphasis on fecundity, which complements the governmental emphasis on fecundity, it comes as no surprise that the Central Asian population growth rate is so high compared to the national average.

In earlier times, before the flush of ideological fervor associated with the Revolution had worn off, the regime sought to populate the unsettled areas by appealing to the patriotic feelings of the citizenry. Komsomolsk on the Amur River in Eastern Siberia, now a city of over a quarter of a million, was originally settled by *Komsomol* members in 1932. The founding of the city was associated with a campaign emphasizing the romantic aspects of capturing the frontier. But exhortations alone have long since lost their effectiveness. Material incentives have also had little success. Settlement in remote areas has been encouraged by paying higher wage rates to workers in the far north regions, Siberia, and the Far East. In unusual circumstances, such as working on the construction of the northern branch of the Trans-Siberian Railroad (the so-called Baikal-Amur Mainline, which was completed in 1984), wages and bonuses could amount to five to six times the average industrial wage. But high wages do not necessarily hold workers. In fact, sociologists have found that it is precisely the highest paid workers in the remote regions who are more likely to quit and leave after saving large amounts of money.[68]

The whole complex of living conditions—including housing, services, climate, educational opportunities, and other factors—work against attracting new settlers to these areas. It has been estimated that the standard of living in Siberia and the Far East is about one quarter lower than that of the Russian Republic as a whole, and Soviet sources frequently point to examples of the hardships of daily existence in remote regions, such as having to travel 400 miles to get a tooth pulled.[69]

The classic Soviet study of labor turnover and population in Siberia is the demographer V. I. Perevedentsev's 1966 book on the subject.[70] Perevedentsev sums up the conditions existing in Siberia by noting that in housing, real wages, retail-trade volume and outlets, medical services, transportation services, level of education and educational opportunities, amount of free time, and average life span, Siberia is worse off than the rest of the RSFSR or the USSR as a whole.[71] What Perevedentsev found in the mid-1960s remains basically true in the 1980s. Then there are the less quantifiable aspects of life, such as air pollution (which Perevedentsev found to be particularly bad in some West Siberian towns) and the annoyance of biting insects. About the latter he writes:

> One of the most difficult conditions of life for the population in the taiga portion of Siberia, and sometimes in the forest steppe (for example, the Baraba), is the prevalence of blood-sucking insects—gadflies, mosquitos, and midges, which locally have the generic name *gnus*. During certain periods in many parts of Siberia, the quantity of *gnus* is so great that it is impossible to work in the open air without taking special protective measures. The use of nets and special clothing involves a number of inconveniences, greatly hinders the work, reducing productivity, and unfavorably affects the workers' state of mind. Siberia's major construction projects have special institutions to combat *gnus*. However this effort is extraordinarily difficult, because these insects cover large areas and are very mobile. There is nothing comparable in the western parts of the country with their labor surplus.[72]

How are the authorities attempting to deal with this complex of problems? It must be said that no overall strategy seems to have emerged. In large part the answers appear to be "the same, only more so," but some of the solutions clearly conflict with others. As mentioned, recommendations concerning increasing the birth rate seem largely to revolve around increased material benefits for children and mothers. It may be that a general improvement in the level of housing, a problem which the system appears slowly to be solving, would be a further incentive to families to have more children.

Regarding labor turnover and the general shortage of labor, a wide-ranging variety of solutions and recommendations has been put forward. Each worker is required to have a "labor booklet" which he takes from job to job. In it are recorded, among other things, the reasons for a worker's leaving a job. It has been suggested that these entries should be used more forcefully to guarantee privileged treatment for conscientious workers and distinguish them from "job flitters." In a number of cities job placement bureaus have been set up to centralize information about vacancies and available workers. Leningrad and other cities have adopted stricter measures, requiring that each person fired for an infraction of labor discipline be assigned to a low-paying job for three months.

Restrictions on garden plots allotted to manual and office workers by factories also aim at reducing job leaving. A regulation adopted in 1974 provides that when a worker gives notice of quitting he loses his right to such a plot.[73]

A regulation long in effect has required graduates of higher educational institutions to, in effect, "pay" for their free education by working at assigned jobs, perhaps in remote parts of the country, for three years. But the reluctance to report to assignments in outlying areas is, as one commentator has put it, "legendary."[74] Many graduates manage to avoid seemingly compulsory moves, and studies show that great numbers of those who do report leave assigned jobs at the earliest possible time.[75]

Then there are the antiparasite laws, which can be used to force work upon able-bodied persons who have been avoiding it, and the all-union labor legislation adopted in 1970, which prescribes priority in housing and other benefits to workers who "successfully and conscientiously perform their duties." Although it does not appear that the regime will return to the restrictive labor legislation of the Stalin period, it is clear that the authorities are attempting to take more aggressive measures to curb labor turnover.

A number of other recommendations aimed at alleviating the labor shortage have been aired. The number of young people entering the labor market will be affected in coming years by the falling birth rate. Efforts are being made, therefore, to bring more young people directly into the labor market by playing down the utility of higher education. Moreover, students in higher education are increasingly attracted into the labor market on a part-time basis. Some "guest workers" from the Soviet Union's neighboring socialist countries have been imported. And there has been some effort to bring about increased employment of housewives in the economy. As made clear at the beginning of the chapter, women already constitute 51 percent of the total labor force, an extraordinarily high proportion when compared with Western countries. Further emphasis on female employment, however, will aggravate the already falling birth rate, as Soviet writers themselves realize.[76] Finally, the authorities have attempted to draw on the increasing number of older people in the country, attracting them back into the labor market through material inducements. Pensioners have been allowed to draw their full pensions and work, as long as their total income does not exceed 300 rubles per month.

The convergence of these three related problems of low birth rate, labor mobility, and population migration stands out most clearly in areas of greatest underpopulation such as Siberia. One Soviet writer summed it up as follows:

> A vicious circle has been created: the rapidly developing industry of Siberia requires millions of new people, and for them much decent housing as well as cultural and supply services are needed . . . You might ask why do you not use the capital investments allocated to you? The first answer is that there are not enough workers on the building sites, just as there are shortages at the machine construction factories and in oil, gas, diamonds and timber . . . Towns are built slowly and poorly. The results are obvious: workers for industrial enterprises become scarce and there is enormous labor turnover.[77]

In other words, labor is not attracted to the area because of the absence of basic comforts and amenities that cannot be provided because of the shortage of labor to build them. This is a complex problem which obviously will not be solved soon. In the meantime, the Soviet leaders must look with some anxiety on the underpopulation of the eastern part of their country, and not just out of economic considerations. Another reason is the contiguity of these regions with China. Large numbers of Soviet troops are stationed at strategic points along the Chinese border,* and China makes open claim to vast amounts of Soviet territory. The Soviet leaders would obviously like to see more Soviet citizens living in these border regions. In yet another move to encourage settlement, the USSR Council of Ministers in 1973 provided increased financial inducements to settlers along the border with China. These incentives are quite clearly related to the political as much as the economic importance of these areas.[78]

NOTES

[1] Much of the data in this chapter are from the annual statistical yearbook published in Moscow, *Narodnoe Khoziastvo v SSSR*. The latest edition available to the authors was the one for 1984, published in 1985. When used in citations this source will be identified as *Narkhoz*, followed by the year covered and the page number. Unless otherwise indicated, comparative figures on the United States are from *Statistical Abstract of the United States, 1984* (104th ed., 1983), Washington, DC: U.S. Department of Commerce.

[2] For numerous examples see: "Women's Rights at Work," *Radio Liberty Research*, No. 107/83, Mar. 8, 1983.

[3] Alastair McAulay, *Women's Work and Wages in the Soviet Union*, (London: George Allen & Unwin, 1981), pp. 96 and 206.

[4] On the quotations and other information in this paragraph see Sergei Voronitsyn, "Soviet Demographers See Signs of a 'Women's Revolt' in the USSR," *Radio Liberty Research*, No. 84/78, Apr. 14, 1978; also "Women in the Labor Force," *Radio Liberty: Current Abstracts and Annotations*, No. 5, 1980, p. 13. A thorough analysis of the subject is Peter H. Juviler's "The Soviet Family in Post-Stalin Perspective," in *The Soviet Union Since Stalin*, eds. Stephen F. Cohen, Alexander Rabinowitch, and Robert Sharlet (Bloomington, IN: Indiana University Press, 1980), pp. 227–51. Juviler's note 15, p. 248, lists many of the recent writings in English on women in the Soviet Union. On underground feminist literature see various issues of the *Radio Liberty Research* reports, including Julia Wishnevsky, "The *Samizdat* Almanac of Soviet Feminists," no. 143/80, Apr. 15, 1980.

[5] See a review of relevant press comments in Yu. Voznesenkaya, "Housework—Soviet Women's Second Shift," *Radio Liberty Research*, no. 448/84, Nov. 23, 1984.

[6] F.J.M. Feldbrugge, ed., *Encyclopedia of Soviet Law, I* (Leiden, the Netherlands: A. W. Sijthoff, 1973), p. 273.

[7] *Itogi Vsesoiuznoi Perepisi Naseleniia 1970 Goda*, VI (Moscow: "Statistika," 1972), p. 165.

[8] *Izvestiia*, Jul. 9, 1975, p. 3.

[9] Ibid., Jul. 10, 1975, p. 4; see also *Vedomosti Verkhovnogo Soveta SSSR*, 1975, No. 11, item 182.

[10] M. Garin and Z. Druzenko, "Vozrast Molodykh," *Izvestiia*, Oct. 25, 1973, p. 2.

[11] N. S. Khrushchev, *Khrushchev Remembers: The Last Testament* (Boston, MA: Little, Brown, 1974), p. 133.

[12] *Izvestiia*, Sept. 21, 1985, p. 2, and Sept. 22, 1985, p. 2–3. Stakhanov died in 1977.

[13] Robert V. Daniels, *The Conscience of the Revolution* (New York: Simon and Schuster, 1960), passim, but especially pp. 119–36 and 156–59.

[14] Reports of strikes by Soviet workers appear in the Western press from time to time. See,

---

*As of 1980 it was estimated that forty-six Soviet divisions were stationed along the Chinese frontier and in Mongolia, as compared with fifteen divisions in 1968. See Robin Edmonds, *Soviet Foreign Policy, 1962–1973* (London: Oxford University Press, 1975), p. 110; *The Military Balance, 1980–1981* (London: The International Institute for Strategic Studies, 1980), p. 11.

for instance, the report of a strike of 70,000 workers at the Togliatti automobile plant in May 1980, *The New York Times,* Jun. 14, 1980, p. 1.

[15]John N. Hazard, *The Soviet System of Government,* 5th ed., rev. (Chicago, IL: The University of Chicago Press, 1980), pp. 70–71 and 221.

[16]*Iuridicheskii Entsiklopedicheskii Slovar'* (Moscow: Sovetskaia Entsiklopediia), 1984, p. 307.

[17]"A Force to be Reckoned With," *Soviet Life,* No. 8 (Aug. 1975), p. 41.

[18]Keith Bush, "Soviet Living Standards: Some Salient Data," *Radio Liberty Research Supplement,* Mar. 7, 1975, p. 4. For reports of unemployment in Soviet Central Asia, see *Radio Liberty Research,* no. 482/83, Dec. 27, 1983.

[19]Various issues of *Narkhoz,* and *Izvestiia,* Jan. 26, 1985, p. 2.

[20]See David Lane, *The End of Inequality?* (Baltimore, MD: Penguin, 1971), p. 32.

[21]The wage data in these pages are based on *Narkhoz,* 1978, pp. 372–73.

[22]David W. Bronson and Barbara S. Severin, "Soviet Consumer Welfare: The Brezhnev Era," in *Soviet Economic Prospects for the Seventies* (Joint Economic Committee, Congress of the United States, Jun. 27, 1973), pp. 379–81.

[23]John Scott, *Detente Through Soviet Eyes* (New York: Radio Liberty Committee, 1974), p. 116.

[24]James R. Millar, *The ABCs of Soviet Socialism* (Urbana, IL: University of Illinois Press, 1981), pp. 189 and 190.

[25]F.J.M. Feldbrugge, "Government and the Shadow Economy in the Soviet Union," *Soviet Studies,* 36, No. 4 (Oct. 1984), p. 542.

[26]In addition to other sources cited, the information in this section is based on discussions with former Soviet citizens.

[27]Zorii Shokhin, "The Caviar Gospel," *Radio Liberty Research Report,* no. 248, June 13, 1975, p. 4; A. Pravdin, "Inside the Central Committee," *Survey,* 20, No. 4 (Autumn 1974), p. 102. See also Alexander Yanov's discussion of "The migration to academe" by high Party officials through the acquisition of higher degrees. Yanov considers this a manifestation of the "aristocratization" of the Soviet political elite. *Detente After Brezhnev: The Domestic Roots of Soviet Foreign Policy* (Policy Papers in International Affairs, Number Two) (Berkely, CA: Institute of International Studies, University of California, 1977), pp. 7–11.

[28]Pravdin, "Inside the Central Committee," p. 102.

[29]Ibid., pp. 102–4, and the authors' conversations with Soviet citizens and former citizens.

[30]*Time,* Jun. 23, 1980, p. 58.

[31]Mervyn Matthews, *Privilege in the Soviet Union* (London: George Allen & Unwin, 1978), p. 33.

[32]Konstantin Simis, *USSR: The Corrupt Society* (New York: Doubleday, 1982), pp. 40–41. Another recent description by an insider of elite privileges, including the *kremlyovka,* may be found in Michael Vozlensky, *Nomenklatura: The Soviet Ruling Class* (New York: Doubleday, 1984), especially Chap. 5, "Privileged Class," pp. 178 ff.

[33]These salaries were raised in 1980 from 150 rubles and 75 rubles, respectively. See *Vedomosti Verkhovnogo Soveta SSSR,* 1980, no. 4, item 66, and *Vedomosti Verkhovnogo Soveta RSFSR,* 1980, no. 5, item 116.

[34]Pravdin, "Inside the Central Committee," p. 104; Shokhin, "The Caviar Gospel," p. 5. U.S. officials and their families are required to turn such gifts over to the government.

[35]The quotation is from the Soviet journal *EKO,* 1978, No. 5, p. 17, as quoted in Andreas Tenson, "The Journal *EKO* Finds Fault with the Soviet Pension System," *Radio Liberty Research,* no. 299/78, Dec. 27, 1978. See also Craig R. Whitney, "Old-Age Pensions in Soviet Leaving Many Impoverished," *The New York Times,* Nov. 19, 1978, p. 1; Andreas Tenson, "The Soviet Pension System: Principles and Rates of Entitlement," *Radio Liberty Research,* no. 288/78, Dec. 14, 1978.

[36]Scott, *Detente,* p. 52; Bronson and Severin, "Soviet Consumer Welfare, p. 379.

[37]Mervyn Matthews, "Poverty in the Soviet Union," *The Wilson Quarterly,* 9, no. 4 (Autumn 1985), 79.

[38]*Narkhoz*, 1984, p. 433.

[39]Andreas Tenson, "A Note on Soviet Family Budget Data," *Radio Liberty Dispatch*, Apr. 24, 1974, p. 3.

[40]*Statistical Abstract*, 1984, pp. 490–93.

[41]*Izvestiia*, Jan. 26, 1985, p. 2. A discussion of the makeup of the payments and benefits from the social consumption fund is found in *Narkhoz*, 1978, p. 597.

[42]Robert J. Osborn cites a 1967 Soviet source which demonstrates that 60 percent of the social consumption fund goes to nonemployed persons. *Soviet Social Policies* (Homewood, IL: The Dorsey Press, 1970), pp. 33–34.

[43]A 1980 attempt to quantify differences in transfer payments produced the following figures for transfer payments as a percentage of GNP: USSR, 26.2; United Kingdom, 26.2; USA, 18.6. Barry Lynch, "A Comparison of Income from Transfer Payments in the USSR, The United Kingdom and the United States," *Radio Liberty Research*, no. 31/80, Jan. 21, 1980, p. 4.

[44]Keith Bush, "Retail Prices in Moscow and Four Western Cities in March 1982," *Radio Liberty Research*, no number, 1982, p. 32.

[45]Ibid., p. 7.

[46]M. Elizabeth Denton, "Soviet Consumer Policy: Trends and Prospects," in *Soviet Economy in a Time of Change*, vol. 1, p. 359; *Statistical Abstract*, 1979, p. 127. Much of the data in this paragraph is confirmed in *Consumption in the USSR: An International Comparison*, a study prepared for the use of the Joint Economic Committee of Congress, Washington, DC: 1981.

[47]Yuri Kanin, "Soviet Living Standards Rise," *Soviet Life*, no. 6 (Jun. 1975), p. 18. See also Alexander Birman, "Why Doesn't the Soviet Union have Inflation?" ibid., no. 8 (Aug. 1978), p. 13.

[48]*Narkhoz*, 1985, p. 462.

[49]"New Models of Soviet Automobiles Under the Eleventh Five Year Plan," *Radio Liberty Research*, no. 208/83, May 26, 1983. See also: Toli Welihozkiy, "Automobiles and the Soviet Consumer," in *Soviet Economy in a Time of Change*, vol. 1, p. 819.

[50]It is reported that turnover tax amounted to 60 percent of the purchase price of the Zhiguli 2101 in 1979. Welihozkiy, "Automobiles and the Soviet Consumer," p. 821.

[51]"Prices of Soviet Automobiles on the Domestic and Foreign Markets," *Radio Liberty Research*, No. 380/82, Sept. 20, 1982.

[52]See, for example, Willard S. Smith, "Housing in the Soviet Union-Big Plans, Little Action," in *Soviet Economic Prospects for the Seventies*, p. 406.

[53]The Soviet Union does not publish figures on living space but by comparing the urban population with published data on "useful housing space" for urban areas and extracting "living space" from "useful space," an estimate can be made. Based on 1982, the latest data available (*Narkhoz*, 1982, pp. 6 and 393), and using a correction factor of 0.7 as used previously by one of the authors (see Donald D. Barry, "Housing in the USSR: Cities and Towns," *Problems of Communism*, 18, no. 3 (May–Jun. 1969), 2, note 6) an average of 9.5 square meters is achieved. Using the factor of 0.67 employed by Henry Morton ("Who Gets What, When and How? Housing in the Soviet Union," *Soviet Studies*, 32, no. 2 (Apr. 1980), p. 256, note 2) yields an average of 9.12 square meters.

[54]The RSFSR Housing Code adopted in 1983 sets the maximum living space at 12 square meters. However, this amounts to a recommendation having little practical significance. See Andreas Tenson, "More Living Space for Soviet City-Dwellers," *Radio Liberty Research*, no. 54/84, Feb. 2, 1984.

[55]Henry W. Morton, "The Soviet Quest for Better Housing—An Impossible Dream?" in *Soviet Economy in a Time of Change*, vol. 1, pp. 791–92. Morton notes that since 1975 Czechoslovakia and Hungary have also exceeded the USSR in per capita housing production. See also Smith, "Housing," pp. 408–10.

[56]Henry W. Morton, "The Housing Game," *The Wilson Quarterly*, 9, no. 4 (Autumn 1985), 62; Keith Bush, "Soviet Housing Target Date Again Deferred," *Radio Liberty Research*, No. 11/85, Jan. 9, 1985. In Jan. 1985, the Soviet authorities stated that over four-fifths of the Soviet people now live in separate apartments.

[57]Morton, "The Soviet Quest," pp. 415–17.

[58]Henry W. Morton, "What Have Soviet Leaders Done About the Housing Crisis?" in

Soviet Politics and Society in the 1970's, ed. Henry W. Morton and Rudolf L. Tokes (New York: Free Press, 1974) p. 172.

[59]Ibid., pp. 174–75.

[60]Barry, "Housing," p. 9; *Izvestiia,* Feb. 25, 1972, p. 3.

[61]This paragraph is based largely on Barry, "Housing," p. 10.

[62]Kanin, "Soviet Living Standards," p. 19.

[63]See Morton, "The Soviet Quest for Better Housing," pp. 803–4.

[64]S. S. Ostroumov and V. E. Chugunov, "Study of the Criminal Personality from the Materials of Criminological Research," *Sovetskoe Gosudarstvo i Pravo,* no. 9 (Sept. 1965), translated in *Soviet Law and Government,* IV, no. 3 (Winter 1965–66), 21. Ostroumov and Chugunov deny a relationship between housing and crime, but some of their data fail to support this position. They indicate that about two-thirds of juvenile lawbreakers surveyed in a Moscow district lived in families with more than 5 square meters of housing space per person, about 35 percent having their own apartments. This is surely a low percentage for one-family apartments in the whole of Moscow at the time, and the figure of 5 square meters of housing space is well below the national urban average of 6.8 square meters at the time of their study. Thus, a high percentage of offenders do seem to have come from below-average housing conditions.

[65]The decree and subsequent implementing decisions are described in *Izvestiia,* Mar. 1, 1981, p. 1, and Sept. 6, 1981, p. 1. For commentaries in English, see *Radio Liberty Research,* no. 158/81, Apr. 10, 1981, and no. 353/81, Sept. 8, 1981.

[66]This passage is based largely on the following sources: Murray Feshbach, "Manpower Management," *Problems of Communism,* 23, no. 6 (Nov.–Dec. 1974), 28, and Feshbach and Rapawy, "Labor Constraints," pp. 538–44; Frederick A. Leedy, "Demographic Trends in the USSR," in *Soviet Economic Prospects for the Seventies,* pp. 451–52. See also Stephen Rapawy, "Regional Employment Trends in the USSR: 1950–1975," in *Soviet Economy in a Time of Change,* vol. 1, p. 600, and Warren Eason, "Demographic Divergences at the Republic Level," in *Regional Development in the USSR* (Newtonville, MA: Oriental Research Partners, 1979), p. 119. This information is largely confirmed by more recent sources. See, Murray Feshbach, "Population and Labor Force," in *The Soviet Economy: Toward the Year 2000,* eds. Abram Bergson and Herbert S. Levine (London: George Allen & Unwin, 1983), p. 78 and Leslie Dienes, "Regional Economic Development," ibid., p. 219, and especially pp. 236 and 249ff.

[67]See Andreas Tenson, "Vain Attempts to Bolster the Labor Force on Soviet Farms," *Radio Liberty Research,* no. 203/80, Jun. 5, 1980. See also Barbara S. Severin and David W. Carey, "The Outlook for Soviet Agriculture," in *The Future of the Soviet Economy: 1978–1985,* ed. Holland Hunter (Boulder, CO: Westview Press, 1978), p. 109.

[68]Allan Kroncher, "Labor Turnover in Siberia," *Radio Liberty Dispatch,* Sept. 3, 1973, p. 3.

[69]This example is cited by Feshbach and Rapawy, "Labor Constraints," p. 539.

[70]Perevedentsev's book *(Population Movement and Labor Supply in Siberia)* was translated in the following issues of *Soviet Sociology:* 8, nos. 1, 2 (Summer and Fall 1969); 9, no. 3 (Winter 1970–71), and 11, nos. 1, 2 (Summer and Fall 1972).

[71]*Soviet Sociology* 11, no. 1 (Summer 1972), 37/56.

[72]Ibid., p. 54.

[73]"New Assault on the Rights of Soviet Workers," *Radio Liberty Research,* no. 188, May 2, 1975, p. 6.

[74]Walter D. Connor, "Education and National Development in the European Socialist States: A Model for the Third World," *Comparative Studies in Society and History,* 17, No. 3 (July 1975), 344.

[75]Ibid., p. 345. See David K. Shipler's observations on the problem of job assignment (referred to as "the distribution"—*raspredelenie*) faced by graduates of Soviet higher educational institutions. *Russia: Broken Idols, Solemn Dreams* (New York: New York Times Books, 1983), pp. 163 ff.

[76]See the sources cited in Allan Kroncher, "The Growing Problem of Labor Resources in the USSR," *Radio Liberty Dispatch,* Dec. 19, 1973, pp. 3–4.

[77]A. Ladinskii, "Chto Zhe Kak Stroit'," *Literaturnaia Gazeta,* Aug. 8, 1973, p. 10.

[78]Andreas Tenson, "New Inducements for Resettlement in Farming Areas," *Radio Liberty Dispatch,* Jan. 2, 1974.

SELECTED BIBLIOGRAPHY

ANDRUSZ, GREGORY D., *Housing and Urban Development in the USSR.* Albany, NY: State University of New York Press, 1985.

BERGSON, ABRAM, and HERBERT S. LEVINE, eds., *The Soviet Economy: Toward the Year 2000.* London: George Allen & Unwin, 1983.

Consumption in the USSR: An International Comparison. A study prepared for the use of the Joint Economic Committee of Congress, Washington, DC: U.S. Government Printing Office, 1981.

DEMAIO, ALFRED JOHN, JR., *Soviet Urban Housing: Problems and Prospects.* New York: Holt, Rinehart & Winston, 1974.

FELDBRUGGE, F.J.M., G.P. VAN DEN BERG, and WILLIAM B. SIMONS, eds., *Encyclopedia of Soviet Law.* Dordrecht, the Netherlands: Martinus Nijhoff Publishers, 1985.

FELDBRUGGE, F.J.M., "Government and Shadow Economy in the Soviet Union," *Soviet Studies,* XXXVI, no. 4 (Oct. 1984), 528–43.

HUNTER, HOLLAND, ed., *The Future of the Soviet Economy: 1978–1985.* Boulder, CO: Westview Press, 1978.

KAHAN, ARCADIUS, and BLAIR A. RUBLE, eds., *Industrial Labor in the U.S.S.R.* New York: Pergamon Press, 1979.

LANE, DAVID, and FELICITY O'DELL, *The Soviet Industrial Worker.* New York: St. Martin's Press, 1978.

MAMONOVA, TATYANA, ed., *Women and Russia: Feminist Writing from the Soviet Union.* Boston: Beacon Press, 1984.

MATTHEWS, MERVYN, *Privilege in the Soviet Union.* London: George Allen & Unwin, 1978.

MCAULAY, ALASTAIR, *Women's Work and Wages in the Soviet Union.* London: George Allen & Unwin, 1981.

MILLAR, JAMES R., *The ABC's of Soviet Socialism.* Urbana, IL: University of Illinois Press, 1981.

MORTON, HENRY W., "Housing Problems and Policies of Eastern Europe and the Soviet Union," *Studies in Comparative Communism,* 12, No. 4 (Winter 1979), 300–21.

————, and ROBERT C. STUART, *The Contemporary Soviet City.* Armonk, NY: M. E. Sharpe, 1984.

NATO (Economic Directorate and Information Directorate, eds.), *Regional Development in the USSR.* Newtonville, MA: Oriental Research Partners, 1979.

NOVE, ALEC, *The Economics of Feasible Socialism.* London: George Allen & Unwin, 1983.

————, "When Is a Price Increase Not a Price Increase?" *Soviet Studies,* XXXIV, no. 3 (July 1982), 440–42.

SCHAPIRO, LEONARD, and JOSEPH GODSON, eds., *The Soviet Worker: Illusions and Realities.* New York: St. Martin's Press, 1981.

SHENFIELD, STEPHEN, "A Note on Data Quality in the Soviet Family Budget Survey," *Soviet Studies,* XXXV, No. 4 (Oct. 1983), 561–68.

SHIPLER, DAVID, K., *Russia: Broken Idols, Solemn Dreams.* New York: New York Times Books, 1983.

SIMIS, KONSTANTIN, *USSR: The Corrupt Society.* New York: Simon and Schuster, 1982.

Soviet Economy in a New Perspective (Prepared for the Joint Economic Committee, U.S. Congress). Washington, DC: U.S. Government Printing Office, 1976.

Soviet Economy in a Time of Change (Prepared for the Joint Economic Committee, U.S. Congress). Washington, DC: U.S. Government Printing Office, Oct. 10, 1979.

VOZLENSKY, MICHAEL, *Nomenklatura: The Soviet Ruling Class.* New York: Doubleday, 1984.

11

PROBLEMS IN THE POLITICAL PROCESS: *"Loyal Opposition," Interest Articulation, and Dissent*

How is policy made in the Soviet Union? This is much too broad a question to be answered with one general statement. But the question gets at the essence of the political process in the USSR, and every serious student of Soviet politics must grapple with it. During Stalin's heyday an easy answer to the policy-making question would have been "by Stalin himself," or "at most by Stalin, a few close advisers, and the Politburo." And during this period of the "personality cult," it is clear that Stalin *did* have enormous personal power and *did* make numerous decisions more or less on his own. But careful research has shown that even during Stalin's time certain specialists had some effect on policy making in that they provided the information that served as the basis for decisions that were made.[1]

No person since Stalin has held the monopoly of power that he exercised; there has been a wider circle of participants in policy making. And numerous studies have shown that specialists and experts have played salient roles in the adoption of particular policies. The extent of this specialist input varies with the policy at issue and with the political atmosphere at the time the decision was being made. But some level of participation of this kind has been evident through most of the post-Stalin period.

How, then, can one generalize about Soviet policy making? It is important to distinguish the kind of policy at issue and the number of potential participants in the policy-making process. We would suggest, as a theory rather than a verifiable statement of fact, two levels of participation: (1)

issues on which decisions are made by a small group of men at the top of the Party-governmental hierarchy plus a few advisers or representatives of strategic elites (such as the armed forces or the secret police), and (2) issues that are open to a wider circle of participants—at least at the stage where policy alternatives are being recommended. The more important issues would obviously tend to fall into the first category. It is difficult to give an exhaustive list of such issues, but it would include the major features of the budget and the production plans, all important personnel decisions, all foreign-policy matters, and a scattering of issues across the remainder of the policy spectrum. Examples of the more open policy areas will be given later, but it is important to note that the wider participation mentioned appears to be limited largely to recommending policy alternatives and arguing for their adoption. If such recommendations come to be adopted, it must be assumed that the top leaders have approved, at least tacitly.

The policy process followed in both of these cases is considered legitimate—politics according to the Soviet "rules of the game." There are, however, other efforts to influence Soviet politics, many of which the authorities consider to be of questionable legality or downright illegal. These activities can be grouped under the general heading of "dissent" and will be discussed later in this chapter.

"LOYAL OPPOSITION"

We have put the term "loyal opposition" in quotation marks because the concept does not exist in Soviet politics. "Her Majesty's loyal opposition" is an institutionalized part of the British system, referring to the party out of power in a stable two-party system, and variations on this British institution exist in other countries in the West.[2]

According to the theory on which the Soviet system is based, there is no need for more than one party because socialism has created a unity of views and an absence of antagonistic interests. As discussed in Chapter 7, not only are other parties prohibited, but factions within the Communist Party are also formally outlawed. Anything identified as internal "opposition" by Soviet spokespersons would be something to be repressed, whether it came from within the Party or not. Other terms of opprobrium, such as "anti-Party group,"* suggest group action that is also subject to repression. This antipathy to opposition has been a recurrent theme during all of Soviet history. Lenin, the Soviet founding father, was highly intolerant of any serious challenge to his authority. And, of course, the severity with which Stalin dealt with his opponents—both real and imagined—is legendary.[3]

Yet we also know that decision making by members of the top leadership group is not the exercise in monolithic unity the Soviet media would

---

*This term was used to refer to Malenkov, Molotov, Kaganovich, and others who opposed Khrushchev in 1957 and were defeated by him. It is another matter, of course, if the opposition group carries the day, as the anti-Khrushchev forces did in 1964.

have us believe. The leaders do disagree over politics, issues, and matters of personality. Most Western analysts now accept the "conflict model" of Soviet leadership politics, which stresses the presence of conflict over both personal power and over policy decisions.[4] Whether such conflicts involve contention between more-or-less permanent factions (for example, the "Pro-Reformist" and "Neo-Stalinist" factions), as some kremlinologists contend, or whether the struggle is characterized by shifting alliances that are more fluid than permanent, as others hold, it is clear that the disputes are there.

Some disputes become serious enough that they take on the characteristics of a struggle for power in which one or more leaders lose their positions. But even such power struggles can have a policy dimension. Aleksandr Shelepin is thought to have lost his Politburo position in 1975 because of his disagreement with Brezhnev on Soviet policy toward China, and Pyotr Shelest's removal in 1972 from the post of Ukrainian Party leader and later from the Politburo is attributed to his opposition to détente and his earlier criticism of the policy toward Czechoslovakia before the invasion of 1968. Even Khrushchev's removal in 1964 appears to have been directly connected with his "hare-brained schemes" in several policy areas, particularly those that earned him the opposition of military and heavy-industry leaders.

But there are great numbers of policy issues that are settled without personnel changes. Many of these are resolved amidst disagreement and contention, and, without doubt, there is some attempt to organize opinion and persuade the undecided prior to the resolution of an issue. Such attempts do not approach the concept of "loyal opposition," but they do suggest that the rules of the game allow some latitude for organized advocacy of policy positions at the top layers of the political elite.

If this assumption is sound, where do these disputes take place, who participates, and what are the policy matters at issue? Let us take up these questions one at a time. Since the Politburo is the top policy-making body of the Party, it is clear that most or all important policy issues receive a hearing there. Such issues probably are framed beforehand and perhaps preliminarily discussed in the Secretariat meeting as a group. Previous to that, the responsible CC secretary and his staff may have done some preliminary work on the issue in question; and the secretary may, in addition, have discussed it with the General Secretary. It is this early initiative and exposure to issues that, among other advantages and powers, gives the secretaries, and particularly the General Secretary, the strategic position that they hold. The ability to present the issues, to set the agenda for Politburo meetings, and perhaps to come to the meetings with prepared draft resolutions on agenda matters must provide the General Secretary considerable advantage over his colleagues who are not on the Secretariat.* Party chief Khrushchev tried to take further advantage of his Politburo (then called Presidium) colleagues by

---

*As noted in Chap. 6, there is no formal position of "chairman of the Politburo." But apparently the General Secretary normally serves in that capacity at Politburo meetings.

holding expanded Politburo meetings to which various experts and specialists were invited. Because Khrushchev's high-level antagonists were inhibited about speaking freely and criticizing the leader's policies in front of so large a group, Khrushchev was thereby able to gain even more leverage over the rest of the Politburo. This practice is seen as one of a large number of factors that led to Khrushchev's ouster by his colleagues.[5]

Some matters may also be taken up in the governmental hierarchy, perhaps going from a minister to the Chairman of the Council of Ministers, with discussion thereafter in the Presidium of the Council of Ministers. From there the Chairman might transfer the issue to the Politburo, of which he is also normally a member. The fact that policy proposals may emanate from two hierarchies, perhaps in drastically different forms, probably enhances the possibility of contention, which is to be expected among the powerful, ambitious men at the top of a political system. Kremlinologists from time to time point to signs of the Party apparatus's taking measures to ensure continued dominance over the governmental apparatus.

Disagreements can, and apparently do, take place at Politburo meetings. Since these meetings receive only superficial coverage in the Soviet press, there is virtually never any public reference to such problems. But differences sometimes show up in the speeches made by the various leaders at public functions and in newspaper articles that appear in papers "representing" various factions (for example, *Pravda,* the organ of the CC CPSU, representing the position of the Party General Secretary; *Izvestiia,* the organ of the USSR Supreme Soviet, representing the government's or the Premier's position). Such differences are rarely expressed in direct terms, however, and thus are not obvious to the uninitiated. The "esoteric communication" of policy differences is the stuff of kremlinology. Since kremlinology is an inexact science, however, it is not uncommon for kremlinologists to disagree, both as to the meaning of the messages expressed and as to the lineups of personalities on one or another side of an issue. Thus, although most specialists agree that conflict at the top level takes place, the shroud of official secrecy applied at this level makes it difficult to describe the conflicts in much detail.

It may also be that the Central Committee takes a hand in policy determination, although it is not likely that this happens on a regular basis. The top fifteen to twenty leaders in the Politburo can easily see the dangers of having the more than four hundred members of the Central Committee come to the conclusion that *their* body should be the forum for regular policy formation. More likely, the short, twice-yearly CC meetings are used to *inform* CC members of Politburo policy determinations, thus keeping the policy initiative clearly in the Politburo. The occasional use of the CC as a forum for the resolution of policy disputes cannot be entirely ruled out, however. Some publicity has been given to such occasions in the past, and since there is minimal press coverage of CC meetings, no one but a CC member knows with any certainty what goes on in CC meetings.

The policy matters that the Politburo discusses are numerous and cut across all areas of Soviet life. A good portion of its time must be spent on economic matters, from the relatively long-term considerations of the main features of the coming Five-Year Plan to the immediate problems of, say, the size of the current grain harvest and the decision as to whether to import more wheat from the West. In other areas, similar long- and short-term problems probably get put on the Politburo agenda: In foreign policy, what strategy to pursue regarding Western protests over the Soviet occupation of Afghanistan and how best to acquire necessary products through foreign trade; on the domestic front, how to deal with rising juvenile crime and what stand to take on an attempt to stage an unauthorized contemporary art show in Moscow. In all these areas and a multitude of others the Politburo probably reaches a consensus on the main lines of policy, and that consensus is then translated into policy execution through the Party or governmental apparatus whose leaders are represented in the Politburo membership.

On some of these general policies, and particularly on the details of proposals designed to implement the policy decisions reached, there is a wider circle of potential participants. Occasionally it even appears that "outside" participants initiate proposals that lead to basic policy changes. A case in point is the so-called "Liberman proposals" and their relation to the economic reform of 1965.* If the actual Politburo deliberations on policy matters are largely hidden from public view, a bit more can be said about some of the examples of extra-Politburo participation in the policy process. This we will refer to as "interest articulation."

INTEREST ARTICULATION

Interest articulation is a concept that has received wide application in political science in recent years. It has been used much more frequently in the analysis of Western political systems that it has in the analysis of the Soviet political system, but it does have utility in the latter context. Students of interest articulation examine the manifestation of points of view on various political issues and the avenues by which these points of view are brought to bear on policy making. Certain people or organizations are seen as being voices for various points of view; they seek access to the policy-making process through their positions in the political hierarchy or their contacts in the hierarchy. Even if the term "interest articulation" is not used, Western analysts of the Soviet system apply the concept in their analyses; thus, that the Minister of Defense was brought into the Politburo in 1973 was widely and no doubt rightly interpreted as giving the military a more direct voice in policy making at the highest level. The same applies to the accession of the

---

*See the section on "Economic Reform" in Chap. 9.

Minister of Foreign Affairs to the Politburo and the elevation of the Chairman of the KGB from candidate to full-member status at the same time. Specialists have argued about whether these changes constituted a strengthening of Brezhnev's hand because the new members were his allies; an attempt to limit and control his foreign policy initiatives because they were his opponents; or a move taken for totally different reasons. But that the new memberships strengthened the access to the hierarchy of the interests these men represented probably would be accepted by everyone. The same could be said, in one way or another, for every member of the Politburo. At all times, the overwhelming majority of members are from the three major Slavic nationalities, and this presumably assures that the predominant interests of these groups are expressed. But a small number of "representatives" from one or another of the minor Soviet nationalities have also gained full or candidate Politburo status in recent years. In this way, then, each member of the Politburo could be identified with at least one interest that he presumably represents and whose point of view he presumably makes known.

But interest articulation is normally used to suggest a broader access to policy making than merely having the interests represented in the membership of the top ruling bodies. The methods and results of interest articulation can be demonstrated by means of case studies of policy making that show, to the extent possible, who participated, at what level and in what way, and how this participation can be related to the resulting policy. Assuming complete access to relevant information, one could theoretically do a case study of any and every example of Soviet policy making. As already emphasized, however, getting accurate information about policy making in the Soviet Union is a great problem. So we will have to content ourselves with the relatively small number of case studies and other analyses that have been made.

Does the attempt to examine *interest articulation* imply the examination of *interest-group* activity? It certainly would if we were discussing U.S. politics or that of another Western country. But there are considerable problems in applying the interest-group approach, which was developed first in the context of American politics, to the Soviet scene. When one thinks of interest-group activity in American politics, it is first and foremost the so-called "associational" interest group that comes to mind. The associational type is "designed specifically to represent the goals of particular groups" and includes such bodies as "trade unions, ethnic associations, organizations for particular businesses or industries, associations organized by religious denominations, and associations organized to promote particular causes, such as civic reform or foreign policy."[6] In the Soviet Union the establishment of such groups is prohibited almost by definition on the basis of the Party's monopoly of legitimate political power. And where formal organizations exist that might conceivably develop into associational groups (for example, the writers' union, the trade unions, the artists' union), the level of Party control is such that they are not allowed to speak in a unified, independent voice. It is only within the dissident movement that the beginnings of genuine associational interest articulation can be found. And, of course, the authorities have moved to break up and eliminate such groups. Thus, what in most developed nations amounts to the foremost type of interest-group activity is largely closed off in the Soviet context.

According to the typology developed by Gabriel Almond, additional kinds of interest articulation that exist in other countries are the following: individual self-representation, anomic interest groups, nonassociational interest groups, and institutional interest groups.[7] Individual self-representation in the Soviet Union might involve submitting a complaint about treatment by a government official to the legal authorities or writing a letter to a newspaper. Although both kinds of action are taken, sometimes with success for the initiator, such activity hardly can be considered a major aspect of policy making. Anomic interest groups include the temporary aggregations of people who join in a demonstration, riot, or similar activity. Spontaneous acts of this kind are rare in the Soviet Union and certainly are discouraged by the authorities. Although several examples (besides those involving dissidents) might be cited, anomic interest articulation is not an important matter. Nonassociational groups include ethnic, religious, regional, class, and status groups; whereas institutional groups may be found within armies, bureaucracies, parties, legislatures, and similar organizations that are established for purposes other than interest articulation. There is some evidence of interest articulation from both these sources in the Soviet Union, but whether it involves interest-*group* activity is open to question.

A number of Soviet Jews favoring emigration and groups of Crimean Tatars pressing for the return of their homeland have taken on some of the characteristics of nonassociational interest groups. The same is true of several religious groups. These will be discussed subsequently under dissent. Beyond these examples, advocacy in favor of an ethnic group, region, or other interest appears to be limited to that of individual representatives for such interests who, because of their place in the hierarchy, can present their group's point of view. Examples might be the Kazakh who sits on the Politburo or the Supreme Soviet deputy from the Latvian Republic who speaks in favor of more investment funds for his republic.

Regarding institutional interests, it is clear that most of the examples of input into the policy process originating outside the high Party leadership that Western scholars have discovered come from this source: individuals or collections of individuals who, on the basis of their occupations and the knowledge and access gained therefrom, are able to participate in the policy-making process in various ways.

But should such aggregations of individuals be referred to as *interest groups*? Such a question may seem irrelevant at this point, and in a sense it is. But it is a question that has generated considerable controversy within the political-science profession, and it should therefore be pursued just a bit further. Since such aggregations seldom speak or claim to speak for the profession or occupation as a whole and, indeed, may be opposed by other aggregations within the profession that hold different points of view, it is said that there is too great a lack of cohesion to talk of interest groups.[8] This is certainly a valid point, and to it may be added the fact that on some issues, aggregations advocating a point of view may cross professional lines—as when "liberal" artists, writers, and other intellectuals press for a loosening of cultural policy. But lack of absolute cohesion is one of the major points that distinguishes the associational from the institutional interest group. Since, unlike the former, the latter is not created to advocate particular points of view, it must be expected that not all of its members will support the same policies. At least to Gabriel Almond, who created the typology of interest articulation used here, it is not necessary for institutional interest groups to speak for the whole profession or larger group within which they are found. Institutional interest groups can operate, he states, "either as whole institutional structures or as subgroups (for example, either the military establishment or special factions within it)."[9]

Many, if not all, of the examples of influence on the Soviet policy process found by Western scholars suggest an effort of two or more persons advocating similar points of view. If this advocacy is not always highly coordinated, neither does it seem to be accidental or to have taken place without knowledge among the participants of others advocating the same policy. Many of the examples, in other words, suggest more than "sets of individuals who share common attitudes."[10] These aggregations, often subgroups in professions or in larger organizations, deserve to be called what Gordon Skilling has referred to as "opinion groups."[11]

What are the opinion groups that have been studied and how have they participated in the policy-making process? Literally dozens of scholars have studied examples of interest-group involvement in policy making. The activities of educational personnel in modifying Khrushchev's proposals for educational reform in 1958 have been analyzed, as have the roles played by various groupings in effecting the repeal of large parts of this educational policy.[12] The participation of economists in the adoption of the economic reform of 1965 has been described, and the role of scientists in reorganizing the Academy of Sciences has been examined.[13] A number of studies have looked into the roles of Soviet jurists in policy making, from their work on the reform of family law to their influence on the norms of civil, criminal, and penal legislation to their resistance (partially successful) to the so-called antiparasite laws.[14] Other studies have examined Party *apparatchiki*, security police, the military, industrial managers, and writers as interest groups.[15] Still other writings have commented on the role of collective-farm chairmen in effecting the abolition of the machine-tractor stations; the work of a set of "noninstitutionalized ad hoc environmental lobbies" in achieving stricter pollution standards; and the efforts of nationality and religious groups in pressing their demands on policy makers.[16]

Recent research has shown that regional Party leaders who have presented their views at Party congresses have been reasonably successful in getting local projects added to national investment plans. Howard Biddulph concluded in studying such Party Congress lobbying that increased efforts by regional leaders in this area have helped to legitimize their role in the process.[17] And, of course, it is not only through speeches at Party and government meetings that such regional interests are promoted. General and specialist newspapers and journals have long been vehicles for interest articulation of this kind. For example, a grandiose plan to divert water from Siberian rivers in order to cope with water shortages in Central Asia and Kazakhstan has been debated in the press for years—with the "Central Asian lobby" vigorously leading the pro-diversion side.[18]

Naturally, not all of these aggregations are equally influential or have equal access to the policy-formation process. Regional Party *apparatchiki* are in a much better position to air their views to higher Party leaders than are, say, a group of like-minded lawyers or economists. Nor are all groups equally close to the top Party leadership in their views. One would expect a greater identity of viewpoint between lower Party *apparatchiki* and Politburo members than between the latter and writers advocating greater freedom of literary expression. William C. Odom has argued persuasively that a "party-military consensus" exists across a wide range of issues; he sees a greater convergence of views between the Party and the military than between the Party and some other groups.[19]

What seems to be common to all these studies of group influence on the policy process is the acknowledgement, tacit or explicit, that the Party leadership sets the ground rules for such participation. It is often responsible for allowing discussions to be initiated, it seeks to control the limits of debate on issues, and it signals when such discussion should end. Participants who go beyond these limits may be subject to criticism. Moreover, it must be assumed that the Party leadership retains ultimate veto power over any policy proposal, no matter how widely discussed. And it is certainly within its capacity to "mobilize bias and otherwise prevent the emergence of some issues."[20] In other words, the groups about which we are here speaking, unlike the dissidents, play by the rules of the game and acknowledge the limitations on legitimate participation set down by the Party.

It should be added that even a policy that has been adopted may remain unimplemented or only implemented in part. If policy making has been opened up to some extent, the same is not necessarily true of administration. Western scholars preoccupied with "inputs" into policy making have to some extent ignored the degree to which such policies can be affected by administrators.[21] The emphasis on inputs also tends to divert attention from a different form of citizen participation: activity aimed not at affecting the *adoption* of general policy but at influencing policy *implementation* in individual cases. In a careful study of ex-Soviet citizens who left the USSR in the late 1970s, DeFranceisco and Gitelman found little belief among respondents in their ability to affect policy making. But a large proportion saw the possibility of influencing the application of policies to them. These Soviet citizens were very open "to entering into formal and even illegal interactions with officials."[22] A variety of approaches, ranging from appealing to an administrative superior and writing letters to officials to the use of personal connections and the offering of bribes (the latter two perceived as generally more effective) were identified as among those that might produce positive results.

Some of the research referred to has suggested that several of the opinion groups grew more autonomous during the 1960s and sought to assert their importance in policy making in their narrow spheres of operation.[23] But such activity did not reach a point where it amounted to a challenge to overall Party supremacy or a lack of acceptance of the Party's leading role.

The ways in which the Party seeks to maintain its position are manifold. One of the most important is the maintenance of Party groups in all other organizations. Some percentage of every institution, professional body, or other organization is made up of Party members who as a group are described by the Constitution as "the leading core of all organizations." Such Party groups tend to mitigate the degree of autonomy from the Party that such bodies might otherwise enjoy. Another way in which the Party maintains its leading role is by its control over the media of communication. This control is accomplished in a number of ways, including the *nomenklatura* system of personnel appointments described in Chapter 7. The media are, of course, crucial instruments both for the development of group attitudes and for the transmission of views and proposals to the policy makers. They are also the major source of information for Western scholars writing case studies of the policy process or of interest-group activity.

One of the characteristics of the post-Stalin period has been the wide use of journals and newspapers for the initiation and discussion of policy recommendations. Within the authority-set limits, scholars, specialists, and other citizens may air their views on draft laws and other proposals. This practice has been in use for many years. The draft of the 1936 Constitution was subject to wide discussion before its final enactment. But such discussions have been much more frequent since Stalin. And it is not just proposed laws that receive such treatment. Jerry Hough has commented, "virtually no official policy is immune" from such discussion, within limits prescribed by the Party.[24]

Evidently these discussions can have an impact on policy proposals, and a number of the case studies of policy development have involved detailed examinations of the course of published commentaries on various issues. Western scholars also are occasionally able to include information based on interviews with opinion-group members, and such information is invariably more revealing than the published information. For instance, the American law professor Harold J. Berman has written of an interview with a Soviet legal scholar in which the latter asserted, in discussing an action of apparent illegality on the Soviet government's part, "we lawyers didn't like that."[25] Needless to say, such comments would not be aired in the Soviet press—which suggests that unpublished or oral communications among members of opinion groups, including discussions at their scholarly conferences and meetings, are important vehicles for the formation of group attitudes. But aside from the occasional interview or informal conversation with knowledgeable Soviet citizens, Western scholars have very little opportunity to learn about this aspect of the policy process and must rely mainly on whatever information is published.

So whether or not one is inclined to say that the processes described amount to interest-group activity, it does seem clear that they involve a wider sphere of consultation and discussion of policy than was once the norm in Soviet politics. Soviet spokespersons are quick to claim that this participation demonstrates the "genuinely democratic character" of the system, but it has little to do with democracy as we understand the term. It has been more accurately described by Western scholars in such terms as "participatory bureaucracy" and a "pluralism of elites."[26] This is not to deny that such participation might turn out to be a stage in the development toward a pluralism akin to that familiar in the West. But a genuine pluralism requires a level of tolerance and responsiveness to the dissident segments of society that the Soviet Union seems far from achieving.

Soviet publications frequently discuss the high degree of citizen participation in various types of public organizations such as trade unions, local soviet committees, and a multitude of other bodies. This activity is distinguishable from the interest articulation already discussed and might more accurately be described as mass political participation. The level of such participation claimed by Soviet authorities is impressive and suggests a considerable increase in recent years in the political activity of the Soviet populace at large. Some Western writers interpret such evidence as manifesting a genuine and significant increase in citizen participation in Soviet political life.[27] Others are more dubious, seeing the data (if they are to be accepted as accurate) as evidence of greater success by the regime in mobilizing and channeling popular participation into acceptable areas of formalized activity but not necessarily as evidence of a higher level of meaningful, genuine participation.[28] As indicated earlier, DiFranceisco and Gitelman found a strong belief among their respondents (recent Soviet emigrés to the West) in the efficacy of informal influence on policy implementation in individual cases. Their conclusion as to the relative importance of this kind of citizen activity on the one hand and ritualized mass participation on the other seems eminently sensible: ". . . the way Soviet people relate to the political administrative system is to go through the motions of participation in the nominally democratic process of making decisions, but to put far more serious effort into trying to influence the way decisions are implemented."[29]

DISSENT

When people speak of the dissident movement in the Soviet Union, they have in mind a phenomenon originating almost entirely in the 1960s. A scattering of expressions of dissent before that time have been documented, but the movement achieved widespread recognition in the outside world only after the 1950s. Its rise at that time seems to have been related to the partial liberalizations of the late 1950s and early 1960s and to frustrations growing out of the return to greater limitations on expression that followed Khrushchev's removal.[30]

In a large sense the dissident movement had its origins in the field of artistic expression, especially that of literature. There are several reasons for this. Among the various ways of expressing dissenting views in the Soviet Union, the written word is the most important. So it is not surprising that some writers would be among the dissenters. But the link between literature and dissonant political views is more basic. Throughout most of Soviet history the authorities have gone to great lengths to control literary expression, and their efforts have been largely successful. Officially published fiction and poetry are by and large supportive of the regime. If little of it amounts to inspired literature, at least it poses no political threat. But a relatively small number of writers and other artists have not conformed to the dictates of official policy. They have sought ways around it.

Literature and poetry can be vehicles for the expression of views by indirection, and they have long provided an outlet for mildly critical assessments of aspects of Soviet life that could not be criticized directly. A poem resounding with double meanings or a play about a foolish king portrayed in a way to remind the audience of a Soviet leader might be published or performed, and its underlying significance would not be lost on the Soviet public. "Getting it past the censor" has a long tradition, going well back into prerevolutionary Russia. This is not to say that anything and everything can be published in this way, or that writers and poets have not been criticized for what they have published. The ambit of acceptable literary expression has been subject to periodic contraction and expansion throughout Soviet history. For instance, Solzhenitsyn's novella about prison camp life, *One Day in the Life of Ivan Denisovich,* could be published in the relatively relaxed year of 1962. But aside from a few short pieces, nothing else by the author has ever been published in the Soviet Union. And Solzhenitsyn was severely criticized for his writings, including *One Day,* after the period of reaction had set in later in the 1960s. Many other writers have been similarly censured when caught beyond the bounds of the permissible. The worst of times for Soviet citizens in general have also been the worst of times for Soviet writers: During the heyday of Stalinism a large number died in prison or labor camps or were shot outright.

Soviet leaders seem to have an inordinate fear of the power of literature to serve as a catalyst in activating antiregime sentiment. Khrushchev was supposed to have said regarding the Hungarian Revolution of 1956, which was ruthlessly suppressed by the Soviet Army: "If ten or so Hungarian writers had been shot at the right moment, the revolution would never have occurred."[31] And as Solzhenitsyn himself has put it, "a great writer is, so to speak, a second government. That is why no regime anywhere has ever loved its great writers, only its minor ones."[32]

So while the writers have had a bit of latitude in expressing mild criticism of the system, they have had their frustrations as well. Fear of reprisal or discouragement at rejection of work submitted for publication has led many to write works in strict conformity with the dictates of official cultural policy. Others have taken to writing "for the desk drawer"—that is, producing work that could not be published because of its political or social content and might be shown at most to a few friends. Writing "for the drawer" has long been practiced in Russia, but only in the 1960s did some such writings make an emergence of sorts in the form of *samizdat*. The word *samizdat* means "self-published." It is an ironic usage, modeled after the acronym *gosizdat*, the term used in the name of official state publishing houses. *Samizdat* refers to underground publications, typescript and mimeographed copies of writings that circulate unofficially among various groups and individuals in the Soviet Union. Some of the contributors to *samizdat* are writers and artists, and a good bit of the early *samizdat* was poetry and fiction.[33] But the bulk of *samizdat* has long since been nonliterary, consisting largely of articles, essays, and other statements about political, economic, social, and religious life in the USSR.

A connection of a different sort between dissent and literary expression is the Siniavskii-Daniel trial of February 1966, an event of watershed importance in the dissident movement. Andrei Siniavskii and Yuli Daniel were Soviet writers whose works were smuggled out of the Soviet Union and published pseudonymously abroad. The writings gained a considerable following, and whether or not they were anti-Soviet in character (as the prosecution charged in the trial), they *were* beyond the bounds of approved Soviet literary expression and would not have been published within the country. Siniavskii and Daniel were finally discovered to be the authors of the works and were tried under Article 70 of the RSFSR Criminal Code, "Anti-Soviet Agitation and Propaganda." Their celebrated trial and subsequent prison sentences stirred liberal sentiment both within the country and outside. Many Soviet dissidents date their participation in the movement from the time of the trial. The unofficial record of this trial, prepared by the young writer Alexander Ginzburg, became a leading *samizdat* document. When Ginzburg and others were tried and sentenced in 1968 for their dissident activities, their trial brought forth even more protest. It was shortly after this trial that publication of the foremost *samizdat* journal, *The Chronicle of Current Events*, was initiated, and the dissident movement was launched in earnest.[34]

One of the marks of the dissident movement is its great diversity.

People dissent and protest for different reasons, and a great number of causes and interests are represented. Many dissenters are mainly interested in freedom of expression and other "democratic" rights. On the other hand, groups of Baptists, Orthodox believers, Catholics, and others stress religious freedom. Some members of minority nationalities protest against restrictions on them imposed by the Russian majority. Among the most well known are groups and individuals from among the Ukrainians, the Lithuanians, and the Crimean Tatars. A large number of Jews have protested in support of Jewish emigration and other causes. There are even dissidents of what might be called the extreme right, who favor a more authoritarian, traditional state, and whose ideology includes strong overtones of anti-Semitism, racism, and Russian nationalism.[35]

Even within these broad groupings diversity exists. Three of the most well known of the dissenters are the writer Aleksandr Solzhenitsyn, the physicist Andrei Sakharov, and the historian Roy Medvedev. They are all preoccupied with freedom of expression and intellectual freedom, among other legal and political rights. But their orientations are vastly different. Medvedev is a Marxian socialist who offers a "Leninist" critique of the Soviet system. He advocates a democratic socialism created by eliminating the abuses of the present system.[36] Sakharov's views are more reformist than Marxian and closely parallel those of Western European liberals and social democrats.[37] Solzhenitsyn thoroughly rejects Marxism-Leninism but is not completely comfortable with Western-type democratic views either. He believes that Russia is not yet ready for democracy and favors a kind of benevolent authoritarianism during the period of development toward democracy.[38]

These three have paid for their dissent in various ways. Solzhenitsyn was seized by Soviet authorities in 1974 and expelled from the country. He now lives in isolation in Vermont. Sakharov was banished from Moscow in January 1980, under an administrative procedure of dubious legality. Since then, he has been detained in Gorky, a city closed to foreigners, which is located 250 miles east of Moscow. Medvedev has remained free to live and continue his writing in Moscow but has been subjected to various forms of harassment by the authorities.

Forms of Dissent

In spite of this diversity, a certain amount of coherence has existed within groups in the dissident community. A number of formal and informal groups have been created, one of the earliest being the Moscow Committee on Human Rights, founded in 1970 by Sakharov and two younger physicists, Valerii Chalidze and André Tverdokhlebov. In 1976 the Moscow branch of the Public Group to Promote the Fulfillment of the Helsinki Accords was created, and parallel groups were founded in several other Soviet republics. What distinguished the efforts of such groups as these from earlier manifestations of dissent was the open acknowledgement of membership by participants. Such groupings have been the focal point for much of the dissident activity about which we in the West have heard.

As mentioned, the foremost manifestation of dissent has been the written word, but such communication has taken several forms. One practice is the "nonpublic protest," such as the signing of petitions addressed to Party and governmental leaders calling for changes in governmental practices or the release of persons held by the authorities. Although some of these petitions later received publicity, their original objective was to appeal to the leadership through nonpublic channels. One analyst has suggested that this form of dissent predominated in the early stages of the movement (that is, until the mid-to-late 1960s) because it was more consonant with the approved Soviet political style of airing grievances in private.[39]

After the pivotal Siniavskii-Daniel trial in 1966, the tendency toward *public* dissent grew. The aforementioned Ginzburg "white book" on the trial was prepared for public dissemination, and when several associates of Ginzburg (Galanskov, Dobrovolsky, and Lashkova) were arrested, a public *demonstration* protesting these arrests was held in Moscow's Pushkin Square. The leading participants in this demonstration (Bukovsky, Khaustov, and others) were duly arrested and tried, as were Ginzburg and his associates. A central figure in publicizing these events was Pavel Litvinov, a young physicist known until then mainly for being the grandson of Maxim Litvinov, a long-time Soviet Foreign Minister during the 1930s. Litvinov, who was converted to the dissident cause by the Siniavskii-Daniel trial, prepared widely circulated accounts of the trials of these two groups of defendants. These compilations were later published in the West as books.[40]

At the end of the trial of Ginzburg and the others in January 1968, Litvinov (with Larisa Bogaraz, wife of Daniel) distributed to foreign correspondents and others a plea to world public opinion protesting the trial.[41] This action illustrates another form of protest used by dissenters, the appeal to the outside world. Such pleas have been widely used by the dissident community and have helped to rally to the cause sympathizers from outside the Soviet Union.

A few months after the Ginzburg trial, on August 25, 1968, Litvinov participated with others in a demonstration against the Soviet invasion of Czechoslovakia. Held in Red Square in the heart of Moscow, only a few yards from the Lenin Mausoleum, the demonstration was quickly put down. The participants were beaten, taken off to jail, and tried shortly thereafter. Litvinov served four months in prison and several years in Siberian exile. The account of the demonstration in Red Square and the subsequent trial became a leading *samizdat* document and was also published in the West as a book.[42]

A kind of institutionalization of protest was evidenced by the initiation in 1968 of the journal *The Chronicle of Current Events*. The *Chronicle* became a regular bimonthly publication of credible, accurate information which provided the dissenters with a reliable channel of communication. As will be shown, the Soviet authorities went to considerable lengths to silence this publication. Although the *Chronicle* was the best known of the journals, a number of others, representing other aspects of the dissent movement, also came into being. Among them have been the *Ukrainian Herald;* the *Chronicle of the Lithuanian Catholic Church; Veche,* which represented a strong Russian nationalist viewpoint; and *Political Diary,* which is said to have circulated among fairly high-placed Party officials.

Another manifestation of the growth of dissent has been its extension to more particular causes. The late 1970s saw the stirrings of efforts to create an unofficial trade-union movement in the USSR, which led in 1978 to the formation of the Free Interprofessional Union of Workers (SMOT).[43] At about the same time, a group of Soviet women began publishing a *samizdat* feminist journal called *Women in the USSR,* and an organization known as the Action Group for the Defense of the Rights of Invalids in the USSR published its first *Bulletin.* Religious groups, especially Catholics in Lithuania, have for a number of years been active in religious dissent. In the late 1970s such new groups as "The Christian Seminar on Problems of Religious Revival," "The Christian Committee for the Defense of the Rights of Believers" (both oriented toward the Russian Orthodox Church), and "The Catholic Committee for the Defense of the Rights of Believers" came into prominence.

There have also been more extreme forms of manifesting dissident views. A bomb explosion in a Moscow subway train in 1977, which killed seven and injured thirty-seven, led to the execution of three Soviet Armenians.[44] Numerous fires in the Georgian Republic, including one at the Georgian Council of Ministers in 1976, have allegedly been politically motivated. In 1970 a dozen persons, ten of whom were Jews, were sentenced to prison for attempting to hijack an airplane in Leningrad in order to flee the country.* Since then, there have been other attempted hijackings, at least one of which has succeeded.[45] A dozen or more self-immolations, several in the Lithuanian SSR, in protest against the Soviet system took place during the late 1960s and 1970s.[46] These are the acts of desperate people. They are not typical forms of dissent. But if the other dissenters cannot be characterized as desperate, it is fair to say that they pursue their objectives against great odds and with little hope of success. As has been noted with regard to demonstrations in other countries, protest is the political resource of the powerless.[47]

No wonder, then, that there are not many dissidents. Estimates of

---

*Two of the defendants in this case, M. Dymshits and E. S. Kuznetsov, were originally sentenced to death, but after a worldwide outcry at the severity of the punishment, the death sentences were commuted. In 1979, Dymshits and Kuznetsov were freed and allowed to leave for the West, along with three other Soviet dissidents, in exchange for two convicted Soviet spies being held in the United States.

the number of dissidents in the "democratic movement" (that is, those advocating increases in democratic rights and freedom of expression) range between several hundred and about three thousand.[48] The number of protesters against Soviet religious and nationality policies may be somewhat higher,[49] but it is still a figure that reaches only to the thousands. There are probably a considerable number of silent sympathizers who approve of the views of the active dissidents.[50] But just as surely, a much higher proportion of the population is indifferent, unsympathetic, or downright hostile. As in other societies, most of the people express little interest in matters political. Given Russia's political history, it seems likely that most Soviet citizens would have even less inclination than their counterparts in many other countries to test their ability to influence governmental policy. This is testimony not so much to the success of Soviet political socialization as to the poverty of citizen experience in genuine political participation, coupled with an appreciation of the consequences in store for those who challenge the system.

For the vast majority of the Soviet population, in other words, the Soviet authorities have succeeded in stifling the inclination to protest. This is not to be equated with creating a completely satisfied populace, however. The leaders must harbor some fear that the dissent movement could grow to proportions that would be difficult to manage. They have sought to discourage dissent in various ways.

Suppressing Dissent

Several of the more publicized trials have been mentioned. Scores of other dissidents have been sent to prison or labor camps after trials that received far less publicity or none at all. A variety of measures of "extra-judicial repression" have silenced many more. Many of the signers of early protest letters either lost their jobs or were threatened with dismissal. Anyone who persisted in dissent after a warning would at least face this prospect. A variety of forms of long-term harassment have also been used, including repeated house searches, frequent summonses for questioning, and constant following and surveillance by secret-police operatives. Nor are the defense lawyers in the political trials immune from sanction for zealous advocacy on behalf of their clients. The Moscow lawyer Boris Zolotukhin was expelled from the Party and removed as head of a legal consultation office after his defense of Alexander Ginzburg. Other defense lawyers have been treated to like forms of harassment.

Samizdat publications have been subjected to varying levels of harassment over the years. The authorities have seemed particularly intent on stamping out the more well-known underground periodicals. Perhaps the most famous of these, *The Chronicle of Current Events,* was edited by a variety of individuals from its inception in 1968 until it ceased publishing in 1982.[51]

For those whose actions appear inappropriate for judicial repression, enforced incarceration in psychiatric hospitals has been used. Several books by dissidents, including Vladimir Bukovsky's *To Build a Castle: My Life as a Dissenter* (1978), Leonid Plyushch's *History's Carnival: A Dissident's Autobiography* (1979), and Peter Grigorenko's *Memoirs* (1982), provide vivid accounts of experiences in psychiatric hospitals. This practice, which has analogs in prerevolutionary Russia, is sometimes accompanied by the compulsory administration of drugs.

Attempts by the regime to suppress dissent appeared to gain momentum in the late 1970s and early 1980s.[52] The crackdown at this time is thought to have been connected with the USSR's hosting of the Moscow Olympics in 1980 and perhaps with the low level of Western protest against the treatment of dissidents due to the distractions of Iran and Afghanistan. Whatever the explanation, the intensification of repression appears to be part of a cyclical pattern of governmental response to dissent.[53] This suggests both that the Soviet leadership has been attuned to world public opinion relative to its treatment of dissidents and that it has not yet found a completely successful policy for containing the dissident movement.

Another regime practice for dealing with troublesome dissidents is banishment from the country. As noted, Solzhenitsyn was simply arrested and forcibly deported to the West in February 1974. A number of others, including the late Andrei Amalrik, Valerii Chalidze, Pavel Litvinov, and Zhores Medvedev, were "invited" to leave, with the clear implication that long prison sentences faced them if they refused. After departure they were deprived of Soviet citizenship. Alexander Ginzburg, Valentyn Moroz, and three others who were serving prison sentences for dissident activities were taken from prison and sent directly to the West (in exchange for two convicted Soviet spies being held in the United States). Such banishment has been successful in removing important dissidents from the scene and has helped weaken some of the protesting groups. In the same way, allowing some of the most vocal dissident Jews to emigrate has undoubtedly eased the pressure that the authorities feel from this area. And, as noted, for his outspoken dissident views Andrei Sakharov in 1980 earned "internal banishment" from Moscow to the city of Gorky.

Finally, in their efforts to combat dissent, the authorities have attempted to manipulate the "hard-hat mentality" and antipathy toward Jews and other minorities that characterizes some working-class Russians. The KGB operatives who beat up Litvinov and his fellow pro-Czechoslovak demonstrators shouted "beat up the Jews," "dirty yids," and other epithets, and in doing so expressed a persistent theme in Russian history—that of "Russian Jew as scapegoat."[54]

As a result of these measures, it appears that in recent years the Soviet leaders have reduced the dissent movement to a more manageable level. But there has been a cost. The efforts of dissenters have not met with complete failure. And this fact brings the discussion of dissent back into the context of the chapter, that is, the influence that the dissenters have had on policy making.

The Impact of Dissent

It is clear that not all dissidents or dissident groups are equally influential. The success of a group of respected scientists in obtaining the release of the biologist Zhores Medvedev from a KGB psychiatric hospital could not have been achieved by an unknown aggregation of protesters. The relatively mild response to the outspoken views of academician Sakharov, even after his banishment from Moscow, and the choice of exile rather than prison for Solzhenitsyn obviously reflect the importance and international following of these two men. On the other hand, the repeated incarcerations of Andrei Amalrik,* the author of the essay "Will the Soviet Union Survive Until 1984?," and the harsh treatment of many other dissenters indicate the attitude of the authorities toward protesters who do not possess significant political resources.

To the extent that the size and authority of one's "constituency" are related to the treatment one is accorded, dissident politics in the Soviet Union resembles politics in general. The political objectives sought by the various dissenters also have a bearing on their success. Certainly the more grandiose aims of some dissenters—to create a multiparty system or to eliminate Marxist-Leninist ideology, for instance—have not been and will not soon be realized. Such dissenters, according to the American political scientist Rudolf Tökés, manifest a "moral absolutist" ideology, and their impact is likely to be minimal. More likely to succeed, according to Tökés, are dissenters who follow an "instrumental-pragmatic" approach, that is, one that emphasizes bargaining or negotiation toward rational ends. This approach has been practiced so far largely by scientists and other specialists. Obtaining the release of Medvedev from the psychiatric hospital is seen as an example of such efforts. Tökés believes that under the right conditions, the influence of the instrumental-pragmatic dissenters could be significant.[55]

Another factor relevant to dissident success involves the basis of one's support, specifically, whether or not it extends beyond the bounds of Soviet territory. The mass emigration of Soviet Jews to Israel and other countries, which took place largely during the 1970s, would have been unthinkable a few years earlier and certainly would not have taken place without pressure from Soviet Jews themselves. But their ability to arouse the support and sympathy of the outside world had much to do with the decision to allow the emigration. One of the strongest weapons in the hands of the dissenters has been the ability to ally themselves with sympathetic public opinion in the West. An unusual communications network has been established which includes the following aspects: Dissidents provide information to Western newsmen, which is publicized in the West; *samizdat* becomes *tamizdat* (*tam* = "over there," that is, abroad), meaning *samizdat* material that is published in

---

*Amalrik was forced to emigrate from the USSR in 1976. He was killed in an automobile accident in Spain late in 1980.

the West; Western public opinion is aroused, resulting in demands on Western governments to press the Soviet government for better treatment of dissidents; Western radio stations broadcast to the Soviet Union, informing Soviet citizens of the developments. It was clearly a pattern of interest articulation of this kind that led the Soviet authorities in 1973 to suspend the "education tax," a charge of thousands of rubles for the costs of higher education that was demanded of departing emigrants who had degrees. And the so-called Jackson Amendment (named after U.S. Senator Henry Jackson, its sponsor), which offered trade concessions to the Soviet Union in exchange for a freer Soviet emigration policy, was also influenced by this communications pattern.

Another effect of dissident activities has been their impact on Moscow's ability to control the world communist movement. A number of communist parties, particularly those in Western Europe, have disassociated themselves from the Soviet policy of handling internal dissent. Seeing the possibility of gaining a share of power in their countries, the Italian and French Communist parties, the two largest in Western Europe, have at times publicly criticized the Soviet treatment of dissidents. French Communist Party leader George Marchais boycotted the Twenty-Fifth Congress of the CPSU in Moscow in 1976, apparently in part because of what he called the Soviet Union's "unjust and unjustifiable acts of repression against Soviet citizens."[56] While relations between the CPSU and the French Communist Party improved after 1976, Soviet policy toward its dissidents continues to be a source of discord between the two parties.

In general it appears that publicity in the West concerning Soviet treatment of dissidents imposes some restraint on the authorities. The release of a number of dissidents from incarceration and the granting of permission to emigrate to a number of others, after repeated refusals of permission, are probably attributable in part to the pressure of Western public opinion. The dissidents themselves appreciate the value of this alliance. They fear détente between the Soviet Union and the United States because they believe that they might be sacrificed in the interests of better relations on the official level. As Pavel Litvinov said after his coerced departure from the USSR in 1974: "I want all of you to understand that we have survived because the West exists and in it a Western press."[57] As corollary to this point, where the presence of Western foreigners in the USSR is infrequent or absent, the treatment of dissenters is perceived to be more harsh.[58]

In conclusion, Soviet dissidents so far have not had much success in effecting reforms within the country. But they have caused problems for the Soviet leaders that are not easily solved and have thereby changed official behavior to some degree. Because the regime is concerned about world public opinion and about its own position as leader of the world communist movement, it has chosen not to eliminate the dissenters with the ruthlessness and abandon used against opponents during the Stalin period. It has been decidedly cautious in its treatment of prominent dissenters and has at times abandoned measures taken against certain others when international protest reached a high level. Such results probably constitute sufficient encouragement so that the small number of citizens inclined to dissent will continue to do so. The leaders should have little trouble containing dissent at this level. But if they wish to improve their international position, they may have to ease up on the treatment of this portion of their citizenry. Such a move would have significant implications for the development of Soviet domestic politics.

NOTES

[1]See, for instance, Peter H. Solomon, Jr., *Soviet Criminologists and Criminal Policy: Specialists in Policy Making* (New York: Columbia University Press, 1978), pp. 19–32. Although Solomon's conclusions are carefully drawn and moderate in tone, there has been some tendency to overstate the meaning of his findings. One reviewer of Solomon's book reaches the following conclusion which, to the authors, is unwarranted: "Neither the character of the criminologists' participation in terms of its scope, quality and effect, nor the political constraints on their capacity to influence policy appears to be significantly different from what is found in the U.S. or Britain." *The American Political Science Review*, 73, No. 3 (June 1980), 573.

[2]See Barbara N. McLennan, ed., *Political Opposition and Dissent* (New York: Dunellen Publishing Co., 1973), pp. 16–21.

[3]The best book on opposition during the periods of Lenin and Stalin is Robert V. Daniels, *The Conscience of the Revolution* (New York: Simon and Schuster, 1960). See also Roland Gaucher, *Opposition in the U.S.S.R., 1917–1967* (New York: Funk and Wagnalls, 1969); George Saunders, *Samizdat: Voices of the Soviet Opposition* (New York: Monad Press, 1974). The last book has a section devoted to early opposition to Stalin.

[4]See on this point the discussion by Carl A. Linden, *Khrushchev and the Soviet Leadership, 1957–1964* (Baltimore: The Johns Hopkins Press, 1966), esp. pp. 1–9.

[5]See Adam B. Ulam, *The Russian Political System* (New York: Random House, 1974), p. 53.

[6]Gabriel Almond and G. Bingham Powell, Jr., *Comparative Politics* (Boston: Little, Brown, 2nd ed., 1978), p. 175.

[7]Ibid., pp. 170–74.

[8]Franklyn Griffiths, "A Tendency Analysis of Soviet Policy Making," in *Interest Groups in Soviet Politics*, ed. H. Gordon Skilling and Franklyn Griffiths (Princeton, NJ: Princeton University Press, 1971), esp. pp. 340–41; and William E. Odom, *The Soviet Volunteers: Modernization and Bureaucracy in a Public Mass Organization* (Princeton, NJ: Princeton University Press, 1973), pp. 318–21.

[9]Almond and Powell, *Comparative Politics*, p. 174. For further discussion see the first edition of Almond and Powell (Boston: Little, Brown, 1966), p. 77, and Almond's earlier writing, for example, his "Introduction" in *The Politics of Developing Areas*, eds. Gabriel Almond and James S. Coleman (Princeton, NJ: Princeton University Press, 1960), p. 33.

[10]Griffiths, "A Tendency Analysis," p. 342.

[11]Ibid. In a 1983 article on interest groups and communist politics, Skilling describes much of the more recent research and reiterates his support for the "opinion group" concept. "Interest Groups and Communist Politics Revisited," *World Politics*, 36, No. 1 (Oct. 1983), 1–27.

[12]Joel J. Schwartz and William R. Keech, "Group Influence and the Policy Process in the Soviet Union," *American Political Science Review*, 62, No. 3 (Sept. 1968), 840; Philip D. Stewart, "Soviet Interest Groups and the Policy Process: The Repeal of Production Education," *World Politics*, 22, No. 1 (Oct. 1969), 29.

[13]Richard W. Judy, "The Economists," in *Interest Groups in Soviet Politics*, p. 209 and especially pp. 233–40; Loren R. Graham, "Reorganization of the USSR Academy of Sciences," in *Soviet Policy Making*, ed. Peter H. Juviler and Henry W. Morton (New York: Holt, Rinehart & Winston, 1967), p. 133.

[14]See Donald D. Barry and Harold J. Berman, "The Jurists," in *Interest Groups in Soviet Politics*, p. 291 and especially pp. 321–30 and sources cited therein; John Gorgone, "Soviet Jurists in the Legislative Arena: The Reform of Criminal Procedure," *Soviet Union*, 3, No. 1 (1976), 1; Solomon, *Soviet Criminologists and Criminal Policy;* Morris A. McCain, Jr., "Soviet Lawyers and the Reform Debate: Cohesion and Efficacy," paper presented at the Eleventh National Convention of the American Association for the Advancement of Slavic Studies, Oct. 1979.

[15]These professions are covered in *Interest Groups in Soviet Politics*.

[16]Theodore H. Friedgut, "Interests and Groups in Soviet Policy-Making: The MTS Reforms," *Soviet Studies*, 28 (1976), 524; Donald R. Kelley, "Environmental Policy-Making in the USSR: The Role of Industrial and Environmental Interest Groups," *Soviet Studies*, 28 (1976), 570, 585–86; Griffiths, "A Tendency Analysis," pp. 361, 407.

[17]Howard L. Biddulph, "Local Interest Articulation at CPSU Congresses," *World Politics*, 36, No. 1 (Oct. 1983), 28–52.

[18]The idea of diverting Siberian rivers southward was proposed during the nineteenth century and revived during the period of Stalin's rule. Much attention has been given to the matter in the Soviet press since the late 1970s. For discussions in English, with references to Soviet sources, see *Radio Liberty Research*, Nos. 189/78 (Aug. 29, 1978), 76/81 (Feb. 20, 1981), 478/81 (Dec. 1, 1981), 154/82 (Apr. 6, 1982), 167/82 (Apr. 20, 1982), 196/83 (May 17, 1983), 260/84 (Jul. 3, 1984), 313/84 (Aug. 20, 1984), and *The New York Times*, May 6, 1983, p. A2, and Feb. 7, 1985, p. A6.

[19]See William E. Odom, "The Party Connection," *Problems of Communism*, 22, No. 6 (Sept.–Oct. 1973), 12, 17.

[20]Griffiths, "A Tendency Analysis," p. 369. A useful survey of the interest-group literature is David E. Powell, "In Pursuit of Interest Groups in the USSR," *Soviet Union*, 6, No. 1 (1979), 99. The authors do not share Powell's conclusion concerning the interest-group approach that (p. 122) "efforts to apply it to the Soviet Union result in a massive distortion of reality." But they do agree with his views (see esp. p. 124) concerning the high level of control exercised by Soviet leaders over the influence of specialists.

[21]On this point see Paul Cocks, "The Policy Process and Bureaucratic Politics," in *The Dynamics of Soviet Politics*, eds. Paul Cocks, Robert V. Daniels, and Nancy Whittier Heer (Cambridge, MA: Harvard University Press, 1976), pp. 161–62. Cocks suggests that the recent use of the "systems approach," which has been gaining favor among some Soviet leaders and technocrats, is intended to strengthen the central Party apparatus "to counter pluralist tendencies and particularist forces" (p. 170), such as those described by scholars studying Soviet interest groups.

[22]Wayne DiFranceisco and Zvi Gitelman, "Soviet Political Culture and 'Covert Participation' in Policy Implementation," *The American Political Science Review*, 78, No. 3 (Sept. 1984), 611.

[23]See, for example, Milton C. Lodge, *Soviet Elite Attitudes Since Stalin* (Columbus, OH: Charles E. Merrill Publishing Co., 1969), especially pp. 27–30.

[24]Jerry F. Hough, "The Soviet System: Petrification or Pluralism?" *Problems of Communism*, 12, No. 2 (Mar.–Apr. 1972), 31.

[25]Harold J. Berman, "The Struggle of Soviet Jurists Against a Return to Stalinist Terror," *Slavic Review*, 22, No. 2 (Jun. 1963), 315. Among other scholars who have made use of interviews in this kind of research see Solomon, *Soviet Criminologists*, passim.

[26]The terms are those of Robert V. Daniels and Gordon Skilling, respectively, as cited in Hough, "The Soviet System," p. 28. Hough uses the term "institutionalized pluralism" as suggestive of this state of development, but he is careful to distinguish it from the democratic pluralism of the West.

[27]See in particular Jerry F. Hough, Chap. 4, "Political Participation in the Soviet Union," p. 109–24, in *The Soviet Union and Social Science Theory* (Cambridge, MA: Harvard University Press, 1977). Hough discusses participation along similar lines at several points in Jerry F. Hough and Merle Fainsod, *How the Soviet Union is Governed* (Cambridge, MA: Harvard University Press, 1979); see esp. pp. 285–319. Another important work, which is more balanced in its conclusions as to the significance of mass participation, is Theodore H. Friedgut, *Political Participation in the USSR* (Princeton, NJ: Princeton University Press, 1979).

[28]See the exchange between Jerry F. Hough and Donald Barry in Samuel Hendel, ed., *The Soviet Crucible: The Soviet System in Theory and Practice* (North Scituate, MA: Duxbury Press, 1980), pp. 221–31; see also George W. Breslauer, "Khrushchev Reconsidered," in *The Soviet*

Union Since Stalin, eds. Stephen F. Cohen, Alexander Rabinowitch, and Robert Sharlet (Bloomington, IN: Indiana University Press, 1980), pp. 50–70. An important article on this subject is Aryeh L. Unger, "Political Participation in the USSR: YCL and CPSU," *Soviet Studies,* 33, No. 1 (Jan. 1981), 107–24. A balanced and interesting view of much of the writing on participation is D. Richard Little, "Political Participation and the Soviet System," *Problems of Communism,* 29 (Jul.–Aug. 1980), 62–67.

²⁹DiFranceisco and Gitelman, "Soviet Political Culture," p. 604. This article contains references to much of the recent literature of Soviet political participation.

³⁰Julia Wishnevsky's analysis, from the vantage point of 1984, of the origins of the dissident movement, is instructive on this point. Among other things, she states: "With some qualifications, it is reasonable to say that the Soviet dissident movement in its traditional form came into being as a reaction to Khrushchev's ouster." "The Fall of Khrushchev and the Birth of the Human Rights Movement in the Soviet Union," *Radio Liberty Research,* No. 382/84, Oct. 8, 1984, p. 1.

³¹Noel Barber, *Seven Days of Freedom: The Hungarian Uprising, 1956* (New York: Stein and Day, 1974), p. 17.

³²Aleksandr I. Solzhenitsyn, *The First Circle,* trans. Thomas P. Whitney (New York: Harper and Row, Bantam Books, 1967), p. 415.

³³See Rudolf F. Tökés, "Varieties of Soviet Dissent: An Overview," in *Dissent in the USSR: Politics, Ideology and People,* ed. Rudolph L. Tökés (Baltimore: The Johns Hopkins University Press, 1975), pp. 11–12; Joseph Langland et al., eds., *Poetry From the Russian Underground* (New York: Harper and Row, 1973), pp. 7–19; F.J.M. Feldbrugge, *Samizdat and Political Dissent in the Soviet Union* (Leiden, the Netherlands: A. W. Sijthoff, 1975), p. 53.

³⁴On the Siniavskii-Daniel trial, see Max Hayward, ed., trans., *On Trial: The Soviet State Versus "Abram Tertz" and "Nikolai Arzhak,"* rev. ed., enl. (New York: Harper and Row, 1967). On the trial of Ginzburg and the others, see Peter Reddaway, ed., *The Trial of the Four* (New York: Viking, 1972). The "trial of the four" was also covered in early issues of *The Chronicle of Current Events.* For an English translation of the first eleven issues of the *Chronicle,* see Peter Reddaway, ed., trans. *Uncensored Russia* (New York: McGraw-Hill, American Heritage Press, 1972).

³⁵See Alexander Yanov, *The Russian New Right* (Berkeley, CA: Institute of International Studies, University of California, 1978); John B. Dunlop, *The New Russian Revolutionaries* (Belmont, MA: Nordland Publishing Co., 1976); *The Political, Social and Religious Thought of Russian "Samizdat"—An Anthology,* eds. Michael Meerson-Aksenov and Boris Shragin (Belmont, MA: Nordland Publishing Co., 1977), part VI, pp. 345–448. A suggestive, if exaggerated, analysis of the influence and plans of dissident rightists working in concert with Russian nationalists in the present Soviet establishment is Elena Klepikova and Vladimir Solovyov, "The Secret Russian Party," *Midstream,* 26, No. 8 (Oct. 1980), 12.

³⁶See Roy A. Medvedev, *On Socialist Democracy* (New York: Knopf, 1975); *On Stalin and Stalinism* (New York: Oxford University Press, 1979).

³⁷See Andrei D. Sakharov, *Sakharov Speaks* (New York: Knopf, 1974); *My Country and the World* (New York: Knopf, 1975); *Alarm and Hope* (New York: Random House, 1978).

³⁸A volume that includes several of Solzhenitsyn's most important political statements is *East and West* (New York: Harper and Row, 1980).

³⁹Howard L. Biddulph, "Protest Strategies of the Soviet Intellectual Opposition," in *Dissent in the USSR,* p. 103.

⁴⁰On the trial of Ginzburg and the others, see *The Trial of the Four;* on the trial of the demonstrators in Pushkin Square see Pavel Litvinov, *The Demonstration in Pushkin Square* (Boston: Gambit, 1969).

⁴¹The text of the plea "To World Public Opinion" is published in Karel Van Het Reve, ed., *Dear Comrade: Pavel Litvinov and the Voices of Soviet Citizens in Dissent* (New York: Pitman, 1969), p. 39; see also p. xv.

⁴²Natalia Gorbanevskaya, *Red Square at Noon* (New York: Holt, Rinehart & Winston, 1972).

⁴³See John C. Michael, "The Independent Trade Union Movement in the Soviet Union," *Radio Liberty Research,* No. 304/79, Oct. 11, 1979.

⁴⁴See Ann Sheehy, "Three Executed for Moscow Metro Bombing," *Radio Liberty Research,*

No. 44/79, Feb. 12, 1979, and Radio Liberty, *Current Abstracts and Annotations,* 1980, No. 10, p. 10.

[45]See "Hijacker Stripped of Soviet Citizenship," *Radio Liberty Research,* No. 108/80, Mar. 10, 1980; also Radio Liberty, *Current Abstracts and Annotations,* 1979, No. 19, p. 15.

[46]See Julia Wishnevsky, "A History of Recent Self-Immolations in the USSR," *Radio Liberty Research,* No. 74/77, Mar. 29, 1977; also Radio Liberty, *Current Abstracts and Annotations,* 1979, No. 8, p. 10.

[47]Biddulph, "Protest Strategies," pp. 96, 101; and see the sources cited in Biddulph's notes 2 and 3, p. 96.

[48]Theodore Friedgut, "The Democratic Movement: Dimensions and Perspectives," in *Dissent in the USSR,* pp 123–24.

[49]For instance, Barbara Wolfe Jancar cites a petition signed by 17,000 Lithuanian Catholics. See "Religious Dissent in the Soviet Union," in *Dissent in the USSR,* p. 196.

[50]One *samizdat* source counts among the dissidents those who refuse to take part in elections or who vote against the single candidate. By this method the author comes up with a figure of 200,000 to 250,000. See Radio Liberty, *Current Abstracts and Annotations,* 1980, No. 15, p. 10.

[51]See Julia Wishnevsky, "Dissent under Three Soviet Leaders: Suppression Continues, The Style Varies," *Radio Liberty Research,* No. 89/85, Mar. 21, 1985, p. 4, and "From Gorbanevskaya to Smirnov: The Fate of the Chroniclers," *Radio Liberty Research,* No. 241/83, Jun. 22, 1983. A thorough analysis in English of the *Chronicle of Current Events* is Mark Hopkins, *Russia's Underground Press: The Chronicle of Current Events* (New York: Praeger Publishers, 1983).

[52]Elizabeth C. Scheetz refers to this period as "doubtless the most severe such crackdown since the Soviet dissident movement took shape in the late 1960's." "Hard Times for Dissent in the USSR," *Radio Liberty Research,* No. 184/80, May 21, 1980, p. 1.

[53]See Peter Reddaway, "Soviet Policy Toward Dissent Since Khrushchev," *Radio Liberty Research,* No. 297/80, Aug. 21, 1980, p. 20.

[54]See Gorbanevskaya, *Red Square,* pp. 28, 33, 37 for the quotations of the KGB operatives who broke up the demonstration, and Harrison Salisbury's "Introduction" in ibid., p. 8, on the Soviet hard-hat mentality.

[55]Rudolph Tökés, "Dissent: The Politics for Change in the USSR," in *Soviet Politics and Society in the 1970's,* ed. Henry W. Morton and Rudolf L. Tökés (New York: Free Press, 1974), pp. 32–33. Another classification of dissident activities is given by Erik Hoffman in "Political Opposition in the Soviet Union," in *Political Opposition,* p. 334.

[56]*The New York Times,* Feb. 5, 1976, p. 1. On Marchais's boycott of the CPSU Congress, see ibid., Feb. 29, 1976, p. 1.

[57]"Press Statement of Pavel Litvinov on March 22, 1974," *Radio Liberty Dispatch,* Apr. 17, 1974, p. 2.

[58]Lev Navrozov in his haunting essay on twentieth-century Russia returns again and again to the difference between "the cities which foreigners are permitted to visit" and those which they are not. *The Education of Lev Navrozov: A Life in the Closed World Once Called Russia* (New York: Harper's Magazine Press, 1975), pp. 9, 19, 22, 23. On this point, also see Frederick C. Barghoorn, "The Post-Khrushchev Campaign to Suppress Dissent: Perspectives, Strategies, and Techniques of Repression," in *Dissent in the USSR,* pp. 76–77.

SELECTED BIBLIOGRAPHY

ALEXEEVA, LUDMILA, "The Movement for Social and Economic Rights in the Soviet Union," *Russia,* No. 5–6 (1982), 81–89.

BARGHOORN, FREDERICK C., *Détente and the Democratic Movement in the USSR.* New York: Free Press, 1976.

BIDDULPH, HOWARD L., "Local Interest Articulation at CPSU Congresses," *World Politics,* XXXVI, No. 1 (Oct. 1983), 28–52.

BLOCH, SIDNEY, and PETER REDDAWAY, *Psychiatric Terror.* New York: Basic Books, 1977.

BUKOVSKY, VLADIMIR, *To Build a Castle: My Life as a Dissenter.* New York: Viking, 1979.

COHEN, STEPHEN F., ed., *An End to Silence: Uncensored Opinion in the Soviet Union* (from Roy Medvedev's Underground magazine *Political Diary*). New York: W. W. Norton & Co., 1982.

CUTLER, ROBERT M., "Soviet Dissent Under Khrushchev: An Analytical Study," *Comparative Politics,* 13, No. 1 (Oct. 1980), 15–35.

DiFRANCEISCO, WAYNE, and ZVI GITELMAN, "Soviet Political Culture and 'Covert Participation' in Policy Implementation," *American Political Science Review,* 78, No. 3 (Sept. 1984), 603–21.

DUNLOP, JOHN B., *The New Russian Revolutionaries.* Belmont, MA: Nordland Publishing Co., 1976.

FELDBRUGGE, F.J.M., *Samizdat and Political Dissent in the Soviet Union.* Leiden, the Netherlands: A. W. Sijthoff, 1975.

FIRESIDE, HARVEY, *Soviet Psychoprisons.* New York: W. W. Norton & Co., 1979.

FRIEDGUT, THEODORE H., *Political Participation in the USSR.* Princeton, NJ: Princeton University Press, 1979.

GORBANEVSKAYA, NATALIA, *Red Square at Noon.* New York: Holt, Rinehart & Winston, 1972.

GRIGORENKO, PETER, *Memoirs.* New York: W. W. Norton & Co., 1982.

HAYWARD, MAX, trans. and ed., *On Trial: The Soviet State Versus "Abram Tertz" and "Nikolai Arzhak,"* rev. ed. enl. New York: Harper & Row, 1967.

HINGLEY, RONALD, *Russian Writers and Soviet Society, 1917–1978.* New York: Random House, 1979.

HOPKINS, MARK, *Russia's Underground Press: The Chronicle of Current Events.* New York: Praeger Publishers, 1983.

HOUGH, JERRY F., *The Soviet Union and Social Science Theory.* Cambridge, MA: Harvard University Press, 1977.

KUZNETSOV, EDWARD, *Prison Diaries.* New York: Stein and Day, 1975.

LITVINOV, PAVEL, *The Demonstration on Pushkin Square.* Boston: Gambit, 1969.

LOWENHARDT, JOHN, *Decision Making in Soviet Politics.* New York: St. Martin's Press, 1981.

MEDVEDEV, ROY A., *On Socialist Democracy.* New York: Knopf, 1975.

———, *On Stalin and Stalinism.* New York: Oxford University Press, 1979.

MEDVEDEV, ZHORES A., *Ten Years After Ivan Denisovich.* New York: Vintage Books, 1974.

MEERSON-AKSENOV, MICHAEL, and BORIS SHRAGIN, eds., *The Political, Social And Religious Thought of Russian "Samizdat"—An Anthology.* Belmont, MA: Nordland Publishing Co., 1977.

NEKIPELOV, VICTOR, *Institute of Fools: Notes from the Serbsky.* New York: Farrar, Straus, & Giroux, 1980.

PLYUSHCH, LEONID, *History's Carnival: A Dissident's Autobiography.* New York: Harcourt Brace Jovanovich, 1979.

REDDAWAY, PETER, ed., *The Trial of the Four.* New York: Viking, 1972.

———, *Uncensored Russia.* New York: McGraw-Hill, American Heritage Press, 1972.

———, "Dissent in the Soviet Union," *Problems of Communism,* 32, No. 6 (Nov./Dec. 1983), pp. 1–15.

SAKHAROV, ANDREI D., *Alarm and Hope,* New York: Knopf, 1978.

———, *My Country and the World.* New York: Knopf, 1976.

———, *Progress, Coexistence and Intellectual Freedom.* New York: W. W. Norton & Co., 1968.

———, *Sakharov Speaks.* New York: Vintage Books, 1974.

SKILLING, H. GORDON, "Interest Groups and Communist Politics Revisited," *World Politics,* XXXVI. No. 1 (Oct. 1983), 1–27.

SKILLING, H. GORDON, and FRANKLYN GRIFFITHS, eds. *Interest Groups in Soviet Politics.* Princeton, NJ: Princeton University Press, 1971.

SOLOMON, PETER H., JR., *Soviet Criminologists and Criminal Policy: Specialists in Policy Making.* New York: Columbia University Press, 1978.

SOLZHENITSYN, ALEKSANDR I., *East and West.* New York: Harper and Row, 1980.

————, *The Gulag Archipelago.* New York: Harper & Row, vol. 1, 1974; vol. 2, 1975; vol. 3, 1976.

————, *Letters to the Soviet Leaders.* New York: Knopf, 1974.

TAYLOR, TELFORD, and others, *Courts of Terror: Soviet Criminal Justice and Jewish Emigration.* New York: Knopf, 1976.

TÖKÉS, RUDOLF L., ed., *Dissent in the USSR: Politics, Ideology and People.* Baltimore, MD: The Johns Hopkins University Press, 1975.

YANOV, ALEXANDER, *The Russian New Right.* Berkeley, CA: Institute of International Studies, University of California, 1978.

12

SOCIAL PROBLEMS I:
Nationality and Religion

In this chapter and the next we will consider several of the major social issues facing the USSR after nearly seven decades of Soviet rule. The Soviet Union is composed of a multiplicity of nationalities and religious groups, many of which were inherited from a Russian Empire that had conquered diverse peoples. Unlike the United States, where everyone but Native Americans immigrated from their ancestral lands, in the USSR the members of the various nationalities in a large proportion still live on the land their forebears occupied for centuries and are still in touch with reminders of their religious and cultural heritages. One need only look at the mosques of Uzbekistan or the churches and monasteries of Armenia to understand how these traditions could not possibly be ignored or forgotten by the people living there. Out of these traditions and the loyalty expected by Moscow to the Communist Party and to the Soviet Union grow many problems, both practical and ideological.

One might consider the alcohol problem an inheritance as well, for the high level of alcohol consumption and its adverse social effects characterized prerevolutionary Russia as well as today's Soviet Union. But the alcohol problem seems more closely related to juvenile delinquency and adult crime. As a matter of fact, Soviet analysts frequently cite excessive alcohol consumption as one of the major factors behind such antisocial behavior. These three matters—alcohol, juvenile delinquency, and crime—along with the minor but apparently growing problem of narcotic drug use, are examined in the next chapter.

Common to all the problems discussed in these two chapters is that according to orthodox Marxian precepts, they should have largely disappeared some time ago. Poverty, deprivation, and social injustice—all associated with the class basis of capitalist society—were said to be at the root of criminal (including juvenile criminal) behavior. Once the Marxian socialist society was created, the objective reasons for this behavior would be absent and crime would wither away. Alcoholism was likewise treated as alien to socialist society. The continued existence of crime and alcohol abuse causes some embarrassment to Soviet authorities. The standard rationale is that they are "survivals of the past" which exist among certain elements of society. After seven decades of Soviet power this explanation hardly seems adequate, and recently some of the more sophisticated Soviet authors have cautiously put forward the idea that psychological factors and even differences in economic conditions within Soviet society may be contributing to these problems.

Nationality and religious problems were also supposed to be eliminated by socialism. The proletarian movement would develop international consciousness, overcoming national differences and antagonisms. Religion, an "opiate" that served to make the exploited classes submissive, would also disappear once changes in the economic system made it unnecessary. Needless to say, neither nationality differences nor religious worship has been eliminated by the Soviet state. In spite of apparently genuine efforts by Lenin to curb Great Russian chauvinism within Soviet territory, the dominance of the Russian nationality continues to be one of the basic facts of life in the Soviet Union today. It is undoubtedly connected with the remarkable persistence of national consciousness among other ethnic groups. The Soviet authorities have even stronger ideological justification for dealing harshly with religious denominations than with nationalism. Their generally negative policy toward religion has undoubtedly undercut its impact, but religious beliefs have not been stamped out. Some would say, in fact, that recent years have seen a revival of religion.

THE NATIONALITY PROBLEM

Igor Shafarevich, the well-known Soviet mathematician and dissident, has written: "Of all the urgent problems that have accumulated in our life, the most painful seems to be that concerning relations between the various nationalities in the USSR. No other question arouses such explosions of resentment, malice, and pain—neither material inequality, nor lack of spiritual freedom, nor even the persecution of religion."[1] This depiction of the situation is scarcely the orthodox one. Soviet authorities have long claimed that the nationality question has been solved, that "national antagonisms have been done away with," and that "national equality is now an integral part of Soviet life."[2] Such contradictory views as these are hardly surprising to anyone familiar with the Soviet scene. Marxist-Leninist ideology teaches that the true internationalism of the doctrine eliminates the national antagonisms that have plagued different peoples in the past, and Soviet officialdom steadfastly treats this article of faith as an accomplished fact. But a frank conversation with a Soviet citizen is likely to contradict this glowing tribute to international toleration. When a Russian girl said to the authors several years ago, "we dislike the Georgians and the Georgians dislike us," she was voicing a variation on a theme we heard numerous times in our travels through the USSR.

What lies behind sentiments such as these? Answering this question involves an analysis of the dimensions of the Soviet nationality problem and the main lines of government policy. With more than 100 different nationalities, the Soviet Union is truly the multinational state that its authorities like to claim it is. Some 130 distinct languages are recognized, and the equality of all languages and nationalities is proclaimed. National diversity is not actually so great as these numbers imply, however. Several of the smallest groups number only in the hundreds, and in the 1970 census* nearly 60 of the nationalities listed had fewer than a quarter million members.[3] The number of nationalities has tended to drop over time, with the smaller groups being assimilated into the larger ones. It is the larger groups that constitute the core of the nationality problem in the USSR. According to the 1979 census, there were 23 ethnic groups in the country with over a million members. These include the 15 nationalities for whom the union republics are named, the Tatars, Germans, Jews, Chuvash, Peoples of Dagestan, Bashkirs, Mordvins, and Poles. Of the last 8, only the Tatars have over 2 million members. Our discussion will be limited to the Tatars, the 15 titular nationalities of the union republics, and the Jews—who constitute an interesting population category for a number of reasons. Together, these 17 nationalities account for more than 90 percent of the total Soviet population.

These seventeen nationalities vary substantially in relative size and rate of growth of their populations. (See Table 12–1.) The generalizations one can make are strong and clear: By and large, the ethnic groups that can be classified as European are growing slowly (that is, well under the national average), whereas the Asian and Caucasian nationalities, but particularly the Moslem groups, are growing at a rate far above the national average. In addition, there is a perceptible shift in population to the more southerly parts of the USSR, namely Central Asia and the Caucasus regions. Further evidence on these points can be shown by looking at the individual groups more closely.

The biggest single nationality is the Russians, with over 137 million people and 52.4 percent of the Soviet population. This figure is down from

---

*The last three censuses in the USSR were done in 1959, 1970, and 1979. Much less information has been made public from the 1979 census than was the case with regard to the previous two. In some cases, therefore, we have had to rely on 1970 data.

53.4 percent in 1970, however, suggesting that a time is coming when the Russians will be a minority nationality. This development is not only symbolic but also points to a time when a relatively smaller number of Russians will find it increasingly difficult to maintain their dominant position among other rapidly growing indigenous groups within the country. One of the ways in which this dominance is maintained is through the settling of a significant number of Russians in non-Russian areas of the USSR. Although over 82 percent of Russians lived in the Russian Republic in 1979, this was a drop of 3.2 percent from 20 years earlier, indicating a continuing effort to settle Russians in the borderlands. This is a point to which we will return.

After the Russians come the Ukrainians, with over 42 million people. This second major Soviet nationality is close to the Russian people in language and cultural traditions, but there has long been considerable enmity between the groups, growing out of Russian efforts at domination. Over 86 percent of the Ukrainians live in the Ukrainian Republic. To indicate something of the size and significance of this republic, with more than 50 million people in 1985, it is about one and one-half times as large as Poland, the largest East European socialist state. The Ukraine contains much of the best farm land and many of the important industrial centers in the USSR.

The other nationalities are considerably smaller than these two giant ethnic groups. The third major Slavic nationality—the Byelorussians—has over nine million people, but in recent years it has been far surpassed as the third largest nationality in the country by the Uzbeks, who numbered more than twelve million in 1979. The Uzbeks, along with the four other major nationalities of Central Asia—the Kazakhs, Tadzhiks, Turkmen, and Kirghiz—amount to some twenty-six million people, almost one tenth of the Soviet population. What is significant about this population figure is that it has almost doubled in twenty years, a growth rate not approached by any other major Soviet nationality or group of nationalities. Except for the Tadzhiks, who are a Persian people, all these nationalities share a common Turkic stock. More important, all five have a common Moslem religious heritage.

Another major Moslem ethnic group is the Azerbaidzhanis, who live mainly in the Azerbaidzhan SSR in the Caucasus Mountains between the Black and Caspian seas. Their growth has been equally impressive, about 87 percent between the 1959 and 1979 censuses.

The Tatars also have a strong Moslem religious tradition. Although there are over six million Tatars in the USSR, they do not qualify for union-republic status because their centers of population concentration are located in the central parts of the country rather than on the borders. Over one-and-one-half million Tatars live in the Tatar ASSR, whose capital is the city of Kazan on the Volga River; most of the remaining members of this ethnic group reside in other parts of the RSFSR.

The two other major nationalities of the Caucasus, in addition to the Azerbaidzhanis, are the Armenians and the Georgians. These two groups have some similarities to the Moslem nationalities in culture and way of life, but they have long Christian traditions. Their recent population growth rate has been above average but not so high as that of the major Moslem ethnic groups.

Slightly more than five million people are members of the major Baltic nationalities: the Lithuanians, Latvians, and Estonians. Their growth rate has been uneven, higher in traditionally Catholic Lithuania, lower in traditionally Protestant Latvia and Estonia. A high proportion of the recent growth of these union republics is based on in-migration of other Soviet citizens, mostly Russians. Lithuania, Latvia, and Estonia are among the newest union republics in the country, having been annexed by the Soviet Union in 1940. The Moldavian SSR also was established in 1940. It was formed from the Moldavian Autonomous Republic and Bessarabia, which was annexed by the USSR from Rumania in that year. Whether Moldavians constitute a distinct ethnic group from Rumanians is a disputed matter. The Soviet authorities claim they do, but many others assert that they are basically ethnic Rumanians.

TABLE 12–1   Major Soviet Nationalities, 1959, 1970, and 1979 (In Descending Order of Size in 1979)

	NUMBER OF PERSONS OF GIVEN NATIONALITY (IN THOUSANDS)			PERCENTAGE INCREASE OR DECREASE		RANK BY 1970–1979 GROWTH
	1959	1970	1979	1959–70	1970–79	
Total population of the USSR	208,827	241,720	262,085	15.8	8.4	
Russians	114,114	129,015	137,397	13.1	6.5	12
Ukrainians	37,253	40,753	42,347	9.4	3.9	14
Uzbeks	6,015	9,195	12,456	52.9	35.5	2
Byelorussians	7,913	9,052	9,463	14.4	4.5	13
Kazaks	3,622	5,299	6,556	46.3	23.7	6
Tatars	4,968	5,931	6,317	19.4	6.5	11
Azeris	2,940	4,380	5,477	49.0	25.0	5
Armenians	2,787	3,559	4,151	27.7	16.6	7
Georgians	2,692	3,245	3,571	20.5	10.0	8
Moldavians	2,214	2,698	2,968	21.9	10.0	9
Tajiks	1,397	2,136	2,898	52.9	35.7	1
Lithuanians	2,326	2,665	2,851	14.6	7.0	10
Turkmen	1,002	1,525	2,028	52.2	33.0	3
Kirghiz	969	1,452	1,906	49.8	31.3	4
Jews	2,263	2,151	1,811	−5.2	−15.8	17
Latvians	1,400	1,430	1,439	2.1	0.6	16
Estonians	980	1,007	1,020	1.8	1.3	15

Source: Based on Ann Sheehy, "The National Composition of the Population of the USSR According to the Census of 1979," *Radio Liberty Research.* No. 123/80, March 27, 1980, pp. 10–11.

The Soviet Jews are in a different situation from the other major nationality groups in several ways. Judaism, which is considered a religion by most people in the West, is officially designated a nationality in the Soviet Union. But it is a nationality that does not have a recognized territory worthy of the name, as do most of the other major nationalities. It is true that there is the Jewish Autonomous Province, a territory surrounding the town of Birobidzhan in far eastern Russia near the Chinese border. This province was created in 1928, but relatively few Jews settled there. In 1970 only 11,000 Jews lived there, 6.6 percent of the province's population. This is thought to be the lowest percentage of a titular nationality within its own territory.[4] Most Soviet Jews live in the RSFSR or the Ukraine, with smaller numbers in the other union republics. Soviet Jews are overwhelmingly city dwellers.

Another distinguishing feature of Soviet Jews is that they are the only major nationality* whose numbers have declined in recent years. To some degree, this decline was noticeable before the substantial Jewish emigration to the West began in the early 1970s, and in this sense the decline may be somewhat overstated. In census-taking, documentary proof of nationality is not supposed to be required, and many Jews may have chosen to identify themselves as being of other nationalities. One estimate put the actual number of Soviet Jews at about 2.7 million in the late 1970s, rather than 1.8 million.[5] Nevertheless, it is unquestionable that there has been a substantial decline in the number of Soviet Jews in recent years, in large part through emigration.

During the decade of the 1970s Soviet authorities allowed substantial numbers of Jews, Germans, and Armenians to leave the country. Of these, the Jews constituted the largest number. The size of Jewish emigration varied considerably from year to year, with the number of "refuseniks" (those denied permission to leave) apparently related to the state of Soviet-American relations. Some 240,000 Soviet Jews emigrated from the USSR during the 1970s, with 51,000 leaving during 1979 alone. But after that year emigration was abruptly curbed. It became virtually nonexistent by the mid-1980s, reflecting the generally poor relationship between Moscow and Washington.

The Soviet claim concerning the elimination of nationality problems has some substance to it. The preservation of cultural and ethnic traditions of the various peoples has to some extent been encouraged. The same is true of the national languages of the minority groups. And considerable effort has been made over the years to diminish the differences in level of economic achievement among the major nationalities. But on each of these matters

---

*Two large nationalities not discussed here who also lost population, both from 1959 to 1970 and from 1970 to 1979, are the Mordvins and the Poles. See Ann Sheehy, "The National Composition of the Population of the USSR According to the Census of 1979," *Radio Liberty Research*, No. 123/80, Mar. 27, 1980, pp. 10–11.

there is another side to the coin. The efforts to encourage national identity have been sufficiently meager to disappoint many members of nationality groups. Fears on the part of the authorities that too loose a policy on these matters could lead to increasing desires for separatism have prompted further restraints. In recent years this tension has produced what some Western observers term the "new nationalism" in the USSR.

Soviet policy has never embraced the concept of the melting pot, and a development of this kind cannot soon be expected. What the various peoples of the USSR would melt into would be some kind of Soviet nationality. Although Soviet leaders have talked at times about such an eventual development, a *sliyanie* (merging) of the various nationalities, which would accompany the achieving of a mature communist society, there is not now sufficient emotional identification with the Soviet state to overcome the nationality attachments of the various ethnic groups that populate the country. In the shorter term, a process identified as *sblizhenie,* which implies the drawing together of nationalities and the achievement of socioeconomic equality while preserving national uniqueness, is seen as taking place.[6] In the meantime, while all subjects of the USSR are Soviet citizens, their self-identification as Russians, Ukrainians, Tatars, Georgians, and so on is at least as strong as their attachment to the Soviet state. And this ethnic identification is formalized in Soviet law. The internal passport which each Soviet citizen must carry from age sixteen lists nationality. Because this document must frequently be shown to authorities for identification or on special occasions, such as for registration when one moves to a new city, the nationality of every Soviet citizen is readily ascertainable.

Linguistic differences also divide the Soviet peoples. Russian is the dominant language of the country, and one can talk with people in Russian in almost every corner of the USSR. Virtually all of the 137 million Russians as well as 16 million other Soviet citizens consider Russian their native tongue. Another 61 million state it to be their second language. Thus, some 82 percent of the Soviet population speak Russian fluently. Soviet authorities cite these figures to demonstrate the significance of Russian "in the convergence of peoples." They also usually cite Lenin on the impermissibility of forcing minorities to study Russian. But in spite of this caution, the pressure to learn Russian, and even to use it in preference to one's native language, is considerable. Many governmental, economic, and Party activities are conducted almost exclusively Russian, even in the non-Russian republics. The same is true of the Soviet armed forces, much of higher education, and other aspects of life. The message, although nowhere spelled out in so many words, is clear: If you want to get anywhere in life, learn Russian. From one point of view, being equipped with knowledge of Russian can be considered a positive achievement for any person of a minority nationality, particularly since Russian is the native language of the majority ethnic group. Those Soviet citizens who complain about the process of linguistic Russification do not object to the acquisition of the Russian lan-

246 Social Problems I

guage per se but to the destructive effects of the preponderant emphasis on Russian on the native language and culture of nearly half of the Soviet population.[7]

In spite of the pressure for learning Russian, a persistence in holding on to the native language is evident. According to the 1979 census, in each of the 17 major nationality groups except the Jews and the Byelorussians, at least 80 percent speak the nationality language as their native tongue.* In most cases the figure is above 90 percent. The bilingualism that has been created among non-Russians is generally strongest among European nationalities (for example, for 57 percent of Byelorussians and 56.7 percent of Latvians, Russian is a second language) and weaker in Central Asia and the Caucasus (the corresponding figures are 25.4 percent for the Turkmen and 26.7 percent for the Georgians). It is fair to say, however, that by virtually any measure, linguistic Russification of all of the major nationalities in the country is increasing from year to year.** For obvious reasons, the nationality that has the lowest percentage of persons who freely speak a second language of the USSR is the Russians. Only about 3 percent of Russians claim this ability.

In addition to language, one of the obvious ways in which Russians influence the peoples of other ethnic groups is through their presence in the various republics. (See Table 12–2.) The Russians constitute the largest nationality group in two of the fifteen republics, their own and the Kazakh SSR. They are second in population in nine republics and third in the other four. Only in four republics was the percentage of Russians under 10 percent in 1979. But an even more important generalization has to do with the dynamics of population developments in the republics, which is also demonstrated in Table 12–2: In each of the European republics (with the exception of Lithuania) the percentage of the nominal population has declined in both the 1970 and 1979 censuses and the percentage of Russians has grown; in each of the Asian and Transcaucasian republics the Russian proportion has dropped and the percentage of the nominal population has

---

*The figure for the Jews is 14.2 percent and that for the Byelorussians is 74.2 percent.

**For instance, between 1970 and 1979 the percentage claiming a good knowledge of Russian as a second language increased for every major nationality group (excluding the Russians) except the Estonians, for whom the percentage went from 29.0 to 24.2. Moreover, among the 16 major nationalities (again excluding the Russians) the percentage regarding the language of the nationality as their native tongue decreased between 1970 and 1979 in every case but one (the Lithuanians, for whom it remained the same, at 97.9 percent). For a discussion of some surprises in the reported census figures on language use (for example, the drop in the percentage of Estonians claiming Russian as a second language), see Ann Sheehy, "Language Affiliation Data from the Census of 1979," *Radio Liberty Research*, No. 130/80, Apr. 2, 1980, esp. p. 4. As Rasma Karklins has shown, actual linguistic Russification may be somewhat understated by responses to the "native-tongue" question in the census, as numerous members of ethnic minorities appear to answer the question on the basis of psychological identification with a given nationality but actually speak mostly in another language, often Russian. See "A Note on 'Nationality' and 'Native Tongue' as Census Categories in 1979," *Soviet Studies*, 32, No. 3 (Jul. 1980), 415, esp. 419–21.

grown. Obviously in the European part of the USSR the Russians are continuing to "colonize" the non-Russian republics. What the table does not show is that an attempt to do the same thing is being made in the other republics but with less success. More Russians were living in each of the five Central Asian republics in 1979 than in 1970, but in each case these increases were more than offset by the high birth rates of the native populations.* What we said earlier about relatively fewer Russians among greater indigenous populations applies primarily to the non-European republics. On the other hand, the increasing presence of Russians in the other European republics has caused great concern among the native populations. This appears to be particularly true in Latvia and Estonia, where the changes between 1959 and 1979 were most dramatic.

Of course political control is not indicated by the mere number of Russians in a given republic. But by a number of other measures, the disproportionate influence of Russians can be shown. Although Russians

TABLE 12–2   Percentage of Titular Nationality's Population and Russian Population in the 15 Union Republics of the USSR, 1959, 1970, and 1979

| | TITULAR NATIONALITY | | | | RUSSIANS | | | |
	1959	1970	1979	1979 Rank	1959	1970	1979	1979 Rank
RSFSR	83.3	82.8	82.6	1	83.3	82.8	82.6	1
Ukraine	76.8	74.9	73.6	1	16.9	19.4	21.1	2
Byelorussia	81.1	81.0	79.4	1	8.2	10.4	11.9	2
Uzbekistan	62.1	65.5	68.7	1	13.5	12.5	10.8	2
Kazakstan	30.0	32.6	36.0	2	42.7	42.4	40.8	1
Tajikistan	53.1	56.2	58.8	1	13.3	11.9	10.4	3
Turkmenistan	60.9	65.6	68.4	1	17.3	14.5	12.6	2
Kirghizia	40.5	43.8	47.9	1	30.2	29.2	25.9	2
Azerbaidzhan	67.5	73.8	78.1	1	13.6	10.0	7.9	2*
Armenia	88.0	88.6	89.7	1	3.2	2.7	2.3	3
Georgia	64.3	66.8	68.8	1	10.1	8.5	7.4	3
Lithuania	79.3	80.1	80.0	1	8.5	8.6	8.9	2
Latvia	62.0	56.8	53.7	1	26.6	29.8	32.8	2
Estonia	74.6	68.2	64.7	1	20.1	24.7	27.9	2
Moldavia	65.4	64.6	63.9	1	10.2	11.6	12.8	3

*The Armenian population of Azerbaidzhan in 1979 was virtually identical with that of the Russian population.

Source: Based on Ann Sheehy, "The National Composition of the Population of the USSR According to the Census of 1979," *Radio Liberty Research,* No. 123/80, Mar. 1980, p. 15.

*Of the fourteen union republics other than the RSFSR, the absolute number of Russians decreased between 1970 and 1979 only in Georgia and Azerbaidzhan.

total only 52.4 percent of the population, over 60 percent of all Party members are Russians. All but one of the ten Secretaries of the CC CPSU (90 percent) chosen in 1986 were Russian, as were eight of the 12 full members of the Politburo (67 percent). In all, 20 or 77 percent of the top twenty-six members of the Party hierarchy chosen in 1986 (that is, full or candidate Politburo members and/or CC Secretaries) were Russians.*

In the union republics other than the RSFSR, the dominance of Russians is not so evident as it is at the all-union level. The Party first secretaryship is usually held by a member of the native ethnic group. But the second secretary is usually a member of one of the three major Slavic nationalities, most often a Russian. The same is true with regard to the head of the republican KGB or security police. By contrast, members of non-Slavic nationality groups are not often represented in the political hierarchies of republics other than their own. But if these critical positions are often controlled by Russians or other Slavs, the native nationalities hold on to all the other posts of significance that they can, a practice that seems to be on the rise—at least in some parts of the country.[8] This frequently gives rise to complaints from Moscow of "localism," meaning that the leaders of the indigenous nationalities overemphasize local interests to the detriment of national interests.

These localism–nationalism tensions on the one hand and the interests of the center on the other involve economic as well as cultural and political dimensions. The overall economic development of the USSR in its 70 years existence has been impressive. The same can be said with regard to all of the regions and ethnic groups of the country. But because the USSR has been composed from its beginnings of territories and national groups at diverse stages of economic development, this impressive economic growth has not meant equalization of economic well-being for all groups. In spite of efforts over several decades on the part of the authorities to close the development gap among the republics, the picture in the 1980s is a mixed one, with the gap apparently widening on some measures relevant to regional wealth.[9]

What this has meant is a considerable variation in economic levels in different parts of the country, with evident effects on the economic well-being of the residents of these parts of the country. The picture of regional differences is quite clear: The European republics (with the exception of Moldavia) consistently rank higher than the Asian and Transcaucasian republics on most of the measures of regional wealth, including per capita income produced, per capita money in savings accounts, and per capita trade turnover. In an overall sense, the Baltic republics are the most affluent, followed by the other European republics (including the RSFSR but ex-

---

*If one considers the members of the 3 major Slavic nationalities, the Russians, Ukrainians, and Byelorussians, in these bodies, the figures are also impressive. These 3 groups accounted for 72.2 percent of the Soviet population in 1979 but comprised 75 percent of full Politburo members, 100 percent of CC Secretaries, and 88 percent of the top 26 members of the Party hierarchy elected in 1986.

cluding Moldavia), then the Armenians and Georgians, with the Moslem republics at the bottom.

To the extent that level of education, opportunity for higher education, and the number of trained scientific workers are related to present and future economic well-being, it can be said that the Central Asian peoples can look forward to continued disadvantages in comparison with their fellow Soviet citizens. On all of these measures the Central Asian ethnic groups (with the Moldavians) rank near the bottom.[10]

As is emphasized elsewhere in this book, the improvements in the economic status of most Soviet citizens has been impressive in recent years. And the growth rates in per capita income in the Central Asian republics, even though below the national average, have been higher than those in most developed and developing countries for the same period. But the peoples from the less affluent republics are not likely to judge their economic status against the rate of development of foreign countries, about which they know little. Rather, they will compare themselves with fellow Soviet citizens from the northern and western parts of the country. And the failure to achieve economic equality, coupled with the antagonisms growing out of Russian political and cultural domination, seem to be at the root of an intensified national feeling evident in recent years. The very existence of a federal system, which provides local elites the opportunity to have some influence on affairs within their territories, creates additional burdens on the Russian-dominated central government and Party apparatus.

But for the near future, at least, the nominal federalism that exists cannot be easily abolished. Instead, the Russian leaders follow a practice of removing indigenous leaders who encourage excessive nationalistic feelings or fail to keep them in check. Another recent practice has been to mitigate the impact of the federal system by reducing republican administrative control: The number of republican-level ministries has been shrinking, their functions being taken over by union-republic ministries, and the number of all-union ministries has been increasing.[11]

Such policies constitute little more than short-term solutions, however. Although occasional official pronouncements will vaguely acknowledge the nationality problem, the more typical response is to assert that the problem does not exist, that it has been solved. The means by which Soviet officialdom practices this self-delusion is illustrated by Grigori Svirski, a Soviet writer who emigrated to the West in the early 1970s. Svirski once objected to anti-Semitic remarks made by a man in a Moscow subway station and sought to have the man arrested. Svirski related what happened after the police lieutenant heard his complaint and took him aside.

> "Look," he said, "if I'll write that this man is an anti-Semite, we wouldn't be able to give him even 24 hours. But if I write that he was disturbing the peace, we can give him 15 days."
> I didn't believe it and went to court to find out if that was true. The judge was very smart; he understood exactly what I wanted and he said, "Tomorrow I

have a similar case. Come and you'll understand everything." The next day in court there was some loose female who had apparently insulted a middle-aged watchman, who was a Tatar, and the judge asks, "What did you call him?"

"Tatar's pig ear." The secretary of the court doesn't write it down.

"What else?"

"All Tatars are speculators." The secretary remains in the sphinx position.

"What else?" the judge asks.

"An old fool," she answers, and the secretary of the court writes it out immediately.

And thus I understood all the mechanics of this uncomplicated lie, and it became clear to me why the statistics of nationalistic crimes do not exist in the Soviet Union. In every court, in every police station there is that cipher through which all those cases are sifted out, and that is the reason there are no files. So that the leaders may quite honestly say, "There isn't any anti-Semitism in the Soviet Union."[12]

RELIGION

The nationality problem is complicated by the religious issue in the USSR. Thus, for example, the manifestations of Lithuanian nationalism are in large part associated with Catholicism in Lithuania; a major factor common to the indigenous peoples of Soviet Central Asia is their Moslem tradition; restrictions on Soviet Jews have included constraints on the practice of the Jewish religion. At the same time, Soviet religious policy can be looked upon as a distinct matter on which the leadership has pursued a number of objectives over the years.

Official attitudes toward religion, according to the Canadian scholar Bohdan Bociurkiw, are based on "the historical memory, the ideological legacy, and the authoritarian aspirations of the regime."[13] Briefly stated, these three factors involve the close connection of the Russian Orthodox Church with tsarist autocracy and its early opposition to the Bolsheviks; the Marxist antagonism toward religion, and the brand of Soviet atheism that grew out of this ideological precept; and the regime's effort to suppress or neutralize any competing focus of loyalty that could not easily be integrated into the political system.

Out of the interplay of these three elements, Soviet policy toward religion has been formed. The general direction of official policy has always been negative, but it has vacillated between extreme hostility and reluctant toleration. In part this inconsistency has to do with differences among Soviet officials about the proper stance toward religion. Again using the terms of Bociurkiw, the "fundamentalists" favor an intense antireligious campaign against all groups in order to rid the country of religion as soon as possible. The "pragmatists" advocate a more selective approach, favoring religious groups that will cooperate with the regime and punishing those that will not.[14] This attempt to "sovietize" religion is aimed at legitimizing the regime in the eyes of Soviet citizens who are believers. Both these tendencies are evident in the official policy toward religion, and to some extent they have competed for ascendancy over time. Thus, there has been an ebb and flow in the zealousness with which antireligious policies have been pursued. A wholesale offensive against religion during the 1930s was followed by a policy of accommodation during World War II in the interests of unifying the country. The Khrushchev years saw a resumption of antireligious activities, marked by the closing of many churches and the initiation of systematic "scientific atheistic" indoctrination. In the post-Khrushchev period this campaign subsided somewhat. This is not to say that a benevolent attitude was taken toward churches and religion, only that antireligious efforts were not pursued with as much zealousness as before. The state remains implacably opposed to religion in any form, and no citizen who manifests overt religious beliefs will have the opportunity to perform any responsible political role. But the effort to "sovietize" the more favored religious groups goes on, which suggests that the pragmatists among the leadership have for the present gained ascendancy.[15]

Maintaining a religious establishment under these circumstances inevitably involves compromises and accommodations. Most organized religions in the Soviet Union have accepted this necessity, however reluctantly. A common practice of Soviet authorities, for instance, is interviewing compliant spokespersons of various faiths, whose pro-regime views can be aired for both internal and foreign consumption. Thus, the Moslem mufti who states that "the crowning glory of nature is man, and the crowning glory of all laws existing on earth is the USSR Constitution" has no doubt thereby earned some cooperation from the authorities in his and his co-religionists' efforts to pursue their faith.[16] The major legal document defining the place of churches in the Soviet system is a resolution of the All-Russian Executive Committee of April 8, 1929 (significantly amended in 1975),[17] which provides for the registration of religious associations. Such registration indicates official recognition by the state. Unregistered groups are considered illegal and are subject to varying degrees of harassment by the government. The largest registered group, the Russian Orthodox Church, reportedly has some thirty million adherents. The Orthodox hierarchy has studiously avoided clashes with state authority. Its Patriarch and other leaders give sermons supporting political and social policies of the state and have rebutted charges from abroad of government suppression of religion. They have silenced, suspended, or transferred parish priests who have been too outspoken. Where these measures have not succeeded, the state has stepped in to silence priests through harassment, arrest, and prison sentences.[18]

The Orthodox Church has the largest number of adherents in the country, but there are other important denominations. Determining the number of believers of any religious group is difficult, since official figures are not available. The figure of 30 million Russian Orthodox is a substantial number —almost twice the number of Party members in the USSR. But some estimates are higher. Spokesmen for the Orthodox Church estimate that 30 to 50 million people regularly attend services, based on the size of Sunday offerings, and other estimates go as high as 70 to 115 million.[19] The Georgian Orthodox Church and the Armenian Church maintain close relations with Russian Orthodoxy. They are both closely linked, however, with the ethnic self-consciousness of their respective nationalities. It is estimated that two thirds of the 3 million Georgians and 60 percent of the 3.5 million Armenians are actively religious.

The number of Moslems is also hard to estimate. One source puts the figure at about 45 million. This writer adds: "In the case of Islam a confusion between religion and nationality is still valid. Islam is more than a religious belief: it is a way of life, a culture, a means of national expression. Nowadays in the USSR there is even the expression 'the non-believing Muslim'."[20]

The Catholics are said to number 3 to 4 million, a great percentage of whom are in Lithuania.[21] Lutherans, mostly living in Estonia and Latvia, are estimated at 850,000. The Baptists are divided into three groups, the members of the All-Union Council of Evangelical Christians and Baptists, the Pentecostalists, and the so-called "Initsiativniki." All the religious groups discussed up to this point have been among those recognized by the government. The split among the Baptists, however, involves a distinction between "legal" and "illegal" groups. The first group, the "registered Baptists," is officially recognized by the state authorities. They number about 535,000 and are concentrated in a few areas in the RSFSR, the Ukraine, and several other republics. Estimates on the other two groups are as high as 600,000.[22] The Pentecostalists have a history in Russia that dates back to the beginning of the century. They are not an officially recognized religion (although a few individual congregations apparently have been officially registered by local authorities in recent years) and are said to number about 100,000.[23] The "Initsiativniki" came into existence in the early 1960s when an "Action Group" (*Initsiativnaia Gruppa*) of dissident Baptists led a breakaway from the registered Baptist Church. At that time the Khrushchev regime was taking a particularly hard line against religion, harassing those who engaged in such practices as "unhealthy missionary tendencies" and illegal baptisms of children. The Initsiativniki are an illegal group and have been subject to much state persecution in recent years. The split is said to have brought about reform within the registered Baptist movement, resulting in greater democracy in the conduct of church affairs.[24]

A notable development among the smaller religious groups in the late 1970s and early 1980s has been the creation of organizations designed to strengthen the groups against state harassment. Examples are the Catholic Committee for the Defense of the Rights of Believers, created in Lithuania in 1978,[25] and the Council of Pentecostalist Churches, created by representatives from six Soviet republics in 1979.[26] It is said that some thirty thousand Pentecostalists wish to emigrate from the USSR to obtain religious freedom but few have been allowed to leave. A symbol of this desire is the so-called "Siberian Seven," members of two families of Pentecostalists from Siberia who staged a sit-in at the U.S. Embassy in Moscow in June 1978 in hopes of persuading the Soviet government to allow them to emigrate. They remained in the embassy for nearly five years, leaving in 1983 with assurances that they would be allowed to emigrate.

Jews in the Soviet Union were discussed in the section on nationalities. Fewer than 100 synagogues remain open in the entire country (as recently as 1956 the number was reportedly 450).[27] The number of practicing Jews in the country is, according to published sources, about 60,000 (out of a population of 1.8 million in 1979), but dissident Jewish sources estimate the number to be higher.[28] There are said to be some 50,000 Buddhists, who live in eastern Siberia, and an undetermined number of members of congregations of Seventh-Day Adventists, Methodists, adherents of the Reformed Church, and other denominations. In addition, there are a number of other illegal sects besides the two Baptist ones mentioned, including the Jehovah's Witnesses, Uniates, True Orthodox Christians, and others.

Dissidents and other critics have charged the registered religions, particularly the Russian Orthodox Church, with "collaborating with atheism," and there is some truth to this accusation. The Council for Religious Affairs, a state agency, has jurisdiction over all church matters and has enforced its views on church leaders in exchange for privileges denied unrecognized religious groups. While condoning religious worship in "sovietized" churches, the state attempts to suppress noncooperating religious groups and goes to great lengths to deter parents from having their children baptized. Organized religious instruction for children is forbidden by law. Priests who have violated this principle have been prosecuted. Some of this harassment clearly violates the constitutional guarantee of freedom of worship for all citizens. And it is likely that overzealous local authorities sometimes carry the persecution even further than the central leadership intends. A common practice is the administrative fining of persons holding unauthorized religious services. A receipt issued by local authorities for the payment of one of these fines was smuggled out of the USSR in 1975. It states: "Fine for belief in God, 50 rubles."[29] In 1980 it was reported that a former instructor in a higher educational institution had her candidate of science degree (roughly equivalent to a Ph.D.) revoked because she "believes in God" and "openly announced to her students that she is a believer."[30]

In spite of such restrictions, religion has not died out in the Soviet Union. A number of observers, in fact, say that a revival of sorts has taken place in recent years. In addition to the little old ladies in black shawls, the typical churchgoer described in countless travelers' reports, more young people are attending services. Increasing numbers of intellectuals and other highly educated Soviet citizens have acknowledged religious beliefs. Reports of known Party members and soldiers in uniform worshiping in church have been published. It is said that "perhaps as many as 50 percent of marriages take place in churches."[31] A survey published in the Soviet press showed that 60 percent of babies born in the city of Gorky in recent years were baptized. Reports from other parts of the country also show a high level of baptism. Untold numbers of Soviet citizens, from all walks of life, practice a double life of public conformity to regime values and private religious piety. *New York Times* correspondent David Shipler wrote of a young Komsomol activist, both of whose parents were Party members, who visited a church, lit a candle, and prayed every day after school. Her response to the question of how she could reconcile the seeming contradictions between her political participation and her practice of religion: " 'It's easy,' she said brightly. 'At the komsomol committee, when they ask if I believe in God, I say no.' "[32] The Ukrainian paper *Pravda Ukrainy* reported in 1973 that while a high Party official was giving a speech on atheism his children were taken to be baptized by his wife and mother-in-law.

Among the numerous factors cited to explain this revival are the following: the pageantry of religious services as compared with the drabness of civil ceremonies; the search for new values; a manifestation of antigovernment protest that stops short of overt dissent; an effort to find a link between the present and a rich cultural heritage that had a strong religious content.[33]

Official reactions to this revival of interest in religion have followed predictable courses: an increased propaganda campaign against religion in general, with harassment and persecution of the illegal groups that resist cooperation with the state authorities. One of the manifestations of the religious revival—and of the state response to it—has been the emergence of the so-called "underground church." The term is usually used to refer to dissident elements among Russian Orthodox believers who resist the degree of state control that the Church hierarchy accepts.[34] But one can also speak of underground religion in a broader sense: worshiping and the propagation of religious views outside of traditional religious buildings or approved religious publications. This practice includes many religious denominations besides the dissident factions of Russian Orthodoxy. The religious services conducted by these groups take place in private apartments or in secluded places in the countryside. Religious literature is distributed by means of an unofficial publication system known as *samizdat* (which means literally "self-publishing" in Russian). *Samizdat* is discussed in detail earlier in this book in connection with political dissent. Suffice it to say here that a large segment of *samizdat* output is religious in content, which suggests an active underground religious movement of considerable proportions.

Neither nationality tensions nor the persistence of religion amounts to a serious threat to the maintenance of the present regime or the traditional form of Soviet rule. They do demonstrate that the facile Marxist pronouncements about the impact of socialism (at least of the Soviet variety) on "unprogressive" social phenomena are of questionable validity. Even the most diehard Party ideologue must realize this. But more important, they are *real* problems which, with the other shortcomings of the Soviet system in areas such as consumer economics, cannot help but have negative effects on citizen satisfaction and feelings of support for the regime. Undoubtedly the nationality problem is the more important of the two discussed in this chapter. The dominant Russian leadership has the physical and organizational power to maintain its position in every corner of the vast Soviet landmass. But have current and past policies assured the loyalty of minority Soviet citizens along the lengthy borders of the USSR? This is a question that must give pause to all thoughtful Soviet officials.

NOTES

[1]Igor Shafarevich, "Separation or Reconciliation? The Nationalities Question in the USSR," in *From Under the Rubble,* Alexandr Solzhenitsyn and others (Boston: Little, Brown, 1975), p. 88.

[2]The quotations are from Bobozhan Gafurov, "The USSR: Equality of Nations," *Soviet Life,* No. 2 (Feb. 1976), 45.

[3]Comparable data for the 1979 census were not available at the time of this writing. The 1970 census data included in this discussion are from *Itogi Vsesoiuznoi Perepisi Naseleniia 1970 Goda* (Moscow: "Statistika," 1973). Unless otherwise indicated, the 1979 census data are from "The All Union Census of 1979 in the USSR: A Collection of Reports Prepared Before and After the Census by the Staff of RL Research," *Radio Liberty Research Bulletin,* Sept. 1980.

[4]Zev Katz, ed., *Handbook of Major Soviet Nationalities* (New York: Free Press, 1975), p. 365. In 1979 Theodore Shabad reported that there were about 10,000 Jews in Birobidzhan, about 5 percent of the province's population. *The New York Times,* Oct. 10, 1979, p. A8.

[5]*The New York Times,* Apr. 3, 1979, p. 1.

[6]On the processes leading to the merger of Soviet nations, see Martha Brill Olcott, "Yuri Andropov and the 'National Question,'" *Soviet Studies,* 37, No. 1 (Jan. 1985), 103–17; Ellen Jones and Fred W. Grupp, "Modernization and Ethnic Equalization in the USSR," *Soviet Studies,* 36, No. 2 (Apr. 1984), 159–84; Roman Solchanyk, "Soviet Author on Contradictions in the National Question," *Radio Liberty Research,* No. 416/84, Oct. 30, 1984; Roman Solchanyk, "Ethnic Processes in the USSR and the Merger of Nations," *Radio Liberty Research,* No. 177/83, May 2, 1983.

[7]On this point, see especially Ivan Dzyuba, *Internationalism or Russification?* (London: Weidenfeld and Nicolson, 1968), pp. 149–65. After serving part of a prison sentence for "anti-Soviet agitation and propaganda," Dzyuba recanted his views on Russification, was released from prison, and resumed his work as a journalist. See "Ivan Dzhuba Warns Against Republication of *Internationalism or Russification?*" *Radio Liberty Research,* No. 224/80, Jun. 20, 1980, and "New Book by Ivan Dzhuba to be Published in Kiev," ibid., No. 244/80, Jul. 9, 1980.

[8]See "The National Composition of the Governments of the Central Asian Republics," *Radio Liberty Research,* No. 313/82, Aug. 14, 1982. This source suggests, p. 1, that in Moscow "there may even be a perception of indigenous nationalities in at least some Central Asian republics having taken over too much of the republican power structure."

[9]Considerable attention has been devoted to this subject by Western scholars for a number of years. Among recent writings, see Jones and Grupp, "Modernization and Ethnic Equalization"; Leslie Dienes, "Regional Economic Development," in *The Soviet Economy: Toward the Year 2000,* eds. Abram Bergson and Herbert S. Levine (London: George Allen & Unwin, 1983), pp. 218–68, esp. p. 244; Gertrude E. Schroeder, 'Consumption' in ibid., pp. 311–49, esp. pp. 338–40; Elizabeth Clayton, "USSR Regional Issues: Growth vs. Equality," *Problems of Communism,* 32, No. 5 (Sept.–Oct. 1983), 75–77 (this source is a book review that surveys several recent writings on the subject); Victor Zaslavsky, *The Neo-Stalinist State: Class, Ethnicity and Consensus in Soviet Society* (Armonk, NY: M. E. Sharpe, Inc., 1982), pp. 108–9.

[10]A composite index of these educational measures, based on data gathered by Zev Katz and associates, shows the following ranking for the fifteen titular nationalities of the union republics: Georgians, Armenians, Russians, Estonians, Latvians, Azerbaidzhanis, Ukrainians, Kazakhs, Lithuanians, Turkmen, Kirghiz, Uzbeks, Byelorussians, Tadzhiks, and Moldavians.

Note the high rankings of the Caucasian nationalities and the low ranking of the Byelorussians in comparison with the rankings on the Index of Economic Development. See *Handbook,* Table A.26, p. 463.

[11]See Boris Lewytskyj, "Sources of Conflict in the Top Levels of Soviet Leadership," *Radio Liberty Dispatch,* No. 3, 1975. The title of this article is misleading, since all seventeen pages concern the distribution of functions between the union and the republics.

[12]Irina Kirk, *Profiles in Russian Resistance* (New York: Quadrangle/The N. Y. Times, 1975), pp. 244–45.

[13]Bohdan Bociurkiw, "The Shaping of Soviet Religious Policy," *Problems of Communism,* 22, No. 3 (May–Jun. 1973), 39.

[14]Ibid., p. 41.

[15]On historical developments in church-state relations, see ibid.; also Gerhard Simon, *Church, State and Opposition in the USSR* (Berkeley, CA: University of California Press, 1974), pp. 64–100.

[16]This statement by mufti A. Isaev, Chairman of the Spiritual Administration of Moslems of the European part of the USSR and Siberia, was published in V. A. Kuroedov, *Religia i Tserkov v Sovetskom Obshchestve* (Moscow: Izdatel'stvo Politicheskoi Literatury, 1984), p. 9. Quotations of this kind from representatives of other faiths in the Soviet Union may be found on pp. 8–11 and elsewhere in the book. Kuroedov is Chairperson of the Council for Religious Affairs of the USSR Council of Ministers.

[17]An English translation of the text of this document, with amendments up to Jun. 23, 1975, may be found in "The Revised Version of the Resolution on Religious Societies," *Radio Liberty Research,* No. 155, Mar. 31, 1976. A listing and discussion of the religious groups known to be registered and those which are unregistered is contained in Simon, *Church, State,* pp. 102–104.

[18]For instance, Father Gleb Yakunin was tried and convicted in Aug. 1980 of "anti-Soviet agitation and propaganda" and sentenced to five years in a labor camp and five years of internal exile. See "The Work and Fate of Father Gleb Yakunin," *Radio Liberty Research,* No. 307/80, Aug. 28, 1980. Father Dmitri Dudko, another Orthodox priest, was arrested in January 1980 by the KGB for anti-Soviet activity. In Jun. 1980, Dudko appeared on Soviet television to confess his guilt, and later he wrote to Patriarch Pimen asking forgiveness for his errors. See the article in *Izvestiia,* Jun. 21, 1980, p. 6, which includes a statement by Dudko on his anti-Soviet activity.

[19]The figures on religious adherents are from a variety of sources, the most important of which are: Paul A. Lucey, "Religion," in *The Soviet Union Today,* ed. James Cracraft (Chicago: Educational Foundation for Nuclear Science, Inc., 1983), pp. 295–303. The larger figure for Russian Orthodox believers is from "Number of Religious Persons in the USSR," *Radio Liberty Research,* No. 58, Feb. 2, 1976, p. 1.

[20]Alexandre Bennigsen, as quoted in "Number of Religious Persons in the USSR," p. 3. In a more recent writing Bennigsen refers to "some 43 million Soviet Muslims." "Soviet Muslims and the World of Islam," *Problems of Communism,* 29 (Mar.–Apr. 1980), p. 40.

[21]V. Stanley Vardys states that the number of Catholics "probably is not larger than three and a half million." "Modernization and Latin Rite Catholics in the Soviet Union," in *Religion and Modernization in the Soviet Union,* ed. Dennis J. Dunn (Boulder, CO: Westview Press, 1977), p. 349.

[22]See "Soviet Pentecostalists Form Church Council," *Radio Liberty Research,* No. 274/79, Sept. 13, 1979. For a discussion of a variety of estimates on the size of these groups and the registered Baptists, see Christel Lane, *Christian Religion in the Soviet Union* (Albany, NY: State University of New York Press, 1978), p. 140.

[23]"The Pentecostalist Movement," *Radio Liberty Research,* No. 42, Jan. 31, 1975.

[24]The development of the split among the Baptists is described in detail in Simon, *Church, State,* pp. 154–75.

[25]Among numerous sources on the Catholic Committee, see "Catholic Committee for the Defense of Believers' Rights Releases Four More Documents," *Radio Liberty Research,* No. 385/80, Oct. 16, 1980.

[26]See "Soviet Pentecostals Form Church Council," ibid., No. 274/79, Sept. 13, 1979.

[27]Kuroedov, *Religia i Tserkov,* p. 108, gives a figure of 120 synagogues, but Lucey, "Religion," p. 300, mentions "between 50 and 60 open synagogues."

[28]See ibid; also Radio Liberty, *Current Abstracts and Annotations*, 1980, No. 1, p. 4.

[29]A photocopy of this receipt is provided by Albert Boiter in "Religious Samizdat in 1975," *Radio Liberty Research*, No. 40, Jan. 24, 1976, p. 10.

[30]Radio Liberty, *Current Abstracts and Annotations*, 1980, No. 6, p. 11.

[31]Nicholas Lupinin, "A Review of Soviet Religious Policies," *Radio Liberty Research*, No. 75, Feb. 21, 1975.

[32]David K. Shipler, *Russia: Broken Idols, Solemn Dreams* (New York: Times Books, 1983), p. 266.

[33]For more detail on these matters and on the examples cited in the previous paragraph, see the following sources: Lupinin, "A Review"; Hendrick Smith, *The Russians* (New York: Quadrangle/The N. Y. Times, 1976), pp. 432–38; Robert G. Kaiser, *Russia* (New York: Atheneum, 1976), pp. 82–86; *The New York Times*, Apr. 14, 1974, p. 1.

[34]See William C. Fletcher, *The Russian Orthodox Church Underground, 1917–1970* (London: Oxford University Press, 1971).

SELECTED BIBLIOGRAPHY

ALLWORTH, EDWARD, ed., *Ethnic Russia in the USSR: The Dilemma of Dominance*. New York: Pergamon Press, 1980.

———, *Nationality Group Survival in Multi-Ethnic States: Shifting Support Patterns in the Soviet Baltic Region*. New York: Holt, Rinehart & Winston, 1977.

AZRAEL, JEREMY R., ed., *Soviet Nationality Policies and Practices*. New York: Holt, Rinehart & Winston, 1978.

BENNINGSEN, ALEXANDRE, and MARIE BROXUP, *The Islamic Threat to the Soviet State*. New York: St. Martin's Press, 1983.

BESSEMERES, JOHN F., *Socialist Population Policies*. White Plains, NY: M. E. Sharpe, Inc., 1980.

BIDDULPH, HOWARD L., "Religious Participation of Youth in the USSR," *Soviet Studies*, 31 (Jul. 1979), 417.

BINYON, MICHAEL, *Life in Russia*. New York: Pantheon Books, 1983.

BOCIURKIW, BOHDAN, and JOHN W. STRONG, eds., *Religion and Atheism in the U.S.S.R. and Eastern Europe*. Toronto, Canada: University of Toronto Press, 1975.

BOITER, ALBERT, *Religion in the Soviet Union*. (The Washington Papers, Vol. VIII, No. 78). Beverly Hills, CA: Sage, 1980.

BOURDEAUX, MICHAEL, *Land of the Crosses: The Struggle for Religious Freedom in Lithuania, 1939–1978*. Devon, England: Keston College, 1979.

CARRÈRE D'ENCAUSE, HÉLÈNE, *Decline of an Empire: The Soviet Socialist Republics in Revolt*. New York: Harper and Row, 1981.

DUNN, DENNIS J., ed., *Religion and Modernization in the Soviet Union*. Boulder, CO: Westview Press, 1977.

FLETCHER, WILLIAM C., *Soviet Believers: The Religious Sector of the Population*. Lawrence, KS: The Regents Press of Kansas, 1981.

FREEDMAN, ROBERT O., ed., *Soviet Jewry in the Decisive Decade, 1971–1980*. Durham, NC: Duke University Press, 1981.

GITELMAN, ZVI, "Are Nations Merging in the USSR?" *Problems of Communism*, 32, No. 5, Sept.–Oct. 1983, 35–47.

KAMENETSKY, IHOR, *Nationalism and Human Rights*. Littleton, CO: Libraries Unlimited, Inc., 1977.

KARKLIN, RASMA, "Islam: How Strong is it in the Soviet Union," *Cahiers du Monde Russe et Soviètique*, 21, No. 1 (Jan.–Mar. 1980), 65.

KATZ, ZEV, ed., *Handbook of Major Soviet Nationalities*. New York: Free Press, 1975.

KERBLAY, BASILE, *Modern Soviet Society*. New York: Pantheon Books, 1983.

KOCHAN, LIONEL, *The Jews in Soviet Russia Since 1917*, 3rd ed. New York: Oxford University Press, 1975.

LANE, CHRISTEL, *Christian Religion in the Soviet Union.* Albany, NY: State University of New York Press, 1978.

LUBIN, NANCY, *Labour and Nationality in Soviet Central Asia.* Princeton: Princeton University Press, 1985.

McCAGG, WILLIAM O., JR., and BRIAN D. SILVER, eds., *Soviet Asian Ethnic Frontiers.* New York: Pergamon Press, 1979.

MILLER, JACK, ed., *Jews in Soviet Culture.* New Brunswick, NJ: Transaction Books, 1984.

"Nationalism and Nationalities in the USSR" (6 articles), Survey, 24, No. 3 (108) (Summer 1979), 1–90.

PARMING, TÖNU and ELMAR ÄRVESOO, eds., *A Case Study of a Soviet Republic: The Estonian SSR.* Boulder, CO: Westview Press, 1978.

RAMET, PEDRO, ed., *Religion and Nationalism in Soviet and East European Politics.* Durham, NC: Duke University Press, 1984.

RYWKIN, MICHAEL, *Moscow's Muslim Challenge: Soviet Central Asia.* New York: M. E. Sharpe, 1982.

SAWYER, THOMAS E., *The Jewish Minority in the Soviet Union.* Boulder, CO: Westview Press, 1979.

SIMMONDS, GEORGE W., ed., *Nationalism in the USSR and Eastern Europe.* Detroit, MI: University of Detroit Press, 1977.

SIMON, GERHARD, *Church, State and Opposition in the USSR.* Berkeley, CA: University of California Press, 1974.

VARDYS, V. STANLEY, "Polish Echoes in the Baltic," *Problems of Communism,* 32, No. 4, Jul.–Aug. 1983, 21–34.

————, *The Catholic Church, Dissent and Nationality in Soviet Lithuania.* Boulder, CO: East European Quarterly, 1978. (Distributed by Columbia University Press, New York.)

ZASLAVSKY, VICTOR, *The Neo-Stalinist State: Class, Ethnicity, and Consensus in Soviet Society.* Armonk, NY: M. E. Sharpe, 1982.

13

SOCIAL PROBLEMS II: Alcohol, Drugs, Juvenile Delinquency, and Crime

In 1961, shortly after we had arrived for our first sojourn in the Soviet Union, the head of the Foreign Students' Office at Moscow University proudly informed us that crime had been eliminated in the Soviet Union. Being newcomers and guests, we kept our skepticism to ourselves—until one Friday night when we arrived home after a delightful evening at the Moscow circus. At first the room seemed a little bare. But why? Nothing looked conspicuously out of place. Or did it? The radio? Our American radio was missing from the windowsill. What else? Turning, we noticed that Don's closet was in disarray and that nearly all his winter clothing was missing (Western tailoring currently commanded premium prices on the Moscow black market). Distressed, we notified the police, who did not even bother to examine the room. Discussions with the police and with our Soviet friends about the theft convinced us that such occurrences were far from rare in the Soviet Union—either inside or outside the university.

Although no responsible Soviet writer has committed to print the proposition that crime has been eliminated in the Soviet Union (the head of the Foreign Students' Office was merely demonstrating his zeal), many Soviet authorities are quick to make the point that in large urban areas the number of crimes committed is declining. Over ten years ago, the Chief of the All-Union Criminal Investigation Board stated, "The streets and parks of Moscow and Leningrad are safe both in the daytime and at night."[1] Verify-

259

ing or disproving this statement was and is impossible, since adequate Soviet crime statistics are difficult to obtain—even for Soviet criminologists.

Certainly it is undeniable that we, and many Western residents in Moscow, feel safer on the streets of Moscow than on the streets of New York. Why? Until recently, there has been little in the mass media or in our own experiences to lead us to feel otherwise. Though this may be about to change,[2] crimes against persons, like plane crashes and other such distressing domestic phenomena, have historically been ignored by the Soviet press. Thus, one must visit the courts or personally experience a crime (as we did) to be aware of the fact that such crimes are reasonably common in the Soviet Union.

Though the streets of Moscow may be free of any obvious manifestations of crime, to date they have not been free of obvious manifestations of another serious Soviet social problem—alcoholism. Heavy drinking or alcoholism is not a purely Soviet phenomenon, though there is evidence that there has been a gradual increase in alcohol consumption during the Soviet period.[3] Heavy drinking among men is a tradition that goes back in Russian experience far beyond the Bolshevik Revolution. The cultural image of the adequate male as a person able and willing to drink both heavily and frequently has proved exceptionally difficult for the Soviet government to eradicate, despite the serious losses in productivity and the other problems that it creates.

On the other hand, although the alcoholism problem is more serious than it is in the United States, the narcotics problem seems less serious. In fact, the only indications that there is any problem with drugs are a small number of media stories and journal articles concerning drug use and the passage in 1974 of an edict by the Presidium of the USSR Supreme Soviet, "Concerning the Strengthening of the Fight Against Drug Addiction."[4] In addition, there are persistent rumors about drug use—especially among university students and soldiers returning from Afghanistan. However, even when the most negative interpretation is placed on the available evidence, it is inescapable that drug abuse is not a major problem in either absolute or relative terms.

Although there appears to be little "drug culture" among Soviet youth, there is a problem with juvenile delinquency, which is of great concern to Soviet authorities. The very persistence of a juvenile delinquency problem indicates a series of failures on the part of the government which has, over the years, been designing and redesigning its programs in a persistent but unsuccessful effort to eradicate it.[5]

Crime, juvenile delinquency, narcotics, and alcoholism are, to a greater or lesser degree, social problems common to the entire developed and urbanized world. The brief outline in the previous paragraphs indicates their relative seriousness as problems in Soviet society. In the following four sections, we will take a more detailed look at the magnitude and consequences of each, as well as the basic measures the Soviet government is using to combat them.

ALCOHOLISM

Alcoholism and drunkenness[6] have long been substantial social problems in Russia.[7] The more serious consequences include alcohol-related crimes, public disorders, loss of productivity, illness, a decreasing male life expectancy, suicide, and death. In spite of this, however, drunkenness has traditionally been regarded with a high degree of tolerance by the majority of the Russian people. An indication of this is the fact that under the criminal law of tsarist Russia, being drunk could be an extenuating circumstance. The lack of similar tolerance on the part of the Soviet leadership is shown by the fact that under Soviet law intoxication is a circumstance aggravating responsibility for certain crimes.[8]

What Walter D. Connor calls "the Russian drinking culture"[9] has, to date, been definitely a gender-associated phenomenon. Historically, drunkenness in men has been taken for granted, whereas drunkenness in women has been condemned. Men cannot abstain without risking slurs on their manhood (or, in the case of one of the authors, on the adequacy of American men); they are expected to drain their glasses with every toast and immediately be ready for more. Women have been freer to choose moderation or abstinence. There is evidence, however, that drinking among women is becoming more of a problem.[10] This has led to increasing official concern because of its effects on the infant mortality rate and the conviction that alcohol abuse among mothers is contributing to a rise in birth defects.[11] In 1983 a Soviet sociologist wrote that 12 to 15 percent of Soviet alcoholics are women and claimed that the incidence of female alcoholism was growing more rapidly than the incidence of male alcoholism.[12] For men and women alike, there is certainly no social pressure to abstain. Even media propaganda has stressed the importance of moderation, as though total abstention were too utopian to be worth considering as a goal. For example, in 1985 at the inception of a major campaign against alcoholism, it was announced that the production of beer would be increased.[13] Presumably, it would be a substitute for the more lethal hard liquor.

Juvenile drinking is also of concern to Soviet authorities. A. Mayurov, a lecturer for the Knowledge Society, states that 90 percent of alcoholics begin drinking before the age of 15, and 33 percent before the age of 10.[14] There are regulations that govern the sale of alcoholic beverages to minors, but they are constantly being violated, due in part to the pressures on distributors and salespersons to fulfill their part of the state plan. Thus, the following comment by the manager of a food store in Moscow:

> Now as before, the regulations for the sale of liquor are being violated. You probably think that Masha standing at the counter in the wine department has no conscience? And that I have none either? We do have a conscience, and we also have children. We do not want them to become drunkards. But we have our plan, and we want to receive a bonus. If we have not fulfilled the plan by the end of the month, do you think they make up the deficit? They give us vodka. As far as the plan is concerned there is no difference between milk and vodka.[15]

The parallel between milk and alcoholic beverages has an even more significant dimension because of what a Soviet scholar calls "breast-milk alcoholism."[16] According to Uglov, many children begin imbibing alcohol via the breast milk of their drinking mothers. This is both supplemented and compounded by the fact that many Soviet parents feed alcohol to fussy babies in order to quiet them at night. This introduction to alcohol is reinforced by adult examples and the mass media, until for many Soviet children there arises the belief that it is impossible to be a proper adult without drinking.[17] In 1985—perhaps in order to counter this attitude among young people—the Soviet government raised the drinking age from 18 to 21.

Most Russians drink their vodka straight and rapidly; sedately sipping mixed drinks is not in the Russian tradition. They tend to drink to get drunk, hardly pausing long enough to taste what they are drinking. As if drinking to get drunk were not enough, the occasions on which heavy drinking is expected are many. There are, of course, the events that are celebrated with alcoholic beverages in most countries: a wedding, a birthday, the birth of a child. However, "it is apparently the custom in the USSR to arrange a party to celebrate one's first payday, the distribution of bonuses, or other occasions that other cultures would not mark by drinking."[18] Then, many see fit to drink in honor of holidays—like Sunday, the anniversary of the October Revolution, May Day, International Women's Day, Red Army Day, New Year's Eve, and so forth. Besides these, there are the holidays that are more limited in scope, but that are often also celebrated alcoholically by certain segments of the population: Builders' Day, Miners' Day, Chemical Workers' Day, and all the other days set aside in honor of somebody or other. Thus, for those who are of a mind to drink, it is usually easy to find an appropriate occasion—frequently.

In fact, for some it is not necessary to find an occasion. A Deputy Minister of Justice of the Latvian SSR related the story of Janis Baris, a bulldozer operator who habitually came to work intoxicated but who was only reprimanded (instead of dismissed) by the factory administration. The culmination of his drinking career came when he organized a collective drinking spree at the factory that resulted in production losses of about 860 rubles.[19] This sort of behavior continues to be quite typical. Factory managers frequently write to Soviet newspapers complaining about drinking among their workers. As of 1985 at only one factory near Irkutsk, 500 person days per year were being lost as a result of drunkenness among the work force. In 1984 in Moscow alone, 51,000 industrial workers and 22,500 construction workers were absent from work because of drunkenness.[20]

Given this attitude toward drinking, it is little wonder that the USSR ranks among the leaders of the world in the consumption of intoxicating beverages. A careful statistical study by a Western scholar places the USSR fourth in the world in per capita consumption of all alcoholic beverages.[21] This estimate excludes illegally made home-brewed alcoholic beverages, which constitute a considerable proportion of Soviet alcohol consumption. Moreover, in spite of Soviet efforts to deal with the problem, the rate of increase in alcohol consumption in recent years has been among the highest in the world.[22]

Some Soviet scholars have examined the production losses that could be attributed to alcohol abuse. The possible magnitude of the problem is indicated by a report of the USSR Anti-Alcohol Committee, which stated that approximately 37 percent of male workers are alcohol abusers and approximately 1 percent per day of all male workers misses work because of drinking.[23] Particularly serious are the effects of payday and holiday drinking. At a group of Leningrad factories which were studied, it was found that 90 percent of the absenteeism and 85 percent of the late arrivals occurred on the day after a payday or holiday. On Mondays, productivity is approximately 12 to 15 percent below productivity on other working days. In addition, drinking is a contributing factor in about one fourth of all industrial accidents. Accidents and injuries double on paydays.[24]

Even agricultural production, chronically a problem area in the Soviet Union, is affected. For example, drunken tractor drivers are a major problem throughout the country. According to Chita radio, drinking is the main cause of the increase in accidents among tractor drivers in Chita Province and is blamed for 90 percent of road deaths and 70 percent of injuries. More than 800 tractor drivers were relieved of their responsibilities in Georgia during 1978, and a spot-check in Moscow Province caused the arrest of over 110 tractor drivers for intoxication.[25]

The Journal *Molodoi Kommunist* (The Young Communist) reported that in one region in Russia, 71.4 percent of all divorces sought by women are attributed to their husbands' drunkenness. Elsewhere it has been estimated that 40 to 50 percent of all divorces in the USSR involve alcohol abuse by one of the spouses.[26] Aside from the obvious unpleasantness and embarrassment of living with someone who drinks excessively, this statistic may implicate alcohol consumption as a factor in family disputes over finances—a point of contention often associated with divorce in the United States. It is certainly true that a substantial portion of the Soviet family budget goes for alcoholic beverages which, unlike wine in Italy and France, are not commonly considered a part of meals.

Just how substantial this budget item is cannot be determined with certainty, but some idea may be gotten from data that have been published. On December 3, 1967, *Izvestiia* reported on page 1 that 93 rubles or 2.85 percent of an average yearly family income of 3,268 rubles was spent on vodka, beer, and other alcoholic beverages. This was approximately the same amount that the same "average family" spent on furniture (96.3 rubles or 2.9 percent) or on the combination of movies, plays, newspapers, and other cultural needs (122 rubles or 3.7 percent). Higher figures were given in a Soviet book published in the 1970s.[27] Although the raw figures were not given, the family, which was comparable in income level to the *Izvestiia* "average family," spent 14.64 percent of its income on alcohol.[28] This was compared to 34.20 percent spent on food and drink combined. If it is assumed that the latter figure includes the former, it implies that approximately 43 percent of what is spent for food and drink is spent for alcoholic beverages. More recently, a study conducted by MVD (Ministry of Internal Affairs) found that "among the families of the alcoholics investigated, more than 40 percent of their monthly incomes are spent on the purchase of spirits."[29] If these figures are even approximately accurate, it is easy to see how the family of an alcoholic might resent the sacrifices required to support one family member's habit.

The figures do not take into account the consumption of *samogon* (home-brewed alcoholic beverages). *Samogon* consumption can be only roughly estimated because official Soviet statistical sources have not published summary statistics since the 1930s. In fact, Vladimir Treml, a Western expert on Soviet alcohol production and consumption, is of the opinion that even Soviet authorities do not have an accurate picture of the situation with regard to *samogon*. Thus, we can do little more than give a tentative indication of overall *samogon* production and consumption based on estimates by Treml and fragmentary information from Soviet sources. Soviet scholars have estimated that 467 million liters of *samogon* were distilled in the Soviet Union in 1972.[30] This is higher than the comparable estimate of legally brewed vodka, which was 446 million liters in 1972. Treml's most recent estimate is that 1,645 million liters of 40 percent *samogon* were consumed by the Soviet people in 1979. In the same year, the domestic production of vodka (which has a comparable alcohol content) was 2,850 million liters.[31]

An indication that *samogon* production may be increasing is the report in a Soviet youth periodical that for some families the production of *samogon* is becoming a major source of income. Using fairly sophisticated equipment, these home distillers can turn out as much as ten liters of *samogon* per day.[32] In rural areas, "moonshining" can account for as much as a third of the total criminal convictions.[33] Even this does not seem to be much of a deterrent, given the indicators of total illegal production. Perhaps one reason is the lenience of the courts, which tend to utilize the relatively mild penalties mandated for the crime of distilling for personal use instead of the harsher penalties for illegal commercial distilling.

"Moonshining" is not the only crime that is alcohol-related. A high proportion of all crimes committed in the Soviet Union are committed by intoxicated persons—more than 50 percent (according to an MVD source), including about 80 percent of all murders. Another scholar reported that "according to data from many criminological studies, about 75 percent to 80 percent of the most common urban crimes are committed by intoxicated persons." The situation among juveniles is, if anything, even worse; 80 percent of all crimes committed by juveniles are committed under the influence of alcohol or with the intent of obtaining money to buy alcoholic beverages. A breakdown of crimes against persons shows that the overwhelming majority of crimes are committed by individuals under the influence of alcohol. Crimes against property, such as thefts from stores, tend to be committed by persons seeking money to buy alcoholic beverages. According to a Soviet newspaper, there is even a tendency for sports events to be marred by the violence of inebriated fans.[34]

Intoxication not only contributes to the commission of crimes by the persons who are intoxicated, but it also contributes by making drunken persons prey for those who are both sober and unscrupulous. For example, an article in *Pravda* in 1975 tells of two policemen in Tambov who discovered that their salaries could be augmented by shaking down drunken drivers. Whenever they found a driver who had been drinking, they reminded him that even a suspicion of alcohol could cost him his license, and they collected 30 rubles "hush money." Fragmentary statistics indicate that a considerable number of the victims of crime are drunk and that many of them had been drinking with the person who subsequently victimized them.

To summarize, the problem of alcohol abuse is a serious one in the Soviet Union, and because of traditional Russian attitudes toward drinking, it is one that is particularly difficult to eradicate. This is a matter of grave concern to the Soviet government, which has devoted substantial resources to the prevention of alcohol abuse and to the rehabilitation of chronic drunkards. The measures that have officially been favored are based on a generally accepted etiological explanation: "Alcoholic behavior is learned behavior."[35] Therefore, alcoholism is treated as a habit that develops from drinking increasing amounts over time. Given this assumption, the way to attack the problem is to discourage drinking in general, to change traditional attitudes toward alcoholic beverages and drunkenness, and to help those who have acquired the habit to break it.

In 1985 the new Gorbachev regime embarked on a massive campaign to discourage the drinking of alcoholic beverages, particularly hard liquor, among the Soviet populace. Simultaneous decrees of the Central Committee of the CPSU, the Soviet of Ministers of the USSR, and the Presidium of the Supreme Soviet of the USSR were published in May 1985.[36] They initiated a series of measures aimed at discouraging the drinking of hard liquor and stopping the production of *samogon*. Among other things, it increased the penalties for being drunk in public, driving while drunk, drinking on the job, giving alcohol to minors, and producing, marketing or storing *samogon*.[37] In addition, the drinking age was raised from 18 to 21, the opening of liquor stores on working days was delayed three hours, and there began a gradual reduction in the production of vodka and other hard liquor. It was further announced that certain fruit-based alcoholic drinks would be completely banned by 1988. On the plus side, the government added some "sweeteners." For example, it promised to begin increasing the production of soft drinks in 1986 and to increase the production of juices, jams, and fresh fruit.[38]

A few months later, the government intensified the campaign by raising the price of vodka 25 percent and announcing that a majority of distilleries would be closed or changed to food production.[39] In addition, the price of baking yeast, which is commonly used to brew illegal liquor, was raised 30 kopeks per 100 grams.[40] All of these changes were accompanied by a considerable media hype and educational efforts. There was evidence, however, that compliance by the Soviet people, particularly salespeople, was not uniformly good. While it is early to attempt an estimate of how successful this effort will be (this is not the first time the Soviet government has embarked on a vigorous campaign against alcohol abuse), it is an indication of the high priority the alcohol problem has in the Gorbachev regime.

The basic method of coping with the problem of changing people's attitudes toward drinking has been education and propaganda. This effort has two aims: (1) the formation of a public attitude that alcohol abuse is foreign to Soviet social goals because of its harmful consequences for the individual, the family, production, and the general welfare; and (2) the involvement and organization of the general public in prevention.[41]

The educational effort begins in school. In 1984 the USSR Deputy Minister of Health announced a stepped-up program to fight childhood alcoholism.[42] First, a new program was instituted, starting at age seven, to educate schoolchildren about the dangers of alcohol. Second, a similar program was begun in vocational-technical schools. Finally, drug abuse clinics are being established specifically to treat teenagers. Adults are the target of lectures, consultations with physicians, and personal exhortations by propagandists, plays, movies, posters, pamphlets, and tape recordings. As an extension of the new crackdown on alcohol consumption, a new journal, *Sobriety and Culture*, began publication in January 1986.

Special educational efforts are sometimes directed at persons thought to be particularly susceptible. For example, the authorities in Minsk identify groups of potential alcoholics and invite them to attend court hearings involving alcohol abuse. Afterward, they are addressed by representatives of the Procuracy, judges, and policemen. The occasion is televised and photographs of it are displayed throughout the city. This has apparently been highly successful in reducing the number of offenses committed by drunkards in Minsk.[43]

Aside from such relatively small-scale experiments, however, the educational campaign against alcohol has not been successful. Walter D. Connor attributes this lack of success to three major problems.[44] First, it is very difficult to change attitudes—especially those that are as ingrained as traditional Russian attitudes toward drinking. Second, there is a basic inconsistency in the picture of drinking that is being presented. Most educational efforts depict alcohol as an unmitigated evil; yet the emphasis is on moderation rather than on total abstinence. Also, the government-controlled entertainment media often treat drinking in ways consistent with traditional attitudes. Finally, the persons most likely to be problem drinkers are those for whom Soviet life offers the fewest rewards and who are least likely to expose themselves to propaganda efforts: the poorly educated and un-skilled. For them, much of life is drab and boring, and alcohol is used as an escape.

Another related method the Soviet government uses in combating alcohol abuse is the mobilization of public pressures via social organizations. Much of this work falls to Party and *Komsomol* groups, comrades' courts, and the people's volunteers *(druzhiny)*. For example, since the mid-1970s special detachments of people's volunteers have been organized to deal with par-ticular problems, including alcohol abuse and the distilling of *samogon*. Also, as we mentioned in Chapter 4, "checklists for lawbreakers" were being distributed to Soviet citizens to encourage them to be informants for the police. One of the infractions listed on these cards is drunken behavior. In 1984 General Secretary Chernenko made a speech at the USSR Conference of People's Controllers urging every Soviet citizen to think and act like a controller. In this connection, he emphasized the importance of such uni-versal surveillance in the campaign against alcoholism.[45] Finally, there is unmistakable symbolism in the fact that the recent Twenty-Seventh Party Congress in 1986 was dry.[46]

The techniques utilized in such efforts seem to be limited only by the imaginations of those involved. Among the more common are ridicule of known drinkers in satirical wall newspapers, the public posting of their pictures, and the discussion of specific alcohol abusers at meetings. Many of these groups also engage in direct preventive work with teenagers. Adults who drink too much in the opinion of such groups can be subjected to measures that go beyond attacks on self-esteem. For example, social organi-zations can suggest to the authorities at the drinker's place of work such measures as nonpayment of bonuses, refusal of annual leave, placement lower on the waiting list for housing, transfer to a lower paid job, and a cut in wages.

In 1972 the Presidium of the Supreme Soviet of the RSFSR issued a decree establishing Commissions for the Struggle with Drunkenness at the local, regional, and union-republic levels. They coordinate the activities of government authorities and social organizations as well as develop and implement preventive measures. On any given commission there may be representatives from diverse official and semiofficial organizations, includ-ing government, social organizations, workers' *kollektivs,* and economic or-ganizations. Because the commissions have fairly comprehensive rights and duties, they may enhance a campaign by providing a coordination of effort which has been lacking in the past. There are some areas, however, where governmental authorities must assume exclusive responsibility. First and foremost is determining what role alcohol production and consumption should play in the national economy.

For decades Soviet authorities have been trying to restrict alcohol consumption by regulating the retail distribution of alcoholic beverages. Since the late 1950s there has been an attempt to reduce consumption by limiting the places where alcoholic beverages could be purchased and by shortening the hours during which they could be sold. These measures had little lasting effect during the 1960s, when the consumption of legal alcoholic beverages continued to rise steadily. Beginning in 1970, these efforts were intensified with the publication of new regulations limiting the sale of vodka to certain stores and allowing sales only between 11 A.M. and 8 P.M. In 1985 the hours became even shorter: 2 P.M. to 8 P.M.

With some minor fluctuations, the prices of all alcoholic beverages have been rising steadily since 1955.[47] When prices were raised in 1981, there was a subsequent increase in the production of *samogon* and in the use of substitutes, such as industrial alcohol, for drinking. Subsequently, there was a decline in the quality of alcohol being consumed by many people, causing a sharp increase in the incidence of alcohol-related health problems and alcohol poisoning, and exacerbating an alcohol-related death rate far above the world average. Also, the increase in *samogon* production diverted grain, potatoes, sugar beets, and sugar away from consumption as food products—a serious matter given the problems the Soviet Union has had recently feeding its population.[48] It is too early to say whether the 1985 reforms will have similar undesirable side-effects, but it is interesting to note that the increase in price and decrease in availability have been accompanied by a vigorous effort to prevent and harshly punish home-brewing.

The reforms have also been accompanied by efforts to encourage people to substitute soft drinks and fruit juices. A 1986 report stated that the sale of alcoholic drinks was reduced by 25 percent during the second half of 1985 and that the number of stores selling wine and hard liquor had been cut in half.[49] Early reports, however, have also indicated that efforts to reduce problem drinking in some locations have had little impact[50] and that alcoholics have begun drinking perfume and industrial fluids, causing increased numbers of poisonings.[51]

In spite of all efforts to change consumption habits, it must be said that the attitude of the authorities with regard to alcohol use had been, at best, ambivalent. Sales of alcoholic beverages yield tax revenues that "contribute in a significant way to the taxation burden in the USSR."[52] According to Treml, in 1979, "taxes of 25.4 billion rubles on alcoholic beverages made up about 29 percent of the total taxes paid by the (Soviet) population." A more recent estimate put the government's earnings from alcohol at approximately 10 percent of the national budget.[53] A Soviet *samizdat* writer, after making some very clever calculations, estimates that 92.4 percent of what the Soviet consumer pays for a bottle of vodka goes directly into the Soviet national treasury.[54] Treml sums up the situation as follows:

> No other industry or economic activity in the USSR comes even close to the alcohol industry in terms of contributions to the state budget. State revenues from production and sales of alcoholic beverages are therefore such an important factor in the administration of fiscal policy in the USSR that it is difficult to

imagine that it would not frustrate or at least constrain any government antidrinking measures and policies.[55]

From some points of view, then, the production of alcohol is very profitable, as is its trade and distribution. From another perspective, however, the cost of alcohol use are extremely high. The Soviet demographer Urlanis estimates that the economic losses sustained by the government through alcohol abuse exceed the income from the sale of alcoholic beverages.[56] That the Gorbachev regime takes the second point of view is evidenced by the fact that the 1985 reforms go further than any previous reforms in restricting the production of alcoholic beverages and, by extension, restricting the government's income from the sale of these beverages.

A further reason why the state has—at least before 1985—been reluctant to restrict alcohol production is that drinking provides a pastime, no matter how destructive, to persons who have little other opportunity for diversion in their lives. This point would appear to be particularly applicable to the rural areas of Russia. Also, there is the ease with which *samogon* can be made. Home brewing of *samogon* requires minimal skill, primitive equipment, little space, and easily obtained raw materials such as potatoes, grain, sugar, sugar beets, or fruit. This fact limits the use of price increases to limit liquor consumption. The more they have to pay, the more likely people are to find it worthwhile to brew their own.

Thus, it can be seen that the 1985 reforms were designed to attack this multi-faceted problem in a complex way. Not only were there measures to increase the cost and inconvenience of drinking, but there were also measures designed to discourage recourse to the brewing of *samogon*. Most notably, the curtailing of the production of hard liquor signaled a decision on the part of the Gorbachev regime that the evils engendered by excessive and inappropriate alcohol consumption outweighed the benefits, such as the contribution of liquor sales to the Soviet budget.

For the person who abuses alcohol in spite of all prevention efforts, there is treatment. In line with the opinion that chronic drunkenness is learned behavior, Soviet treatment stresses: (1) the use of drugs, vitamins, and hypnosis to detoxify and negatively condition the patient toward alcoholic beverages; (2) psychotherapy and autogenic training;[57] (3) work therapy to make the patient able to cope more effectively with daily life outside the treatment institution; and (4) early treatment at the work site.

In urban areas, the first institution the drunkard may encounter might be the "sobering-up station" of the local militia. These receive drunks off the streets, get them cleaned up, give them symptomatic treatment, and furnish a place to sleep it off—all for a nominal fee. This, of course, is not treatment; it is custodial care. For treatment, the alcoholic may be cared for in any of several medical and rehabilitative institutions, either on an inpatient or an outpatient basis.

A recent innovation is the establishment of fee-charging treatment centers call "narcological units," where a person may seek treatment anonymously to avoid the label "alcoholic"—a designation that could be detrimental to an individual, especially at work. In an effort to put greater emphasis on early treatment, "narcological departments" have been established at construction sites, enterprises, and agroindustrial complexes. At these centers individuals can get treatment for a period of between one and two months while continuing to work as usual. Part of the person's paycheck is deducted to cover treatment expenses and the rest is sent to his or her family. During the treatment period the patient stays at the hospital when he is not working and receives a combination of medicinal, psychotherapeutic and physiotherapeutic treatments. Authorities claim that this approach is quite effective in decreasing the number of persons with serious forms of alcoholism.[58] The overall rate of success in all forms of treatment is difficult to ascertain, but there is little reason at present to assume that it is any better or worse than in other countries with major alcoholism problems.

Alcohol abusers who create substantial problems for the authorities either by criminal activities or by noncriminal forms of social disruption can be subjected to compulsory treatment in special institutions under the jurisdiction of the Ministry of Internal Affairs. These institutions, called *profilaktorii* or treatment-labor institutions, were first created by a 1967 decree of the RSFSR Supreme Soviet. The system was expanded in 1972 by a decree of the Central Committee of the CPSU and the Council of Ministers of the USSR. Finally, in the mid-1970s, an RSFSR Supreme Soviet decree established a system of medical-labor institutions where alcoholics could be confined for as much as two years.

The problem is not to get the law on the books but to get the responsible authorities to enforce it as strictly as the Soviet leadership would like. Thus, the courts are constantly being exhorted to pay attention to intoxication as a factor in crime and to make use of compulsory treatment statutes. One can find complaints like the following, taken from the *Bulletin of the Supreme Court of the USSR:*

> Mirakhmetov was convicted of hooliganistic activities under art. 200 (3) of the Criminal Code of the Kazakh SSR by the city people's court of Chimkent. From the record of the case it can be ascertained that the convicted person was a chronic alcoholic. The wife of Mirakhmetov requested that he be referred for compulsory treatment, but the court did not even give consideration to the question.[59]

Thus, the Soviet government is using a wide variety of measures to cope with a serious problem that has proved too deeply ingrained to be solved quickly or easily. It is certainly clear that all past efforts to solve the alcoholism problem have, at best, met with limited success. The 1985 reforms seem more comprehensive than any tried within recent memory.

They also seem designed with past setbacks in mind. More time is needed before it will be possible to assess their impact.

DRUG ABUSE

It is difficult to write about the problem of drug abuse in the Soviet Union because virtually no data are available to indicate the nature and magnitude of the problem. Although Soviet sources repeatedly stress that this problem is not very widespread, they do not support this assertion with facts and figures. Thus, one is left to infer what one can from fragmentary reports of drug abuse in the Soviet media and from published legislation, as well as published judicial interpretations of that legislation. In addition, one can get occasional unofficial information such as the assertion by Zemtsov that "according to the USSR Public Prosecutor's Office, 18 percent of young people in the major cities and 7 percent of young people in rural areas take drugs."[60]

Laws on drug abuse generally have paralleled laws on alcohol abuse. There has been periodic revision of the applicable laws aimed at making them more comprehensive and increasing the penalties.[61] Also, compulsory treatment for narcotics addicts in treatment-labor institutions, or *profilaktorii,* was established in 1972 by the Presidium of the Supreme Soviet of the RSFSR.[62] In 1974, the Soviet government banned the cultivation of the opium poppy. Even the use of heroin in pharmaceutics is forbidden. The legislative effort, however, has not been as comprehensive, nor has it been accompanied by as much media coverage as measures concerning alcoholism. Thus, it is clear that there is enough of a drug-abuse problem to warrant substantial and continuing governmental activity, but the absence of a concerted media "campaign" against drug abuse indicates that the problem is not one of major proportions.

In a statement on narcotics laws, the Plenum of the Supreme Court of the USSR[63] stated that although drug abuse is not a major problem, the court must give it particular attention because of the serious social danger it poses and because drug-related crimes are severely punished under Soviet law. The Supreme Court put special emphasis on the identification and punishment of persons pushing drugs. It also ordered lower courts to pay more attention to reasons why persons commit drug-related crimes as well as the sources from which illegal narcotics are obtained. A subsequent decree issued by the Plenum of the Supreme Court[64] indicated considerable dissatisfaction with the work of the lower courts in handling drug-related cases. In some detail, it outlined the available laws that can be applied to such cases and the circumstances under which they can be applied. The overall message of the decree seems to be that the lower courts are being too lenient in drug-related cases.

Such decrees also may be interpreted as indications that there is a sufficiently heavy caseload of drug cases to warrant such attention by the Supreme Court to what the lower courts are doing. More recently, the USSR Supreme Soviet Presidium made a change in the law which would also seem to indicate a growing drug problem. The change eliminates the possibility of a reduction in punishment for certain crimes. Among these is "theft of narcotics." Dina Kaminskaya, a noted Soviet defense lawyer now living in the West, interprets this change to mean that "the spread of drug abuse and the consequent expansion of criminal organizations dealing in the theft and sale of narcotics have reached such proportions that the state has been forced to step up its campaign to combat the problem."[65]

One person who has studied the Soviet drug problem is Boris M. Segal, who was Director of the Department of Clinical Psychology and psychotherapy at the Moscow Institute of Psychiatry before he emigrated to the United States.[66] On the basis of various sources, Dr. Segal asserts that narcotics abuse, especially among juveniles, has become a significant social and medical problem. This is due—at least in part—to the ease with which drugs can be purchased on the black market. A major source of illegal drugs seems to be those pharmacies that are specially designated to dispense narcotics for medical purposes.[67] Drugs disappear into the illegal market because of serious violations of the rules for inventorying, storing, prescribing, and dispensing them. The causes of these violations are, no doubt, many; but some are as simple as a shortage of metal safes and files.

A particular problem has arisen among Soviet soldiers serving in Afghanistan. Recent interviews with Soviet army defectors have indicated that hashish use is widespread among Soviet troops in Afghanistan. If so, this raises a question as to the extent to which these soldiers will carry this habit back with them when they return to the USSR.[68]

Treatment seems also to be a problem. A major handicap is the shortage of doctors to staff treatment centers and the inadequate qualifications of those physicians who do work with addicts. Also, there are shortages of laboratory facilities and of beds for inpatient treatment. Some drug-treatment centers do not even have permanent quarters in which to carry out their function.

In short, although it can be said that there is a drug-abuse problem in the Soviet Union, the only verifiable indicators of its magnitude are the facts that a legal apparatus has been set up to handle drug-related crimes, that a medico-correctional system has been set up to treat drug abusers, and that drug abuse has been the topic of relatively frequent official pronouncements in recent years. That this effort is meeting with less than complete success is indicated by scattered indicators, such as a recent statement by Edward Shevardnadze, while he was still the Georgian Communist Party leader. In the newspaper *Zarya Vostoka* he asserted that drug abuse is increasing and that official efforts to fight this trend have been inadequate.[69]

JUVENILE DELINQUENCY

What to do with delinquent and wayward youth has long been a problem in the Soviet Union. In fact, A. Makarenko—sometimes rather inaccurately referred to as the "Soviet Dr. Spock"—made his reputation by doing innovative rehabilitative work with homeless and delinquent young people. Historically, much of the problem has been a result of the creation of large numbers of orphaned children by such upheavals as the 1917 Revolution, the subsequent civil war, and World War II. The absence of such major crises, however, has not meant the absence of problem youth. It has meant that the problem of delinquency has assumed more manageable proportions because of the effective functioning of most families, as well as the numerous agencies of socialization and control.

The overwhelming majority of juvenile offenders whose cases are processed by the regular courts are sixteen or seventeen years of age and have committed relatively serious offenses, such as homicide or theft. Juveniles who have committed less serious offenses, such as truancy, or who are under the age of fourteen (regardless of offense) end up under the jurisdiction of one of the Commissions for Minors' Affairs. These are composed of representatives of the community as well as of the police and the legal profession.

Commissions for Minors' Affairs have jurisdiction over the parents of juvenile delinquents as well as over the youths themselves. In most such cases, the parents are censured (70 percent) or fined (25 percent).[70] Other measures, however, such as referral of the parents to a comrades' court are possible, though apparently seldom taken. In deciding what to do with the juveniles themselves, the Commissions consider such factors as the social danger of the offense, the reasons why it was committed, and the background of the juvenile. The last factor includes age, health, education, attitude toward work and school, prior behavior, home environment, and upbringing. Frequently, the decision is made to issue a warning and then pardon the offenses of those youths who seem to realize the implications of what they did and who are likely to avoid such behavior in the future.

Local Commissions for Minors' Affairs also function as probation offices. They supervise juvenile delinquents who have been sentenced to measures that do not necessitate their removal from the community. Also, they function as parole supervisors, keeping an eye on youths who have been discharged from correctional institutions. This supervision includes making sure that the young person either has a job or is attending school.

What sort of people become juvenile delinquents in the Soviet Union? The overwhelming majority are male; approximately 5 percent of delinquents are female.[71] In addition, 78 percent live in urban areas.[72] The home environment of these youths is frequently substandard. For example, Connor reports[73] that more juvenile delinquents come from one-parent families than could be predicted from the number of broken homes in the population. Also, parents of juvenile delinquents tend to be poorly educated, to have drinking problems or criminal records, and to engage in disruptive behavior in the home.[74] Whether or not these families can be termed "disadvantaged" in terms of the income and employment status of their parents is unclear. Soviet sources seem to indicate that delinquents come disproportionately from families with relatively low income and employment status.[75] On the other hand, Zemtsov, an emigré sociologist, asserts that more than 60 percent of juvenile delinquents come from relatively prosperous family backgrounds and that many come from the families of professionals, scientists, and Communist Party officials.[76]

What about the educational level and employment status of the juvenile delinquents themselves? Senchin[77] reports that in the Ukraine only 45 percent of those studied were at the proper educational level for their age; the rest lagged behind by two or three classes. This lag was caused by dropping out of school and repeating classes. As might be expected from this statistic, working youth are much more likely to commit offenses than students in trade school or academic schools, and school dropouts are about twenty-four times more likely to commit crimes than those still in school. The nonworker and nonstudent, the idle youth, is most likely to become delinquent. Thus, Gendrikh Minkovsky, an eminent Sovient criminologist, asserts, "What they need is the businesslike atmosphere of a collective of working people with well-organized facilities. For instance, the inclusion of difficult teenagers in student building detachments has been completely successful."[78]

Finally, in the area of juvenile delinquency, as in many other areas of Russian life, the pervasive alcohol problem plays a role. Eighty percent of juvenile crime is committed by persons who are drunk or who are trying to get money to buy alcoholic beverages.[79] The job is made more complex by the fact that drinking by parents affects the home environment and parenting to which the potential delinquent is exposed from an early age. For example, a study in Leningrad indicated that in 88 out of 100 "problem families" one or both parents had a drinking problem.[80] It was estimated that in 60 to 82 percent of the cases, the parents were instrumental in introducing their chidren to the use of alcohol. It was also found that a very high percentage of the crimes committed by juveniles was related to drunkenness.

In summary, Soviet juvenile delinquents, not unlike juvenile delinquents in other countries, tend to be youths who are male, urban, less educated, from substandard families, and prone to drink to excess. However, to list their characteristics does not really answer the "why?" of juvenile delinquency. Soviet orthodoxy on this subject is that "deviant behaviors are survivals of an outgrown, but tenacious presocialist past; they are not, cannot be, symptoms of a 'sick' society, for ideology decrees that Soviet society is not sick."[81]

Within this framework of orthodoxy it is possible to distinguish two principal approaches that Soviet criminologists use in analyzing the causes of juvenile delinquency. The first, and currently most prevalent in official pronouncements, is the assertion that delinquency stems from a breakdown in the functioning of some of the basic socializing institutions in Soviet society: family, school, youth organizations, and places of employment. The second, which enjoys increasing popularity among Soviet criminologists, focuses on the personality of the adolescent as it dynamically interacts with the environment. In both cases, juvenile delinquency is seen as a basically social—not a psychological or biological—problem, and individuals are held to be responsible for their acts.[82]

How do Soviet socializing institutions break down or malfunction? In the case of the home, the problem may be that both parents work (which is usually the case) and the child does not get proper supervision. Or, as suggested previously, the alcohol problems of family members may interfere with the proper parenting of the child and, subsequently, become the problem of the child as well. The tendency for juvenile delinquents to be under-achievers or school dropouts is taken by Soviet authorities as an indication that the schools have failed in their responsibilities toward these young people. Malfunctioning of social institutions at the workplace may involve many things, ranging from an unwillingness to hire young people to a tradition of periodic drunkenness in the workers' *kollektiv*.

Usually the problem is seen as resulting from a complex of antecedents. For example, after reciting the crimes of a pair of delinquent youth, A. Satarov, the procurator of the Kirghiz SSR, concluded, "The finale to which they proceeded was a result of many causes: trouble in the family, the irresponsibility and neglect of parents, the indifference of the surrounding people, yes, and let us be frank, of the local government organs."[83] He later asserts, "Only we are guilty: fathers and mothers, teachers, Communists and *Komsomols*, police, procurators and courts." In all such cases, analysis of the problem proceeds on the assumption that the institution itself is basically sound and that the problem is to get it functioning properly. For example, there is little effort to create a situation that will do away with the necessity for two working parents in every family. Rather, the labor of both parents is assumed, and the issue is seen as the provision of adequate facilities for the care and supervision of the child while the parents are at work.

The current interest among Soviet criminologists in the personality of the child seems to supplement, rather than substitute for, an analysis based on institutional malfunctioning. This comes across very clearly in the following breakdown of juvenile delinquents into four groups by Professor Minkovsky and his colleagues.[84]

1. The youth actively seeks criminal activities (10 to 15 percent of juvenile delinquents). These delinquents are the most difficult to change but are not regarded as incorrigible.

2.   The youth has no sense of social responsibility and is inclined towards idleness: he becomes involved in crime through inertia (30 to 40 percent). The solution here is a sharp change in the environment and living situation.

3.   The youth has an unstable personality which is easily swayed both by positive and negative influences (25 to 35 percent). The remedy in this case is to strengthen the positive influences.

4.   The youth has a positively oriented personality but commits a crime accidentally, often through ignorance of the law (25 to 30 percent). Compulsory education measures or suspended sentences are the preferred approach with these.

Such standard interpretations of juvenile crime as those based entirely on institutional failures and on personality-related problems have become less satisfactory as the Soviet Union has experienced a growth in the number of juvenile crimes committed for no clear reason. Research in the South and Central Urals by Soviet criminologists indicates that the number of offenses falling in this category is approaching 50 percent.[85] This analysis is profoundly disquieting to Soviet authorities because it suggests that the USSR, like other developed countries, is vulnerable to affluence-related crime—something that official ideologues have long dismissed as impossible. There are also suggestions of a growing recognition by Soviet criminologists that they may have to pay more attention to the possibility that some crimes may be related to such factors as defects of character or "purely biological peculiarities."[86]

This position has been argued by three scholars associated with the MVD Academy.[87] Stating that "(i)t is wrong to view human behavior as the result of social causes alone," they assert that Soviet criminology does not pay sufficient attention "to the role of mental abnormalities—short of those which render persons legally incompetent—in forming the criminal personality and criminal behavior." The effect is to hamper the efforts of Soviet specialists in preventive, corrective, and rehabilitative work. There is virtually no scientifically substantiated body of information that can be used as a basis for deciding how best to assess psychophysiological abnormality. With specific reference to juveniles, they state that:

> Chronic alcoholism and a number of mental illnesses and pathological character traits may have an unfavorable effect on one's offspring. Hence, the regular medical observation of children whose parents suffer from such problems and the taking of corrective therapeutic, pedagogical, and—in the case of antisocial behavior—preventive action may help to eliminate or lessen the effect of pathological character traits and to prevent or alleviate mental illness, thereby lowering the risk that such persons will commit crimes.

They subsequently note that 57.4 percent of a group of juvenile delinquents studied manifested "mental abnormalities."

They too, however, were constrained to defer to the mainstream position: "Medical, biological and genetic disorders cannot, in and of themselves, be the causes of criminal behavior; they can only provide a background that makes it easier for illegal behavior to occur, given unfavorable social conditions." Thus, the foot is in the door—but just barely. The primacy of social factors in crime is qualified but basically unchallenged.

The psychological and physical changes associated with adolescence are also beginning to be seen as significant. In an article in *Literaturnaia Gazeta*,[88] A. Portnov, M.D., expressed the opinion that, while "(l)aw breaking is a social phenomenon," more attention should be paid to "certain biological and psychophysiological patterns that govern much of a person's behavior":

> [W]e must not forget that adolescence is a time of swift physiological changes. During this period there is an abrupt and rapid increase in the production of hormones that, by acting upon certain brain structures, stimulate in the adolescent an irresistible desire for physical activity, for creativity, for seeking out adventure and danger. It has been established that these same hormones raise the level of aggressiveness. At the same time, the adolescent's psyche is still immature; he has not yet fully developed firm moral convictions, notions of what is impermissible, or norms of social behavior. This disharmony makes adolescence the most difficult time in a person's entire life. This same disharmony, I am convinced, is one of the specific causes of juvenile misdemeanors and crimes—above all, of "motiveless" crimes. . . .

What kinds of crimes are most typical of Soviet juvenile delinquents? Basing his report on unpublished data from 1,200 towns, Zemtsov reports that "in 1971 people below the age of 20 accounted for 12 percent of all murder, 22 percent of gang robberies with violence, 59 percent of the burglaries, 52 percent of the thefts and 49 percent of all rapes."[89] These figures, though somewhat old, are particularly interesting because little data on juvenile crime is published. But they must be approached with some caution because it is impossible to verify Zemtsov's assertions. Walter Connor, whose data are limited to published information, concluded that most juvenile crimes that end up in the courts involve either property offenses (especially theft and stealing) or hooliganism.[90]

As was noted previously, there is a strong emphasis on the prevention of juvenile delinquency. Quite often the measures taken are closely related to the basic socialization process (see Chapter 4). The themes are familiar: the creation of the "new Soviet person" and the improvement of the standard of living and cultural level of the general population. Once a person has shown a proclivity for delinquent behavior, the preventive measures become more specifically directed at what are perceived as the problem areas: (1) aid to children who live in damaging home environments; (2) measures to prevent recidivism in cases where minor offenses have been committed; and (3) corrective and educational efforts directed at youths involved in serious crimes.[91] In short, prevention efforts are based on the idea "First, that delinquency is a socially caused phenomenon, to be coped with by manipulation and improvement of the social environment; and second, that the individual is, by and large, perfectible, given the proper social environment and a correct approach to influencing his behavior."[92]

When prevention efforts fail, the correctional system takes over.[93] Approximately one half of juvenile cases are disposed of without a court trial. Most of the cases that do go to trial involve youths who are 16 to 17 years old. Although the courts have a range of correctional measures from which to choose, there seems to be a strong tendency in practice to favor deprivation of freedom. Thus, approximately 60 to 70 percent are sentenced to a term in a juvenile labor colony.

There are three basic types of juvenile labor colonies: (1) "Standard-regime" colonies for males; (2) "standard-regime" colonies for females; and (3) "intensified-regime" colonies for males. The last type is reserved for juveniles who have already served a term in a colony or who have committed certain serious offenses. While all types of juvenile colonies are undoubtedly punitive in character, they do emphasize education more than do adult correctional institutions.

The average sentence is three years. The average amount of time a youth actually spends in the juvenile colony, however, is about nine months. There are three basic reasons for this. First, there is a law that allows conditional early release when a juvenile has served a third of his sentence. This is predicated on good behavior. Second, the time a person spends in jail during his pretrial investigation and the time he spends waiting to be sent to the juvenile colony are both credited to his sentence. Finally, youths are usually transferred to an adult correctional institution to complete their sentences if they become eighteen years old while in a juvenile correctional institution.

What are these institutions like? Usually there is strong peripheral security in the form of fences, armed guards, and watchtowers. Conditions inside are more relaxed, minimizing such jaillike attributes as barred windows. There are limits on the number of visits and packages an inmate may receive, and letters are subject to censorship. All inmates are required to work, usually in metalworking, woodworking, or construction. They are paid on a piecework basis, with a deduction for the colony's operating expenses. Thirty-three percent is put in the inmate's personal account.

Both general and vocational educational programs are offered. Because of the relatively short period of time a youth usually spends in the colony and because the entry of most youths into the colony does not coincide with the beginning of a school term, however, there is the perennial problem of giving the youths a block of education that will have meaning in the outside world. Also, there is the constant problem of finding personnel who are willing to work with inmate populations and who possess the necessary training and aptitudes to work in this rather unusual situation.

Finally, Soviet juvenile correctional institutions, like similar institutions elsewhere in the world, have constant problems coping with inmate subcultures. These include the curbing of exploitation and bullying of some inmates by other inmates. And, of course, the familiar prison problem of sexual attack seems to exist to some extent—although it is not mentioned frequently in Soviet literature on the subject. Correctional authorities try to organize the inmates into *kollektivs,* but this tactic has not been overwhelmingly successful—often for reasons that are beyond the control of the colony's staff, such as the brutalizing experiences inmates may have experienced from fellow prisoners while awaiting transfer to the colony. Also, the inmate–staff ratio, although better than those in many other countries, is far from ideal.

As in the United States and many other countries, the inmate may simply experience the juvenile labor colony as a way station on the road to an adult correctional facility. This may come about through transfer when the youth becomes eighteen, or it may come about because the youth becomes a recidivist.

ADULT CRIME

Unlike the juvenile delinquent, the adult criminal must be regarded as a finished product—however imperfect—of the Soviet system of socialization. He has been "processed" by all the formative institutions to which Soviet youth are subject and he has emerged "flawed." Not only does he fall short of the ideal embodied in the "new Soviet person," but he also falls short of the accepted minimum standards of behavior considered acceptable. Thus, the adult criminal is a much more serious problem, not only for the legal and correctional systems, but also for those who would like to be able to assert the superiority of the Soviet system over all others.

As in most societies, it is the relatively youthful segment of the adult population that commits a disproportionate number of crimes—especially crimes of violence.[94] And, as was the case with alcoholism,[95] crime seems to be mainly a masculine occupation. Female criminals are a decided minority and tend to commit nonviolent crimes, such as speculation (buying and reselling scarce goods). Finally, there is evidence that the propensity to commit crimes (except certain economic crimes) is strongly associated with lower educational achievement and occupational status.

What is the magnitude of the crime problem? The most accurate answer to this is probably that no one knows for certain—not even Soviet criminologists.[96] First of all, there is the problem endemic to criminological studies everywhere in the world: Are the crime statistics reported by the police more an effort to project a desirable image of police work than they are a reflection of the actual crimes committed and criminals apprehended? There is evidence that this happens in the Soviet Union. Second, a problem characteristic of closed societies like the Soviet Union is extreme secrecy. Most crime statistics are treated as classified information, and those that do find their way into print are usually so incomplete and without context that few conclusions, if any, can be drawn from them. Therefore, while some official and semiofficial Soviet sources assert that crime is on the wane, other fragmentary and circumstantial evidence indicates that it may be increasing.[97]

The only thing that can be said with any degree of certainty is that the Soviet people seem to feel safer in their parks and on their streets than do Americans, though much of this atmosphere of security may be created by the failure of the media to report much crime news. But, given the efficiency with which news seems to spread by word of mouth, the safe feeling may also reflect a somewhat lower incidence of crime. In addition, all major sources of information seem to agree that there is no substantial problem of organized crime, although some of the activities that are carried out by syndicates in other countries exist on a more modest scale in the Soviet Union.[98]

Much Soviet crime is similar to crime elsewhere, but some types are of particular interest because of what they indicate about Soviet society and government. Those that will be discussed here are hooliganism, parasitism, and economic crimes.[99]

Hooliganism is defined in the RSFSR Criminal Code as "intentional actions violating public order in a coarse manner and expressing a clear disrespect toward society."[100] This crime is the one most frequently committed in the USSR, accounting for approximately 25 to 30 percent of recorded offenses.[101] The term "hooliganism" derives from the name of a notorious Irish family of nineteenth-century London and came into use in Russian legal literature before the Revolution. It was not until after the Revolution, however, in the 1922 Criminal Code, that it became an official crime. Now hooliganism is a widely discussed topic in Soviet popular and scholarly legal literature and, apparently, a frequently adjudicated crime.

Soviet authorities view hooliganism as a serious matter, claiming that approximately half of those persons involved in instances of petty hooliganism sooner or later commit serious crimes. Thus, they see the struggle against hooliganism as a key element in the fight against crime. As a result, there are periodic "campaigns" designed to involve the whole populace in the effort to cut down on the incidence of hooliganism. These campaigns have not been notably successful, however, and there are perennial accusations that the authorities have not been harsh enough in dealing with hooligans. Although this may be a problem in some jurisdictions, it is also clear that hooliganism is closely related to the seemingly insoluble problem of alcoholism. For example, in 1971, 91 percent of those convicted of hooliganism had been drunk at the time of the hooliganistic incident.[102] Therefore, no matter how harsh the treatment, it seems unlikely that the problem will be significantly alleviated until the prior problem of alcohol abuse is dealt with more successfully. This may be another reason why the Gorbachev regime seems so determined to make some headway against alcoholism—even at substantial cost to the national budget.

Parasitism is "the reluctance to work and study, the striving to live at the expense of another."[103] Soviet authorities take such matters seriously, regarding such a lifestyle as a threat to the work ethic (which is at the base of the Soviet social and economic system) and as a breeder of crime. Soviet studies indicate that a significant proportion of criminals and juvenile delinquents were neither working nor studying at the time of their criminal activities. For example, in the Georgian SSR the proportion of criminals classed as parasites has risen as high as every third adult criminal and every fourth juvenile delinquent.[104] In the Ukraine, "parasites" have been accused of committing 30 to 35 percent of the total number of law violations.[105]

Simply leading a parasitic existence is not, per se, against the law—a person has to put up a determined effort to resist reform. The first step in the process is the issuing of an official warning to the individual that such a way of life is impermissible; the individual is then given fifteen days to find a job. If this warning is ignored, more pressure is applied. If this further pressure meets with recalcitrance, the matter is turned over to criminal investigation authorities and Article 209-1 of the Criminal Code of the RSFSR or its equivalent comes into play. The punishment specified by Article 209-1 is deprivation of freedom for up to one year or correctional tasks for the same period. For the recidivist, the punishment is deprivation of freedom for not more than two years.

Economic crimes present a particular problem to authorities in a country where all economic activity is supposed to be under the control of the government and where all the economic resources are supposed to belong to "the people." In such a milieu, the type of individual initiative that is widely considered praiseworthy in the United States can be criminal. In fact, increasing success in individual economic endeavors tends to bring increasingly severe penalties, culminating in the death penalty for persons who are exceptionally successful. An example is found in Article 88 of the Criminal Code of the RSFSR:

> Speculation in currency or securities as a form of business or on a large scale . . . shall be punished by deprivation of freedom for a term of five to fifteen years with confiscation of property, with or without additional exile for a term of two to five years, or by death with confiscation of property.[106]

More commonly, economic crimes involve such matters as graft, embezzlement, and swindling.

Many economic crimes, of course, would be illegal or at least unethical in other legal systems. In the USSR, however, they pose a serious threat to government control over the economy. This is at least one reason why they can carry severe punishments—particularly the death penalty.[107] Although the men and women executed have clearly not led exemplary lives by any standard, a death sentence seems excessively severe. Thus, two officials of an Azerbaijan knitwear factory and two law enforcement officials were sentenced to death for setting up a private enterprise operation that netted them more than two million rubles.[108] More spectacularly, the director of

Moscow's best grocery store was sentenced to death for bribe-taking and "various illegal machinations with food products."[109] The use of the death penalty in the fight against crime appeared to have diminished during the earlier part of the 1970s. But the late 1970s and 1980s have apparently seen a significant rise in death sentences imposed largely but not exclusively for economic crimes.

Death-penalty cases are spectacular instances of economic crime. In the final analysis, however, the more serious threat to the Soviet economy probably is posed by crimes of a much more modest nature, such as petty pilfering, small-scale embezzlement, and the hoarding of scarce goods for resale. This kind of crime is hard to detect and prosecute successfully, not only because any one infraction seems insignificant, but because it is widespread—so widespread that it is considered acceptable by a broad segment of the populace. Unaware of how such minor crimes can add up to serious economic loss for the state, the average Soviet citizen can see no great harm in them. Also, to many Soviet citizens, "socialist" property belongs to everyone and therefore to no one. If it seems necessary—and Soviet citizens are continually in need of things of one sort or another—it does little *apparent* harm if they help themselves from "the common pot."

As part of its fight against corruption, the Andropov regime instituted new fines and stiffer prison terms for a wide range of economic crimes such as profiteering and stealing public property. Habitual offenders were denied parole, and mandatory sentences were set for more serious crimes.[110] Gorbachev has continued his mentor's effort by prosecuting many highly placed officials for economic crimes and by giving these trials widespread media coverage.

When a crime is petty or when, in the opinion of the authorities, it does not represent sufficient "social danger" to be worth prosecuting, the accused may be turned over to a comrades' court or released "on surety" to his *kollektiv*. This usually happens only in cases of first offenders who give evidence of acknowledging their guilt and resolving to reform. The rationale is that the social pressure exerted on the accused will be sufficient to prevent further wrongdoing, and it seems reasonably successful with this kind of criminal. But using the *kollektiv* to influence the behavior of lawbreakers is relatively rare.[111]

Most adult offenders—approximately three fourths—go on to a trial at the People's Court level and to some form of criminal punishment.[112] Although the courts have a fairly wide range of possibilities, they tend to sentence most adult criminals either to correctional tasks or to deprivation of freedom. Other punishments—such as fines, dismissal from office, and exile—are available but are seldom used.

"Correctional tasks" is a punishment that does not involve isolation from society. In some cases the person serves his sentence while working at his regular job. This is the form of correctional task used in the overwhelming majority of the cases. In certain situations, however, the court can and does require the offender to work at a job that is different from his regular employment and perhaps even outside his vocational or professional competence. Sentences to correctional tasks range from one month to one year; 5 to 20 percent of the person's earnings is deducted from his pay. During the period of the sentence, the individual is subjected to checks on his behavior by the *inspeksiia,* which is a government organ with responsibility for supervision of such offenders. Also, the time of the sentence is not counted as part of the person's labor record for purposes of seniority, pension, and other social-insurance provisions. It is simply noted in his record that he served a correctional-tasks sentence.

Deprivation of freedom is a much more severe form of punishment involving incarceration in a penal institution. The maximum term of imprisonment is fifteen years. Soviet penal institutions have inherited a particularly bad reputation from the Stalin era. There certainly has been some improvement in the situation for criminals—political prisoners have traditionally been treated more severely. The nature and extent of the improvement are virtually impossible to determine, however, because of the prevailing practice of extreme secrecy concerning what actually happens within the walls of Soviet penal institutions or even how many persons are in the penal system.[113] All we can do here is to outline some of the more formal characteristics of these institutions and, where feasible, give some indication of what the actual situation is most likely to be.

There are two basic types of penal institutions: corrective-labor colonies (*ispravitel'no-trudovye kolonii*) and prisons (*tiurmy*). Since the latter contain a relatively small proportion of the correctional population, we will concentrate on the former.

Corrective-labor colonies come in four degrees of harshness: (1) standard regime, (2) intensified regime, (3) strict regime, and (4) special regime. Prisoners are assigned to them according to their past records and the seriousness of their crime. First offenders who are convicted of crimes viewed as "not grave" are sent to standard-regime colonies. At the other end of the spectrum, special-regime colonies are intended for convicts adjudged "especially dangerous recidivists" and for those with commuted death sentences. There are, of course, also differences in living conditions, with progressively stricter regimes implying increasing limits on the number of visitors an inmate may have, the number of packages he may receive, the number of letters he may send, and his freedom of movement within the institution. Prisoners in special-regime colonies are housed in cells, the rest are in dormitories. The amount of food allowed prisoners also varies according to climatic conditions, the kind of work being done, and each individual inmate's attitude toward the labor required of him.

Adult colonies are similar to juvenile institutions in their emphasis on the creation of stable *kollektivs.* Work is seen as having a healthy influence on the convict's personality—an attitude that is undoubtedly related to the fact that parasitism is regarded as a factor predisposing individuals to the commission of crime. Inmates who do not have work skills are required to take vocational-technical instruction. Those without eight years of education must study in the colony school in order to complete their education.[114] Finally, inmates in the corrective-labor colonies are not exempt from the general Soviet requirement to be politically active. In colonies, political activity usually consists of lectures and discussions that are set up according to a schedule established by the MVD administration in charge of the colonies.

As in the case of juvenile correctional institutions, this program is not always carried out precisely as intended by higher authorities. A number of factors are involved, including administrative difficulties, simple incompetence, abuses, and a lack of cooperation on the part of the inmates. Noncooperation stems mainly from the dynamics of informal attitudes, such as a lack of interest in studying, or from the dynamics of the informal group structure that develops among the inmates. Group leaders, more often than not, are the incorrigible members of the group, and their attitudes can be very infectious.

In all of this, however, the Soviet penal system is not particularly unusual. Anyone who takes a close look at the penal system of any country meets with similar tales of incompetence, bureaucracy, inmate subcultures, and unrealized rehabilitative goals. Whether the difference in degree is sufficient to amount to a difference in kind is a function of whom you choose to believe about what actually happens within the walls of Soviet correctional institutions. As with so many elements of Soviet life, a thick blanket of secrecy totally precludes verification of any version of what constitutes the truth.

Release from a corrective-labor colony may come after an inmate has served his or her entire sentence—or it may come earlier. There is provision in the law for conditional early release after a person has served half his sentence. The decision is supposed to be made on merit, although there seems to be some disagreement among Soviet jurists on how to apply the criteria of merit. "Exemplary conduct" is a term subject to many interpretations.

A recommendation for conditional early release can be made jointly by the colony administration and a public inspection commission. The final decision is made by the local court. In practice, the key role is played by the colony administration when it decides whom to recommend for consideration. Persons so released appear to be subject either to no supervision or, at best, minimal supervision by a public organization or *kollectiv*. On the other hand, "especially dangerous recidivists" are automatically subject to supervision by the police. A 1985 amendment to Soviet corrective-labor legislation excluded from early release or commutation of term those persons who because of their crimes pose a special danger to society.[115] Examples of such crimes are banditry, theft of arms, and gang rape.

In addition to the penal institutions described, there are settlement colonies, which were set up in 1966 by the Soviet government for persons who were clearly on the path to reform. In 1977 similar colonies were created for persons who had committed crimes through negligence. Finally, in 1985, colonies were set up for persons serving their first term for an intentional crime that is less than a felony and for which they have been sentenced to five years or less.

These settlement colonies have a regime that is very different from that in other types of penal institutions. They do not have guards, fences, or barbed wire. Men and women share the facilities and marriage between inmates is permitted. Prisoners may also be allowed to live in family units and travel without supervision within the bounds of the local autonomous republic, krai, or oblast. Such prisoners can wear civilian clothing, have money and valuables, and receive an unlimited number of parcels and letters. This regime is thought to aid in combating recidivism and to make inmates more productive during their time in custody.

The ultimate test for any correctional system is the recidivism rate. Among persons sentenced to correctional tasks, the overall rate is relatively low. Connor estimates it to be somewhere in the neighborhood of 9.2 percent. This is fairly good, even when one takes into consideration that the type of criminals who most likely would be sentenced to correctional tasks are those least likely to be recidivists. This optimistic assessment, however, must be tempered by the considerable variation that occurs in the rate when one takes into account factors such as the seriousness of the crime, prior criminal activity, and the amount of supervision the convict has while serving his sentence and afterward.

Relatively little information is available concerning recidivism rates among persons released from corrective-labor colonies or settlement colonies. Connor, after studying the available evidence, concludes that the rates reported by Soviet sources are lower than those generally reported in the studies of American penal practices. Whether the actual rate is lower is another question. Also, there is the predictable pattern of increasing incidence of recidivism with increasing strictness of colony type. Finally, persons on conditional release seem to have a lower recidivism rate than those serving their full sentences. Again, as in the case of persons sentenced to corrective tasks, this description of the situation with respect to recidivism is in accord with common-sense notions as to what one might expect from different classes of criminals and as a result of different types of correctional treatment. Thus, it possesses at least a superficial plausibility.

Most recidivists are persons who have been convicted of hooliganism or property offenses such as theft. Murderers in the Soviet Union, as elsewhere, are unlikely to repeat their crime because crimes such as murder are usually committed in the heat of passion and are highly related to circumstances that are not likely to be repeated. On the other hand, stealing is quite likely to be a calculated act and is much more prone to develop into a "profession" for some persons. Thus, the typical recidivist tends to have a background of recurrent and frequent violations of the law—perhaps mixed with a strong propensity to alcohol abuse. As a result, some recidivists may spend substantial portions of their lives inside correctional institutions. They tend to be leaders within the inmate subculture and, thus, to do their part in perpetuating recidivism from generation to generation of convicts—much to the frustration of police, courts, and penal authorities.

NOTES

[1] Igor Karpets, "Preventing Crime, Rehabilitating the Offender," *Soviet Life*, No. 10 (Oct. 1974), 44.

[2] Vera Tolz, "Gorbachev's Speech to the Twenty-Seventh Party Congress: Reaffirmation of *'Glasnost'*," *Radio Liberty Research*, No. 102/86, Feb. 26, 1986.

[3] Walter D. Connor, *Deviance in Soviet Society* (New York: Columbia University Press, 1972), pp. 345–38; Vladimir G. Treml, "Alcohol in the USSR: A Fiscal Dilemma," *Soviet Studies*, 27, No. 2 (Apr. 1975), 162–63; Sergei Voronitsyn, "Increasing Concern over Effects of Alcoholism in the USSR," *Radio Liberty Research*, No. 156/80, Apr. 28, 1980, p. 1, and Vladimir G. Treml, *Alcohol in the USSR: A Statistical Study*, (Durham, NC: Duke University Press, 1982), p. 16.

[4] *Biulleten' Verkhovnogo Suda, SSSR*, No. 3 (1974), 43–46.

[5] This effort began with the birth of the Soviet state. For an account of its origins, see: Peter H. Juviler, "Contradictions of Revolution: Juvenile Crime and Rehabilitation," in *Bolshevik Culture*, eds. Abbott Gleason, Peter Kenez, and Richard Stites (Bloomington, IN: Indiana University Press, 1985), pp. 261–78.

[6] Soviet writers make no sharp distinction between the terms "drunkenness" (p'ianstvo) and "alcoholism" (alkogolizm). Therefore, in the following discussion we will follow the Soviet practice of not maintaining a clear differentiation.

[7] The cultural factors discussed here apply to the Russian portion of the Soviet people. Because the Soviet government is reluctant to release systematic data on ethnic differences in drinking behavior, it is impossible to say to what extent traditional Russian attitudes toward alcohol have spread to more abstemious Soviet cultures. There is evidence, however, of some diffusion, so that it is clear that a Soviet problem exists but unclear what its magnitude is. See, e.g., *The Washington Post*, July 8, 1985, p. A17.

[8] Article 39, Criminal Code of the RSFSR, *Soviet Criminal Law and Procedure: The RSFSR Codes*, 2nd ed., trans. Harold J. Berman and James W. Spindler (Cambridge, MA: Harvard University Press, 1972), p. 139.

[9] Connor, *Deviance*, p. 39.

[10] "Alcoholism Growing Among Women," *Soviet Analyst*, 8, No. 4 (Jan. 11, 1979), 7–8, and "Aspects of Crime: More Women Drinkers," ibid., 9, No. 6 (Mar. 19, 1980), 8.

[11] F. Uglov, "Daleko upali iabolki," *Izvestiia*, July 4, 1984, p. 3, and S. Tutorskaia, "Trudnoe vozrashchenie," *Izvestiia*, July 24, 1984, p. 6. Also see: Christopher Davis and Murray Feshbach, *Rising Infant Mortality in the USSR in the 1970s* (Washington, DC: U.S. Bureau of the Census), Series p-95, No. 74, Sept. 1980, and Murray Feshbach, "Soviet Health Problems," *The Soviet Union in the 1980s*, ed. Erik P. Hoffmann (New York: The Academy of Political Science, 1984), pp. 81–97.

[12] G. G. Zaigraev, as cited in Dana Townsend, "Soviet Concern about Alcoholism among Women," *Radio Liberty Research*, No. 321/84, Aug. 24, 1984, p. 2.

[13] *The Washington Post*, May 31, 1985, p. A22.

[14] A. Mayurov, writing in *Selskaya zhizn'*, Dec. 17, 1983, as quoted in: Yu. Vosnesenskaya, "Alcoholism among Children and Teenagers," *Radio Liberty Research*, No. 307/84, Aug. 13, 1984, p. 1.

[15] *Komsomolskaya Pravda*, Oct. 11, 1978, as quoted in Sergei Voronitsyn, "Alcoholism Among Soviet Youth," *Radio Liberty Research*, No. 291/78, Dec. 18, 1978, p. 3. See also *Izvestiia*, *Oct. 24, 1979, p. 3, and I. Lychagin, "Bormotukha' dlia podrostkov," Nedelia*, No. 12, 1984.

[16] Uglov, "Daleko upali iabloki," p. 3.

[17]Vosnesenskaya, "Alcoholism."

[18]David E. Powell, "Alcoholism in the USSR," *Survey*, 16, No. 1 (Winter 1971), 125, and "Annotations," *Radio Liberty Research*, No. 374/84, Oct. 2, 1984, p. 6.

[19]A Riga radio broadcast, May 29, 1974, reported in *Soviet Analyst*, No. 3 (Jul. 18, 1974), 8.

[20]*The Washington Post*, May 17, 1985, p. A26; June 1, 1985, p. A22.

[21]Treml, "Alcohol . . . Statistical Study," p. 70.

[22]Approximately 50 percent since 1965 and 100 percent since 1955, *ibid*, p. 68.

[23]Michael Binyon, *Life in Russia* (New York: Pantheon Books, 1983), pp. 58–59.

[24]Ibid, p. 59.

[25]*Soviet Analyst*, 8, No. 17 (Aug. 30, 1979), 8.

[26]*Molodoi Kommunist*, No. 9 (Sept. 1975), 102: Boris Segal, "Drinking and Alcoholism in Russia," *Psychiatric Opinion*, 12, No. 9 (Nov. 1975), 23.

[27]See the collection of various reports in "How Much Does the Soviet Family Spend on Alcoholic Drink?" *Radio Liberty Research*, No. 390, Sept. 16, 1975, p. 1.

[28]This is in rough agreement with Vladimir Treml's more recent estimate of 13 percent for the entire USSR. In a breakdown by union republic, the highest is the RSFSR with 15.8 percent, the lowest is Georgia with 6.3 percent. Vladimir Treml, *Alcohol in the USSR*. (Durham, NC: Duke University Press, 1982), p. 81.

[29]B. T. Shumilin, *P'ianstvo i Pravonarushenie* (Moscow: "Znanie," 1979), p. 14. Also see: Treml, "Alcohol . . . Statistical Study," pp. 70–80.

[30]S.G. Shumilin and M. Ya. Sonin. "Alkogol'nye Poteri i Bor'ba s Nimi," EKO, No. 4 (1974), 36–39, as reported in *Abstracts of Soviet and East European Studies,* Jan. 1975, p. 69. This estimate is well below Treml's minimum estimate for the same year, which was 1,108 million liters. Treml, "Alcohol in the USSR," p. 176.

[31]Treml, "Alcohol . . . Statistical Study," pp. 5, 55.

[32]"Annotations," *Radio Liberty Research*, No. 374/84, Oct. 2, 1984, p. 2.

[33]S. S. Ostroumov, *Sovetskaia Sudebnaia Statistika* (Moscow: Izdatel'stvo Moskovskogo Universiteta, 1970), p. 248, and Connor, *Deviance*, p. 38.

[34]The sources used in this paragraph were Shumilin, P'ianstvo, pp. 6 and 19; V.K. Zvirbul', *Rol' Sotsial'nogo Planirovaniia v Preduprezhdenii Pravonarushenii* (Moscow: "Znanie," 1977), p. 48; *Sovetskii Sport*, Sept. 23, 1973, p. 2; "Annotations," *Radio Liberty Research*, No. 374/84, Oct. 2, 1984, p. 3, and David K. Shipler, *Russia: Broken Idols, Solemn Dreams* (New York: Penguin Books, 1984), p. 237.

[35]Connor, *Deviance*, p. 54.

[36]*Izvestiia*, May 17, 1985.

[37]Valerii Konovalov, "Stiffer Penalties Decreed for Abuse of Alcohol and Production of Home-brew," *Radio Liberty Research*, No. 257/85, Aug. 7, 1985; *Izvestiia*, May 17, 1985, pp. 1–2, May 18, 1985, p. 1.

[38]*The Washington Post*, May 17, 1985, pp. A1, A26.

[39]*The Washington Post*, Aug. 28, 1985, pp. A21, A24.

[40]*Radio Liberty Research*, No. 286/85, p. 3.

[41]Connor, *Deviance*, p. 69.

[42]*Pravda*, Jun. 20, 1974, p. 6.

[43]*Pravda*, Jun. 20, 1974, p. 6.

[44]Connor, *Deviance*, pp. 71–73.

[45]Allan Kroncher, "Chernenko's Speech to the People's Controllers: Universal Surveillance is the Watchword," *Radio Liberty Research*, No. 389/84, Oct. 11, 1984, pp. 1–2.

[46]*The New York Times*, Feb. 27, 1986, p. A8.

[47]Treml, "Alcohol . . . Statistical Study," p. 26.

[48]It has recently been estimated that Soviet citizens use more than one million tons of sugar per year to make *samogon* and wine. *The Washington Post*, Aug. 28, 1985, p. A24.

[49]These statistics were reproduced in: Keith Bush, "Soviet Plan Fulfillment in 1985," *Radio Liberty Research*, No. 47/86, Jan. 27, 1986, p. 2.

⁵⁰"Soviet Antialcohol Drive Failing," *Radio Liberty Research,* No. 27/86, Jan. 10, 1986, p. 10.

⁵¹*The Washington Post,* Aug. 28, 1985, p. A24.

⁵²This and the following quotations are from Treml, "Alcohol . . . Statistical Study," p. 30.

⁵³*The Washington Post,* May 17, 1985, p. A26.

⁵⁴A. Krasikov, "Commodity Number One," in *The Samizdat Register,* ed. Roy Medvedev (New York: W. W. Norton, 1977), p. 106.

⁵⁵Treml, "Alcohol . . . Statistical Study," p. 33.

⁵⁶Segal, "Drinking and Alcoholism," p. 23.

⁵⁷A form of therapy usually combining relaxation with suggestion and autosuggestion.

⁵⁸Roman Solchanyk, "Ukrainian Minister of Health Outlines the Struggle against Alcoholism," *Radio Liberty Research,* No. 256/85, Aug. 6, 1985.

⁵⁹On this quotation and other information in this paragraph see "Sudebnaia Praktika po Delam o Khuliganstve," *Biulleten' Verkhovnogo Suda SSSR,* No. 1 (1973), p. 38, and "Priznanie Ogranichenno Deesposobnymi Grazhdan, Zloupotrebliaiushchikh Sprit'nymi," in ibid., No. 3 (1976), pp. 35–41.

⁶⁰Il'ya Zemtsov, "Problems of Soviet Youth," *Radio Liberty Research,* No. 125, Mar. 21, 1975, p. 10. Zemtsov is a Soviet sociologist who emigrated to Israel.

⁶¹For example, compare *Soviet Criminal Law and Procedure,* pp. 191–92, with Ukaz Presidiuma Verkhovnogo Soveta SSSR, "Ob Usilenii Bor'by s Narkomaniei," *Biulleten' Verkhovnogo Suda SSSR,* No. 3 (1974), pp. 43–45.

⁶²Ukaz Presidiuma Verkhovnogo Soveta RSFSR, "O Prinuditel'nom Lechenii i Trudovom Perevospitanii Bol'nykh Narkomaniei," *Vedomosti Verkhovnogo Soveta RSFSR,* No. 35 (Aug. 31, 1972), pp. 574–75.

⁶³*Izvestiia,* Oct. 9, 1974, p. 4.

⁶⁴Postanovleni No. 7 Plenuma Verkhovnogo Suda SSSR ot 26 Sentiabria 1975, g. "O Sudebnoi Praktike po Delam o Khishchenii Narkoticheskikh Veshchestv, Nezakonnom Izgotovlenii i Rasprostranenii Narkoticheskikh, Sil'nodeistvuiushchikh i Iadovitykh Veshchestv," *Biulleten' Verkhovnogo Suda SSSR,* No. 6 (1975), pp. 17–20. Also see "Primenenie Sudami Zakonodatel'stva o Bor'be s Narkomaniei i Rasprostraneniem Sil'nodeistvuiushchikh i Iadovitykh Veshchestv," *Biulleten' Verkhovnogo Suda SSSR,* No. 5 (1976), pp. 29–37.

⁶⁵Dina Kaminskaya, "Changes in the Fundamentals of Criminal and Corrective-Labor Legislation," *Radio Liberty Research,* No. 283/85, Aug. 29, 1985, pp. 3–4.

⁶⁶Boris M. Segal, "Soviet Studies on the Effects of Hashish," *Radio Liberty Research,* No. 142/77, Jun. 10, 1977.

⁶⁷The information that follows in this and the next paragraph is based on T. Abramova, "Drug Treatment Center Hurt by Poor Staffing, Facilities," *Current Digest of the Soviet Press,* 31, No. 48 (Dec. 26, 1979), 47–48. T. Abramova also discussed this problem in *Zarya Vostoka,* Oct. 13, 1979, cited in Radio Liberty, *Current Abstracts and Annotations,* No. 23 (1979), pp. 1–2.

⁶⁸See, for example, "Interviews with Two Soviet Defectors—Igor Rykov and Oleg Khlan'," *Radio Liberty Background Report,* No. 220/84, June 1, 1984, pp. 4–5; "Why One Soviet Soldier Defected in Afghanistan," *U.S. News & World Report,* Sept. 24, 1984, p. 32.

⁶⁹*The Washington Post,* Jan. 26, 1984, p. A20.

⁷⁰A. V. Senchin, "Komissii po Delam Nesovershennoletnikh: Nekotorye Rezul'taty Izucheniia Deiatel'nosti," *Sovetskoe Gosudarstvo i Pravo,* No. 7 (July 1974), p. 121. These statistics are based on research done in the Ukraine. Also see: Shipler, "Russia," p. 242.

⁷¹Il'ya Zeldes, *The Problems of Crime in the USSR* (Springfield, IL: Charles C. Thomas, 1981), p. 95.

⁷²Zeldes, *Problems of Crime,* pp. 96–97.

⁷³Connor, *Deviance,* pp. 87–89.

⁷⁴Zeldes, *Problems of Crime,* p. 92.

⁷⁵For a summary, see ibid., pp. 89–90. Also see: *Soviet Studies Information Supplement,* Oct. 1969, p. 25. Also see: Shipler, "Russia," pp. 232–33, 237–38.

[76]"Juvenile Delinquency in the USSR," *Soviet Analyst,* No. 4 (Sept. 4, 1975), p. 8, and Zemtsov, "Problems of Soviet Youth," pp. 3–4.

[77]Senchin, "Komissii," p. 120.

[78]Alexei Flerovsky, "Crime Drops: Criminologists Look at Their Jobs," *Soviet Life,* No. 10 (Oct. 1974), p. 33.

[79]Shumilin, *P'ianstvo,* p. 19.

[80]*Molodoi Kommunist,* No. 9 (Sept. 1975), p. 102.

[81]Connor, *Deviance,* p. 94, and Shipler, *Russia,* p. 230. Michael Binyon notes that public debate on the causes of crime is freer than it used to be. *Life in Russia* (New York: Pantheon Books, 1983), p. 249.

[82]Zeldes, *Problems of Crime,* Chap. 2, pp. 90–94.

[83]*Izvestiia,* Oct. 16, 1975, p. 5.

[84]Flerovsky, "Crime Drops," p. 33.

[85]Book review by V. N. Kudriavtsev, *Sovetskoe Gosudarstvo i Pravo,* No. 4 (Apr. 1973), p. 143.

[86]*Nash Sovremennik,* No. 2 (1972), p. 105, as quoted in Sergei Voronitsyn, "The Problem of 'Unmotivated' Juvenile Delinquency," *Radio Liberty Dispatch,* Feb. 25, 1974, p. 41. See also: Connor, *Deviance,* pp. 182–89. For insights into recent Soviet thinking about the biological bases of aggressiveness, see: T. G. Rumiantseva, *Kriticheskii Analiz Kontseptsii "Chelovecheskoi Agressivnoisti"* (Minsk: Izdatel'stvo BGU im, V. I. Lenina, 1982).

[87]The information and quotations in this paragraph are from Yu. M. Antonyan, M. V. Vinogradov, and Ts. A. Golumb, "Criminal Behavior Tied to Mental Problems," *Current Digest of the Soviet Press,* 31, No. 40 (Oct. 31, 1979), 4–6.

[88]The quotations in the paragraph from A. Portnov, "Drugs to Tame 'Aggressive' Teenagers?" *Digest of the Soviet Press,* 32, No. 4 (Feb. 27, 1980), 18.

[89]Zemtsov, "Problems of Soviet Youth," p. 2.

[90]Connor, *Deviance,* pp. 81–84.

[91]Connor, *Deviance,* pp. 115–24; *Izvestiia,* Sept. 12, 1975, p. 3; *Izvestiia,* Oct. 16, 1975, p. 5, and Zeldes, *Problems of Crime,* pp. 109–10.

[92]Connor, *Deviance,* p. 116.

[93]The authors are indebted to Connor, *Deviance,* pp. 125–41, for much of the material used in discussing the juvenile correctional system.

[94]Most of the statistical information in this and the following paragraph is based on the excellent summary in ibid, pp. 148–61.

[95]No doubt the correspondence between the characteristics of alcoholics and criminals is, to some extent, accounted for by the strong relationship between alcoholism and crime.

[96]For an insight into the problems associated with making such a determination, see: Zeldes, *Problems of Crime,* pp. 59–75.

[97]Connor, *Deviance,* pp. 158–59, *The Washington Post,* Mar. 15, 1976, pp. 1, 10, and Kaminskaya. "Changes," pp. 3–4.

[98]Yuri Brokhin, *Hustling on Gorky Street: Sex and Crime in Russia Today,* (New York: Dial Press, 1975); Konstantin Simis, *USSR: The Corrupt Society,* (New York: Simon & Schuster, 1982).

[99]Economic crime, because of its close relationship to the "second economy," also receives attention in Chapter 10. Another type of Soviet crime, which is mentioned only briefly here but is treated more extensively in Chapter 11, is political crime.

[100]*Soviet Criminal Law Procedure,* p. 186.

[101]Ostroumov, *Sovetskaia Sudebnaia Statisika,* p. 248, and Zeldes, *Problems of Crime,* p. 62.

[102]"Sudebnaia Praktika po Delam o Khuliganstve," p. 38.

[103]Kuznetsova and others, "Neobkhodimo," p. 33.

[104]"Nekotorye Rezul'taty Izucheniia Del o Sovestnom Sovershenii Prestuplenii Nesovershennoletnimi i Vzroslymi," *Biulleten' Verkhovnogo Suda SSSR,* No. 4 (1969), 44, and "Upholding Socialist Legality in Georgia: An Uphill Struggle," *Radio Liberty Research,* No. 142/82, Mar. 29, 1982, p. 2.

[105]*Radyans'ka Ukrayina,* September 23, 1973, p. 4, as cited in *Abstracts of Soviet and East European Studies,* Jan. 1974, p. 50.

[106]*Soviet Criminal Law and Procedure,* p. 157.

[107]For a listing of those crimes, including economic crimes, for which the death penalty is a possible, not mandatory, sentence, see: Ger P. Van den Berg, "The Soviet Union and the Death Penalty," *Soviet Studies* 35 (1983), 160.

[108]*The New York Times,* Aug. 3, 1983, p. A1.

[109]*The New York Times,* Nov. 25, 1983, p. A1.

[110]*The Washington Post,* Dec. 19, 1983, p. A40.

[111]Zvirbul', *Rol' Planirovaniia,* p. 41.

[112]For the material in the following section on the penal system, the authors have depended heavily on the excellent analysis of available data in Connor, *Deviance,* pp. 198–235. Connor translates the term *ispravitel'nye raboty* as "corrective works." We have chosen to follow Berman and Spindler's translation of it as "correctional tasks" in *Soviet Criminal Law and Procedure,* p. 361.

[113]Recent reports on Soviet prison conditions have compared them unfavorably with penal institutions in the West. See, e.g., "Estimates of the Prison Population of the USSR," *Radio Liberty Research,* No. 351/82, Aug. 31, 1982, p. 1, and Julia Wishnevsky, "The Use of Torture in Soviet Penal Institutions: The 'Pressure Cell,' " *Radio Liberty Research,* No. 329/83, Sept. 6, 1983. Because of the Soviet government's practice of extreme secrecy, it is impossible to determine how accurate such descriptions are. The same difficulty arises with reference to estimating the size of the penal population. See, e.g., "Estimates," and *The New York Times,* Nov. 7, 1982, p. 3. Of special significance are political prisoners. A 1984 estimate of the number of political prisoners confined in camps, prisons, special psychiatric hospitals, or sentenced to exile or banishment was approximately 900. Galina Salova, "Soviet Political Prisoners Today: Types of Punishment and Places of Detention," *Radio Liberty Research,* No. 410/84, Oct. 24, 1984. A broader and less precisely defined category of detainees that carries with it strong ideological and emotional connotations is that of "forced laborers." Some Western critics advocate that Western countries not cooperate with the Soviet Union in activities that involve the use of "forced labor." For example, this controversy surfaced in the early 1980s in connection with the pipelines being built to bring Soviet petroleum to Western Europe. Recent Western estimates appear to put the number of people in this category at 4 to 6 million (i.e., perhaps more than 2 percent of the total Soviet population). See Catherine Cosman, "Forced Labor in the USSR." *Russia,* No. 10, 1984, pp. 1–20.

[114]Exceptions are made for convicts who are over forty years of age and in poor health.

[115]This material and the information in the next paragraph are taken mainly from Kaminskaya, "Changes."

SELECTED BIBLIOGRAPHY

BERMAN, HAROLD J., and JAMES W. SPINDLER, trans. and eds., *Soviet Criminal Law and Procedure,* 2nd ed. Cambridge, MA: Harvard University Press, 1972.

BROKHIN, YURI, *Hustling on Gorky Street: Sex and Crime in Russia Today.* New York: Dial Press, 1975.

CHALIDZE, VALERII, *Criminal Russia: A Study of Crime in the Soviet Union.* New York: Random House, 1977.

———, and LEON LIPSON, eds., *Documents on Soviet Criminal Procedure.* New York: Institute on Socialist Law, 1979.

CLAWSON, ROBERT W., and DAVID L. NORRGARD, "National Responses to Urban Crime: The Soviet Union, the United Kingdom, and the United States," in *Police in Urban Society,* ed. Harlan Hahn. Beverly Hills, CA: Sage Publications, 1971.

CONNOR, WALTER D., *Deviance in Soviet Society.* New York: Columbia University Press, 1972.

FELDBRUGGE, F.J.M., ed., *Encyclopedia of Soviet Law.* 2 vols., Leiden, the Netherlands: A. W. Sijthoff, 1973.

FELDBRUGGE, F.J.M., "Soviet Penitentiary Law," *Review of Socialist Law,* 1 (1975), 123.

JUVILER, PETER, "Crime and Its Study," in *Soviet Politics and Society in the 1970s,* eds. Henry W. Morton and Rudolf L. Tokes. New York: Free Press, 1974.

KELLER, MARK, and VERA AFRON, "Alcohol Problems in Yugoslavia and Russia," *Quarterly Journal of Studies on Alcohol,* 35 (1974), 260.

KRASIKOV, A., "Commodity Number One," in *The Samizdat Register,* ed. Roy A. Medvedev, New York: W. W. Norton & Co., 1977.

POWELL, DAVID E., "Alcoholism in the USSR," *Survey,* 16, No. 1 (Winter 1971), 123.

SEGAL, BORIS M., "Drinking and Alcoholism in Russia," *Psychiatric Opinion,* 12, No. 9 (Nov. 1975), 21.

SHELLEY, LOUISE, "The Geography of Soviet Criminality," *American Sociological Review,* 45 (Feb. 1980), 111.

———, "Soviet and Yugoslavian Criminology," *International Journal of Comparative and Applied Criminal Justice,* 3, No. 2 (Fall 1979), 143.

SIMIS, KONSTANTIN M., *USSR: The Corrupt Society.* New York: Simon and Schuster, 1982.

TREML, VLADIMIR G., "Alcohol in the USSR: A Fiscal Dilemma," *Soviet Studies,* 18, No. 2 (Apr. 1975), 161.

VAN DEN BERG, GER P., "The Soviet Union and the Death Penalty," *Soviet Studies,* 35 (1983), 154–74.

ZELDES, ILYA, *The Problem of Crime in the USSR.* Springfield, IL: Charles C. Thomas, 1981.

14

SOVIET FOREIGN POLICY:
Internal and External Dimensions

This book has to do primarily with domestic politics in the Soviet Union. Foreign policy is generally considered a subject of equal importance and complexity and is often treated in separate textbooks and separate university courses. Our aim in this chapter is a modest one: to provide a brief sketch of the major features of Soviet foreign policy in recent years and to relate foreign policy making to the internal political scene.

CHARACTERISTICS OF SOVIET FOREIGN POLICY

Some scholars see in Soviet foreign policy certain persistent themes which they trace beyond the Soviet period into prerevolutionary Russian history. Usually such themes are geopolitical in nature. They emerge from the fact that the USSR covers roughly the same territory as its tsarist predecessor and thus, it is argued, faces the same problems. One such theme is the preoccupation with acquiring and controlling ice-free ports which give access to warm-water oceans. Another is the securing of the western border of the country, a plain without natural boundaries that has been a problem for the Russian authorities throughout the centuries.[1]

There is undoubtedly something to these ideas. Russia is a vast country crossed with sprawling rivers whose banks are dotted with settlements.

Control is vital over the coastal areas where the rivers empty into the sea. Since many of these outlets are icebound for part of the year, it has been imperative to acquire and protect ice-free ports in order to maintain the country's status as a maritime nation. The European border in the west is of equal import from the point of view of defense. Long before Napoleon's invasion in the nineteenth century and Hitler's invasion in the twentieth, Russia was facing hostile adversaries to the west. Gaining security against incursions from this direction has had to be of utmost importance. The buffer zone of East European satellite states created by Stalin after World War II was a partial solution to this longstanding problem.

But explaining foreign-policy behavior exclusively on the basis of geo-political considerations is too simplistic. Technological achievements of the twentieth century have to some extent tempered the significance of space and geography. Although borders must still be protected, aircraft, missiles, and nearly self-sufficient fleets of ships and submarines range far beyond national borders. In other words, although geopolitical factors continue to be of importance, they constitute only a part of a much more complex set of larger foreign-policy considerations. For a country such as the Soviet Union, a global power that has shown interest in political developments in many parts of the world, it is necessary now to pursue policy objectives of global scope.

This is one reason why the traditional explanation of Russian foreign-policy objectives is inadequate for the present-day Soviet Union. A second factor that distinguishes Soviet foreign policy from its prerevolutionary counterpart has to do with the ideological content of policy objectives. Prerevolutionary Russian foreign policy was not strongly guided by ideological considerations.[2] But the Soviet regime is based on an overt allegiance to the code of Marxism-Leninism, which naturally raises the question of the extent of that doctrine's effect on foreign policy. This has been a matter of dispute among Western scholars over the years. Put most bluntly, specialists have argued over whether "doctrine" or "national interest" determines Soviet foreign-policy behavior.[3] This controversy is a rehearsal of the question raised in Chapter 3 on the impact of ideology on policy in general. And the answer here must be the same as in Chapter 3: In spite of the presence of doctrinal *ornamentation* in Soviet foreign-policy pronouncements, the policies themselves are largely determined by national interests as perceived by the contemporary Soviet leadership.

Although it may be true that earlier in the seven-decade history of the Soviet state doctrinal considerations were more important (and some would even doubt this), they have become increasingly less so in recent years. This is not to say that Soviet foreign-policy moves are *never* based on ideological considerations. As suggested in Chapter 3, Soviet ideology possesses an extremely broad body of doctrine. It provides a general framework which allows for both antagonism and cooperation with countries having different social and economic systems. Soviet ideology recognizes the propriety of support for "wars of national liberation," a concept that has some relation to the precept of fomenting world revolution. The Soviet Union supports such wars selectively, which demonstrates the flexibility of the leaders' attitude toward doctrine in foreign policy making. Recent examples include Soviet support for a Marxist faction in the conflict in Angola in 1976 and its backing of Ethiopia in its war with Somalia in 1977 and 1978. These moves were motivated in part by the leadership's desire to establish further influence in Africa—and to reduce Western leverage in the process. At least in the case of Angola, however, it is also clear that they were competing with Communist China for a presence in Africa. That such adventures were pursued within the context of détente with the West is what makes dealing with the Soviet Union so difficult. The possibility cannot be excluded that such seemingly contradictory policies emanate from disputes in the top leadership over the role ideology should play and the relationship of short-term to long-term goals. In short, although it cannot be said that ideological considerations play no role, foreign-policy actions based on ideological motives will not be pursued to the point where they threaten genuine national interests. Recent Soviet history is quite clear on this point.

Although not mainly based on ideological considerations, Soviet foreign-policy behavior has resulted in basic conflicts with the United States and the other countries of the Western alliance. Why? One reason is the existence of the possibly misleading ideological rhetoric mentioned. The very fact that Soviet leaders discuss foreign policy in Marxist-Leninist terms, with that ideology's emphasis on the irreconcilable differences between the camps of socialism and capitalism, is bound to generate antagonism; to the extent that Western foreign-policy views are also couched in ideological language, this antagonism can only be heightened. Perhaps more importantly, however, the USSR and the United States are the two foremost global powers. With their divergent value systems and social systems, their interests are often not in harmony in the various parts of the world where they exercise influence. But to state this is a far cry from saying that the Soviets have an ideological blueprint for world revolution and global conquest that guides their basic foreign-policy moves. A more realistic appraisal would be that they pursue a foreign policy designed to expand their sphere of influence, guided not by predetermined doctrine but by their own conceptions of self-interest. In other words, as several commentators have put it, Soviet foreign policy has largely been "deideologized" in recent years, allowing the USSR to pursue the aims of *realpolitik* largely unfettered by doctrinal considerations.[4] Having said this, let us emphasize again that the language and tone of much Soviet foreign-policy rhetoric—if not the foreign-policy behavior itself—is ideological in nature. This ideological rhetoric is one of the factors that makes dealing with the Soviet Union so difficult for the countries of the West. But just as the language of ideology performs a legitimizing function in Soviet internal politics (as discussed in Chapter 3), so too ideological language helps legitimize the USSR in one of its foremost foreign-policy roles, that of leader of the international communist movement. This role will be discussed in more detail subsequently.

In summary, the Soviet Union's present status as a global superpower overshadows traditional geopolitical considerations in its foreign-policy behavior; the Soviet leadership's pursuit of perceived national interest is far more important than Marxist-Leninist ideology in determining foreign-policy goals, although ideological rhetoric remains the language of overt foreign-policy communication. What are the other characteristics of recent Soviet foreign policy? We will discuss this matter under four headings: relations with the West; the communist nations; the world communist movement; and the Third World.

Relations with the West

During the 1970s undoubtedly the major foreign-policy development involved the pursuit of détente with the West, a policy that has affected many other aspects of Soviet foreign and domestic activity. Détente did not begin in the Khrushchev era, although Khrushchev laid the groundwork for it by his adoption of the principle of "peaceful coexistence." Whether peaceful coexistence was a Leninist principle, as Soviet authorities maintain, or was contrary to Lenin's view, as both the Chinese Communists and Western analysts of the Soviet system conclude, is not a matter that need detain us here. What is important is that Khrushchev in 1956 stated that war between the camps of capitalism and communism was not fatalistically inevitable, modifying a well-known Leninist view on this subject. The alternative was peaceful coexistence, which involves, on the one hand, the avoidance of major wars and of direct participation in wars of national liberation and, on the other, the desirability of negotiating and reaching politically and economically advantageous agreements with the capitalist world. As all Soviet authorities since Khrushchev have emphasized, peaceful coexistence does not extend to the ideological sphere. The ideological purity of the Soviet system must be maintained, and each system will try to demonstrate its superiority through competition in the production of material goods and the development of culture.

In spite of Khrushchev's popularizing of the term, his record of accomplishments regarding peaceful coexistence was not impressive. Tough and combative by nature, Khrushchev initiated policies such as the placement of strategic missiles in Cuba in 1962 that brought the United States and the USSR close to military confrontation. And he made relatively little headway on the second part of peaceful coexistence, negotiating agreements with the West.* In the early years after his ouster, Khrushchev's successors were more cautious than he was. They avoided major confrontations with the West. Perhaps as a result, their progress in formal negotiations during these years was considerably greater. The Treaty on the Non-Proliferation of Nuclear Weapons was signed with Great Britain and the United States on July 1, 1968, less than two months before the Soviet invasion of Czechoslovakia. That event cooled Soviet-Western relations temporarily, but 1969 saw a renewal of negotiations. During that year Strategic Arms Limitation Talks began in Helsinki between the United States and the USSR, and after West Germany signed the Non-Proliferation Treaty, Soviet–German talks aimed at a relaxation of tensions between the two countries began. In addition, 1969 saw the first moves by the two great alliances, the Warsaw Pact headed by the USSR and NATO headed by the United States, toward a European Security Conference. The "turning point" was 1969.[5]

Thereafter followed several years' negotiation culminating in results that just a few years before would have been considered impossible by all but the most optimistic observers. In August 1970 came the treaty between West Germany and the USSR on the mutual renunciation of force. This paved the way for a West Germany–Polish treaty later in the year on the normalization of relations between the two countries, which allowed for diplomatic relations to be reestablished (the two countries had not had diplomatic relations since the creation of West Germany in 1949). A similar treaty was signed between West Germany and Czechoslovakia in 1973, followed shortly thereafter by West Germany's establishment of formal diplomatic relations with Hungary and Bulgaria. For the first time since World War II, West Germany had formal ties with virtually all the countries of socialist East Europe.

Concurrently, the United States, France, and Great Britain were working with the Soviet Union on a new agreement on Berlin, which was announced in 1971. This allowed East and West Germany to negotiate a transit agreement regulating Western access to West Berlin. The generally favorable atmosphere led to the establishment of diplomatic relations between the United States and East Germany in 1974. The culmination of these years of diplomatic efforts was the agreement signed at the thirty-five–nation European Security Conference in Helsinki, Finland, in August 1975. This agreement covered three basic matters: security in Europe; cooperation in the fields of economics, science, technology, and the environment; and cooperation in humanitarian and other fields. Part One involves a recognition of Europe's post-World War II boundaries, including the divided Germany, a recognition that the Soviet Union had been seeking for many years.

*Among the important negotiating accomplishments during the Khrushchev period were the establishment of a "hot line" between Washington and Moscow to improve communications during crisis periods; the partial Nuclear Test Ban Treaty signed by Great Britain, the USSR, and the United States; and the agreement made at the United Nations not to place weapons of mass destruction in outer space (this was adopted as a treaty in 1967). On this "temporary détente" see Robin Edmonds, *Soviet Foreign Policy, 1962–1973* (London: Oxford University Press, 1975), pp. 31–32.

Part Two was not particularly controversial, since it involves matters on which the concerned nations had already been cooperating. Part Three was the most difficult to achieve and was the result of hard, intensive negotiations on the part of the West. Its general aim was to achieve "a freer flow of information, people and ideas," and it contained a number of more specific statements on how these goals should be accomplished. This far-reaching provision has been the most objectionable one from the standpoint of the Soviet authorities since the adoption of the agreement.

While these developments did much for security on the European continent, even more important agreements took place between the United States and the Soviet Union. The Strategic Arms Limitation Treaty (SALT) as well as a number of less important agreements were signed during President Nixon's visit to Moscow in May 1972. A series of other agreements, including a general Agreement on the Prevention of Nuclear War, was signed during Brezhnev's trip to the United States a year later. All these developments were preceded by a treaty signed in 1971 by the United States, Great Britain, and the USSR banning emplacement of nuclear weapons on the ocean floor. In the mid-1970s still other agreements were reached. For instance, in May 1976, Brezhnev and President Ford signed a treaty restricting peaceful nuclear explosions.

The latter part of the 1970s saw the beginning of a considerable deterioration in Soviet-American relations, however. In early 1975 Moscow cancelled the 1972 bilateral trade agreement act with the United States. It had linked most-favored-nation status for the USSR with the adoption by that country of relaxed emigration policies. President Carter came into office in 1977 with criticism of Soviet human-rights violations, which led to a public rebuff of American initiatives for arms-limitation talks a short time later. The United States, in other words, was pursuing a policy of "linkage," that is, tying arms limitation and trade agreements to Soviet concessions on other political matters such as human rights and emigration. The Soviet authorities reacted angrily to these moves, saying that they transformed détente into "political extortion."

Soviet activities in Africa from 1976 to 1978 worsened relations further, but the event that definitively sent détente into deep freeze was the Soviet invasion of Afghanistan in December 1979. Condemned in many parts of the world, including thirty-four Moslem nations and a number of Western communist parties, the invasion was seen by many as a new kind of Soviet military initiative: Content theretofore to see its cause advanced by proxy armies of Cuba and Vietnam, the Soviet Union was now applying the Brezhnev Doctrine (see p. 299) to a Third World country by committing its own troops to the effort. The invasion may indeed have signaled a new departure or been merely another example of "the relentless opportunism of Soviet expansion."[6] Perhaps it could be explained in part by other considerations, such as Soviet fear of the possibility of growing Chinese influence in Afghanistan.[7] Whatever the reason, it is clear that it was a serious blow to

Soviet-American relations and to détente in general, at least in the short run. Almost immediately President Carter imposed embargoes on the shipment of grain, fertilizer, and other products to the Soviet Union and asked the Senate to defer indefinitely consideration of the Strategic Arms Limitation Treaty (SALT II), which had been completed after painstaking negotiations over the previous seven years. These actions, in turn, had ripple effects over an expanding range of cultural exchanges, scientific contacts, and other ties. A notable example was the boycott of the 1980 Moscow Olympics by a number of Western and Third World nations.

It has been suggested that the Soviet authorities considered the invasion of Afghanistan a "safe gamble" because they felt that the SALT II treaty would not pass the U.S. Senate in any case.[8] Certainly as far as the United States was concerned, Salt II was dead when the Reagan administration took over in 1981. Nor did things go any better in other aspects of Soviet-American relations during this period. "Détente in decline"[9] appropriately describes Soviet-United States relations during most of President Reagan's first term, which ended within months of the boycott of the Los Angeles Olympics by the USSR and its allies (but not China and Rumania) in the summer of 1984. The low point during this period was undoubtedly the September, 1983 shooting down of a South Korean airliner that had intruded into Soviet air space, killing all 269 people on board.

Yet, as the 1984 U.S. presidential election neared, a few signs of a possible improvement in relations were observable. The Korean airliner incident did not prevent the implementation of a five-year grain agreement between the United States and the Soviet Union, signed a few days before, and by the end of 1984 record amounts of grain were being imported by the Soviet Union from the United States. The year 1985 saw renewed talks on expanded trade and arms reduction and a much-publicized summit meeting in Geneva between President Reagan and General Secretary Gorbachev. It is clear that whatever their long-term aims, the Soviet authorities do have a genuine interest in improving relations with the West. Given the economic and social problems within their country and the political difficulties within the communist bloc, particularly with China, they no doubt welcome the prospect of a respite with the West. There are also clear economic motivations for improved relations. They have many trade objectives, particularly in technology, machinery, and certain other industrial products that they find difficult to produce themselves. The more wary or suspicious observers in the West see in Soviet actions an attempt to lull the West into dropping its guard, making it easier for the communist camp to pursue its traditional aim of world conquest. As noted, Soviet authorities make no secret of their view that there can be no ideological coexistence. They profess to believe that their system will triumph in the end, albeit by peaceful means.

Throughout the period of détente the United States continued its military spending at a high level and urged its allies to do likewise. Détente proceeded, therefore, with the expectation on both sides that some sort of rough military parity would be maintained. If the two sides return to a policy of "relaxation of international tensions" (as the Soviet call détente), then it is likely that efforts to continue such parity will be made on each side.

The Communist Nations

The communist world includes all of the countries with ruling communist regimes. These numbered fourteen until 1975, when pro-Western or neutralist regimes collapsed in Vietnam, Cambodia, and Laos. In the 1980s Afghanistan could be added to this number, although stiff opposition to Moscow's hand-picked regime and to Soviet occupation forces had gone on for years. As the first Marxian socialist state, the Soviet Union claims leadership among the communist countries. Its foreign-policy objectives are to maintain that leadership position and to achieve the support and cooperation of other communist countries in its foreign-policy operations. Its closest allies are several East European states, namely, Bulgaria, Czechoslovakia, East Germany, Hungary, and Poland. With varying degrees of Soviet help, these five countries, along with Rumania, Yugoslavia, and Albania, became Marxist socialist countries in the years immediately after World War II.

Securing this zone of influence was a long-term objective of Russian and Soviet foreign policy as a protection against incursions from the West. It is unquestionable that maintaining this area as a part of the socialist bloc is considered by Soviet leaders to be among their most important foreign-policy objectives, as their invasions of Hungary in 1956 and Czechoslovakia in 1968 showed. But they have not been able to maintain a uniform level of control throughout East Europe. Yugoslavia was expelled from the Cominform* in 1948 and since then has pursued a "separate road to socialism." Albania sided with Communist China in the Sino–Soviet dispute in the early 1960s as a manifestation of its departure from the Soviet sphere of control. Since then it has pursued a policy of isolation from most other countries, even the fraternal socialist states. Rumania in the mid-1960s began following a path somewhat separate from Moscow's, particularly in the area of foreign policy. In spite of these exceptions, the USSR has been able to maintain a high level of influence in East Europe. Its five closest allies in this group can be counted on to support the USSR in all its foreign-policy actions. Its invasion of two of the five and its strong presence or influence in the other three make it clear that the Soviet Union will not willingly permit a lessening of its control over this area. It was on the basis of the invasion of Czechoslovakia that what Westerners call the "doctrine of limited sovereignty" was pronounced. Alternatively known as the "Brezhnev Doctrine," this concept holds that (as Brezhnev put it) "the borders of the socialist commonwealth

---

*The Cominform, or Communist Information Bureau, was established in 1947 as an organ for the exchange of information and experience among communist nations. It was disbanded in 1956.

are inviolable" and that the Soviet Union will decide when its intervention is needed to repel dangers to socialism.

The Soviet Union's primary military pact, the Warsaw Treaty Organization, is with the East European communist states. Yugoslavia was never a member. Albania, as a result of the invasion of Czechoslovakia, withdrew in 1968 after several years of nonparticipation. Rumania refused to participate in the invasion of Czechoslovakia but remains in the Warsaw Pact. Technically, the invasion of Czechoslovakia was by the Warsaw Pact, for token forces from Bulgaria, East Germany, Hungary, and Poland participated in the action along with large numbers of Soviet troops. The Soviet Union also maintains bilateral alliances with each of the other members of the Warsaw Pact. Soviet or East European proposals to abolish the Warsaw Pact along with NATO would have no effect on these separate bilateral arrangements.

The Council of Mutual Economic Assistance (CMEA or Comecon) was established in 1949. Its members include the USSR, Bulgaria, Czechoslovakia, Hungary, Poland, Rumania, Albania (largely inactive in recent years), East Germany, Mongolia, Cuba, and Vietnam. Yugoslavia was granted associate status in 1965. The CMEA seeks coordination of economic planning of member states and other measures aimed at maximizing economic efficiency and production. Some resistance to decisions taken by CMEA has been manifested in recent years, particularly by Rumania, because of the perception of unfair economic advantages being gained by the Soviet Union as a result of such agreements.

The Soviet Union maintains close ties with Cuba and has given large amounts of economic aid to that country over the years. Cuba is a sometimes difficult ally for the USSR because the Castro regime's zeal for exporting revolution impedes correct relations between the Soviet Union and the other countries of Latin America. Moreover, Cuba has failed to take the strong anti-China stand that Moscow would like. But the USSR's influence in Cuba remains strong. Its influence in Mongolia, the first communist state to be created (in 1924) after the USSR, is even greater. Mongolia has consistently and strongly supported the Soviet Union in its dispute with China. After North Vietnam's victory over South Vietnam in 1975, Soviet influence increased in that now-unified country. Vietnam joined the CMEA and signed long-term economic and friendship agreements with the USSR, a great step toward the containment of China in Southeast Asia. North Korea has tried to maintain a neutral position between the USSR and China and has been quite successful in playing off the two giants against each other. It is, of course, the longstanding dispute between the two communist superpowers that allows this neutrality.

The Sino-Soviet rift burst fully into the open in 1961, but it had been simmering for years before that time and had been evident to close observers. Differences between the two countries can be traced to several sources: Stalin's shabby treatment of the Chinese communists both before and after their accession to power, the differing interpretations of Marxism-Leninism that had evolved in the two countries, and the suspicion among Chinese leaders that Khrushchev's campaign for peaceful coexistence implied an accommodation with the United States at the expense of China. One can also trace the causes of the antagonism to deeper cultural and historical factors. The Russians, members of a European civilization built by white men, were bound to be viewed with suspicion by the Chinese. And the Russo-Chinese territorial disputes of the 1850s and 1860s settled by treaties that China considered coerced did not help to engender Chinese trust of the Russians. A number of border disputes, the most bloody in 1969, followed by a series of less serious confrontations throughout the 1970s indicates that China still does not consider these border matters settled.[10]

In all, then, there was no particular reason why the Chinese and the Soviets should have become close allies other than their common commitment to communism. But this tie has not been strong enough to overcome the other antagonisms, and the Chinese—a much more formidable force than the USSR's East European neighbors—have challenged the Soviets on a number of fronts: on the correct interpretation of Marxism-Leninism; on whether China should be a nuclear power (China achieved this status, largely without Soviet help, in 1964); on the very leadership of the world communist movement. Expectations that the rift would soon be healed after the demise of Khrushchev went unrealized, and the dispute has continued since then at varying levels of intensity. The thirty-year treaty of alliance between the two communist superpowers was allowed to expire in 1980, but by mid-decade signs that both sides were actively seeking an improvement in relations were evident. The Soviet policy stance regarding China remains one of overt willingness to patch up differences while at the same time working to contain Chinese influence both within the communist sphere and in the world at large.

The World Communist Movement

The world communist movement is made up of party organizations from countries having ruling communist parties together with communist parties from other nations of the world. To call this aggregation of parties a movement may be somewhat misleading. The Soviet Union seeks to form it into a movement with itself at the head; it gives shape to efforts toward this goal through meetings and other contacts with foreign communist leaders, as well as with other political and economic inducements and threats. China challenges the Soviet Union for leadership or at least disputes the Soviet claim to primacy in the movement; and a number of other foreign communist parties manifest varying degrees of resistance to Soviet attempts to dictate policy for other communist parties.

The high points of recent developments in the movement have been meetings of delegations from the various communist parties. The two most important of these were the eighty-one–party Moscow meeting in 1960 and the seventy-five–party Moscow conference in 1969. Although the Sino-Soviet dispute had already commenced at the time of the 1960 meeting, and indeed was a dominant topic of discussion there, the rift was not widely known to the world at large. A pretense of unity, with the USSR as unchallenged leader of the movement, was maintained for domestic purposes. But the meeting had been "an important watershed in the history of the Communist camp."[11] The vilification of the Soviet leadership by the Chinese, and particularly by the Albanians, demonstrated a startling departure from the position accorded the Soviets in the previous four decades of international communism. And the significant participation by other foreign communists in the discussions, most notably the French and Italian leaders, presaged the development of more equal status for other parties in international communist councils.[12]

Since that meeting the Soviet Union has had to contend with increasing dissent and unwillingness to submit to Soviet dictation from a number of foreign communist parties. During the 1960s it tried repeatedly to convene another world meeting of communist parties, the main purpose of which was to censure and isolate the Chinese Communists and restore its own unchallenged position in the international communist movement. These objectives met with little success. The 1969 Moscow meeting was convened only after several preconditions demanded by certain dissenting parties were met: that no party, whether present or absent, be condemned or expelled in conference documents; that each party have the right to determine the content of its own statements at the conference; and that an accurate summary of the debates appear in the Soviet press. The latter concession gave an opportunity to Soviet citizens to read of dissident views, including some critical of the Soviet Union. But even these concessions did not satisfy all parties. Only seventy-five of the eighty-eight parties invited attended, and among the absentees were five of the fourteen ruling parties: the Chinese, Albanian, Yugoslav, North Korean, and North Vietnamese contingents. Delegations from the Cuban and Swedish parties came only as "observers." Fourteen delegations refused to sign the final conference document or signed with reservations, even though the Soviet Union had made important concessions, including the statement that "there is no leading center of the international communist movement."[13]

Since 1969 the USSR has agitated for another world party conference to further its traditional goals of condemning the Chinese and resuming its hegemonic position in the movement. But by the mid-1980s more than fifteen years had passed and no such conference had been convened. In the meantime, smaller gatherings, such as the meeting of European communist parties in 1976, have taken place. It is with the European group of communist parties that the Soviet Union has the most trouble. Generally it can count on the unquestioning support of nearly two thirds of the ninety-odd communist parties in the world. Aside from the Chinese opposition, the greatest amount of dissidence comes from Europe. This point does not apply, of course, to the USSR's closest East European allies. They are sufficiently under Soviet control to cause little trouble. But others, including particularly the Yugoslavs, Rumanians, Italians, Spaniards, and French, have increasingly opposed Soviet dictation. The Yugoslavs and Rumanians have consistently resisted Soviet efforts to dominate other communist parties. They have refused to participate in meetings in which China was the major issue or which involved dictation of policies rather than the seeking of consensus. The Italian Communists have also taken an independent line for some years. But in 1975 the French Communists showed signs of drawing away from the Soviet position as well. Domestic political developments in France and Italy enhanced the chances of communist participation in governing these countries, and the communist parties were anxious to show that they were independent of Moscow. This independence was manifested in numerous ways, notably by joining other communists in frustrating Soviet attempts to dictate to the European communist party conference in 1976 and by pursuing more moderate courses in their domestic-policy statements and actions.

The French and Italian Communists have often been critical of internal political repression in the USSR—and here they go beyond the Rumanians and the Yugoslavs. But "Eurocommunism," as this independent line among West European communist parties is known, is by no means a unified movement. The French Communist Party, for instance, has long been more attuned to the USSR's views than the Italian Communist Party, and by the end of the 1970s the French Communists had become less problematical for Moscow than other Western communist parties.

Another forum for the assembling of delegations of communists is the various party congresses, particularly the congresses of the CPSU. The Twenty-Fifth and Twenty-Sixth Congresses (in 1976 and 1981, respectively) have been occasions for minor manifestations of controversy. Again, this has come mostly from the Eurocommunists and has included criticism of certain Soviet policies, such as the invasion of Afghanistan and the treatment of Soviet dissidents, as well as the advocacy of greater pluralism within the world communist movement.

Soviet authorities have not remained silent in the face of these developments. But their condemnation of all of this "revisionism" has been muted rather than direct. They have denounced "ideological divergence" and attempts to "modernize" Marxism and have urged adherence to the principle of "proletarian internationalism," meaning mutual support of communists rallying behind the Soviet lead. But their leverage with regard to West European dissenters is not great. The invasions of Hungary in 1956 and Czechoslovakia in 1968 show what the Soviet Union can do within its unquestioned sphere of influence, and the dissident Rumanians and Yugoslavs are undoubtedly in a somewhat vulnerable position with regard to the threat of invasion. Dispatching an army to put down the dissenting views of a nonruling communist party is quite another matter. The Soviet Union can probably look forward to considerable long-term difficulties in its objective of controlling this part of the world communist movement.

The Third World

It may be too much to say that the USSR has a single policy toward Third World countries. It has a series of policies, depending on the country, the time, and other factors; but the single objective is to enhance Soviet influence in pursuit of its aspirations as a global power. Soviet policy toward the Third World changed considerably after Stalin's death when the USSR began to demonstrate increasing interest in the Arab Near East and other parts of the world. It has trained an impressive number of specialists in the developing areas of the world. The volume of literature it produces on these areas is large.

One of the advantages the Soviet Union enjoys in these countries is that not having been a colonial power (except with regard to countries located on its border) it has had no economic assets to protect. The friction caused by the nationalizing of mines, plantations, and other property does not visit the Soviet Union. Indeed, it can benefit from such developments by acting as the friend of the reformist regime in the developing country, supporting the reformers' activities against the interests of the "imperialist' power.

Marxist-Leninist ideology does not seem to play a large role in Soviet relations with developing countries. The political orientation of a regime is not of great importance. Nor does the presence of strong religious beliefs in a country mean the Soviet Union will not support its devout leaders. The willingness to maintain friendly relations with the Soviet Union is the key to Soviet policy in this regard. This stance has required a willingness on the part of Soviet leaders to stand by while local communist leaders in countries they are wooing are repressed or neutralized, as has happened more than once.

There have been some spectacular failures in Soviet foreign policy in the Third World. The suppressing of the abortive communist coup in Indonesia in 1965 led to the slaughter of 100,000 members of the Indonesian Communist Party. Politically, this was more of a blow to China than to the Soviet Union, but the financial loser was the USSR, which had invested heavily in military hardware for the Sukarno regime and in the end came up with nothing to show for the investment. Other disappointments came with the fall of the Soviet-supported regimes of Lumumba in the Congo, Nkrumah in Ghana, and Ben Bella in Algeria. More recently, Egypt's order in 1972 that the Soviet Union remove its military advisers from the country was a substantial blow to the Soviet military presence in the Middle East. There has been no host of spectacular foreign-policy successes in the Third World, but the Soviet presence in several areas is conspicuous. The cultivation of several countries and support of the Arab cause in its confrontation with Israel have greatly complicated the political situation in the Middle East. The longstanding Soviet friendship with India has been helpful in Soviet attempts to isolate China and has impeded Western efforts to influence Indian developments. Its friendly relations with North Vietnam throughout the long years of the United States' involvement in Southeast Asia undoubtedly strengthened the resolve of the North Vietnamese and limited some-what the influence of China in the area.

The Soviet Union has been more cautious in areas of the world such as Africa and Latin America. In Africa it had given strong support to the Nkrumah regime in Ghana and the Keita regime in Mali, both of which were overthrown in the 1960s. After these overthrows, Soviet involvement on the continent was scaled down. But during the 1970s the USSR aided forces opposing the white rulers of southern Africa and became involved—in an indirect confrontation with China and the United States—in the struggle for power in Angola. And it has lately supported new regimes in Ethiopia, Mozambique, and other African states. The USSR has taken a strong stand against the post-Allende dictatorship in Chile and has provided economic and military aid, through its Cuban ally, to the Sandinistas in Nicaragua and the Marxist rebels in El Salvador.

A particular tool of Soviet foreign policy worth noting is its economic and military aid. Such assistance has been a useful vehicle for establishing Soviet presence in certain parts of the world. Although far smaller than that of the United States, the Soviet aid program is more concentrated in its areas of distribution. The bulk of such aid now goes to two categories of developing countries: those with communist governments—such as Cuba, Mongolia, Vietnam, Cambodia, Laos, and North Korea—and certain client states where Marxist-oriented administrations have gained control. Among the latter are Angola, Ethiopia, Mozambique, Afghanistan, and South Yemen. The choice of countries to receive major aid indicates the close line between aid and political objectives. But it cannot be said that political aims have always been achieved. For instance, the USSR provided the equivalent of billions of dollars in military and economic aid to Egypt from the 1960s to the mid-1970s. But in 1976, President Sadat abrogated agreements of cooperation and eliminated the impressive and costly Soviet presence there.

By far the largest amount of Third World Soviet aid goes to its close ally Cuba. This aid takes various forms, including a sizable subsidy to prop up the Cuban sugar industry. A 1983 NATO study revealed that the Soviet Union had been buying Cuban sugar at 42 percent above world prices while supplying Cuba with oil at well under world prices.[14]

In sum, the Soviet foreign-policy strategy in the Third World appears to follow no grand design. It is selective and emphasizes some areas of the world over others. It is also opportunistic and amenable to change where new opportunities for extending Soviet influence present themselves.

THE CONDUCT OF SOVIET FOREIGN POLICY

It is said that Stalin's foreign policy was conducted in a highly personal, almost intimate style. Through the "Special Sector" of the Party Central Committee, "Stalin directed the foreign Communist parties, received reports on the work of military and political services abroad, gave directions to ambassadors, guided the fifth columns and issued instructions to them. . . . Foreign policy was made in the Kremlin by Stalin and transmitted downward through the Special Sector."[15]

With the passing of the Stalin era, foreign policy making has become increasingly formalized and institutionalized, especially since the departure from the scene of the impulsive Khrushchev. Individual leaders still play a visible role in Soviet foreign policy, just as is the case in the United States. The gradual assumption of a primary role in foreign-policy matters by Brezhnev in the late 1960s and 1970s was easily discernible. But this was accomplished within the context of a foreign-policy apparatus of considerable proportions. The 1980s saw Brezhnev's successors make important contributions to foreign policy. But the professional foreign-policy bureaucracy was also much in evidence.

As in other branches of Soviet policy making, the Party occupies a crucial position in the formulation and execution of foreign policy. One of the ways in which this is accomplished is by staffing with Party members those positions affecting foreign policy. This tactic will be discussed subsequently. In addition, however, the higher Party organs, particularly the Politburo and the Secretariat, become intimately involved in foreign-policy decision making and in overseeing foreign-policy administration.

As mentioned, the growth of Brezhnev's role in foreign policy during the course of his career as General Secretary is easily documented, and it has been commented on by many observers. Obviously, then, the opportunity is available for the Party leader who wishes to assert himself in the foreign-policy arena. But in addition, a regularized role for Party organs exists. Several departments of the Secretariat are concerned with foreign-policy matters. The most important of these are the Department for Liaison with Communist and Workers' Parties of Socialist Countries and the International Department. The latter has a general responsibility for supervising relations with the West and the Third World and a particular concern with nonruling communist parties. In addition, the Department of Organizational Party Work supervises personnel appointments, including those having to do with foreign policy and diplomacy. The Department of Cadres Abroad is responsible for staffing embassies and trade missions abroad. And the International Information Department (created in 1978) plays a visible role in publicizing the USSR's foreign-policy positions.[16]

The responsibilities of the Politburo in foreign policy are more general, but it is fair to say that all foreign-policy actions of importance receive (or should receive*) Politburo consideration. The Politburo appears to have met

---

*One of the numerous motivations for the ouster of Khrushchev was said to have been his efforts to bypass the Politburo on foreign-policy matters. Toward the end of his career Khrushchev appeared to be creating a personal secretariat of consultants on foreign-policy matters as a substitute for Politburo consultations. Brezhnev appeared to have consistently followed a practice of regular consultation with the Politburo on foreign-policy matters.

very frequently in the days just prior to the invasion of Czechoslovakia in August 1968, and the policy of détente had continuous Politburo review and discussion over a period of several years. A development that emphasized the Politburo role in foreign affairs was the addition in 1973 of three "national security"[17] ministers, the Ministers of Defense and Foreign Affairs and the Chairman of the KGB, to full Politburo membership. It had been fifteen years since every one of these government positions had been represented on the Politburo, but since 1973 they have been accorded Politburo status most of the time.[18]

By contrast, the role of the Central Committee in foreign policy is a modest one. During the post-Khrushchev period only minimal press coverage has been given to CC plenary meetings. It is clear that foreign-policy matters are frequently reviewed at CC meetings, but one gains the impression that these sessions are largely "for information only," that is, to keep the important Party leaders below the level of Politburo-Secretariat abreast of developments. If providing information on foreign-policy decisions is one of the important occurrences at CC sessions, it is relevant to inquire as to which of the insiders in the CC occupy other positions associated with foreign-policy operations. We indicated in Chapter 7 that a high percentage of CC members are from the central or regional Party apparatus or from the central governmental apparatus. A significant but smaller number come from the foreign-policy field as well. For instance, thirteen Soviet ambassadors to foreign countries were elected to full membership on the Central Committee at the Twenty-Sixth Party Congress in March 1981, as were three other officials from the Ministry of Foreign Affairs. In addition, another six from the "diplomatic establishment" were elected to candidate CC membership and several more to the Central Auditing Commission. There is a fairly consistent pattern to the representation of Soviet diplomats on these central Party bodies: Full CC membership normally goes to the Minister of Foreign Affairs and his top deputies and to ambassadors to the main Marxian socialist countries and several of the top "capitalist" countries; candidate CC membership and Central Auditing Commission membership goes to ambassadors to the other socialist states and some other capitalist countries. As often as not these ambassadors have as much or more political experience in their backgrounds as they do diplomatic work.

An even larger contingent from the armed forces is represented in the high Party organs. In 1981 twenty-four high military people were elected full CC members. Thirteen more were chosen candidate members, and four were elected to the Central Auditing Commission.[19] The KGB and the Ministry of Internal Affairs (MVD) have smaller representation on the CC (their Chairmen are normally full members and one or more deputy chairmen receives candidate member status). Finally, miscellaneous other officials associated with foreign affairs also are commonly members of the Central Committee, either with full or candidate status. Among these are the Minister of Foreign Trade, the Permanent Representative to Comecon, and the Chairman of the USSR State Committee for Foreign Economic Relations.

If the broad principles of foreign policy are made by the Politburo, overseen by the Party apparatus, and "received" by the Central Committee, what other institutions have a role to play? Several organizations on the governmental side of the ledger are relevant to discuss. Some of these institutions are responsible for execution of foreign policy or for gathering information on which policy is made. Their leaders may also provide input to the policy-making process, advocating one or another point of view based on the interests they represent or the knowledge and expertise they bring to bear on particular problems. The standing commissions on foreign affairs of the two houses of the Supreme Soviet appear to serve mainly as sounding boards for policies already made. Likewise, the Presidium of the Supreme Soviet, though it has a formal role in the ratification of treaties, does not exercise any substantial authority. Of more importance is the Ministry of Foreign Affairs, an institution that is structured in roughly similar fashion to analogous organs in the West such as the U.S. State Department. Below the Minister and several deputy ministers (eight in 1982) is a large number of departments covering fields such as press relations, treaty and legal affairs, protocol, cultural relations, archives, and others. In addition, there are some eighteen departments ("desks," in the U.S. State Department jargon) that cover one or more countries or regions of the world: one for the United States, six for Europe (one of these includes several former British Commonwealth countries such as Canada, Australia, and New Zealand), three for Africa, two for the Far East, two for Latin America, and one each for the Near East, the Middle East, South Asia, and Southeast Asia.[20] Then there are the ambassadors to foreign countries and their staffs. At present the USSR maintains diplomatic relations at the ambassadorial level with some 120 countries.[21] In addition, it has a large mission at the United Nations in New York and maintains consular offices in a number of cities around the world. Some of the employees in these diplomatic outposts are professional diplomats and a few have a largely domestic political background. A considerable number also belong to the ranks of the KGB or Committee for State Security.

The KGB has the dual function of protecting the state from internal subversion or other political disturbances and carrying out various foreign operations. It is equally well known for both. In addition to maintaining an undisclosed number of secret or "illegal" agents abroad, the KGB and its sister agency the GRU (military intelligence) have several thousand "legal" agents working under diplomatic cover at Soviet missions around the world.[22] The KGB also is in charge of the border troops around the USSR, which number some 190,000. Although established for purposes of maintaining the border, these troops are capable of engaging in more ambitious military activities, for they are equipped with tanks, armored fighting vehicles, aircraft, and ships.*

Of course the main responsibility for military operations lies with the armed forces. In 1983 the Soviet Union had a total of over 3.7 million persons in the armed forces (compared with more than 2 million for the United States). More than half of these were in the army, with the remainder spread among the other branches—the navy, air force, and strategic rocket forces. That the armed forces play a role in foreign policy (aside from the obvious one of overt military action) can be shown from the deployment of some of their forces: In 1980, 30 divisions (about 565,000 troops) were maintained in the East European countries of East Germany, Poland, Hungary, and Czechoslovakia, including some 10,500 medium and heavy tanks. In addition, there were four tactical air armies and about 2,000 combat aircraft in Eastern Europe. So much for the possibility of revolt against Soviet domination. Another 52 divisions were stationed in the Soviet Far East, many of them along or near the Sino-Soviet border, including several divisions in Mongolia. The presence of these troops clearly signals to the Chinese the Soviet intention of keeping the borders as they are. In addition, the Soviet navy shows the flag on all of the major seas of the world, with some 288 major surface combat ships and more than 250 submarines.[23]

THE IMPACT OF THE MILITARY ON FOREIGN AND DOMESTIC POLITICS

As such an important arm of foreign policy, it is a wonder that the military does not play a more dominating role in Soviet internal politics. Through the device of political controls in the armed forces and other means, the Party leaders have succeeded in maintaining their ascendance over the military. Among the reasons Marshal Zhukov was removed as Minister of Defense and as a Politburo member in 1957 were his reported "Bonapartist tendencies" and his "curtailment of the work of Party organizations" in the armed forces. No Minister of Defense again sat on the Politburo from 1957 until 1973. The Minister of Defense has usually been a career military officer, the only recent exception being Dmitrii Ustinov (1976–1984), who had close ties with the military through his long Party and governmental work in the defense industry field. It is important for the Party, therefore, to keep the military from adopting too independent a stance. In 1984 the Chief of

---

*The MVD or Ministry of Internal Affairs has control over normal police activities, among other functions. In addition, it is said to have 260,000 security troops equipped with tanks and armored fighting vehicles. The figures on the KGB and the MVD are from *The Military Balance 1983–1984* (London: International Institute for Strategic Studies. 1983). p. 18.

the General Staff of the Armed Forces and First Deputy Minister of Defense, Nikolai Ogarkov, was abruptly dismissed for what were rumored to be "unpartylike tendencies."[24]

The influence of the military on foreign and domestic policy making remains significant, however. As shown, it often has direct representation on the Politburo and consistently maintains a large contingent on the Central Committee. On strictly military and military-political matters its voice is undoubtedly respected and listened to. One of the forums for the articulation of military views is the Defense Council *(Sovet Oborony)*, a body composed of high military and civilian leaders who develop basic military policy. The General Secretary of the Party serves as Chairman of the Defense Council, but military representation on the body is significant. And reports on international negotiations on military-political matters indicate the central role played by participants from the Soviet military.[25] Some observers detected a more assertive stance by the military during the somewhat unstable period of political leadership after Brezhnev's death.[26]

Whether this military representation means that there is an inherent tension between the military and the civilian leadership, with the military often acting as an interest group or lobby for its points of view, as some scholars have contended, is open to question. William E. Odom has argued persuasively that there is a "party-military consensus" on a wide range of issues which places the military ideologically closer to the political leaders than are other potential groups.[27] Odom adds that the nature of the military as an institution leads to a situation where the military acts mainly as an "executant" of policies or responds to issues framed from above, rather than initiating policy proposals. If this reasoning is sound, then the civilian political leaders have little to fear from the military as a potential rival for power: It is not in a good position to outmaneuver the Party professionals in general policy making, and there is a general identity of views between the military and political leaders as to the general line that Soviet domestic and foreign policy should take. But it is implied at least that it is important for the civilian leaders to maintain this identity of views with the military by paying close attention to the latter's most strongly felt needs: a continuing large portion of the budget for military expenditures; a continuing balance in investments favoring heavy (especially defense-related) industries; and a continuation of material perquisites for elite groups (including the military elite). Khrushchev's failure to satisfy the "military-industrial complex" on these matters is cited as being among the reasons for this downfall.[28] His successors' pursuit of a more traditional course in this area has proved more acceptable. And within this context they have found support for a foreign policy that Khrushchev envisaged but was unable to carry out—one that pursues Soviet global interests while at the same time seeking the fruits of accommodation with the West.

NOTES

[1] A source that stresses geopolitical themes is Robert G. Wesson, *The Russian Dilemma: A Political and Geopolitical View* (New Brunswick, NJ: Rutgers University Press, 1974). See especially pp. 3–12. A scholar who has taken a more critical view of geopolitical factors is Uri Ra'anan in "The U.S.S.R. in World Affairs: Problems of a 'Communist' Foreign Policy," in *The U.S.S.R. After 50 Years: Promise and Reality,* eds. Samuel Hendel and Randolph L. Braham (New York: Knopf, 1967), pp. 251–55.

[2] Ibid., p. 252.

[3] On this matter, see R. N. Carew-Hunt, "The Importance of Doctrine," and Samuel L. Sharp, "National Interest: Key to Soviet Politics," in *Soviet Conduct in World Affairs,* ed. Alexander Dallin (New York: Columbia University Press, 1960), pp. 37–58.

[4] Among those who have discussed deideologizing of Soviet foreign policy in recent years, see Vernon V. Aspaturian, "Foreign Policy Perspectives in the Sixties," in *Soviet Politics Since Khrushchev,* eds. Alexander Dallin and Thomas B. Larson (Englewood Cliffs, NJ: Prentice-Hall, 1968), pp. 129, 130–33; Morton Schwartz, *The Foreign Policy of the USSR; Domestic Factors* (Encino, CA: Dickenson Publishing Co., 1975), pp. 109–12. A generally similar position is taken by W. W. Kulski in *The Soviet Union in World Affairs* (Syracuse, NY: Syracuse University Press, 1973), pp. ix, 18–22; and Robin Edmonds, *Soviet Foreign Policy 1962–1973: The Paradox of Super Power* (London: Oxford University Press, 1975), pp. 153–55. Among those who accord a more important place to ideology in foreign policy making are Robert G. Wesson, *Soviet Foreign Policy in Perspective* (Homewood, IL: Dorsey Press, 1969), pp. 396–433, and Richard F. Rosser, *An Introduction to Soviet Foreign Policy* (Englewood Cliffs, NJ: Prentice-Hall, 1969), pp. 62–85. A source containing the writings of a number of other authors, with views on one or the other side of this issue, is Erik P. Hoffmann and Frederic J. Fleron, Jr., eds., *The Conduct of Soviet Foreign Policy,* 2nd ed. (New York: Aldine, 1980), pp. 91–216.

[5] The phrase is Edmonds', *Soviet Foreign Policy,* p. 77.

[6] Stanley Hoffman, "Reflections on the Present Danger," *The New York Review,* Mar. 6, 1980, p. 19.

[7] See *The New York Times,* Mar. 13, 1980, p. A3.

[8] See ibid., Jan. 3, 1980, p. 1.

[9] The phrase is Joseph L. Nogee's and Robert H. Donaldson's in *Soviet Foreign Policy Since World War II.* (New York: Pergamon Press, 1981), p. 267.

[10] See "Another Flare-up on the Sino-Soviet Frontier," *Radio Liberty Research,* No. 104/78, May 13, 1978.

[11] Zbigniew K. Brzezinski, *The Soviet Bloc: Unity and Conflict,* rev. and enlarged ed. (Cambridge, MA: Harvard University Press, 1967), p. 412.

[12] See ibid., pp. 410–13; also Kevin Devlin, "The Interparty Drama," *Problems of Communism,* 24 (Jul.–Aug. 1975), 18.

[13] Cited in ibid., p. 22.

[14] See *The New York Times,* Jan. 23, 1983, p. 7. Also see: "Soviet Economic Assistance to the Third World," *Radio Liberty Research,* No. 290/82, Jul. 19, 1982.

[15] Geoffrey Stern, "The Foreign Policy of the Soviet Union," in *The Foreign Policies of the Powers,* ed. F. S. Northedge (London: Faber and Faber, 1968), p. 85.

[16] See Elizabeth Teague, "The Foreign Departments of the Central Committee of the CPSU," A Supplement to the *Radio Liberty Research Bulletin,* Oct. 27, 1980, 47 pp. On the Party foreign-policy apparatus see also Jerry F. Hough, *Soviet Leadership in Transition* (Washington, DC: The Brookings Institution, 1980), pp. 109–30. See also: "The Apparatus of the Central Committee of the CPSU," *Radio Liberty Research,* No. 21/85, Jan. 22, 1985; Robert W. Kitrinos, "International Department of the CPSU," *Problems of Communism,* 33, No. 5 (Sept.–Oct. 1984), pp. 47–67.

[17] The phrase is Schwartz's, *The Foreign Policy of the USSR,* p. 173.

[18] At the time of this writing (early 1986) Foreign Minister Shevardnadze and KGB

Chairman Chebrikov were full Politburo members, and Defense Minister Sokolov was a Candidate Politburo member.

[19]Peter Kruzhin, "Military Representation in the Leading Organs of the CPSU Following the Twenty-Sixth Congress," *Radio Liberty Research,* No. 116/81, Mar. 16, 1981.

[20]See "The Apparatus of the USSR Ministry of Foreign Affairs," *Radio Liberty Research,* No. 484/82, Dec. 2, 1982.

[21]Ibid.

[22]John Barron, *KGB: The Secret Works of Soviet Secret Agents* (New York: Reader's Digest Press, 1974), p. 509. Schwartz, *The Foreign Policy of the USSR,* p. 176, citing reports by "former Soviet officials," states that "about 60 percent of the diplomatic staffs in Soviet embassies are full-time intelligence officers working for either the KGB or GRU (Military intelligence)." For a brief recent discussion of KGB organization, with estimates of the numbers of various kinds of KGB operatives, see John E. Carlson, "The KGB," in *The Soviet Union Today,* ed. James G. Cracraft (Chicago, IL: Educational Foundation for Nuclear Science, Inc., 1983), pp. 81–94.

[23]The figures in this paragraph are from *The Soviet Military Balance, 1983–1984* (London: The International Institute for Strategic Studies, 1983), pp. 4, 14–18.

[24]See *The New York Times,* Sept. 13, 1984, p. A1, and Bill Murphy, "Chief of Soviet General Staff Removed," *Radio Liberty Research,* No. 338/84, Sept. 7, 1984.

[25]See Mackintosh, "The Soviet Military," pp. 8–10, on the SALT negotiations; and Raymond L. Garthoff, "SALT and the Soviet Military," *Problems of Communism,* 24, No. 1 (Jan.–Feb. 1975), 21, 35–37.

[26]Bill Murray, "Political-Military Relations in the USSR," *Radio Liberty Research,* No. 397/84, Oct. 23, 1984.

[27]William E. Odom, "The Party Connection," *Problems of Communism,* 22, No. 5 (Sept.–Oct. 1973), 12. Others have maintained that Soviet domestic and foreign policy is dominated by a "military-industrial complex" composed of the Party's dominant faction, the KGB, the military, the managers of heavy industry, and others. See Schwartz, *The Foreign Policy of the USSR,* p. 184; Michel Tatu, "Decision Making in the USSR," in *Soviet Strategy,* ed. p. 53.

[28]The dissident Soviet physicist Andrei Sakharov lists among Khrushchev's positive accomplishments his "trying to limit the privileges of the *nomenklatura*" and his "proposing cuts in excessive military expenditures," adding that these two efforts "were the chief cause of his downfall in 1964." Andrei D. Sakharov, *My Country and the World* (New York: Knopf, 1975), p. 28.

SELECTED BIBLIOGRAPHY

ADOMEIT, HANNES, and ROBERT BOARDMAN, eds., *Foreign Policy Making in Communist States: A Comparative Approach.* New York: Holt, Rinehart & Winston, 1979.

BARRON, JOHN, *KGB: The Secret Works of Soviet Secret Agents.* New York: Reader's Digest Press, 1974.

BIALER, SEWERYN, ed., *The Domestic Context of Soviet Foreign Policy.* Boulder, CO: Westview Press, 1981.

BLASIER, COLE, *The Giant's Rival: The USSR and Latin America.* Pittsburgh: University of Pittsburgh Press, 1983.

BRADSHER, HENRY A., *Afghanistan and the Soviet Union.* Durham, NC: Duke Press Policy Studies, 1983.

EDMONDS, ROBIN, *Soviet Foreign Policy: The Brezhnev Years.* Oxford: Oxford University Press, 1983.

ELLISON, HERBERT J., ed., *The Sino-Soviet Conflict: A Global Perspective.* Seattle: University of Washington Press, 1982.

FEUCHTWANGER, E. J., and PETER NAILOR, eds., *The Soviet Union and the Third World.* New York: St. Martin's Press, 1981.

FREEDMAN, ROBERT O., *Soviet Policy Toward the Middle East Since 1970,* 2nd ed. New York: Holt, Rinehart & Winston, 1978.

GINSBURG, GEORGE, and ALVIN Z. RUBENSTEIN, eds., *Soviet Foreign Policy Towards Western Europe.* New York: Holt, Rinehart & Winston, 1978.

HOFFMANN, ERIK P., and FREDERICK J. FLERON, JR., eds., *The Conduct of Soviet Foreign Policy,* 2nd ed. New York: Aldine, 1980.

HOSMER, STEPHEN T., and THOMAS W. WOLFE, *Soviet Policy and Practice Toward Third World Conflicts.* Lexington, MA: Lexington Books, 1983.

JONNSSON, CHRISTER, *Soviet Bargaining Behavior: The Nuclear Test Ban Case.* New York: Columbia University Press, 1979.

KANET, ROGER E., ed., *Soviet Foreign Policy in the 1980's.* New York: Praeger, 1982.

LABRIE, ROGER P., ed., *SALT Handbook: Key Documents and Issues 1972–1979.* Washington, DC: American Enterprise Institute for Public Policy Research, 1980.

LEIKEN, ROBERT S., *Soviet Strategy in Latin America.* New York: Praeger, 1982.

NATION, R. CRAIG, and MARK V. KAUPPI, eds., *The Soviet Impact in Africa.* Lexington, MA: Lexington Books, 1984.

NOGEE, JOSEPH L., and ROBERT H. DONALDSON, *Soviet Foreign Policy Since World War II.* New York: Pergamon Press, 1981.

RO'I, YAACOV, ed., *The Limits of Power: Soviet Policy in the Middle East.* New York: St. Martin's Press, 1979.

RUBENSTEIN, ALVIN Z., *Soviet Foreign Policy Since World War II: Imperial and Global,* 2nd ed. Boston: Little, Brown and Co., 1985.

SCHWARTZ, MORTON, *Soviet Perceptions of the United States.* Berkeley, CA: University of California Press, 1978.

SEGAL, GERALD, ed., *The Soviet Union in East Asia.* London: Heinemann, 1983.

SETON-WATSON, HUGH, *The Imperial Revolutionaries: Trends in World Communism in the 1960's and 1970's.* Stanford, CA: Hoover Institution Press, 1978.

SHEVCHENKO, ARKADY N., *Breaking With Moscow.* New York: Knopf, 1985.

SPECHLER, DINA ROME, *Domestic Influences on Soviet Foreign Policy.* Washington, DC: University Press of America, Inc., 1978.

STAAR, RICHARD F., *USSR Foreign Policies After Détente.* Stanford, CA: Hoover Institution Press, 1985.

STEELE, JONATHAN, *Soviet Power: The Kremlin's Foreign Policy—Brezhnev to Andropov.* New York: Simon and Schuster, 1983.

TERRY, SARAH MEIKLEJOHN, ed., *Soviet Policy in Eastern Europe.* New Haven, CT: Yale University Press, 1984.

ULAM, ADAM B., *Dangerous Relations: The Soviet Union in World Politics, 1970–1982.* New York: Oxford University Press, 1983.

VALENTA, JIRI, *Soviet Intervention in Czechoslovakia, 1968.* Baltimore: Johns Hopkins University Press, 1979.

VALKENIER, ELIZABETH KRIDL, *The Soviet Union and the Third World: An Economic Bind.* New York: Praeger, 1983.

WHETTEN, LAWRENCE L., ed., *The Present State of Communist Internationalism.* Lexington, MA: Lexington Books, 1983.

WICH, RICHARD, *Sino-Soviet Crisis Politics: A Study of Political Change and Communication.* Cambridge, MA: Harvard University Press, 1980.

YANOV, ALEXANDER, *Détente After Brezhnev: The Domestic Roots of Soviet Foreign Policy* (Policy Papers in International Affairs, No. 2). Berkeley, CA: Institute of International Studies, University of California, 1977.

ZAGORIA, DONALD S., ed., *Soviet Policy in East Asia.* New Haven, CT: Yale University Press, 1982.

15

WHAT DO WE REALLY KNOW ABOUT SOVIET POLITICS?

The American political scientist Austin Ranney tells the story of talking with Lord Morrison* about the number of scholars doing research on the British Parliament. The Peer said: "There are so many of you Americans hanging about Parliament asking us how we do the work of Parliament that it is getting difficult to get the work of Parliament done!" No Western political scientist studying the Soviet system need worry about a comment of this sort from a Soviet official, for none would have such easy access to the corridors of power. The difficulty of getting reliable information about the Soviet Union is one of the great problems of studying the political system of the USSR. It makes the analysis of Soviet politics more difficult, and the conclusions one can draw more tenuous, than is the case in analogous studies of Western political systems. What we aim to do in this final chapter is to examine the problems involved in getting data about Soviet politics, the reliability of the information obtained, and the techniques developed by Western students to analyze the information it is possible to get.

Since the so-called "behavioral revolution" in the discipline of political science, a steadily increasing number of Western political scientists, especially those in the United States, have come to rely on various highly systematic techniques of data collection and analysis. Most popular among the data collection techniques has been survey research in all its various forms,

*Lord Morrison was formerly Herbert Morrison, an important Labor Party politician.

ranging from the interviewing of randomly selected political leaders to mass-opinion polling. Correspondingly, there has been a steady increase in the use of mathematical techniques, most notably statistics, to analyze these data. Although these, as well as other currently popular systematic and empirical techniques for doing research, are far from flawless, they have influenced the standards by which scholarly work is judged. When a researcher presents information on a given political system, both his colleagues and his students are increasingly apt to inquire about the method by which he found out what he claims to know. When he gives answers like, "I talked to anyone who would talk to me," or, "I tried to make a guess of relative power based on the position of the leaders on a reviewing stand," colleagues, not to mention students, are bound to look a bit askance. Yet the scholar specializing in the Soviet Union may well use just such techniques. No matter how much more credible his work might seem if he could, he simply is not going to be able to give answers like, "I administered a questionnaire to a random sample of Central Committee members," or "I sat in on the Politburo discussion of that issue and recorded the proceedings which I later content-analyzed."

To serious Western scholars familiar with such techniques who have struggled with the problems of collecting and analyzing data on the Soviet Union, these latter two answers sound almost whimsical. Survey research and related empirical methods of doing research are out of the question for Westerners. Soviet scholars do a little better in this respect, as will be shown. For foreigners, however, access of the sort needed to do such research is not just difficult, it is impossible and probably will remain so for the foreseeable future. Thus, the study of Soviet politics lags behind much of the rest of contemporary political research.

Basically, information about Soviet politics, as well as economics and other social phenomena, comes from two sources. First, there is the information that is released by official Soviet sources, usually in written form, to the general public (including foreigners). Second, there is the information provided by various sources outside the network of official dissemination. This information includes informal statements by governmental or Party officials; information from emigrés and dissidents (including works published in *samizdat*); data from other insiders or quasi-insiders such as members of political communist parties who have conferred with Soviet officials; and information gathered by outsiders such as diplomats, correspondents, and scholars making on-the-scene observations of the Soviet system.

There are problems with both these kinds of sources. Official information is often selective and represented as typical when it may not be; it is usually less complete than information published in the West. Even Soviet writers sometimes lack access to information which would be everyday news in the West (for example, crime statistics) and, as noted in Chapter 4, there is a large number of topics not covered by the press because of censorship (for example, plane crashes and earthquakes). Even systematic data released by official agencies, such as census figures and economic reports, are of limited usefulness because of gaps or distortions

None of the post-World War II censuses (done in 1959, 1970, and 1979) has been particularly comprehensive. Western scholars have pointed out numerous omissions and distortions in the published data from these surveys. But the least amount of information released has been from the most recent census—that of 1979. This is consistent with a general move in recent years toward increasing secrecy with regard to official information. In addition to population information published in newspapers and journals, 1970 census figures were released in seven special volumes amounting to about 3,000 pages of data. No separate volumes of this kind were issued for the 1979 census.[1] Similar problems with the quality and amount of official economic and social information have also been evident in recent years.*[2]

Quite a different question which must be considered is the deliberate falsification of systematic data. Are the figures that *are* published accurate, even if selective, or have they been manufactured to give desirable results where such were not in fact obtained? Most Western analysts appear to agree that the data-collection agencies, such as Gosplan and the Central Statistical Administration, do not deliberately falsify the figures they use in the sense that they do not engage in outright invention or double bookkeeping (one set of books for internal use and another for public consumption.)** The statistics issued by these agencies are often selective and methodologically deficient and have certain other biases, however, requiring considerable efforts by Western economists to come up with useful data or comparative purposes.[3] On the other hand, it seems clear that some data-reporting agencies, such as industrial plants, collective farms, ministries, and republican governments falsify the data that they report to the central agencies. This falsification often takes the form of inflating production and other figures. The Soviet press occasionally cites examples of "cooking" the figures and double-counting at lower economic levels, and there is no reason to believe that some of this deception does not find its way into the final nationwide production figures.[4] The success of economic administrators is judged so much on volume of production, and the pressure for success is so great, that attempts to falsify would be understandably human. Nor are higher administrators likely to push for correction of falsification, if they detected it. They also are judged by production success. In the economic sector there is great pressure to say "plan fulfilled"; all efforts are marshalled in that direction. Soviet authorities go to great lengths, including sometimes

---

*For example, according to the official Soviet figures, infant mortality increased considerably between 1970 and 1975. After 1975, however, the USSR ceased publishing such figures. See Christopher Davis and Murray Feshbach, *Rising Infant Mortality in the USSR in the 1970s* (Washington, DC: U.S. Bureau of the Census), Series P-95, No. 74, September 1980. Similarly, in the early 1980s, after a series of poor harvests, figures on annual grain production simply stopped being included among officially released statistics.

**One exception may be data on Soviet defense spending. The problem of determining the size of the Soviet defense budget is reviewed in Chapter 9.

revising plan targets downward in mid-plan, to be able to report fulfillment and overfulfillment. In the political sector, there is evidence that the figures on public participation in voting for the Supreme Soviet are inflated.[5] The reason for this falsification is the same: pressure from above to show a desired result—human plan fulfillment in the form of a nearly unanimous level of public involvement and support for the regime.

Unofficial sources of information also can be a problem because the people involved often have some ax to grind. In other words, they tend to espouse a definite point of view, and no matter how laudable that point of view might seem to the readers of this text, it can still constitute a source of systematic bias. Focusing on *samizdat,* in particular, one finds a wide range of variation. *The Chronicle of Current Events,* which was finally suppressed by the authorities in the mid-1980s, was long regarded by Western experts as a reliable source of information on dissident activities. But a significant proportion of *samizdat* is produced by persons less willing or able to be balanced or accurate. For example, Abraham Brumberg has characterized a *samizdat* writer whom he met in the following manner: ". . . one was struck by his courage, by his intellectual brilliance, as well as by his hysterical tone, by his proselytizing zeal which was sometimes a far cry from reality . . ."[6]

Samizdat is not the only unofficial source of information. In any Western country, one of the prime sources of information from unofficial sources is the statements that governmental or political officials are willing to make to persons who are serious scholars. Although such statements are not official, and in some cases they are not even for publication (at least with an indication of the source), they can be quite illuminating on the real functioning of the political system within which that official works. It is putting it mildly to say that Soviet officials are not very forthcoming in informal conversations regarding matters political. To carry it a bit further, it might be said that conversations with Soviet officials about matters Soviet are rare indeed. There are those Western scholars who have had the immense good fortune to have talked with Soviet officials (usually of the more obscure variety) and to have gotten information unavailable elsewhere, but this is not an everyday occurrence. Somewhat less rare and often more useful are contacts with non-Soviet communists who provide useful information. An example of such information is the text of Khrushchev's secret speech of February 1956 in which he denounced Stalin. This text has still not been published in the Soviet Union and is thought to have reached the West through members of the Polish Communist Party.

Good information can also be gained from regular Soviet citizens and former citizens. The American scholar doing research in the Soviet Union can pick up bits of data from Soviet friends and acquaintances; but more important perhaps is being able to sense the general mood of the people, to get a "feel" of what is important and unimportant that may not be possible to get from reading Soviet newspapers back in New York or Chicago. More systematic data have been collected from Soviet citizens, however. For example, for a number of years Soviet visitors to Europe have been questioned about their listening habits, level of information, and preferences regarding Western radio broadcasts into the Soviet Union.[7] One of the most ambitious projects involving former Soviet citizens was the Harvard Project on the Soviet Social System. Begun in 1950, this project involved interviews and questionnaires administered to hundreds of former Soviet citizens living in the West. The project produced a great many articles and several books which, even though now dated, contain thought-provoking and important generalizations.[8] More recently, a new wave of emigrants from the Soviet Union has been providing valuable information and insights on the political system. For the most part these are Jews who have been allowed to go to Israel and other countries, but they also include some people of other nationalities, among them a number of political dissidents. Unlike most of the subjects in the Harvard Project who had not had contact with the Soviet Union for a number of years, this group has come with up-to-date information on the Soviet political system. Another way in which they differ from their Harvard Project counterparts is that they themselves have produced an impressive body of writing on the Soviet system. Since many held important and well-placed positions in the USSR, their contribution has been invaluable.

Another way in which data collection has been facilitated in the past several decades has been through the Western scholar's ability to go to the USSR. Only since the mid-1950s, after Stalin's death, have tourists been allowed to visit the USSR in great numbers. At the end of the 1950s the USSR began exchange agreements with a number of Western countries, which allowed not just ballet dancers and technological exhibitions into the country but which also provided for research visits by scholars who were permitted to reside in Soviet cities for months at a time. Even though these scholars have faced difficulties, some of our best analyses of the Soviet system have been aided by such visits. Foreign scholars have been able to get at more published sources in the Soviet Union than at home. Some historians have gained better understanding of aspects of Russian and Soviet history because of access to archives. Certain aspects of Soviet politics and social life can now be vividly described by Western scholars who have had personal experience with them. One of the best of numerous examples of this kind of work is Andrea Lee's *Russian Journal*.[9] Lee spent a year in Moscow as the spouse of an American exchange graduate student. Her book is a series of vivid sketches which show the fascination and frustration of living in the USSR.

But the barriers to social science research in the Soviet Union are still formidable. This is particularly a problem for those scholars who are interested in a subject that has political ramifications. A scholar who wants to study an obscure eighteenth-century poet is most likely to have few or no problems. But even a twentieth-century poet presents substantial problems because of the prevailing necessity for literature to contain an acceptable component of "socialist realism." There are few subjects outside of the "hard" natural sciences that are permitted by Soviet authorities to be devoid of political content.

At one time, it seemed as if the mere ability of serious scholars to live and work in the Soviet Union would open up an era of greatly increased understanding of the Soviet system. And, in some ways, it has. The gains, however, are hard won. Upon arriving in the Soviet Union, the scholar finds that the Soviets greatly restrict his or her ability to travel and choose where to live. Consequently, most end up living and working mainly in Leningrad or Moscow. Once settled, the scholar finds that it is impossible to go everywhere the research plan calls for. For example, a foreign researcher living in Moscow may not go more than 50 kilometers (about 35 miles) away from Red Square in any direction without special permission, which is usually difficult or impossible to get—depending on the proposed destination. Wide areas of the Soviet Union are closed to all foreigners, and a researcher who needs to see someone or something in a "closed area" is most likely out of luck. Aside from travel, one of the most important things a scholar goes to another country to get are fruitful contacts with native scholars working in the same or similar areas. Although such contacts are not impossible, a chilling effect on the free interchange of ideas and information is created by the authorities' systematic attempts to discourage Soviet citizens from talking to foreigners, visiting them in their apartments, or entertaining them. Correspondingly, many of the most important scholarly meetings in the country are closed, as are all important government and Party meetings.

Access to research institutes and archives is difficult, and at times impossible, to obtain. When access is gotten, full use of the facilities is not always possible. For example, one of the authors had the following experience in Moscow's Lenin Library, an institution that is easier than most to gain access to and utilize fully: A book containing some interesting Soviet legal statistics from the 1920s was found. Rather than hand copying the mass of data, which would have taken a great deal of time, he decided to submit a request to have several pages of the book photostated. The photostating service had been used without incident before. When this request was made, however, the reading-room librarian refused to process it, saying that the data in the book "don't reflect reality." In such cases, protest is almost invariably futile and, since there was the possibility that further use of the book might have been denied, the requestor kept the book and hand copied the data.

How do students of Soviet politics and government cope with these formidable problems in getting information about their subject? Put most bluntly, they try to squeeze every possible drop of information out of whatever data they can get. Then they put it all together and try to make sense of it—to find salient patterns. We know what we know about Soviet politics, therefore, because the specialists in the field have painstakingly assembled many small bits of evidence and have found what seem to them to be reasonable and useful patterns. Much of this work goes under the comprehensive title "kremlinology."

Kremlinology is a much-maligned art. It has been ridiculed as "the effort to do archival research without access to the archives."[10] In the heyday of détente in the 1970s, it was predicted that kremlinology, like the state in the Marxian vision, would wither away. It is true that the Soviet Union, along with the United States and thirty-three other countries, pledged when it signed the European Security Conference agreement in 1975 to provide for "a freer flow of people, information and ideas." But in the years since 1975 it has become clear that this agreement has had little or no effect on accessibility of information; indeed, a good case can be made that less information has been available.[11] Thus, the prospects for a continuation of kremlinology remain good.

The heart of kremlinology is the study of subtle variations in several forms of communication. It is based on certain assumptions about Soviet behavior. The most important of these is that little or nothing happens by chance in official communications or formal Party and governmental activities. Soviet authorities, operating under the Marxist-Leninist ideology, which claims to be the key to understanding social processes, are fond of using the phrase "it is not accidental" *(ne sluchaino)*. They might say, for instance, "it is not accidental that the ruling circles in the United States oppose the Sandinistas in Nicaragua." In effect, the kremlinologist makes this kind of assumption about Soviet behavior, reasoning that slight changes in wording or alterations in the ordering of things or people imply more significant changes behind the scenes, perhaps in power relationships or policy stances at the top. These communication clues often appear to be directed at key subelites within the Soviet Union.

As was suggested in Chapter 3, the ability to manipulate the language of ideology is crucial to political success in the Soviet Union. The expression of ideological precepts follows such a conformist pattern that very small deviations from the set formulas can signal serious disagreements or changes in relative power among the top leaders. If these deviations are accompanied by rationales of current policies which are justified defensively against nameless critics, the combination is treated as additional evidence of conflict, and the kremlinologists turn their efforts to guessing what the real issues are and who the nameless critics are. In a like fashion, history is manipulated to give important roles to persons on the ascent and to downgrade the roles of persons on the decline. Students of Soviet politics spend many hours poring over tedious ideological or historical writings in search of just such clues.

The nonverbal indicator that has achieved the most notoriety outside scholarly circles is the order in which the top leaders line up on the reviewing stand for the annual May Day and November 7 parades. But kremlinologists have gone far beyond this rather primitive level of analysis and have had many successes in determining or predicting policy and personnel changes from the clues they have gathered. Any listing or ordering of the leaders that is not alphabetical is treated as possibly meaningful. For instance, when on the occasion of national holidays huge pictures of the top leaders are hung on the façade of Lenin Library, everyone notes the order in which they are hung. And when in 1974 Brezhnev greeted Nixon before the ceremonial head of state, Podgornyi, greeted him, the break in normal protocol was considered important. (Podgornyi had greeted Nixon first during the latter's visit in 1972.) Nothing of this nature is assumed to happen by accident or by chance.

Considerable significance is attributed to changes in personnel in key governmental and Party organs such as the Central Committee or the Presidium of the Supreme Soviet. This extends not only to members of the top leadership group (where Politburo membership is most significant) but to their protégés as well. If a leader's protégés are on the rise, the leader's power is also assumed to be increasing. For example, it has been asserted that "Khrushchev in 1953–1957 was more successful than any of his rivals in posting adherents to the various switchboards of power."[12] These are only some of the clues that kremlinologists use and are intended to give the flavor of the enterprise rather than a comprehensive description of it. They are most useful to the scholar who is trying to determine who is wielding how much power in the Kremlin, and—when used skillfully and with discretion—they have had a rather good "batting average" in giving at least gross indications of what is going on in the inner circles of the Soviet leadership.

There are, of course, a number of problems with the kremlinological approach. Long on assumptions and short on evidence as it must be, the judgments based on this technique are highly subjective and frequently turn out to be wrong. The approach is practiced by specialists long conversant with Soviet politics whose conclusions may be based largely on hunch, "feel," or idiosyncratic data-gathering techniques. These characteristics do not take away from the skill and accomplishments of kremlinologists, but they mean that such work is usually neither replicable nor suitable for the creation of large data bases or broader theories. Kremlinology does not yield the systematic data that political scientists consider necessary for progress in the field. The American Sovietologist Marshall Shulman puts the kremlinological enterprise in proper perspective in the following statement: "Kremlinology is a legitimate and useful function. It helps to sharpen our perspectives, helps keep in suspension in our minds a range of possible developments—providing, however, it is properly labeled as speculation. The danger comes when the distinction between guesswork and knowledge is blurred."[13]

A refinement on kremlinological research has come closer, however. For some time various researchers have kept detailed personnel records on a great many Soviet officials, including Politburo members, Central Committee members, and a number of other officeholders and important individuals around the country. Out of this collection of data have been developed fairly detailed career patterns of individuals who have risen in the Soviet power hierarchy. These career patterns convey a reasonably good idea of some of the factors favoring a person's success in Soviet politics. Systematic records are kept on the comings and goings of Soviet officials and on whom they meet. Out of such records, for instance, it was possible to document the fact (suggested as an impression by several analysts) that from the early 1970s Brezhnev increasingly turned his attention to foreign-policy matters, particularly in terms of contacts with noncommunist foreigners.[14]

Such information can also serve as the basis for speculation concerning the rising or falling fortunes of political leaders and the state of their health. Brezhnev, Andropov, and Chernenko, while holding the top Party post of General Secretary, were absent from public view during large parts of their last months in office. Although Soviet spokesmen downplayed the health problems that Western analysts suspected, in all three cases the Soviet leaders were suffering terminal illnesses.[15] In these instances, it required little kremlinological insight to conclude that something was amiss; these leaders simply ceased to be seen in public. The attempts to cover up this fact—which obviously could not succeed for long—provide useful examples of the irrational passion for secrecy that characterizes the system.

The techniques just described are used largely to examine leadership groups and the power relationships among them. There is much more to Soviet politics, however, than such groups and their interrelations, and scholars have addressed themselves to a number of other topics. Several other techniques of analysis, as well as the subjects on which they have been used, should be mentioned.

Official sources such as newspapers and journals are not used only by kremlinologists. They are the stock-in-trade of scholars studying other aspects of Soviet politics. Several studies of local government have been based in large part on Soviet local newspapers.[16] The work of scholars in such fields as economics, education, law, and history makes use of specialized journals in these fields. As noted in Chapter 11, considerable attention has been devoted since the 1960s to the roles played by interest groups and opinion groups in Soviet policy making. Numerous case studies of group processes have been based largely on the specialized publications of the various Soviet professions. These case studies reach their conclusions through traditional, nonquantitative methods. A technique which has received limited use is the content analysis of specialized publications. This systematic, quantitative examination of published materials is thought by some scholars to provide a more scientific and objective basis for analyzing communications. Numerous content analyses have been made of a variety of Soviet publications, which are assumed to speak both for and to various Soviet elites. The results of these analyses purport to show attitudinal differences among Soviet elites on certain policy issues.[17]

Research in archives was mentioned earlier. This is an activity usually undertaken by historians. Archives located in the Soviet Union on contemporary or even early twentieth-century political subjects are not easily accessible to the foreigner. One set of documents constituting an archive that has been available to Western scholars is the "Smolensk Archive." This archive contains records (including those of the Party organization) that were taken by the Germans when they overran Smolensk in 1941. These records were acquired by the American forces at the end of the war and became available for scholarly examination thereafter. The most comprehensive analysis of the documents in the archive is Merle Fainsod's *Smolensk Under Soviet Rule* (1958).

An important source of information that has been used by many Western scholars is the large number of opinion questionnaires and other sociological surveys that have been done in the Soviet Union in recent years. The write-ups of these studies may be considered official data, and are, therefore, subject to the selectiveness and potential biases of all such information. Moreover, opinion polling does not serve precisely the same purposes that it does in the West. In the revival of sociology in the USSR that began in the 1960s, emphasis is placed on what has been referred to as "practical empiricism,"[18] that is, sociological research designed to aid in the solution of practical problems. Thus, there is no polling of attitudes toward political leaders in the country or other overtly political issues, a staple of the pollster's activity in the West.

A great deal of emphasis is placed on matters of less interest to political scientists, such as how people use their leisure time, satisfaction with one's job and reasons for changing jobs, and the aspirations of youth. The few surveys that deal with Party and governmental organizations involve workers at the lower level. But thousands of polls and other surveys have been conducted in the USSR in recent years, and Western analysts have mined a number of nuggets of information from them. Survey data with information on the conditions of life in Siberia, for instance, have helped us to understand why it is so difficult to induce settlers to remain in that part of the country. Other surveys on sensitive matters or containing results not welcomed by the regime have never seen the light of day. Occasionally, emigré reports have contained information from such secret surveys.[19]

Scholars use fiction to gain insights into the Soviet system. The orthodox novel, story, or poem often suggests the ideal political stance of the subject or characters depicted according to the tenets of socialist realism, the guiding formula for correct Soviet creative writing. Such writing may also contain allowable criticism of shortcomings. The literary criticism of such writings by Soviet authors can supplement the analyst's understanding of these matters. Alexander Gerschenkron, among others, has described the many insights into contemporary Soviet economics and politics to be gained from this "neglected source of information."[20]

The strictures placed by the state on literary expression make literature a focus of political activity in its own right. A more-or-less constant struggle goes on between some Soviet writers striving for freer expression in their creative work and other writers and officials who want to keep such expression within prescribed bounds. The publishing of a liberal poem or story may presage the coming of a more relaxed literary and political climate, and many Western scholars have traced the ups and downs of literary expression over the years.

This somewhat different kind of relationship between politics and literature in the Soviet Union is not always fully grasped by the beginning student. As Crouch and Porter put it in their anthology *Understanding Soviet Politics Through Literature* (1984), "the authorities today take literature seriously, both as a potentially explosive phenomenon that needs to be controlled and censored and as a vehicle for positively inculcating regime values and attitudes. Politics and literature are thus inextricably intertwined."[21] Their collection of readings is designed to demonstrate this "indivisibility of literature and politics" through representative selections from official and unofficial writings.

While Westerners, including Americans, have produced numerous fictional accounts of the Soviet scene, the prose works of Soviet and former Soviet authors bear the stamp of greater authenticity. Even the person casually interested in the USSR is familiar with the historical panorama of the Soviet period covered in the works of Solzhenitsyn, both his fictionalized accounts and his nonfiction. But the "third wave" of emigrés since the 1970s has brought great numbers of talented fiction writers and poets to the West. In continuing to ply their trade, they have produced a rich emigré literature which provides insights on political, social, and economic problems in their native land. The topics covered range widely, from broad ones such as the oppressive weight of ideology on the Soviet populace (Aleksander Zinoviev, *The Yawning Heights,* 1978) to more mundane subjects like the strictures on practicing the journalist's trade (Sergei Dovaltov, *The Compromise,* 1983) or the problems of keeping one's apartment from being given to a politically influential adversary (Vladimir Voinovich, *The Ivankiad,* 1976) to scores of other topical subjects. As the late Carl Proffer put it in discussing this emigré writing: "A large part, in many ways the best part, of Soviet Russian literature simply moved abroad for one stage of its existence—the printing stage."[22]

The student would do well to employ all of these resources in attempting to understand Soviet politics. But what kind of framework can be used to reconcile their diversity? It is a commonplace of scholarly endeavor that in order to make sense out of social phenomena, some overall pattern or theory must be posited against which random facts, observations, and impressions may be set. In the confrontation of facts and theory, either the former fit the latter or the latter is modified or discarded, with a new theory taking its place. By this procedure higher levels of generalization in the social sciences are sought. The study of the USSR has been rich with attempts to suggest a general theory or framework within which Soviet politics can be best understood. Perhaps the most often cited writing on the Soviet Union in recent years is Daniel Bell's 1958 article "Ten Theories in Search of Reality: The Prediction of Soviet Behavior in the Social Sciences."[23] The title is adapted from a 1921 work by the Italian dramatist Luigi Pirandello, "Six Characters in Search of an Author," which is a play about the confusion of illusion and reality. In his article, Bell demonstrates the confusion resulting from the plethora of theories about Soviet behavior and the inadequacy of any one framework for analyzing the Soviet system. In the nearly thirty years since Bell's article, little progress has been made in reducing this confusion.

Undoubtedly the single most-discussed general concept used to characterize the Soviet system is that of totalitarianism. The totalitarian model has been described and defined in various ways, but the conception most commonly used with regard to the Soviet system is the one associated with Carl J. Friedrich and Zbigniew Brzezinski. The concept of totalitarianism as applied to the Soviet Union has adherents and opponents. The latter say that it is conceptually vague, that its supposed characteristics are too open-ended. Thus, there is no measureable way for discussing trends, for determining whether a regime is becoming more or less totalitarian. As a result, its critics assert, creating an empirical theory of totalitarianism is impossible.[24] Out of such dissatisfactions have come attempts to create other theories, and one can read in recent writings on the Soviet Union about authoritarian, bureaucratic, oligarchic, modernization, and other models of the Soviet system.[25] Others have used terms such as "administered society,"[26] "monohierarchical polity,"[27] and "corporatist politics"[28] to distinguish newer concepts from the old totalitarian paradigm. Particularly after the late 1950s and early 1960s, when the country seemed for a time to be pursuing a more liberal, relaxed course in internal politics, the idea of totalitarianism, with its implications of *total* control, seemed inappropriate.

Still, the totalitarian model has had remarkable staying power and continues to elicit both positive and negative assessments.[29] Let us look more closely at the concept. As employed here, totalitarianism is what the sociologist Max Weber called an "ideal type." An ideal type "is never, or only very rarely, encountered in all its purity in real life." Rather, it amounts to a "rational blueprint," a representative of "logical organization as distinct from the fluctuations of reality."[30] Thus, the salient characteristics of the totalitarian model may not be fully achieved in practice, even though the system's leaders strive for their achievement.

What are these characteristics? As suggested above, Friedrich and Brzezinski are most closely associated with the application of the concept of totalitarianism to the Soviet Union. Their version has gone through several stages of development since originally stated in their 1956 book *Totalitarian Dictatorship and Autocracy.* (Actually, Friedrich has been responsible for the later alterations of the concept.) In the latest version Friedrich describes six features that distinguish totalitarian regimes from other systems:

(1) a totalist ideology; (2) a single party committed to this ideology and usually led by one man, the dictator; (3) a fully developed secret police; and (4) three kinds of monopoly or, more precisely, monopolistic control: namely that of (a) mass communications; (b) operational weapons; (c) all organizations, including economic ones, thus involving a centrally planned economy.[31]

The rest of Friedrich's analysis involves an elaboration of these features.

It is worth noting that nothing in the totalitarian model rules out conflict within the ruling elite. Indeed, enough has been learned about Soviet politics over the years that most Western analysts now embrace the so-called "conflict model."[32] But such conflict is played out within the single party, and all participants appear implicitly to agree not to allow it to expand beyond a narrowly circumscribed group of players. Moreover, a certain amount of interest-group activity, or at least "interest articulation," by like-minded individuals is not inconsistent with totalitarianism. It is only when such activity breaks through the bounds of the permissible (as defined by the authorities) that sanctions are imposed. Thus, dissidents are punished for going beyond the officially imposed limits, for (in Walter Connor's phrase) "enter[ing] politics without a license."[33] Those who work within the system may contribute to policy making, but only under conditions established by a leadership group that is insulated from any kind of popular control.

As we have already noted, one of the major criticisms of the totalitarian model is its static quality. Development, trends, and change are not considerations that can be readily accommodated by the model. And yet, virtually every serious observer of the Soviet Union would agree that substantial changes have taken place in the system over the past several decades (the controversy often involves the question of whether or not these changes have fundamentally affected the basic nature of the system). Even Brzezinski, whose earlier work on totalitarianism has been cited, came to the conclusion during the 1970s that the Soviet system had changed enough to warrant the consideration of a different descriptive label:

> . . . by the mid-seventies the Soviet system had become in some respects more akin to traditional authoritarian regimes, but with an enormous and increasingly dysfunctional totalitarian residue inherent in the doctrinal and political system of controls still bureaucratically, ritualistically, and occasionally coercively imposed on society. The contemporary Soviet system thus combines residual elements of revolutionary totalitarianism with features reminiscent of the more traditional autocracy.[34]

The work of a number of analysts of the Soviet system who have rejected or moved away from the totalitarian model can be categorized under the general rubric of political development or, more simply, "change." This orientation has found expression in the study of comparative politics for some time but only came to Soviet studies in the late 1960s and early 1970s. There are now numerous such analyses, and they vary widely both in approach and in conclusions reached.[35] What they have in common is the attempt to assess the degree of change in the political system (starting from some landmark point such as the death of Stalin) and the capacity for further development toward a more rationally organized (though not necessarily democratic) political-social-economic system. Since the original impetus for studying political change came from comparative politics, a number of analyses have attempted to place Soviet developments in a comparative framework. This, in turn, has generated objections from those who think it best to "focus on the uniqueness of Soviet politics."[36]

The study of political change can emphasize various aspects of politics, and a diverse literature on this subject has developed in recent years. Stephen Cohen's seminal article on "the friends and foes of change" sees Soviet development as involving "a social and political confrontation between reformism and conservatism," which is played out "within the parameters of the existing order." In this struggle, the reformers have achieved some successes that have typically been "followed by a conservative backlash." Thus continuing reform, Cohen concludes, is hindered by the "profound conservatism" that generally characterizes the USSR, a country he calls "one of the most conservative . . . in the world."[37] Alexander Yanov, a former Soviet journalist now living in the United States, takes a longer historical view and concludes that numerous Russian reform efforts going back over the centuries have met a similar fate: "whenever a reform threatened to move Russia irreversibly toward political modernization, a counterreform was there to reverse the process." This particular Russian pattern, Yanov found, applied fully to the agricultural reform of the 1960s which he analyzed in detail.[38]

Change, then, is an important consideration for those attempting to analyze and explain the Soviet system. But it is more than this, of course. It has a reality beyond the intellectual perceptions of the sovietologist. To one degree or another, all recent Soviet leaders have been trying to achieve change in the system. The subject matter of much of this book, and particularly of Part IV, has been the problems of the Soviet system and the need to find new ways to cope with them. The change the leaders seek would preserve the essential or desirable (from the standpoint of the leaders) characteristics of the system while providing better mechanisms for confronting the social and economic pressures the system faces.

When he was chosen Party General Secretary, Mikhail Gorbachev was the fourth man to hold that post in twenty-nine months. Brezhnev is remembered as a leader who ran out of initiatives and provided little new impetus for the system during the last years of his rule. Chernenko clearly operated in the Brezhnev tradition during his thirteen months in the top position. Between these two men, Andropov served as General Secretary of the party. He was widely seen as intent on shaking up the system and moving it in new directions, but poor health cut short his work long before his sixteen months in office were completed. Gorbachev came to power in March 1985 as the youngest man to occupy the top position since Stalin. He has been described by journalists as "impatient" and "a man in a hurry." His early statements suggested the possibility of bold new initiatives; shortly before his accession to power he called for "profound transformations" in the economy and social system.[39] As of this writing, however, his actual reform efforts have been more cautious than bold.

Thus, there is a considerable difference between Soviet political rhetoric and Soviet political action. Cohen, Yanov, and others have discussed historical patterns that seem related to the current difficulty of overcoming conservative opposition to change.[40] Even a relatively young and vigorous leader like Gorbachev, fully aware of the need for reform, may find the inertia of the system difficult to overcome. New leaders *can* make a difference, even in Soviet-type systems, as the political scientist Valerie Bunce has amply documented.[41] Her research suggests, however, that they need to move quickly, to take advantage of the honeymoon period immediately after their ascent to power, in order to maximize the impact of the innovations they seek to introduce. From this standpoint, the early period of the Gorbachev regime may constitute an important situation of opportunity in the recurrent efforts of the Soviet leadership to effect genuine change in the Soviet system.

NOTES

[1] On these matters, see Murray Feshbach, "Census Censored," *Problems of Communism*, 31, No. 6 (Nov.–Dec. 1982), p. 87; "The All-Union Census of 1979 in the USSR," (A Collection of Reports Prepared Before and After the Census by the Staff of RL Research), *Radio Liberty Research Bulletin*, Sept. 1980, pp. i–iii; Sergei Voronitsyn, "Demographic Information Under Wraps," *Radio Liberty Research*, No. 359/83, Sept. 27, 1983.

[2] See, for example, "Signs of Further Deterioration of Soviet Economic Statistics Since the Helsinki Agreements," *Radio Liberty Research*, No. 453/80, Dec. 2, 1980.

[3] On the reliability of Soviet economic statistics, see *USSR: Measures of Economic Growth and Development, 1950–1980*, Studies Prepared for the Joint Economic Committee, Congress of the United States, Washington, DC: Dec. 8, 1982, pp. 260–68.

[4] The extent to which this practice has been deterred by the 1961 law making it a crime to make inflated statements of plan-fulfillment figures is not known. See ibid., p. 263.

[5] Robert G. Kaiser, *Russia: The People and the Power* (New York: Atheneum, 1976), pp. 154–55, and Hedrick Smith, *The Russians* (New York: Quadrangle/The N.Y. Times, 1976), pp. 286–87. Also Victor Zaslavsky and Robert J. Brym, "The Functions of Elections in the USSR," *Soviet Studies*, 30 (Jul. 1978), 365.

[6] Abraham Brumberg, "The Future of Samizdat: Significance and Prospects," London, England, Apr. 23, 1971, full transcript, p. 46, as cited in Paige Bryan, "Concerning Economic Grievances From Samizdat," *Radio Liberty Dispatch*, July 7, 1972, p. 2.

[7] See Maury Lisann, *The Impact of Foreign Broadcasting in the USSR* (New York: Holt, Rinehart & Winston, 1975).

[8] The major volume from the Harvard Project was Alex Inkeles and Raymond A. Bauer, *The Soviet Citizen: Daily Life in a Totalitarian Society* (Cambridge, MA: Harvard University Press, 1969). A list of publications based on the Harvard Project is found on p. 464.

[9] New York: Random House, 1981.

[10] David Joravsky, *The Lysenko Affair* (Cambridge, MA: Harvard University Press, 1970), p. 329.

[11]See, for example, "Signs of Further Deterioration of Soviet Economic Statistics."

[12]Sidney I. Ploss, "Techniques of Analysis: What Soviet Politics Looks and Sounds Like," in *The Soviet Political Process*, ed. Sidney I Ploss (Waltham, MA: Ginn and Co., 1971), p. 70.

[13]Marshall D. Shulman, "Kremlinologizing," *The New York Times*, Nov. 19, 1982, p. A35.

[14]See Jerry F. Hough, "The Brezhnev Era: The Man and the System," *Problems of Communism*, 25, No. 2 (Mar.–Apr. 1976), 4, note 9. Hough cites a U.S. government periodical, *Appearances of Soviet Leaders* (Washington, DC).

[15]On the Soviet preoccupation with secrecy regarding the health of leaders and other matters, see Leslie H. Gelb, "What We Really Know about the Soviet Union," *The New York Times Magazine*, Oct. 28, 1984, 22.

[16]See, for instance, Jerry F. Hough, *The Soviet Prefects: The Local Party Organs in Industrial Decision-Making* (Cambridge, MA: Harvard University Press, 1969), Philip Stewart, *Political Power in the Soviet Union* (New York: Bobbs-Merrill, 1968), Joel C. Moses. *Regional Party Leadership and Policy-Making in the USSR* (New York: Holt, Rinehart & Winston, 1974), and Theodore H. Friedgut, "Community Structure, Political Participation, and Soviet Local Government: The Case of Kutaisi," in *Soviet Politics and Society in the 1970's*, ed. Henry W. Morton and Rudolf L. Tokes (New York: Free Press, 1974); Ronald J. Hill, *Soviet Political Elites: The Case of Tiraspol* (New York: St. Martin's Press, 1977).

[17]The work of Milton Lodge is perhaps the most comprehensive in this area. See *Soviet Elite Attitudes since Stalin* (Columbus, OH: Charles E. Merrill, 1969). A recent example, involving the examination of varying Soviet elite viewpoints on the Cyprus conflict, is Robert M. Cutler, "Domestic and Foreign Influences on Policy Making: The Soviet Union in the 1974 Cyprus Conflict," *Soviet Studies*, 37 No. 1 (Jan. 1985), 60.

[18]Robert K. Merton and Henry W. Riecken, "Notes on Sociology in the U.S.S.R.," in *Current Problems in Social-Behavior Research*, Synposia Studies Series No. 10 (Washington, DC: National Institute of Social and Behavioral Science, Mar. 1962), p. 10.

[19]See, e.g., the description of unpublished poll results in Victor Zaslavsky, *The Neo-Stalinist State: Class, Ethnicity, and Consensus in Soviet Society* (Armonk, NY: M. E. Sharpe, 1982), pp. 22–43.

[20]Alexander Gerschenkron, "A Neglected Source of Economic Information on Soviet Russia," and "Reflections on Soviet Novels," in *Economic Backwardness in Historical Perspective: A Book of Essays* (Cambridge, MA: The Belknap Press of Harvard University Press, 1962), pp. 296 and 318. See also Nadine Natov, "Daily Life and Individual Psychology in Soviet Russian Prose of the 1970's," *Russian Review*, 33, No. 4 (Oct. 1974), 357; Vera S. Dunham, "The Waning Theme of the Worker as Hero in Recent Soviet Literature," in *Industrial Labor in the U.S.S.R.*, eds. Arcadius Kahan and Blair A. Ruble (New York: Pergamon, 1979), pp. 399–412. On fiction in the Stalin period see Dunham's *In Stalin's Time: Middleclass Values in Soviet Fiction* (Cambridge, MA: Cambridge University Press, 1976). See also George Gibian. "New Aspects of Soviet Russian Literature," in *The Soviet Union Since Stalin*, eds. Stephen F. Cohen, Alexander Rabinowitch, and Robert Sharlet (Bloomington, IN: Indiana University Press, 1980), pp. 252–75.

[21]Martin Crouch and Robert Porter, *Understanding Soviet Politics Through Literature: A Book of Readings* (London: George Allen & Unwin, 1984), p. ix.

[22]Carl R. Proffer, "The Remarkable Decade That Destroyed Russian Emigre Literature," *Russia*, No. 3 (1981), p. 34. This article provides a good overview of Russian emigre literature. Ardis Publishers of Ann Arbor, Michigan, which was founded by Proffer, has published much of this literature.

[23]Daniel Bell, "Ten Theories in Search of Reality," *World Politics*, 10, No. 3 (Apr. 1958), 327.

[24]One of the most cogent criticisms of the concept of totalitarianism is that of Frederic J. Fleron, Jr. See his "Soviet Area Studies and the Social Sciences: Some Methodological Problems in Communist Studies," in *Communist Studies and the Social Sciences: Essays on Methodology and Empirical Theory*, ed. Frederic J. Fleron, Jr. (Chicago, IL: Rand McNally, 1969), pp. 15–19. More recently, Jerry F. Hough has made a detailed analysis and criticism of the totalitarian model within the context of a discussion of several other models. See Jerry F. Hough and Merle Fainsod, *How the Soviet Union is Governed* (Cambridge, MA: Harvard University Press, 1979), pp. 518–29.

[25] A good summary of these and other models may be found in John S. Reshetar, Jr., *The Soviet Polity,* 2nd ed. (New York: Harper and Row, 1978), pp. 336–61.

[26] Allen Kassof, "The Administered Society: Totalitarianism Without Terror," *World Politics,* 16, No. 4 (July 1964), 558.

[27] Roy D. Laird, *The Soviet Paradigm: An Experiment in Creating a Monohierarchical Polity* (New York: Free Press, 1970).

[28] Valerie Bunce and John M. Echols, III, "Soviet Politics in the Brezhnev Era: 'Pluralism' or 'Corporatism,'" in *Soviet Politics in the Brezhnev Era,* ed. Donald R. Kelley (New York: Holt, Rinehart & Winston, 1980), p. 1.

[29] The most thorough recent analysis of the concept, which contains views both pro and con, is: Earnest A. Menze, ed., *Totalitarianism Reconsidered* (Port Washington, NY: Kennikat Press, 1981). A recent argument against the totalitarian model may be found in Stephen F. Cohen's *Rethinking the Soviet Experience* (New York: Oxford University Press, 1985). Cohen's analysis of totalitarianism is in Chapter 1, "Scholarly Missions: Sovietology as a Vocation," pp. 3–38. See also Maurice Cranston, "Should We Cease to Speak of Totalitarianism?" *Survey,* 23, No. 3 (Summer 1977/78), 62.

[30] The quotations are from Julien Freund, *The Sociology of Max Weber* (New York: Pantheon, 1968), pp. 62–63. See also H. H. Gerth and C. Wright Mills, eds. and trans., *From Max Weber: Essays in Sociology* (New York: Oxford University Press, 1956), pp. 59–61.

[31] Friedrich, op. cit., p. 126.

[32] On the "conflict model" see Carl A. Linden, *Khrushchev and the Soviet Leadership 1957–1964* (Baltimore, MD: The Johns Hopkins Press, 1966), pp. 1–9.

[33] Walter D. Connor, "Generations and Politics in the USSR," *Problems of Communism,* 25, No. 5 (Sept.–Oct. 1975), 24.

[34] Zbigniew Brzezinski, "Soviet Politics: From the Future to the Past?" in *The Dynamics of Soviet Politics,* eds. Paul Cocks, Robert V. Daniels, and Nancy Whittier Heer (Cambridge, MA: Harvard University Press, 1976), p. 342.

[35] The best work on the subject is William Taubman, "The Change to Change in Communist Systems: Modernization, Post Modernization, and Soviet Politics," in *Soviet Politics and Society in the 1970s,* eds. Henry W. Morton and Rudolf L. Tokes (New York: Free Press, 1974), pp. 369–91.

[36] The quotation is that of Susan Gross Solomon, who proposes "a temporary suspension of the passion for comparison and a new focus on the uniqueness of Soviet politics." Quoted by T. H. Rigby in a review of Solomon, ed., *Pluralism in the Soviet Union: Essays in Honour of H. Gordon Skilling,* in *Soviet Studies,* 36, No. 3 (July 1984), 450. Others who have urged treating the Soviet Union as unique include Alain Besançon, *The Soviet Syndrome* (New York: Harcourt, Brace, Jovanovich, 1978) and Mark Raeff, "Some Remarks on the Pipes-Nove Exchange," *Russia* No. 5–6 (1982), 124–26.

[37] Stephen F. Cohen, "The Friends and Foes of Change: Reformism and Conservatism in the Soviet Union," *The Soviet Union Since Stalin,* eds. Stephen F. Cohen, Alexander Rabinowitch and Robert Sharlet (Bloomington, IN: Indiana University Press, 1980), pp. 11–31. The quotations are from pp. 12, 13, 17, and 22.

[38] Alexander Yanov, *The Drama of the Soviet 1960s: A Lost Reform* (Berkeley, CA: Institute of International Studies, 1984), p. xii.

[39] The quotations are from *The New York Times,* Mar. 12, 1985, pp. 1 and 16, and Mar. 15, 1985, p. 1. Gorbachev's speech appeared in *Pravda,* Dec. 10, 1984.

[40] Another recent writing of this genre is Timothy J. Colton, *The Dilemma of Reform in the Soviet Union* (New York: Council on Foreign Relations, Inc., 1984). See especially the section of this book entitled "The Improbability of Fundamental Change," pp. 58–63. Colton believes that the most realistic scenario for change will involve what he calls moderate reform.

[41] Valerie Bunce, *Do New Leaders Make a Difference? Executive Succession and Public Policy Under Capitalism and Socialism* (Princeton, NJ: Princeton University Press, 1981). See esp. pp. 222–56.

SELECTED BIBLIOGRAPHY

BELL, DANIEL, "Ten Theories in Search of Reality." *World Politics,* 10, No. 3 (Apr. 1958), 327–65.

BESANÇON, ALAIN, *The Soviet Syndrome.* New York: Harcourt Brace Jovanovich, 1978.

BUNCE, VALERIE *Do New Leaders Make a Difference? Executive Succession and Public Policy Under Capitalism and Socialism.* Princeton, NJ: Princeton University Press, 1981.

CARRÈRE D'ENCAUSSE, HÉLÈNE, *Confiscated Power: How Soviet Russia Really Works.* New York: Harper & Row, 1982.

COHEN, STEPHEN F., ALEXANDER RABINOWITCH, and ROBERT SHARLET, eds., *The Soviet Union Since Stalin.* Bloomington, IN: Indiana University Press, 1980.

———, *Rethinking the Soviet Experience.* New York: Oxford University Press, 1985.

COLTON, TIMOTHY J., *The Dilemma of Reform in the Soviet Union.* New York: Council on Foreign Relations, Ind., 1984.

CRANKSHAW, EDWARD *Putting up with the Russians: Commentary and Criticism, 1947–1984.* New York: Viking Penguin, 1984.

CROUCH, MARTIN, and ROBERT PORTER, *Understanding Soviet Politics Through Literature: A Book of Readings.* London: George Allen & Unwin, 1984.

DEWHIRST, MARTIN, and ROBERT FARRELL, eds., *The Soviet Censorship.* Metuchen, NJ: Scarecrow, 1973.

FLERON, FREDERIC J., JR., ed., *Communist Studies and the Social Sciences: Essays on Methodology and Empirical Theory.* Chicago: Rand McNally, 1969.

FRIEDRICH, CARL J., MICHAEL CURTIS, and BENJAMIN R. BARBER, *Totalitarianism in Perspective:* (rev. Carl J. Friedrich). New York: Holt, Rinehart & Winston, 1966.

FRIEDRICH, CARL J., MICHAEL CURTIS, and BENJAMIN R. BARBER, *Totalitarianism in Perspective: Three Views,* New York: Holt, Rinehart & Winston, 1969.

GELB, LESLIE H., "What We Really Know About the Soviet Union," *The New York Times Magazine* (Oct. 28, 1984), 22.

HOUGH, JERRY F., and MERLE FAINSOD, *How the Soviet Union is Governed.* Cambridge, MA: Harvard University Press, 1979.

HOUGH, JERRY F., *The Soviet Union and Social Science Theory.* Cambridge, MA: Harvard University Press, 1977.

INKELES, ALEX, and RAYMOND A. BAUER, *The Soviet Citizen.* Cambridge, MA: Harvard University Press, 1959.

KANET, ROGER E., ed., *The Behavioral Revolution and Communist Studies.* New York: Free Press, 1971.

KELLEY, DONALD R., ed., *Soviet Politics in the Brezhnev Era.* New York: Holt, Rinehart & Winston, 1980.

MCCREA, BARBARA P., JACK C. PLANO, and GEORGE KLEIN, *The Soviet and East European Political Dictionary.* Santa Barbara, CA: ABC Clio Information Services, 1984.

MENZE, ERNEST A., ed., *Totalitarianism Reconsidered.* Port Washington, NY: Kennikat Press, 1981.

MURPHY, CULLEN, "Watching the Russians," *The Atlantic Monthly,* 251, No. 2 (February 1983), 33.

TARSCHYS, DANIEL, *The Soviet Political Agenda: Problems and Priorities, 1950–1970.* White Plains, NY: M. E. Sharpe, Inc., 1979.

YANOV, ALEXANDER, *The Drama of the 1960s: A Lost Reform.* Berkeley, CA: Institute of International Studies, 1984.

ZASLAVSKY, VICTOR, *The Neo-Stalinist State: Class, Ethnicity, and Consensus in Soviet Society.* Armonk, NY: M. E. Sharpe, 1982.

Appendix A

CONSTITUTION (FUNDAMENTAL LAW) OF THE UNION OF SOVIET SOCIALIST REPUBLICS*

The Great October Socialist Revolution, fought by the workers and peasants of Russia under the leadership of the Communist Party headed by Lenin, overthrew capitalist and landowner rule, broke the fetters of oppression, established the dictatorship of the proletariat, and created the Soviet state, a new type of state, the basic instrument for defending the gains of the revolution and for building socialism and communism. Humanity thereby began the epoch-making turn from capitalism to socialism.

After achieving victory in the Civil War and repulsing imperialist intervention, the Soviet government carried through far-reaching social and economic transformations and put an end once and for all to exploitation of man by man, antagonisms between classes, and strife between nationalities. The unification of the Soviet Republics in the Union of Soviet Socialist Republics multiplied the forces and opportunities of the peoples of the country in the building of socialism. Social ownership of the means of production and genuine democracy for the working masses were established. For the first time in the history of humanity a socialist society was created.

The strength of socialism was vividly demonstrated by the immortal feat of the Soviet people and their Armed Forces in achieving their historic victory in the Great Patriotic War. This victory consolidated the influence and international standing of the Soviet Union and created new opportunities for growth of the forces of socialism, national liberation, democracy, and peace throughout the world.

Continuing their creative endeavors, the working people of the Soviet Union have ensured rapid, all-round development of the country and steady improvement of the socialist system. They have consolidated the alliance of the working class, collective-farm peasantry, and people's intelligentsia and the friendship between the nations and nationalities of the USSR. The socio-political and ideological unity of

*Adopted at the Seventh (Special) Session of the Supreme Soviet of the USSR, Ninth Convocation, on Oct. 7, 1977.

Soviet society, in which the working class is the leading force, has been achieved. The aims of the dictatorship of the proletariat having been fulfilled, the Soviet state has become a state of the whole people. The leading role of the Communist Party, the vanguard of all the people, has grown.

In the USSR a developed socialist society has been built. At this stage, when socialism is developing on its own foundations, the creative forces of the new system and the advantages of the socialist way of life are becoming increasingly evident, and the working people are more and more widely enjoying the fruits of their great revolutionary gains.

It is a society in which powerful productive forces and a progressive science and culture have been created, in which the well-being of the people is constantly rising, and more and more favorable conditions are being provided for the all-round development of the individual.

It is a society of mature socialist social relations, in which, on the basis of the drawing together of all classes and social strata and the juridical and factual equality of all its nations and nationalities and their fraternal cooperation, a new historical community of people has been formed—the Soviet people.

It is a society of high organizational capacity, ideological commitment, and consciousness of the working people, who are patriots and internationalists.

It is a society in which the law of life is the concern of all for the good of each and concern of each for the good of all.

It is a society of true democracy, the political system of which ensures effective management of all public affairs, ever more active participation of the working people in running the state, and the combining of citizens' real rights and freedoms with their obligation and responsibility to society.

Developed socialist society is a necessary stage on the road to communism.

The supreme goal of the Soviet state is the building of a classless communist society in which there will be public, communist self-government. The main aims of the people's socialist state are: to lay the material and technical foundation of communism, to perfect socialist social relations and transform them into communist relations, to mold the citizen of communist society, to raise the people's living and cultural standards, to safeguard the country's security, and to further the consolidation of peace and development of international cooperation.

The Soviet people,

guided by the ideas of scientific communism and true to their revolutionary traditions,

relying on the great social, economic, and political gains of socialism,

striving for the further development of social democracy,

taking into account the international position of the USSR as part of the world system of socialism, and conscious of their internationalist responsibility,

preserving continuity of the ideas and principles of the first Soviet Constitution of 1918, the 1924 Constitution of the USSR and the 1936 Constitution of the USSR,

hereby affirm the principles of the social structure and policy of the USSR, and define the rights, freedoms, and obligations of citizens, and the principles of the organization of the socialist state of the whole people, and its aims, and proclaim these in this Constitution.

I. PRINCIPLES OF THE SOCIAL STRUCTURE AND POLICY OF THE USSR

Chapter 1 The Political System

ARTICLE 1. The Union of Soviet Socialist Republics is a socialist all-people's state expressing the will and interests of the workers, peasants, and intelligentsia, the working people of all the nations and nationalities of the country.

ARTICLE 2. All power in the USSR belongs to the people.

The people exercise state power through Soviets of People's Deputies, which constitute the political foundation of the USSR.

All other state bodies are under the control of, and accountable to, the Soviets of People's Deputies.

ARTICLE 3. The Soviet state is organized and functions on the principle of democratic centralism, namely the election of all bodies of state authority from the lowest to the highest, their accountability to the poeple, and the obligation of lower bodies to observe the decisions of higher ones. Democratic centralism combines central leadership with local initiative and creative activity and with the responsibility of each state body and official for the work entrusted to them.

ARTICLE 4. The Soviet state and all its bodies function on the basis of socialist legality, ensure the maintenance of law and order, and safeguard the interests of society and the rights and freedoms of citizens.

State organizations, social organizations and officials shall observe the Constitution of the USSR and Soviet laws.

ARTICLE 5. Major matters of state shall be submitted to nationwide discussion and put to a popular vote (referendum).

ARTICLE 6. The leading and guiding force of Soviet society and the nucleus of its political system, of state and social organizations, is the Communist Part of the Soviet Union. The CPSU exists for the people and serves the people.

The Community Party, armed with Marxism-Leninism, determines the general perspectives of the development of society and the line of domestic and foreign policy of the USSR, directs the great constructive work of the Soviet people, and imparts a planned, systematic, and theoretically substantiated character to their struggle for the victory of communism.

All party organizations shall function within the framework of the Constitution of the USSR.

ARTICLE 7. Trade unions, the All-Union Leninist Young Communist League, cooperatives, and other public organizations participate, in accordance with the aims laid down in their rules, in managing state and public affairs and in deciding political, economic, and social and cultural matters.

ARTICLE 8. Labor collectives take part in discussing and deciding state and public affairs, in planning production and social development, in training and placing personnel, and in discussing and deciding matters pertaining to the management of enterprises and institutions, the improvement of working and living conditions, and the use of funds allocated for developing production and for social and cultural purposes and financial incentives.

Labor collectives promote socialist competition, the spread of progressive methods of work, and the strengthening of discipline, educate their members in the spirit of communist morality and strive to enhance their political consciousness and raise their cultural level and skills and qualifications.

ARTICLE 9. The principal direction of the developing of the political system of Soviet society is the extension of socialist democracy, namely ever broader participation of citizens in managing the affairs of society and the state, continuous improvement of the machinery of state, heightening of the activity of public organizations, strengthening of the system of people's control, consolidation of the legal foundations of the functioning of the state and of public life, greater openness and publicity, and constant responsiveness to public opinion.

Chapter 2   The Economic System

ARTICLE 10. The foundation of the economic system of the USSR is socialist ownership of the means of production in the form of state property (belonging to all the people) and collective-farm and cooperative property.

Socialist ownership also embraces the property of trade unions and other public organizations which is necessary to carry out its statutory functions.

The state protects socialist property and provides conditions for its growth.

No one has the right to use socialist property for personal gain or other selfish ends.

ARTICLE 11. State property, that is, the common property of the Soviet people, is the principal form of socialist property.

The land, its minerals, waters, and forests are the exclusive property of the state. The state owns the basic means of production in industry, construction, and agriculture; means of transport and communication; the banks; the property of state-run trade organizations and public utilities and other state-run undertakings; most urban housing; and other property necessary for state purposes.

ARTICLE 12. The property of collective farms and other cooperative organizations and of their joint undertakings comprises the means of production and other assets which they require for the purposes laid down in their rules.

The land held by collective farms is secured to them for their free use in perpetuity.

The state promotes development of collective-farm and cooperative property and its drawing together with state property.

Collective farms, like other land users, are obliged to make effective and thrifty use of the land and to increase its fertility.

ARTICLE 13. Earned income forms the basis of the personal property of Soviet citizens. The personal property of citizens of the USSR may include articles of everyday use, personal consumption and convenience, the implements and other objects of a small holding, a house, and earned savings. The personal property of citizens and the right to inherit it are protected by the state.

Citizens may be granted the use of plots of land, made available in the manner prescribed by law, for a subsidiary small holding (including the keeping of livestock and poultry), for fruit and vegetable growing or for building an individual dwelling. Citizens are required to make rational use of the land allotted to them. The state and collective farms provide assistance to citizens in working their small holdings.

Property owned or used by citizens shall not serve as a means of deriving unearned income or be employed to the detriment of the interests of society.

ARTICLE 14. The source of the growth of social wealth and of the well-being of the people, and of each individual, is the labor, free from exploitation, of Soviet people.

The state exercises control over the measure of labor and of consumption in accordance with the principle of socialism: "From each according to his ability, to each according to his work." It fixes the rate of taxation on taxable income.

Socially useful work and its results determine the person's status in society. By combining material and moral incentives and encouraging innovation and a creative attitude to work, the state helps transform labor into the prime vital need of every Soviet citizen.

ARTICLE 15. The supreme goal of social production under socialism is the fullest possible satisfaction of the people's growing material and cultural and intellectual requirements.

Relying on the creative initiative of the working people, socialist emulation, and scientific and technological progress, and by improving the forms and methods of economic management, the state ensures the growth of the productivity of labor, raising of the efficiency of production and of the quality of work, and dynamic, planned, proportionate development of the economy.

ARTICLE 16. The economy of the USSR is an integral economic complex comprising all the elements of social production, distribution, and exchange on its territory.

The economy is managed on the basis of state plans for economic and social development, with due account of the sectoral and territorial principles, and by combining centralized direction with the managerial independence and initiative of enterprises, associations, and other organizations for which active use is made of economic accountability, profit cost, and other economic levers and incentives.

ARTICLE 17. In the USSR, the law permits individual labor in handicrafts, farming, the provision of services for the public, and other forms of activity based exclusively on the personal work of individual citizens and members of their families. The state makes regulations for such work to ensure that it serves the interests of society.

ARTICLE 18. In the interests of the present and future generations, the necessary steps are taken in the USSR to protect and make scientific, rational use of the land and its mineral and water resources and the plants and animals, to preserve the purity of air and water, ensure reproduction of natural wealth, and improve the human environment.

Chapter 3   Social Development and Culture

ARTICLE 19. The social basis of the USSR is the unbreakable alliance of the workers, peasants, and intelligentsia.

The state helps enhance the social homogeneity of society, namely the elimination of class differences and of the essential distinctions between town and country and between mental and physical labor and the all-round development and drawing together of all the nations and nationalities of the USSR.

ARTICLE 20. In accordance with the communist ideal—"The free development of each is the condition of the free development of all"—the state pursues the aim of giving citizens more and more real opportunities to apply their creative energies, abilities, and talents and to develop their personalities in every way.

ARTICLE 21. The state concerns itself with improving working conditions, safety and labor protection, and the scientific organization of work, and with reducing and ultimately eliminating all arduous physical labor through comprehensive mechanization and automation of production processes in all branches of the economy.

ARTICLE 22. A program is being consistently implemented in the USSR to convert agricultural work into a variety of industrial work, to extend the network of educational, cultural, and medical institutions, and of trade, public catering, service, and public utility facilities in rural localities, and transform hamlets and villages into well-planned and well-appointed settlements.

ARTICLE 23. The state pursues a steady policy of raising people's pay levels and real incomes through increase in productivity.

In order to satisfy the needs of the Soviet people more fully, social consumption funds are created. The state, with the broad participation of public organizations and work collectives, ensures the growth and just distribution of these funds.

ARTICLE 24. In the USSR, state systems of health protection, social security, trade and public catering, communal services and amenities, and public utilities operate and are being extended.

The state encourages cooperatives and other public organizations to provide all types of services for the population. It encourages the development of mass physical culture and sport.

ARTICLE 25. In the USSR there is a uniform system of public education, which is being constantly improved, that provides general education and vocational training for citizens, serves the communist education and intellectual and physical development of the youth, and trains them for work and social activity.

ARTICLE 26. In accordance with society's needs the state provides for the planned development of science and the training of scientific personnel and organizes introduction of the results of research into the economy and other spheres of life.

ARTICLE 27. The state concerns itself with protecting, augmenting, and making extensive use of society's cultural wealth for the moral and aesthetic education of the Soviet people, for raising their cultural level.

In the USSR, development of the professional, amateur, and folk arts is encouraged in every way.

Chapter 4 Foreign Policy

ARTICLE 28. The USSR steadfastly pursues a Leninist policy of peace and stands for the strengthening of the security of nations and broad international cooperation.

The foreign policy of the USSR is aimed at ensuring international conditions favorable for building communism in the USSR, safeguarding the state interests of the Soviet Union, consolidating the positions of world socialism, supporting the struggle of peoples for national liberation and social progress, preventing wars of aggression, achieving universal and complete disarmament, and consistently implementing the principle of the peaceful coexistence of states with different social systems.

In the USSR, war propaganda is banned.

ARTICLE 29. The USSR's relations with other states are based on observance of the following principles: sovereign equality; mutual renunciation of the use or threat of force; inviolability of frontiers; territorial integrity of states; peaceful settlement of disputes; noninterference in internal affairs; respect for human rights and fundamental freedoms; the equal rights of peoples and their right to decide their own destiny; cooperation among states; and fulfillment in good faith of obligations arising from the generally recognized principles and rules of international law and from the international treaties signed by the USSR.

ARTICLE 30. The USSR, as part of the world system of socialism and of the socialist community, promotes and strengthens friendship, cooperation, and comradely mutual assistance with other socialist countries on the basis of the principle of socialist internationalism and takes an active part in socialist economic integration and the socialist international division of labor.

Chapter 5 Defense of the Socialist Motherland

ARTICLE 31. Defense of the Socialist Motherland is one of the most important functions of the state and is the concern of the whole people.

In order to defend the gains of socialism, the peaceful labor of the Soviet people, and the sovereignty and territorial integrity of the state, the USSR maintains armed forces and has instituted universal military service.

The duty of the Armed Forces of the USSR to the people is to provide reliable defense of the Socialist Motherland and to be in constant combat readiness, guaranteeing that any aggressor is instantly repulsed.

ARTICLE 32. The state ensures the security and defense capability of the country, and supplies the Armed Forces of the USSR with everything necessary for that purpose.

The duties of state bodies, public organizations, officials, and citizens in regard to safeguarding the country's security and strengthening its defense capacity are defined by the legislation of the USSR.

II. THE STATE AND THE INDIVIDUAL

Chapter 6   Citizenship of the USSR Equality of Citizens' Rights

ARTICLE 33. Uniform federal citizenship is established for the USSR. Every citizen of a Union Republic is a citizen of the USSR.

The grounds and procedures for acquiring or forfeiting Soviet citizenship are defined by the Law on Citizenship of the USSR.

When abroad, citizens of the USSR enjoy the protection and assistance of the Soviet state.

ARTICLE 34. Citizens of the USSR are equal before the law, without distinction of origin, social or property status, race or nationality, sex, education, language, attitude to religion, type and nature of occupation, domicile, or other circumstances.

The equal rights of citizens of the USSR are guaranteed in all fields of economic, political, social, and cultural life.

ARTICLE 35. Women and men have equal rights in the USSR.

Exercise of these rights is ensured by according women equal access with men to education and vocational and professional training, equal opportunities in employment, remuneration, and promotion, and in social and political and cultural activity, and by special labor and health protection measures for women; by providing conditions enabling mothers to work; by legal protection and material and moral support for mothers and children, including paid leaves and other benefits for expectant mothers and mothers, and the gradual reduction of working time for mothers with small children.

ARTICLE 36. Citizens of the USSR of different races and nationalities have equal rights.

Exercise of these rights is ensured by a policy of all-round development and drawing together of all the nations and nationalities of the USSR, by educating citizens in the spirit of Soviet patriotism and socialist internationalism, and by the possibility to use their native language and the languages of other peoples of the USSR.

Any direct or indirect limitation of the rights of citizens or establishment of direct or indirect privileges on grounds of race or nationality and any advocacy of racial or national exclusiveness, hostility, or contempt are punishable by law.

ARTICLE 37. Citizens of other countries and stateless persons in the USSR are guaranteed the rights and freedoms provided by law, including the right to apply to a court and other state bodies for the protection of their personal, property, family, and other rights.

Citizens of other countries and stateless persons, when in the USSR, are obliged to respect the Constitution of the USSR and observe Soviet laws.

ARTICLE 38. The USSR grants the right of asylum to foreigners persecuted for defending the interests of the working people and the cause of peace, or for participation in the revolutionary and national-liberation movement, or for progressive social and political, scientific, or other creative activity.

Chapter 7   The Basic Rights, Freedoms, and Duties of Citizens of the USSR

ARTICLE 39. Citizens of the USSR enjoy in full the social, economic, political and personal rights and freedoms proclaimed and guaranteed by the Constitution of the USSR and by Soviet laws. The socialist system ensures enlargement of the rights and freedoms of citizens and continuous improvement of their living standards as social, economic, and cultural development programs are fulfilled.

Enjoyment by citizens of their rights and freedoms must not be to the detriment of the interests of society or the state or infringe the rights of other citizens.

ARTICLE 40. Citizens of the USSR have the right to work (that is, to guaranteed employment and pay in accordance with the quantity and quality of their work and not below the state-established minimum), including the right to choose their trade or profession, type of job, and work in accordance with their inclinations, abilities, training, and education, taking into account the needs of society.

This right is ensured by the socialist economic system, steady growth of the productive forces, free vocational and professional training, improvement of skills, training in new trades or professions, and development of the systems of vocational guidance and job placement.

ARTICLE 41. Citizens of the USSR have the right to rest and leisure.

This right is ensured by the establishment of a working week not exceeding forty-one hours for workers and other employees, a shorter working day in a number of trades and industries, and shorter hours for night work; by the provision of paid annual holidays, weekly days of rest, extension of the network of cultural, educational, and health-building institutions, and the development on a mass scale of sport, physical culture, camping, and tourism; by the provision of neighborhood recreational facilities and of other opportunities for rational use of free time.

The length of collective-farmers' working and leisure time is established by their collective farms.

ARTICLE 42. Citizens of the USSR have the right to health protection.

This right is ensured by free, qualified medical care provided by state health institutions; by extension of the network of therapeutic and health-building institutions; by the development and improvement of safety and hygiene in industry; by carrying out broad prophylactic measures; by measures to improve the environment; by special care for the health of youth, including prohibition of child labor, excluding the work done by children as part of the school curriculum; and by developing research to prevent and reduce the incidence of disease and ensure citizens a long and active life.

ARTICLE 43. Citizens of the USSR have the right to maintenance in old age, in sickness, and in the event of complete or partial disability or loss of the breadwinner.

This right is guaranteed by social insurance of workers and other employees and collective farmers; by allowances for temporary disability; by the provision by the state or by collective farms of retirement pensions, disability pensions, and pensions for loss of the breadwinner; by providing employment for the partially disabled; by care for the elderly and the disabled; and by other forms of social security.

ARTICLE 44. Citizens of the USSR have the right to housing.

This right is ensured by the development and upkeep of state and socially owned housing; by assistance for cooperative and individual house building; by fair distribution, under public control, of the housing that becomes available through fulfillment of the program of building well-appointed dwellings; and by low rents and low charges for utility services. Citizens of the USSR shall take good care of the housing allocated to them.

ARTICLE 45. Citizens of the USSR have the right to education.

This right is ensured by the free provision of all forms of education, by the institution of universal, compulsory secondary education, and the broad development of vocational, specialized secondary, and higher education, in which instruction is oriented toward practical activity and production; by the development of extramural, correspondence, and evening courses; by the provision of state scholarships and grants and privileges for students; by the free issue of school textbooks; by the opportunity to attend a school where teaching is in the native language; and by the provision of facilities for self-education.

ARTICLE 46. Citizens of the USSR have the right to enjoy cultural benefits.

This right is ensured by broad access to the cultural treasures of their own land and of the world, which are preserved in state and other public collections; by the development and fair distribution of cultural and educational institutions throughout the country; by the development of television and radio broadcasting and the publishing of books, newspapers, and periodicals, and by the extension of the free library service; and by the expansion of cultural exchanges with other countries.

ARTICLE 47. Citizens of the USSR, in accordance with the aims of building communism, are guaranteed freedom of scientific, technical, and artistic work. This freedom is ensured by broadening scientific research, encouraging invention and innovation, and developing literature and the arts. The state provides the necessary material conditions for this and support for voluntary societies and unions of workers in the arts, organizes introduction of inventions and innovations in production and other spheres of activity.

The rights of authors, inventors, and innovators are protected by the state.

ARTICLE 48. Citizens of the USSR have the right to take part in the management and administration of state and public affairs and in the discussion and adoption of laws and measures of All-Union and local significance.

This right is ensured by the opportunity to vote and to be elected to Soviets of People's Deputies and other elective state bodies and to take part in nationwide discussions and referendums, in people's control, in the work of state bodies, public organizations, and local community groups, and in meetings at places of work or residence.

ARTICLE 49. Every citizen of the USSR has the right to submit proposals to state bodies and public organizations for improving their activity and to criticize shortcomings in their work.

Officials are obliged, within established time limits, to examine citizens' proposals and requests, to reply to them, and to take appropriate action.

Persecution for criticism is prohibited. Persons guilty of such persecution shall be called to account.

ARTICLE 50. In accordance with the interests of the people and in order to strengthen and develop the socialist system, citizens of the USSR are guaranteed freedom of speech, of the press, and of assembly, meetings, street processions, and demonstrations.

Exercise of these political freedoms is ensured by putting public buildings, streets, and squares at the disposal of the working people and their organizations, broad dissemination of information; and by the opportunity to use the press, television, and radio.

ARTICLE 51. In accordance with the aims of building communism, citizens of the USSR have the right to associate in public organizations that promote their political activity and initiative and satisfaction of their various interests.

Public organizations are guaranteed conditions for successfully performing the functions defined in their rules.

ARTICLE 52. Citizens of the USSR are guaranteed freedom of conscience, that is, the right to profess or not to profess any religion and to conduct religious worship or atheistic propaganda. Incitement of hostility or hatred on religious grounds is prohibited.

In the USSR, the church is separated from the state and the school from the church.

ARTICLE 53. The family enjoys the protection of the state.

Marriage is based on the free consent of the woman and the man; the spouses are completely equal in their family relations.

The state helps the family by providing and developing a broad system of child-care institutions, by organizing and improving communal services and public catering, by paying grants on the birth of a child, by providing children's allowances and benefits for large families, and other forms of family allowances and assistance.

A RTICLE 54. Citizens of the USSR are guaranteed inviolability of the person. No one may be arrested except by a court decision or on the warrant of a procurator.

ARTICLE 55. Citizens of the USSR are guaranteed inviolability of the home. No one may, without lawful grounds, enter a home against the will of those residing in it.

ARTICLE 56. The privacy of citizens, and of their correspondence, telephone conversations, and telegraphic communications, is protected by law.

ARTICLE 57. Respect for the individual and protection of the rights and freedoms of citizens are the duty of all state bodies, public organizations, and officials.

Citizens of the USSR have the right to protection by the courts against encroachments on their honor and reputation, life and health, and personal freedom and property.

ARTICLE 58. Citizens of the USSR have the right to lodge a complaint against the actions of officials, state bodies, and public bodies. Complaints shall be examined according to the procedure and within the time limit established by law.

Actions by officials that contravene the law or exceed their powers and infringe the rights of citizens may be appealed against in a court in the manner prescribed by law.

Citizens of the USSR have the right to compensation for damage resulting from unlawful actions by state organizations and public organizations or by officials in the performance of their duties.

ARTICLE 59. The exercise of rights and freedoms is inseparable from the performance by the citizens of their duties.

Citizens of the USSR are obliged to observe the Constitution of the USSR and Soviet laws, comply with the rules of socialist community life, and uphold the honor and dignity of Soviet citizenship.

A RTICLE 60. It is the duty of, and a matter of honor for, every able-bodied citizen of the USSR to work conscientiously in his chosen, socially useful occupation and strictly to observe labor discipline. Evasion of socially useful work is incompatible with the principles of socialist society.

ARTICLE 61. Citizens of the USSR are obliged to preserve and protect socialist property. It is the duty of a citizen of the USSR to combat misappropriation and squandering of state and socially owned property and to make thrifty use of the people's wealth.

Persons encroaching in any way on socialist property shall be punished according to the law.

ARTICLE 62. Citizens of the USSR are obliged to safeguard the interests of the Soviet state and to enhance its power and prestige.

Defense of the Socialist Motherland is the sacred duty of every citizen of the USSR.

Betrayal of the Motherland is the gravest of crimes against the people.

A RTICLE 63. Military service in the ranks of the Armed Forces of the USSR is an honorable duty of Soviet citizens.

ARTICLE 64. It is the duty of every citizen of the USSR to respect the national dignity of other citizens and to strengthen friendship of the nations and nationalities of the multinational Soviet state.

A RTICLE 65. A citizen of the USSR is obliged to respect the rights and lawful interests of other persons, to be uncompromising toward antisocial behavior, and to help maintain public order.

ARTICLE 66. Citizens of the USSR are obliged to concern themselves with the upbringing of children, to train them for socially useful work, and to raise them as worthy members of socialist society. Children are obliged to care for their parents and help them.

ARTICLE 67. Citizens of the USSR are obliged to protect nature and conserve its riches.

ARTICLE 68. Concern for the preservation of historical monuments and other cultural values is a duty and obligation of citizens of the USSR.

ARTICLE 69. It is the internationalist duty of citizens of the USSR to promote friendship and cooperation with peoples of other lands and help maintain and strengthen world peace.

III. THE NATIONAL-STATE STRUCTURE OF THE USSR

Chapter 8 The USSR—A Federal State

ARTICLE 70. The Union of Soviet Socialist Republics is a unitary, federal, multinational state formed on the principle of socialist federalism as a result of the free self-determination of nations and the voluntary association of equal Soviet Socialist Republics.

The USSR embodies the state unity of the Soviet people and draws all its nations and nationalities together for the purpose of jointly building communism.

ARTICLE 71. The Union of Soviet Socialist Republics unites:

the Russian Soviet Federative Socialist Republic,
the Ukrainian Soviet Socialist Republic,
the Byelorussian Soviet Socialist Republic,
the Uzbek Soviet Socialist Republic,
the Kazakh Soviet Socialist Republic,
the Georgian Soviet Socialist Republic,
the Azerbaidzhan Soviet Socialist Republic,
the Lithuanian Soviet Socialist Republic,
the Moldavian Soviet Socialist Republic,
the Latvian Soviet Socialist Republic,
the Kirghiz Soviet Socialist Republic,
the Tajik Soviet Socialist Republic,
the Armenian Soviet Socialist Republic,
the Turkmen Soviet Socialist Republic,
the Estonian Soviet Socialist Republic.

ARTICLE 72. Each Union Republic shall retain the right freely to secede from the USSR.

ARTICLE 73. The jurisdiction of the Union of Soviet Socialist Republics, as represented by its highest bodies of state authority and administration, shall cover:

1. the admission of new republics to the USSR; endorsement of the formation of new autonomous republics and autonomous regions within Union Republics;
2. determination of the state boundaries of the USSR and approval of changes in the boundaries between Union Republics;
3. establishment of the general principles for the organization and functioning of republican and local bodies of state authority and administration;

4. the ensurance of uniformity of legislative norms throughout the USSR and establishment of the fundamentals of the legislation of the Union of Soviet Socialist Republics and Union Republics;

5. pursuance of a uniform social and economic policy; direction of the country's economy; determination of the main lines of scientific and technological progress and the general measures for rational exploitation and conservation of natural resources; the drafting and approval of state plans for the economic and social development of the USSR, and endorsement of reports on their fulfillment;

6. the drafting and approval of the consolidated Budget of the USSR and endorsement of the report on its execution; management of a single monetary and credit system; determination of the taxes and revenues forming the Budget of the USSR; and the formulation of prices and wages policy;

7. direction of the sectors of the economy and of enterprises and amalgamations under Union jurisdiction, and general direction of industries under Union-Republican jurisdiction;

8. issues of war and peace, defense of the sovereignty of the USSR and safeguarding of its frontiers and territory, and organization of defense; direction of the Armed Forces of the USSR;

9. state security;

10. representation of the USSR in international relations; the USSR's relations with other states and with international organizations; establishment of the general procedure for, and coordination of, the relations of Union Republics with other states and with international organizations; foreign trade and other forms of external economic activity on the basis of state monopoly;

11. control over observance of the Constitution of the USSR, and insurance of conformity of the Constitutions of Union Republics to the Constitution of the USSR;

12. and settlement of other matters of All-Union importance.

ARTICLE 74. The laws of the USSR shall have the same force in all Union Republics. In the event of a discrepancy between a Union-Republic law and an All-Union law, the law of the USSR shall prevail.

ARTICLE 75. The territory of the Union of Soviet Socialist Republics is a single entity and comprises the territories of the Union Republics.

The sovereignty of the USSR extends throughout its territory.

Chapter 9   The Union Soviet Socialist Republic

ARTICLE 76. A Union Republic is a sovereign Soviet socialist state that has united with other Soviet Republics in the Union of Soviet Socialist Republics.

Outside the spheres listed in Article 73 of the Constitution of the USSR, a Union Republic exercises independent authority on its territory.

A Union Republic shall have its own Constitution conforming to the Constitution of the USSR with the specific features of the Republic being taken into account.

ARTICLE 77. Union Republics take part in decision making in the Supreme Soviet of the USSR, the Presidium of the Supreme Soviet of the USSR, the Government of the USSR, and other bodies of the Union of Soviet Socialist Republics in matters that come within the jurisdiction of the Union of Soviet Socialist Republics.

A Union Republic shall ensure comprehensive economic and social development on its territory, facilitate exercise of the powers of the USSR on its territory, and implement the decisions of the highest bodies of state authority and administration of the USSR.

In matters that come within its jurisdiction, a Union Republic shall coordinate and control the activty of enterprises, institutions, and organizations subordinate to the Union.

ARTICLE 78. The territory of a Union Republic may not be altered without its consent. The boundaries between Union Republics may be altered by mutual agreement of the Republics concerned, subject to ratification by the Union of Soviet Socialist Republics.

ARTICLE 79. A Union Republic shall determine its division into territories, regions, areas, and districts and decide other matters relating to its administrative and territorial structure.

ARTICLE 80. A Union Republic has the right the enter into relations with other states, conclude treaties with them, exchange diplomatic and consular representatives, and take part in the work of international organizations.

ARTICLE 81. The sovereign rights of Union Republics shall be safeguarded by the USSR.

Chapter 10   The Autonomous Soviet Socialist Republic

ARTICLE 82. An Autonomous Republic is a constituent part of a Union Republic.

In spheres not within the jurisdiction of the Union of Soviet Socialist Republics and the Union Republic, an Autonomous Republic shall deal independently with matters within its jurisdiction.

An Autonomous Republic shall have its own Constitution conforming to the Constitutions of the USSR and the Union Republic with the specific features of the Autonomous Republic being taken into account.

ARTICLE 83. An Autonomous Republic takes part in decision making through the highest bodies of state authority and administration of the USSR and of the Union Republic, respectively, in matters that come within the jurisdiction of the USSR and the Union Republic.

An Autonomous Republic shall ensure comprehensive economic and social development on its territory, facilitate exercise of the powers of the USSR and the Union Republic on its territory, and implement decisions of the highest bodies of state authority and administration of the USSR and the Union Republic.

In matters within its jurisdiction, an Autonomous Republic shall coordinate and control the activity of enterprises, institutions, and organizations subordinate to the Union or the Union Republic.

ARTICLE 84. The territory of an Autonomous Republic may not be altered without its consent.

ARTICLE 85. The Russian Soviet Federative Socialist Republic includes the Bashkir, Buryat, Daghestan, Kabardin-Balkar, Kalmyk, Karelian, Komi, Mari, Mordovian, North Ossetian, Tatar, Tuva, Udmurt, Chechen-Ingush, Chuvash, and Yakut Autonomous Soviet Socialist Republics.

The Uzbek Soviet Socialist Republic includes the Kara-Kalpak Autonomous Soviet Socialist Republic.

The Georgian Soviet Socialist Republic includes the Abkhasian and Adzhar Autonomous Soviet Socialist Republics.

The Azerbaidzhan Soviet Socialist Republic includes the Nakhichevan Autonomous Soviet Socialist Republic.

Chapter 11   The Autonomous Region and Autonomous Area

ARTICLE 86. An Autonomous Region is a constituent part of a Union Republic or Territory. The Law on an Autonomous Region, upon submission by the Soviet of

People's Deputies of the Autonomous Region concerned, shall be adopted by the Supreme Soviet of the Union Republic.

ARTICLE 87. The Russian Soviet Federative Socialist Republic includes the Adygei, Gorno-Altai, Jewish, Karachai-Circassian, and Khakass Autonomous Regions.

The Georgian Soviet Socialist Republic includes the South Ossetian Autonomous Region.

The Azerbaidzhan Soviet Socialist Republic includes the Nagorno-Karabakh Autonomous Region.

The Tajik Soviet Socialist Republic includes the Gorno-Badakhshan Autonomous Region.

ARTICLE 88. An Autonomous Area is a constituent part of a Territory or Region. The Law on an Autonomous Area shall be adopted by the Supreme Soviet of the Union Republic concerned.

IV. SOVIETS OF PEOPLE'S DEPUTIES AND ELECTORAL PROCEDURE

Chapter 12   The System of Soviets of People's Deputies and the Principles of Their Work

ARTICLE 89. The Soviets of People's Deputies, that is, the Supreme Soviet of the USSR, the Supreme Soviets of Union Republics, the Supreme Soviets of Autonomous Republics, the Soviets of People's Deputies of Territories and Regions, the Soviets of People's Deputies of Autonomous Regions and Autonomous Areas, and the Soviets of People's Deputies of districts, cities, city districts, settlements, and villages shall constitute a single system of bodies of state authority.

ARTICLE 90. The term of the Supreme Soviet of the USSR, the Supreme Soviets of Union Republics, and the Supreme Soviets of Autonomous Republics shall be five years.

The term of local Soviets of People's Deputies shall be two-and-a-half years.

Elections to Soviets of People's Deputies shall be called not later than two months before the expiration of the term of the Soviet concerned.

ARTICLE 91. The most important matters within the jurisdiction of the respective Soviets of People's Deputies shall be considered and settled at their sessions.

Soviets of People's Deputies shall elect standing commissions and form executive-administrative and other bodies accountable to them.

ARTICLE 92. Soviets of People's Deputies shall form people's control bodies combining state control with control by the working people at enterprises, collective farms, institutions, and organizations.

People's control bodies shall check on the fulfillment of state plans and assignments, combat breaches of state discipline, localistic tendencies, narrow departmental attitudes, mismanagement, extravagance and waste, red tape and bureaucracy, and help improve the working of the state machinery.

ARTICLE 93. Soviets of People's Deputies shall direct all sectors of state, economic, and social and cultural development, either directly or through bodies instituted by them, take decisions and ensure their execution, and verify their implementation.

ARTICLE 94. Soviets of People's Deputies shall function publicly on the basis of collective, free, constructive discussion and decision making of systematic reporting back to them and the people by their executive-administrative and other bodies, and of involving citizens on a broad scale in their work.

Soviets of People's Deputies and the bodies set up by them shall systematically inform the public about their work and the decisions taken by them.

Chapter 13   The Electoral System

ARTICLE 95. Deputies to all Soviets shall be elected on the basis of universal, equal, and direct suffrage by secret ballot.

ARTICLE 96. Elections shall be universal: All citizens of the USSR who have reached the age of eighteen shall have the right to vote and to be elected, with the exception of persons who have been legally certified insane.

To be eligible for election to the Supreme Soviet of the USSR a citizen of the USSR must have reached the age of twenty-one.

ARTICLE 97. Elections shall be equal: Each citizen shall have one vote; all voters shall exercise the franchise on an equal footing.

ARTICLE 98. Elections shall be direct: Deputies to all Soviets of People's Deputies shall be elected by citizens by direct vote.

ARTICLE 99. Voting at elections shall be secret: Control over voters' exercise of the franchise is inadmissible.

ARTICLE 100. The following shall have the right to nominate candidates: branches and organizations of the Communist Party of the Soviet Union, trade unions, and the All-Union Leninist Young Communist League; cooperatives and other public organizations; work collectives and meetings of servicemen in their military units.

Citizens of the USSR and public organizations are guaranteed the right to free and all-round discussion of the political and personal qualities and competence of candidates and the right to campaign for them at meetings, in the press and on television and radio.

The expenses involved in holding elections to Soviets of People's Deputies shall be met by the state.

ARTICLE 101. Deputies to Soviets of People's Deputies shall be elected by constituencies.

A citizen of the USSR may not, as a rule, be elected to more than two Soviets of People's Deputies.

Elections to the Soviets shall be conducted by electoral commissions consisting of representatives of public organizations and work collectives and of meetings of servicemen in military units.

The procedure for holding elections to Soviets of People's Deputies shall be defined by the laws of the USSR and of Union and Autonomous Republics.

ARTICLE 102. Electors give mandates to their Deputies.

The appropriate Soviets of People's Deputies shall examine electors' mandates, take them into account in drafting economic and social development plans and in drawing up the budget, organize implementation of the mandates, and inform citizens about it.

Chapter 14   People's Deputies

ARTICLE 103. Deputies are the plenipotentiary representatives of the people in the Soviets of People's Deputies.

In the Soviets, Deputies deal with matters relating to state, economic, and social and cultural development, organize implementation of the decisions of the Soviets, and exercise control over the work of state bodies, enterprises, institutions, and organizations.

Deputies shall be guided in their activities by the interests of the state and shall take the needs of their constituents into account and work to implement their electors' mandates.

ARTICLE 104. Deputies shall exercise their powers without discontinuing their regular employment or duties.

During sessions of the Soviet, and so as to exercise their deputy's powers in other cases stipulated by law, Deputies shall be released from their regular employment or duties, with retention of their average earnings at their permanent place of work.

ARTICLE 105. A Deputy has the right to address inquiries to the appropriate state bodies and officials, who are obliged to reply to them at a session of the Soviet.

Deputies have the right to approach any state or public body, enterprise, institution, or organization on matters arising from their work as Deputies and to take part in considering the questions raised by them. The heads of the state or public bodies, enterprises, institutions, or organizations concerned are obliged to receive Deputies without delay and to consider their proposals within the time limit established by law.

ARTICLE 106. Deputies shall be ensured conditions for the unhampered and effective exercise of their rights and duties.

The immunity of Deputies, and other guarantees of their activity as Deputies, are defined in the Law on the Status of Deputies and other legislative acts of the USSR and of Union and Autonomous Republics.

ARTICLE 107. Deputies shall report on their work and on that of the Soviet to their constituents and to the work collectives and public organizations that nominated them.

Deputies who have not justified the confidence of their constituents may be recalled at any time by decision of a majority of the electors in accordance with the procedure established by law.

V. HIGHER BODIES OF STATE AUTHORITY AND ADMINISTRATION OF THE USSR

Chapter 15 The Supreme Soviet of the USSR

ARTICLE 108. The highest body of state authority of the USSR shall be the Supreme Soviet of the USSR.

The Supreme Soviet of the USSR is empowered to decide all questions within the jurisdiction of the Union of Soviet Socialist Republics, as defined by this Constitution.

The adoption and amendment of the Constitution of the USSR; admission of new Republics to the USSR; endorsement of the formation of new Autonomous Republics and Autonomous Regions; approval of the state plans for economic and social development of the Budget of the USSR and of reports on their execution; and the institution of bodies of the USSR accountable to it are the exclusive prerogatives of the Supreme Soviet of the USSR.

Laws of the USSR shall be enacted by the Supreme Soviet of the USSR or by a nationwide vote (referendum) held by decision of the Supreme Soviet of the USSR.

ARTICLE 109. The Supreme Soviet of the USSR shall consist of two chambers: the Soviet of the Union and the Soviet of Nationalities.

The two chambers of the Supreme Soviet of the USSR shall have equal rights.

ARTICLE 110. The Soviet of the Union and the Soviet of Nationalities shall have equal numbers of deputies.

The Soviet of the Union shall be elected by constituencies with equal populations.

The Soviet of Nationalities shall be elected on the basis of the following representation: thirty-two deputies from each Union Republic, eleven deputies from each Autonomous Republic, five deputies from each Autonomous Region, and one deputy from each Autonomous Area.

The Soviet of the Union and the Soviet of Nationalities, upon submission by the credentials commissions elected by them, shall decide on the validity of Deputies' credentials and, in cases in which the election law has been violated, shall declare the election of the Deputies concerned null and void.

ARTICLE 111. Each chamber of the Supreme Soviet of the USSR shall elect a Chairman and four Vice-Chairmen.

The Chairmen of the Soviet of the Union and of the Soviet of Nationalities shall preside over the sittings of the respective chambers and conduct their affairs.

Joint sittings of the chambers of the Supreme Soviet of the USSR shall be presided over alternately by the Chairman of the Soviet of the Union and the Chairman of the Soviet of Nationalities.

ARTICLE 112. Sessions of the Supreme Soviet of the USSR shall be convened twice a year.

Special sessions shall be convened by the Presidium of the Supreme Soviet of the USSR at its discretion or on the proposal of a Union Republic or of not less than one third of the Deputies of one of the chambers.

A session of the Supreme Soviet of the USSR shall consist of separate and joint sittings of the chambers, and of meetings of the standing commissions of the chambers, or commissions of the Supreme Soviet of the USSR held between the sittings of the chambers. A session may be opened and closed at either separate or joint sittings of the chambers.

ARTICLE 113. The right to initiate legislation in the Supreme Soviet of the USSR is vested in the Soviet of the Union and the Soviet of Nationalities, the Presidium of the Supreme Soviet of the USSR, the Council of Ministers of the USSR, Union Republics through their highest bodies of state authority, commissions of the Supreme Soviet of the USSR and standing commissions of its chambers, Deputies of the Supreme Soviet of the USSR, the Supreme Court of the USSR, and the Procurator-General of the USSR.

The right to initiate legislation is also vested in public organizations through their All-Union bodies.

ARTICLE 114. Bills and other matters submitted to the Supreme Soviet of the USSR shall be debated by its chambers at separate or joint sittings. Where necessary, a bill or other matter may be referred to one or more commissions for preliminary or additional consideration.

A law of the USSR shall be deemed adopted when it has been passed in each chamber of the Supreme Soviet of the USSR by a majority of the total number of its Deputies. Decisions and other acts of the Supreme Soviet of the USSR are adopted by a majority of the total number of Deputies of the Supreme Soviet of the USSR.

Bills and other very important matters of state may be submitted for nation-wide discussion by a decision of the Supreme Soviet of the USSR or its Presidium, taken on their own initiative or on the proposal of a Union Republic.

ARTICLE 115. In the event of disagreement between the Soviet of the Union and the Soviet of Nationalities, the matter at issue shall be referred for settlement to a conciliation commission formed by the chambers on a parity basis, after which it shall be considered for a second time by the Soviet of the Union and the Soviet of Nationalities at a joint sitting. If agreement is again not reached, the matter shall be postponed for debate at the next session of the Supreme Soviet of the USSR or submitted by the Supreme Soviet to a nationwide vote (referendum).

ARTICLE 116. Laws of the USSR and decisions and other acts of the Supreme Soviet of the USSR shall be published in the languages of the Union Republics over the signatures of the Chairman and Secretary of the Presidium of the Supreme Soviet of the USSR.

ARTICLE 117. A Deputy of the Supreme Soviet of the USSR has the right to address inquiries to the Council of Ministers of the USSR and to Ministers and the heads of other bodies formed by the Supreme Soviet of the USSR. The Council of Ministers of the USSR, or the official to whom the inquiry is addressed, is obliged to give a verbal or written reply within three days at the given session of the Supreme Soviet of the USSR.

ARTICLE 118. A Deputy of the Supreme Soviet of the USSR may not be prosecuted or arrested or incur a court-imposed penalty without the sanction of the Supreme Soviet of the USSR or, between its sessions, of the Presidium of the Supreme Soviet of the USSR.

ARTICLE 119. The Supreme Soviet of the USSR, at a joint sitting of its chambers, shall elect a Presidium of the Supreme Soviet of the USSR which shall be a standing body of the Supreme Soviet of the USSR, accountable to it for all its work and exercising the functions of the highest body of state authority of the USSR between sessions of the Supreme Soviet, within the limits prescribed by the Constitution.

ARTICLE 120. The Presidium of the Supreme Soviet of the USSR shall be elected from among the Deputies and shall consist of a Chairman, First Vice-Chairman, fifteen Vice-Chairmen (one from each Union Republic), a Secretary, and 21 members.

ARTICLE 121. The Presidium of the Supreme Soviet of the USSR shall:

1. name the date of elections to the Supreme Soviet of the USSR;
2. convene sessions of the Supreme Soviet of the USSR;
3. coordinate the work of the standing commissions of the chambers of the Supreme Soviet of the USSR;
4. ensure observance of the Constitution of the USSR and conformity of the Constitutions and laws of Union Republics to the Constitution and laws of the USSR;
5. interpret the laws of the USSR;
6. ratify and denounce international treaties of the USSR;
7. revoke decrees and resolutions of the Council of Ministers of the USSR and of the Councils of Ministers of Union Republics should they fail to conform to the law;
8. institute military and diplomatic ranks and other special titles and confer the highest military and diplomatic ranks and other special titles;
9. institute orders and medals of the USSR and honorific titles of the USSR, award orders and medals of the USSR, and confer honorific titles of the USSR;
10. grant citizenship of the USSR and rule on matters of the renunciation or deprivation of citizenship of the USSR and of granting asylum;
11. issue All-Union acts of amnesty and exercise the right of pardon;
12. appoint and recall diplomatic representatives of the USSR to other countries and to international organizations;
13. receive the letters of credence and recall of the diplomatic representatives of foreign states accredited to it;
14. form the Council of Defense of the USSR and confirm its composition; appoint and dismiss the high command of the Armed Forces of the USSR;

15. proclaim martial law in particular localities or throughout the country in the interests of defense of the USSR;
16. order general or partial mobilization;
17. between sessions of the Supreme Soviet of the USSR, proclaim a state of war in the event of an armed attack on the USSR or when it is necessary to meet international treaty obligations relating to mutual defense against aggression;
18. and exercise other powers vested in it by the Constitution and laws of the USSR.

ARTICLE 122. The Presidium of the Supreme Soviet of the USSR, between sessions of the Supreme Soviet of the USSR and subject to submission for its confirmation at the next session, shall:

1. amend existing legislative acts of the USSR when necessary;
2. approve changes in the boundaries between Union Republics;
3. form and abolish Ministries and State Committees of the USSR on the recommendation of the Council of Ministers of the USSR;
4. relieve individual members of the Council of Ministers of the USSR of their responsibilities and appoint persons to the Council of Ministers on the recommendation of the Chairman of the Council of Ministers of the USSR.

ARTICLE 123. The Presidium of the Supreme Soviet of the USSR promulgates edicts and adopts decrees.

ARTICLE 124. On expiration of the term of the Supreme Soviet of the USSR, the Presidium of the Supreme Soviet of the USSR shall retain its powers until the newly elected Supreme Soviet of the USSR has elected a new Presidium.

The newly elected Supreme Soviet of the USSR shall be convened by the outgoing Presidium of the Supreme Soviet of the USSR within two months of the elections.

ARTICLE 125. The Soviet of the Union and the Soviet of Nationalities shall elect standing commissions from among the Deputies to make a preliminary review of matters coming within the jurisdiction of the Supreme Soviet of the USSR, to promote execution of the laws of the USSR and other acts of the Supreme Soviet of the USSR and its Presidium, and to check on the work of state bodies and organizations. The chambers of the Supreme Soviet of the USSR may also set up joint commissions on a parity basis.

When it deems it necessary, the Supreme Soviet of the USSR sets up commissions of inquiry and audit and commissions on any other matter.

All state and public bodies, organizations, and officials are obliged to meet the requests of the commissions of the Supreme Soviet of the USSR and of its chambers and submit the requisite materials and documents to them.

The commissions' recommendations shall be subject to consideration by state and public bodies, institutions, and organizations. The commissions shall be informed, within the prescribed time limit, of the results of such consideration or of the action taken.

ARTICLE 126. The Supreme Soviet of the USSR shall supervise the work of all state bodies accountable to it.

The Supreme Soviet of the USSR shall form a Committee of People's Control of the USSR to head the system of people's control.

The organization and procedure of people's control bodies are defined by the Law on People's Control in the USSR.

ARTICLE 127. The procedure of the Supreme Soviet of the USSR and of its bodies shall be defined in the Rules and Regulations of the Supreme Soviet of the

USSR and other laws of the USSR enacted on the basis of the Constitution of the USSR.

Chapter 16   The Council of Ministers of the USSR

ARTICLE 128. The Council of Ministers of the USSR, that is, the Government of the USSR, is the highest executive and administrative body of state authority of the USSR.

ARTICLE 129. The Council of Ministers of the USSR shall be formed by the Supreme Soviet of the USSR at a joint sitting of the Soviet of the Union and the Soviet of Nationalities and shall consist of the Chairman of the Council of Ministers of the USSR, First Vice-Chairmen and Vice-Chairmen, Ministers of the USSR, and Chairmen of the State Committees of the USSR.

The Chairmen of the Council of Ministers of Union Republics shall be *ex officio* members of the Council of Ministers of the USSR.

The Supreme Soviet of the USSR, on the recommendation of the Chairman of the Council of Ministers of the USSR, may include in the Government of the USSR the heads of other bodies and organizations of the USSR.

The Council of Ministers of the USSR shall tender its resignation to a newly elected Supreme Soviet of the USSR at its first session.

ARTICLE 130. The Council of Ministers of the USSR shall be responsible and accountable to the Supreme Soviet of the USSR and, between sessions of the Supreme Soviet of the USSR, to the Presidium of the Supreme Soviet of the USSR.

The Council of Ministers of the USSR shall report regularly on its work to the Supreme Soviet of the USSR.

ARTICLE 131. The Council of Ministers of the USSR is empowered to deal with all matters of state administration within the jurisdiction of the Union of Soviet Socialist Republics insofar as, under the Constitution, they do not come within the competence of the Supreme Soviet of the USSR or the Presidium of the Supreme Soviet of the USSR.

Within its powers the Council of Ministers of the USSR shall:

1.   ensure direction of economic, social, and cultural development; draft and implement measures to promote the well-being and cultural development of the people, to develop science and engineering, to ensure rational exploitation and conservation of natural resources, to consolidate the monetary and credit system, to pursue a uniform prices, wages, and social security policy, and to organize state insurance and a uniform system of accounting and statistics; and organize the management of industrial, constructional, and agricultural enterprises and amalgamations, transport and communications undertakings, banks, and other organizations and institutions of All-Union subordination;

2.   draft current and long-term state plans for the economic and social development of the USSR and the Budget of the USSR and submit them to the Supreme Soviet of the USSR; take measures to execute the state plans and Budget; and to report to the Supreme Soviet of the USSR on the implementation of the plans and Budget;

3.   implement measures to defend the interests of the state, protect socialist property and maintain public order, and guarantee and protect citizens' rights and freedoms;

4.   take measures to ensure state security;

5.   exercise general direction of the development of the Armed Forces of the

USSR and determine the annual contingent of citizens to be called up for active military service;

6. provide general direction in regard to relations with other states, foreign trade, and economic, scientific, technical, and cultural cooperation of the USSR with other countries; take measures to ensure fulfillment of the USSR's international treaties; and ratify and denounce intergovernmental international agreements;

7. and when necessary, form committees, central boards, and other departments under the Council of Ministers of the USSR to deal with matters of economic, social, and cultural development and defense.

ARTICLE 132. A Presidium of the Council of Ministers of the USSR, consisting of the Chairman, the First Vice-Chairmen, and Vice-Chairmen of the Council of Ministers of the USSR, shall function as a standing body of the Council of Ministers of the USSR to deal with questions relating to guidance of the economy and with other matters of state administration. Upon a decision of the Council of Ministers of the USSR, other members of the Government of the USSR may also be included in the Presidium of the Council of Ministers of the USSR.

ARTICLE 133. The Council of Ministers of the USSR, on the basis of and in pursuance of, the laws of the USSR and other decisions of the Supreme Soviet of the USSR and its Presidium, shall issue decrees and resolutions and verify their execution. The decrees and resolutions of the Council of Ministers of the USSR shall be binding throughout the USSR.

ARTICLE 134. The Council of Ministers of the USSR has the right, in matters within the jurisdiction of the Union of Soviet Socialist Republics, to suspend execution of decisions and resolutions of the Councils of Ministers of the USSR and of other bodies subordinate to it.

ARTICLE 135. The Council of Ministers of the USSR shall coordinate and direct the work of All-Union and Union-Republican ministries, state committees of the USSR, and other bodies subordinate to it.

All-Union ministries and state committees of the USSR shall direct the work of the branches of administration entrusted to them, or exercise interbranch administration, throughout the territory of the USSR directly or through bodies set up by them.

Union-Republican ministries and state committees of the USSR direct the work of the branches of administration entrusted to them, or exercise interbranch administration, as a rule, through the corresponding ministries and state committees and other bodies of Union Republics, and directly administer individual enterprises and amalgamations of Union subordination. The procedure for transferring enterprises and amalgamations from Republic or local subordination to Union subordination shall be defined by the Presidium of the Supreme Soviet of the USSR.

Ministries and state committees of the USSR shall be responsible for the condition and development of the spheres of administration entrusted to them; within their competence, they issue orders and other acts on the basis of, and in execution of, the laws of the USSR and other resolutions of the Supreme Soviet of the USSR and its Presidium, and of decisions and ordinances of the Council of Ministers of the USSR, and organize and verify their implementation.

ARTICLE 136. The competence of the Council of Ministers of the USSR and its Presidium, the procedure for their work, relationships between the Council of Ministers and other state bodies, and the list of All-Union and Union-Republican ministries and state committees of the USSR are defined, on the basis of the Constitution, in the Law on the Council of Ministers of the USSR.

VI. BASIC PRINCIPLES OF THE STRUCTURE OF THE BODIES OF STATE AUTHORITY AND ADMINISTRATION IN UNION REPUBLICS

Chapter 17 Higher Bodies of State Authority and Administration of a Union Republic

ARTICLE 137. The highest body of state authority of a Union Republic shall be the Supreme Soviet of that Republic.

The Supreme Soviet of a Union Republic is empowered to deal with all matters within the jurisdiction of the Republic under the Constitutions of the USSR and the Republic.

Adoption and amendment of the Constitution of a Union Republic; endorsement of state plans for economic and social development, of the Republic's Budget, and of reports on their fulfillment; and the formation of bodies accountable to the Supreme Soviet of the Union Republic are the exclusive prerogative of that Supreme Soviet.

Laws of a Union Republic shall be enacted by the Supreme Soviet of the Union Republic or by a popular vote (referendum) held by decision of the Republic's Supreme Soviet.

ARTICLE 138. The Supreme Soviet of a Union Republic shall elect a Presidium, which is a standing body of that Supreme Soviet and accountable to it for all its work. The composition and powers of the Presidium of the Supreme Soviet of a Union Republic shall be defined in the Constitution of the Union Republic.

ARTICLE 139. The Supreme Soviet of a Union Republic shall form a Council of Ministers of the Union Republic, that is, the Government of that Republic, which shall be the highest executive and administrative body of state authority in the Republic.

The Council of Ministers of a Union Republic shall be responsible and accountable to the Supreme Soviet of that Republic or, between sessions of the Supreme Soviet, to its Presidium.

ARTICLE 140. The Council of Ministers of a Union Republic issues decisions and ordinances on the basis of, and in pursuance of, the legislative acts of the USSR and of the Union Republic, and of decisions and resolutions of the Council of Ministers of the USSR, and shall organize and verify their execution.

ARTICLE 141. The Council of Ministers of a Union Republic has the right to suspend the execution of decisions and resolutions of the Councils of Ministers of Autonomous Republics, to rescind the decisions and orders of the Executive Committees of Soviets of People's Deputies of Territories, Regions, and cities (that is, cities under Republic jurisdiction), and of Autonomous Regions, and in Union Republics not divided into regions, of the Executive Committees of district and corresponding city Soviets of People's Deputies.

ARTICLE 142. The Council of Ministers of a Union Republic shall coordinate and direct the work of the Union-Republican and Republican ministries and of state committees of the Union Republic and other bodies under its jurisdiction.

The Union-Republican ministries and state committees of a Union Republic shall direct the branches of administration entrusted to them, or exercise interbranch control, and shall be subordinate to both the Council of Ministers of the Union Republic and the corresponding Union-Republican ministry or state committee of the USSR.

Republican ministries and state committees shall direct the branches of administration entrusted to them, or exercise interbranch control, and shall be subordinate to the Council of Ministers of the Union Republic.

Chapter 18   Higher Bodies of State Authority and Administration of an Autonomous Republic

ARTICLE 143.   The highest body of state authority of an Autonomous Republic shall be the Supreme Soviet of that Republic.

Adoption and amendment of the Constitution of an Autonomous Republic; endorsement of state plans for economic and social development and of the Republic's Budget; and the formation of bodies accountable to the Supreme Soviet of the Autonomous Republic are the exclusive prerogative of that Supreme Soviet.

Laws of an Autonomous Republic shall be enacted by the Supreme Soviet of the Autonomous Republic.

ARTICLE 144.   The Supreme Soviet of an Autonomous Republic shall elect a Presidium of the Supreme Soviet of the Autonomous Republic and shall form a Council of Ministers of the Autonomous Republic, that is, the Government of that Republic.

Chapter 19   Local Bodies of State Authority and Administration

ARTICLE 145.   The bodies of state authority in Territories, Regions, Autonomous Regions, Autonomous Areas, districts, cities, city districts, settlements, and rural communities shall be the corresponding Soviets of People's Deputies.

ARTICLE 146.   Local Soviets of People's Deputies shall deal with all matters of local significance in accordance with the interests of the whole state and of the citizens residing in the area under their jurisdiction, implement decisions of higher bodies of state authority, guide the work of lower Soviets of People's Deputies, take part in the discussion of matters of Republican and All-Union significance, and submit their proposals concerning them.

Local Soviets of People's Deputies shall direct state, economic, social and cultural development within their territory; endorse plans for economic and social development and the local budget; exercise general guidance over state bodies, enterprises, institutions, and organizations subordinate to them; ensure observance of the laws, maintenance of law and order, and protection of citizens' rights; and help strengthen the country's defense capacity.

ARTICLE 147.   Within their powers, local Soviets of People's Deputies shall ensure the comprehensive, all-round economic and social development of their areas; exercise control over the observance of legislation by enterprises, institutions, and organizations subordinate to higher authorities and located in their area; and coordinate and supervise their activity as regards land use, nature conservation, building, employment of manpower, production of consumer goods, and social, cultural, communal, and other services and amenities for the public.

ARTICLE 148.   Local Soviets of People's Deputies shall decide matters within the powers accorded them by the legislation of the USSR and of the appropriate Union Republic and Autonomous Republic. Their decisions shall be binding on all enterprises, institutions, and organizations located in their areas and on officials and citizens.

ARTICLE 149.   The executive-administrative bodies of local Soviets shall be the Executive Committees elected by them from among their deputies.

Executive Committees shall report on their work at least once a year to the

Soviets that elected them and to meetings of citizens at their places of work or residence.

ARTICLE 150. Executive Committees of local Soviets of People's Deputies shall be directly accountable both to the Soviet that elected them and to the higher executive and administrative body.

VII. JUSTICE, ARBITRATION, AND PROCURATOR'S SUPERVISION

Chapter 20   Courts and Arbitration

ARTICLE 151. In the USSR justice is administered only by the courts.

In the USSR there are the following courts: the Supreme Court of the USSR; the Supreme Courts of Union Republics; the Supreme Courts of Autonomous Republics; Territorial, Regional, and city courts; courts of Autonomous Regions; courts of Autonomous Areas; district (city) people's courts; and military tribunals in the Armed Forces.

ARTICLE 152. All courts in the USSR shall be formed on the principle of the election of judges and people's assessors.

People's judges of district (city) people's courts shall be elected for a term of five years by the citizens of the district (city) on the basis of universal, equal, and direct suffrage by secret ballot. People's assessors of district (city) people's courts shall be elected for a term of two-and-a-half years at meetings of citizens at their places of work or residence by a show of hands.

Higher courts shall be elected for a term of five years by the corresponding Soviet of People's Deputies.

The judges of military tribunals shall be elected for a term of five years by the Presidium of the Supreme Soviet of the USSR and people's assessors for a term of two-and-a-half years by meetings of servicemen.

Judges and people's assessors are responsible and accountable to their electors or the bodies that elected them, shall report to them, and may be recalled by them in the manner prescribed by law.

ARTICLE 153. The Supreme Court of the USSR is the highest judicial body in the USSR and supervises the administration of justice by the courts of the USSR and Union Republics within the limits established by law.

The Supreme Court of the USSR shall be elected by the Supreme Soviet of the USSR and shall consist of a Chairman, Vice-Chairmen, members, and people's assessors. The Chairmen of the Supreme Courts of Union Republics are *ex officio* members of the Supreme Court of the USSR.

The organization and procedure of the Supreme Court of the USSR are defined in the Law on the Supreme Court of the USSR.

ARTICLE 154. The hearing of civil and criminal cases in all courts is collegial; in courts of first instance, cases are heard with the participation of people's assessors. In the administration of justice, people's assessors have all the rights of a judge.

ARTICLE 155. Judges and people's assessors are independent and subject only to the law.

ARTICLE 156. Justice is administered in the USSR on the principle of the equality of citizens before the law and the court.

ARTICLE 157. Proceedings in all courts shall be open to the public. Hearings *in camera* are only allowed in cases provided for by law, with observance of all the rules of judicial procedure.

ARTICLE 158. A defendant in a criminal action is guaranteed the right to defense.

ARTICLE 159. Judicial proceedings shall be conducted in the language of the Union Republic, Autonomous Republic, Autonomous Region, or Autonomous Area, or in the language spoken by the majority of the people in the locality. Persons participating in court proceedings who do not know the language in which they are being conducted shall be ensured the right to become fully acquainted with the materials in the case, the services of an interpreter during the proceedings, and the right to address the court in their own language.

ARTICLE 160. No one may be adjudged guilty of a crime and subjected to punishment as a criminal except by the sentence of a court and in conformity with the law.

ARTICLE 161. Colleges of advocates are available to give legal assistance to citizens and organizations. In cases provided for by legislation, citizens shall be given legal assistance free of charge.

The organization and procedure of the bar are determined by legislation of the USSR and Union Republics.

ARTICLE 162. Representatives of public organizations and of work collectives may take part in civil and criminal proceedings.

ARTICLE 163. Economic disputes between enterprises, institutions, and organizations are settled by state arbitration bodies within the limits of their jurisdiction.

The organization and manner of functioning of state arbitration bodies are defined in the Law on State Arbitration in the USSR.

Chapter 21   The Procurator's Office

ARTICLE 164. Supreme power of supervision over the strict and uniform observance of laws by all ministries, state committees and departments, enterprises, institutions and organizations, executive-administrative bodies of local Soviets of People's Deputies, collective farms, cooperatives and other public organizations, officials and citizens is vested in the Procurator-General of the USSR and procurators subordinate to him.

ARTICLE 165. The Procurator-General of the USSR is appointed by the Supreme Soviet of the USSR and is responsible and accountable to it and, between sessions of the Supreme Soviet, to the Presidium of the Supreme Soviet of the USSR.

ARTICLE 166. The procurators of Union Republics, Autonomous Republics, Territories, Regions and Autonomous Regions are appointed by the Procurator-General of the USSR. The procurators of Autonomous Areas and district and city procurators are appointed by the Procurators of Union Republics, subject to confirmation by the Procurator-General of the USSR.

ARTICLE 167. The term of office of the Procurator-General of the USSR and all lower-ranking procurators shall be five years.

ARTICLE 168. The agencies of the Procurator's Office exercise their powers independently of any local bodies whatsoever and are subordinate solely to the Procurator-General of the USSR.

The organization and procedure of the agencies of the Procurator's Office are defined in the Law on the Procurator's Office of the USSR.

VIII.   THE EMBLEM, FLAG, ANTHEM, AND CAPITAL OF THE USSR

ARTICLE 169. The State Emblem of the Union of Soviet Socialist Republics is a hammer and sickle on a globe depicted in the rays of the sun and framed by ears of wheat, with the inscription "Workers of All Countries, Unite!" in the languages of the Union Republics. At the top of the Emblem is a five-pointed star.

ARTICLE 170. The State Flag of the Union of Soviet Socialist Republics is a rectangle of red cloth with a hammer and sickle depicted in gold in the upper corner next to the staff and with a five-pointed red star edged in gold above them. The ratio of the width of the flag to its length is 1 to 2.

ARTICLE 171. The State Anthem of the Union of Soviet Socialist Republics is confirmed by the Presidium of the Supreme Soviet of the USSR.

ARTICLE 172. The Capital of the Union of Soviet Socialist Republics is the city of Moscow.

IX. THE LEGAL FORCE OF THE CONSTITUTION OF THE USSR AND PROCEDURE FOR AMENDING THE CONSTITUTION

ARTICLE 173. The Constitution of the USSR shall have supreme legal force. All laws and other acts of state bodies shall be promulgated on the basis of and in conformity with it.

ARTICLE 174. The Constitution of the USSR may be amended by a decision of the Supreme Soviet of the USSR adopted by a majority of not less than two-thirds of the total number of Deputies of each of its chambers.

Appendix B

RULES OF THE COMMUNIST PARTY OF THE SOVIET UNION*

The Communist Party of the Soviet Union is the militant, tested vanguard of the Soviet people, uniting on a voluntary basis the advanced, most socially conscious part of the working class, the collective farm peasantry and the intelligentsia of the USSR.

Founded by V. I. Lenin as the vanguard of the working class, the Communist Party has traversed a glorious path of struggle; it led the working class and the working peasantry to the victory of the Great October Socialist Revolution and to the establishment of the dictatorship of the proletariat in our country. Under the leadership of the Communist Party, the exploiter classes were eliminated in the Soviet Union, and the social, political and ideological unity of the multinational Soviet society has taken shape and is constantly growing stronger. Socialism has triumphed completely and finally. The proletarian state has developed into the state of all the people.

The CPSU, while remaining in its class essence and ideology a Party of the working class, has become a Party of all the people.

The Party exists for the people and serves the people. It is the highest form of sociopolitical organization, the nucleus of the political system, and the leading and guiding force of Soviet society. The Party defines the general prospects for the country's development, ensures scientific guidance for the people's constructive activity, and imparts an organized, planned and purposeful nature to their struggle to achieve the ultimate goal—the victory of communism.

The CPSU organizes its work on the basis of unswerving observance of the Leninist norms of Party life and the principles of democratic centralism, collective leadership, the comprehensive development of inner-Party democracy, the creative activeness of Communists, criticism and self-criticsm, and broad public openness.

Ideological and organizational unity, the monolithic solidarity of the Party's

*As adopted by the Twenty-Seventh Party Congress, Mar. 1, 1986.

ranks and a high degree of conscious discipline on the part of all Communists are an inviolable law of the life of the CPSU. Any manifestation of factionalism or cliquishness is incompatible with Marxist-Leninist Party spirit and with Party membership. The Party expels persons who violate the CPSU's Program and Statutes and who, by their behavior, compromise the lofty name of Communist.

In all its activity, the CPSU is guided by the Marxist-Leninist teaching and by its Program, which defines the tasks of the systematic and comprehensive improvement of socialism and of the further advance of Soviet society toward communism on the basis of the acceleration of the country's social and economic development.

While creatively developing Marxist-Leninism, the CPSU resolutely combats all manifestations of revisionism and dogmatism, which are profoundly alien to revolutionary theory.

The Communist Party of the Soviet Union is a component part of the international Communist movement. It firmly adheres to the tested Marxist-Leninist principles of proletarian, socialist internationalism, actively promotes the strengthening of the cooperation and cohesion of the fraternal socialist countries, the consolidation of the world system of socialism and the unity of the international Communist and workers' movement, and displays solidarity with the peoples that are struggling for national and social liberation, against imperialism and for the preservation of peace.

I. Party Members, Their Duties and Rights

1. Any citizen of the Soviet Union who accepts the Party Program and Statutes, actively participates in the construction of communism, works in one of the Party organizations, carries out Party decisions and pays membership dues may be a member of the CPSU.

2. It is the duty of a Party member:

(a) to firmly and steadfastly carry out the Party's general line and directives, to explain the CPSU's domestic and foreign policy to the masses, to organize the working people for its implementation, and to facilitate the strengthening and expansion of the Party's ties with the people;

(b) to set an example of a conscientious, creative attitude toward labor and a high level of organization and discipline, and to safeguard and increase socialist property—the economic basis of the Soviet social system. To persistently strive for an increase in production efficiency, steady growth in labor productivity, and the introduction in the national economy of the achievements of present-day science and technology; to improve his qualifications, to support and disseminate advanced experience, and to be an active champion of everything new and progressive;

(c) to actively participate in the political life of the country and in the administration of state and public affairs, to set an example in the performance of civic duty, and to actively facilitate the ever fuller implementation of the socialist self-government of the people;

(d) to master Marxist-Leninist theory, to expand his political and cultural horizons, and to promote in every way an increase in Soviet people's consciousness and their ideological and moral growth. To wage a resolute struggle against all manifestations of bourgeois ideology, private-property mentality, religious prejudices and other views and customs that are alien to the socialist way of life;

(e) to strictly observe the norms of communist morality, to affirm the principle of social justice that is inherent in socialism, to place public interests above personal ones, to show modesty, decency, sensitivity and attention toward people, to respond promptly to the needs of the working people, and to be truthful and honest with the Party and the people;

(f) to consistently propagate the ideas of proletarian, socialist internationalism and Soviet patriotism among the masses of the working people, to wage a struggle against manifestations of nationalism and chauvinism, to actively promote the strengthening of friendship among the peoples of the USSR and fraternal ties with the socialist countries and with the proletarians and working people of the whole world;

(g) to promote in every way the strengthening of the defensive might of the USSR, and to wage a tireless struggle for peace and friendship among peoples;

(h) to strengthen the ideological and organizational unity of the Party, to safeguard the Party against the infiltration into its ranks of people unworthy of the lofty title of Communist, to display vigilance, and to keep Party and state secrets;

(i) to develop criticism and self-criticism, to boldly disclose shortcomings and strive for their removal, to combat ostentation, conceit, complacency, parochialism, departmentalism and hoodwinking, to administer a resolute rebuff to all attempts to suppress criticism, to oppose all actions detrimental to the Party and the state and to report them to Party bodies, up to and including the CPSU Central Committee;

(j) to steadfastly carry out the Party line in the selection of cadres according to their political, business and moral qualities. To be uncompromising in all cases in which the Leninist principles of the selection and upbringing of cadres are violated;

(k) to observe Party and state discipline, which is equally binding on all Party members. The Party has one discipline and one law for all Communists, regardless of their services or the positions they hold.

3.   A Party member has the right:

(a) to elect and be elected to Party bodies;

(b) to freely discuss questions of the Party's policy and practical activity at Party meetings, conferences and Congresses, at meetings of Party committees and in the Party press, to submit proposals, and to openly express and uphold his opinion until the organization has adopted a decision;

(c) to criticize any Communist, regardless of the position he holds, at Party meetings, conferences and Congresses and at plenary sessions of the committees of any Party body. Persons guilty of suppressing criticism or persecuting anyone for criticism are to be held to strict Party accountability, up to and including expulsion from the ranks of the CPSU;

(d) to personally participate in Party meetings and bureau and committee meetings when the question of his activity or conduct is under discussion;

(e) to address questions, statements or proposals to Party bodies at any level, up to and including the CPSU Central Committee, and to demand an answer on the substance of his address.

4.   Admission to Party membership is conducted exclusively on an individual basis. Membership in the Party is open to socially conscious and active workers, peasants and representatives of the intelligentsia who are devoted to the cause of communism. New members are admitted from among candidate members who have completed the established period as candidates.

Persons who have reached the age of 18 may be admitted to the Party. Young people up to 25 years of age may join the Party only through the Young Communist League.

The procedure for the admission of candidate members to full Party membership is as follows:

(a) applicants for Party membership are to submit recommendations from three CPSU members who have been Party members for at least five years and who know the applicants from having worked with them on the job or in public activity for at least one year.

Note 1. YCL members applying for admission to the Party present a recommendation from the district or city YCL committee, which is equivalent to a recommendation from one Party member.

Note 2. Members and candidate members of the CPSU Central Committee are to refrain from making recommendations;

(b) the question of admission to the Party is discussed and decided by a general meeting of the primary Party organization; its decision is considered to be adopted if at least two-thirds of the Party members present at the meeting vote for it, and it goes into effect after confirmation by the district Party committee or, in cities that are not divided into boroughs, by the city Party committee.

Those who have recommended an applicant are not required to be present during the discussion of the person's admission to the Party. Admission to the Party is conducted at open meetings, as a rule;

(c) citizens of the USSR who were previously members of Communist and Workers' Parties of other countries are admitted to the Communist Party of the Soviet Union on the basis of the rules established by the CPSU Central Committee.

5. Those who recommend applicants are responsible to the Party organizations for the objectivity of their description of the recommended individuals' political, business and moral qualities, and for providing them with assistance in their ideological-political growth.

6. The length of Party service for individuals admitted to Party membership is calculated from the day on which the general meeting of the primary Party organization decides to admit a given candidate to Party membership.

7. The procedure for registering Party members and candidate members and for transferring them from one organization to another is determined by relevant instructions of the CPSU Central Committee.

8. The question of a Party member or candidate member who has not paid his membership dues for three months without valid reason is subject to discussion in the primary Party organization. Should it turn out that the Party member or candidate member has in effect lost contact with the Party organization, he shall be considered to have dropped out of the Party; the primary Party organization shall adopt a decision to this effect and submit it to the district or city Party committee for ratification.

9. A Party member or candidate member who fails to perform his statutory duties or commits other offenses shall be called to account, and the following penalties may be imposed on him: admonition, reprimand (or severe reprimand), or reprimand (or severe reprimand) to be entered in his permanent record. The highest Party penalty is expulsion from the Party.

For minor offenses, measures of Party upbringing and influence in the form of comradely criticism, Party censure, warnings or reproof should be taken.

A Communist who has committed an offense must answer for it, first of all, to his primary Party organization. When a Communist is called to Party account by a higher agency, the primary Party organization is to be informed.

In examining the question of calling a Communist to Party account, maximum attention and a thorough analysis of the grounds for the charges brought against him must be ensured.

No later than one year after a penalty is imposed on a Party member, the Party organization gives him a hearing to learn how he has rectified his shortcomings.

10. The question of expelling a Communist from the Party is decided by a general meeting of the primary Party organization. A decision of the primary Party organization on expulsion from the Party is considered adopted if at least two-thirds of the Party members present at the meeting vote for it, and it comes into force after the district or city Party committee ratifies it.

Until a district or city Party committee ratifies a decision to expel a Communist from the CPSU, his Party card or candidate's card remains in his hands, and he has the right to attend closed Party meetings.

A person expelled from the Party retains the right to submit an appeal within two months to higher Party bodies, up to and including the CPSU Central Committee.

11. The question of calling to Party account members and candidate members of the Union-Republic Communist Party Central Committees and of territory, province, region, city and district Party committees, as well as members of inspection commissions, is discussed in the primary Party organization.

Decisions of Party organizations to impose penalties on members and candidate members of these Party committees and members of inspection commissions are adopted by the regular procedure.

The proposals of Party organizations regarding expulsion from the CPSU are reported to the Party committee of which the Communist in question is a member. A decision to expel from the Party a member or candidate member of a Union-Republic Communist Party Central Committee or a territory, province, region, city or district Party committee or a member of an inspection commission is adopted at a plenary session of the appropriate committee by a two-thirds majority vote of its members.

The question of expelling from the Party a member or candidate member of the CPSU Central Committee or a member of the CPSU Central Auditing Commission is decided by a Party Congress or, in the interval between Congresses, by a plenary session of the Central Committee, with a two-thirds majority of the Central Committee members voting to expel.

12. A Party member has a twofold responsibility for violating Soviet laws—to the state and to the Party. Individuals who have committed offenses punishable under criminal procedure are expelled from the ranks of the CPSU.

13. Appeals by those who have been expelled from the Party or who have received penalties, as well as decisions of Party organizations to expel Party members, are reviewed by the appropriate Party agencies no later than two months from the date of their receipt.

II. Candidates for Party Membership

14. Those joining the Party pass through a candidate stage, which is essential in order that the candidate may more thoroughly acquaint himself with the CPSU Program and Statutes and prepare for Party membership. The Party organization is to help the candidate prepare for admission to Party membership and is to verify his personal qualities through practical deeds and the performance of Party and public assignments.

The period of candidacy is set at one year.

15. The procedure for admitting candidates (individual admission, presentation of recommendations, the decision of the primary organization on admission and its ratification) is identical with that for admission to Party membership.

16. Upon expiration of the period of candidacy, the primary Party organization examines and decides the question of admitting the candidate to Party membership. If during his period of candidacy the candidate has not proved himself and, because of his personal qualities, cannot be admitted to CPSU membership, the Party organization decides to refuse him admission to Party membership, and after this decision is ratified by the district or city Party committee, he is considered dropped from candidacy for CPSU membership.

17. Candidates for Party membership participate in all the activities of the Party organization and enjoy the right to a consultative voice at Party meetings. Candidates for Party membership may not be elected to executive Party bodies or as delegates to Party conferences and Congresses.

18. Candidates for CPSU membership pay the same Party dues as Party members.

III. The Organizational Structure of the Party, Inner-Party Democracy

19. The guiding principle of the organizational structure and of the entire life and activity of the Party is democratic centralism, which means:

(a) the election of all Party executive bodies, from bottom to top;

(b) periodic reporting by Party agencies to their Party organizations and to higher bodies;

(c) strict Party discipline and subordination of the minority to the majority;

(d) the unconditionally binding nature of the decisions of higher bodies on lower ones.

20. The Party is built on a territorial-production basis: Primary organizations are created at the Communists' places of work and are united in district organizations, city organizations, etc., on a territorial basis. The organization uniting the Communists of a given territory is higher than all of its component Party organizations.

21. All Party organizations are autonomous in deciding local questions, provided that these decisions are not at variance with Party policy.

22. The highest executive body of a Party organization is: the general meeting or conference (for primary organizations), the conference (for district, city, region, province and territory organizations), and the Congress (for the Union-Republic Communist Parties and the Communist Party of the Soviet Union). A meeting, a conference or a Congress is legally competent if over half the members of the Party organization or elected delegates are present.

23. The general meeting, conference or Congress elects a bureau or a committee, which is the executive body and directs all of the current work of the Party organization.

An apparatus is set up with the CPSU Central Committee, the Union-Republic Communist Party Central Committees and the territory, province, region, city and district Party committees for current work with respect to organizing Party decisions and verifying their fulfillment and providing assistance to lower-level organizations of their activity.

The CPSU Central Committee determines the structure and staff of the Party apparatus.

24. Elections to Party bodies are conducted by closed (secret) ballot. At meetings in primary and shop organizations having fewer than 15 Party members and in Party groups, elections of secretaries and deputy secretaries of Party organizations and Party group organizers may be conducted by open ballot, with the Communists' agreement.

In elections, all Party members have the unrestricted right to challenge candidates and to criticize them. Voting is conducted separately on each candidate. Candidates who receive more than one-half of the vote of the participants in the meeting, conference or Congress are considered elected.

The principle of the systematic renewal of the membership of Party bodies and the continuity of leadership is observed in elections to all Party bodies—from primary organizations to the CPSU Central Committee.

25. A member or candidate member of the CPSU Central Committee, a Union-Republic Communist Party Central Committee or a territory, province, region, city or district Party committee must by his entire activity justify the high trust placed in him. If a member or candidate member of a Party committee has sullied his honor and dignity, he cannot remain a member of that committee.

The question of removing a member or candidate member of a Party committee from that body is decided at a plenary session of that committee. The decision is considered adopted if at least two-thirds of the members of the Party committee vote for it by closed (secret) ballot.

The question of removing members of the CPSU Central Auditing Commission and the auditing commissions of local Party organizations from these commissions is decided at their meetings, under the procedure stipulated for members and candidate members of Party committees.

26.   The free and businesslike discussion of questions of Party policy in individual Party organizations or in the Party as a whole is an inalienable right of the Party member and an important principle of inner-Party democracy. The high creative activeness of Communists, open criticism and self-criticism and strong Party discipline, which should be conscious and not mechanical, can be ensured only on the basis of inner-Party democracy.

Discussions on disputed or insufficiently clear questions are possible within the framework of individual organizations or of the Party as a whole.

General Party discussion is necessary:

(a) if this need is recognized by several Party organizations at the province or republic level;

(b) if there is not a sufficiently firm policy within the Central Committee on major questions of Party policy;

(c) if the CPSU Central Committee deems it necessary to consult with the entire Party on specific questions of policy.

Broad discussion, especially discussion on an all-union scale, of questions of Party policy should be conducted in such a way as to ensure the free expression of the views of Party members and to exclude the possibility of attempts to form factional groupings destructive to Party unity or of attempts to split the Party.

27.   The highest principle of Party leadership is collectivity of leadership—an indispensable condition for the normal activity of Party organizations, the correct upbringing of cadres and the development of the activeness and independence of Communists, and a reliable guarantee against the adoption of willful, subjectivist decisions, the manifestation of a cult of personality, and the violation of Leninist norms of Party life.

Collective leadership does not absolve officials of personal responsibility for their assigned tasks.

28.   In the intervals between Congresses and conferences, the CPSU Central Committee, the Union-Republic Communist Party Central Committees and the territory, province, region, city and district Party committees are to provide Party organizations with regular information about their work.

29.   Meetings of the aktivs of district, city, region, province and territory Party organizations and of the Union-Republic Communist Parties are convened to discuss major Party decisions and to work out measures for implementing them, as well as to consider questions of local life.

30.   Permanent or temporary commissions and working groups for various questions of Party work may be created in the Party committees, and other forms of enlisting Communists in the activy of Party bodies on a voluntary basis may also be used.

IV.   Higher Party Bodies

31.   The supreme body of the Communist Party of the Soviet Union is the Party Congress. Regular Congresses are convened by the Central Committee at least once every five years. The convocation of a Party Congress and its agenda are announced at least one and one-half months before the Congress. Extraordinary

Congresses are convened by the Party Central Committee on its own initiative or on the demand of at least one-third of the total number of Party members represented at the preceding Party Congress. Extraordinary Congresses are convened on two-months' notice. A Congress is considered valid if at least one-half of all Party members are represented at it.

The norms of representation at a Party Congress are fixed by the Central Committee.

32.   If no extraordinary Congress is convened by the Party Central Committee within the term indicated in Art. 31, the organizations demanding the convocation of an extraordinary Congress have the right to form an organizational committee enjoying the rights of the Party Central Committee with respect to convening an extraordinary Congress.

33.   The Congress:

(a) hears and approves reports of the Central Committee, the Central Auditing Commission and other central organizations;

(b) reviews, amends and approves the Party Program and Statutes;

(c) determines the Party line on questions of domestic and foreign policy, and considers and decides major questions of Party and state life and communist construction;

(d) elects the Central Committee and the Central Auditing Commission.

34.   The number of members of the Central Committee and the Central Auditing Commission is determined, and their members are elected, by the Congress. In the event of vacancies in the membership of the Central Committee, they are filled from among the candidate members of the CPSU Central Committee elected by the Congress.

35.   In the intervals between Congresses, the Central Committee of the Communist Party of the Soviet Union directs all activity of the Party and of local Party agencies, carries out the selection and placement of executive cadres, directs the work of central state and public organizations of the working people, creates various agencies, institutions and enterprises of the Party and directs their activity, appoints the editorial boards of the central newspapers and magazines that operate under its control, distributes the funds in the Party budget and supervises its implementation.

The Central Committee represents the CPSU in its relations with other parties.

36.   The CPSU Central Auditing Commission checks on compliance with the established procedure for handling matters; work relating to the examination of letters, applications and complaints from working people by central Party bodies, and the correct fulfillment of the Party budget, including the payment, receipt and accounting of Party members' dues, as well as on the financial and economic activity of enterprises and institutions of the CPSU Central Committee.

37.   The CPSU Central Committee holds at least one plenary session every six months. Candidate members of the Central Committee attend plenary sessions of the Central Committee with the right to a consultative voice.

38.   The Central Committee of the Communist Party of the Soviet Union elects a Politburo to direct the work of the Party between plenary sessions of the Central Committee and a Secretariat to direct current work, chiefly in selecting cadres and organizing the verification of fulfillment of Party decisions. The Central Committee elects the General Secretary of the CPSU Central Committee.

39.   The Central Committee of the Communist Party of the Soviet Union organizes a Party Control Committee under the Central Committee.

The Party Control Committee under the CPSU Central Committee:

(a) verifies the observance of Party discipline by CPSU members and candidate members, and calls to account Communists who are guilty of violating the Party Program and Statutes or Party and state discipline, as well as violators of Party morality;

(b) examines appeals against decisions of the Union-Republic Communist Party Central Committees and territory and province Party committees concerning expulsion from the Party and Party penalties.

40.   In the interval between Party Congresses, the CPSU Central Committee may, when necessary, convene an All-Union Party Conference to discuss urgent questions of Party policy. The procedure for holding an All-Union Party Conference is determined by the CPSU Central Committee.

V.   The Party's Republic, Territory, Province, Region, City and District Organizations

41.   The republic, territory, province, region, city and district Party organizations and their committees are guided in their activity by the CPSU Program and Statutes, conduct all work relating to the implementation of Party policy within the given republic, territory, province, region, city or district, and organize the fulfillment of the CPSU Central Committee's directives.

42.   The basic duties of the republic, territory, province, region, city and district Party organizations and their executive agencies are:

(a)   political and organizational work among the masses and their mobilization for the accomplishment of the tasks of communist construction, the all-round development of industrial and agricultural production and an increase in its efficiency, the fulfillment and overfulfillment of state plans, and the ensuring of steady growth in the material welfare and cultural level of the working people;

(b)   the organization of ideological work, the propaganda of Marxism-Leninism, an increase in the communist awareness of the working people, guidance of the local press, radio and television, and supervision over the activity of scientific, cultural and public education institutions;

(c)   guidance of the Soviets of People's Deputies, the trade unions, the Young Communist League, the cooperatives and other public organizations through the Communists who work in them, the ever broader enlistment of the working people in the work of these organizations, and the development of the independent activity and activeness of the masses as a necessary condition for the further deepening of socialist democracy;

(d)   strict observance of the Leninist principles and methods of leadership, the establishment of a Leninist style in Party work and in all spheres of state and economic management, the ensuring of the unity of ideological, organizational and economic activity, and the strengthening of state and labor discipline, order and organization in all sectors;

(e)   the implementation of personnel policy and the cultivation in cadres of a spirit of communist ideological conviction, moral purity and lofty responsibility to the Party and the people for assigned tasks;

(f)   the organization of various Party institutions and enterprises within the bounds of their republic, territory, province, region, city or district and the guidance of their activity; the distribution of Party funds in their organizations; the regular provision of information to the higher Party agency, and accountability to it for their work.

The Executive Bodies of Republic, Territory and Province Party Organizations

43.   The highest body of the province, territory or republic Party organization is the province or territory Party conference or the Congress of the Union-Republic

Communist Party, and, in the intervals between them, the province committee, the territory committee or the Union-Republic Communist Party Central Committee.

44.   A regular province or territorial conference is convened by the province or territory committee once every two or three years. A regular Congress of a Union-Republic Communist Party is convened by the Communist Party Central Committee at least once every five years. Extraordinary conferences and Congresses are convened by a decision of a province or territory committee or of a Union-Republic Communist Party Central Committee or at the demand of one-third of the total number of members of the organizations belonging to a province, territory or republic Party organization.

The norms of representation at province and territorial conferences and at Congresses of Union-Republic Communist Parties are fixed by the appropriate Party committees.

Province and territory conferences and Congresses of Union-Republic Communist Parties hear reports of the province and territory committees, the Union-Republic Communist Party Central Committees and auditing commissions, discuss at their discretion other questions of Party, economic and cultural construction, and elect province and territory committees, Union-Republic Communist Party Central Committees, auditing commissions and delegates to the CPSU Congress.

In the intervals between Congresses of the Union-Republic Communist Parties, the Communist Party Central Committees, when necessary, may convene republic Party conferences to discuss major questions of the activity of Party organizations. The procedure for holding republic Party conferences is determined by the Union-Republic Communist Party Central Committees.

45.   Province and territory committees and Union-Republic Communist Party Central Committees elect bureaus, which include the secretaries of the committees. Secretaries are required to have been Party members for at least five years. The plenary sessions of committees confirm the chairmen of Party control commissions, the heads of the committees' departments and the editors of Party newspapers and magazines.

Secretaries are set up in province and territory Party committees and Union-Republic Communist Party Central Committees to examine current questions and to check on fulfillment.

46.   Plenary sessions of province and territory committees and Union-Republic Communist Party Central Committees are convened at least once every four months.

47.   The province and territory committees and the Union-Republic Communist Party Central Committees direct the region, city and district Party organizations, check on their activity, and regularly hear reports of region, city and district Party committees.

The Party organizations of the autonomous republics, as well as of autonomous and other provinces forming parts of territories and Union republics, work under the direction of the territory committees or the Union-Republic Communist Party Central Committees.

The Executive Bodies of Region, City, District (Rural and Urban) Party Organizations

48.   The highest body of the region, city or district Party organization is the region, city or district Party conference or the general meeting of Communists convened by the region, city or district committee once every two or three years; extraordinary conferences are convened by decision of the committee or at the

request of one-third of the total number of Party members in the Party organization in question.

The region, city or district conference (meeting) hears reports of the committee and the auditing commission, discusses at its discretion other questions of the Party, economic and cultural construction, elects the region, city or district committee, the auditing commission, and delegates to the province or territory conference or the Congress of the Union-Republic Communist Party.

The norms of representation at the region, city or district conference are fixed by the appropriate Party committee.

49.   The region, city or district committee elects the bureau, which includes the secretaries of the committee, and also approves the heads of the committees' departments, the chairmen of Party commissions and the editors of newspapers. The secretaries of region, city and district committees are required to have been Party members for at least five years. The committees' secretaries are confirmed by the province or territory Party committee or by the Union-Republic Communist Party Central Committee.

50.   The region, city and district committees create the primary Party organizations, direct their activity, regularly hear reports on the work of Party organizations, and keep registers of Communists.

51.   Plenary sessions of region, city and district committees are convened at least once every three months.

VI. The Party's Primary Organizations

52.   The primary organizations are the foundation of the Party.

Primary Party organizations are set up at the places of work of Party members—at plants and factories, on state farms and other enterprises, on collective farms, in units of the Armed Forces, institutions, educational establishments, etc., provided that there are at least three Party members. When necessary, territorial primary Party organizations may also be set up at the places of residence of Communists.

In individual cases, and with the authorization of the province or territory Party committee or the Union-Republic Communist Party Central Committee, Party organizations may be set up within the framework of several enterprises that make up a production association and are located, as a rule, on the territory of a single borough or of several boroughs of the same city.

53.   At enterprises, on collective farms and in institutions where there are more than 50 CPSU members and candidate members, Party organizations may be set up within the overall primary Party organization in shops, sectors, livestock sections, brigades, departments, etc., with the authorization of the district, city or region Party committee.

Party groups by brigades and other production units may be set up within shop, sector and other organizations, as well as within primary Party organizations having fewer than 50 members and candidate members.

54.   The highest body of the primary Party organization is the Party meeting, which is held at least once a month. In Party organizations that have shop organizations, both general and shop meetings are held at least once every two months.

In large Party organizations with more than 300 Communists, the general Party meeting is convened, when necessary, at times fixed by the Party committee or on the demand of several shop Party organizations.

55.   The primary or shop Party organization elects a bureau, with the number of its members fixed by the Party meeting, for a term of two or three years to conduct current work. Primary and shop Party organizations with fewer than 15 Party

members elect a secretary and a deputy secretary of the Party organization instead of a bureau.

At least one year's membership in the Party is mandatory for secretaries of primary and shop Party organizations.

Posts for Party officials released from their regular work are not set up in primary Party organizations with fewer than 150 Party members, as a rule.

56. At large enterprises and in institutions with over 300 Party members and candidate members, and also in organizations with over 100 Communists, in cases in which special production conditions or territorial dispersion make it necessary, Party committees may be set up, with the authorization of the province or territory Party committee, or the Union-Republic Communist Party Central Committee, and the shop Party organizations of these enterprises and institutions are granted the rights of primary Party organizations.

The Party organizations of collective farms, state farms and other agricultural enterprises may set up Party committees, provided that they have 50 Communists.

In Party organizations with over 500 Communists, in individual cases and with the authorization of the province or territory Party committee or the Union-Republic Communist Party Central Committee, Party committees may be set up in large shops, and the Party organizations of production sectors may be given the rights of primary Party organizations.

Party committees are elected for terms of two or three years, and the number of their members is fixed by the general Party meeting or conference.

At Party meetings, Party committees, Party bureaus and the secretaries of primary and shop Party organizations provide the Communists with regular information about their work.

57. The Party committees of primary organizations with over 1,000 Communists may, with the authorization of the Union-Republic Communist Party Central Committee, be granted the rights of district Party committees with respect to questions of admission to the CPSU, keeping a register of Party members and candidate members, and hearing personal cases involving Communists.

These organizations may elect expanded Party committees, within which a bureau is formed to direct current work.

58. The primary Party organization is guided in its activity by the CPSU Program and Statutes. It is the political nucleus of the labor collective, it conducts work directly among the working people, rallies them around the Party, organizes them for the fulfillment of the tasks of communist construction, and takes an active part in implementing the Party's personnel policy.

The primary Party organization:

(a) admits new members to the CPSU;

(b) instills in Communists a spirit of devotion to the cause of the Party, ideological conviction and communist morality;

(c) organizes the study by Communists of Marxist-Leninist theory in close connection with the practice of communist construction, and combats all attempts at revisionist distortions of Marxism-Leninism and its dogmatic interpretation and all manifestations of bourgeois ideology and backward views and sentiments;

(d) concerns itself with enhancing the vanguard role of the Communists in labor and in the sociopolitical and economic life of enterprises, collective farms, institutions, educational establishments, etc.;

(e) acts as the organizer of the working people in accomplishing the tasks of economic and social development, heads socialist competition for the fulfillment of state plans and the pledges of the working people, the intensification of production, the raising of labor productivity and output quality and the wide-scale introduction in production of scientific and technical achievements and advanced experience, mobilizes the working people for finding internal reserves, strives for the rational and economical use of material, labor and financial resources, and shows concern for protecting and multiplying public wealth and for improving people's working and living conditions;

(f) conducts mass-agitation and propaganda work; instills in the working people a spirit of devotion to the ideas of communism and the friendship of peoples; helps them to develop high political standards; ensures, in accordance with the law, the enhancement of the labor collective's role in managing enterprises and institutions; and promotes the development of activeness in trade union, YCL and other public organizations;

(g) on the basis of the broad development of criticism and self-criticism, combats manifestations of red tape, parochialism and departmentalism and violations of state, labor and production discipline, thwarts attempts to deceive the state, and takes measures against laxity, mismanagement and waste at enterprises, on collective farms and in institutions;

(h) assists the region, city and district Party committees in all their activity, and is accountable to them for its work.

59.   The primary Party organizations of enterprises in industry, transportation, communications, construction, material and technical supply, trade, public catering and communal and consumer services of collective farms, state farms and other agricultural enterprises, of design organizations, design bureaus, research institutes, educational institutions and cultural enlightenment and medical institutions enjoy the right to supervise the activity of management.

The Party organizations of ministries, state committees and other central and local Soviet and economic institutions and departments exercise supervision over the work of the administrative apparatus in fulfilling directives of the Party and the government and observing Soviet laws. They should actively influence the improvement of the work of the apparatus, instill in staff members a spirit of lofty responsibility for their assigned tasks, take measures to strengthen state discipline and to improve services to the population, wage a resolute struggle against bureaucracy and red tape, and promptly inform the appropriate Party bodies of shortcomings in the work of institutions, as well as of individual personnel, regardless of the posts they occupy.

Note. Primary Party organizations may form commissions to exercise the right of supervision over the activity of management and over the work of the apparatus in certain areas of production activity.

VII.   The Party and State and Public Organizations

60.   The CPSU exercises guidance of state and public organizations through the Communists who work in them. The Party strives to ensure that state and public organizations fully exercise their constitutional powers and statutory rights and duties and facilitate the broad enlistment of the working people in their work. Party organizations operate within the framework of the USSR Constitution; they do not supplant Soviet, trade union, cooperative and other public organizations, and they do not permit the commingling of the functions of the Party and other agencies or unneeded parallelism in work.

61.   Party groups are organized at congresses, conferences and meetings convened by state and public organizations, as well as in the elective bodies of these organizations, if there are at least three Party members. The tasks of these groups are an all-round increase in the influence of the Party and the implementation of its policy in the corresponding non-Party organizations, the development of the activeness of Communists and an increase in their responsibility for the state of affairs in these organizations, the strict observance of democratic norms in their activity, the

strengthening of Party and state discipline, the combating of red tape, and verification of the fulfillment of Party and Soviet directives.

62.   The work of Party groups in non-Party organizations is directed by the appropriate Party body: the CPSU Central Committee, a Union-Republic Communist Party Central Committee, or a territory, province, region, city or district Party committee.

VIII.   The Party and the Young Communist League

63.   The All-Union Leninist Young Communist League is an independent public and political organization of young people and an active assistant and reserve of the Party. The YCL helps the Party to instill a spirit of communism in young people, to enlist them in the practical construction of a new society and in the administration of state and public affairs, and to mold a generation of comprehensively developed people.

64.   YCL organizations enjoy the right of broad initiative in discussing and submitting to the appropriate Party organizations questions of the work of enterprises, collective farms or institutions, and they take a direct part in the resolution of these questions, especially if they concern the labor, everyday life, instruction and upbringing of young people. YCL organizations are called upon to be active champions of Party directives in all spheres of production and public life.

65.   The YCL works under the guidance of the Communist Party of the Soviet Union. The work of local YCL organizations is directed and supervised by the appropriate republic, territory, province, region, city and district Party organizations.

In their work in the communist upbringing of young people, local Party agencies and primary Party organizations rely on YCL organizations, support their useful undertakings and provide all possible assistance to their activity.

66.   YCL members who are admitted to the CPSU leave the YCL from the moment they join the Party, unless they are members of elective YCL bodies and are doing YCL work.

IX.   Party Organizations In the Armed Forces

67.   The Party organizations of the Armed Forces are guided in their activity by the CPSU Program and Statutes and work on the basis of instructions approved by the Central Committee. They ensure the implementation of Party policy in the Armed Forces, rally their personnel around the Communist Party, instill in fighting men the spirit of the ideas of Marxism-Leninism and selfless devotion to the socialist homeland, actively help to consolidate the unity of the Army and the people, concern themselves with increasing the combat readiness of troops and strengthening military discipline, and mobilize personnel to fulfill the tasks of combat and political training, master new equipment and weapons, and irreproachably carry out their military duty and the orders and instructions of the command.

68.   The guidance of Party work in the Armed Forces is exercised by the CPSU Central Committee through the Chief Political Administration of the Soviet Army and Navy, which operates with the powers of a department of the CPSU Central Committee.

Party membership of five years is mandatory for the directors of the political administrations of military districts and fleets and the heads of the political departments of armies, flotillas and formations.

69.   The Party organizations and political agencies of the Armed Forces

maintain close connections with local Party committees and regularly provide them with information about political work in the military units. The secretaries of military Party organizations and the heads of political agencies participate in the work of the local Party committees.

X. Party Funds

70. The financial resources of the Party and its organizations consist of membership dues, income from Party undertakings and other revenue.

The procedure for using the Party's financial resources is established by the CPSU Central Committee.

71. The monthly membership dues for Party members and the CPSU candidate members are established as follows:

Monthly Earnings	Dues
up to 70 rubles	10 kopeks
from 71 to 100 rubles	20 kopeks
from 101 to 150 rubles	1.0% of monthly earnings
from 151 to 200 rubles	1.5% of monthly earnings
from 201 to 250 rubles	2.0% of monthly earnings
from 251 to 300 rubles	2.5% of monthly earnings
over 300 rubles	3.0% of monthly earnings

72. An entrance fee in the amount of 2% of monthly earnings is assessed upon admission as a candidate member of the Party.

Appendix C

SELECTED PERIODICALS

New writing on Soviet politics and government is published constantly. The following periodicals are devoted largely or exclusively to material on the Soviet Union.

TRANSLATIONS OF SOVIET WRITINGS OR SOVIET PUBLICATIONS IN ENGLISH

Current Digest of the Soviet Press
International Affairs
New Times
Problems of Economics
Soviet and East European Foreign Trade
Soviet Anthropology and Archeology
Soviet Education
Soviet Law and Government
Soviet Life
Soviet Literature
Soviet Military Review
Soviet Psychology
The Soviet Review
Soviet Sociology
Soviet Statutes and Decisions

Soviet Studies in History
Soviet Studies in Literature
Soviet Studies in Philosophy
Sputnik

WESTERN PERIODICALS

ABSEES-Soviet and East European Abstracts Series
Canadian-American Slavic Studies
Canadian Slavonic Papers
Current Soviet Leaders
Problems of Communism
Review of Socialist Law
Russia
Russian Review
Slavic Review
Slavonic and East European Review
Soviet Analyst
Soviet Nationality Survey
Soviet Studies
Soviet Union
Studies in Soviet Thought
Survey

In addition to these sources, a valuable set of publications which is not a periodical is issued by Radio Liberty Research (1 Englischer Garten, 8 Munich 22, Germany). These papers and bibliographic annotations, of varying lengths, are prepared for the use of the Radio Liberty programming and policy staffs and may be purchased by the general public.

GLOSSARY

Agitprop. Department of Agitation and Propaganda of the CPSU Central Committee.

Agitpunkt. (Agitation point). Agitation and propaganda centers which furnish materials and facilities for neighborhood political activities and which serve as polling places in Soviet elections.

Aktiv. The most active members of the Party or other organizations.

Antiparasite Laws. Laws designed to curb the leading of an "anti-social parasitic way of life." These laws were quasicriminal "administrative" sanctions in the 1950s and 1960s but were incorporated into the republican criminal codes during the 1970s.

Apparat. The bureaucracy or administrative apparatus of the CPSU or the Soviet state.

Apparatchik. A member of the *apparat.*

Blat. "Pull" or influence. Often associated with illegal or questionable economic activity.

Bolshevik. Lenin's wing of the Russian Social Democratic Labor Party, which took power in Russia after the November 1917 Revolution.

CC. Central Committee.

CPSU. Communist Party of the Soviet Union.

Comrades' Courts. Tribunals outside the regular court system set up in places of work or residence to judge minor offenses. Made up of laymen, these courts may assess a variety of minor penalties against persons brought before them. A type of *obshchestvennyi* organization.

Council of Ministers. Cabinet-level agency of the Soviet government. The Chairman is the equivalent of a Prime Minister or Premier in a West European system.

Defense Council *(Sovet Oborony).* A high governmental body for planning military strategy made up of a small number of political and military leaders.

Detskie Sady.   Child-care centers accepting children from four to six years of age.

Druzhiny.   Volunteer people's detachments; semiofficial organizations serving as aides to the police; an *obshchestvennyi* organization.

Glavlit.   Chief Administration for Literary and Publishing Affairs. The term is used to denote the Chief Administration and successor bodies which exercise censorship functions over Soviet publications.

Gosarbitrazh.   The system of state arbitration tribunals which resolve disputes between state enterprises.

Heroine Mother.   A woman who has borne and raised ten more more children.

Initsiativniki.   A breakaway group from the registered Baptists in the Soviet Union.

Izvestiia (The News).   The official newspaper of the Soviet government.

Jurisconsult.   Legal adviser to an enterprise, government agency, or other organization.

KGB.   Committee for State Security.

Khozraschet.   The principle of economic accountability used in Soviet economic enterprises.

Kolkhoz.   Collective farm.

Kolkhoznik.   Collective farmer.

Kollektiv.   The collective or peer group to which every Soviet citizen belongs at his place of work, study, or residence. The *kollektiv* often imposes group values on the individual.

Komsomol (Communist Youth League).   Youth organization of the CPSU for persons fifteen to twenty-seven years of age.

Komsomolskaia Pravda (Komsomol Truth).   The official newspaper of the Communist Youth League.

Krai.   Territorial unit in the USSR.

Krasnaia Zvezda (Red Star).   Newspaper of the Soviet military.

Literaturnaia Gazeta (Literary Gazette).   Newspaper of the Union of Soviet Writers.

MVD.   Ministry of Internal Affairs.

Menshevik.   Wing of the Russian Social Democratic Labor Party which opposed Lenin's Bolsheviks. The Mensheviks were eliminated from participation in government in Soviet Russia after the Bolsheviks consolidated their power.

NKVD.   People's Commissariat of Internal Affairs. Predecessor to the MVD and KGB. Until 1946, government ministries were called people's commissariats.

Negotiated Planning *(vstrechnoe planirovanie).*   Also referred to as "counterplanning." The process by which enterprises provide production estimates to counter the production quotas suggested by planning agencies. Out of negotiation based on these figures the final planning figures are said to emerge.

Nomenklatura.   Lists of positions, governmental and nongovernmental, which can only be filled by certain persons designated by responsible Party organs.

Novosti.   A soviet news agency which is technically nongovernmental but which is subject to government control.

Obkom *(oblastnoi komitet).*   CPSU committee of the *Oblast'* or province.

Oblast'.   Province, a territorial subdivision within the larger union republics.

Obshchestvennost'.   An important term translated generally as "the public" or "society." The term has to do with organized public opinion or public action (as opposed to official or governmental opinion or action) mobilized to achieve desired ends. The term was popular in Khrushchev's time but has decreased somewhat in importance since then. The objectives of *obshchestvennost'* are often carried out by *obshchestvennye* organizations.

Obshchestvennye Organizations.   "Public" or "social" organization. Any approved Soviet organization that is not governmental. Supposedly voluntary, *obshchestvennye* organizations include comrades' courts, the *druzhiny,* and others. Even the CPSU is technically such an organization. These bodies are often directed toward the achievement of officialy inspired ends, though they are not governmental bodies themselves.

PPO (Primary party organization).   The lowest level of Party organization.

Parasitism.   Unwillingness to hold a job or perform socially useful work, or use of a job as a cover for carrying out illegal activity. Punishable by Article 209-1 of the RSFSR Criminal Code.

Partiinost'.   Communist Party-mindedness.

People's Assessor.   Lay member of a Soviet court of original jurisdiction.

People's Court.   The lowest level of the Soviet court system.

Plenum of the USSR Supreme Court.   The full membership of the Supreme Court. The Supreme Court sometimes sits in plenary session (as a plenum) and sometimes is broken down into civil, criminal, and military collegia, all three of which may hear and decide cases on their own.

Politburo (Political Bureau).   The most important policy-making body in the CPSU.

Pravda (The Truth).   The newspaper of the CC CPSU and the most important newspaper in the country.

Presidium.   An executive body—Presidium of the Supreme Soviet, Presidium of the Council of Ministers. From 1952 to 1966 the Party Politburo was known as the Presidium.

Procuracy (Prokuratura).   The branch of the legal system responsible for prosecution in criminal cases and for guaranteeing "socialist legality" in the system as a whole. Procurators perform functions somewhat analogous to those performed by district attorneys in the United States.

Profilaktorii.   Medico-correctional institutions for alcohol and drug abusers.

Samizdat.   Literally, "self-publishing." The underground literature circulated in the USSR by dissidents.

Samogon.   Home-distilled alcoholic beverages.

Secretariat.   Organ of the Central Committee of the CPSU charged with overseeing the execution of Party policy. Headed by the General Secretary.

Shefstvo.   Patronage; system of political alliances based on personal connections.

Socialist Realism.   The standard for orthodox artistic expression in the Soviet Union.

Sovkhoz.   State farm.

Speculation *(spekuliatsiia).*   Private buying and selling of goods for profit. Prohibited by Soviet law. May be punished by the death penalty if engaged in on a large scale.

Subbotnik.   A time of voluntary unpaid labor which is usually done on Saturdays (from the Russian word *subbota*—Saturday).

The "Talmud."   An informal name for the *Index of Information Not to Be Published in The Open Press.*

Tamizdat.   *Samizdat* publications that have reached the West and have been published there (from *tam,* meaning "over there," and *izdat,* an abbreviation for the Russian word meaning "publishing house").

TASS (Telegraph Agency of the Soviet Union).   The Soviet government's official news agency.

Turnover Tax.   An indirect tax levied largely on consumer goods; one of the most important sources of Soviet budget revenues.

Yasli.   Child-care centers accepting children up to the age of four.

Young Octobrists.   A youth organization for children seven to ten years of age.

Young Pioneers.   A youth organization for children ten to fifteen years of age.

Zhurnalist (Journalist).   The trade magazine of the journalism profession.

INDEX